THE COMPLETE PREFACES
VOLUME 1: 1889–1913

Bernard Shaw

===

The Complete Prefaces
Volume 1: 1889–1913

===

Edited by Dan H. Laurence
and Daniel J. Leary

ALLEN LANE
THE PENGUIN PRESS

ALLEN LANE
THE PENGUIN PRESS

Published by the Penguin Group
Penguin Books Ltd, 27 Wrights Lane, London W8 5TZ, England
Penguin Books USA Inc., 375 Hudson Street, New York, New York 10014, USA
Penguin Books Australia Ltd, Ringwood, Victoria, Australia
Penguin Books Canada Ltd, 10 Alcorn Avenue, Toronto, Ontario, Canada M4V 3B2
Penguin Books (NZ) Ltd, 182–190 Wairau Road, Auckland 10, New Zealand

Penguin Books Ltd, Registered Offices: Harmondsworth, Middlesex, England

First published 1993
1 3 5 7 9 10 8 6 4 2

Typeset by Datix International Limited, Bungay, Suffolk
Set in 11/13 pt Lasercomp Bembo
Printed in England by Clays Ltd, St Ives plc

A CIP catalogue record for this book is available from the British Library

ISBN 0-713-990562

Contents

═══

Contents

Introduction

═══

I

I have never aimed at style in my life: style is a sort of melody that comes into my sentences by itself. If a writer says what he has to say as accurately and effectively as he can, his style will take care of itself, if he has a style.

(Preface to *Immaturity*, 1930)

Shaw has a style in his prefaces that is both a melody and a message: a combination of rhythm and verbal communication immediately recognizable as the Shavian voice. It ranges from intimate chamber music to full brass band, from arias and recitatives to dithyrambic cadences. It can be heard in any of the modes of his verbal expression; but each mode has its own pronounced orchestration: his speeches can be songs of persuasion; his letter-writing, chamber-music confidences; his journalism, brassy argument-ation; his plays and novels, vital visualizations, symphonic in structure, operatic in their arias, duets, and ensembles. Moreover, the circularity of that final clause in the passage above sounds the Irish penny whistle of anticlimax that can at any moment top these scorings.

Each of the more than one hundred prefaces in this three-volume collec-tion incorporates one or more of these cadencings; but in the prefatory mode, which is an amalgam of all the modes, the libretto is dominant. In Shaw the sounds of the melody and the words of the song blend into one; but in the prefaces what is being said – the message – is underscored. Whether the preface is about a Fabian position, a colonial scandal of government, a photographic exhibit, a Dickens novel, or a new English alphabet, Shaw's motive is the conveying of information – information, admittedly, passed through the prism of a remarkable personality. The same is true of all the extended prefaces to his plays. As Shaw explains, 'When the subject of a play is a large one, there is a great deal about it that cannot be put on the stage though it can be said in an essay.' The earliest of the play prefaces – *Widowers' Houses*, *Plays Unpleasant* and *Pleasant*, *Three Plays for Puritans*, *Mrs Warren's Profession* – have the immediacy and unbroken flow of epistolary essays and are essentially autobiographical. With *John Bull's Other Island* and after, the emphasis shifts to an argumentative, journalistic style, dramatized by capitalized subheadings as in newspapers. Whether personal or journalistic, there is in Shaw a drive to express himself 'as accurately and effectively as [I] can'. To read these prefaces is to experience Shaw over the decades achieving the same synthesis of message and art he achieves in the plays, combining the information he feels compelled to share with a music that emerges from the mode in which he works.

In the prefatory mode, the melody or rhythm is not impersonal, mechanical, or routine. It is Shaw we experience: as we hear the inflexions of his living voice we feel him working on us. Shaw was simultaneously the last of the nineteenth century's prophetic seers, in the tradition of Carlyle, Emerson, and Ruskin, and the first of the twentieth century's troubled questioners. The message he conveys in any of his longer prefaces reveals the tension between, on the one hand, his Life Force hyper-energetic, messianic optimism and futuristic vision, and, on the other, his penny whistle self-mockery, self-doubts, and wryness about the possibilities of real progress.

The prophet is without solemnity in his tone: his prose is swift, his voice lively. His phrases and clauses fall into natural, rhythmic groupings and build to a satisfying periodic close: Shaw the seer is a deft carpenter aligning his boards and driving home his nails. The questioner is equally vigorous, but with a difference. There is no sign of fatigue – at least for the first fifty years of his career – but in the most characteristic prefaces the forward thrust gives way to a more tentative circling motion. There are moments when he admits he is contradicting or undercutting himself. Far from routine, the message is evolving as it is being written. This conflict in Shaw's style – the seer and the questioner – comes out of the depths of his personality. It is the voice of an authentic human being reminding us of our authentic selves, of our role as members of a developing community: the vision is there, as is the struggle to find motivating words and viable means.

If the melody is personal, the message, the information to be conveyed, is encyclopaedic. Recognizing the professions as a conspiracy against the laity, Shaw sought to express in non-specialized language what the specialists were now doing in medicine, law, theology, anthropology, photography, biology, physics, sociology, and economics. Like a modern Dante, Shaw had a world of new knowledge to convey and a perennial dream to share, and he did both by stretching old words, coining new ones, combining old and new in fresh ways, reinventing clichés, and couching all in a vulgate that was reassuringly accessible even while it was disturbingly transformed.

II

In his prefaces Shaw, the lecturer-debater, projects for himself a listening and responding live audience and relates to it. In the preface to *Mrs Warren's Profession* (1902), for instance, he places questions into the mouths of his personified readers: 'It will be asked', 'What was the result?', 'Is it more enlightened, more liberal . . .?' These are more than rhetorical questions. They are ones that a reasonable and intelligent person might ask who was gradually becoming familiar with the issues. Another of Shaw's strategies is to address the reader in the imperative: 'Ask yourself whether', 'Read the first report of the Commission', 'Now let us consider how'. The commands are actually requests for co-operation in following the argument; they are, however, also stimulating, suggesting that action is within the power of the audience. A third Shavian technique is to project the anti-audience, so hopelessly sunk in its false idealisms and its prejudices that, by contrast, the reader-audience appears enlightened. In the *Mrs Warren* preface Shaw dramatizes his opponent – by this time the reader's opponent too – by transforming his voice into that of the British monarch: 'the Lord Chamberlain's Examiner . . . places the King in the position of saying to the dramatist "Thus, and thus only, shall you present . . ."'

Shaw, the lecturer-teacher, is also a Socialist, using strategies on his audience with the Fabians' famous motto in mind: 'Educate, Agitate, Organize.' He seeks to educate his readers about 'the new theatre', about the play of ideas, about how the stage is 'the most effective instrument of moral propaganda in the world . . . because it works by exhibiting examples of personal conduct made intelligible and moving to crowds of unobservant unreflecting people to whom real life means nothing'. But the *world* is a stage: 'the influence of the theatre in England is growing so great that private conduct, religion, law . . . morals are becoming more and more theatrical.' His preface, a podium performance, is a variation of that theatre. Shaw stands before just such an unformed, uninformed crowd, demonstrating through 'the example of personal conduct' what an observant, reflecting person is. There is an absence of verbal decoration, which underscores his pose of sweet reasonableness. The audience witnesses a demonstration of plain home truths about censorship, receiving an education in the absurdities of a system that censors without knowing what is immoral, until at last it can answer questions for itself and judge more judicially than the judges.

Education and agitation overlap. The reader is agitated into moral choice by a histrionic presentation of information. Strategies of discomposure pervade the preface. The cool prose with which Shaw introduces us to the respectability of Mrs Warren, 'her vitality, her thrift . . . her wise care of her daughter, and . . . [her] managing capacity', is calculated to disturb the 'unreflecting' respectability of his readers. There is, too, the objectivity, the anthropological distancings, with which Shaw observes the curious creatures around him, including the reader. In one section he uses the word 'tapu' – more eye-catching than the variant 'tabu' or 'taboo' – seven times as he studies the 'tribal customs' of licensing plays. One has the sensation of Shaw the lecturer holding up to the light an unusual specimen, but the specimen, unsettlingly, is of one's own society. Again, his subsequent framing of the 1902 preface with a 1930 introduction and conclusion aims to disturb by suggesting that more than a generation of passing time has made little difference, with action yet to be taken in 1930 for the 1902 problem. We may now be dealing with cinema, but the same obfuscated censoring mentality remains at work.

In Shaw's characteristic development of similarities into patterns, climaxed by a hard-hitting compressed clause or phrase, there is more than just the deft carpenter of words at work. There is a drive to make disturbing 'connexion[s] between things that seem apart and unrelated in the haphazard order of events' (preface to *Major Barbara*): the connections between life and drama; between Mrs Warren's profession and respectable life; between primitive tribes and modern society; between 'two sorts of immorality', poverty and prostitution. The connections and juxtaposings often prompt Shaw's piercing, laugh-provoking undercuttings, but they have the intent of reorganizing society. It is a way of 'mak[ing] people so extremely uncomfortable . . . that they finally stop blaming "human nature" . . . and begin to support measures for their reform'. Shaw drove home his messages by heightening to a striking metaphor or memorable aphorism, as when, after an extended report of an editor excising from a Shaw article on dramatic censorship all examples of immoral scenes accepted by the censor, Shaw concludes: 'He fired my broadside after withdrawing the cannon balls.' Again, after pages devoted to the ineptitudes of the drama critics, Shaw sums up his position aphoristically: 'The critics who accuse me of sacrificing nature to logic are so sophisticated by their profession that to them logic is nature, and nature absurdity.'

By 'Organize' the Fabians were thinking, of course, not of prose style but of political action. And in the prefaces, as on the podium, the presence and voice of Shaw comprised a form of political statement. Just as the theatre reflects the world, so Shaw the lecturer reflected an organized community. A melodious and coherent style is a projection of moral and intellectual order, a counterstatement to the flattened conventions of the unshaped or pre-shaped vulgate. Shaw's reader-audience experiences simultaneously a stirring of heightened intelligence and communal emotions resulting from his play of logic and wit and his disciplined words marching in metrical pattern and cadenced order. On his podium, in his prefaces, Shaw spoke and wrote into being a climate of opinion, a city of reason, a virtual world that his audience could enter, if only while hearing that melody and voice.

III

Through the confiding immediacy of his epistolary style Shaw's audience becomes a single listener, as in *Major Barbara*'s 'First Aid to Critics' and the 'Preface for Politicians' to *John Bull's Other Island*. In the 'Epistle Dedicatory' to *Man and Superman* Shaw constantly addresses a singular 'you': 'You meant me', 'You once asked me', 'You know your man'. The pronoun appears a dozen times in the first paragraph alone. Ostensibly Shaw is addressing Arthur Bingham Walkley, drama reviewer of *The Times*; but Shaw endows Walkley with, and himself assumes, a persona in the manner of Alexander Pope in the 'Epistles'. He presents Walkley, the voice of the establishment, as a witty, stylistic revolutionary, full of 'levities and auda- cities', constantly upsetting staid society, and himself as 'a reasonable, patient, consistent, apologetic, laborious person, with the temperament of a schoolmaster and the pursuits of a vestryman'. Shaw has transformed his dedicatee into GBS and projected himself into the respectable, steady, well-above-average A. B. W., who is capable of carrying on a dialogue with him. But GBS was – as Shaw admitted more than once – already a very consciously constructed mask for the innately 'reasonable, patient, consistent', etc., private Bernard Shaw. A friend is – as Francis Bacon would have it – 'another self'. Shaw confides to this other self that it is this other self who is responsible for *Man and Superman*, since it was his sugges- tion that began it and his meticulous sensibility that informed the sanitized modern depiction of Don Juan. Implicitly the playful transference of iden- tities involves Walkley, not only in the authorship of the play, but in the penning of the epistle, which is a public self-exploration in the guise of a private confession.

Why this extreme instance of one of Shaw's standardized techniques, the shifting of responsibility and masks (a sort of Edwardian prelude to deconstruction)? To involve *you*, dear reader, in the processes of his thought.

After a dozen pages of the epistle, the ubiquitous 'you' has become a free-floating pronoun that now includes you, caught in a verbal construct, a play of mirrors. The reflections are sometimes the real Shaw, the real Walkley, sometimes their masks, and increasingly you experience yourself as the Reader; but then, of course, you have been reading the text into consciousness from the beginning: yet another author! This ingenuity does not interfere with Shaw's standard practice: he still manages to put himself on a level with his readers, or vice versa, with whom the continuity of his rhythm keeps him in a point-for-point relation. Much of the tone is ordinary conversation with the reader; there is easy use of parenthetical interjection, of casually inserted dashes, of unforced repetitive circling of key ideas and words.

In the first half of the *Man and Superman* preface one of the repeated key ideas is that of rejection – rejection of the authorship of Shaw's play and its inspiration; rejection of his political pamphleteering and 'our political experiment'; rejection of the standard play of sex; rejection of Byron, Goethe, Mozart and, in general, the romantic hero; rejection of the whole democratic dream; rejection of Shakespeare for his unphilosophical ideas and Dickens for his sentimentality; rejection of his own art, which 'is only the self-consciousness of certain abnormal people who have the specific artistic talent and temperament' for revealing a world that is not 'the main world' at all.

In this, Shaw had a double aim. He was involving Walkley and the reader in his exploration, confession, self-doubt; requiring them to experience the rejections while preparing them to participate personally in the long countermovement that would follow, when the air on a penny whistle gives place to an assured string section on style leading to a celebratory trumpet voluntary: the Bunyan-inspired rejection of rejection. The preface's descent into the Slough of Despond and its eventual ascent to the Celestial City anticipate the play's interlude – the 'Don Juan in Hell' sequence – in which a devil questions and a seer, Don Juan, affirms. But that pattern was too neat for Shaw's purpose. After the rhapsody, again the whistle, a rejection of the rejection of the rejection: a whispered admission that he sometimes dislikes himself so much he feels 'unspeakably relieved and obliged' when attacked by a reviewer – a reviewer, perhaps, like Walkley, who actually never did understand what Shaw was doing in his plays. This concluding undercutting was part of Shaw's second aim, to put the critic Walkley in a position to experience what he, Shaw, was seeking to do in his plays, cajoling him into identifying both with author and reader and, by extension, playwright and audience. The 'Epistle Dedicatory' concludes with a conjecture and a wink at the two you's: '[W]e are both critics of life as well as of art; and you have perhaps said to yourself when I have passed your windows "There, but for the grace of God, go I."'

IV

The insistence and immediacy of Shaw's journalistic drum and trumpet were also orchestrated into the melody of his prefaces. As a reviewer of books, art, music, drama, he prepared newspaper readers for the cultural elements they might soon experience. As a perennial letter-to-the-editor 'headmaster to the universe', he daily prepared himself for his audience by skimming through a large number of London's principal newspapers, including those of the halfpenny 'new journalism' variety. This simultaneous shaping and sharing resulted in a feedback of information, an immediate relationship between Shaw and an audience as extensive and diversified as the world had seen to that time. Shaw, the twentieth-century ironist-questioner, was quick to recognize the oxymoron in 'mass culture' and to manipulate that mob of readers with all the communication techniques he was discovering. At the same time the nineteenth-century 'seer' in him fought that mass flattening of values with a message that reintroduced the theological, the aesthetic, the philosophic, in a language alive to the rich peculiarities of the vernacular and sustained by vividly concrete images and similes. The agenda was ambitious: from the mass and mob, through communication, to consciousness and community.

Consider the journalistically oriented preface to *Major Barbara*. The initial subheading is 'First Aid to Critics', which, in the mind's eye, creates an audience within an audience. The reader-audience sits beside Shaw on the podium, overhearing him genially but firmly correct the obtuse, misinformed critics he has assembled in a semicircle of grammar-school chairs before him. The reader-audience shares Shaw's elevated position, made to feel that they have seen the play and scanned the reviews Shaw refers to in the opening segment and throughout the preface.

Thereafter, the text teems with allusions to newspaper-worthy happenings: the Chicago meat-packing atrocity reported in Upton Sinclair's just-published novel *The Jungle*; 'our commercial millionaires today'; a quotation from Commissioner Howard of the Salvation Army; 'American trusts'; 'the exploitation of African gold, diamonds, ivory, and rubber'; Americans refusing to share a hotel with the scandalous Maxim Gorky. At last, in the preface's penultimate moments, we find such hot-off-the-wire announcements as 'at this very moment there appears the biography of one of our dukes' and 'As I write these lines . . . [a] royal marriage has been celebrated'.

This Stop Press element is characteristic of Shaw's style. As evidenced by his notebooks there was rarely any outlining, no drafting, and, usually, minimal insertion or revision, aside from the occasional deletion of an extraneous adjective or phrase or the insertion of a clarifying or refining one. Yet, in the midst of the apparent journalistic rush of the *Major Barbara* preface, there *is* an outline – a plan. The melody, complicated but clear, is in three overlapping, circling movements: a lecture to critics on the real sources of his revolutionary ideas; a probing of the revolutionary implications of those ideas in the play; and citation of revolutionary actions or revolution-provoking events throughout the world. The three strands appear in all seven subdivisions of the preface, from 'First Aid to Critics' through 'Christianity and Anarchism' to 'Sane Conclusions'.

The reader, as he examines Shaw's conclusions, finds he must 'look evil in the face without illusion' and must share in blood-letting – as executioner of the criminal unwilling to recognize his moral responsibility and the hard fact that 'his life depends on his usefulness'. The reader, as executioner of the useless, must also, of course, judge himself. Later, in *The Simpleton of the Unexpected Isles* (1934), Shaw would have all those who were not useful 'removed' by angelic decree. In 1907 there is just a chill in the air. The reader, who had been ensconced in his seat of judgement alongside Shaw, catches a peripheral reflection of evil and develops an uncomfortable suspicion of himself as a guilty creature sitting at a preface. Shaw, waving current newspaper cuttings, steps down from the podium, bringing the reader down with him: 'Cain took care not to commit another murder, unlike our railway shareholders (I am one) who kill and maim shunters by hundreds to save the cost of automatic couplings, and make atonement by annual subscriptions to deserving charities.' Bill Walker and Bodger (in the play), Commissioner Howard, Shaw, and the reader bear the mark of Cain.

V

Most of Shaw's prefaces are in some way dramatic, often (like the plays) bordering on the operatic. As early as the preface to *Plays Pleasant* (1898) the modern questioner in Shaw was conscious of society's growing manipulation of the theatrical: 'the modern [leader] is nothing if not an effective actor; all newspapers are now edited histrionically'. We have just seen Shaw being a journalistic manipulator himself, but in that same preface the seer in him comes to the more striking insight that drama is a form of thinking: 'The truth is that dramatic invention is the first effort of man to become intellectually conscious. No frontier can be marked between drama and history or religion, or between acting and conduct.' Limiting ourselves to the three prefaces we have already used to demonstrate Shaw's rhetorical, epistolary, and journalistic modes, let us examine three dramatic techniques he uses to become 'intellectually conscious' himself and to raise consciousness in his reader.

1. *Characters in the preface to* Mrs Warren's Profession.

Shaw peoples his prefaces with 'characters', whose handling provides us with some evidence of how his imagination works in the plays themselves. The preface to *Mrs Warren's Profession* could also have had a 'First Aid to Critics' subheading, for there are references to and quotations from a score of reviewers throughout. In this instance the intended effect is more farcical than journalistic: as one critic's unthinking reaction is disposed of, another reviewer pops up with his rehearsed response. Still, these straw men come alive in the very first paragraph of the preface: 'a pallid crowd of critics . . . shrieking that the pillars of society are cracking'; 'an hysterical tumult of protest'; 'rushed from my play to declare furiously'. Shaw at this point is sketching in the real villain in his preface-play. The critics are a choric antagonist; they are the voice of the mass culture they both reflect and make. Shaw dismisses their nameless sameness in the final pages with a weary wave of his headmaster hand: 'I am tired of playing the preceptor . . . the eager thirst of my pupils for improvement does not console me for the slowness of their progress.' But their comic inability, their bull-headed unwillingness to imagine what his play is really about, is the burden of his melody.

'Dramatic invention', to repeat, 'is the first effort of man to become intellectually conscious.' The critic may be dismissed as hopeless, but you, the reader, must become conscious of the three-dimensional non-idealistic reality of the dramatist's characters. Shaw works to accomplish this by having you share in his compensating imagination (his power of understanding and assimilating the motivations of the characters in the plays with the 'characters' that surround him in life). There are no villains; to understand all is to begin remedying some. He introduces a race-track bookmaker, whose character and profession are juxtaposed with those of Mrs Warren.

The man lives for half a page as we are told of his 'strength of character' in 'handling large sums of money', some of which is 'subscribed' to 'public work'. Moving from prostitution to the sporting world and to making our little donation to charity, Shaw involves our imaginations.

Elsewhere, our attention is called to 'the poorer girls in the gallery', watching a fashionable play featuring an attractive prostitute. So long as the exquisite courtesans of these romantic plays die at the end through consumption or suicide they are acceptable to the censor and to the stalls. To the gallery girls, however, aware that 'the drudgeries of ... honest work' available to them lead only to 'lung disease, premature death, and domestic desertion or brutality', the 'primrose path' holds no greater terrors. Examine the parliamentary bluebooks on the subject, Shaw advises the reader, and 'ask yourself whether, if the lot in life therein described were your lot in life, you would not rather be a jewelled Vamp'. Once we can see into the minds of these young women, to whom 'the lot of the stage courtesan is heavenly in comparison with their own', we are ready for Kitty Warren.

The compensating imagination becomes more prominent in space and stress as Shaw vitalizes the ostensible knave of the piece, the King's Reader of Plays, who has refused to license *Mrs Warren's Profession*. In the 1930 revision the Reader's name is excluded, for he is long dead and forgotten, and it is the idea of censorship itself Shaw is addressing. In 1902, however, Shaw has him gradually come alive. At first he is identified only by his title of King's Reader; next as 'our Censor'; then Shaw breathes upon him and gives him a name, 'Mr Redford'. We now are permitted to know the workings of his mind: he is 'compelled to maintain the present compromise of a partial tapu, applied, to the best of his judgment, with a careful respect to person and to public opinion'. There can be no doubt that Mr Redford is an obtuse functionary, but Shaw with sweet, compensating reasonableness insists, 'Let nobody conclude ... that Mr Redford is a monster.' Like the other native islanders he is struggling to come of age; he is the victim of an ancient social taboo. It's a demonstration of the same imaginative power that on stage gives us Sir George Crofts as a living human being.

One critic emerges from the straw-man chorus and is given a name and a local habitation. He is J. T. Grein of the Independent Theatre, producer of Shaw's *Widowers' Houses*, and dramatic critic of the *Sunday Special*, in which he 'complains that Mrs Warren is not wicked enough'. His complaint, in fact, extended to Shaw's compensating imagination, as he enumerated 'several romancers who would have clothed [Mrs Warren's] black soul with all the terrors of tragedy'. '[T]hat,' said Shaw, 'is just what

I did not want to do', as he embarked on a three-page tirade on how 'the whole aim of my play is to throw that guilt on the British public itself.' Shaw needs the imagined – almost the palpable – presence of his wrong-headed friend Grein before him to initiate the flow of his impassioned utterance, and certainly uses that presence as a way of making the reader become 'intellectually conscious' of the central concern of the preface and the play.

Redford, Grein, the Critics, all seem to be striving to speak. Time after time in the prefaces Shaw is on the verge of abandoning the essay for dramatic dialogue. Later in his career he would actually do it in the preface to *On the Rocks* (1933), where his thinking about Christ and Pilate material-izes as the seer and the questioner shift from indirect to direct discourse. In the 1902 preface to *Mrs Warren* Shaw moved in that direction by intro-ducing a passage of dialogue from the fifth chapter of Dickens's *Our Mutual Friend*. He omitted the extract in the 1930 revision, perhaps because he could no longer assume an audience would share his own knowledge of and delight in Dickens, or perhaps because he had had second thoughts about so direct a demonstration of the Dickensian encoding of his imagina-tion. It was, however, an early and prime example of Shaw's theatrical mode of prose writing. In the passage from Dickens, Wegg, a slow-witted bumpkin, attempts to conceal his ignorance by claiming that he does not wish to offend the female sensibility. It is the very argument the farcical figures of the London press use to excuse themselves from discussing in detail *Mrs Warren's Profession*. We have the sensation that one of the benighted critics has shambled stage-front-centre in the guise of Dickens's half-educated blusterer to represent the whole straw-man assemblage. Farce it is, but laughter, as in the plays, opens a door to heightened consciousness. The iterative pounding of Shaw's sentence (retained in 1930) that im-mediately follows the deleted Dickens dialogue – 'for women . . . for women . . . of women . . . of women . . . these women' – drives home the seriousness of the content (and the male conspiracy to hush it up) even while the smile elicited by the Dickensian demurral stiffens on one's face.

2. *Concrete images in the preface to* Major Barbara.

In all his plays Shaw excels in the use of vivid, concrete props and settings that make a direct, memorable statement, and which become, as the play unfolds, part of an organic structure. As with other aspects of Shaw's style, this imagery seems to be conceived and arranged in a musical manner. Stage images are not isolated; they interrelate, forming clusters of Wagner-inspired leitmotifs radiating out through the work. Shaw's manner of thinking – like Shakespeare's – seems to be circularly associational rather than linearly developmental, with one image being called into being by another and linking laterally with it. In *Major Barbara*, when the millionaire ironically holds twopence up to the light in the shelter, he is commenting on the fragility of the structure in which he stands and on its whitewashed dependence on his 'tainted' money. The drum that separates and unites Barbara and Cusins as they lean over it to kiss is cumbersome and fragile, but it is also a dithyrambic summoner to the Army's war of Blood and Fire, a motto and an agenda the millionaire recognizes as his own. The coin, the drum, the shelter interweave; they become a visual dialectic of competitive compatibility. In Act II Undershaft's tuppence becomes Bill Walker's sovereign; becomes the millionaire's cheque for £5,000; becomes once again, at the close, a few pennies that Barbara searches out for her tea with Peter Shirley. The drum recalls the first act's performance of 'Onward Christian Soldiers' on a concertina, with tambourine accompaniment; prepares for the thundering irony of the Cusins–Undershaft drum-and-trombone rendition of 'Immenso Giubilo' that closes the second act; and anticipates Cusins 'flourishing imaginary drumsticks' in the play's closing moments, when he discovers that his cumbersome and fragile dealings with Undershaft have not come between Barbara and himself.

Something like this symphonic use of concrete imagery is happening in the preface to the play as Shaw conjures up a book (of 'about half a century ago'), a millionaire and a pauper, and a bullfight. Each of these three foci begins as a vividly presented image that becomes the radiating centre of one of the preface's three circling, interweaving revolutionary movements: the book and Shaw's home-grown sources of revolutionary ideas; money and the revolutionary implications of its presence in Undershaft and its absence in Peter Shirley; the bullfight and immediate manifestations of revolt. Now, of course, we are not on the stage: we are dealing with words, not enacted events. We are dealing with developing ideas; and yet these substantives are so vigorously and concretely 'dramatized' that we see them as well as follow their sequence – or better, watch the expanding circles of their associations.

The specificity of 'the book', Charles Lever's *A Day's Ride*, is established as Shaw tells us that he first read it as a child in Dickens's journal *Household Words* and saw the title 'the other day in the catalogue of Tauchnitz'. Alluded to on the opening page of the preface, it foreshadows what became Shaw's revolutionary message and method: the message manifested by a 'very romantic hero' constantly grounded by reality; and the method the 'throwing [of] a stone ... that ... hits each of us full in the conscience'. 'The book' is always there. Though it changes author and title, the message and method remain the same in Belfort Bax's anti-idealistic view of woman; Stuart-Glennie's dismissal of 'the white-man's burden'; Samuel Butler's advanced morality and clear-eyed respect for money as evidenced in *The Way of All Flesh*; Dickens's *Little Dorrit*, demonstrating that Christianity encourages submissiveness; the 'Enthusiasts' among the Salvationists, finding in their King James Version the message of Blood and Fire.

One English source-book goes further than the others in its contrast and shock. Linking William Morris with John Ruskin and the anarchist Peter Kropotkin as one of those 'with a developed sense of life', Shaw holds up Morris's Kelmscott *Chaucer*. The real revolution will not be equitable distribution of a nation's wealth, but what may follow: the transformed expectations of what life can be, the unifying of ideal and reality symbolized by this product of Morris's taste and workmanship.

After 'the book' comes 'Money', which is not only concretized, but is conveyed by Shaw as an all-pervading atmosphere that oozes into every corner of our lives, like Dickens's fog of Chancery in *Bleak House*. 'MONEY' (as it is finally set, in uniform capitals) materializes only after an extended passage in which the word (and pronoun references to it) has occurred a score of times. The word's ubiquitous presence – at least a hundred citations in the course of the essay – takes more concrete form in references to 'rent', 'interest', 'profit', 'penny', 'tips', 'pensions', '£365 a year'; but it is always a frame of mind, a climate of opinion. Shaw is exploring the 'mercanto-Christian morality' of our world, in which 'money is the counter that enables life to be distributed socially: it *is* life as truly as sovereigns and bank notes are money.' In the preface he capitalizes, as it were, on the characters in the play, on their dramatic vitality that here also shimmers in allegorical outline. Undershaft and Shirley are not dramatic characters; they are the presence and absence of MONEY. They are the poles of Shaw's revolutionary claim that Undershaft's religion recognizes in 'Money the first need and in poverty the vilest sin of man and society' and that 'the great mass of men act and believe as Peter Shirley acts and believes.'

In this atmosphere and between these poles are heard a dozen symphonic variations on the monetary theme: how to live with money, without it, in spite of it, on it, above it, how to control it, use it, apportion it, steal it. Each of the play's characters sets forth the theme allegorically: MONEY as Undershaft's 'mystic nexus', Barbara's necessary corruption, Bill Walker's psychic pay-off, Mrs Baines's devilish charity, Rummy Mitchens's retributive justice, Cusins's moral checks and balances. All, in some way, are paying the piper in vital compromises and the tune they call is an ironic one on the big bass drum. The accountant mentality is the way of the world and shapes the secular and the sacred: it accounts for Bodger's buying social absolution; it accounts for the Salvationists postulating a spiritual treasury wherein their good deeds are banked away, eventually to be cashed in for celestial security.

Is there an answer to the failure of Christian cut-throat Capitalism? Shaw introduces the third movement of his symphony. It flows from the themes of his English sources – the juxtaposing of idealism and reality – and develops graphically the Blood and Fire motif introduced both by the Salvation Army and Undershaft. The bullfight, which is introduced in the section 'Christianity and Anarchism', is at the centre of this third cluster of images and associations, 'having for its main amusement the spectacle of horses gored and disembowelled by the bull, after which, when the bull is ... exhausted ... he is killed by a cautious matador'. The first association, thereafter, is the spectacle of a royal wedding that is the target of an anarchist's bomb, which kills and injures scores of people and horses. The marzipan bride (an English princess) and groom (the young Spanish monarch) stand on the entrails of innocent creatures such as the anarchist and are totally unaware of their involvement. Associations – wider implications – begin to circle around the two bloody events. The English princess has been 'broken in' to accept the slaughter in the bullring just as the young king and his subjects have been accustomed to 'the morality of militarism ... at which our newspapers have been working so hard for years past'. The lack of compensating imagination in those at the bullring ends in the spattering of blood at the nuptials. Earlier images now begin to link laterally to the events: Shaw alludes to 'a Chicago meat King', recalling for us two earlier references to the inhumanly cruel slaughter of animals and the victimization of workers reported by Upton Sinclair, events that could ignite anarchism.

The blood-letting at the bullfight, the carnage at the marriage, the slaughterhouses, 'the whiff of grapeshot', the battlefields of the world, all thematically swirl around Christianity's 'chief sensation', which is 'a sanguinary execution after torture'. About this image of Christ on the Cross, Shaw confesses, 'I loathe [it] as I loathe all gibbets', for he associates it with the Church of Crosstianity, which preaches vengeance for the convicted and vicarious atonement for the convicters. His final image of Blood and Fire is the gallows – the gibbet without Christ – where men fired with a dream of a useful community and free of 'systems of conscience banking' will shed the blood of the incorrigibly useless without vengeance and 'with many apologies and expressions of sympathy'.

In that gallows Shaw evokes the three major images of his 'Revolutionary Symphony', which lead to a final assertion, in 'Sane Conclusions', of his answers to the failure of our 'mercato-Christian morality' that he has been shaping and developing all through the preface. The first has to do with MONEY: in 'dividing the wealth of the country' nothing shall go to those able-bodied adults 'not producing by their personal exertions'. Not unlike the French Revolution's guillotine, the gallows is for those among the one per cent of a nation who do nothing for the one-third of that nation's income they receive each year. The second answer has to do with the merciful blood-letting of the 'incorrigibly useless' we have just discussed above. In his third answer Shaw stresses that 'Creeds must become intellectually honest.' It is not sufficient to be 'Dickens, Carlyle, Ruskin, Butler, and Morris all rolled into one'; nor to give lip-service to the battle against the false creed of Crosstianity. Anti-Crosstianity will be honest only in the 'true and inspired action it leads to'.

3. Dramatic cadencing in the preface to Man and Superman.

Shaw emphasizes in 'The Play of Ideas' (*New Statesman*, XXXIX, 6 May 1950) the similarity of his long dramatic speeches to that of operatic solos, confessing that in his dreams he 'was going back . . . to the forms of my idol Mozart'. The big speeches are built up like arias, which repeat a major theme through variations until the cumulative effect demands a dramatic close. We, in turn, find similar aria-like cadencing and building to climax in many of Shaw's prefaces. Here let us focus on the 'Epistle Dedicatory' of *Man and Superman*. Verbal cadencing is an inadequate way of putting it. It is not just a voice we experience; it's a body. The song and dance rituals that are part of drama's beginnings enter into these prefatory exhortations, reflections, agitations, dramatizations, about human well-being and self-realization.

The year is 1903. Shaw knows that in his writing of *Man and Superman* he has been involved in the creation of a masterwork. And now that highly complex mind probes the question of its authorship. We have earlier noted Shaw's whimsical strategy of conferring the authorship on A. B. Walkley. Amidst the laughter and proliferating reference to 'you', we recall, Shaw slyly slipped in a confession/denial of the real authorship that he seemed compelled to acknowledge/repudiate. We now draw the reader's attention to a lengthy passage in which Shaw starts with the experience of having seen *Everyman* and closes with a justly celebrated verbal flight ('This is the true joy in life') inspired by *Pilgrim's Progress*; you will find it on pp. 158–62.

Early in the passage Shaw volunteers that Plato and Boswell, seized with vision, became 'dramatists who invented' Socrates and Dr Johnson, thus surpassing their inventions and becoming true artist-philosophers rather than 'romantic playwrights'. Mozart, Shaw tells us, has invented Shaw by transporting him from such romantic foolishness into 'transcendental regions'. Aside from music he admits to being invented by four non-dramatists, 'Bunyan, Blake, Hogarth, and Turner', and at a distance by the romantic Shelley and the art-for-art sympathizer Morris, as well as the continentals Goethe, Schopenhauer, Wagner, Ibsen, Tolstoy and Nietzsche, 'whose peculiar sense of the world I recognize as more or less akin to my own'.

Peculiar? 'Mark the word,' says Shaw. The Peculiar People were a Christian sect (founded in London, 1838) distinguished by their non-conformity to the world – particularly the world of science and medicine – and their sense of community. These Peculiars are contrasted by Shaw with Dickens and Shakespeare, the obvious inventors – the real fathers – of Shaw, whose work, he tells us, is 'not co-ordinated into any philosophy or religion' and is ridden with personal sentiment or pessimism. As Shaw overcomes his 'fathers' his own inner convictions rise to the surface and an increasingly triumphant voice and rhythm, song and dance, whirl us along for two full pages till in his exuberance of rejection he thinks on John Bunyan, and then his soul, like to the lark at break of day, arising from the sullen 'tragedy of . . . disappointment' and the shallow 'comedy of . . . incongruity', sings a hymn at Heaven's Gate.

This paraphrase of the passage and characterization of its conflict, however, fails to address itself to the issue of Shaw's word music. There is much feeling, highly poetic and highly dramatic, which cannot be expressed by words – the markers of thought – but which can be expressed in music. Admitting that in Shaw thought and music cannot be separated, let us endeavour to shift the emphasis from sense by taking one section of the prose aria and outlining the pattern, with comment on the way that rhythm echoes and augments the verbal message, just as it does on Shaw's stage. The passage is short and the commentary brief, as we are aware that we come perilously close to what Shaw in his criticism described as 'pars[ing] in the most edifying academic manner', and which he devastatingly parodied in an 'academic' analysis of Hamlet's suicide soliloquy (in a review of H. H. Statham, *Form and Design in Music*, 1893; in *Shaw's Music*, Vol. 2, p. 898, London, 1981).

The passage as we have dissected and arranged it is divided into seven units:

1 Both [Shakespeare and Dickens] have
    the specific genius of the fictionist and
    the common sympathies of human feeling and thought
        in pre-eminent degree.
2 They are often saner and shrewder than the philosophers
    just as Sancho Panza was often saner and shrewder than Don Quixote.
3 They clear away vast masses of oppressive gravity
    by their sense of the ridiculous,
    which is at bottom
    a combination of sound moral judgment
    with lighthearted good humor.
4 But they are concerned with the diversities of the world
    instead of with its unities:
5 they are so irreligious
    that they exploit popular religion
        for professional purposes without delicacy or scruple
        (for example, Sydney Carton and the ghost in Hamlet!):
6 they are anarchical,
    and cannot balance their exposures of Angelo and Dogberry,
        Sir Leicester Dedlock and Mr Tite Barnacle
    with any portrait of a prophet or a worthy leader:
7 they have no constructive ideas:
    they regard those who have them as dangerous fanatics:
    in all their fictions there is no leading thought or inspiration
        for which any man could conceivably risk
        the spoiling of his hat in a shower,
        much less his life.

Shaw's sentences as here arranged illustrate how naturally they break into balanced clauses, much as do the lengthier speeches of his stage characters. In moments of emotional climax, as at the close of the section a few pages later, the parallels become a series of phrases with an even more pronounced accentual pattern, not unlike verse. The vocabulary, however, is simple and direct, for example closing the section with a characteristic Shavian verbal shrug 'and the like', or here concluding unit 7 with the contrast of 'risk[ing] the spoiling of his hat ... much less his life'. Six paralleling units open with 'they', the pronoun referring always to Shakespeare and Dickens. The middle unit, which is the central statement of this section and of the extended passage, begins with the balancing yet shifting 'But they'. All seven units reflect Shaw's associational structuring in that the first three and the last three radiate back and forth across the central sentence: the negative import of 5, 6, 7 tend to cancel the positive assertions of 3, 2, 1, and in that order.

This conflict reflects a larger one in the passage and in the preface, a conflict of positive identification and negative rejection. We have seen already Shaw's manipulation of personae and 'you', and his three strands of rejection forming the preface's warp and woof. Here we see that Shaw has drawn so much from Shakespeare's musical imagery and Dickens's allegorical characters that, in his anxiety about influence, in his need to establish his own ground as a 'fictionist', he feels a necessity to reject them. He is more comfortable with the two 'fathers' who provide the frame for this passage, the author of *Everyman* and the allegorist Bunyan, since the one is anonymous and the other 'reinvented', drawn from obscurity by the pen of Shaw.

This self-cancelling, parallel cadencing reflects the essential Shaw music, which is the assertion of similarities in the world through similarities in prose form. In this instance the form tells more than the words, for in the subtext the assertion and rejection merge, having, all of them, positive and negative, been applied to Shaw by Shaw. The negative units 5, 6, 7, moreover, emerge in quite the same fashion again in the preface to *Major Barbara*, in which Shaw exploits Christianity by labelling it Crosstianity; leads his readers to the verge of anarchy and extols the anarchists; and rejects his art, politics, and self. The charges against Shakespeare and Dickens, which can also be self-accusations, continue through the cited passage in the 'Epistle Dedicatory': Shaw, who refers to the frame plot of *Man and Superman* as 'a trumpery story of modern London life', accuses Dickens and Shakespeare of raiding 'the common stockpot of melodramatic plots'; Shaw, who on numerous occasions admitted being inspired by puppet shows, accuses them of producing human figures that became 'puppet[s] on their hands'; Shaw, who hid behind the comic mask of 'G. B. S.', accuses them of veering toward comedy with characters like Coriolanus and Micawber because 'comedy neither compromises the author nor reveals him'.

This tracing of conflicts in the text is decidedly not meant to be a demonstration of Shaw's prefaces as messages calculated to self-destruct upon reading. The conflict is an essential part of the 'melody that comes into [Shaw's] sentences by itself' (which, you will recall, is from the epigraph to our introduction) and reflects his dialectical orientation toward life. As a lecturer, letter-writer, journalist, dramatist, he is always writing beyond the mode he is in because the selfless Socialist is also an egotistical

VIKING

375 HUDSON STREET, NEW YORK, N.Y. 10014
Review Copy

TITLE:

THE COMPLETE PREFACES:
VOLUME I, 1889-1913

AUTHOR:

Bernard Shaw, ed. by Dan H.
Laurence and Daniel J. Leary

PRICE:

$39.95

PUBLICATION DATE:

February 2, 1993

*Kindly send two copies of your review to the
Viking Publicity Department.*

individualist, the seer is a questioner, the entertainer is a propagandist, the drum is a penny whistle, the encyclopaedic know-it-all has a compensating imagination.

Compensating imagination! Chesterton said somewhere that the best way to win a debate with Shaw was to present your argument so incompetently that he would feel obliged to take your side. On the stage this compensating conflict meant Mrs Warren, Undershaft, the Devil might at any moment sing one of the best tunes. It certainly increases dramatic tension. On the page the conflict in his clauses and phrases – apparent or subliminal – meant that the tenor could abruptly shift, circle, reverse, permitting the counter-tenor to be heard, this possibility again increasing dramatic tension.

Return to unit 4. It is the shortest of the units, but the central one in position and importance: 'they are concerned with the diversities of the world instead of with its unities'. If you ignore the 'instead of', an omission already realized in the self-cancelling interaction of the six framing units, you have a paradigm for creation. All three – Dickens, Shakespeare, Shaw – seem to be sustained, sometimes tortured, by a vision of community, a vision of sameness (projected, respectively, as Christmas, a Green World, a Garden City), while unblinkingly admitting the diverse in the forms of the eccentric, the outsider, the questioner. Shaw confesses to this unity/diversity in a striking simile in the preface's closing paragraph. He compares himself to an electrical system in which 'heat and light' are produced when the free-flowing current, indistinguishably the same all along the line, is blocked by 'a scrap of intensely . . . resistant material'. In unit 4 we have the artist as a resistor in a unified field.

The antitheses, balances, parallels, repetitions that surround this creative centrality spread through the four pages and finally convey a message in the preface that is not quite articulated because it cannot be put into words. Shaw tries to articulate it in his musings on the moral passion and the Life Force, but it comes through better in his persistent verbal attempts in these prefaces to communicate with an audience, to prepare the way for a community, to make a harmonious whole out of national, social, specialist parts. The subtextual, unheard but overheard, message of dialectical wholeness that we have focused on in this one section permeates Shaw's work. The trumpet, drum, concertina – what have you – are the strategies, the conscious left-brain cerebration, but in these essays and plays that were written – like Shakespeare's work – without blotting a line, there is an unconscious right-brain celebration, a song of oneness, whose insights, contradictions, instinctive balancings combine with the cerebration to produce the extraordinary Shavian world that we enter if only while hearing that voice and overhearing that melody.

All of these harmonic balancings presumably owe much to Mozart, whom Shaw identifies as his primary 'inventor'. But there are four others whom Shaw admits have been primary influences: Bunyan, Hogarth, Blake, and Turner. The first two are allegorists attempting through their art to make the world experience its ways of sin. It is what we have seen Shaw attempting to do through his four prose modes. Blake's and Turner's transcending of time and place in their final works seems to balance the realistic message-oriented art of the first two. It is the ultimate Shavian dialectic, providing a possible clue to the significance of this rejection/accept-ance passage and its placement in the context of a preface that questions the concept of self. It is a significance that goes beyond matters of style and that should be explored at length elsewhere. Here, perhaps, it is enough to suggest that this cadenced self-cancelling is the vital pulse of Shaw's style and a major element in his characteristically ebullient spirit. No matter what human experience Shaw is writing of in these prefaces – the work experience, the political experience, the sexual experience, the aesthetic experience – they all turn into versions of the same thing, which is, activity through which the human organism realizes itself. It is the individual self that is having these experiences, but it is in the human organism – in the collective – that the individual attains his completest development: 'Unless you break through the shell of "self" you shall not truly realize yourself.'

A self-realizing community encourages a compensating mind in the individual, encourages compassion toward the other illusory egos whose aggregate of illusions is the society of which the individual is a part. In short, the dialectic rhythm whose synthesis is nothing reflects not only the non-existence of self, but the non-existence of the society in which that non-self experiences consciousness. Little wonder that Shaw lists the non-realist Turner and the cosmic mythologist Blake as two of his primary 'inventors'. To experience non-self can be heartbreak as the familiar world of restless, perpetual grasping gives ground to nihilism. But Shaw's style tells us he has moved beyond nihilism to a compassionate awareness and a sense of realization. His freedom from anxiety about self and benevolence toward his kindred illusions accounts for his singing voice and dancing feet. Shaw's denial of Shakespeare paradoxically puts us in mind of Prospero's 'We are such stuff as dreams are made on'.

At the close of the passage we have been examining, when John Bunyan, Shaw's artist-philosopher and *Heldentenor*, sings his way on to the stage, he provides the dramatic climax and the ultimate explanation for the vitality that is Shaw's melody. '[I]dentifying himself with the purpose of the world', he is one with the Life Force. His is the heroic spirit: '[M]y sword to him that shall succeed me in my pilgrimage.' And Shaw's spirit takes wing as he finds an inspiration for and an echo of his own mental, emotional and dramatic optimism. We often hear that Shaw waged a calculated campaign against Shakespeare in the early years to make room on the boards for his own kind of drama, for the 'new' theatre. Probably it is true. But the energy, the moral passion of this passage and others like it, testify to something more than a left-brain strategy. The aria closes in a dramatic climax that any of Shaw's Supermen, from Caesar to Saint Joan, or, in the minor key, from William the waiter to Private Meek, might have sung. It is a song of life usefully lived in the context of death and the unreality of worldly appearance. This section needs no scansion by us to reveal the cadence, no commentary to affirm its sincerity.

VI

So, then, the melody lingers on. And what of the message? Have we long since been educated, agitated, organized beyond a need for these prefaces? In his essay 'To Introduce the Prefaces' in a single-volume edition in 1934, Shaw declares that, rather than being 'left . . . behind [in] the march of our supposedly progressive civilization . . . the prefaces are still rather ahead of the times than behind them.' What was true in 1934 remains true today. This edition of the prefaces is crammed with material exasperatingly pertinent to ourselves. *Mrs Warren's Profession* and its preface on economic realities, *Man and Superman*'s preface on evolution, *Major Barbara*'s preface on revolution, summarize Shaw's concern about the human condition at the turn of the century, a concern that continues to trouble our 'progressive civilization' as it approaches a millennial turn.

We have seen how the plays and the prefaces develop by association. Prostitution is the selling of the human body; but by association all the professions are involved in prostitution through the selling of the human spirit, mind, talents, potentialities. The Rev. Samuel Gardner's Christianity prostitutes itself by accepting the morality of whatever war happens to be advocated by the prevailing big business of the time. Praed's sentimental ineffectuality is a betrayal of the humanistic concerns of the artistic imagination. (In the preface Shaw admits a missed opportunity in not making Praed a theatrical critic prostituting human values into romantic fudge.) Vivie's rejection of the life of the heart and the spirit for the Victorian equivalent of an MBA can be read as a death in life. Shaw probes the subject from the surface level of hypocrisy, posturing, sentimentality, to the abysses of international lust and greed in plays and prefaces that range from *Widowers' Houses* to *Too True to be Good*.

By discouraging prostitution in all its forms, mankind may have a chance for continued evolution. In the preface to *Man and Superman*, Shaw focuses on the dance of sex, the conscious female and unconscious male desire to produce the most promising offspring. According to Freud and Shaw's Don Juan, sublimation of the sexual drive furnishes the energy for the development of human culture. Thus, in the same preface, Shaw's tracing of sources of the Don Juan myth becomes a presentation of the evolution of authorship, a questioning of the fatherhood of written material. Shaw seeks to neutralize the ruthless conflict for survival and dominance postulated by Darwinism, which in its capitalist form prostitutes surplus sexual energy by directing it toward money-making. If we are part of a biological intentionality, part of a racial drive with a governing end, then there is no real conflict: our experience of a coherent, continuous 'self' and competing 'you' is an illusion; we are one, we are a community. This vision of the evolutionary community in sex, in art, in daily life informs many of the prefaces: the one to *Back to Methuselah*, of course, but really any that discuss Supermen like Caesar or Joan (what evolutionists refer to as 'hopeful monsters' – mutants – born slightly before their time into an environment that may or may not be ready for them).

A 'revolution' can be defined as a motion of any figure about a centre or axis. The revolution of Shaw's mind seems to have had a double axis. The prefaces – especially the early ones – attest to the persistent revolution of Shaw's mind about the idea of the French Revolution and the possibility of an English variation on the same theme. In essay after essay, we find references to the Paris Commune, the Royalists, the Girondists, Napoleon, the writings of Edmund Burke and Thomas Paine on the French Revolution. Shaw was meditating on the renunciation and overthrow of a government that prostituted and victimized its people and prevented their natural evolution into a truly human community. In the preface to *Man and Superman*, as we have seen, he sympathizes with terrorists who destroy in order to draw attention to the ruthless, competitive unfairness, the inhumanity of the establishment. That section, though, is succeeded immediately by one headed 'Sane Conclusions'.

The 'revolution' of Shaw's mind has a double centre: one reflects Tom Paine's *Rights of Man*, which advocates overthrow of all tradition and sentiment, and the other Edmund Burke's *Thoughts on the French Revolution*, with its sense of the sacred, evolving nature of human groups. Shaw's Fabianism was prompted by Burkian conservatism. The revolution was one that would take place in individual minds in his various audiences as they surrendered private self to communal entity. The alternate contrapuntal revolution came more and more to the fore in Shaw's writings as the rich grew richer and found ever more effective ways to mute the masses or set them quarrelling with each other. Shaw the seer had a Life Force vision of the destiny of man; Shaw the questioner had a clear awareness of the man-made distortions blocking that destiny. Shaw's prefaces are perennial because of such polarities. Though they often begin as journalistic or lecturing exhortations, their true value is found in their epistolary intimacy and dramatic objectivity.

Dan H. Laurence
Daniel J. Leary

Editors' Note

This edition, in three volumes, contains in chronological order every Shaw preface, introduction, or foreword known to us. In keeping with Shaw's testamentary wishes we have reproduced the texts from the last printing authorized by him in his lifetime. It was not uncommon for Shaw to revise prefatory materials (or add postscripts to them) when a reprint or new edition was called for, removing references to 'events which have lost their interest or been forgotten', and sometimes tossing in allusions to events occurring many years after the original publication of the preface, to the bewilderment of the reader. We have sought to clarify the discrepancies unobtrusively in headnotes. Occasionally, when we have thought them significant, we have not scrupled to restore deleted passages, clearly identifying them as such.

The texts Shaw included in his collected edition (1930–32) are set as he restyled them, with the assistance of his wife Charlotte. Those texts he did not collect have been styled by the editors uniformly with the others. In our editorial apparatus we have followed house style. Occasional typographical errors or misreadings in the Shaw texts have been silently corrected, as have a few factual errors overlooked by Shaw, such as his misdating of the year he commenced *Widowers' Houses* (1884, not 1885). Archaic spelling of place-names is retained, though updated in the notes. In those instances in which Shaw has mischievously indulged in exaggeration or misrepresentation of events, we have, at the risk of committing what he labelled 'editorial impertinences', provided a counterbalance in our annotations. In no instance has there been any tampering with Shaw's texts.

Many of Shaw's prefaces were (despite his vegetarianism) heavily larded with topical references, incorporating newspaper reports he had devoured that morning with his breakfast. We have tended to concentrate our annotative efforts on the now obscure allusions as expansively as necessary, while limiting, often drastically, biographical information readily accessible in dictionaries and desk encyclopaedias. Electing to treat the three volumes of this edition as a single unit, we have provided identifications (as far as possible within the text, in square brackets) and footnotes only at their first need. The inclusion in each volume of a comprehensive index by David Bowron (in which we have inserted years of birth and death for individuals mentioned in the prefaces) eliminates annotative clutter and extraneous cross-referencing.

In the preparation of the edition we have been supported by a number of generous colleagues and friends who have given extensively of their time and efforts, considerably lightening our task. We especially wish to thank Nicholas Boyle, Bernard F. Dukore, the Eisner Scholar Award John Geary, Maureen Halligan, Sir Rupert Hart-Davis, Cathy Henderson (Research Librarian, Harry Ransom Humanities Research Center), Marshall Horowitz, Leon Hugo, Mary Ann Ignatius (Cultural Affairs Officer, US Embassy, Brussels), Thomas Postlewait, Nancy Sadek (Special Collections Librarian, University of Guelph Library), Ann Simmons (The Irish Architectural Archive, Dublin), as well as the staffs of the Library of the City University of New York, the Performing Arts Research Center of the New York Public Library, and the Elizabeth Coates Maddux Library of Trinity University, San Antonio.

We acknowledge with gratitude permission from the Henry W. and Albert A. Berg Collection, New York Public Library, Astor, Lenox and Tilden Foundations, for use of three discarded fragments of Shaw's preface to *Three Plays for Puritans*; permission from the Harry Ransom Humanities Research Center, University of Texas at Austin, to use the fragmentary draft of a preface provisionally titled by Shaw 'Irish Mountains'.

D. H. L.

D. J. L.

THE COMPLETE PREFACES
1889–1913

Fabian Essays in Socialism

*A collection of essays by members of the Fabian Society
first published in 1889, edited by Shaw*

=====

The essays in this volume were prepared last year as a course of lectures for delivery before mixed audiences in London and the provinces.[1] They have been revised for publication, but not recast. The matter is put, not as an author would put it to a student, but as a speaker with only an hour at his disposal has to put it to an audience. Country readers may accept the book as a sample of the propaganda carried on by volunteer lecturers in the workmen's clubs and political associations of London.* Metropolitan readers will have the advantage of making themselves independent of the press critic by getting face to face with the writers, stripping the veil of print from their personality, cross-examining, criticising, calling them to account amid surroundings which inspire no awe, and before the most patient of audiences. For any Sunday paper which contains a lecture list will shew where some, if not all, of the seven essayists may be heard for nothing; and on all such occasions questions and discussion form part of the procedure.

The projection and co-ordination of these lectures is not the work of any individual. The nominal editor is only the member told off to arrange for the publication of the papers, and see them through the press with whatever editorial ceremony might be necessary. Everything that is usually implied by the authorship and editing of a book has in this case been done by the seven essayists, associated as the Executive Council of the Fabian

---

* In the year ending April, 1889, the number of lectures delivered by members of the Fabian Society alone was upwards of 700. [GBS]

1. Delivered to the Fabian Society between 21 September and 21 December 1888. The Fabian Society, founded late in 1883 (its first meeting was on 4 January 1884), was one of Britain's earliest socialist organizations, consisting of middle-class radical reformers who believed in moderation: evolution rather than revolution. The Fabians sought social change by constitutional means, patiently practising elusive tactics to win an ultimate victory over stronger forces. Led by Sidney Webb and Shaw (who joined in September 1884) it soon became the most influential reformist group in Britain.

Society;[2] and not one of the essays could be what it is had the writer been a stranger to his six colleagues and to the Society. But there has been no sacrifice of individuality—no attempt to cut out every phrase and opinion the responsibility for which would not be accepted by every one of the seven. Had the sections been differently allotted, they would have been differently treated, though the net result would probably have been the same. The writers are all Social Democrats, with a common conviction of the necessity of vesting the organization of industry and the material of production in a State identified with the whole people by complete Democracy. But that conviction is peculiar to no individual bias: it is a Capitol to which all roads lead; and at least seven of them are represented in these Fabian Essays; so that the reader need not fear oppression here, any more than in the socialized State of the future, by the ascendancy of one particular cast of mind.

There are at present no authoritative teachers of Socialism. The essayists make no claim to be more than communicative learners.

LONDON.
December, 1889.

---

2. The Executive Council and authors of these Fabian essays were Bernard Shaw, Sidney Webb, Graham Wallas, Sydney Olivier, William Clarke, Annie Besant and Hubert Bland.

The Quintessence of Ibsenism

First published in 1891

═══

In the spring of 1890, the Fabian Society, finding itself at a loss for a course of lectures to occupy its summer meetings, was compelled to make shift with a series of papers put forward under the general heading of Socialism in Contemporary Literature. The Fabian Essayists, strongly pressed to do "something or other," for the most part shook their heads; but in the end Sydney Olivier consented to "take Zola"; I consented to "take Ibsen"; and Hubert Bland undertook to read all the Socialist novels of the day, an enterprise the desperate failure of which resulted in the most amusing paper of the series. William Morris, asked to read a paper on himself, flatly declined, but gave us one on Gothic Architecture. Stepniak[1] also came to the rescue with a lecture on modern Russian fiction; and so the Society tided over the summer without having to close its doors, but also without having added anything whatever to the general stock of information on Socialism in Contemporary Literature. After this I cannot claim that my paper on Ibsen, which was duly read at the St James's Restaurant on the 18th July 1890, under the presidency of Mrs Annie Besant,[2] and which was the first form of this little book, is an original work in the sense of being the result of a spontaneous internal impulse on my part. Having purposely couched it in the most provocative terms (of which traces may be found by the curious in its present state), I did not attach much importance to the somewhat lively debate that arose upon it; and I had laid it aside as a *pièce d'occasion* which had served its turn, when the production of [Ibsen's] Rosmersholm [1886] at the Vaudeville Theatre [1891] by Florence Farr, the inauguration of the Independent Theatre by Mr J. T. Grein[3] with a performance of Ghosts, and the sensation created by the experiment of Elizabeth

1. Sergei Mikhailovich Stepniak (real name, Kravchinski), Russian nihilist and author, resident in London.
2. English political radical and theosophist.
3. The Independent Theatre (1891–9), founded by J. T. Grein, dramatic critic of the *Sunday Special* and Consul-General of the Netherlands, was inaugurated with a performance of Ibsen's *Ghosts* (1881) at the Royalty Theatre, London, on 13 March 1891.

Robins and Marion Lea[4] with Hedda Gabler, started a frantic newspaper controversy, in which I could see no sign of any of the disputants having ever been forced by circumstances, as I had, to make up his mind definitely as to what Ibsen's plays meant, and to defend his view face to face with some of the keenest debaters in London. I allow due weight to the fact that Ibsen himself has not enjoyed this Fabian advantage; but I have also shewn that the existence of a discoverable and perfectly definite thesis in a poet's work by no means depends on the completeness of his own intellectual consciousness of it. At any rate, the controversialists, whether in the abusive stage, or the apologetic stage, or the hero-worshipping stage, by no means made clear what they were abusing, or apologizing for, or going into ecstasies about; and I came to the conclusion that my explanation might as well be placed in the field until a better could be found.

With this account of the origin of the book, and a reminder that it is not a critical essay on the poetic beauties of Ibsen, but simply an exposition of Ibsenism, I offer it to my readers to make what they can of.

LONDON.
June, 1891.

4. American actress-managers who presented Ibsen's *Hedda Gabler* (1890) at the Vaudeville Theatre, London, on 20 April 1891.

The Author's Preface

First published in Widowers' Houses, *Independent Theatre Series, 1893*

===

The early history of the play which forms this first volume of the "Independent Theatre Series"[1] has been given by Mr William Archer[2] in The World of the 14th December 1892, in the following terms:

"Partly to facilitate the labors of Mr George Bernard Shaw's biographers, and partly by way of relieving my own conscience, I think I ought to give a short history of the genesis of Widowers' Houses. Far away back in the olden days, while as yet the Independent Theatre slumbered in the womb of Time, together with the New Drama, the New Criticism, the New Humor, and all the other glories of our renovated world, I used to be a daily frequenter of the British Museum Reading Room. Even more assiduous in his attendance was a young man of tawny complexion and attire, beside whom I used frequently to find myself seated. My curiosity was piqued by the odd conjunction of his subjects of research. Day after day for weeks [February–March 1883] he had before him two books, which he studied alternately, if not simultaneously—Karl Marx's Das Kapital (in French), and an orchestral score of [Wagner's] Tristan und Isolde. I did not know then how exactly this quaint juxtaposition symbolized the main interests of his life. Presently I met him at the house of a common acquaintance, and we conversed for the first time. I learned from himself that he was the author of several unpublished masterpieces of fiction. Construction, he owned with engaging modesty, was not his strong point, but his dialogue was incomparable. Now, in those days, I had still a certain hankering after the rewards, if not the glories, of the playwright. With a modesty in no way inferior to Mr Shaw's, I had realized that I could not write dialogue a

---

1. *Widowers' Houses*, the first home-grown play produced by the Independent Theatre, was presented on 9 December 1892; only two performances were scheduled. The play was published in 1893 as the first volume in J. T. Grein's 'Independent Theatre Series', with appendices dealing with the discussions it had provoked. Shaw revised the play when he reprinted it in *Plays Pleasant and Unpleasant* (1898), deleting the preface and appendices.

2. Distinguished dramatic critic, remembered principally for his translating and editing of the plays of Ibsen.

bit; but I still considered myself a born constructor. So I proposed, and Mr Shaw agreed to, a collaboration. I was to provide him with one of the numerous plots I kept in stock, and he was to write the dialogue. So said, so done. I drew out, scene by scene, the scheme of a twaddling cup-and-saucer comedy vaguely suggested by [Guillaume-Victor-Émile] Augier's Ceinture Dorée.[3] The details I forget, but I know it was to be called Rhinegold, was to open, as Widowers' Houses actually does, in a hotel-garden on the Rhine, and was to have two heroines, a sentimental and a comic one, according to the accepted Robertson-Byron-Carton formula.[4] I fancy the hero was to propose to the sentimental heroine, believing her to be the poor niece instead of the rich daughter of the sweater, or slum landlord, or whatever he may have been; and I know he was to carry on in the most heroic fashion, and was ultimately to succeed in throwing the tainted treasure of his father-in-law, metaphorically speaking, into the Rhine. All this I gravely propounded to Mr Shaw, who listened with no less admirable gravity. Then I thought the matter had dropped, for I heard no more of it for many weeks. I used to see Mr Shaw at the Museum, laboriously writing page after page of the most exquisitely neat shorthand at the rate of about three words a minute; but it did not occur to me that this was our play. After about six weeks he said to me, 'Look here, I've written half the first act of that comedy, and I've used up all your plot. Now I want some more to go on with.' I told him that my plot was a rounded and perfect organic whole, and that I could no more eke it out in this fashion than I could provide him or myself with a set of supplementary arms and legs. I begged him to extend his shorthand and let me see what he had done; but this would have taken him far too long. He tried to decipher some of it orally, but the process was too lingering and painful for endurance. So he simply gave me an outline in narrative of what he had done; and I saw that, so far from having used up my plot, he had not even touched it. There the matter rested for months and years. Mr Shaw would now and then hold out vague threats of finishing 'our play,' but I felt no serious alarm. I thought (judging from my own experience in other cases) that when he came to read over in cold blood what he had written, he would see what impossible stuff it was. Perhaps my free utterance of this

3. French poet and dramatist, whose realistic 'Comédies des moeurs', like the 1855 play *La Ceinture dorée* (*The Golden Girdle*), were skilfully constructed studies of class conflict and the money question, which achieved great popularity.
4. Successful English playwrights: Thomas William Robertson, Henry James Byron, Richard Claude Carton.

view piqued him; perhaps he felt impelled to remove from the Independent Theatre the reproach of dealing solely in foreign products. The fire of his genius, at all events, was not to be quenched by my persistent applications of the wet-blanket. He finished his play; Mr Grein, as in duty bound, accepted it; and the result was the performance of Friday last at the Independent Theatre."

To this history I have little to add. The circumstances occurred, in the main, as Mr Archer states them. But I most strenuously deny that there is any such great difference between his Rhinegold and Widowers' Houses as he supposes. I appeal to the impartial public, which has now both my play and Mr Archer's story before it, to judge whether I did not deal faithfully with him. The Rhine hotel garden, the hero proposing to the heroine in ignorance of the source of her father's wealth, the "tainted treasure of the father-in-law," the renunciation of it by the lover: all these will be found as prominently in the following pages as in Mr Archer's description of the fable which he persists in saying I did "not even touch." As a matter of fact the dissolution of partnership between us came when I told him that I had finished up the renunciation and wanted some more story to go on with, as I was only in the middle of the second act. He said that according to his calculation the renunciation ought to have landed me at the end of the play. I could only reply that his calculation did not work out, and that he must supply further material. This he most unreasonably refused to do; and I had eventually to fish up the tainted treasure out of the Rhine, so to speak, and make it last out another act and a half, which I had to invent all by myself. Clearly, then, he was the defaulter; and I am the victim.

It will have been noted by the attentive reader that what I have called a story, Mr Archer calls a plot; and that he mentions two heroines, introduced for the sole purpose of being mistaken for one another. Now, I confess to discarding the second daughter. She was admittedly a mere joist in the plot; and I had then, have now, and have always had, an utter contempt for "constructed" works of art. How any man in his senses can deliberately take as his model the sterile artifice of Wilkie Collins or [Eugène] Scribe,[5] and repudiate the natural artistic activity of [Henry] Fielding,[6] Goldsmith, Defoe and Dickens, not to mention Eschylus and Shakespear, is beyond

5. French playwright identified with the well-made play.
6. Considered by Shaw to be 'the greatest practising dramatist, with the single exception of Shakespear, produced by England between the Middle Ages and the nineteenth century'. (See preface to *Plays Pleasant and Unpleasant*, p. 30.)

argument with me: those who entertain such preferences are obviously incapable people, who prefer a "well made play" to King Lear exactly as they prefer acrostics to sonnets. As a fictionist, my natural way is to imagine characters and spin out a story about them, whether I am writing a novel or a play; and I please myself by reflecting that this has been the way of all great masters of fiction. At the same time I am quite aware that a writer with the necessary constructive ingenuity, and the itch for exercising it for its own sake, can entertain audiences or readers very agreeably by carefully constructing and unravelling mysteries and misunderstandings; and that this ingenuity may be associated with sufficient creative imagination to give a considerable show of humanity and some interest of character to the puppets contrived for the purpose of furthering the plot. The line between the authors who place their imagination at the service of their ingenuity and those who place their ingenuity at the service of their imagination may be hard to draw with precise justice (to Edgar Allan Poe, for instance!); but it is clear that if we draw it as an equator, Scribe and the plot constructors will be at the south pole, and Eschylus and the dramatic poets at the north. Now, Archer's Rhinegold, in the absence of any convincing evidence that I was an Eschylus, was designed for the southern hemisphere; and Widowers' Houses was built for the north. I told the story, but discarded the plot; and Archer at once perceived that this step made the enterprise entirely my own, since the resultant play, whether good or bad, must on my method be a *growth* out of the stimulated imagination of the actual writer, and not a manufactured article constructed by an artisan according to plans and specifications supplied by an inventor. The collaboration was therefore dropped; and after finishing the second act, so as to avoid leaving a loose end, and noting such beginnings of the third as had already sprouted, I left the work aside for seven years and thought no more of it. Last August, having been rather overworked by the occurrence of a General Election at the busiest part of the journalistic season in London, I could do nothing for a while but potter aimlessly over my old papers, among which I came across the manuscript of the play; and it so tickled me that I there and then sat down and finished it. But for Mr Grein and the Independent Theatre Society it would probably have gone back to its drawer and lain there for another seven years, if not for ever.

Some idea of the discussion which followed the performance may be gathered from the appendices which will be found at the end of this volume. The entire novelty on the stage of the standpoint taken, which is impartially Socialistic, greatly confused the critics, especially those who are in the habit of accepting as Socialism that spirit of sympathy with the poor and indignant protest against suffering and injustice which, in modern literature, culminated in Victor Hugo's Les Miserables, and has lately been forced into the theatre by the pressure of the Socialist propaganda outside. This "stage Socialism" is represented in my play by the goodnatured compunction of my hero, who conceives the horrors of the slums as merely the result of atrocious individual delinquency on the part of the slum landlord. In spite of the unanswerable way in which the shallowness and impracticability of this view are exposed at once by a single speech from a practical business man, many of my critics were unable to rid themselves of it. They dismissed the man of business as a sophistical villain, and so got hopelessly astray as to the characterization in the piece. My portraiture of Lickcheese, the slum rent collector, an effective but quite common piece of work, pleased better than any of the rest. My technical skill as a playwright sustained many attacks, all based on the assumption that the only admissible stage technique is the technique of plot construction, an assumption which excludes Shakespear and Goethe from the ranks of competent stage workmen, and which therefore appears to me to reduce itself to absurdity, although I am well aware that many of our critics look on Shakespear and Goethe as literary men who were unfortunately disabled from producing good acting plays by their deficiency in the stage craft of the ordinary farcical comedy writer and melodramatist. It was further objected that my play, being didactic, was therefore not a work of art—a proposition which, if examined, will be found to mean either that the world's acknowledged masterpieces are not works of art, or else exactly nothing at all. Now, I submit that I could not reasonably be expected to defer to the authority of canons of art which no artist acknowledges, and in subjection to which no art would be possible, even if I had not, by my practice in the profession of music critic during the remarkable development effected both in that art and in its criticism by Richard Wagner, been sufficiently trained in critical processes to recognize the objections I have cited as nothing more than the common fallacies and ineptitudes into which all critics fall when first confronted with a progressive movement. I have also practised picture criticism, and have had to make up my mind as to the pre-Raphaelite movement and the Impressionist movement, with the result that I have come to suspect dramatic critics of never having had to make up their minds about anything, owing to the fact that until the advent of Ibsen the other day there had not for many years been anything worth calling a movement in dramatic art. I by no means undervalued their like or dislike of my work, which was written as much to please them as any one else; but, as an expert, I found their critical analysis anything but skilful, and their power of imposing on themselves by phrase-making, boundless. Even the best of the younger school will occasionally be satisfied that he has quite accounted for an unexpected speech by dismissing it as a wanton paradox (without any consciousness of having insulted the author); or he will dispose of an incident by pointing out that it is "inconsistent"; or, if he wishes to be specially ingenious, he will say of a character—a red-haired one, for instance—that it is not a human being at all, but a type of the red-haired variety of mankind. I make free to criticize my critics thus because some of them are my personal friends; others have dealt so handsomely by me that I cannot very well except them without a ridiculous appearance of returning the compliment; and the rest will be all the better for being brought to book. Besides, I may offer my Quintessence of Ibsenism, written and published before there was any question of finishing or producing Widowers' Houses, as a substantial proof that my interest in the art of criticism is not at bottom merely the protest of my own sensitiveness against the very disrespectful way in which my work has been handled in various quarters. There must, however, be no mistake as to the ground upon which I challenge criticism for the play, now that I submit it in print to the public. It is a propagandist play—a didactic play—a play with a purpose; but I do not therefore claim any special indulgence for it from people who go to the theatre to be entertained. I offer it as a technically good practicable stage play, one which will, if adequately acted, hold its proper audience and drive its story home to the last word.

But in claiming place for my play among works of art, I must make a melancholy reservation. One or two friendly readers may find it interesting, amusing, even admirable, as far as a mere topical farce can excite admiration; but nobody will find it a beautiful or lovable work. It is saturated with the vulgarity of the life it represents: the people do not speak nobly, live gracefully, or sincerely face their own position: the author is not giving expression in pleasant fancies to the underlying beauty and romance of happy life, but dragging up to the smooth surface of "respectability" a handful of the slime and foulness of its polluted bed, and playing off your laughter at the scandal of the exposure against your shudder at its blackness. I offer it as my own criticism of the author of Widowers' Houses that the disillusion which makes all great dramatic poets tragic has here made him only derisive; and derision is by common consent a baser atmosphere than that of tragedy. I had better have written a beautiful play, like Twelfth Night, or a grand play, like the tragic masterpieces; but, frankly, I was not able to: modern commercialism is a bad art school, and cannot, with all its robberies, murders and prostitutions, move us in the grand manner to pity and terror: it is squalid, futile, blundering, mean, ridiculous, for ever uneasily pretending to be the wide-minded, humane, enterprising thing it is not. It is not my fault, reader, that my art is the expression of my sense of moral and intellectual perversity rather than of my sense of beauty. My life has been passed mostly in big modern towns, where my sense of beauty has been starved whilst my intellect has been gorged with problems like that of the slums in this play, until at last I have come, in a horrible sort of way, to relish them enough to make them the subjects of my essays as an artist. Such art as can come out of these conditions for a man of my endowment I claim to have put into my work; and therefore you will please judge it, not as a pamphlet in dialogue, but as in intention a work of art as much as any comedy of Molière's is a work of art, and as pretending to be a better made play for actual use and long wear on the boards than anything that has yet been turned out by the patent constructive machinery. And I claim that its value in both respects is enhanced by the fact that it deals with a burning social question, and is deliberately intended to induce people to vote on the Progressive side at the next County Council election in London. So, as the clown says in All's Well, "Spare not me" [II: ii]. I am no novice in the current critical theories of dramatic art; and what I have done I have done on purpose.

LONDON.
March, 1893.

The Theatrical 'World' of 1894

Preface to a collection of theatre reviews by William Archer, 1895

My qualification for introducing this annual record is, as I have vainly urged upon my friend the author, the worst qualification possible. For years past those readers of The World whose interest in art gave them an appetite for criticism, turned every Tuesday from a page on the drama by W. A. to a page on music by G. B. S.[1] Last year the death of [the editor] Edmund Yates closed a chapter in the history of the paper; and G. B. S., having exhausted his message on the subject of contemporary music, took the occasion to write "Finis" at the end of his musical articles. But the old association was so characteristic, and is still so recent, that we have resolved to try whether the reader will not, just this once more, turn over the page and pass from G. B. S. to W. A., by mere force of habit, without noticing the glaring fact that the musical duties of G. B. S., by cutting him off almost entirely from the theatre, have left him, as aforesaid, quite the most unsuitable person to meddle in a book about the theatre and nothing else.

However, one can learn something about the theatre even at the opera: for instance, that there are certain permanent conditions which have nothing to do with pure art, but which deeply affect every artistic performance in London. No journalist, without intolerable injustice to artists and managers whose livelihood is at stake, can pass judgment without taking these conditions into account; and yet he may not mention them, because their restatement in every notice would be unbearable. The journalist is therefore forced to give his reader credit for knowing the difficulties under which plays are produced in this country, just as the writer of the leading article is forced to assume that his reader is acquainted with the British constitution and the practical exigencies of our system of party government. And it is because the reader hardly ever does know these things that newspapers so often do more harm than good.

Obviously, Mr Archer, in reprinting his weekly articles exactly as they appeared, and thereby preserving all their vividness and actuality, preserves

1. Shaw contributed music criticism, signed with his initials, to the *World* from 28 May 1890 to 4 August 1894.

also this dependence of the journalist on the public for a considerate and well-informed reading of his verdicts. I need hardly add that he will not get it, because his readers, though interested in the art of the theatre, neither know nor care anything about the business of the theatre; and yet the art of the theatre is as dependent on its business as a poet's genius is on his bread and butter. Theatrical management in this country is one of the most desperate commercial forms of gambling. No one can foresee the fate of a play: the most experienced managers carefully select failure after failure for production; and the most featherheaded beginners blunder on successes. At the London West End theatres, where all modern English dramas are born, the minimum expense of running a play is about £400 a week, the maximum anything you please to spend on it. And all but the merest fraction of it may be, and very frequently is, entirely lost. On the other hand, success may mean a fortune of fifty thousand pounds accumulated within a single year. Very few forms of gambling are as hazardous as this. At roulette you can back red or black instead of yellow. On the turf you can take the low odds against the favorite instead of the high odds against the outsider. At both games you can stake as much or as little as you choose. But in the theatre you must play a desperate game for high stakes, or not play at all. And the risk falls altogether on the management. Everybody, from the author to the charwoman, must be paid before the management appropriates a farthing.

The scientific student of gambling will see at once that these are not the conditions which permanently attract the gambler. They are too extreme, too inelastic; besides, the game requires far too much knowledge. Consequently, the gambler pure and simple never meddles with the theatre: he has ready to his hand dozens of games that suit him better. And what is too risky for the gambler is out of the question for the man of business. Thus, from the purely economic point of view, the theatre is impossible. Neither as investment nor speculation, enterprise nor game, earnest nor jest, can it attract a single sovereign of capital. You must disturb a man's reason before he will even listen to a proposal to run a playhouse.

It will now be asked why, under these circumstances, have we a couple of dozen West End theatres open in London. Are they being run by people whose reason is disturbed? The answer is, emphatically, Yes. They are the result of the sweeping away of all reasonable economic prudence by the immense force of an artistic instinct which drives the actor to make opportunities at all hazards for the exercise of his art, and which makes the theatre irresistibly fascinating to many rich people who can afford to keep theatres just as they can afford to keep racehorses, yachts, or newspapers.

The actor who is successful enough to obtain tolerably continuous employment as "leading man" in London at a salary of from twenty to forty
pounds a week, can in a few years save enough to try the experiment of
taking a theatre for a few months and producing a play on his own
account. The same qualities which have enabled him to interest the public
as an actor will help him, as actor-manager, to interest the rich theatre
fanciers, and to persuade them to act as his "backers." If the enterprise thus
started be watered now and then by the huge profits of a successful play, it
will take a great deal to kill it. With the help of these profits and occasional
subsidies, runs of ill-luck are weathered with every appearance of brilliant
prosperity, and are suspected only by experienced acting-managers, and by
shrewd observers who have noticed the extreme scepticism of these gentlemen as to the reality of any apparently large success.

This system of actor-manager and backer is practically supreme in
London. The drama is in the hands of Mr [Henry] Irving, Mr [George]
Alexander, Mr [Herbert] Beerbohm Tree, Mr Lewis Waller, Mrs John
Wood [Matilda Vining], Mr [John] Hare, Mr [Edward O'Connor] Terry,
Mr [Charles] Wyndham, Mr [William Sydney] Penley, and Mr [John
Lawrence] Toole. Nearly all the theatres other than theirs are either devoted,
like the Adelphi and Drury Lane, to the routine of those comparatively
childish forms of melodrama which have no more part in the development
of the theatre as one of the higher forms of art than Madame Tussaud's or
the Christy Minstrels,[2] or else they are opera houses.

We all know by this time that the effect of the actor-manager system is
to impose on every dramatic author who wishes to have his work produced
in firstrate style, the condition that there shall be a good part for the actor-
manager in it. This is not in the least due to the vanity and jealousy of the
actor-manager: it is due to his popularity. The strongest fascination at a
theatre is the fascination of the actor or actress, not of the author. More
people go to the Lyceum Theatre to see Mr Irving and Miss Ellen Terry
than to see Shakespear's plays; at all events, it is certain that if Mr Irving
were to present himself in as mutilated a condition as he presented King
Lear, a shriek of horror would go up from all London. If Mr Irving were
to produce a tragedy, or Mr Wyndham a comedy, in which they were cast
for subordinate parts, the public would stay away; and the author would
have reason to curse the self-denial of the actor-manager. Mr Hare's person-

2. The Christy Minstrels was the most famous of the blackface minstrel troupes,
thus becoming a generic name for all the groups flourishing in London from 1862
to the turn of the century.

ally modest managerial policy is anything but encouraging to authors and critics who wish that all actor-managers were even as he. The absence of a strong personal interest on his part in the plays submitted to him takes all the edge off his judgment as to their merits; and except when he is falling back on old favorites like [T. W. Robertson's] Caste and [Victorien Sardou's] Diplomacy, or holding on to [Sydney Grundy's] A Pair of Spectacles, which is as much a one-part actor-manager's play as Hamlet is, he is too often selecting all the failures of the modern drama, and leaving the successes to the actor-managers whose selective instincts are sharpened by good parts in them. We thus see that matters are made worse instead of mended by the elimination of personal motives from actor-management; whilst the economic conditions are so extremely unfavorable to anyone but an actor venturing upon the management of any but a purely routine theatre, that in order to bring up the list of real exceptions to the London rule of actor-management to three, we have to count Mr Daly and Mr Grein of the Independent Theatre along with Mr Comyns Carr.[3] Mr Grein, though his forlorn hopes have done good to the drama out of all apparent proportion to the show they have been able to make, tells us that he has lost more by his efforts than anybody but a fanatic would sacrifice; whilst Mr Daly, as the manager and proprietor of a London theatre (New York is his centre of operations), has had little success except in the Shakespearean revivals which have enabled him to exploit Miss Ada Rehan's unrivaled charm of poetic speech.

Taking actor-management, then, as inevitable for the moment, and dismissing as untenable the notion that the actor-manager can afford to be magnanimous any more than he can afford to be lazy, why is it that, on the whole, the effect of the system is to keep the theatre lagging far behind the drama? The answer is, that the theatre depends on a very large public, and the drama on a very small one. A great dramatic poet will produce plays for a bare livelihood, if he can get nothing more. Even if a London theatre would perform them on the same terms, the sum that will keep the poet for a year—or five years at a pinch—will not keep the theatre open for more than a week. Ibsen, the greatest living dramatic poet, produces a play in two years. If he could sell twenty thousand copies of it at five shillings apiece within the following two years, he would no doubt consider

3. Augustin Daly, American theatre manager and dramatist, leased a London theatre for his company in 1893. Joseph Comyns Carr, popular dramatist, frequently adapted novels or French plays for the English stage, notably Henri Meilhac's *Frou Frou* (1881).

himself, for a poet, a most fortunate man in his commercial relations. But unless a London manager sees some probability of from 50,000 to 75,000 people paying him an average five shillings apiece within three months, he will hardly be persuaded to venture. In this book the reader will find an account of the production for the first time in England of Ibsen's Wild Duck, a masterpiece of modern tragi-comedy, famous throughout Europe. It was by no means lacking in personal appeal to the actor-manager; for it contains two parts, one of which, old Ekdal, might have been written for Mr Hare, whilst the other, Hjalmar Ekdal, would have suited Mr Beerbohm Tree to perfection. What actually happened, however, was that no London manager could afford to touch it; and it was not until a few private persons scraped together a handful of subscriptions that two modest little representations [actually three performances, by the Independent Theatre, May 1894] were given by Mr Grein under great difficulties. Mr Tree had already, by the experiment of a few matinées [June 1893] of An Enemy of the People, ascertained that such first-rate work as Ibsen's is still far above the very low level represented by the average taste of the huge crowd of playgoers requisite to make a remunerative run for a play. The Wild Duck, therefore, had to give place to commoner work. This is how the theatre lags behind its own published literature. And the evil tends to perpetuate itself in two ways: first, by helping to prevent the formation of a habit of playgoing among the cultivated section of the London community; and second, by diverting the best of our literary talent from the theatre to ordinary fiction and journalism, in which it becomes technically useless for stage purposes.

The matter is further complicated by the conditions on which the public are invited to visit the theatre. These conditions, in my opinion, are sufficient by themselves to make most reasonable people regard a visit to the theatre rather as a troublesome and costly luxury to be indulged in three or four times a year under family pressure, than as the ordinary way of passing an unoccupied evening. The theatrical managers will not recognize that they have to compete with the British fireside, the slippers, the easy chair, the circulating library, and the illustrated press. They persist in expecting a man and his wife to leave their homes after dinner, and, after worrying their way to the theatre by relays of train and cab or omnibus, pay seven-and-sixpence or half-a-guinea apiece for comfortable seats. In the United States, where prices are higher in other things, the same accommodation can be had for five and six shillings. The cheaper parts of the London theatre are below the standard of comfort now expected by third-class travellers on our northern railway lines. The result is, not that people refuse to go to the theatre at all, but that they go very seldom, and then only to some house of great repute, like Mr Irving's, or to see some play which has created the sort of mania indicated by the term "catching on." No doubt, when this mania sets in, the profits are, as we have seen, enormous. But when it does not—and this is the more frequent case—the acting-manager is at his wit's end to find people who will sit in his half-guinea stalls and seven-and-sixpenny balcony seats for nothing, in order to persuade the provincial playgoer, when his turn comes to see the piece "on tour" from an excellent seat costing only a few shillings, that he is witnessing a "great London success." In the long run this system will succumb to the action of competition, and to the growing discrepancy between the distribution of income in the country and the distribution of prices in the theatre; but the reader who wishes to intelligently understand the failures and successes recorded in this book, must take account of the fact that, with the exception of the shilling gallery, every seat in a West End London theatre is at present charged for at a rate which makes it impossible for theatrical enterprise to settle down from a feverish speculation into a steady industry.

Among other effects of this state of things is an extreme precariousness of employment for actors, who are compelled to demand unreasonably high salaries in order that they may earn in the course of the year discouragingly small incomes. As we have seen, the few who have sufficient adaptable ability and popularity to be constantly employed, save rapidly enough to become actor-managers and even to build theatres for themselves. The result is that it becomes more and more difficult to obtain a fine cast for a play. The "star system," which is supposed to have disappeared in London, is really rampant there as far as acting is concerned. Compare, for example, the Opera, where the actor-manager is unknown, with the Lyceum Theatre.[4] Sir Augustus Harris can present an opera with a whole constellation of stars in it.[5] One of the greatest operas in the world, sung by half a dozen of the greatest dramatic singers in the world, is a phenomenon, which, as a musical critic, I have seen, and found fault with, at Covent Garden. Now try to imagine Mr Irving attempting to do for a masterpiece of Shakespear's what Sir Augustus Harris does for Lohengrin. All the other stars are like Mr Irving: they have theatres of their own, and are competing with him as men of business, instead of co-operating with him as artists. The old receipt for an opera company, "[Angelica] Catalani[6] and a few

4. Home of Henry Irving's productions.
5. In 1887 Augustus Harris inaugurated a series of operas at Covent Garden with due attention to every artistic element rather than to the *prima donna* alone.
6. Italian opera singer who, from 1806 to 1813, reigned in England as a *prima donna* without rival.

dolls," is, leaving scenery and mounting out of the question, as applicable to a Shakespearean performance at the Lyceum today as it was to the provincial starring exploits of the late Barry Sullivan.[7] One expects every month to hear that Mr [Herbert] Waring, Mr Fred Terry, Mr Yorke Stephens, Mr [Johnston] Forbes Robertson, Mr Brandon Thomas, and Mr [Charles] Hawtrey are about to follow Mr Alexander and Mr Waller into actor-management. We should then have sixteen actor-managers competing with one another in sixteen different theatres, in a metropolis hardly containing good actors enough to cast three good plays simultaneously, even with the sixteen actor-managers counted in. No doubt such an increased demand for actors and plays as six additional managers would set up might produce an increased and improved supply if the demand of the public for theatrical amusements kept pace with the ambition of actors to become actor-managers; but is there, under existing conditions as to growth of population and distribution of income, the slightest likelihood of such an upward bound of public demand without a marked reduction of prices?

There is yet another momentous prospect to be taken into consideration. We have at present nine actor-managers and only one actress-manageress— Mrs John Wood. So far, our chief actresses have been content to depend on the position of "leading lady" to some actor-manager. This was sufficient for all ordinary ambitions ten years ago; but since then the progress of a revolution in public opinion on what is called the Woman Question has begun to agitate the stage. In the highest class of drama the century has produced, the works of Richard Wagner, we find the Elsa of Lohengrin, the most highly developed of the operatic "prima donnas" whose main function it was to be honored with the love of the hero, supplanted by a race of true heroines like Brynhild and Isolde, women in no sense secondary to the men whose fate is bound up with their own, and indeed immeasurably superior in wisdom, courage, and every great quality of heart and mind, to the stage heroes of the middle Victorian period of Romance. The impulse felt in heroic music drama has now reached domestic prose comedy; and Esther Eccles[8] and Diplomacy Dora[9] are succeeded by [Ibsen's] Nora Helmer, Rebecca West, Hedda Gabler and Hilda Wangel. The change is so

7. Irish actor-manager. After losing money in productions in London, he successfully and profitably toured the provinces playing Shakespeare. As a boy in Dublin, Shaw saw his Hamlet and never forgot Sullivan's bravura style and delivery.
8. Character in T. W. Robertson's *Caste* (1867).
9. Sardou's *Dora* was adapted by B. C. Stephenson and Clement Scott (1878) as *Diplomacy*, a London success.

patent, that one of the plays criticized by Mr Archer in the pages which follow is called The New Woman.[10] Now it is not possible to put the new woman seriously on the stage in her relation to modern society, without stirring up, both on the stage and in the auditorium, the struggle to keep her in her old place. The play with which Ibsen conquered the world, A Doll's House, allots to the "leading man" the part of a most respectable bank manager, exactly the sort of person on whose quiet but irresistible moral superiority to women Tom Taylor insisted with the fullest public applause in his Still Waters Run Deep [1855]. Yet the play ends with the most humiliating exposure of the vanity, folly, and amorous beglamorment of this complacent person in his attitude towards his wife, the exposure being made by the wife herself. His is not the sort of part that an actor-manager likes to play. Mr Wyndham has revived Still Waters Run Deep: he will not touch A Doll's House. The one part that no actor as yet plays willingly is the part of a hero whose heroism is neither admirable nor laughable. A villain if you like, a hunchback, a murderer, a kicked, cuffed, duped pantaloon by all means; but a hero *manqué*, never. Man clings to the old pose, the old cheap heroism; and the actor in particular, whose life aspiration it has been to embody that pose, feels, with inexpressible mis-giving, the earth crumbling beneath his feet as the enthusiasm his heroism once excited turns to pity and ridicule. But this misgiving is the very material on which the modern dramatist of the Ibsen school seizes for his tragi-comedy. It is the material upon which I myself have seized in a play of my own criticized in this book, to which I only allude here to gratify my friend the author, who has begged me to say something about Arms and the Man. I comply by confessing that the result was a misunderstanding so complete, that but for the pleasure given by the acting, and for the happy circumstance that there was sufficient fun in the purely comic aspect of the piece to enable it to filch a certain vogue as a novel sort of extravaganza, its failure would have been as evident to the public as it was to me when I bowed my acknowledgments before the curtain to a salvo of entirely mistaken congratulations on my imaginary success as a convention-ally cynical and paradoxical castigator of "the seamy side of human nature." The whole difficulty was created by the fact that my Bulgarian hero, quite as much as Helmer in A Doll's House, was a hero shewn from the modern woman's point of view. I complicated the psychology by making him catch glimpse after glimpse of his own aspect and conduct from this point

10. A play by Sydney Grundy, produced at the Comedy Theatre, London, on 1 September 1894.

of view himself, as all men are beginning to do more or less now, the result, of course, being the most horrible dubiety on his part as to whether he was really a brave and chivalrous gentleman, or a humbug and a moral coward. His actions, equally of course, were hopelessly irreconcilable with either theory. Need I add that if the straightforward Helmer, a very honest and ordinary middle-class man misled by false ideals of womanhood, bewildered the public, and was finally set down as a selfish cad by all the Helmers in the audience, *a fortiori* [all the more] my introspective Bulgarian never had a chance, and was dismissed, with but moderately spontaneous laughter, as a swaggering impostor of the species for which contemporary slang has invented the term "bounder"?

But what bearing have the peculiarities of Helmer and my misunderstood Bulgarian on the question of the actress-manageress? Very clearly this, that it is just such peculiarities that make characteristically modern plays as repugnant to the actor as they are attractive to the actress, and that, consequently, the actress who is content to remain attached to an actor-manager as "leading lady," forfeits all chance of creating any of the fascinating women's parts which come at intervals of two years from the Ibsen mint. Among the newest parts open to the leading lady, Paula Tanqueray[11] counts as "advanced," although she would be perfectly in her place in a novel by Thackeray or Trollope, to either of whom Nora Helmer would have been an inconceivable person. A glance at our theatres will shew that the higher artistic career is practically closed to the leading lady. Miss Ellen Terry's position at the Lyceum Theatre may appear an enviable one;[12] but when I recall the parts to which she has been condemned by her task of "supporting" Mr Irving, I have to admit that Miss Janet Achurch,[13] for instance, who made for herself the opportunity of "creating" Nora Helmer in England by placing herself in the position virtually of actress-manageress, is far more to be envied. Again, if we compare Miss Elizabeth Robins, the creator of Hedda Gabler and Hilda Wangel, with Miss Kate Rorke at the Garrick Theatre, or the records of Miss Florence Farr and Miss Marion Lea with that of Miss Mary Moore at the Criterion,[14] we cannot but see that

11. In Arthur W. Pinero's *The Second Mrs Tanqueray* (1893).
12. Shaw waged a long campaign to free the actress Ellen Terry (associated for much of her career with Irving at the Lyceum) – and the theatre-going public – from what he considered to be the traditional and reactionary art of Irving.
13. Janet Achurch and her husband Charles Charrington had independently produced a number of plays, notably Ibsen's *A Doll's House*.
14. Florence Farr in 1894 undertook a season of plays at the Avenue Theatre that included Shaw's *Arms and the Man* and W. B. Yeats's *The Land of Heart's Desire* on

the time is ripe for the advent of the actress-manageress, and that we are on the verge of something like a struggle between the sexes for the dominion of the London theatres, a struggle which, failing an honorable treaty, or the breakup of the actor-manager system by the competition of new forms of theatrical enterprise, must in the long run end disastrously for the side which is furthest behind the times. And that side is at present the men's side.

The reader will now be able to gratify his impatience, and pass on to Mr Archer's criticisms (if he has not done so long ago), with some idea of the allowances that must be made for circumstances in giving judgment on the curious pageant which passes before the dramatic critic as he sits in his stall night after night. He has had to praise or blame, advocate or oppose, always with a human and reasonable regard to what is possible under existing conditions. Most of his readers, preoccupied with pure ideals of the art of the theatre, know nothing of these conditions, and perhaps imagine that all that lies beyond their ken is the working of the traps and the shifting of the scenery. Perhaps these few hints of mine may help them to understand that the real secrets of the theatre are not those of the stage mechanism, but of the box office, the acting-manager's room, and the actor-manager's soul.

G. B. S.

---

a double bill. Kate Rorke was leading lady to John Hare, manager of the Garrick Theatre. Mary Moore was wife of, and leading lady to, Charles Wyndham, manager of the Criterion Theatre.

Mainly about Myself (Plays Unpleasant)

First published in 1898

=====

There is an old saying that if a man has not fallen in love before forty, he had better not fall in love after. I long ago perceived that this rule applied to many other matters as well: for example, to the writing of plays; and I made a rough memorandum for my own guidance that unless I could produce at least half a dozen plays before I was forty, I had better let playwriting alone. It was not so easy to comply with this provision as might be supposed. Not that I lacked the dramatist's gift. As far as that is concerned, I have encountered no limit but my own laziness to my power of conjuring up imaginary people in imaginary places, and finding pretexts for theatrical scenes between them. But to obtain a livelihood by this insane gift, I must have conjured so as to interest not only my own imagination, but that of at least some seventy or a hundred thousand contemporary London playgoers. To fulfil this condition was hopelessly out of my power. I had no taste for what is called popular art, no respect for popular morality, no belief in popular religion, no admiration for popular heroics. As an Irishman I could pretend to patriotism neither for the country I had abandoned nor the country that had ruined it. As a humane person I detested violence and slaughter, whether in war, sport, or the butcher's yard. I was a Socialist, detesting our anarchical scramble for money, and believing in equality as the only possible permanent basis of social organization, discipline, subordination, good manners, and selection of fit persons for high functions. Fashionable life, open on indulgent terms to unencumbered "brilliant" persons, I could not endure, even if I had not feared its demoralizing effect on a character which required looking after as much as my own. I was neither a sceptic nor a cynic in these matters: I simply understood life differently from the average respectable man; and as I certainly enjoyed myself more—mostly in ways which would have made him unbearably miserable—I was not splenetic over our variance.

Judge then, how impossible it was for me to write fiction that should delight the public. In my nonage I had tried to obtain a foothold in literature by writing novels, and had actually produced five long works in that form[1] without getting further than an encouraging compliment or two from the most dignified of the London and American publishers, who unanimously declined to venture their capital upon me. Now it is clear that a novel cannot be too bad to be worth publishing, provided it is a novel at all, and not merely an ineptitude. I was not convinced that the publishers' view was commercially sound until I got a clue to my real condition from a friend of mine, a physician [J. Kingston Barton] who had devoted himself specially to ophthalmic surgery. He tested my eyesight one evening, and informed me that it was quite uninteresting to him because it was normal. I naturally took this to mean that it was like everybody else's; but he rejected this construction as paradoxical, and hastened to explain to me that I was an exceptional and highly fortunate person optically, normal sight conferring the power of seeing things accurately, and being enjoyed by only about ten per cent of the population, the remaining ninety per cent being abnormal. I immediately perceived the explanation of my want of success in fiction. My mind's eye, like my body's, was "normal": it saw things differently from other people's eyes, and saw them better.

This revelation produced a considerable effect on me. At first it struck me that I might live by selling my works to the ten per cent who were like myself; but a moment's reflection shewed me that these must all be as penniless as I, and that we could not live by taking in oneanother's literary washing. How to earn daily bread by my pen was then the problem. Had I been a practical commonsense moneyloving Englishman, the matter would have been easy enough: I should have put on a pair of abnormal spectacles and aberred my vision to the liking of the ninety per cent of potential bookbuyers. But I was so prodigiously self-satisfied with my superiority, so flattered by my abnormal normality, that the resource of hypocrisy never occurred to me. Better see rightly on a pound a week than squint on a million. The question was, how to get the pound a week. The matter, once I gave up writing novels, was not so very difficult. Every despot must have one disloyal subject to keep him sane. Even Louis the Eleventh [founder in 1480–81 of the absolute monarchy of France] had to tolerate his confessor, standing for the eternal against the temporal throne. Democracy has now handed the sceptre of the despot to the sovereign people; but they, too, must have their confessor, whom they call Critic. Criticism is not only

---

1. Titled *Immaturity*, 1879; *The Irrational Knot*, 1880; *Love Among the Artists*, 1881; *Cashel Byron's Profession*, 1882; *An Unsocial Socialist*, 1883. With the exception of the first (unpublished until 1930), all were serialized, in 1884–8, prior to book publication.

medicinally salutary: it has positive popular attractions in its cruelty, its gladiatorship, and the gratification given to envy by its attacks on the great, and to enthusiasm by its praises. It may say things which many would like to say, but dare not, and indeed for want of skill could not even if they durst. Its iconoclasms, seditions, and blasphemies, if well turned, tickle those whom they shock; so that the critic adds the privileges of the court jester to those of the confessor. Garrick, had he called Dr Johnson Punch, would have spoken profoundly and wittily; whereas Dr Johnson, in hurling that epithet at him, was but picking up the cheapest sneer an actor is subject to.[2]

It was as Punch, then, that I emerged from obscurity. All I had to do was to open my normal eyes, and with my utmost literary skill put the case exactly as it struck me, or describe the thing exactly as I saw it, to be applauded as the most humorously extravagant paradoxer in London. The only reproach with which I became familiar was the everlasting "Why can you not be serious?" Soon my privileges were enormous and my wealth immense. I had a prominent place reserved for me on a prominent journal [*The World* and the *Saturday Review*] every week to say my say as if I were the most important person in the kingdom. My pleasing toil was to report upon all the works of fine art the capital of the world can attract to its exhibitions, its opera house, its concerts and its theatres. The classes eagerly read my essays: the masses patiently listened to my harangues. I enjoyed the immunities of impecuniosity with the opportunities of a millionaire. If ever there was a man without a grievance, I was that man.

But alas! the world grew younger as I grew older: its vision cleared as mine dimmed: it began to read with the naked eye the writing on the wall which now began to remind me that the age of spectacles was at hand. My opportunities were still there: nay, they multiplied tenfold; but the strength and youth to cope with them began to fail, and to need eking out with the shifty cunning of experience. I had to shirk the platform; to economize my health; even to take holidays. In my weekly columns, which I once filled full from a magic well that never ran dry or lost its sparkle provided I pumped hard enough, I began to repeat myself; to fall into a style which, to my great peril, was recognized as at least partly serious; to find the

2. David Garrick, perhaps the greatest English actor of the eighteenth century, was the quondam student of Dr Samuel Johnson, author, critic and lexicographer. Hester Lynch Thrales in 1777 reported in her diary that Garrick, distressed during his performance of *Lear* by Johnson's noisiness behind the scenes, begged him to 'have done with all this Rattle – it spoyles my Thoughts, it destroys my Feelings.' 'No Sir,' Johnson replied, loud enough to be overheard by the general company, 'Punch has no feelings.'

pump tiring me and the water lower in the well; and, worst symptom of all, to reflect with little tremors on the fact that my mystic wealth could not, like the money for which other men threw it away, be stored up against my second childhood. The younger generation, reared in an enlightenment unknown to my schooldays, came knocking at the door too: I glanced back at my old columns and realized that I had timidly botched at thirty what newer men do now with gay confidence in their cradles. I listened to their vigorous knocks with exultation for the race, with penurious alarm for my own old age. When I talked to this generation, it called me Mister, and, with its frank, charming humanity, respected me as one who had done good work in my time. A famous playwright wrote a long play [Arthur Pinero, *The Princess and the Butterfly*, 1897] to shew that people of my age were on the shelf; and I laughed at him with the wrong side of my mouth.

It was at this bitter moment that my fellow citizens, who had previously repudiated all my offers of political service, contemptuously allowed me to become a vestryman:[3] *me*, the author of Widowers' Houses! Then, like any other harmless useful creature, I took the first step rearward. Up to that fateful day I had never penuriously spooned up the spilt drops of my well into bottles. Time enough for that when the well was empty. But now I listened to the voice of the publisher for the first time since he had refused to listen to mine. I turned over my articles again; but to serve up the weekly paper of five years ago as a novelty! no: I had not yet fallen so low, though I see that degradation looming before me as an agricultural laborer sees the workhouse. So I said "I will begin with small sins: I will publish my plays."

How! you will cry: plays! What plays?

Let me explain. One of the worst privations of life in London for persons of serious intellectual and artistic interests is the want of a suitable playhouse. I am fond of the play, and am, as intelligent readers of this preface will have observed, myself a bit of an actor. Consequently, when I found myself coming across projects of all sorts for the foundation of a theatre which should be to the newly gathered intellectual harvest of the XIX century what Shakespear's theatre was to the harvest of the Renascence, I was warmly interested. But it soon appeared that the languid demand of a small and uppish group for a form of entertainment which it had become thoroughly accustomed to do without, could never provide the intense energy necessary for the establishment of the New Theatre (we

3. Shaw was elected to the St Pancras Vestry in May 1897, serving as a vestryman and, later, as a borough councillor until October 1903.

of course called everything advanced "the New" at that time: see The
Philanderer, the second play in this volume). That energy could be set free
only by the genius of the actor and manager finding in the masterpieces of
the New Drama its characteristic and necessary mode of expression, and
revealing their fascination to the public. Clearly the way to begin was to
pick up a masterpiece or two. Masterpieces, however, do not grow on the
bushes. The New Theatre would never have come into existence but for
the plays of Ibsen, just as the Bayreuth Festival Playhouse would never
have come into existence but for Wagner's Nibelungen tetralogy. Every
attempt to extend the repertory proved that it is the drama that makes the
theatre and not the theatre the drama. Not that this needed fresh proof,
since the whole difficulty had arisen through the drama of the day being
written for the theatres instead of from its own inner necessity. Still, a
thing that nobody believes cannot be proved too often.

Ibsen, then, was the hero of the new departure. It was in 1889 that the
first really effective blow was struck by the production of A Doll's House
by Charles Charrington and Janet Achurch. Whilst they were taking that
epoch making play round the world, Mr Grein followed up the campaign
in London with his Independent Theatre. It got on its feet by producing
Ibsen's Ghosts; but its search for unacted native dramatic masterpieces was
so complete a failure that in the autumn of 1892 it had not yet produced a
single original piece of any magnitude by an English author. In this humiliating national emergency, I proposed to Mr Grein that he should boldly
announce a play by me. Being an extraordinarily sanguine and enterprising
man, he took this step without hesitation. I then raked out, from my
dustiest pile of discarded and rejected manuscripts, two acts of a play I had
begun in 1884, shortly after the close of my novel writing period, in
collaboration with my friend William Archer.

Archer has himself described how I proved the most impossible of
collaborators. Laying violent hands on his thoroughly planned scheme for a
sympathetically romantic "well made play" of the Parisian type then in
vogue, I perversely distorted it into a grotesquely realistic exposure of slum
landlordism, municipal jobbery, and the pecuniary and matrimonial ties
between them and the pleasant people with "independent" incomes who
imagine that such sordid matters do not touch their own lives. The result
was revoltingly incongruous; for though I took my theme seriously
enough, I did not then take the theatre quite seriously, even in taking it
more seriously than it took itself. The farcical trivialities in which I followed
the fashion of the times became silly and irritating beyond all endurance
when intruded upon a subject of such depth, reality, and force as that into

which I had plunged my drama. Archer, perceiving that I had played the fool both with his plan and my own theme, promptly disowned me; and the project, which neither of us had much at heart, was dropped, leaving me with two abortive acts of an unfinished and condemned play. Exhuming this as aforesaid eight years later, I saw that the very qualities which had made it impossible for ordinary commercial purposes in 1884 might be exactly those needed by the Independent Theatre in 1892. So I completed it by a third act; gave it the farfetched Scriptural title of Widowers' Houses; and handed it over to Mr Grein, who launched it at the public in the Royalty Theatre with all its original tomfooleries on its head. It made a sensation out of all proportion to its merits or even its demerits; and I at once became infamous as a playwright. The first performance was sufficiently exciting: the Socialists and Independents applauded me furiously on principle; the ordinary playgoing first-nighters hooted me frantically on the same ground; I, being at that time in some practice as what is impolitely called a mob orator, made a speech before the curtain; the newspapers discussed the play for a whole fortnight not only in the ordinary theatrical notices and criticisms, but in leading articles and letters; and finally the text of the play was published with an introduction by Mr Grein, an amusing account by Archer of the original collaboration, and a long preface and several elaborate controversial appendices in my most energetically egotistic fighting style. The volume, forming number one of the Independent Theatre series of plays, now extinct, is a curious relic of that nine days wonder; and as it contains the original text of the play with all its silly pleasantries, I can recommend it to collectors of quarto Hamlets, and of all those scarce and superseded early editions which the unfortunate author would so gladly annihilate if he could.

I had not achieved a success; but I had provoked an uproar; and the sensation was so agreeable that I resolved to try again. In the following year, 1893, when the discussion about Ibsenism, "the New Woman," and the like, was at its height, I wrote for the Independent Theatre the topical comedy called The Philanderer. But even before I finished it, it was apparent that its demands on the most expert and delicate sort of high comedy acting went beyond the resources then at the disposal of Mr Grein. I had written a part which nobody but Charles Wyndham[4] could act, in a play which was impossible at his theatre: a feat comparable to the building of

4. Wyndham had distinguished himself as a light comedian in such plays as James Albery's *The Pink Dominoes* (1877), R. C. Carton's *The Home Secretary* (1895), and Henry Arthur Jones's *The Liars* (1897).

Robinson Crusoe's first boat. I immediately threw it aside, and, returning to the vein I had worked in Widowers' Houses, wrote a third play, Mrs Warren's Profession, on a social subject of tremendous force. That force justified itself in spite of the inexperience of the playwright. The play was everything that the Independent Theatre could desire: rather more, if anything, than it bargained for. But at this point I came upon the obstacle that makes dramatic authorship intolerable in England to writers accustomed to the freedom of the Press. I mean, of course, the Censorship.

In 1737, Henry Fielding, the greatest practising dramatist, with the single exception of Shakespear, produced by England between the Middle Ages and the XIX century, devoted his genius to the task of exposing and destroying parliamentary corruption, then at its height. [The Prime Minister Robert] Walpole, unable to govern without corruption, promptly gagged the stage by a censorship which is in full force at the present moment. Fielding, driven out of the trade of Molière and Aristophanes, took to that of Cervantes; and since then the English novel has been one of the glories of literature, whilst the English drama has been its disgrace. The extinguisher which Walpole dropped on Fielding descends on me in the form of the Lord Chamberlain's Examiner of Plays, a gentleman who robs, insults, and suppresses me as irresistibly as if he were the Tsar of Russia and I the meanest of his subjects. The robbery takes the form of making me pay him two guineas for reading every play of mine that exceeds one act in length. I do not want him to read it (at least officially: personally he is welcome): on the contrary, I strenuously resent that impertinence on his part. But I must submit in order to obtain from him an insolent and insufferable document, which I cannot read without boiling of the blood, certifying that in his opinion—*his* opinion!—my play "does not in its general tendency contain anything immoral or otherwise improper for the stage," and that the Lord Chamberlain therefore "allows" its performance (confound his impudence!). In spite of this certificate he still retains his right, as an ordinary citizen, to prosecute me, or instigate some other citizen to prosecute me, for an outrage on public morals if he should change his mind later on. Besides, if he really protects the public against my immorality, why does not the public pay him for the service? The policeman does not look to the thief for his wages, but to the honest man whom he protects against the thief. And yet, if I refuse to pay, this tyrant can practically ruin any manager who produces my play in defiance of him. If, having been paid, he is afraid to license the play: that is, if he is more afraid of the clamor of the opponents of my opinions than of their supporters, then he can suppress it, and impose a mulct [a fine] of £50 on everybody who takes part in a representation of it, from the callboy to the principal tragedian. And there is no getting rid of him. Since he lives, not at the expense of the taxpayer, but by blackmailing the author, no political party would gain ten votes by abolishing him. Private political influence cannot touch him; for such private influence, moving only at the promptings of individual benevolence to individuals, makes nice little places to job nice little people into instead of doing away with them. Nay, I myself, though I know that the Examiner is necessarily an odious and mischievous official, and that if I were appointed to his post (which I shall probably apply for at the next vacancy) I could no more help being odious and mischievous than a ramrod could if it were stuck into the wheels of a steam engine, am loth to stir up the question lest the Press, having now lost all tradition of liberty, and being able to conceive no alternative to the Lord Chamberlain's Examiner than a Home Secretary's Examiner or some other sevenheaded devil to replace the oneheaded one, should make the remedy worse than the disease. Thus I cling to the Censorship as many Radicals cling to the House of Lords or the Throne, or as domineering women shun masterful men, and marry weak and amiable ones. Until the nation is prepared for Freedom of The Stage on the same terms as it now enjoys Freedom of The Press, by allowing the playwright and manager to perform anything they please and take the consequences before the ordinary law as authors and editors do, I shall cherish the Lord Chamberlain's Examiner as the apple of my eye. I once thought of organizing a Petition of Right from all the managers and authors to the Prime Minister; but as it was obvious that nine out of ten of these victims of oppression, far from daring to offend their despot, would promptly extol him as the most salutary of English institutions, and spread themselves with unctuous flattery on the perfectly irrelevant question of his estimable personal character, I abandoned the notion. What is more, many of them, in taking this safe course, would be pursuing a sound business policy, since the managers and authors to whom the existing system has brought success not only have no incentive to change it for another which would expose them to wider competition, but have for the most part the greatest dread of the "New" ideas which the abolition of the Censorship would let loose on the stage. And so long live the Lord Chamberlain's Examiner!

In 1893 this post was occupied by a gentleman [E. Smyth Pigott], now deceased, whose ideas had in the course of nature become quite obsolete. He was openly hostile to the New movement; and his evidence before the Select Committee of the House of Commons on Theatres and Places of Entertainment in 1892 (Blue Book No. 240, pp. 328–335) is probably the best compendium in existence of every fallacy that can make a Censor obnoxious. In dealing with him Mr Grein was at a heavy disadvantage. Without a license, Mrs Warren's Profession could only be performed in some building not a theatre, and therefore not subject to reprisals from the Lord Chamberlain. The audience would have to be invited as guests only; so that the support of the public paying money at the doors, a support with which the Independent Theatre could not afford to dispense, was out of the question. To apply for a license was to court a practically certain refusal, entailing the £50 penalty on all concerned in any subsequent performance whatever. The deadlock was complete. The play was ready; the Independent Theatre was ready; and the cast was ready; but the mere existence of the Censorship, without any action or knowledge of the play on its part, was sufficient to paralyze all these forces. So I threw Mrs Warren's Profession aside too, and, like another Fielding, closed my career as playwright in ordinary to the Independent Theatre.

Fortunately, though the Stage is bond, the Press is free. And even if the Stage were freed, none the less would it be necessary to publish plays as well as perform them. Had the two performances of Widowers' Houses achieved by Mr Grein been multiplied by fifty, it would still have remained unknown to those who either dwell out of reach of a theatre, or, as a matter of habit, prejudice, comfort, health or age, abstain altogether from playgoing. Many people who read with delight all the classic dramatists, from Eschylus to Ibsen, only go to the theatre on the rare occasions when they are offered a play by an author whose work they have already learnt to value as literature, or a performance by an actor of the first rank. Even our habitual playgoers have no true habit of playgoing. If on any night at the busiest part of the theatrical season in London, the audiences were cordoned by the police and examined individually as to their views on the subject, there would probably not be a single house-owning native among them who would not conceive a visit to the theatre, or indeed to any public assembly, artistic or political, as an exceptional way of spending an evening, the normal English way being to sit in separate families in separate houses, each person silently occupied with a book, a paper, or a game of halma,[5] cut off equally from the blessings of society and solitude. You may make the acquaintance of a thousand streets of middle-class English families without coming on a trace of any consciousness of citizenship, or any artistic cultivation of the senses. The condition of the men is bad enough, in spite of their daily escape into the city, because they carry the exclusive

5. Halma is a board game for two or four players, resembling Chinese checkers.

and unsocial habits of "the home" with them into the wider world of their business. Amiable and companionable enough by nature, they are, by home training, so incredibly ill-mannered, that not even their interest as men of business in welcoming a possible customer in every inquirer can correct their habit of treating everybody who has not been "introduced" as a stranger and intruder. The women, who have not even the city to educate them, are much worse: they are positively unfit for civilized intercourse: graceless, ignorant, narrow-minded to a quite appalling degree. In public places these homebred people cannot be taught to understand that the right they are themselves exercising is a common right. Whether they are in a second-class railway carriage or in a church, they receive every additional fellow-passenger or worshipper as a Chinaman receives the "foreign devil" who has forced him to open his ports.

In proportion as this horrible domestic institution is broken up by the active social circulation of the upper classes in their own orbit, or its stagnant isolation made impossible by the conditions of working class life, manners improve enormously. In the middle classes themselves the revolt of a single clever daughter (nobody has yet done justice to the modern clever Englishwoman's loathing of the very word Home), and her insistence on qualifying herself for an independent working life, humanizes her whole family in an astonishingly short time; and such communal enjoyments as a visit to the suburban theatre once a week, or to the Monday Popular Concerts, or both, softens the worst symptoms of its unsociableness. But none of these breaches in the English survival of the hareem can be made without a cannonade of books and pianoforte music. The books and music cannot be kept out, because they alone can make the hideous boredom of the hearth bearable. If its victims may not live real lives, they may at least read about imaginary ones, and perhaps learn from them to doubt whether a class that not only submits to home life, but actually boasts about it, is really a class worth belonging to. For the sake of the unhappy prisoners of the home, then, let my plays be printed as well as acted.

But the dramatic author has reasons for publishing his plays which would hold good even if English families went to the theatre as regularly as they take in the newspaper. A perfectly adequate and successful stage representation of a play requires a combination of circumstances so extraordinarily fortunate that I doubt whether it has ever occurred in the history of the world. Take the case of the most successful English dramatist of the first rank: Shakespear. Although he wrote three centuries ago, he still holds his own so well that it is not impossible to meet old playgoers who have witnessed public performances of more than thirty out of his thirty-seven reputed plays, a dozen of them fairly often, and half a dozen over and over again. I myself, though I have by no means availed myself of all my opportunities, have seen twenty-three of his plays publicly acted. But if I had not read them as well, my impression of them would be not merely incomplete, but violently distorted and falsified. It is only within the last few years that some of our younger actor-managers have been struck with the idea, quite novel in their profession, of performing Shakespear's plays as he wrote them, instead of using them as a cuckoo uses a sparrow's nest. In spite of the success of these experiments, the stage is still dominated by Garrick's conviction that the manager and actor must adapt Shakespear's plays to the modern stage by a process which no doubt presents itself to the adapter's mind as one of masterly amelioration, but which must necessarily be mainly one of debasement and mutilation whenever, as occasionally happens, the adapter is inferior to the author. The living author can protect himself against this extremity of misrepresentation; but the more unquestioned his authority is on the stage, and the more friendly and willing the co-operation of the manager and the company, the more completely does he get convinced of the impossibility of achieving an authentic representation of his piece as well as an effective and successful one. It is quite possible for a piece to enjoy the most sensational success on the basis of a complete misunderstanding of its philosophy: indeed, it is not too much to say that it is only by a capacity for succeeding in spite of its philosophy that a dramatic work of serious poetic import can become popular. In the case of the first part of Goethe's Faust we have this frankly avowed by the extraction from the great original of popular entertainments like Gounod's opera or the Lyceum version [by W. G. Wills], in which poetry and philosophy are replaced by romance, which is the recognized spurious substitute for both and is destructive of them. Not even when a drama is performed without omission or alteration by actors who are enthusiastic disciples of the author does it escape transfiguration. We have lately seen some remarkably sympathetic stage interpretations of poetic drama, from the experiments of Charles Charrington with Ibsen, and of [A. F.] Lugné Poe[6] with Maeterlinck, under comparatively inexpensive conditions, to those of the Wagner Festival Playhouse at Bayreuth on the costliest scale; and readers of Ibsen and Maeterlinck, and pianoforte students of Wagner, are rightly warned that they cannot fully appreciate the force of a dramatic masterpiece without the aid of the theatre. But I have never found an acquaintance with a dramatist founded on the theatre alone, or

6. French actor, founder and manager of the Théâtre de l'Œuvre in Paris.

with a composer founded on the concert room alone, a really intimate and accurate one. The very originality and genius of the performers conflicts with the originality and genius of the author. Imagine Shakespear confronted with Sir Henry Irving at a rehearsal of The Merchant of Venice,[7] or Sheridan with Miss Ada Rehan[8] at one of The School for Scandal. It is easy to imagine the speeches that might pass on such occasions. For example "As I look at your playing, Sir Henry, I seem to see Israel mourning the Captivity and crying, 'How long, O Lord, how long?' It is a little startling to see Shylock's strong feelings operating through a romantic intellect instead of through an entirely commercial one; but pray dont alter your conception, which will be abundantly profitable to us both." Or "My dear Miss Rehan: let me congratulate you on a piece of tragic acting which has made me ashamed of the triviality of my play, and obliterated Sir Peter Teazle from my consciousness, though I meant him to be the hero of the scene. I foresee an enormous success for both of us in this fortunate misrepresentation of my intention." Even if the author had nothing to gain pecuniarily by conniving at the glorification of his play by the performer, the actor's excess of power would still carry its own authority and win the sympathy of the author's histrionic instinct, unless he were a Realist of fanatical integrity. And that would not save him either; for his attempts to make powerful actors do less than their utmost would be as futile as his attempts to make feeble ones do more.

In short, the fact that a skilfully written play is infinitely more adaptable to all sorts of acting than available acting is to all sorts of plays (the actual conditions thus exactly reversing the desirable ones) finally drives the author to the conclusion that his own view of his work can only be conveyed by himself. And since he could not act the play singlehanded even if he were a trained actor, he must fall back on his powers of literary expression, as other poets and fictionists do. So far, this has hardly been seriously attempted by dramatists. Of Shakespear's plays we have not even complete prompt copies: the folio gives us hardly anything but the bare lines. What would we not give for the copy of Hamlet used by Shakespear at rehearsal, with the original stage business scrawled by the prompter's pencil? And if we had in addition the descriptive directions which the author gave on the stage: above all, the character sketches, however brief, by which he tried to

7. Irving had infuriated Shaw by distorting Shakespeare's text in his 1879 production of *The Merchant of Venice*.
8. A much admired actress, who was leading lady to Augustin Daly, another notorious embroiderer and distorter of the classics.

convey to the actor the sort of person he meant him to incarnate, what a light they would shed, not only on the play, but on the history of the XVI century! Well, we should have had all this and much more if Shakespear, instead of merely writing out his lines, had prepared the plays for publication in competition with fiction as elaborate as that of [George] Meredith.[9] It is for want of this elaboration that Shakespear, unsurpassed as poet, storyteller, character draughtsman, humorist, and rhetorician, has left us no intellectually coherent drama, and could not afford to pursue a genuinely scientific method in his studies of character and society, though in such unpopular plays as All's Well, Measure for Measure, and Troilus and Cressida, we find him ready and willing to start at the twentieth century if the XVII would only let him.

Such literary treatment is much more needed by modern plays than by Shakespear's, because in his time the acting of plays was very imperfectly differentiated from the declamation of verses; and descriptive or narrative recitation did what is now done by scenery, furniture, and stage business. Anyone reading the mere dialogue of an Elizabethan play understands all but half a dozen unimportant lines of it without difficulty; whilst many modern plays, highly successful on the stage, are not merely unreadable but positively unintelligible without visible stage business. Recitation on a platform, with the spectators seated round the reciter in the Elizabethan fashion, would reduce them to absurdity. The extreme instance is a pure pantomime, like L'Enfant Prodigue,[10] in which the dialogue, though it exists, is not spoken. If a dramatic author were to publish a pantomime, it is clear that he could make it intelligible to a reader only by giving him the words which the pantomimist is supposed to be uttering. Now it is not a whit less impossible to make a modern practical stage play intelligible to an audience by dialogue alone, than to make a pantomime intelligible to a reader without it.

Obvious as this is, the presentation of plays through the literary medium has not yet become an art; and the result is that it is very difficult to induce the English public to buy and read plays. Indeed, why should they, when they find nothing in them except the bare words, with a few carpenter's and costumier's directions as to the heroine's father having a grey beard, and the drawing room having three doors on the right, two doors and an

9. English novelist, poet and critic, who employed the novel as a vehicle for character analysis and constructive philosophy.
10. A musical play without words by Michel Carré, music by André Wormser, produced in London in 1891.

entrance through the conservatory on the left, and a French window in the middle? It is astonishing to me that Ibsen, devoting two years to the production of a three-act play, the extraordinary quality of which depends on a mastery of character and situation which can only be achieved by working out a good deal of the family and personal history of the individuals represented, should nevertheless give the reading public very little more than the technical memorandum required by the carpenter, the electrician, and the prompter. Who will deny that the resultant occasional mysteriousness of effect, enchanting though it may be, is produced at the cost of intellectual obscurity? Ibsen, interrogated as to his meaning, replied "What I have said, I have said." Precisely; but the point is that what he hasnt said, he hasnt said. There are perhaps people (though I doubt it, not being one of them myself) to whom Ibsen's plays, as they stand, speak sufficiently for themselves. There are certainly others who could not understand them on any terms. Granting that on both these classes further explanations would be thrown away, is nothing to be done for the vast majority to whom a word of explanation makes all the difference?

Finally, may I put in a plea for the actors themselves? Born actors have a susceptibility to dramatic emotion which enables them to seize the moods of their parts intuitively. But to expect them to be intuitive as to intellectual meaning and circumstantial conditions as well, is to demand powers of divination from them: one might as well expect the Astronomer Royal to tell the time in a catacomb. And yet the actor generally finds his part full of emotional directions which he could supply as well or better than the author, whilst he is left quite in the dark as to the political or religious conditions under which the character he impersonates is supposed to be acting. Definite conceptions of these are always implicit in the best plays, and are often the key to their appropriate rendering; but most actors are so accustomed to do without them that they would object to being troubled with them, although it is only by such educative trouble that an actor's profession can place him on the level of the lawyer, the physician, the churchman, and the statesman. Even as it is, Shylock as a Jew and usurer, Othello as a Moor and a soldier, Cæsar, Cleopatra and Antony as figures in defined political circumstances, are enormously more real to the actor than the countless heroes as to whom nothing is ever known except that they wear nice clothes, love the heroine, baffle the villain, and live happily ever after.

The case, then, is overwhelming not only for printing and publishing the dialogue of plays, but for a serious effort to convey their full content to the reader. This means the institution of a new art; and I daresay that before these two volumes are ten years old, the bald attempt they make at it will be left far behind, and that the customary brief and unreadable scene specification at the head of an act will have expanded into a chapter, or even a series of chapters. No doubt one result of this will be the production, under cover of the above arguments, of works of a mixture of kinds, part narrative, part homily, part description, part dialogue, and (possibly) part drama: works that could be read, but not acted. I have no objection to such works; but my own aim has been that of the practical dramatist: if anything my eye has been too much on the stage. At all events, I have tried to put down nothing that is irrelevant to the actor's performance, and, through it, to the audience's comprehension of the play. I have of course been compelled to omit many things that a stage representation could convey, simply because the art of letters, though highly developed grammatically, is still in its infancy as a technical speech notation: for example, there are fifty ways of saying Yes, and five hundred of saying No, but only one way of writing them down. Even the use of spaced letters instead of italics for underlining, though familiar to foreign readers, will have to be learned by the English public before it becomes effective. But if my readers do their fair share of the work, I daresay they will understand nearly as much of the plays as I do myself.

Finally, a word as to why I have labelled the three plays in this first volume Unpleasant. The reason is pretty obvious: their dramatic power is used to force the spectator to face unpleasant facts. No doubt all plays which deal sincerely with humanity must wound the monstrous conceit which it is the business of romance to flatter. But here we are confronted, not only with the comedy and tragedy of individual character and destiny, but with those social horrors which arise from the fact that the average homebred Englishman, however honorable and goodnatured he may be in his private capacity, is, as a citizen, a wretched creature who, whilst clamoring for a gratuitous millennium, will shut his eyes to the most villainous abuses if the remedy threatens to add another penny in the pound to the rates and taxes which he has to be half cheated, half coerced into paying. In Widowers' Houses I have shewn middle-class respectability and younger son gentility fattening on the poverty of the slum as flies fatten on filth. That is not a pleasant theme.

In The Philanderer I have shewn the grotesque sexual compacts made between men and women under marriage laws which represent to some of us a political necessity (especially for other people), to some a divine ordinance, to some a romantic ideal, to some a domestic profession for women, and to some that worst of blundering abominations, an institution which society has outgrown but not modified, and which "advanced"

individuals are therefore forced to evade. The scene with which The
Philanderer opens, the atmosphere in which it proceeds, and the marriage
with which it ends, are, for the intellectually and artistically conscious
classes in modern society, typical; and it will hardly be denied, I think, that
they are unpleasant.

In Mrs Warren's Profession I have gone straight at the fact that, as Mrs
Warren puts it, "the only way for a woman to provide for herself
decently is for her to be good to some man that can afford to be good to
her." There are certain questions on which I am, like most Socialists, an
extreme Individualist. I believe that any society which desires to found
itself on a high standard of integrity of character in its units should organize itself in such a fashion as to make it possible for all men and all
women to maintain themselves in reasonable comfort by their industry
without selling their affections and their convictions. At present we not
only condemn women as a sex to attach themselves to breadwinners,
licitly or illicitly, on pain of heavy privation and disadvantage; but we
have great prostitute classes of men: for instance, the playwrights and
journalists, to whom I myself belong, not to mention the legions of
lawyers, doctors, clergymen, and platform politicians who are daily using
their highest faculties to belie their real sentiments: a sin compared to
which that of a woman who sells the use of her person for a few hours is
too venial to be worth mentioning; for rich men without conviction are
more dangerous in modern society than poor women without chastity.
Hardly a pleasant subject, this!

I must, however, warn my readers that my attacks are directed against
themselves, not against my stage figures. They cannot too thoroughly understand that the guilt of defective social organization does not lie alone on the
people who actually work the commercial makeshifts which the defects
make inevitable, and who often, like Sartorius and Mrs Warren, display
valuable executive capacities and even high moral virtues in their administration, but with the whole body of citizens whose public opinion, public
action, and public contribution as ratepayers, alone can replace Sartorius's
slums with decent dwellings, Charteris's intrigues with reasonable marriage
contracts, and Mrs Warren's profession with honorable industries guarded
by a humane industrial code and a "moral minimum" wage.

How I came, later on, to write plays which, dealing less with the crimes
of society, and more with its romantic follies and with the struggles of
individuals against those follies, may be called, by contrast, Pleasant, is a
story which I shall tell on resuming this discourse for the edification of the
readers of the second volume.

Plays Pleasant

First published in 1898; amended in 1930

———

Readers of the discourse with which the preceding volume commences will remember that I turned my hand to playwriting when a great deal of talk about "the New Drama," followed by the actual establishment of a "New Theatre" (the Independent), threatened to end in the humiliating discovery that the New Drama, in England at least, was a figment of the revolutionary imagination. This was not to be endured. I had rashly taken up the case; and rather than let it collapse I manufactured the evidence.

Man is a creature of habit. You cannot write three plays and then stop. Besides, the New movement did not stop. In 1894, Florence Farr, who had already produced Ibsen's Rosmersholm, was placed in command of the Avenue Theatre in London for a season on the new lines by Miss A. E. F. Horniman,[1] who had family reasons for not yet appearing openly as a pioneer-manageress. There were, as available New Dramatists, myself, discovered by the Independent Theatre (at my own suggestion); Dr John Todhunter,[2] who had been discovered before (his play The Black Cat had been one of the Independent's successes); and Mr W. B. Yeats, a genuine discovery. Dr Todhunter supplied A Comedy of Sighs: Mr Yeats, The Land of Heart's Desire. I, having nothing but unpleasant plays in my desk, hastily completed a first attempt at a pleasant one, and called it Arms and the Man, taking the title from the first line of Dryden's Virgil. It passed for a success, the applause on the first night being as promising as could be wished; and it ran from the 21st of April to the 7th of July. To witness it the public paid £1777:5:6, an average of £23:2:5 per representation (including nine matinées). A publisher receiving £1700 for a book would have made a satisfactory profit: experts in West End theatrical management will contemplate that figure with a grim smile.

In the autumn of 1894 I spent a few weeks in Florence, where I occupied

1. Wealthy patron of theatre, remembered particularly for her financial backing of the Abbey Theatre, Dublin, beginning in 1904. In 1894, she hid her love of theatre from her Puritan family behind the management of Florence Farr.
2. Dublin physician and author of several inconsequential plays.

myself with the religious art of the Middle Ages and its destruction by the Renascence. From a former visit to Italy on the same business I had hurried back to Birmingham to discharge my duties as musical critic at the Festival there. On that occasion a very remarkable collection of the works of our British "pre-Raphaelite" painters was on view. I looked at these, and then went into the Birmingham churches to see the windows of William Morris and [Edward] Burne-Jones.[3] On the whole, Birmingham was more hopeful than the Italian cities; for the art it had to shew me was the work of living men, whereas modern Italy had, as far as I could see, no more connection with Giotto than Port Said has with Ptolemy.[4] Now I am no believer in the worth of any mere taste for art that cannot produce what it professes to appreciate. When my subsequent visit to Italy found me practising the playwright's craft, the time was ripe for a modern pre-Raphaelite play. Religion was alive again, coming back upon men, even upon clergymen, with such power that not the Church of England itself could keep it out. Here my activity as a Socialist had placed me on sure and familiar ground. To me the members of the Guild of St Matthew[5] were no more "High Church clergymen," Dr [John] Clifford[6] no more "an eminent Nonconformist divine," than I was to them "an infidel." There is only one religion, though there are a hundred versions of it. We all had the same thing to say; and though some of us cleared our throats to say it by singing revolutionary lyrics and republican hymns, we thought nothing of singing them to the music of [Arthur] Sullivan's Onward Christian Soldiers or Haydn's God Preserve the Emperor.

Now unity, however desirable in political agitations, is fatal to drama; for every drama must present a conflict. The end may be reconciliation or destruction; or, as in life itself, there may be no end; but the conflict is indispensable: no conflict, no drama. Certainly it is easy to dramatize the prosaic conflict of Christian Socialism with vulgar Unsocialism: for instance, in Widowers' Houses, the clergyman, who does not appear on the

3. Member of the Pre-Raphaelite Brotherhood and partner of Morris, both being noted for stained-glass designs.
4. Port Said, a seaport in Egypt founded in 1860 during the building of the Suez Canal, is contrasted with the antiquity of the Egyptian dynasty of the Ptolemies. Giotto di Bondone, Italian painter, is generally considered the leader of the early Renaissance in Italy.
5. Founded by The Revd Stewart D. Headlam, Christian-Socialist minister and Fabian, to support worthy social causes.
6. English Baptist minister, who directed church thought towards contemporary social problems.

stage at all, is the real antagonist of the slum landlord. But the obvious conflicts of unmistakeable good with unmistakeable evil can only supply the crude drama of villain and hero, in which some absolute point of view is taken, and the dissentients are treated by the dramatist as enemies to be piously glorified or indignantly vilified. In such cheap wares I do not deal. Even in my unpleasant propagandist plays I have allowed every person his or her own point of view, and have, I hope, to the full extent of my understanding of him, been as sympathetic with Sir George Crofts as with any of the more genial and popular characters in the present volume. To distil the quintessential drama from pre-Raphaelitism, medieval or modern, it must be shewn at its best in conflict with the first broken, nervous, stumbling attempts to formulate its own revolt against itself as it develops into something higher. A coherent explanation of any such revolt, addressed intelligibly and prosaically to the intellect, can only come when the work is done, and indeed *done with*: that is to say, when the development, accomplished, admitted, and assimilated, is a story of yesterday. Long before any such understanding can be reached, the eyes of men begin to turn towards the distant light of the new age. Discernible at first only by the eyes of the man of genius, it must be focussed by him on the speculum of a work of art, and flashed back from that into the eyes of the common man. Nay, the artist himself has no other way of making himself conscious of the ray: it is by a blind instinct that he keeps on building up his masterpieces until their pinnacles catch the glint of the unrisen sun. Ask him to explain himself prosaically, and you find that he "writes like an angel and talks like poor Poll,"[7] and is himself the first to make that epigram at his own expense. John Ruskin [in his *Modern Painters*, 1843–60] has told us clearly enough what is in the pictures of Carpaccio and Bellini: let him explain, if he can, where we shall be when the sun that is caught by the summits of the work of his favorite Tintoretto, of his aversion Rembrandt, of Mozart, of Beethoven and Wagner, of Blake and of Shelley, shall have reached the valleys. Let Ibsen explain, if he can, why the building of churches and happy homes is not the ultimate destiny of Man, and why, to thrill the unsatisfied younger generations, he must mount beyond it to heights that now seem unspeakably giddy and dreadful to him, and from which the first climbers must fall and dash themselves to pieces.[8] He cannot explain it:

7. 'Here lies Nolly Goldsmith, for shortness called Noll, / Who wrote like an angel, but talked like poor Poll': David Garrick's 'Impromptu Epitaph on Goldsmith'.
8. The allusion is to Ibsen's *The Master Builder*.

he can only shew it to you as a vision in the magic glass of his artwork; so that you may catch his presentiment and make what you can of it. And this is the function that raises dramatic art above imposture and pleasure hunting, and enables the playwright to be something more than a skilled liar and pandar.

Here, then, was the higher but vaguer and timider vision, the incoherent, mischievous, and even ridiculous unpracticalness, which offered me a dramatic antagonist for the clear, bold, sure, sensible, benevolent, salutarily shortsighted Christian Socialist idealism. I availed myself of it in Candida, the drunken scene in which has been much appreciated, I am told, in Aberdeen. I purposely contrived the play in such a way as to make the expenses of representation insignificant; so that, without pretending that I could appeal to a very wide circle of playgoers, I could reasonably sound a few of our more enlightened managers as to an experiment with half a dozen afternoon performances. They admired the play generously: indeed I think that if any of them had been young enough to play the poet, my proposal might have been acceded to, in spite of many incidental difficulties. Nay, if only I had made the poet a cripple, or at least blind, so as to combine an easier disguise with a larger claim for sympathy, something might have been done. Richard Mansfield,[9] who had, with apparent ease, made me quite famous in America by his productions of my plays, went so far as to put the play actually into rehearsal before he would confess himself beaten by the physical difficulties of the part. But they did beat him; and Candida did not see the footlights until my old ally the Independent Theatre, making a propagandist tour through the provinces with A Doll's House, added Candida to its repertory, to the great astonishment of its audiences.

In an idle moment in 1895 I began the little scene called The Man of Destiny, which is hardly more than a bravura piece to display the virtuosity of the two principal performers.

In the meantime I had devoted the spare moments of 1896 to the composition of two more plays, only the first of which appears in this volume. You Never Can Tell was an attempt to comply with many requests for a play in which the much paragraphed "brilliancy" of Arms and the Man should be tempered by some consideration for the requirements of managers in search of fashionable comedies for West End theatres. I had no difficulty in complying, as I have always cast my plays in the

9. American actor-manager, the first to present Shaw's plays in the United States (*Arms and the Man*, 1894, and *The Devil's Disciple*, 1897, both in New York).

ordinary practical comedy form in use at all the theatres; and far from taking an unsympathetic view of the popular preference for fun, fashionable dresses, a little music, and even an exhibition of eating and drinking by people with an expensive air, attended by an if-possible-comic waiter, I was more than willing to shew that the drama can humanize these things as easily as they, in the wrong hands, can dehumanize the drama. But as often happens it was easier to do this than to persuade those who had asked for it that they had indeed got it. A chapter in Cyril Maude's history of the Haymarket Theatre records how the play was rehearsed there, and why I withdrew it.[10] And so I reached the point at which, as narrated in the preface to the Unpleasant volume, I resolved to avail myself of my literary expertness to put my plays before the public in my own way.

It will be noticed that I have not been driven to this expedient by any hostility on the part of our managers. I will not pretend that the modern actor-manager's talent as player can in the nature of things be often associated with exceptional critical insight. As a rule, by the time a manager has experience enough to make him as safe a judge of plays as a Bond Street dealer is of pictures, he begins to be thrown out in his calculations by the slow but constant change of public taste, and by his own growing conservatism. But his need for new plays is so great, and the few accredited authors are so little able to keep pace with their commissions, that he is always apt to overrate rather than to underrate his discoveries in the way of new pieces by new authors. An original work by a man of genius like Ibsen may, of course, baffle him as it baffles many professed critics; but in the beaten path of drama no unacted works of merit, suitable to his purposes, have been discovered; whereas the production, at great expense, of very faulty plays written by novices (not "backers") is by no means an unknown event. Indeed, to anyone who can estimate, even vaguely, the complicated trouble, the risk of heavy loss, and the initial expense and thought, involved by the production of a play, the ease with which dramatic authors, known and unknown, get their works performed must needs seem a wonder.

10. Maude, actor-manager of the Haymarket Theatre, contracted in 1897 to present *You Never Can Tell*, with staging by Shaw. Unable to obtain the results he wanted, Shaw cancelled the production and the agreement in mid-rehearsal, later contributing anonymously the chapter on the fiasco published in Maude's *The Haymarket Theatre* (1903). The presence of this latter reference in a preface ostensibly composed in 1897 serves as reminder that Shaw frequently (and silently) amended his work for later editions whenever he felt the inclination to do so.

Only, authors must not expect managers to invest many thousands of pounds in plays, however fine (or the reverse), which will clearly not attract perfectly commonplace people. Playwriting and theatrical management, on the present commercial basis, are businesses like other businesses, depending on the patronage of great numbers of very ordinary customers. When the managers and authors study the wants of these customers, they succeed: when they do not, they fail. A public-spirited manager, or an author with a keen artistic conscience, may choose to pursue his business with the minimum of profit and the maximum of social usefulness by keeping as close as he can to the highest marketable limit of quality, and constantly feeling for an extension of that limit through the advance of popular culture. An unscrupulous manager or author may aim simply at the maximum of profit with the minimum of risk. These are the opposite poles of our system, represented in practice by our first rate managements at the one end, and the syndicates which exploit pornographic farces at the other. Between them there is plenty of room for most talents to breathe freely: at all events there is a career, no harder of access than any cognate career, for all qualified playwrights who bring the manager what his customers want and understand, or even enough of it to induce them to swallow at the same time a great deal that they neither want nor understand; for the public is touchingly humble in such matters.

For all that, the commercial limits are too narrow for our social welfare. The theatre is growing in importance as a social organ. Bad theatres are as mischievous as bad schools or bad churches; for modern civilization is rapidly multiplying the class to which the theatre is both school and church. Public and private life become daily more theatrical: the modern Kaiser, Dictator, President or Prime Minister is nothing if not an effective actor; all newspapers are now edited histrionically; and the records of our law courts shew that the stage is affecting personal conduct to an unprecedented extent, and affecting it by no means for the worse, except in so far as the theatrical education of the persons concerned has been romantic: that is, spurious, cheap, and vulgar. The truth is that dramatic invention is the first effort of man to become intellectually conscious. No frontier can be marked between drama and history or religion, or between acting and conduct, nor any distinction made between them that is not also the distinction between the masterpieces of the great dramatic poets and the commonplaces of our theatrical seasons. When this chapter of science is convincingly written, the national importance of the theatre will be as unquestioned as that of the army, the fleet, the Church, the law, and the schools.

For my part, I have no doubt that the commercial limits should be overstepped, and that the highest prestige, with a financial position of reasonable security and comfort, should be attainable in theatrical management by keeping the public in constant touch with the highest achievements of dramatic art. Our managers will not dissent to this: the best of them are so willing to get as near that position as they can without ruining themselves, that they can all point to honorable losses incurred through aiming "over the heads of the public," and will no doubt risk such loss again, for the sake of their reputation as artists, as soon as a few popular successes enable them to afford it. But even if it were possible for them to educate the nation at their own private cost, why should they be expected to do it? There are much stronger objections to the pauperization of the public by private doles than were ever entertained, even by the Poor Law Commissioners of 1834,[11] to the pauperization of private individuals by public doles. If we want a theatre which shall be to the drama what the National Gallery and British Museum are to painting and literature, we can get it by endowing it in the same way. In the meantime there are many possibilities of local activity. Groups of amateurs can form permanent societies and persevere until they develop into professional companies in established repertory theatres. In big cities it should be feasible to form influential committees, preferably without any actors, critics, or playwrights on them, and with as many persons of title as possible, for the purpose of approaching one of the leading local managers with a proposal that they shall, under a guarantee against loss, undertake a certain number of afternoon performances of the class required by the committee, in addition to their ordinary business. If the committee is influential enough, the offer will be accepted. In that case, the first performance will be the beginning of a classic repertory for the manager and his company which every subsequent performance will extend. The formation of the repertory will go hand in hand with the discovery and habituation of a regular audience for it; and it will eventually become profitable for the manager to multiply the number of performances at his own risk. It might even become worth his while to take a second theatre and establish the repertory permanently in it. In the event of any of his classic productions proving a fashionable success, he could transfer it to his fashionable house and make the most of it there. Such managership would carry a knighthood with it; and such a theatre

11. The objective of the Commission was to stop the immense expenses of caring for the poor by making it standard policy to assume that the indigent could become self-reliant.

would be the needed nucleus for municipal or national endowment. I make the suggestion quite disinterestedly; for as I am not an academic person, I should not be welcomed as an unacted classic by such a committee; and cases like mine would still leave forlorn hopes like the Independent Theatre its reason for existing. The committee plan, I may remind its critics, has been in operation in London for two hundred years in support of Italian opera.[12]

Returning now to the actual state of things, it is clear that I have no grievance against our theatres. Knowing quite well what I was doing, I have heaped difficulties in the way of the performance of my plays by ignoring the majority of the manager's customers: nay, by positively making war on them. To the actor I have been more considerate, using all my cunning to enable him to make the most of his technical methods; but I have not hesitated on occasion to tax his intelligence very severely, making the stage effect depend not only on *nuances* of execution quite beyond the average skill produced by the routine of the English stage in its present condition, but on a perfectly sincere and straightforward conception of states of mind which still seem cynically perverse to most people, and on a goodhumoredly contemptuous or profoundly pitiful attitude towards ethical conventions which seem to them validly heroic or venerable. It is inevitable that actors should suffer more than most of us from the sophistication of their consciousness by romance; and my view of romance as the great heresy to be swept off from art and life—as the food of modern pessimism and the bane of modern self-respect, is far more puzzling to the performers than it is to the pit. It is hard for an actor whose point of honor it is to be a perfect gentleman, to sympathize with an author who regards gentility as a dishonest folly, and gallantry and chivalry as treasonable to women and stultifying to men.

The misunderstanding is complicated by the fact that actors, in their demonstrations of emotion, have made a second nature of stage custom, which is often very much out of date as a representation of contemporary life. Sometimes the stage custom is not only obsolete, but fundamentally wrong: for instance, in the simple case of laughter and tears, in which it deals too liberally, it is certainly not based on the fact, easily enough discoverable in real life, that we only cry now in the effort to bear happiness,

12. Covent Garden depended on committees of wealthy patrons for fund-raising to meet its deficits, as well as encouraging wealthy individuals to become 'guarantors' of traditional opera by 'requiring an opera-box in the season just as they require a carriage' (Shaw, *Music in London*, 1931: Vol. I, p. 250).

whilst we laugh and exult in destruction, confusion, and ruin. When a comedy is performed, it is nothing to me that the spectators laugh: any fool can make an audience laugh. I want to see how many of them, laughing or grave, are in the melting mood. And this result cannot be achieved, even by actors who thoroughly understand my purpose, except through an artistic beauty of execution unattainable without long and arduous practice, and an intellectual effort which my plays probably do not seem serious enough to call forth.

Beyond the difficulties thus raised by the nature and quality of my work, I have none to complain of. I have come upon no ill will, no inaccessibility, on the part of the very few managers with whom I have discussed it. As a rule I find that the actor-manager is over-sanguine, because he has the artist's habit of underrating the force of circumstances and exaggerating the power of the talented individual to prevail against them; whilst I have acquired the politician's habit of regarding the individual, however talented, as having no choice but to make the most of his circumstances. I half suspect that those managers who have had most to do with me, if asked to name the main obstacle to the performance of my plays, would unhesitatingly and unanimously reply "The author." And I confess that though as a matter of business I wish my plays to be performed, as a matter of instinct I fight against the inevitable misrepresentation of them with all the subtlety needed to conceal my ill will from myself as well as from the manager.

The main difficulty, of course, is the incapacity for serious drama of thousands of playgoers of all classes whose shillings and half guineas will buy as much in the market as if they delighted in the highest art. But with them I must frankly take the superior position. I know that many managers are wholly dependent on them, and that no manager is wholly independent of them; but I can no more write what they want than Joachim[13] can put aside his fiddle and oblige a happy company of beanfeasters with a marching tune on the German concertina. They must keep away from my plays: that is all.

There is no reason, however, why I should take this haughty attitude towards those representative critics whose complaint is that my talent, though not unentertaining, lacks elevation of sentiment and seriousness of purpose. They can find, under the surface-brilliancy for which they give me credit, no coherent thought or sympathy, and accuse me, in various terms and degrees, of an inhuman and freakish wantonness; of preoccupation with "the seamy side of life"; of paradox, cynicism, and eccentricity,

13. Celebrated Hungarian violinist, a principal attraction at London concerts for nearly half a century.

reducible, as some contend, to a trite formula of treating bad as good and good as bad, important as trivial and trivial as important, serious as laughable and laughable as serious, and so forth. As to this formula I can only say that if any gentleman is simple enough to think that even a good comic opera can be produced by it, I invite him to try his hand, and see whether anything resembling one of my plays will reward him.

I could explain the matter easily enough if I chose; but the result would be that the people who misunderstand the plays would misunderstand the explanation ten times more. The particular exceptions taken are seldom more than symptoms of the underlying fundamental disagreement between the romantic morality of the critics and the natural morality of the plays. For example, I am quite aware that the much criticized Swiss officer in Arms and the Man is not a conventional stage soldier. He suffers from want of food and sleep; his nerves go to pieces after three days under fire, ending in the horrors of a rout and pursuit; he has found by experience that it is more important to have a few bits of chocolate to eat in the field than cartridges for his revolver. When many of my critics rejected these circumstances as fantastically improbable and cynically unnatural, it was not necessary to argue them into common sense: all I had to do was to brain them, so to speak, with the first half dozen military authorities at hand, beginning with the present Commander in Chief.[14] But when it proved that such unromantic (but all the more dramatic) facts implied to them a denial of the existence of courage, patriotism, faith, hope, and charity, I saw that it was not really mere matter of fact that was at issue between us. One strongly Liberal critic, the late Moy Thomas,[15] who had, in the teeth of a chorus of dissent, received my first play with the most generous encouragement, declared, when Arms and the Man was produced, that I had struck a wanton blow at the cause of liberty in the Balkan Peninsula by mentioning that it was not a matter of course for a Bulgarian in 1885 to wash his hands every day. He no doubt saw soon afterwards the squabble, reported all through Europe, between Stambouloff[16] and an eminent lady of the Bulgarian court who took

14. Garnet Joseph Wolseley, First Viscount, Commander-in-Chief of the British Army 1895–1901. In Shaw's essay 'A Dramatic Realist to His Critics' (*New Review*, July 1894) he cites Wolseley, who at the time was a field marshal.
15. English novelist and journalist. As dramatic critic of the *Daily News* and the *Graphic*, he was one of the few journalists in the early years who gave positive reviews to Shaw's plays.
16. Stefan Stambolov, premier of Bulgaria under Prince Ferdinand. A despotic ruler, he yet was considered to be the most remarkable man produced by modern Bulgaria.

exception to his neglect of his fingernails. After that came the news of his ferocious assassination, with a description of the room prepared for the reception of visitors by his widow, who draped it with black, and decorated it with photographs of the mutilated body of her husband. Here was a sufficiently sensational confirmation of the accuracy of my sketch of the theatrical nature of the first apings of western civilization by spirited races just emerging from slavery. But it had no bearing on the real issue between my critic and myself, which was, whether the political and religious idealism which had inspired Gladstone[17] to call for the rescue of these Balkan principalities from the despotism of the Turk, and converted miserably enslaved provinces into hopeful and gallant little States, will survive the general onslaught on idealism which is implicit, and indeed explicit, in Arms and the Man and the naturalist plays of the modern school. For my part I hope not; for idealism, which is only a flattering name for romance in politics and morals, is as obnoxious to me as romance in ethics or religion. In spite of a Liberal Revolution or two, I can no longer be satisfied with fictitious morals and fictitious good conduct, shedding fictitious glory on robbery, starvation, disease, crime, drink, war, cruelty, cupidity, and all the other commonplaces of civilization which drive men to the theatre to make foolish pretences that such things are progress, science, morals, religion, patriotism, imperial supremacy, national greatness and all the other names the newspapers call them. On the other hand, I see plenty of good in the world working itself out as fast as the idealists will allow it; and if they would only let it alone and learn to respect reality, which would include the beneficial exercise of respecting themselves, and incidentally respecting me, we should all get along much better and faster. At all events, I do not see moral chaos and anarchy as the alternative to romantic convention; and I am not going to pretend I do merely to please the people who are convinced that the world is held together only by the force of unanimous, strenuous, eloquent, trumpet-tongued lying. To me the tragedy and comedy of life lie in the consequences, sometimes terrible, sometimes ludicrous, of our persistent attempts to found our institutions on the ideals suggested to our imaginations by our half-satisfied passions, instead of on a genuinely scientific natural history. And with that hint as to what I am driving at, I withdraw and ring up the curtain.

17. Prime Minister of England (1868–74; 1880–85; 1886; 1892–4); author of *Bulgarian Horrors* (1876–7).

The Perfect Wagnerite

First published in 1898

===

This book is a commentary on The Niblung's Ring, Richard Wagner's chief work. I offer it to those enthusiastic admirers of Wagner who are unable to follow his ideas, and do not in the least understand the dilemma of Wotan, though they are filled with indignation at the irreverence of the Philistines who frankly avow that they find the remarks of the god too often tedious and nonsensical. Now to be devoted to Wagner merely as a dog is devoted to his master, sharing a few elementary ideas, appetites and emotions with him, and, for the rest, reverencing his superiority without understanding it, is no true Wagnerism. Yet nothing better is possible without a stock of ideas common to master and disciple. Unfortunately, the ideas of the revolutionary Wagner of 1848 are taught neither by the education nor the experience of English and American gentleman-amateurs, who are almost always political mugwumps, and hardly ever associate with revolutionists. The earlier attempts to translate his numerous pamphlets and essays into English resulted in ludicrous mixtures of pure nonsense with the absurdest distortions of his ideas into the ideas of the translators. We now have a translation which is a masterpiece of interpretation and an eminent addition to our literature; but that is not because its author, Mr [William] Ashton Ellis,[1] knows the German dictionary better than his predecessors. He is simply in possession of Wagner's ideas, which were to them inconceivable.

All I pretend to do in this book is to impart the ideas which are most likely to be lacking in the conventional Englishman's equipment. I came by them myself much as Wagner did, having learnt more about music than about anything else in my youth, and sown my political wild oats subsequently in the revolutionary school. This combination is not common in England; and as I seem, so far, to be the only publicly articulate result of it, I venture to add my commentary to what has

---

1. A physician who devoted himself to the translation into English of Richard Wagner's prose works.

already been written by musicians who are no revolutionists, and revolutionists who are no musicians.

PITFOLD, HINDHEAD, 1898.   G. B. S.

Fabianism and the Empire

A manifesto issued by the Fabian Society, edited by Shaw, 1900

———

As the word editor is not a term of precision, it is necessary to explain that it means, in this instance, only the draughtsman employed by the eight hundred members of the Fabian Society to produce their Election Manifesto. The Society is alive to the importance of making its utterances readable; and this can only be done by leaving the manner of their expression to a literary expert, and confining its dictation to the matter to be expressed.

Further, it will be understood that the greatest common measure of the opinions of eight hundred persons is not the same thing as the opinion of every individual member, and that on certain points a wholly dissentient minority has been small enough to submit to being voted down. For example, some members regard the South African expedition[1] as a foreseen and deliberate act on the part of the Government; and of these, some consider it a political crime, and others a justifiable stroke of Imperial Statesmanship. Again, on the point of Army Reform, many members disapprove so strongly of war that they desire it to be understood that they endorse the pages which follow on that subject only as a Tolstoyan opponent of our criminal system might nevertheless provisionally advocate prison reform, or as a vegetarian might advocate municipal abattoirs. There are Fabian teetotalers, too, who refuse to say anything more for the municipal public house than to admit, doubtfully and reluctantly, that it is a more controllable evil than a brewer's tied house,[2] and will not go even so far as that without an explicit affirmation that a more excellent way is not to have drinkshops of any sort. All reservations made, however, it may be taken that what is said in this Manifesto is what the great majority of the members of the Fabian Society desire to have said at the present moment.

It must not be inferred from the restriction of the Manifesto to the general lines of the reforms advocated that these have been but superficially

---

1. The English expedition into South Africa began on 11 October 1899 after rejection of a Boer ultimatum by the British Government.
2. A tavern under exclusive contract with a particular brewery.

considered. Our allusion to the Drink Question, for instance, clearly does not exhaust it, since a considerable interval of regulation of private enterprise lies between us and complete municipalization. But the tracts prepared by Mr Edward Pease,[3] and already issued by the Society, supply the lacking proposals. Again, the inevitableness of the Minimum Wage, which is no mere theoretic remedy, but the irresistible conclusion from a century of labor organization, has come out in the course of a unique investigation, the most elaborate and severe yet undertaken by individual Fabians, by Mr & Mrs Sidney Webb. It is recorded in their volumes entitled The History of Trade Unionism and Industrial Democracy. The suggestion as to the provision of a Militia by raising the half-time age was first mooted by them in a letter to The Times last year. The important proposals as to the consular service are the outcome of a series of discussions initiated by Mr S. G. Hobson,[4] who was the first Fabian to see the value, as an illustration of the need for State organization of foreign trade, of the contrast between the imbecility and paralysis of English commercial diplomacy in the valley of the Yang-tse, and the victorious alertness and efficiency of Russia.[5] As to Municipal Trading, those who are not yet alive to the fact that we are in the throes of a struggle—quite as important as the South African one— between the new local authorities, representing the citizenship of England, and the company promoters, for the control of our common life industries, will find in the Fabian tract on The Economics of Direct Employment, and that on The Growth of Monopoly by Mr H. W. Macrosty,[6] a mass of facts which cannot be detailed in an Election Manifesto. The elector who votes in ignorance of these facts will vote on assumptions which, though they are unfortunately still the prevalent assumptions of our educated classes, have long ceased to have any relation to contemporary reality.

For many valuable amendments and certain chastening criticisms, I am indebted to several members of the Society; but those named above, with Mr Gilbert Slater,[7] have contributed as well as criticized.

3. Founder-member and long-serving secretary of the Fabian Society.
4. Member of the Fabian Society since 1891, on its Executive Committee 1900–1909, when he resigned from the Society in protest over its policies.
5. A reference to the Russian, German and English attempts to establish spheres of influence in China. In October 1899 Britain signed a convention with Germany to maintain an open-door policy in the Yang-tse Valley, while Russia remained free to establish a monopoly in Manchuria.
6. Director of the first Census of Production, member of the Fabian Executive 1898–1907, and author of eight Fabian tracts.
7. Fabian economist, who later wrote Currency, Credit and the Unemployment Crisis,

One of the reasons for issuing this Manifesto in the form of a shilling book is that the custom of the Society, which is to sell for a penny a quantity of literary matter and political and statistical information which could not be commercially produced and sold for less than half-a-crown, has resulted in an undue specialization of its market. The richer classes in England read nothing but what their booksellers sell; and booksellers cannot afford to sell penny pamphlets. It is one of the oddities of our competitive system that, out of the multitude of useful things that are sold for a penny, the millionaire can only obtain the penny stamp and the penny newspaper: if he wants the penny Fabian Tract he must either join one of the political or social organizations by which such wares are distributed (and their articles of faith are seldom such as a conscientious millionaire can subscribe), or else the Society must come to his rescue by charging him at least a shilling. It does so in this instance with many apologies for the smallness of the sum, which is, nevertheless, an exclusive one—how exclusive the reader will best appreciate after a reference to our Facts for Socialists,[8] facts which unfortunately remain facts from edition to edition, in spite of our sixteen years' struggle to awaken social compunction concerning them.

G. B. S.

Fabian Tract No. 239 (1932) and *The Growth of Modern England* (1932).
8. Fabian Tract No. 5 (1887) by Sidney Webb. In it distinguished British statisticians are cited to prove the scandalous injustice in the distribution of British wealth and – by implication – the drastic transformation that reform must implement.

Love among the Artists

Prefatory letter: 'The Author to the Reader'
first published in 1900

Dear Sir or Madam:

Will you allow me a word of personal explanation now that I am, for the second time, offering you a novel which is not the outcome of my maturer experience and better sense? If you have read my Irrational Knot to the bitter end, you will not accuse me of mock modesty when I admit that it was very long; that it did not introduce you to a single person you could conceivably have been glad to know; and that your knowledge of the world must have forewarned you that no satisfactory ending was possible. You may, it is true, think that a story teller should not let a question of mere possibility stand between his audience and the satisfaction of a happy ending. Yet somehow my conscience stuck at it; for I am not a professional liar: I am even ashamed of the extent to which in my human infirmity I have been an amateur one. No: my stories were meant to be true *ex hypothesi* [according to the hypothesis]: the persons were fictitious; but had they been real, they must (or so I thought at the time) have acted as I said. For, if you can believe such a prodigy, I was but an infant of twenty-four when, being at that time one of the unemployed, I sat down to mend my straitened fortunes by writing The Irrational Knot. I had done the same thing once before; and next year, still unemployed, I did it again. That third attempt of mine is about to see the light in this volume. And now a few words of warning to you before you begin it.

1. Though the wisdom of the book is the fruit of a quarter century's experience, yet the earlier years of that period were much preoccupied with questions of bodily growth and nutrition; so that it may be as well to bear in mind that "even the youngest of us may be wrong sometimes."[1]

2. Love among the Artists is what is called a novel with a purpose. I will

---

1. Variation of a remark, 'We are none of us infallible – not even the youngest of us', made in 1878 by W. H. Thompson, Master of Trinity College, Cambridge, in reference to a junior fellow, the Rt. Hon. Gerald William Balfour, later Second Earl of Balfour.

not undertake to say at this distance of time what the main purpose was; but I remember that I had a notion of illustrating the difference between that enthusiasm for the fine arts which people gather from reading about them, and the genuine artistic faculty which cannot help creating, interpreting, or at least unaffectedly enjoying music and pictures. 3. This book has no winding-up at the end. Mind: it is not, as in The Irrational Knot, a case of the upshot being unsatisfactory! There is absolutely no upshot at all. The parties are married in the middle of the book; and they do not elope with or divorce one another, or do anything unusual or improper. When as much is told concerning them as seemed to me at the time germane to my purpose, the novel breaks off. But if you prefer something more conclusive, pray do not scruple to add a final chapter of your own invention. 4. If you find yourself displeased with my story, remember that it is not I, but the generous and appreciative publisher of the book, who puts it forward as worth reading.

I shall polish it up for you the best way I can, and here and there remove some absurdity out of which I have grown since I wrote it, but I cannot substantially improve it, much less make it what a novel ought to be; for I have given up novel writing these many years, during which I have lost the impudence of the apprentice without gaining the skill of the master.

There is an end to all things, even to stocks of unpublished manuscript. It may be a relief to you to know that when this Love among the Artists shall have run its course, you need apprehend no more furbished-up early attempts at fiction from me. I have written but five novels in my life; and of these there will remain then unpublished only the first—a very remarkable work, I assure you, but hardly one which I should be well advised in letting loose whilst my livelihood depends on my credit as a literary workman.

I can recall a certain difficulty, experienced even whilst I was writing the book, in remembering what it was about. Twice I clean forgot the beginning, and had to read back, as I might have read any other man's novel, to learn the story. If I could not remember then, how can I presume on my knowledge of the book now so far as to make promises about it? But I suspect you will find yourself in less sordid company than that into which The Irrational Knot plunged you. And I can guarantee you against any plot. You will be candidly dealt with. None of the characters will turn out to be somebody else in the last chapter: no violent accidents or strokes of pure luck will divert events from their normal course: [no] forger, long lost heir, detective, nor any commonplace of the police court or of the realm of romance shall insult your understanding, or tempt you to read on when you might better be in bed or attending to your business.

By this time you should be eager to be at the story. Meanwhile I must not forget that it is only by your exceptional indulgence that I have been suffered to detain you so long about a personal matter; and so I thank you and proceed to business.

29, FITZROY SQUARE, LONDON, W.

Three Plays for Puritans

First published in 1901

═══

WHY FOR PURITANS?

Since I gave my Plays, Pleasant and Unpleasant, to the world two years ago, many things have happened to me. I had then just entered on the fourth year of my activity as a critic of the London theatres. They very nearly killed me. I had survived seven years of London's music, four or five years of London's pictures, and about as much of its current literature, wrestling critically with them with all my force and skill. After that, the criticism of the theatre came to me as a huge relief in point of bodily exertion. The difference between the leisure of a Persian cat and the labor of a cockney cab horse is not greater than the difference between the official weekly or fortnightly playgoings of the theatre critic and the restless daily rushing to and fro of the music critic, from the stroke of three in the afternoon, when the concerts begin, to the stroke of twelve at night, when the opera ends. The pictures were nearly as bad. An Alpinist once, noticing the massive soles of my boots, asked me whether I climbed mountains. No, I replied: these boots are for the hard floors of the London galleries. Yet I once dealt with music and pictures together in the spare time of an active young revolutionist, and wrote plays and books and other toilsome things into the bargain. But the theatre struck me down like the veriest weakling. I sank under it like a baby fed on starch. My very bones began to perish, so that I had to get them planed and gouged by accomplished surgeons.[1] I fell from heights and broke my limbs in pieces. The doctors said: This man has not eaten meat for twenty years: he must eat it or die. I said: This man has been going to the London theatres for three years; and the soul of him has become inane and is feeding unnaturally on his body. And I was right. I did not change my diet; but I had myself carried up into a mountain where there was no theatre; and there I began to revive. Too weak to work, I wrote books and plays: hence the second

1. For most of 1898 Shaw suffered from a necrosed bone in his foot, over which a number of surgeons laboured.

and third plays in this volume. And now I am stronger than I have been at any moment since my feet first carried me as a critic across the fatal threshold of a London playhouse.

Why was this? What is the matter with the theatre, that a strong man can die of it? Well, the answer will make a long story; but it must be told. And, to begin, why have I just called the theatre a playhouse? The well-fed Englishman, though he lives and dies a schoolboy, cannot play. He cannot even play cricket or football: he has to work at them: that is why he beats the foreigner who plays at them. To him playing means playing the fool. He can hunt and shoot and travel and fight: he can, when special holiday festivity is suggested to him, eat and drink, dice and drab [go wenching], smoke and lounge. But play he cannot. The moment you make his theatre a place of amusement instead of a place of edification, you make it, not a real playhouse, but a place of excitement for the sportsman and the sensualist.

However, this well-fed grown-up-schoolboy Englishman counts for little in the modern metropolitan audience. In the long lines of waiting playgoers lining the pavements outside our fashionable theatres every evening, the men are only the currants in the dumpling. Women are in the majority; and women and men alike belong to that least robust of all our social classes, the class which earns from eighteen to thirty shillings a week in sedentary employment, and lives in lonely lodgings or in drab homes with nagging relatives. These people preserve the innocence of the theatre: they have neither the philosopher's impatience to get to realities (reality being the one thing they want to escape from), nor the longing of the sportsman for violent action, nor the full-fed, experienced, disillusioned sensuality of the rich man, whether he be gentleman or sporting publican. They read a good deal, and are at home in the fool's paradise of popular romance. They love the pretty man and the pretty woman, and will have both of them fashionably dressed and exquisitely idle, posing against backgrounds of drawing room and dainty garden; in love, but sentimentally, romantically; always ladylike and gentlemanlike. Jejunely insipid, all this, to the stalls, which are paid for (when they *are* paid for) by people who have their own dresses and drawing rooms, and know them to be a mere masquerade behind which there is nothing romantic, and little that is interesting to most of the masqueraders except the clandestine play of natural licentiousness.

The stalls cannot be fully understood without taking into account the absence of the rich evangelical English merchant and his family, and the presence of the rich Jewish merchant and *his* family. I can see no validity whatever in the view that the influence of the rich Jews on the theatre is any worse than the influence of the rich of any other race. Other qualities being equal, men become rich in commerce in proportion to the intensity and exclusiveness of their desire for money. It may be a misfortune that the purchasing power of men who value money above art, philosophy, and the welfare of the whole community, should enable them to influence the theatre (and everything else in the market); but there is no reason to suppose that their influence is any nobler when they imagine themselves Christians than when they know themselves Jews. All that can fairly be said of the Jewish influence on the theatre is that it is exotic, and is not only a customer's influence but a financier's influence: so much so, that the way is smoothest for those plays and those performers that appeal specially to the Jewish taste. English influence on the theatre, as far as the stalls are concerned, does not exist, because the rich purchasing-powerful Englishman prefers politics and church-going: his soul is too stubborn to be purged by an avowed make-believe. When he wants sensuality he practises it: he does not play with voluptuous or romantic ideas. From the play of ideas—and the drama can never be anything more—he demands edification, and will not pay for anything else in that arena. Consequently the box office will never become an English influence until the theatre turns from the drama of romance and sensuality to the drama of edification.

Turning from the stalls to the whole auditorium, consider what is implied by the fact that the prices (all much too high, by the way) range from half a guinea to a shilling, the ages from eighteen to eighty, whilst every age, and nearly every price, represents a different taste. Is it not clear that this diversity in the audience makes it impossible to gratify every one of its units by the same luxury, since in that domain of infinite caprice, one man's meat is another man's poison, one age's longing another age's loathing? And yet that is just what the theatres kept trying to do almost all the time I was doomed to attend them. On the other hand, to interest people of divers ages, classes, and temperaments by some generally momentous subject of thought, as the politicians and preachers do, would seem the most obvious course in the world. And yet the theatres avoided that as a ruinous eccentricity. Their wiseacres persisted in assuming that all men have the same tastes, fancies, and qualities of passion; that no two have the same interests; and that most playgoers have no interests at all. This being precisely contrary to the obvious facts, it followed that the majority of the plays produced were failures, recognizable as such before the end of the first act by the very wiseacres aforementioned, who, quite incapable of understanding the lesson, would thereupon set to work to obtain and produce a play applying their theory still more strictly, with proportionately more disastrous results. The sums of money I saw thus transferred from the pockets of theatrical speculators and syndicates to those of wigmakers, costumiers, scene painters, carpenters, doorkeepers, actors, theatre landlords, and all the other people for whose exclusive benefit most London theatres seem to exist, would have kept a theatre devoted exclusively to the highest drama open all the year round. If the Browning and Shelley Societies were fools, as the wiseacres said they were, for producing Strafford, Colombe's Birthday, and The Cenci; if the Independent Theatre, the New Century Theatre, and the Stage Society are impracticable faddists for producing the plays of Ibsen and Maeterlinck,[2] then what epithet is contemptuous enough for the people who produce the would-be popular plays?

The actor-managers were far more successful, because they produced plays that at least pleased themselves, whereas Commerce, with a false theory of how to please everybody, produced plays that pleased nobody. But their occasional personal successes in voluptuous plays, and, in any case, their careful concealment of failure, confirmed the prevalent error, which was exposed fully only when the plays had to stand or fall openly by their own merits. Even Shakespear was played with his brains cut out. In 1896, when Sir Henry Irving was disabled by an accident at a moment when Miss Ellen Terry was too ill to appear, the theatre had to be closed after a brief attempt to rely on the attraction of a Shakespearean play performed by the stock company. This may have been Shakespear's fault: indeed Sir Henry later on complained that he had lost a princely sum by Shakespear. But Shakespear's reply to this, if he were able to make it, would be that the princely sum was spent, not on his dramatic poetry, but on a gorgeous stage ritualism superimposed on reckless mutilations of his text, the whole being addressed to a public as to which nothing is certain except that its natural bias is towards reverence for Shakespear and dislike and distrust of ritualism. No doubt the Irving ritual appealed to a far more cultivated sensuousness and imaginativeness than the musical farces in which

2. *Strafford* (1837), a tragedy by Robert Browning, was staged by the Browning Society in 1886. *Colombe's Birthday* (1844), also by Browning, was presented by the Society in 1885. *The Cenci* (1819), a tragedy by Percy Bysshe Shelley, was staged by the Shelley Society in 1886. The Incorporated Stage Society, which presented many first performances of Shaw's plays during its forty-year existence (1899–1939), was an offshoot of the Independent Theatre. The New Century Theatre (1897–1904) offered only four productions. All of these groups were private subscription societies, legally able to avoid restrictions of the censor.

our stage Abbots of Misrule[3] pontificated (with the same financially disastrous result); but in both there was the same intentional brainlessness, founded on the same theory that the public did not want brains, did not want to think, did not want anything but pleasure at the theatre. Unfortunately, this theory happens to be true of a certain section of the public. This section, being courted by the theatres, went to them and drove the other people out. It then discovered, as any expert could have foreseen, that the theatre cannot compete in mere pleasuremongering either with the other arts or with matter-of-fact gallantry. Stage pictures are the worst pictures, stage music the worst music, stage scenery the worst scenery within reach of the Londoner. The leading lady or gentleman may be as tempting to the admirer in the pit as the dishes in a cookshop window are to the penniless tramp on the pavement; but people do not, I presume, go to the theatre to be merely tantalized.

The breakdown on the last point was conclusive. For when the managers tried to put their principle of pleasing everybody into practice, Necessity, ever ironical towards Folly, had driven them to seek a universal pleasure to appeal to. And since many have no ear for music or eye for color, the search for universality inevitably flung the managers back on the instinct of sex as the avenue to all hearts. Of course the appeal was a vapid failure. Speaking for my own sex, I can say that the leading lady was not to everybody's taste: her pretty face often became ugly when she tried to make it expressive; her voice lost its charm (if it ever had any) when she had nothing sincere to say; and the stalls, from racial prejudice, were apt to insist on more Rebecca and less Rowena[4] than the pit cared for. It may seem strange, even monstrous, that a man should feel a constant attachment to the hideous witches in Macbeth, and yet yawn at the prospect of spending another evening in the contemplation of a beauteous young leading lady with voluptuous contours and longlashed eyes, painted and dressed to perfection in the latest fashions. But that is just what happened to me in the theatre.

I did not find that matters were improved by the lady pretending to be "a woman with a past," violently oversexed, or the play being called a problem play, even when the manager, and sometimes, I suspect, the very

3. The Abbot of Misrule was the 'King' of the Christmas revels (late fifteenth and early sixteenth centuries), who lorded over the proceedings with unreasonable abandon.
4. Rebecca and Rowena, Jewish and Christian maidens in Scott's *Ivanhoe* (1820): a reminder that stalls patrons in London consisted predominantly of prosperous bourgeois Jews.

author, firmly believed the word problem to be the latest euphemism for what Justice Shallow called a bona roba,[5] and certainly would not either of them have staked a farthing on the interest of a genuine problem. In fact these so-called problem plays invariably depended for their dramatic interest on foregone conclusions of the most heartwearying conventionality concerning sexual morality. The authors had no problematic views: all they wanted was to capture some of the fascination of Ibsen. It seemed to them that most of Ibsen's heroines were naughty ladies. And they tried to produce Ibsen plays by making their heroines naughty. But they took great care to make them pretty and expensively dressed. Thus the pseudo-Ibsen play was nothing but the ordinary sensuous ritual of the stage become as frankly pornographic as good manners allowed.

I found that the whole business of stage sensuousness, whether as Lyceum Shakespear, musical farce, or sham Ibsen, finally disgusted me, not because I was Pharisaical, or intolerantly refined, but because I was bored; and boredom is a condition which makes men as susceptible to disgust and irritation as headache makes them to noise and glare. Being a man, I have my share of the masculine silliness and vulgarity on the subject of sex which so astonishes women, to whom sex is a serious matter. I am not an archbishop, and do not pretend to pass my life on one plane or in one mood, and that the highest: on the contrary, I am, I protest, as accessible to the humors of The Rogue's Comedy or The Rake's Progress as to the pious decencies of The Sign of the Cross.[6] Thus Falstaff, coarser than any of the men in our loosest plays, does not bore me: Doll Tearsheet,[7] more abandoned than any of the women, does not shock me. I admit that Romeo and Juliet would be a duller play if it were robbed of the solitary fragment it has preserved for us of the conversation of the husband of Juliet's nurse. No: my disgust was not mere thinskinned prudery. When my moral sense revolted, as it often did to the very fibres, it was invariably at the nauseous compliances of the theatre with conventional virtue. If I despised the musical farces, it was because they never had the courage of their vices. With all their labored efforts to keep up an understanding of furtive naughtiness between the low comedian on the stage and the drunken undergraduate in the stalls, they insisted all the time on their virtue and

5. A 'bona roba' is a showy prostitute. Justice Shallow declares in Shakespeare's *Henry IV, Part 2* (III: ii) that 'we knew where the bona-robas were'.
6. *The Rogue's Comedy* (1896) is by Henry Arthur Jones; *The Rake's Progress* (1837) by W. Leman Rede; *The Sign of the Cross* (1895) by Wilson Barrett.
7. Falstaff's frowsy companion in *Henry IV, Part 2*.

patriotism and loyalty as pitifully as a poor girl of the pavement will pretend to be a clergyman's daughter. True, I may have been offended when a manager, catering for me with coarse frankness as a slave dealer caters for a Pasha, invited me to forget the common bond of humanity between me and his company by demanding nothing from them but a gloatably voluptuous appearance. But this extreme is never reached at our better theatres. The shop assistants, the typists, the clerks, who, as I have said, preserve the innocence of the theatre, would not dare to let themselves be pleased by it. Even if they did, they would not get it from our reputable managers, who, when faced with the only logical conclusion from their principle of making the theatre a temple of pleasure, indignantly refuse to change the theatrical profession for Mrs Warren's. For that is what all this demand for pleasure at the theatre finally comes to; and the answer to it is, not that people ought not to desire sensuous pleasure (they cannot help it) but that the theatre cannot give it to them, even to the extent permitted by the honor and conscience of the best managers, because a theatre is so far from being a pleasant or even a comfortable place that only by making us forget ourselves can it prevent us from realizing its inconveniences. A play that does not do this for the pleasure-seeker allows him to discover that he has chosen a disagreeable and expensive way of spending the evening. He wants to drink, to smoke, to change the spectacle, to get rid of the middle-aged actor and actress who are boring him, and to see shapely young dancing girls and acrobats doing more amusing things in a more plastic manner. In short, he wants the music hall; and he goes there, leaving the managers astonished at this unexpected but quite inevitable result of the attempt to please him. Whereas, had he been enthralled by the play, even with horror, instead of himself enthralling with the dread of his displeasure the manager, the author and the actors, all had been well. And so we must conclude that the theatre is a place which people can endure only when they forget themselves: that is, when their attention is entirely captured, their interest thoroughly aroused, their sympathies raised to the eagerest readiness, and their selfishness utterly annihilated. Imagine, then, the result of conducting theatres on the principle of appealing exclusively to the instinct of self-gratification in people without power of attention, without interests, without sympathy: in short, without brains or heart. That is how they were conducted whilst I was writing about them; and that is how they nearly killed me.

Yet the managers mean well. Their self-respect is in excess rather than in defect; for they are in full reaction against the Bohemianism of past generations of actors, and so bent on compelling social recognition by a blameless respectability, that the drama, neglected in the struggle, is only just beginning to stir feebly after standing still in England from Tom Robertson's time in the sixties until the first actor was knighted in the nineties [Henry Irving, in 1895]. The manager may not want good plays; but he does not want bad plays: he wants nice ones. Nice plays, with nice dresses, nice drawing rooms and nice people, are indispensable: to be ungenteel is worse than to fail. I use the word ungenteel purposely; for the stage presents life on thirty pounds a day, not as it is, but as it is conceived by the earners of thirty shillings a week. The real thing would shock the audience exactly as the manners of the public school and university shock a Board of Guardians. In just the same way, the plays which constitute the genuine aristocracy of modern dramatic literature shock the reverence for gentility which governs our theatres today. For instance, the objection to Ibsen is not really an objection to his philosophy: it is a protest against the fact that his characters do not behave as ladies and gentlemen are popularly supposed to behave. If you adore Hedda Gabler in real life, if you envy her and feel that nothing but your poverty prevents you from being as exquisite a creature, if you know that the accident of matrimony (say with an officer of the guards who falls in love with you across the counter whilst you are reckoning the words in his telegram) may at any moment put you in her place, Ibsen's exposure of the worthlessness and meanness of her life is cruel and blasphemous to you. This point of view is not caught by the clever ladies of Hedda's own class, who recognize the portrait, applaud its painter, and think the fuss against Ibsen means nothing more than the conventional disapproval of her discussions of a *ménage à trois* with Judge Brack. A little experience of popular plays would soon convince these clever ladies that a heroine who atones in the last act by committing suicide may do all the things that Hedda only talked about, without a word of remonstrance from the press or the public. It is not murder, not adultery, not rapine that is objected to: quite the contrary. It is an unladylike attitude towards life: in other words, a disparagement of the social ideals of the poorer middle class and of the vast reinforcements it has had from the working class during the last twenty years. Let but the attitude of the author be gentlemanlike, and his heroines may do what they please. Mrs Tanqueray was received with delight by the public: Saint Teresa would have been hissed off the same stage for her contempt for the ideal represented by a carriage, a fashionable dressmaker, and a dozen servants.

Here, then, is a pretty problem for the manager. He is convinced that plays must depend for their dramatic force on appeals to the sex instinct; and yet he owes it to his own newly conquered social position that they shall be perfectly genteel plays, fit for churchgoers. The sex instinct must therefore proceed upon genteel assumptions. Impossible! you will exclaim. But you are wrong: nothing is more astonishing than the extent to which, in real life, the sex instinct does so proceed, even when the consequence is its lifelong starvation. Few of us have vitality enough to make any of our instincts imperious: we can be made to live on pretences, as the masterful minority well know. But the timid majority, if it rules nowhere else, at least rules in the theatre: fitly enough too, because on the stage pretence is all that can exist. Life has its realities behind its shows: the theatre has nothing but its shows. But can the theatre make a show of lovers' endearments? A thousand times no: perish the thought of such unladylike, ungentlemanlike exhibitions. You can have fights, rescues, conflagrations, trials-at-law, avalanches, murders and executions all directly simulated on the stage if you will. But any such realistic treatment of the incidents of sex is quite out of the question. The singer, the dramatic dancer, the exquisite declaimer of impassioned poesy, the rare artist who, bringing something of the art of all three to the ordinary work of the theatre, can enthral an audience by the expression of dramatic feeling alone, may take love for a theme on the stage; but the prosaic walking gentleman of our fashionable theatres, realistically simulating the incidents of life, cannot touch it without indecorum.

Can any dilemma be more complete? Love is assumed to be the only theme that touches all your audience infallibly, young and old, rich and poor. And yet love is the one subject that the drawing room drama dare not present.

Out of this dilemma, which is a very old one, has come the romantic play: that is, the play in which love is carefully kept off the stage, whilst it is alleged as the motive of all the actions presented to the audience. The result is, to me at least, an intolerable perversion of human conduct. There are two classes of stories that seem to me to be not only fundamentally false but sordidly base. One is the pseudo-religious story, in which the hero or heroine does good on strictly commercial grounds, reluctantly exercising a little virtue on earth in consideration of receiving in return an exorbitant payment in heaven: much as if an odalisque were to allow a cadi to whip her for a couple of millions in gold. The other is the romance in which the hero, also rigidly commercial, will do nothing except for the sake of the heroine. Surely this is as depressing as it is unreal. Compare with it the treatment of love, frankly indecent according to our notions, in oriental fiction. In The Arabian Nights we have a series of stories, some of them very good ones, in which no sort of decorum is observed. The result is that they are infinitely more instructive and enjoyable than our romances, because love is treated in them as naturally as any other passion. There is no cast iron convention as to its effects; no false association of general depravity of character with its corporealities or of general elevation with its sentimentalities; no pretence that a man or woman cannot be courageous and kind and friendly unless infatuatedly in love with somebody (is no poet manly enough to sing The Old Maids of England?): rather, indeed, an insistence on the blinding and narrowing power of lovesickness to make princely heroes unhappy and unfortunate. These tales expose, further, the delusion that the interest of this most capricious, most transient, most easily baffled of all instincts, is inexhaustible, and that the field of the English romancer has been cruelly narrowed by the restrictions under which he is permitted to deal with it. The Arabian storyteller, relieved of all such restrictions, heaps character on character, adventure on adventure, marvel on marvel; whilst the English novelist, like the starving tramp who can think of nothing but his hunger, seems to be unable to escape from the obsession of sex, and will rewrite the very gospels because the originals are not written in the sensuously ecstatic style. At the instance of Martin Luther we long ago gave up imposing celibacy on our priests; but we still impose it on our art, with the very undesirable and unexpected result that no editor, publisher, or manager, will now accept a story or produce a play without "love interest" in it. Take, for a recent example, Mr H. G. Wells's War of the Worlds [1898], a tale of the invasion of the earth by the inhabitants of the planet Mars: a capital story, not to be laid down until finished. Love interest is impossible on its scientific plane: nothing could be more impertinent and irritating. Yet Mr Wells has had to pretend that the hero is in love with a young lady manufactured for the purpose, and to imply that it is on her account alone that he feels concerned about the apparently inevitable destruction of the human race by the Martians. Another example. An American novelist [Edward Bellamy], recently deceased, made a hit some years ago by compiling a Bostonian Utopia [*Looking Backward*, 1888] from the prospectuses of the little bands of devout Communists who have from time to time, since the days of [François] Fourier and [Robert] Owen, tried to establish millennial colonies outside our commercial civilization. Even in this economic Utopia we find the inevitable love affair. The hero, waking up in a distant future from a miraculous sleep, meets a Boston young lady, provided expressly for him to fall in love with. Women have by that time given up wearing skirts; but she, to spare his delicacy, gets one out of a museum of antiquities to wear in his presence until he is hardened to the customs of the new age. When I came to that touching incident, I became as Paolo and Francesca: "in that book I read no more." I will not multiply examples: if such unendurable follies occur in the sort of story made by working out a meteorological or economic hypothesis, the extent to which it is carried in sentimental romances needs no expatiation.

The worst of it is that since man's intellectual consciousness of himself is derived from the descriptions of him in books, a persistent misrepresentation of humanity in literature gets finally accepted and acted upon. If every mirror reflected our noses twice their natural size, we should live and die in the faith that we were all Punches; and we should scout a true mirror as the work of a fool, madman, or jester. Nay, I believe we should, by Lamarckian adaptation [theory of a pre-Darwinian environmental adaptation by animals and plants, propounded by French naturalist Jean-Baptiste Lamarck], enlarge our noses to the admired size; for I have noticed that when a certain type of feature appears in painting and is admired as beautiful, it presently becomes common in nature; so that the Beatrices and Francescas in the picture galleries of one generation, to whom minor poets address verses entitled To My Lady, come to life as the parlormaids and waitresses of the next. If the conventions of romance are only insisted on long enough and uniformly enough (a condition guaranteed by the uniformity of human folly and vanity), then, for the huge compulsorily schooled masses who read romance or nothing, these conventions will become the laws of personal honor. Jealousy, which is either an egotistical meanness or a specific mania, will become obligatory; and ruin, ostracism, breaking up of homes, duelling, murder, suicide and infanticide will be produced (often have been produced, in fact) by incidents which, if left to the operation of natural and right feeling, would produce nothing worse than an hour's soon-forgotten fuss. Men will be slain needlessly on the field of battle because officers conceive it to be their first duty to make romantic exhibitions of conspicuous gallantry. The squire who has never spared an hour from the hunting field to do a little public work on a parish council will be cheered as a patriot because he is willing to kill and get killed for the sake of conferring himself as an institution on other countries. In the courts cases will be argued, not on juridical but on romantic principles; and vindictive damages and vindictive sentences, with the acceptance of nonsensical, and the repudiation or suppression of sensible testimony, will destroy the very sense of law. Kaisers, generals, judges, and prime ministers will set the example of playing to the gallery. Finally the people, now that their compulsory literacy enables every penman to play on their romantic illusions, will be led by the nose far more completely than they ever were by playing on their former ignorance and superstition. Nay, why should I say will be? they *are*. Ten years of cheap reading have changed the English from the most stolid nation in Europe to the most theatrical and hysterical.

Is it clear now, why the theatre was insufferable to me; why it left its black mark on my bones as it has left its black mark on the character of the nation; why I call the Puritans to rescue it again as they rescued it before when its foolish pursuit of pleasure sunk it in "profaneness and immorality"? I have, I think, always been a Puritan in my attitude towards Art. I am as fond of fine music and handsome building as Milton was, or Cromwell, or Bunyan; but if I found that they were becoming the instruments of a systematic idolatry of sensuousness, I would hold it good statesmanship to blow every cathedral in the world to pieces with dynamite, organ and all, without the least heed to the screams of the art critics and cultured voluptuaries. And when I see that the XIX century has crowned the idolatry of Art with the deification of Love, so that every poet is supposed to have pierced to the holy of holies when he has announced that Love is the Supreme, or the Enough, or the All, I feel that Art was safer in the hands of the most fanatical of Cromwell's major generals than it will be if ever it gets into mine. The pleasures of the senses I can sympathize with and share; but the substitution of sensuous ecstasy for intellectual activity and honesty is the very devil. It has already brought us to Flogging Bills in Parliament, and, by reaction, to androgynous heroes on the stage; and if the infection spreads until the democratic attitude becomes thoroughly Romanticist, the country will become unbearable for all realists, Philistine or Platonic. When it comes to that, the brute force of the strongminded Bismarckian man of action, impatient of humbug, will combine with the subtlety and spiritual energy of the man of thought whom shams cannot illude or interest. That combination will be on one side; and Romanticism will be on the other. In which event, so much the worse for Romanticism, which will come down even if it has to drag Democracy down with it. For all institutions have in the long run to live by the nature of things, and not by childish pretendings.

ON DIABOLONIAN ETHICS

There is a foolish opinion prevalent that an author should allow his works to speak for themselves, and that he who appends and prefixes explanations to them is likely to be as bad an artist as the painter cited by Cervantes, who wrote under his picture This is a Cock, lest there should be any mistake about it. The pat retort to this thoughtless comparison is that the painter invariably does so label his picture. What is a Royal Academy catalogue but a series of statements that This is The Vale of Rest, This The Shaving of Samson, This Chill October, This H.R.H. The Prince of Wales, and so on? The reason most playwrights do not publish their plays with prefaces is that they cannot write them, the business of intellectually conscious philosopher and skilled critic being no necessary part of their craft. Naturally, making a virtue of their incapacity, they either repudiate prefaces as shameful, or else, with a modest air, request some popular critic to supply one, as much as to say, Were I to tell the truth about myself I must needs seem vainglorious: were I to tell less than the truth I should do myself an injustice and deceive my readers. As to the critic thus called in from the outside, what can he do but imply that his friend's transcendent ability as a dramatist is surpassed only by his beautiful nature as a man? Now what I say is, why should I get another man to praise me when I can praise myself? I have no disabilities to plead: produce me your best critic, and I will criticize his head off. As to philosophy, I taught my critics the little they know in my Quintessence of Ibsenism; and now they turn their guns—the guns I loaded for them—on me, and proclaim that I write as if mankind had intellect without will, or heart, as they call it. Ingrates: who was it that directed your attention to the distinction between Will and Intellect? Not Schopenhauer, I think, but Shaw.

Again, they tell me that So-and-So, who does not write prefaces, is no charlatan. Well, I am. I first caught the ear of the British public on a cart in Hyde Park, to the blaring of brass bands, and this not at all as a reluctant sacrifice of my instinct of privacy to political necessity, but because, like all dramatists and mimes of genuine vocation, I am a natural-born mountebank. I am well aware that the ordinary British citizen requires a profession of shame from all mountebanks by way of homage to the sanctity of the ignoble private life to which he is condemned by his incapacity for public life. Thus Shakespear, after proclaiming that Not marble nor the gilded monuments of Princes should outlive his powerful rhyme, would apologize, in the approved taste, for making himself a motley to the view; and the British citizen has ever since quoted the apology and ignored the fanfare. When an actress writes her memoirs, she impresses on you in every chapter how cruelly it tried her feelings to exhibit her person to the public gaze; but she does not forget to decorate the book with a dozen portraits of herself. I really cannot respond to this demand for mock-modesty. I am ashamed neither of my work nor of the way it is done. I like explaining its merits to the huge majority who dont know good work from bad. It does them good; and it does me good, curing me of nervousness, laziness, and snobbishness. I write prefaces as Dryden did, and treatises as Wagner, because I *can*; and I would give half a dozen of Shakespear's plays for one of the prefaces he ought to have written. I leave the delicacies of retirement to those who are gentlemen first and literary workmen afterwards. The cart and trumpet for me.

This is all very well; but the trumpet is an instrument that grows on one; and sometimes my blasts have been so strident that even those who are most annoyed by them have mistaken the novelty of my shamelessness for novelty in my plays and opinions. Take, for instance, the first play in this volume, entitled The Devil's Disciple. It does not contain a single even passably novel incident. Every old patron of the Adelphi pit would, were he not beglamored in a way presently to be explained, recognize the reading of the will, the oppressed orphan finding a protector, the arrest, the heroic sacrifice, the court martial, the scaffold, the reprieve at the last moment, as he recognizes beefsteak pudding on the bill of fare at his restaurant. Yet when the play was produced in 1897 in New York by Mr Richard Mansfield, with a success that proves either that the melodrama was built on very safe old lines, or that the American public is composed exclusively of men of genius, the critics, though one said one thing and another another as to the play's merits, yet all agreed that it was novel— *original*, as they put it—to the verge of audacious eccentricity.

Now this, if it applies to the incidents, plot, construction, and general professional and technical qualities of the play, is nonsense; for the truth is, I am in these matters a very old-fashioned playwright. When a good deal of the same talk, both hostile and friendly, was provoked by my last volume of plays, Mr Robert Buchanan,[8] a dramatist who knows what I know and remembers what I remember of the history of the stage, pointed out that the stage tricks by which I gave the younger generation of playgoers an exquisite sense of quaint unexpectedness, had done duty years ago in Cool as a Cucumber, Used Up, and many forgotten farces and comedies of the Byron-Robertson school, in which the imperturbably impudent comedian, afterwards shelved by the reaction to brainless sentimentality, was a stock figure.[9] It is always so more or less: the novelties

---

8. British poet, novelist and playwright. Buchanan noted Shaw's 'stage tricks' in two open letters ('The Jester as Moral Pioneer' and 'The "Translation" of Bottom the Realist') in the *Sunday Special*, 3 and 24 April 1898.
9. *Cool as a Cucumber* (1851) is a farce by W. B. Jerrold. *Used Up* (1855) is a comic drama by Dion Boucicault.

of one generation are only the resuscitated fashions of the generation before last.

But the stage tricks of The Devil's Disciple are not, like some of those of Arms and the Man, the forgotten ones of the sixties, but the hackneyed ones of our own time. Why, then, were they not recognized? Partly, no doubt, because of my trumpet and cartwheel declamation. The critics were the victims of the long course of hypnotic suggestion by which G. B. S. the journalist manufactured an unconventional reputation for Bernard Shaw the author. In England as elsewhere the spontaneous recognition of really original work begins with a mere handful of people, and propagates itself so slowly that it has become a commonplace to say that genius, demanding bread, is given a stone after its possessor's death. The remedy for this is sedulous advertisement. Accordingly, I have advertized myself so well that I find myself, whilst still in middle life, almost as legendary a person as the Flying Dutchman. Critics, like other people, see what they look for, not what is actually before them. In my plays they look for my legendary qualities, and find originality and brilliancy in my most hackneyed claptraps. Were I to republish [J. W.] Buckstone's Wreck Ashore [1837 farce] as my latest comedy, it would be hailed as a masterpiece of perverse paradox and scintillating satire. Not, of course, by the really able critics— for example, you, my friend, now reading this sentence. The illusion that makes *you* think me so original is far subtler than that. The Devil's Disciple has, in truth, a genuine novelty in it. Only, that novelty is not any invention of my own, but simply the novelty of the advanced thought of my day. As such, it will assuredly lose its gloss with the lapse of time, and leave The Devil's Disciple exposed as the threadbare popular melodrama it technically is.

Let me explain (for, as Mr A. B. Walkley[10] has pointed out in his disquisitions on Frames of Mind, I am nothing if not explanatory). Dick Dudgeon, the devil's disciple, is a Puritan of the Puritans. He is brought up in a household where the Puritan religion has died, and become, in its corruption, an excuse for his mother's master passion of hatred in all its phases of cruelty and envy. This corruption has already been dramatized for us by Charles Dickens in his picture of the Clennam household in Little Dorrit: Mrs Dudgeon being a replica of Mrs Clennam with certain circumstantial variations, and perhaps a touch of the same author's Mrs

10. Dramatic critic of the *Star*, 1888–1900, a selection of whose articles from various journals was collected as *Frames of Mind* (1899). In 1900 Walkley was appointed dramatic critic of *The Times*.

Gargery in Great Expectations. In such a home the young Puritan finds himself starved of religion, which is the most clamorous need of his nature. With all his mother's indomitable selffulness, but with Pity instead of Hatred as his master passion, he pities the devil; takes his side; and champions him, like a true Covenanter, against the world. He thus becomes, like all genuinely religious men, a reprobate and an outcast. Once this is understood, the play becomes straightforwardly simple.

The Diabolonian position is new to the London playgoer of today, but not to lovers of serious literature. From Prometheus to the Wagnerian Siegfried, some enemy of the gods, unterrified champion of those oppressed by them, has always towered among the heroes of the loftiest poetry. Our newest idol, the Superman, celebrating the death of godhead, may be younger than the hills; but he is as old as the shepherds. Two and a half centuries ago our greatest English dramatizer of life, John Bunyan, ended one of his stories [*Pilgrim's Progress*, Part I] with the remark that there is a way to hell even from the gates of heaven, and so led us to the equally true proposition that there is a way to heaven even from the gates of hell. A century ago William Blake was, like Dick Dudgeon, an avowed Diabolonian: he called his angels devils and his devils angels. His devil is a Redeemer. Let those who have praised my originality in conceiving Dick Dudgeon's strange religion read Blake's Marriage of Heaven and Hell, and I shall be fortunate if they do not rail at me for a plagiarist. But they need not go back to Blake and Bunyan. Have they not heard the recent fuss about Nietzsche and his Good and Evil Turned Inside Out?[11] Mr Robert Buchanan has actually written a long poem [*The Devil's Case: A Bank Holiday Interlude*, 1896] of which the Devil is the merciful hero, which poem was in my hands before a word of The Devil's Disciple was written. There never was a play more certain to be written than The Devil's Disciple at the end of the XIX century. The age was visibly pregnant with it.

I grieve to have to add that my old friends and colleagues the London critics for the most part shewed no sort of connoisseurship either in Puritanism or in Diabolonianism when the play was performed for a few weeks at a suburban theatre (Kennington) in October 1899 by Mr Murray Carson.[12] They took Mrs Dudgeon at her own valuation as a religious woman

11. Friedrich Nietzsche's *Beyond Good and Evil* (1886), in Helen Zimmern's translation, was not published in England until 1907.
12. *The Devil's Disciple* was first performed in England on 26 September 1899, by the actor-manager Murray Carson, at the Princess Theatre, Kennington.

because she was detestably disagreeable. And they took Dick as a blackguard on her authority, because he was neither detestable nor disagreeable. But they presently found themselves in a dilemma. Why should a blackguard save another man's life, and that man no friend of his, at the risk of his own? Clearly, said the critics, because he is redeemed by love. All wicked heroes are, on the stage: that is the romantic metaphysic. Unfortunately for this explanation (which I do not profess to understand) it turned out in the third act that Dick was a Puritan in this respect also: a man impassioned only for saving grace, and not to be led or turned by wife or mother, Church or State, pride of life or lust of the flesh. In the lovely home of the courageous, affectionate, practical minister who marries a pretty wife twenty years younger than himself, and turns soldier in an instant to save the man who has saved him, Dick looks round and understands the charm and the peace and the sanctity, but knows that such material comforts are not for him. When the woman nursed in that atmosphere falls in love with him and concludes (like the critics, who somehow always agree with my sentimental heroines) that he risked his life for her sake, he tells her the obvious truth that he would have done as much for any stranger—that the law of his own nature, and no interest nor lust whatsoever, forbad him to cry out that the hangman's noose should be taken off his neck only to be put on another man's.

But then, said the critics, where is the motive? *Why* did Dick save Anderson? On the stage, it appears, people do things for reasons. Off the stage they dont: that is why your penny-in-the-slot heroes, who only work when you drop a motive into them, are so oppressively automatic and uninteresting. The saving of life at the risk of the saver's own is not a common thing; but modern populations are so vast that even the most uncommon things are recorded once a week or oftener. Not one of my critics but has seen a hundred times in his paper how some policeman or fireman or nursemaid has received a medal, or the compliments of a magistrate, or perhaps a public funeral, for risking his or her life to save another's. Has he ever seen it added that the saved was the husband of the woman the saver loved, or was that woman herself, or was even known to the saver as much as by sight? Never. When we want to read of the deeds that are done for love, whither do we turn? To the murder column; and there we are rarely disappointed.

Need I repeat that the theatre critic's professional routine so discourages any association between real life and the stage, that he soon loses the natural habit of referring to the one to explain the other? The critic who discovered a romantic motive for Dick's sacrifice was no mere literary dreamer, but a clever barrister. He pointed out that Dick Dudgeon clearly did adore Mrs Anderson; that it was for her sake that he offered his life to save her beloved husband; and that his explicit denial of his passion was the splendid mendacity of a gentleman whose respect for a married woman, and duty to her absent husband, sealed his passion-palpitating lips.[13] From the moment that this fatally plausible explanation was launched, my play became my critic's play, not mine. Thenceforth Dick Dudgeon every night confirmed the critic by stealing behind Judith, and mutely attesting his passion by surreptitiously imprinting a heart-broken kiss on a stray lock of her hair whilst he uttered the barren denial. As for me, I was just then wandering about the streets of Constantinople, unaware of all these doings. When I returned all was over. My personal relations with the critic and the actor forbad me to curse them. I had not even the chance of publicly forgiving them. They meant well by me; but if they ever write a play, may I be there to explain!*

BETTER THAN SHAKESPEAR?

As to the other plays in this volume, the application of my title is less obvious, since neither Julius Cæsar, Cleopatra, nor Lady Cicely Waynflete have any external political connexion with Puritanism. The very name of Cleopatra suggests at once a tragedy of Circe, with the horrible difference that whereas the ancient myth rightly represents Circe as turning heroes into hogs, the modern romantic convention would represent her as turning

* As I pass these pages through the press (September 1900), the critics of Yorkshire are struggling, as against some unholy fascination, with the apparition of Dick Dudgeon on their stage in the person of [Johnston] Forbes Robertson. "A finished scoundrel" is the description which one of them gives of Dick. This is worth recording as an example of the extent to which the moral sense remains dormant in people who are content with the customary formulas for respectable conduct. [GBS]

13. The one barrister-critic in London was H. Spenser Wilkinson of the *Morning Post*. His notice (27 September 1899) bears little resemblance, however, to Shaw's description, his sole remarks on the subject being: 'Richard's love for the heroine is left just as open to doubt as are his sins. He seems to have nice if peculiar feelings, but he neither has nor strikes one as capable of developing an atom of passion beyond a passion for Mr Shaw. Yet without love for Judith his sacrifice is wholly unintelligible.' Although it is conceivable that Shaw confused the source, an examination of more than twenty reviews in principal daily and weekly papers for the offending interpretation of the play as worded by Shaw proved fruitless.

hogs into heroes. Shakespear's Antony and Cleopatra must needs be as intolerable to the true Puritan as it is vaguely distressing to the ordinary healthy citizen, because, after giving a faithful picture of the soldier broken down by debauchery, and the typical wanton in whose arms such men perish, Shakespear finally strains all his huge command of rhetoric and stage pathos to give a theatrical sublimity to the wretched end of the business, and to persuade foolish spectators that the world was well lost by the twain. Such falsehood is not to be borne except by the real Cleopatras and Antonys (they are to be found in every public house) who would no doubt be glad enough to be transfigured by some poet as immortal lovers. Woe to the poet who stoops to such folly! The lot of the man who sees life truly and thinks about it romantically is Despair. How well we know the cries of that despair! Vanity of vanities, all is vanity! [Ecclesiastes 1: 2; 12: 8] moans the Preacher, when life has at last taught him that Nature will not dance to his moralist-made tunes. Thackeray, scores of centuries later, was still baying the moon in the same terms. Out, out, brief candle! cries Shakespear, in his tragedy of the modern literary man as murderer and witch consulter. Surely the time is past for patience with writers who, having to choose between giving up life in despair and discarding the trumpery moral kitchen scales in which they try to weigh the universe, superstitiously stick to the scales, and spend the rest of the lives they pretend to despise in breaking men's spirits. But even in pessimism there is a choice between intellectual honesty and dishonesty. Hogarth drew the rake [*A Rake's Progress*, 1735] and the harlot [*A Harlot's Progress*, 1732] without glorifying their end. Swift, accepting our system of morals and religion, delivered the inevitable verdict of that system on us [*Gulliver's Travels*, 1726] through the mouth of the king of Brobdingnag, and described Man as the Yahoo, shocking his superior the horse by his every action. Strindberg, the only genuinely Shakespearean modern dramatist, shews that the female Yahoo, measured by romantic standards, is viler than her male dupe and slave [in *The Father*]. I respect these resolute tragi-comedians: they are logical and faithful: they force you to face the fact that you must either accept their conclusions as valid (in which case it is cowardly to continue living) or admit that their way of judging conduct is absurd. But when your Shakespears and Thackerays huddle up the matter at the end by killing somebody and covering your eyes with the undertaker's handkerchief, duly onioned with some pathetic phrase, as The flight of angels sing thee to thy rest, or Adsum [I am present], or the like, I have no respect for them at all: such maudlin tricks may impose on tea-drunkards, not on me.

Besides, I have a technical objection to making sexual infatuation a tragic theme. Experience proves that it is only effective in the comic spirit. We can bear to see Mrs Quickly pawning her plate for love of Falstaff, but not Antony running away from the battle of Actium for love of Cleopatra. Let realism have its demonstration, comedy its criticism, or even bawdry its horse-laugh at the expense of sexual infatuation, if it must; but to ask us to subject our souls to its ruinous glamor, to worship it, deify it, and imply that it alone makes our life worth living, is nothing but folly gone mad erotically—a thing compared to which Falstaff's unbeglamored drinking and drabbing is respectable and right-minded. Whoever, then, expects to find Cleopatra a Circe and Cæsar a hog in these pages, had better lay down my book and be spared a disappointment.

In Cæsar, I have used another character with which Shakespear has been beforehand. But Shakespear, who knew human weakness so well, never knew human strength of the Cæsarian type. His Cæsar is an admitted failure: his Lear is a masterpiece. The tragedy of disillusion and doubt, of the agonized struggle for a foothold on the quicksand made by an acute observation striving to verify its vain attribution of morality and respectability to Nature, of the faithless will and the keen eyes that the faithless will is too weak to blind: all this will give you a Hamlet or a Macbeth, and win you great applause from literary gentlemen; but it will not give you a Julius Cæsar. Cæsar was not in Shakespear, nor in the epoch, now fast waning, which he inaugurated. It cost Shakespear no pang to write Cæsar down for the merely technical purpose of writing Brutus up. And what a Brutus! A perfect Girondin,[14] mirrored in Shakespear's art two hundred years before the real thing came to maturity and talked and stalked and had its head duly cut off by the coarser Antonys and Octaviuses of its time, who at least knew the difference between life and rhetoric.

It will be said that these remarks can bear no other construction than an offer of my Cæsar to the public as an improvement on Shakespear's. And in fact, that is their precise purport. But here let me give a friendly warning to those scribes who have so often exclaimed against my criticisms of Shakespear as blasphemies against a hitherto unquestioned Perfection and Infallibility. Such criticisms are no more new than the creed of my Diabolonian Puritan or my revival of the humors of Cool as a Cucumber. Too much surprise at them betrays an acquaintance with Shakespear criti-

14. The Girondists were a moderate French republican party (1791–3), whose idealism and predilection for theory in their opposition to the monarchy led to their overthrow.

cism so limited as not to include even the prefaces of Dr Johnson and the utterances of Napoleon.[15] I have merely repeated in the dialect of my own time and in the light of its philosophy what they said in the dialect and light of theirs. Do not be misled by the Shakespear fanciers who, ever since his own time, have delighted in his plays just as they might have delighted in a particular breed of pigeons if they had never learnt to read. His genuine critics, from Ben Jonson to Mr Frank Harris, have always kept as far on this side idolatry as I.

As to our ordinary uncritical citizens, they have been slowly trudging forward these three centuries to the point which Shakespear reached at a bound in Elizabeth's time. Today most of them have arrived there or thereabouts, with the result that his plays are at last beginning to be performed as he wrote them; and the long line of disgraceful farces, melodramas, and stage pageants which actor-managers, from [David] Garrick and [Colley] Cibber to our own contemporaries, have hacked out of his plays as peasants have hacked huts out of the Coliseum, are beginning to vanish from the stage. It is a significant fact that the mutilators of Shakespear, who never could be persuaded that Shakespear knew his business better than they, have ever been the most fanatical of his worshippers. The late Augustin Daly thought no price too extravagant for an addition to his collection of Shakespear relics; but in arranging Shakespear's plays for the stage, he proceeded on the assumption ·that Shakespear was a botcher and he an artist. I am far too good a Shakespearean ever to forgive Henry Irving for producing a version of King Lear so mutilated that the numerous critics who had never read the play could not follow the story of Gloster. Both these idolators of the Bard must have thought Forbes Robertson mad because he restored Fortinbras to the stage and played as much of Hamlet as there was time for instead of as little.[16] And the instant success of the experiment probably altered their minds no further than to make them think the public mad. Mr Benson[17] actually gives the play

15. Napoleon based 'the superiority of Corneille to Shakespear on the ground of Corneille's power of grasping a political situation, and of seeing men in their relation to the State' (Shaw to Victor Tchertkoff, n.d. [2 August 1905], in *Collected Letters 1898–1910*, 1972.
16. The *Hamlet* of actor-manager Johnston Forbes-Robertson, reviewed by Shaw in the *Saturday Review* on 2 October 1897, is one of the most celebrated Shakespearian productions in British theatre history.
17. F. R. (later Sir Frank) Benson formed a touring company in 1883, visiting Stratford-upon-Avon annually 1886–1916 with a large repertory of plays performed during the summer months as a Shakespeare Festival. He made theatrical history with an uncut *Hamlet*, performed at Stratford in 1899 and in London a year later.

complete at two sittings, causing the aforesaid numerous critics to remark with naïve surprise that Polonius is a complete and interesting character. It was the age of gross ignorance of Shakespear and incapacity for his works that produced the indiscriminate eulogies with which we are familiar. It was the revival of serious attention to those works that coincided with the movement for giving genuine instead of spurious and silly representations of his plays. So much for Bardolatry!

It does not follow, however, that the right to criticize Shakespear involves the power of writing better plays. And in fact—do not be surprised at my modesty—I do not profess to write better plays. The writing of practicable stage plays does not present an infinite scope to human talent; and the playwrights who magnify its difficulties are humbugs. The summit of their art has been attained again and again. No man will ever write a better tragedy than Lear, a better comedy than Le Festin de Pierre[18] or Peer Gynt, a better opera than Don Giovanni, a better music drama than The Niblung's Ring, or, for the matter of that, better fashionable plays and melodramas than are now being turned out by writers whom nobody dreams of mocking with the word immortal. It is the philosophy, the outlook on life, that changes, not the craft of the playwright. A generation that is thoroughly moralized and patriotized, that conceives virtuous indignation as spiritually nutritious, that murders the murderer and robs the thief, that grovels before all sorts of ideals, social, military, ecclesiastical, royal and divine, may be, from my point of view, steeped in error; but it need not want for as good plays as the hand of man can produce. Only, those plays will be neither written nor relished by men in whose philosophy guilt and innocence, and consequently revenge and idolatry, have no meaning. Such men must rewrite all the old plays in terms of their own philosophy; and that is why, as Stuart-Glennie[19] has pointed out, there can be no new drama without a new philosophy. To which I may add that there can be no Shakespear or Goethe without one either, nor two Shakespears in one philosophic epoch, since, as I have said, the first great comer in that epoch reaps the whole harvest and reduces those who come after to the rank of mere gleaners, or, worse than that, fools who go laboriously through all the motions of the reaper and binder in an empty field. What is the use of writing plays or painting frescoes if you have nothing more to say or shew than was said and shewn by Shakespear, Michael Angelo, and Raphael? If these had not seen things differently, for

18. *Don Juan ou Le Festin de Pierre* (1665) is by Molière.
19. Scots historical philosopher, author of *The New Theory of History* (1876).

better or worse, from the dramatic poets of the Townley mysteries, or from Giotto, they could not have produced their works: no, not though their skill of pen and hand had been double what it was. After them there was no need (and *need* alone nerves men to face the persecution in the teeth of which new art is brought to birth) to redo the already done, until in due time, when their philosophy wore itself out, a new race of XIX century poets and critics, from Byron to William Morris, began, first to speak coldly of Shakespear and Raphael, and then to rediscover, in the medieval art which these Renascence masters had superseded, certain forgotten elements which were germinating again for the new harvest. What is more, they began to discover that the technical skill of the masters was by no means superlative. Indeed, I defy anyone to prove that the great epoch makers in fine art have owed their position to their technical skill. It is true that when we search for examples of a prodigious command of language and of graphic line, we can think of nobody better than Shakespear and Michael Angelo. But both of them laid their arts waste for centuries by leading later artists to seek greatness in copying their technique. The technique was acquired, refined on, and elaborated over and over again; but the supremacy of the two great exemplars remained undisputed. As a matter of easily observable fact, every generation produces men of extraordinary special faculty, artistic, mathematical and linguistic, who for lack of new ideas, or indeed of any ideas worth mentioning, achieve no distinction outside music halls and class rooms, although they can do things easily that the great epoch makers did clumsily or not at all. The contempt of the academic pedant for the original artist is often founded on a genuine superiority of technical knowledge and aptitude: he is sometimes a better anatomical draughtsman than Raphael, a better hand at triple counterpoint than Beethoven, a better versifier than Byron. Nay, this is true not merely of pedants, but of men who have produced works of art of some note. If technical facility were the secret of greatness in art, Swinburne would be greater than Browning and Byron rolled into one, Stevenson greater than Scott or Dickens, Mendelssohn than Wagner, [Daniel] Maclise than [Ford] Madox Brown.[20] Besides, new ideas make their technique as water makes its channel; and the technician without ideas is as useless as the canal constructor without water, though he may do very skilfully what the Mississippi does very rudely. To clinch the argument, you have only to

20. Maclise, Irish historical painter, designed book illustrations for Tennyson and some of Dickens's Christmas books. Madox Brown, English historical painter, was allied with the Pre-Raphaelite Brotherhood.

observe that the epoch maker himself has generally begun working professionally before his new ideas have mastered him sufficiently to insist on
constant expression by his art. In such cases you are compelled to admit
that if he had by chance died earlier, his greatness would have remained
unachieved, although his technical qualifications would have been well
enough established. The early imitative works of great men are usually
conspicuously inferior to the best works of their forerunners. Imagine
Wagner dying after composing Rienzi, or Shelley after Zastrozzi! Would
any competent critic then have rated Wagner's technical aptitude as high as
Rossini's, Spontini's, or Meyerbeer's; or Shelley's as high as Moore's? Turn
the problem another way: does anyone suppose that if Shakespear had
conceived Goethe's or Ibsen's ideas, he would have expressed them any worse
than Goethe or Ibsen? Human faculty being what it is, is it likely that in
our time any advance, except in external conditions, will take place in the
arts of expression sufficient to enable an author, without making himself
ridiculous, to undertake to say what he has to say better than Homer or
Shakespear? But the humblest author, and much more a rather arrogant
one like myself, may profess to have something to say by this time that
neither Homer nor Shakespear said. And the playgoer may reasonably ask
to have historical events and persons presented to him in the light of his
own time, even though Homer and Shakespear have already shewn them
in the light of their time. For example, Homer presented Achilles and Ajax
as heroes to the world in the Iliads. In due time came Shakespear, who said,
virtually: I really cannot accept this spoilt child and this brawny fool as
great men merely because Homer flattered them in playing to the Greek
gallery. Consequently we have, in Troilus and Cressida, the verdict of
Shakespear's epoch (our own) on the pair. This did not in the least involve
any pretence on Shakespear's part to be a greater poet than Homer.

When Shakespear in turn came to deal with Henry V and Julius Cæsar,
he did so according to his own essentially knightly conception of a great
statesman–commander. But in the XIX century comes the German
historian [Theodor] Mommsen,[21] who also takes Cæsar for his hero, and
explains the immense difference in scope between the perfect knight
Vercingetorix[22] and his great conqueror Julius Cæsar. In this country,
Carlyle, with his vein of peasant inspiration, apprehended the sort of

21. Author of *Die Römische Chronologie bis auf Cäsar* (1858), credited by Shaw as
a major influence on *Cæsar and Cleopatra*.
22. The Arverian Vercingetorix was the most famous of the Celtic chieftains who
fought against Cæsar's Romans.

greatness that places the true hero of history so far beyond the mere *preux chevalier* [perfect knight], whose fanatical personal honor, gallantry, and self-sacrifice, are founded on a passion for death born of inability to bear the weight of a life that will not grant ideal conditions to the liver. This one ray of perception became Carlyle's whole stock-in-trade; and it sufficed to make a literary master of him. In due time, when Mommsen is an old man, and Carlyle dead, come I, and dramatize the by-this-time familiar distinction in Arms and the Man, with its comedic conflict between the knightly Bulgarian and the Mommsenite Swiss captain. Whereupon a great many playgoers who have not yet read Cervantes, much less Mommsen and Carlyle, raise a shriek of concern for their knightly ideal as if nobody had ever questioned its sufficiency since the middle ages. Let them thank me for educating them so far. And let them allow me to set forth Cæsar in the same modern light, taking the platform from Shakespear as he from Homer, and with no thought of pretending to express the Mommsenite view of Cæsar any better than Shakespear expressed a view which was not even Plutarchian, and must, I fear, be referred to the tradition in stage conquerors established by Marlowe's Tamerlane as much as to the chivalrous conception of heroism dramatized in Henry V.

For my own part, I can avouch that such powers of invention, humor and stage ingenuity as I have been able to exercise in Plays Pleasant and Unpleasant, and in these Three Plays for Puritans, availed me not at all until I saw the old facts in a new light. Technically, I do not find myself able to proceed otherwise than as former playwrights have done. True, my plays have the latest mechanical improvements: the action is not carried on by impossible soliloquys and asides; and my people get on and off the stage without requiring four doors to a room which in real life would have only one. But my stories are the old stories; my characters are the familiar harlequin and columbine, clown and pantaloon (note the harlequin's leap in the third act of Cæsar and Cleopatra); my stage tricks and suspenses and thrills and jests are the ones in vogue when I was a boy, by which time my grandfather was tired of them. To the young people who make their acquaintance for the first time in my plays, they may be as novel as Cyrano's nose to those who have never seen Punch; whilst to older playgoers the unexpectedness of my attempt to substitute natural history for conventional ethics and romantic logic may so transfigure the eternal stage puppets and their inevitable dilemmas as to make their identification impossible for the moment. If so, so much the better for me: I shall perhaps enjoy a few years of immortality. But the whirligig of time will soon bring my audiences to my own point of view; and then the next Shakespear that comes along will turn these petty tentatives of mine into masterpieces final for their epoch. By that time my XX century characteristics will pass unnoticed as a matter of course, whilst the XVIII century artificiality that marks the work of every literary Irishman of my generation will seem antiquated and silly. It is a dangerous thing to be hailed at once, as a few rash admirers have hailed me, as above all things original: what the world calls originality is only an unaccustomed method of tickling it. Meyerbeer seemed prodigiously original to the Parisians when he first burst on them. Today, he is only the crow who followed Beethoven's plough. I am a crow who has followed many ploughs. No doubt I seem prodigiously clever to those who have never hopped, hungry and curious, across the fields of philosophy, politics, and art. Karl Marx said of Stuart Mill that his eminence was due to the flatness of the surrounding country. In these days of Free Schools, universal reading, cheap newspapers, and the inevitable ensuing demand for notabilities of all sorts, literary, military, political and fashionable, to write paragraphs about, that sort of eminence is within the reach of very moderate ability. Reputations are cheap nowadays. Even were they dear, it would still be impossible for any public-spirited citizen of the world to hope that his reputation might endure; for this would be to hope that the flood of general enlightenment may never rise above his miserable high-watermark. I hate to think that Shakespear has lasted 300 years, though he got no further than Koheleth the Preacher [Ecclesiastes], who died many centuries before him; or that Plato, more than 2000 years old, is still ahead of our voters. We must hurry on: we must get rid of reputations: they are weeds in the soil of ignorance. Cultivate that soil, and they will flower more beautifully, but only as annuals. If this preface will at all help to get rid of mine, the writing of it will have been well worth the pains.

Surrey, 1900.

(DELETED PASSAGES: *Reproduced from manuscript fragments of the original holograph draft, in the Henry W. and Albert A. Berg Collection, New York Public Library, Astor, Lenox and Tilden Foundations. The headings were added by a London bookseller, Harry Mushlin, in 1953.*]

[Adelphi Melodrama and William Terriss]

. . . the Adelphi, where popular melodramas were presented to popular audiences on the frank understanding that people who could not or would not read or write could understand every word of them. There was plenty of convention in the Adelphi drama; but it was sounder than the fashionable drama, because it exhibited conduct as founded on character, not upon motives. The virtue of the hero and the vice of the villain were conventional to an extent which often suggested doubts as to whether either the dramatist or the audience had a ray of perception; no matter: the hero was virtuous and the villain vicious because they were respectively built that way, and not on purely commercial grounds.

The principal actor at the Adelphi then was William Terriss. Terriss in his early days had succeeded on the stage namely because his good looks, vitality, and determination made him personally attractive. Later on he became a skilful actor: in fact, during the last years of his life he was for straightforward popular work, executed without affectation or mannerism in terms of a natural and audible personality, by far the best actor in London. One day to my astonishment, Terriss asked me to call on him. I did so, and he, hailing me as a man of intellect and learning, proposed that I should combine these qualities with his experience of the stage, and write a melodrama on a scenario of his own which he would take round the world. The scenario contained incident enough for half a dozen melodramas; but I had to point out to him that a star actor in strange lands must present character as well as incident. He therefore very frankly put his scenario in the fire; and the interview closed with a promise on my part to try my hand at melodrama, coupled with the observation that though a successful melodrama is not the highest feat of the dramatist, it is perhaps the most conclusive proof of his vocation.

In a very short time and with great ease to myself, I produced the first play in this volume, The Devil's Disciple. It does not contain a single original or even passably novel incident. Every old patron of the Adelphi pit would, were he not beglamored in a way presently to be explained, recognize the reading of the will, the arrest, the heroic sacrifice, the court martial, the scaffold, the reprieve at the last moment, as he recognizes beefsteak pudding on the bill of fare at his restaurant. The play was produced in 189[7] in New York by Mr Richard Mansfield.

[W. S. GILBERT AND WILLIAM MORRIS]

... Cervantes, Larochefoucauld[1] and a long line of cynical paradoxers, the last of whom, our contemporary Mr W. S. Gilbert, brought the English stage so close to the new drama—that is, to the new philosophy in drama, that it is astonishing that he should have remained completely dominated by the Shakespearean moral system whose incongruities and absurdities were his stock-in-trade, and lavished on comic operas, as mere topsy turvy funniments, the true observations of life that, taken seriously, might have enabled him to anticipate Ibsen's Wild Duck. This curious situation has been successfully analyzed by Mr A. B. Walkley in his Frames of Mind. Strange that a dramatist with the faculty of seeing things as they are should yet, like Pelpay's Brahmin,[2] allow himself to be persuaded that he saw them upside down!

Morris, it will be remembered, could find no employment for his literary talent except the translation of ancient epics, and the retelling of old stories in verse. In this no doubt he did great social service to English-speaking children, who can now read the Odyssey and the Eneids of Virgil, the story of Jason and Medea, and the legends of the Earthly Paradise, in fit words and graceful measures. But what grown man with serious business on his hands, reading for genuine recreation and not for the mere killing of heavy-hanging time, reads The Earthly Paradise, or knows it save by the famous phrase in which the author slighted himself as an idle singer of an empty day? In those days, Morris was an artist: an artist driven to pure handicraft because he had no gospel to preach. He could not say what Tennyson was saying; because he did not believe it. He could get nothing modern into the Jason epic except a description of the Thames and the tunnel on the Thames and Severn canal, through which he boldly made the Argo pass. When the poem was finished, it was only a piece of word

1. French maxim writer and courtier, author of *Réflexions ou sentences et maximes morales* (1665–78).
2. Pilpay (Ruzeh Abd-Allâh ibn-Almokaffa) was the eighth-century Arabic translator of a Pahlavi (Old Persian) translation of a sixth-century Sanskrit collection of fables and tales, the Panchatantra. The version known to Shaw was *The Fables of Pilpay* in the Chandos Classics edition (1886).

handicraft; for the story had been told before. There was nothing to be done but some apprenticeship to the XII and XV centuries, and revive the decorative arts. Hence the word weaver of The Earthly Paradise and Jason becomes the famous tapestry weaver, stained glass mosaicist, book printer, textile block printer and so forth. He is reduced to such an abjection of handicraft that he sometimes does not even paraphrase the old poems, but sits down and copies them out like a medieval scribe. At last discovering that all this beauty mongering is acting as a propaganda of a voluptuousness which, in deference to Victorian scruples, lacks the one virtue of voluptuousness, a robustly vital carnality, and is consistently melancholy and sickly, he goes into the streets with the common people, just then arrived at the window-breaking pitch of unemployment and starvation, and definitely breaks with the Shakespearean (or Renascence) philosophy in life as he had already broken with its art. Immediately and with hardly any effort to himself, he produces, for the columns of a paper (The Commonweal) which people are begged to give a penny for at street corners, his Dream of John Ball and News from Nowhere, excellent reading for Puritans both of them, and likely to live with the tenacity of More's Utopia, Bunyan's Pilgrim, and Swift's Gulliver.

[A NOTE ON THE REALITY OF MODERN WAR]

One advantage these plays have which was denied to those earlier Pleasant Plays which touched on military matters, the South African War, whilst it has upset my explanation of the schoolboyishness of the critics as an effect of the theatre on them, by proving that the whole nation, from the cabinet minister to the humblest volunteer, is just as schoolboyish, nevertheless has rubbed in, in a very grim manner, the views of Captain Bluntschli in Arms and the Man as to the professional value of high spirited officers who think that war is a matter of plucky charges on modern artillery, and as to the relative importance a prudent soldier would give to chocolate and cartridges in a campaign where men have been twenty-one hours on the field of battle without food. We have the Queen's chocolate [a personal gift of Queen Victoria in November 1899] sent to our troops, and a week of terror caused by a series of defeats of our men under the command of our British Sergius Saranoffs.[3] In fact, a performance of Arms and the

3. In a series of head-on assaults against the Boers in December 1899 and early 1900, the English lost some 5000 men. In March 1900 the newly appointed

Man at this moment would be resented as a satire on our operations in the Orange State before Lord Roberts, with his Irish common sense, went to the front. Just before the war broke out, a performance of The Devil's Disciple shewed by the comments of the critics on General Burgoyne's remarks on the marksmanship of the British soldier, that they were still untaught and unteachable as to the realities of war. But indeed, if war was a reality to us, we would give up making it. Captain Bluntschli's observations would perhaps be received with more respect now than they were in 1894; but Napoleon's saying (in The Man of Destiny) that fear is the mainspring of war, is still as dark as ever to our modern militarist amateurs, who conceive that they have reached the Imperial summit of courage when the terror of every other nation but their own has reached murder point.

---

supreme commander, Frederick Sleigh, First Earl Roberts, with sound strategy, occupied the centre of Boer resistance, Bloemfontein, capital of the Orange Free State.

Socialism for Millionaires

First published in the Contemporary Review, *February 1896;
revised for publication in 1901 as Fabian Tract No. 107*

═══

Since the appearance of the following essay in the Contemporary Review
(February 1896) a Millionaire Movement has taken place, culminating in
the recent expression of opinion by Mr Andrew Carnegie that no man
should die rich.[1] A reference to Fabian Tract No. 5, "Facts for Socialists,"
will convince Mr Carnegie that the danger he warns us against is still far
from widespread. Nor is the doctrine new: John Ruskin "unloaded" and
published his accounts with the public years ago;[2] and Mr [John] Passmore
Edwards's annual investments for the common good[3] have come to be
regarded as an ordinary asset, like the established Parliamentary Grants in
Aid. But the modern substitution of Combination for Competition as the
principle of capitalism is producing a new crop of individual fortunes so
monstrous as to make their possessors publicly ridiculous. Unloading is, for
the moment, the order of the day. The problem is, how to unload without
the waste, pauperization, and demoralization that are summed up in
England under the word charity. It seems clear from some late sensational
disbursements that the Millionaires have not solved this problem. For this
they cannot be blamed, because the problem is fundamentally insoluble
under the social conditions which produce it; but they can at least do their
best instead of their worst with their superfluity; and, so far, they seem to
prefer, with the best intentions, to do their worst. In the hope that my
essay may prove suggestive to them, the Fabian Society has decided to
reprint it, with the permission of the Editor of the Contemporary Review,
as a Fabian Tract.

LONDON, 1901.   G. B. S.

1. The views of multimillionaire industrialist Andrew Carnegie on the responsibilities of making use of a great fortune are set forth in his book *The Gospel of Wealth*
(1900).
2. John Ruskin founded the St George's Guild for channelling a substantial inheritance into a model industrial and social movement.
3. English editor and philanthropist, who established hospitals and free libraries.

Novels of My Nonage

Preface to 1901 edition of Cashel Byron's Profession
(with a few revisions made in 1930)

=====

I never think of Cashel Byron's Profession without a shudder at the narrowness of my escape from becoming a successful novelist at the age of twenty-six. At that moment an adventurous publisher might have ruined me. Fortunately for me, there were no adventurous publishers at that time; and I was forced to fight my way, instead of being ingloriously bought off at the first brush. Not that Cashel Byron's Profession was my very first novel. It was my fourth, and was followed by yet another. I recall these five remote products of my nonage as five heavy brown paper parcels which were always coming back to me from some publisher, and raising the very serious financial question of the sixpence to be paid to Messrs Carter, Paterson, and Co., the carriers, for passing them on to the next publisher. Eventually, Carter, Paterson, and Co. were the only gainers; for the publishers had to pay their readers' fees for nothing but a warning not to publish me; and I had to pay the sixpences for sending my parcels on a bootless errand. At last I grew out of novel-writing, and set to work to find out what the world was really like. The result of my investigations, so far, entirely confirms the observation of Goethe as to the amazement, the incredulity, the moral shock with which the poet discovers that what he supposed to be the real world does not exist, and that men and women are made by their own fancies in the image of the imaginary creatures in his youthful fictions, only much stupider.[1]

Unfortunately for the immature poet, he has not in his nonage the satisfaction of knowing that his guesses at life are true. Bring a peasant into a drawing-room, and though his good sense may lead him to behave very properly, yet he will suffer torments of misgiving that everything he does must be a solecism. In my earlier excursions into literature I confess I felt like the peasant in the drawing-room. I was, on the whole, glad to get out

---

1. There is probably no passage in Goethe to which Shaw refers explicitly; but two passages, one in *Wilhelm Meister's Apprenticeship* (Book II, Chapter 1) and another in *Poetry and Truth* (Part III, Book 13) convey the impact on a writer of discovering that 'what he supposed to be the real world does not exist'.

of it. Looking back now with the eyes of experience, I find that I certainly did make blunders in matters outside the scope of poetic divination. To take a very mild example, I endowed the opulent heroine of this very book with a park of thirty acres in extent, being then fully persuaded that this was a reasonable estimate of the size of the Isle of Wight or thereabouts. But it is not by the solecisms of ignorance that the young man makes himself most ridiculous. Far more unnatural than these were my proprieties and accuracies and intelligences. I did not know my England then. I was young, raw from XVIII century Ireland, modest, and anxious lest my poverty and provinciality should prevent me from correctly representing the intelligence, refinement, conscience, and good breeding which I supposed to be as natural and common in English society as in Scott's novels. I actually thought that educated people conscientiously learnt their manners and studied their opinions—were really educated, in short—instead of merely picking up the habits and prejudices of their set, and confidently presenting the resultant absurd equipment of class solecisms to the world as a perfect gentility. Consequently the only characters which were natural in my novels were the comic characters, because the island was (and is) populated exclusively by comic characters. Take them seriously in fiction, and the result is the Dickens heroine or the Sarah Grand[2] hero: pathetically unattractive figments both of them. Thus my imaginary persons of quality became quite unlike any actual persons at large in England, being superior to them in a priggish manner which would nowadays rouse the humor of our younger publishers' readers very inopportunely. In 1882, however, the literary fashion which distinguished the virtuous and serious characters in a novel by a decorous stylishness and scrupulousness of composition, as if all their speeches had been corrected by their governesses and schoolmasters, had not yet been exploded by the "New Journalism" of 1888[3] and the advent of a host of authors who had apparently never read anything, catering for a proletariat newly made literate by the Education Act. The distinction between the naturalness of Caleb Balderstone and the artificiality of Edgar and Lucy[4] was still regarded as one of the social decencies by the seniors of literature; and this probably explains the fact that the only

2. Popular English novelist and feminist, whose novel *The Heavenly Twins* was a runaway bestseller in 1893.
3. In 1888 halfpenny evening newspapers such as the *Star* were introduced, resulting in a proliferation of journals directed to lower middle and working class readers.
4. In Scott's *The Bride of Lammermoor* (1819) Balderstone is the old servant of the Master of Ravenswood. Edgar Ravenswood and Lucy Ashton are the young lovers.

intimations I received that my work had made some impression, and had even been hesitatingly condemned, were from the older and more august houses whose readers were all grave elderly lovers of literature. And the more I progressed towards my own individual style and ventured upon the freer expression of my own ideas, the more I disappointed them. As to the regular novel-publishing houses, whose readers were merely on the scent of popularity, they gave me no quarter at all. And so between the old stool of my literary conscientiousness and the new stool of a view of life that did not reach publishing-point in England until about ten years later, when Ibsen drove it in, my novels fell to the ground.

I was to find later on that a book is like a child: it is easier to bring it into the world than to control it when it is launched there. As long as I kept sending my novels to the publishers, they were as safe from publicity as they would have been in the fire, where I had better, perhaps, have put them. But when I flung them aside as failures they almost instantly began to shew signs of life.

The Socialist revival of the eighties, into which I had plunged, produced the usual crop of propagandist magazines, in the conduct of which payment of the printer was the main problem, payment of contributors being quite out of the question. The editor of such a magazine can never count on a full supply of live matter to make up his tale of pages. But if he can collect a stock of unreadable novels, the refuse of the publishing trade, and a stock of minor poems (the world is full of such trash), an instalment of serial novel and a few verses will always make up the magazine to any required size. And this was how I found a use at last for my brown paper parcels. It seemed a matter of no more consequence than stuffing so many broken windowpanes with them; but it had momentous consequences; for in this way four of the five got printed and published in London, and thus incidentally became the common property of the citizens of the United States of America.[5] These pioneers did not at first appreciate their new acquisition; and nothing particular happened except that the first novel (No. 5; for I ladled them out to the Socialist magazine editors in inverse order of composition) made me acquainted with William Morris, who, to my surprise, had been reading the monthly instalments with a certain relish. But that only proved how much easier it is to please a great man

5. The Congress of the United States did not officially accept the principles of international copyright until 1891. Prior to that, the works of foreigners could be reproduced in the United States for purposes of financial gain without authorization.

than a little one, especially when you share his politics. No. 5, called An Unsocial Socialist, was followed by No. 4, Cashel Byron's Profession; and Cashel Byron would not lie quiet in his serial grave, but presently rose and walked as a book.

It happened in this way. The name of the magazine was To-Day, not the present paper of that name, but one of the many To-days which are now Yesterdays. It had several editors, among them Mr Belfort Bax and the late James Leigh Joynes; but all the editors were in partnership with Mr Henry Hyde Champion[6] who printed the magazine, and consequently went on for ever, whilst the others came and went. It was a fantastic business, Joynes having thrown up an Eton mastership, and Champion a commission in the army, at the call of Socialism. But Champion's pugnacity survived his abdicated adjutancy: he had an unregenerate taste for pugilism, and liked Cashel Byron so much that he stereotyped the pages of To-Day which it occupied, and in spite of my friendly remonstrances, hurled on the market a misshapen shilling edition. My friend Mr William Archer reviewed it prominently; the Saturday Review, always susceptible in those days to the arts of self-defence, unexpectedly declared it the novel of the age; Mr W. E. Henley[7] wanted to have it dramatized; [Robert Louis] Stevenson wrote a letter about it, of which more presently; the other papers hastily searched their waste-paper baskets for it and reviewed it, mostly rather disappointedly; and the public preserved its composure and did not seem to care.

That shilling edition began with a thousand [2,500] copies; but it proved immortal. I never got anything out of it; and Mr Champion never got anything out of it; for he presently settled in Australia, and his printing presses and stereo plates were dispersed. But from that time forth the book was never really out of print; and though Messrs Walter Scott soon placed a revised shilling edition on the market, I suspect that still, in some obscure printing office, those old plates of Mr Champion's from time to time produce a "remainder" of the original Modern Press edition, which is to the present what the Quarto Hamlet is to the Folio.

On the passing of To-Day, I became novelist in ordinary to a magazine called Our Corner, edited by Mrs Annie Besant. It had the singular habit

6. Bax, Joynes, and Champion were Socialist colleagues and friends of Shaw. The latter two were members of the Social-Democratic Federation, with which Shaw flirted before rejecting it as 'pseudo-Marxist' and joining the Fabians. The SDF later metamorphosed into the British Communist Party.
7. Poet, dramatist, and editor of the *Scots* (later *National*) *Observer*.

of paying for its contributions, and was, I am afraid, to some extent a device of Mrs Besant's for relieving necessitous young propagandists without wounding their pride by open almsgiving. She was an incorrigible benefactress, and probably revenged herself for my freely expressed scorn for this weakness by drawing on her private account to pay me for my jejune novels. At last Our Corner went the way of all propagandist magazines, completing a second nonage novel and its own career at the same moment. This left me with only one unprinted masterpiece, my Opus 1, which had cost me an unconscionable quantity of paper, and was called, with merciless fitness, Immaturity. Part of it had by this time been devoured by mice, though even they had not been able to finish it. To this day it has never escaped from its old brown paper travelling suit; and I only mention it because some of its characters appear, Trollope fashion, in the later novels. I do not think any of them got so far as Cashel Byron's Profession; but the Mrs Hoskyn and her guests who appear in that absurd Chapter VI are all borrowed from previous works.

The unimportance of these particulars must be my apology for detailing them to a world that finds something romantic in what are called literary struggles. However, I must most indignantly deny that I ever struggled. I wrote the books: it was the publishers who struggled with them, and struggled in vain. The public now takes up the struggle, impelled, not by any fresh operations of mine, but by Literary Destiny. For there is a third act to my tragedy.

Not long ago, when the memory of the brown paper parcels of 1879–1883 had been buried under twenty years of work, I learnt from the American papers that the list of book sales in one of the United States was headed by a certain novel called An Unsocial Socialist, by Bernard Shaw. This was unmistakably Opus 5 of the Novels of My Nonage. Columbia was beginning to look after her hitherto neglected acquisition. Apparently the result was encouraging; for presently the same publisher produced a new edition of Cashel Byron's Profession (Opus 4), in criticizing which the more thoughtful reviewers, unaware that the publisher was working backwards through the list, pointed out the marked advance in my style, the surer grip, the clearer form, the finer art, the maturer view of the world, and so forth. As it was clearly unfair that my own American publishers should be debarred by delicacy towards me from exploiting the new field of derelict fiction, I begged them to make the most of their national inheritance; and with my full approval, Opus 3, called Love among the Artists (a paraphrase of the forgotten line Love Among the

Roses)[8] followed. No doubt it will pay its way: people who will read An Unsocial Socialist will read anything. But the new enthusiasm for Cashel Byron did not stop here. American ladies were seized with a desire to go on the stage and be Lydia Carew for two thrilling hours. American actors "saw themselves" as Cashel. Mr James Corbett[9] has actually appeared on the New York stage in the part. There can be no doubt now that my novels, so long left for dead in the forlorn-hope magazines of the eighties, have arisen and begun to propagate themselves vigorously throughout the new world at the rate of a dollar and a half per copy, free of all royalty to the flattered author.

Blame not me, then, reader, if these exercises of a raw apprentice break loose again and insist on their right to live. The world never did know chalk from cheese in matters of art; and, after all, since it is only the young and the old who have time to read, the rest being too busy living, my exercises may be fitter for the market than my masterpieces.

Cashel Byron's Profession is not a very venturesome republication, because, as I have said, the story has never been really out of print. But for some years after the expiration of my agreement with Messrs Walter Scott I did my best to suppress it, though by that time it had become the subject of proposals from a new generation of publishers. The truth is, the preference for this particular novel annoyed me. In novel-writing there are two trustworthy dodges for capturing the public. One is to slaughter a child and pathosticate over its deathbed for a whole chapter. The other is to describe either a fight or a murder. There is a fight in Cashel Byron's Profession: that profession itself is fighting; and here lay the whole schoolboy secret of the book's little vogue. I had the old grievance of the author: people will admire him for the feats that any fool can achieve, and bear malice against him for boring them with better work. Besides, my conscience was not quite easy in the matter. In spite of all my pains to present the prizefighter and his pursuits without any romantic glamor (for indeed the true artistic material of the story is the comedy of the contrast between the realities of the ring and the common romantic glorification or sentimental abhorrence of it), yet our non-combatant citizens are so fond of setting other people to fight that the only effect of such descriptions as I

8. In the *Love Among the Roses Songster* (1869) 'Love Among the Roses' is the title of a 'Song and Dance': words by W. H. Delehanty, music by E. H. Catlen.
9. American boxer, who won the world's heavyweight championship from John L. Sullivan (1892).

have incidentally given of Cashel's professional performances is to make people want to see something of the sort and take steps accordingly. This tendency of the book was repugnant to me; and if prizefighting were a sleeping dog, I should certainly let it lie, in spite of the American editions.

Unfortunately the dog is awake, barking and biting vigorously. Twenty years ago prizefighting was supposed to be dead. Few living men remembered the palmy days when Tom and Jerry went to Jackson's rooms (where Byron—not Cashel, but the poet—studied "the noble art") to complete their education as Corinthians;[10] when Cribb fought Molyneux and was to Tom Spring what Skene was to Cashel Byron;[11] when Kemble engaged Dutch Sam to carry on the war with the O.P. rioters;[12] when [James] Sharples' portraits of leading bruisers were engraved on steel; when Bell's Life was a fashionable paper, and Pierce Egan's Boxiana a more expensive publishing enterprise than any modern Badminton volume.[13] The sport was supposed to have died of its own blackguardism by the second quarter of the century; but the connoisseur who approaches the subject without moral bias will, I think, agree with me that it must have lived by its blackguardism and died of its intolerable tediousness; for all prizefighters are not Cashel Byrons, and in barren dreariness and futility no spectacle on earth can contend with that of two exhausted men trying for hours to tire one another out at fisticuffs for the sake of their backers. The Sayers revival in the sixties only left the ring more discredited than ever, since the injuries formerly reserved for the combatants began, after their

10. 'And men unpractised in exchanging knocks / Must go to Jackson ere they dare to box': Lord Byron, 'Hints from Horace' (published posthumously, 1831). 'Gentleman' John Jackson, English boxing champion (1795–1800) founded the Pugilistic Club, where a 'Corinthian', a man of fashion about town, could learn 'the noble art'. The sporting reporter Pierce Egan in 1821 began publication of a monthly journal, *Life in London or The Day and Night Scenes of Jerry Hawthorn, Esq., and His Elegant Friend, Corinthian Tom, Accompanied by Bob Logic, the Oxonian, in Their Rambles and Sprees Through the Metropolis.*
11. Tom Cribb, English champion pugilist, defeated the American-born former slave Tom Molineaux (misspelled by Shaw). On his retirement in 1821 Cribb handed over the belt to Tom Spring. Cashel Byron's manager, Ned Skene, in Shaw's novel, educated him to view prize-fighting as an art and science.
12. J. P. Kemble, English actor-manager, hired the 'bruiser' Dutch Sam to help quell the O.P. (Old Prices) riots by theatre-goers in 1808 that ensued when he abolished the shilling gallery at Covent Garden.
13. *Boxiana; or Sketches of ancient and modern pugilism from the days of the renowned Broughton and Slack, to the heroes of the present milling era*, a monthly (1818–24) written and published by Pierce Egan. *The Badminton Library of Sports and Pastimes*, edited by Henry Somerset, was published (1886–1920) in 72 volumes.

culmination in the poisoning of Heenan,[14] to be showered on the referee; and as the referee was usually the representative of the Bell's Life type of paper, which naturally organized the prizefights it lived by reporting, the ring went under again, this time undoubtedly through its blackguardism and violence driving away its only capable organizers.

In the eighties many apparently lost causes and dead enthusiasms unexpectedly revived: Imperialism, Patriotism, Religion, Socialism, and many other things, including prizefighting in an aggravated form, and on a scale of commercial profit and publicity which soon made its palmy days insignificant and ridiculous by contrast. A modern American pugilist makes more by a single defeat than Cribb made by all his victories.[15] It is this fact that has decided me to give up my attempt to suppress Cashel Byron's Profession. Silence may be the right policy on a dropped subject; but on a burning one every word that can cool the fervor of idolatry with a dash of cold fact has its value.

I need not postpone a comment on the vast propaganda of pugnacity in modern fiction: a propaganda that must be met, not by shocked silence, but by counter-propaganda. And this counter-propaganda must not take the usual form of "painting the horrors." Horror is fascinating: the great criminal is always a popular hero. People are seduced by romance because they are ignorant of reality; and this is as true of the prize ring as of the battlefield. The intelligent prizefighter is not a knight-errant: he is a disillusioned man of business trying to make money at a certain weight and at certain risks, not of bodily injury (for a bruise is soon cured), but of pecuniary loss. When he is a Jew, a negro, a gypsy, or a recruit from that gypsified, nomadic, poaching, tinkering, tramping class which exists in all countries, he differs from the phlegmatic John Bull pugilist (an almost extinct species) exactly as he would differ from him in any other occupation: that is, he is a more imaginative liar, a more obvious poser, a more plausible talker, a vainer actor, a more reckless gambler, and more easily persuaded that he is beaten or even killed when he has only received an unusually hard punch. The unintelligent prizefighter is often the helpless tool of a gang of gamblers, backers, and showmen, who set him on to fight as they might set on a dog. And the spectacle of a poor human animal

14. The fight between the English pugilist Tom Sayers and the American national champion John C. Heenan in 1860 is perhaps the most famous in the history of the English prize-ring.
15. Shaw may have had in mind John L. Sullivan's profitable loss to James Corbett in 1892.

fighting faithfully for his backers, like a terrier killing rats, or a racehorse doing its best to win a race for its owner, is one which ought to persuade any sensible person of the folly of treating the actual combatants as "the principals" in a prizefight. Cockfighting was not suppressed by imprisoning the cocks; and prizefighting will not be suppressed by imprisoning the pugilists. But, intelligent or unintelligent, first rate like Cashel Byron, second rate like Skene, or third rate like William Paradise [Byron's last ring opponent] in this story, the prizefighter is no more what the spectators imagine him to be than the lady with the wand and star in the pantomime is really a fairy queen. And since Cashel Byron's Profession, on its prizefighting side, is an attempt to take the reader behind the scenes without unfairly confusing professional pugilism with the blackguardly environment which is no more essential to it than to professional cricket, and which is now losing its hold on the pugilist through the substitution of gate-money at boxing exhibitions for stakes at prizefights as his means of living, I think I may let it go its way with a reasonable prospect of seeing it do more good than harm.

It may even help in the Herculean task of eliminating romantic fisticuffs from English novels, and so clear them from the reproach of childishness and crudity which they certainly deserve in this respect. Even in the best XIX century novels the heroes knock the villains down. [Edward] Bulwer Lytton's Kenelm Chillingly [*Kenelm Chillingly: His Adventures and Opinions*, 1873] was a "scientific" pugilist, though his technique will hardly be recognized by experts. Thackeray, who, when defeated in a parliamentary election, publicly compared himself to Gregson beaten by Gully,[16] loved a fight almost as much as he loved a fool. Even the great Dickens himself never quite got away from this sort of schoolboyishness; for though Jo Gargery knocking down Orlick is much more plausible than Oliver Twist punching the head of Noah Claypole, still the principle is the same: virtue still insists on victory, domination, and triumphant assault and battery. It is true that Dombey and Son contains a pious attempt to caricature a prizefighter; but no qualified authority will pretend that Dickens caught the Chicken's point of view, or did justice to the social accomplishments of the ring. Mr Toots's silly admiration of the poor boxer, and the manner in which the Chicken and other professors of the art of self-defence used to sponge on him, is perfectly true to life; but in the real pugilistic world so profitable a gull would soon have been taken out of the hands of the Chicken and preyed upon by much better company. It is true that if

16. John Gully, later a Member of Parliament, defeated Bob Gregson in October 1807 in a fight that lasted thirty-six rounds.

the Chicken had been an unconquerable fighter, he might have maintained a gloomy eminence in spite of his dulness and disagreeable manners; but Dickens gave away this one possible excuse by allowing The Larky Boy to defeat the Chicken with ignominy.[17] That is what is called poetic justice. It is really poetic criminal law; and it is almost as dishonest and vindictive as real criminal law. In plain fact the pugilistic profession is like any other profession: common sense, good manners, and a social turn count for as much in it as they do elsewhere; and as the pugilist makes a good deal of money by teaching gentlemen to box, he has to learn to behave himself, and often succeeds very much better than the average middle-class professional man. Shakespear was much nearer the mark when he made Autolycus better company, and Charles the Wrestler a better-mannered man, than Ajax or Cloten.[18] If Dickens had really known the ring, he would have made the Chicken either a Sayers in professional ability or a Sam Weller [in *Pickwick Papers*] in sociability. A successful combination of personal repulsiveness with professional incompetence is as impossible there as at the bar or in the faculty. The episode of the Chicken, then, must be dismissed, in spite of its hero's tempting suggested remedy for Mr Dombey's stiffness,[19] as a futile atonement for the heroic fisticuffs of Oliver Twist and Co.

There is an abominable vein of retaliatory violence all through the literature of the XIX century. Whether it is [Thomas] Macaulay describing the flogging of Titus Oates [in *History of England*, 1849–61], or Dickens inventing the scene in which old Martin Chuzzlewit bludgeons Pecksniff,[20] the curious childishness of the English character, its naughty relish for

17. In *Great Expectations* (1860–61) the blacksmith, Joe Gargery, strikes his apprentice, Dolge Orlick, after the latter attacks Mrs Gargery. In *Oliver Twist* (1837–9) Oliver hits the undertaker's apprentice Noah Claypole when the latter insults the memory of Oliver's dead mother. In *Dombey and Son* (1846–8) the Game Chicken, a professional fighter, tutors the slow-witted Mr Toots, knocking him about the head thrice weekly at half a guinea a visit. The Larkey Boy in the same novel is a fighter who trounces the Chicken.

18. All are Shakespearian characters: Autolycus, a rogue in *The Winter's Tale*; Charles, a wrestler in *As You Like It*; Ajax, a Grecian commander in *Troilus and Cressida*; Cloten, a son of the queen in *Cymbeline*.

19. The Chicken suggests to the lovelorn Mr Toots that 'you could knock . . . the stiff'un [Mr Dombey] . . . dead out o' wind and time . . .' (*Dombey and Son*, Chapter 56).

20. Seth Pecksniff, a moralizing hypocrite, is a fawning cousin of old Martin Chuzzlewit, who gives Pecksniff a comeuppance at the end of the novel *Martin Chuzzlewit* (1843–4).

primitive brutalities and tolerance of physical indignities, its unreasoning destructiveness when incommoded, crop up in all directions. The childishness has its advantages: its want of foresight prevents the individual from carrying weapons, as it prevents the nation from being prepared for war; its forgetfulness prevents vendettas and prolonged malice-bearing; its simplicity and transparency save it from the more ingenious and complicated forms of political corruption. In short, it has those innocences of childhood which are a necessary result of its impotences. But it has no true sense of human dignity. The son of a Russian noble is not flogged at school, because he commits suicide sooner than survive the outrage to his self-respect. The son of an English noble has no more sense of dignity than the master who flogs him: flogging may be troublesome to the flogger and painful to the floggee; but the notion that the transaction is disgusting to the public and dishonorable and disgraceful to the parties is as unintelligible and fantastic in England as it is in a nursery anywhere. The moment the Englishman gets away from Eton, he begins to enjoy and boast of flogging as an institution. A school where boys are flogged and where they settle their quarrels by fighting with their fists he calls, not, as one might expect, a school of childishness, but a school of manliness. And he gradually persuades himself that all Englishmen can use their fists, which is about as true as the parallel theory that every Frenchman can handle a foil and that every Italian carries a stiletto. And so, though he himself has never fought a pitched battle at school, and does not, pugilistically speaking, know his right hand from his left; though his neighbors are as peaceful and as nervous as he; though if he knocked a man down or saw one of his friends do it, the event would stand out in his history like a fire or a murder; yet he not only tolerates unstinted knockings-down in fiction, but actually founds his conception of his nation and its destiny on these imaginary outrages, and at last comes to regard a plain statement of the plain fact that the average respectable Englishman knows rather less about fighting than he does about flying, as a paradoxical extravagance.

And so every popular English novel becomes a gospel of pugilism. Cashel Byron's Profession, then, is like any other novel in respect of its hero punching people's heads. Its novelty consists in the fact that an attempt is made to treat the art of punching seriously, and to detach it from the general elevation of moral character with which the ordinary novelist persists in associating it.

Here, therefore, the prizefighter is not idolized. I have given Cashel Byron every advantage a prizefighter can have: health and strength and pugilistic genius. But by pugilistic genius I mean nothing vague, imaginary, or glamorous. In all walks of life men are to be found who seem to have powers of divination. For example, you propound a complicated arithmetical problem: say the cubing of a number containing four digits. Give me a slate and half an hour's time, and I can produce a wrong answer. But there are men to whom the right answer is instantly obvious without any consciousness of calculation on their part. Ask such a man to write a description or put a somewhat complicated thought into words; and he will take my slate and blunder over it in search of words for half an hour, finally putting down the wrong ones; whilst for a Shakespear the words are there in due style and measure as soon as the consciousness of the thing to be described or the formation of the thought. Now there are pugilists to whom the process of aiming and estimating distance in hitting, of considering the evidence as to what their opponent is going to do, arriving at a conclusion, and devising and carrying out effective counter-measures, is as instantaneous and unconscious as the calculation of the born arithmetician or the verbal expression of the born writer. This is not more wonderful than the very complicated and deeply considered feats of breathing and circulating the blood, which everybody does continually without thinking; but it is much rarer, and so has a miraculous appearance. A man with this gift, and with no physical infirmities to disable him, is a born prizefighter. He need have no other exceptional qualities, courage least of all: indeed there are instances on record of prizefighters who have only consented to persevere with a winning fight when a mirror has been brought to convince them that their faces were undamaged and their injuries and terrors imaginary. "Stage fright" is as common in the ring as elsewhere: I have myself seen a painful exhibition of it from a very rough customer who presently knocked out his opponent without effort, by instinct. The risks of the ring are limited by rules and conditions to such an extent that the experienced prizefighter is much more afraid of the blackguardism of the spectators than of his opponent: he takes care to have a strong body of supporters in his corner, and to keep carefully away from the opposite corner. Courage is if anything rather scarcer, because less needed, in the ring than out of it; and there are civil occupations which many successful prizefighters would fail in, or fear to enter, for want of nerve. For the ring, like all romantic institutions, has a natural attraction for hysterical people.

When a pugilistic genius of the Cashel Byron type appeared in the ring of his day, it soon became evident to the betting men on whom the institution depended, that it was useless to back clever boxers against him;

for, as the second Lytton (Owen Meredith) wrote ['Talent and Genius', 1870] —

> Talk not of genius baffled: genius is master of man.
> Genius does what it must; and Talent does what it can.

But there is a well-known way of defeating the pugilistic genius. There are hard-fisted, hard-hitting men in the world, who will, with the callousness of a ship's figurehead, and almost with its helplessness in defence, take all the hammering that genius can give them, and, when genius can hammer no more from mere exhaustion, give it back its blows with interest and vanquish it. All pugilism lies between these two extremes typified by Cashel Byron and William Paradise; and it is because the Paradises are as likely to win as the Byrons, and are by no means so scarce, that the case for fist fighting, with gloves or without, as a discipline in the higher athletic qualities, moral and physical, imposes only on people who have no practical knowledge of the subject.

On a previous page I have alluded to a letter from Robert Louis Stevenson to Mr William Archer about Cashel Byron's Profession. Part of that letter has been given to the public in the second volume of Mr Sidney Colvin's edition of Stevenson's letters (Methuen, 1900). But no document concerning a living person of any consequence (by which I mean a person with money enough to take an action for libel) is ever published in England unless its contents are wholly complimentary. Stevenson's letters were probably all unfit for publication in this respect. Certainly the one about Cashel Byron's Profession was; and Mr Sidney Colvin, out of consideration for me and for his publishers and printers, politely abbreviated it. Fortunately the original letter is still in the hands of Mr Archer. I need not quote the handsome things which Mr Colvin selected, as they have been extensively reprinted in America to help the sale of the reprints there. But here is the suppressed portion, to which I leave the last word, having no more to say than that the book is now reprinted, not from the old Modern Press edition which Stevenson read, but from the revised text issued afterwards by Messrs Walter Scott, from which certain "little bits of Social-ism daubed in" for the edification of the readers of To-Day were either painted out or better harmonized with the rest. I had intended to make no further revision; and I have in fact made none of any importance; but in reading the proofs my pen positively jumped to humanize a few passages in which the literary professionalism with which my heroine expresses herself (this professionalism is usually called "style" in England) went past all bearing. I have also indulged myself by varying a few sentences, and inserting one or two new ones, so as to enable the American publisher to secure copyright in this edition. But I have made no attempt to turn an 1882 novel into a twentieth century one; and the few alterations are, except for legal purposes, quite negligible.

And now for the suppressed part of Stevenson's verdict, which is in the form of an analysis of the book's composition.

"Charles Reade . . . . 1 part
Henry James or some kindred author, badly assimilated . . 1 part
Disraeli (perhaps unconscious) . . . . $\frac{1}{2}$ part
Struggling, overlaid original talent . . . . . . $1\frac{1}{2}$ part
Blooming gaseous folly . . . . 1 part

"That is the equation as it stands. What it may become, I dont know, nor any other man. *Vixere fortes*[21]—O, let him remember that—let him beware of his damned century: his gifts of insane chivalry and animated narration are just those that might be slain and thrown out like an untimely birth by the Dæmon of the Epoch.

"And if he only knew how I had enjoyed the chivalry! Bashville—O Bashville! *j'en chortle!*[22] (which is finely polygot).''

1901.

POSTSCRIPT TWENTYNINE YEARS LATER. Pages [93] and [94] of this preface must be read with some reservations. Belfort Bax, Henry Hyde Champion, William Archer, and W. E. Henley are no longer Misters: they are all dead. And the novel that "never escaped from its brown travelling suit" has at last escaped, to be published for the first time in the Collected Edition of my works fifty years after I wrote Finis on its last page.

1930.

21. '*Vixere fortes ante Agamemnona*': Horace, *Odes* IV: ix. Rendered by Byron in *Don Juan* (I: v) as: 'Brave men were living before Agamemnon/And since, exceeding valorous and sage'.
22. 'I chuckle/snort at it'. The portmanteau 'chortle' was coined by Lewis Carroll in *Through the Looking Glass* (1872). Apparently Stevenson continues the playfulness with 'polygot' rather than 'polyglot'.

The Admirable Bashville

A dramatization of Shaw's novel Cashel Byron's Profession, 1882

———

This is the final version of a preface written originally for the 1901 publication of the play, abridged and revised for the 1926 Globe Edition of Shaw's plays, and expanded for the Collected Edition, 1930.

It may be asked why I wrote The Admirable Bashville in blank verse. My answer is that the operation of the copyright law of that time (now happily superseded) left me only a week to write it in.[1] Blank verse is so childishly easy and expeditious (hence, by the way, Shakespear's copious output), that by adopting it I was enabled to do within the week what would have cost me a month in prose.

Besides, I am fond of blank verse. Not XIX century blank verse, of course, nor indeed, with a very few exceptions, any post-Shakespearean blank verse. Nay, not Shakespearean blank verse itself later than the histories. I am quite sure that anyone who is to recover the charm of blank verse must go back frankly to its beginnings, and start a literary pre-Raphaelite Brotherhood. I like the melodious sing-song, the clear simple one-line and two-line sayings, and the occasional rhymed tags, like the half closes in an XVIII century symphony, in [George] Peele, [Thomas] Kyd, [Robert] Greene, and the histories of Shakespear. Accordingly, I poetasted The Admirable Bashville in the primitive Elizabethan style. And lest the literary connoisseurs should declare that there was not a single correct line in all my three acts, I stole or paraphrased a few from Marlowe and Shakespear (not to mention Henry Carey [poet and musician]); so that if any man dared quote me derisively, he should do so in peril of inadvertently lighting on a purple patch from Hamlet or Faustus.

---

1. *Cashel Byron's Profession* was dramatized and performed in the United States in 1900 without authorization or payment of royalties. To establish his copyright and prevent further productions, it was necessary under the new American copyright law for Shaw to make his own dramatization and 'stage it' by way of a copyright-reading performance in London.

I also endeavored in this little play to prove that I was not the heartless creature some of my critics took me for. I observed the established laws of stage popularity and probability. I simplified the character of the heroine, and summed up her sweetness in the one sacred word: Love. I gave consistency to the heroism of Cashel. I paid to Morality, in the final scene, the tribute of poetic justice. I restored to Patriotism its usual place on the stage, and gracefully acknowledged The Throne as the fountain of social honor. I paid particular attention to the construction of the play, which will be found equal in this respect to the best contemporary models.

And the result was that the British playgoer, to whom Elizabethan English is a dead language, only half understood nine tenths of the play, and applauded the other tenth (the big speeches) with a seriousness that was far funnier than any burlesque.

The play, by the way, should be performed on an Elizabethan stage, with traverses for the indoor scenes, and with only one interval after the second act.

★

On reading over the above after a lapse of thirty years I am not quite so sure as I was that Elizabethan English may not again become a living language to the ordinary playgoer. To people who never read anything but newspapers and popular magazines, a good deal of Shakespear's more euphuistic blank verse is hardly more intelligible than classical Greek. Even actors may be heard repeating it by rote with an air that persuades the public that they understand what they are saying; but it cannot impose any such illusion on a professionally skilled listener.

Then there are the people who do not go to Protestant churches nor read anything at all, and consequently understand no English except modern vernacular English. This class is by no means a negligible one even in the theatre; for it includes a large body of intelligent manual and open air workers and sportsmen who, though after their day's exertions they fall asleep in less than a minute if they sit down with an open book in their hands, can be kept awake and alert very effectually in the theatre by a play. Only, it must be a play in the vernacular. Otherwise it does not exist for them except as an incomprehensible bore.

There was a time when not only the theatres but the newspapers addressed themselves to the literate alone. Hunt up an old melodrama (say [F. Hazelton's] Sweeney Todd the Demon Barber of Fleet Street) or an old newspaper file; and you will at once see that the writers of the play and of the contemporary leading articles, though they may have been the seediest

of Bohemians, had learnt Latin grammar and read books written by persons
similarly schooled. They had literally the benefit of clergy, and wrote
accordingly. With the advent of compulsory education sixty years ago, and
the creation thereby of a class which could read and write, but had no
Latin and less Greek, newspapers and plays alike soon came to be written
by illiterate masters of the vernacular; and I myself welcomed the change
and discarded my early very classical style for a vernacular one. Nowadays,
when I read typewritten plays by young authors, as I sometimes have
occasion to do, I find in them such illiteracies as He exits, She exits, They
exit etc. etc. [George] Chapman, who wrote all his stage directions in
Latin, or Ben Jonson, who deplored the slenderness of Shakespear's classical
education, would have risen up and roared for a birchrod to castigate such
execrable solecisms.[2] By the end of the XIX century the press and the
theatre had lost all their Latinity; and this was why, whenever The
Admirable Bashville was performed, men of letters like Maurice Hewlett[3]
would chuckle delightedly over it almost line by line, whilst the ordinary
playgoers would listen with a puzzled and troubled stare, wondering what
on earth it was all about and how they ought to take it, and the unfortunate
persons who had been forced to "get up Shakespear" as part of an academic
course on English literature, sat with a scowl of malignant hatred that
poisoned the atmosphere. When Bashville was followed by a piece in the
vernacular the relief of the audience was so great that there was always a
burst of applause at the very first sentence.

And yet, whenever the meaning of the words was clear, the listeners
shewed unmistakably that they liked hyperbolical rhetoric and deliberately
artificial language. My parodies of the Elizabethan mannerism, and funny
echoes of pet lines from the Elizabethan playwrights were, as such, quite
lost on them; but Ben Webster brought down the house [Stage Society
production, London, 1903] with Cashel Byron's declamatory repudiation
of the name of gentleman, and James Hearn's lamentation over the tragedy
of Cetewayo came off, not as a mockery, but as genuine tragedy, which
indeed it also is. It was the literary fun that proved a mere puzzle, in spite
of the acting of casts which included such accomplished comedians as
Charles Quatermaine, William Wyes, Lennox Pawle, Henrietta Watson,
Marie Lohr, and Fanny Brough.

2. Chapman and Jonson would have used the third person singular (*exit*) or plural
(*exeunt*) of the Latin verb *exire* (to go out) sans pronouns.
3. English writer, Foreign Office diplomat, and unsuccessful playwright, whom
Shaw befriended and advised.

Another significant fact pointed in the same direction. In no country is the worship of the old authorized version of the Bible carried to greater lengths than in the United States of America. To alter a single word of it was, it was believed, to incur the curse in the last chapter of Revelation. Even in England the very timid official revision of 1885[4] shocked our native Fundamentalists (a ridiculous but convenient name not then invented). Yet it was in the United States that the ministers of religion first found themselves compelled to produce versions in modern vernacular and journalese under stress of the flat fact that their flocks often could not understand the old authorized version, and always found the style so artificial that though it could produce an unintelligent reverence it brought no intimate conviction to the reader.

Sometimes, however, the simple and direct passages were not sentimental enough to satisfy people whose minds were steeped in modern literary sob stuff. For instance, such bald statements about Barabbas as that he was a robber, or that he had killed a certain man in a sedition, quite failed to interest anyone in him; but when Marie Corelli expanded this concise information into a novel [*Barabbas*, 1893] in her own passionate and richly colored style it sold like hot cakes.

I must make a personal confession in this matter. Though I was saturated with the Bible and with Shakespear before I was ten years old, and the only grammar I ever learned was Latin grammar, so that Elizabethan English became a mother tongue to me, yet when I first read such vivid and unaffected modern versions as Dr James Moffatt's New Translation of the New Testament [1901] I at once got from them so many lights on the Bible narratives which I had missed in the authorized version that I said to myself "Some day I will translate Hamlet into modern vernacular English." But indeed if the alienation of our young from Elizabethan English continues it will be necessary to produce revised versions not only of Shakespear but of Sir Walter Scott and even of my own early novels.

Still, a revival of Elizabethan literature may be possible. If I, as an Irish child in the eighteen-sixties, could without enforced study become so familiar with it that I had some difficulty as a journalist later on in getting rid of it, it must be possible for the same thing to occur to an English child in the nineteen-sixties. The Elizabethan style has many charms for imaginative children. It is bloody, bombastic, violent, senselessly pretentious,

4. In 1870 the Convocation of Canterbury appointed two teams of scholars to revise the Authorized Version of the Bible. The English Revised Version was published, of the New Testament in 1881, of the Old Testament in 1885.

barbarous and childish in its humor, and full of music. In short, the taste for it, as anyone can observe at the Old Vic or the Stratford Festivals, is essentially half childish, half musical. To acquire it, all that is necessary is access to it. Now the opportunities for such access are enormously wider than they used to be. Of course as long as we persist in stuffing Shakespear and the Bible down our children's throats with threats of condign punishment if they fail to answer silly questions about them, they will continue to be loathed as they very largely are at present. But if our children, when they have been simply taught to read, have plenty of dramatically illustrated Bibles and Shakespears left in their way, with the illustrated passages printed under the pictures, it will soon be possible to find a general audience which can laugh at The Admirable Bashville as heartily as Maurice Hewlett did, and for repertory theatres to amuse themselves and their congregations with occasional performances of Carey's Chrononhotonthologos [1734], Fielding's Tom Thumb [1730], and even [W. B. Rhodes's] Bombastes Furioso [1810].

I shall not here raise the question of whether such a revival is desirable. It would carry me too far and plunge me too deep for a volume of trifles and tomfooleries. But as the Elizabethan style is unquestionably both musical and powerful, I may at least say that it is better to have a sense of it and a fancy for it than to have no sense of style or literary fancy at all.

The Perfect Wagnerite

Preface to the second English edition, 1902

━━━━

The preparation of a Second Edition of this booklet is quite the most unexpected literary task that has ever been set me. When it first appeared I was ungrateful enough to remonstrate with its publisher for printing, as I thought, more copies than the most sanguine Wagnerite could ever hope to sell. But the result proved that exactly one person buys a copy on every day in the year, including Sundays; and so, in the process of the suns, a reprint has become necessary.

Save a few verbal slips of no importance, I have found nothing to alter in this edition. As usual, the only protests the book has elicited are protests, not against the opinions it expresses, but against the facts it records. There are people who cannot bear to be told that their hero was associated with a famous Anarchist [Mikhail Bakunin] in a rebellion; that he was proclaimed as "wanted" by the police;[1] that he wrote revolutionary pamphlets; and that his picture of Niblunghome under the reign of Alberic is a poetic vision of unregulated industrial capitalism as it was made known in Germany in the middle of the XIX century by Engels's Condition of the Laboring Classes in England. They frantically deny these facts, and then declare that I have connected them with Wagner in a paroxysm of senseless perversity. I am sorry I have hurt them; and I appeal to charitable publishers to bring out a new life of Wagner, which shall describe him as a court musician of unquestioned fashion and orthodoxy, and a pillar of the most exclusive Dresden circles. Such a work would, I believe, have a large sale, and be read with satisfaction and reassurance by many lovers of Wagner's music.

As to my much demurred-to relegation of Night Falls on The Gods to the category of grand opera, I have nothing to add or withdraw. Such a classification is to me as much a matter of fact as the Dresden rising or the police proclamation; but I shall not pretend that it is a matter of such fact as everybody's judgment can grapple with. People who prefer grand opera to

1. Socialist revolutions in Naples and Paris in 1848 soon spread throughout Europe. Wagner was 'wanted' because he had been a leader of the Dresden uprising.

serious music–drama naturally resent my placing a very grand opera below a very serious music–drama. The ordinary lover of Shakespear would equally demur to my placing his popular catchpenny plays, of which As You Like It is an avowed type, below true Shakespearean plays like Measure for Measure. I cannot help that. Popular dramas and operas may have overwhelming merits as enchanting make-believes; but a poet's sincerest vision of the world must always take precedence of his prettiest fool's paradise.

As many English Wagnerites seem to be still under the impression that Wagner composed Rienzi in his youth, Tannhäuser and Lohengrin in his middle age, and The Ring in his later years, may I again remind them that The Ring was the result of a political convulsion which occurred when Wagner was only thirty-six, and that the poem was completed when he was forty, with thirty more years of work before him? It is as much a first essay in political philosophy as Die Feen[2] is a first essay in romantic opera. The attempt to recover its spirit twenty years later, when the music of Night Falls on The Gods was added, was an attempt to revive the barricades of Dresden in the Temple of the Grail. Only those who have never had any political enthusiasms to survive can believe that such an attempt could succeed.

LONDON, 1901.   G. B. S.

2. *Die Feen* (*The Fairies*) was Wagner's first opera, completed in 1833 at the age of twenty.

The Author's Apology
(Mrs Warren's Profession)

Preface to 1902 Stage Society edition; revised and expanded for
Collected Edition, 1930, incorporating most of the original preface to
How He Lied to Her Husband, *1907*

———

Mrs Warren's Profession was written in 1894 to draw attention to the truth that prostitution is caused, not by female depravity and male licentiousness, but simply by underpaying, undervaluing, and overworking women so shamefully that the poorest of them are forced to resort to prostitution to keep body and soul together. Indeed all attractive unpropertied women lose money by being infallibly virtuous or contracting marriages that are not more or less venal. If on the large social scale we get what we call vice instead of what we call virtue it is simply because we are paying more for it. No normal woman would be a professional prostitute if she could better herself by being respectable, nor marry for money if she could afford to marry for love.

Also I desired to expose the fact that prostitution is not only carried on without organization by individual enterprise in the lodgings of solitary women, each her own mistress as well as every customer's mistress, but organized and exploited as a big international commerce for the profit of capitalists like any other commerce, and very lucrative to great city estates, including Church estates, through the rents of the houses in which it is practised.

I could not have done anything more injurious to my prospects at the outset of my career. My play was immediately stigmatized by the Lord Chamberlain, who by Act of Parliament has despotic and even supermonarchical power over our theatres, as "immoral and otherwise improper for the stage." Its performance was prohibited, I myself being branded by implication, to my great damage, as an unscrupulous and blackguardly author. True, I have lived this defamation down, and am apparently none the worse. True too that the stage under the censorship became so licentious after the war that the ban on a comparatively prudish play like mine became ridiculous and had to be lifted. Also I admit that my career as a revolutionary critic of our most respected social institutions kept me so continually in hot water that the addition of another jugful of boiling fluid by the Lord Chamberlain troubled me too little to entitle me to personal commiseration, especially as the play greatly strengthened my repute among serious readers. Besides, in 1894 the ordinary commercial theatres would have nothing to say to me, Lord Chamberlain or no Lord Chamberlain. None the less the injury done me now admittedly indefensible, was real and considerable, and the injury to society much greater; for when the White Slave Traffic, as Mrs Warren's profession came to be called, was dealt with legislatively, all that Parliament did was to enact that prostitutes' male bullies and parasites should be flogged, leaving Mrs Warren in complete command of the situation, and its true nature more effectually masked than ever. It was the fault of the Censorship that our legislators and journalists were not better instructed.

In 1902 the Stage Society, technically a club giving private performances for the entertainment of its own members, and therefore exempt from the Lord Chamberlain's jurisdiction, resolved to perform the play. None of the public theatres dared brave his displeasure (he has absolute power to close them if they offend him) by harboring the performance; but another club [New Lyric Club] which had a little stage, and which rather courted a pleasantly scandalous reputation, opened its doors for one night and one afternoon. Some idea of the resultant sensation may be gathered from the following polemic, which appeared as a preface to a special edition of the play, and was headed:

THE AUTHOR'S APOLOGY

Mrs Warren's Profession has been performed at last [5 January 1902], after a delay of only eight years; and I have once more shared with Ibsen the triumphant amusement of startling all but the strongest-headed of the London theatre critics clean out of the practice of their profession. No author who has ever known the exultation of sending the Press into an hysterical tumult of protest, of moral panic, of involuntary and frantic confession of sin, of a horror of conscience in which the power of distinguishing between the work of art on the stage and the real life of the spectator is confused and overwhelmed, will ever care for the stereotyped compliments which every successful farce or melodrama elicits from the newspapers. Give me that critic who rushed from my play to declare furiously that Sir George Crofts ought to be kicked. What a triumph for the actor, thus to reduce a jaded London journalist to the condition of the simple sailor in the Wapping gallery, who shouts execrations at Iago and warnings to Othello not to believe him![1] But dearer still than such simplicity is that sense of the sudden earthquake shock to the foundations of morality which sends a pallid crowd of critics into the street shrieking that the pillars of society are cracking and the ruin of the State at hand. Even the Ibsen champions of ten years ago remonstrate with me just as the veterans of those brave days remonstrated with them. Mr Grein, the hardy iconoclast who first launched my plays on the stage alongside Ghosts and The Wild Duck, exclaims that I have shattered his ideals [*Sunday Special*, 12 January 1902]. Actually his ideals! What would Dr Relling say?[2] And Mr William Archer himself disowns me because I "cannot touch pitch without wallowing in it [the *World*, 15 January 1902]." Truly my play must be more needed than I knew; and yet I thought I knew how little the others know.

Do not suppose, however, that the consternation of the Press reflects any consternation among the general public. Anybody can upset the theatre critics, in a turn of the wrist, by substituting for the romantic commonplaces of the stage the moral commonplaces of the pulpit, the platform, or the library. Play Mrs Warren's Profession to an audience of clerical members of the Christian Social Union and of women well experienced in Rescue, Temperance, and Girls' Club work,* and no moral panic will arise: every man and woman present will know that as long as poverty makes virtue hideous and the spare pocket-money of rich bachelordom makes vice dazzling, their daily hand-to-hand fight against prostitution with prayer and persuasion, shelters and scanty alms, will be a losing one. There was a time when they were able to urge that though "the white-lead factory where Anne Jane was poisoned"[3] may be a far more terrible place than Mrs Warren's house, yet hell is still more dreadful. Nowadays they no

---

* Many a specialist of the stalls will shudder at his own dreary conception of such an audience; but I can assure him that he would hardly know where he was on such an occasion, so much more vital would the atmosphere be, and so much jollier and better-looking the people. [GBS] [The note was deleted in 1930.]

1. The gallery (popularly known as 'the Gods') contains a theatre's cheapest seats. Shaw's tale is apocryphal, for there was no theatre in Wapping, a dock area of London's East End, and the theatres that thrived in other low-income districts of the city specialized in melodrama for their working-class audiences.
2. Dr Relling is a character in Ibsen's *The Wild Duck* (1884), ironically aware of the comforting nature of ideals..
3. The fate of Anne Jane, half-sister of Mrs Warren, is recounted in Act II of the play.

longer believe in hell; and the girls among whom they are working know that they do not believe in it, and would laugh at them if they did. So well have the rescuers learnt that Mrs Warren's defence of herself and indictment of society is the thing that most needs saying, that those who know me personally reproach me, not for writing this play, but for wasting my energies on "pleasant plays" for the amusement of frivolous people, when I can build up such excellent stage sermons on their own work. Mrs Warren's Profession is the one play of mine which I could submit to a censorship without doubt of the result; only, it must not be the censorship of the minor theatre critic, nor of an innocent court official like the Lord Chamberlain's Examiner,[4] much less of people who consciously profit by Mrs Warren's profession, or who personally make use of it, or who hold the widely whispered view that it is an indispensable safety-valve for the protection of domestic virtue, or, above all, who are smitten with a sentimental affection for our fallen sister, and would "take her up tenderly, lift her with care, fashioned so slenderly, young, and *so* fair [Thomas Hood, 'The Bridge of Sighs', 1844]." Nor am I prepared to accept the verdict of the medical gentlemen who would compulsorily examine and register Mrs Warren, whilst leaving Mrs Warren's patrons, especially her military patrons, free to destroy her health and anybody else's without fear of reprisals. But I should be quite content to have my play judged by, say, a joint committee of the Central Vigilance Society and the Salvation Army. And the sterner moralists the members of the committee were, the better.

Some of the journalists I have shocked reason so unripely that they will gather nothing from this but a confused notion that I am accusing the National Vigilance Association and the Salvation Army of complicity in my own scandalous immorality. It will seem to them that people who would stand this play would stand anything. They are quite mistaken. Such an audience as I have described would be revolted by many of our fashionable plays. They would leave the theatre convinced that the Plymouth Brother[5] who still regards the playhouse as one of the gates of hell is

4. Reader for the Lord Chamberlain. By a law of 1843 the Lord Chamberlain, senior officer of the royal household, became censor of plays. On the recommendation of his reader he could ban a play 'for the preservation of good manners, decorum, or of the public peace'. A negative report by the reader, George Alexander Redford, in 1897 resulted in the denial of a licence for production of *Mrs Warren's Profession*.
5. A religious body that had its inception in that city in 1830, recognizing no official order of ministers and lacking any formal creed.

perhaps the safest adviser on the subject of which he knows so little. If I do not draw the same conclusion, it is not because I am one of those who claim that art is exempt from moral obligations, and deny that the writing or performance of a play is a moral act, to be treated on exactly the same footing as theft or murder if it produces equally mischievous consequences. I am convinced that fine art is the subtlest, the most seductive, the most effective instrument of moral propaganda in the world, excepting only the example of personal conduct; and I waive even this exception in favor of the art of the stage, because it works by exhibiting examples of personal conduct made intelligible and moving to crowds of unobservant unreflecting people to whom real life means nothing. I have pointed out again and again that the influence of the theatre in England is growing so great that private conduct, religion, law, science, politics, and morals are becoming more and more theatrical, whilst the theatre itself remains impervious to common sense, religion, science, politics, and morals. That is why I fight the theatre, not with pamphlets and sermons and treatises, but with plays; and so effective do I find the dramatic method that I have no doubt I shall at last persuade even London to take its conscience and its brains with it when it goes to the theatre, instead of leaving them at home with its prayer-book as it does at present. Consequently, I am the last man to deny that if the net effect of performing Mrs Warren's Profession were an increase in the number of persons entering that profession or employing it, its performance might well be made an indictable offence.

Now let us consider how such recruiting can be encouraged by the theatre. Nothing is easier. Let the Lord Chamberlain's Examiner of Plays, backed by the Press, make an unwritten but perfectly well understood regulation that members of Mrs Warren's profession shall be tolerated on the stage only when they are beautiful, exquisitely dressed, and sumptuously lodged and fed; also that they shall, at the end of the play, die of consumption to the sympathetic tears of the whole audience, or step into the next room to commit suicide, or at least be turned out by their protectors, and passed on to be "redeemed" by old and faithful lovers who have adored them in spite of all their levities. Naturally, the poorer girls in the gallery will believe in the beauty, in the exquisite dresses, and the luxurious living, and will see that there is no real necessity for the consumption, the suicide, or the ejectment: mere pious forms, all of them, to save the Censor's face. Even if these purely official catastrophes carried any conviction, the majority of English girls remain so poor, so dependent, so well aware that the drudgeries of such honest work as is within their reach are likely enough to lead them eventually to lung disease, premature death, and domestic desertion or brutality, that they would still see reason to prefer the primrose path to the stony way of virtue, since both, vice at worst and virtue at best, lead to the same end in poverty and overwork. It is true, that the Elementary School mistress will tell you that only girls of a certain kind will reason in this way. But alas! that certain kind turns out on inquiry to be simply the pretty, dainty kind: that is, the only kind that gets the chance of acting on such reasoning. Read the first report of the Commission on the Housing of the Working Classes (Bluebook C 4402, 1889); read the Report on Home Industries (sacred word, Home!) issued by the Women's Industrial Council (Home Industries of Women in London, 1897, 1s); and ask yourself whether, if the lot in life therein described were your lot in life, you would not rather be a jewelled Vamp. If you can go deep enough into things to be able to say no, how many ignorant half-starved girls will believe you are speaking sincerely? To them the lot of the stage courtesan is heavenly in comparison with their own. Yet the Lord Chamberlain's Examiner, being an officer of the Royal Household, places the King in the position of saying to the dramatist "Thus, and thus only, shall you present Mrs Warren's profession on the stage, or you shall starve. Witness Shaw, who told the untempting truth about it, and whom We, by the Grace of God, accordingly disallow and suppress, and do what in Us lies to silence." Fortunately, Shaw cannot be silenced. "The harlot's cry from street to street" [William Blake, 'Auguries of Innocence'] is louder than the voices of all the kings. I am not dependent on the theatre, and cannot be starved into making my play a standing advertisement of the attractive side of Mrs Warren's business.

Here I must guard myself against a misunderstanding. It is not the fault of their authors that the long string of wanton's tragedies, from Antony and Cleopatra to Iris,[6] are snares to poor girls, and are objected to on that account by many earnest men and women who consider Mrs Warren's Profession an excellent sermon. Pinero is in no way bound to suppress the fact that his Iris is a person to be envied by millions of better women. If he made his play false to life by inventing fictitious disadvantages for her, he would be acting as unscrupulously as any tract-writer. If society chooses to provide for its Irises better than for its working women, it must not expect honest playwrights to manufacture spurious evidence to save its credit. The mischief lies in the deliberate suppression of the other side of the case: the refusal to allow Mrs Warren to expose the drudgery and repulsiveness of plying for hire among coarse tedious drunkards. All that, says the Examiner

6. Arthur W. Pinero, *Iris* (1901).

in effect, is horrifying, loathsome. Precisely: what does he expect it to be? would he have us represent it as beautiful and gratifying? His answer to this question amounts, I fear, to a blunt Yes; for it seems impossible to root out of an Englishman's mind the notion that vice is delightful, and that abstention from it is privation. At all events, as long as the tempting side of it is kept towards the public, and softened by plenty of sentiment and sympathy, it is welcomed by our Censor, whereas the slightest attempt to place it in the light of the policeman's lantern or the Salvation Army shelter is checkmated at once as not merely disgusting, but, if you please, unnecessary.

Everybody will, I hope, admit that this state of things is intolerable; that the subject of Mrs Warren's profession must be either tapu [taboo] altogether, or else exhibited with the warning side as freely displayed as the tempting side. But many persons will vote for a complete tapu, and an impartial clean sweep from the boards of Mrs Warren and Gretchen [in Goethe's *Faust*] and the rest: in short, for banishing the sexual instincts from the stage altogether. Those who think this impossible can hardly have considered the number and importance of the subjects which are actually banished from the stage. Many plays, among them Lear, Hamlet, Macbeth, Coriolanus, Julius Cæsar, have no sex complications: the thread of their action can be followed by children who could not understand a single scene of Mrs Warren's Profession or Iris. None of our plays rouse the sympathy of the audience by an exhibition of the pains of maternity, as Chinese plays constantly do. Each nation has its particular set of tapus in addition to the common human stock; and though each of these tapus limits the scope of the dramatist, it does not make drama impossible. If the Examiner were to refuse to license plays with female characters in them, he would only be doing to the stage what our tribal customs already do to the pulpit and the bar. I have myself written a rather entertaining play [*Captain Brassbound's Conversion*] with only one woman in it, and she quite heartwhole; and I could just as easily write a play without a woman in it at all. I will even go as far as to promise the Examiner my support if he will introduce this limitation for part of the year, say during Lent, so as to make a close season for that dullest of stock dramatic subjects, adultery, and force our managers and authors to find out what all great dramatists find out spontaneously: to wit, that people who sacrifice every other consideration to love are as hopelessly unheroic on the stage as lunatics or dipsomaniacs. Hector and Hamlet are the world's heroes; not Paris and Antony.

But though I do not question the possibility of a drama in which love should be as effectively ignored as cholera is at present, there is not the slightest chance of that way out of the difficulty being taken by the Examiner. If he attempted it there would be a revolt in which he would be swept away, in spite of my singlehanded efforts to defend him. A complete tapu is politically impossible. A complete toleration is equally impossible to the Examiner, because his occupation would be gone if there were no tapu to enforce. He is therefor compelled to maintain the present compromise of a partial tapu, applied, to the best of his judgment, with a careful respect to persons and to public opinion. And a very sensible English solution of the difficulty, too, most readers will say. I should not dispute it if dramatic poets really were what English public opinion generally assumes them to be during their lifetime: that is, a licentiously irregular group to be kept in order in a rough and ready way by a magistrate who will stand no nonsense from them. But I cannot admit that the class represented by Eschylus, Sophocles, Aristophanes, Euripides, Shakespear, Goethe, Ibsen, and Tolstoy, not to mention our own contemporary playwrights, is as much in place in the Examiner's office as a pickpocket is in Bow Street [Police Court]. Further, it is not true that the Censorship, though it certainly suppresses Ibsen and Tolstoy, and would suppress Shakespear but for the absurd rule that a play once licensed is always licensed (so that Wycherley is permitted and Shelley prohibited), also suppresses unscrupulous play-wrights. I challenge the Examiner to mention any extremity of sexual misconduct which any manager in his senses would risk presenting on the London stage that has not been presented under his licence and that of his predecessor. The compromise, in fact, works out in practice in favor of loose plays as against earnest ones.

To carry conviction on this point, I will take the extreme course of narrating the plots of two plays witnessed within the last ten years by myself at London West End theatres, one licensed under Queen Victoria, the other under her successor. Both plots conform to the strictest rules of the period when [Alexandre Dumas fils'] La Dame aux Camélias was still a forbidden play, and when The Second Mrs Tanqueray would have been tolerated only on condition that she carefully explained to the audience that when she met Captain Ardale she sinned "but in intention."

Play number one.[7] A prince is compelled by his parents to marry the daughter of a neighboring king, but loves another maiden. The scene represents a hall in the king's palace at night. The wedding has taken place that day; and the closed door of the nuptial chamber is in view of the

---

7. Actually a comic opera, *Incognita* (1892), with music by Alexandre Lecocq and Hamilton Clarke, libretto by Francis Burnand, and lyrics by Harry Greenbank.

audience. Inside, the princess awaits her bridegroom. A duenna is in attendance. The bridegroom enters. His sole desire is to escape from a marriage
which is hateful to him. A means occurs to him. He will assault the
duenna, and be ignominiously expelled from the palace by his indignant
father-in-law. To his horror, when he proceeds to carry out this stratagem,
the duenna, far from raising an alarm, is flattered, delighted, and compliant.
The assaulter becomes the assaulted. He flings her angrily to the ground,
where she remains placidly. He flies. The father enters; dismisses the duenna;
and listens at the keyhole of his daughter's nuptial chamber, uttering various
pleasantries, and declaring, with a shiver, that a sound of kissing, which he
supposes to proceed from within, makes him feel young again.

Story number two.[8] A German officer finds himself in an inn with a
French lady who has wounded his national vanity. He resolves to humble
her by committing a rape upon her. He announces his purpose. She
remonstrates, implores, flies to the doors and finds them locked, calls for
help and finds none at hand, runs screaming from side to side, and, after a
harrowing scene, is overpowered and faints. Nothing further being possible
on the stage without actual felony, the officer then relents and leaves her.
When she recovers, she believes that he has carried out his threat; and
during the rest of the play she is represented as vainly vowing vengeance
upon him, whilst she is really falling in love with him under the influence
of his imaginary crime against her. Finally she consents to marry him; and
the curtain falls on their happiness.

This story was certified by the Examiner, acting for the Lord
Chamberlain, as void in its general tendency of "anything immoral or
otherwise improper for the stage." But let nobody conclude therefore that
the Examiner is a monster, whose policy it is to deprave the theatre. As a
matter of fact, both the above stories are strictly in order from the official
point of view. The incidents of sex which they contain, though carried in
both to the extreme point at which another step would be dealt with, not
by the Examiner, but by the police, do not involve adultery, nor any
allusion to Mrs Warren's profession, nor to the fact that the children of any
polyandrous group will, when they grow up, inevitably be confronted, as
those of Mrs Warren's group are in my play, with the insoluble problem
of their own possible consanguinity. In short, by depending wholly on
the coarse humors and the physical fascination of sex, they comply with
all the formulable requirements of the Censorship, whereas plays in which

8. *The Conquerors* (1898), a play by Paul M. Potter, reviewed by Shaw in the
Saturday Review, 23 April 1898.

these humors and fascinations are discarded, and the social problems created by sex seriously faced and dealt with, inevitably ignore the official formula and are suppressed. If the old rule against the exhibition of illicit sex relations on the stage were revived, and the subject absolutely barred, the only result would be that Antony and Cleopatra, Othello (because of the Bianca episode), Troilus and Cressida, Henry IV, Measure for Measure, Timon of Athens, La Dame aux Camélias, The Profligate, The Second Mrs Tanqueray, The Notorious Mrs Ebbsmith, The Gay Lord Quex, Mrs Dane's Defence, and Iris would be swept from the stage, and placed under the same ban as Tolstoy's Dominion of Darkness and Mrs Warren's Profession, whilst such plays as the two described above would have a monopoly of the theatre as far as sexual interest is concerned.[9]

What is more, the repulsiveness of the worst of the certified plays would protect Censorship against effective exposure and criticism. Not long ago an American Review [*North American Review*] of high standing asked me for an article on the Censorship of the English Stage. I replied that such an article would involve passages too disagreeable for publication in a magazine for general family reading. The editor persisted nevertheless; but not until he had declared his readiness to face this, and had pledged himself to insert the article unaltered (the particularity of the pledge extending even to a specification of the exact number of words in the article) did I consent to the proposal. What was the result? The editor, confronted with the two stories given above, threw his pledge to the winds, and, instead of returning the article, printed it [August 1899] with the illustrative examples omitted, and nothing left but the argument from political principle against the Censorship. In doing this he fired my broadside after withdrawing the cannon balls; for neither the Censor nor any other Englishman, except perhaps a few veterans of the dwindling old guard of Benthamism, cares a dump about political principle. The ordinary Briton thinks that if every other Briton is not under some form of tutelage, the more childish the better, he will abuse his freedom viciously. As far as its principle is concerned, the Censorship is the most popular institution in England; and the playwright who criticizes it is slighted as a blackguard agitating for impunity. Consequently nothing can really shake the confidence of the

9. The non-Shakespearian plays not previously mentioned are Pinero's *The Profligate* (1889), *The Notorious Mrs Ebbsmith* (1895), and *The Gay Lord Quex* (1899); Henry Arthur Jones's *Mrs Dane's Defence* (1900); and Tolstoy's *Dominion of Darkness* (1886; first performed in 1895).

public in the Lord Chamberlain's department except a remorseless and unbowdlerized narration of the licentious fictions which slip through its net, and are hallmarked by it with the approval of the royal household. But as such stories cannot be made public without great difficulty, owing to the obligation an editor is under not to deal unexpectedly with matters that are not *virginibus puerisque* [that is, not fit for children to read], the chances are heavily in favor of the Censor escaping all remonstrance. With the exception of such comments as I was able to make in my own critical articles in The World and the Saturday Review when the pieces I have described were first produced, and a few ignorant protests by churchmen against much better plays which they confessed they had not seen nor read, nothing has been said in the press that could seriously disturb the easygoing notion that the stage would be much worse than it admittedly is but for the vigilance of the Examiner. The truth is, that no manager would dare produce on his own responsibility the pieces he can now get royal certificates for at two guineas per piece.

I hasten to add that I believe these evils to be inherent in the nature of all censorship, and not merely a consequence of the form the institution takes in London. No doubt there is a staggering absurdity in appointing an ordinary clerk to see that the leaders of European literature do not corrupt the morals of the nation, and to restrain Sir Henry Irving from presuming to impersonate Samson or David on the stage,[10] though any other sort of artist may daub these scriptural figures on a signboard or carve them on a tombstone without hindrance. If the General Medical Council, the Royal College of Physicians, the Royal Academy of Arts, the Incorporated Law Society, and Convocation were abolished, and their functions handed over to the Examiner, the Concert of Europe would presumably certify England as mad. Yet, though neither medicine nor painting nor law nor the Church moulds the character of the nation as potently as the theatre does, nothing can come on the stage unless its dimensions admit of its first passing through the Examiner's mind! Pray do not think that I question his honesty. I am quite sure that he sincerely thinks me a blackguard, and my play a grossly improper one, because, like Tolstoy's Dominion of Darkness, it produces, as they are both meant to produce, a very strong and very painful impression of evil. I do not doubt for a moment that the rapine play which I have described, and which he licensed, was quite incapable in manuscript of producing any particular effect on his mind at all, and that

10. At this time the Lord Chamberlain's office forbade stage depiction of God or Biblical personages.

when he was once satisfied that the ill-conducted hero was a German and not an English officer, he passed the play without studying its moral tendencies. Even if he had undertaken that study, there is no more reason to suppose that he is a competent moralist than there is to suppose that I am a competent mathematician. But truly it does not matter whether he is a moralist or not. Let nobody dream for a moment that what is wrong with the Censorship is the shortcoming of the gentleman who happens at any moment to be acting as Censor. Replace him tomorrow by an Academy of Letters and an Academy of Dramatic Poetry, and the new filter will still exclude original and epoch-making work, whilst passing conventional, old-fashioned, and vulgar work. The conclave which compiles the expurgatory index of the Roman Catholic Church is the most august, ancient, learned, famous, and authoritative censorship in Europe. Is it more enlightened, more liberal, more tolerant than the comparatively unqualified office of the Lord Chamberlain? On the contrary, it has reduced itself to a degree of absurdity which makes a Catholic university a contradiction in terms. All censorships exist to prevent anyone from challenging current conceptions and existing institutions. All progress is initiated by challenging current conceptions, and executed by supplanting existing institutions. Consequently the first condition of progress is the removal of censorships. There is the whole case against censorships in a nutshell.

It will be asked whether theatrical managers are to be allowed to produce what they like, without regard to the public interest. But that is not the alternative. The managers of our London music-halls are not subject to any censorship. They produce their entertainments on their own responsibility, and have no two-guinea certificates to plead if their houses are conducted viciously. They know that if they lose their character, the County Council will simply refuse to renew their licence at the end of the year; and nothing in the history of popular art is more amazing than the improvement in music-halls that this simple arrangement has produced within a few years. Place the theatres on the same footing, and we shall promptly have a similar revolution: a whole class of frankly blackguardly plays, in which unscrupulous low comedians attract crowds to gaze at bevies of girls who have nothing to exhibit but their prettiness, will vanish like the obscene songs which were supposed to enliven the squalid dulness, incredible to the younger generation, of the music-halls fifteen years ago. On the other hand, plays which treat sex questions as problems for thought instead of as aphrodisiacs will be freely performed. Gentlemen of the Examiner's way of thinking will have plenty of opportunity of protesting against them in Council; but the result will be that the Examiner will find his natural level; Ibsen and Tolstoy theirs; so no harm will be done.

This question of the Censorship reminds me that I have to apologize to those who went to the recent performance of Mrs Warren's Profession expecting to find it what I have just called an aphrodisiac. That was not my fault: it was the Examiner's. After the specimens I have given of the tolerance of his department, it was natural enough for thoughtless people to infer that a play which overstepped his indulgence must be a very exciting play indeed. Accordingly, I find one critic so explicit as to the nature of his disappointment as to say candidly that "such airy talk as there is upon the matter is utterly unworthy of acceptance as being a representation of what people with blood in them think or do on such occasions." Thus am I crushed between the upper millstone of the Examiner, who thinks me a libertine, and the nether popular critic, who thinks me a prude. Critics of all grades and ages, middle-aged fathers of families no less than ardent young enthusiasts, are equally indignant with me. They revile me as lacking in passion, in feeling, in manhood. Some of them even sum the matter up by denying me any dramatic power: a melancholy betrayal of what dramatic power has come to mean on our stage under the Censorship! Can I be expected to refrain from laughing at the spectacle of a number of respectable gentlemen lamenting because a playwright lures them to the theatre by a promise to excite their senses in a very special and sensational manner, and then, having successfully trapped them in exceptional numbers, proceeds to ignore their senses and ruthlessly improve their minds? But I protest again that the lure was not mine. The play had been in print for four years; and I have spared no pains to make known that my plays are built to induce, not voluptuous reverie but intellectual interest, not romantic rhapsody but humane concern. Accordingly, I do not find those critics who are gifted with intellectual appetite and political conscience complaining of want of dramatic power. Rather do they protest, not altogether unjustly, against a few relapses into staginess and caricature which betray the young playwright and the old playgoer in this early work of mine. As to the voluptuaries, I can assure them that the playwright, whether he be myself or another, will always disappoint them. The drama can do little to delight the senses: all the apparent instances to the contrary are instances of the personal fascination of the performers. The drama of pure feeling is no longer in the hands of the playwright: it has been conquered by the musician, after whose enchantments all the verbal arts seem cold and tame. Romeo and Juliet with the loveliest Juliet is dry, tedious, and rhetorical in comparison with Wagner's Tristan, even though Isolde be both fourteen stone and forty, as she often is in Germany. Indeed, it needed no Wagner to convince the public of this. The voluptuous sentimentality of Gounod's

Faust and Bizet's Carmen has captured the common playgoer; and there is, flatly, no future now for any drama without music except the drama of thought. The attempt to produce a genus of opera without music (and this absurdity is what our fashionable theatres have been driving at for a long time past without knowing it) is far less hopeful than my own determination to accept problem as the normal material of the drama.

That this determination will throw me into a long conflict with our theatre critics, and with the few playgoers who go to the theatre as often as the critics, I well know; but I am too well equipped for the strife to be deterred by it, or to bear malice towards the losing side. In trying to produce the sensuous effects of opera, the fashionable drama has become so flaccid in its sentimentality, and the intellect of its frequenters so atrophied by disuse, that the reintroduction of problem, with its remorseless logic and iron framework of fact, inevitably produces at first an overwhelming impression of coldness and inhuman rationalism. But this will soon pass away. When the intellectual muscle and moral nerve of the critics has been developed in the struggle with modern problem plays, the pettish luxuriousness of the clever ones, and the sulky sense of disadvantaged weakness in the sentimental ones, will clear away; and it will be seen that only in the problem play is there any real drama, because drama is no mere setting up of the camera to nature: it is the presentation in parable of the conflict between Man's will and his environment: in a word, of problem. The vapidness of such drama as the pseudo-operatic plays contain lies in the fact that in them animal passion, sentimentally diluted, is shewn in conflict, not with real circumstances, but with a set of conventions and assumptions half of which do not exist off the stage, whilst the other half can either be evaded by a pretence of compliance or defied with complete impunity by any reasonably strong-minded person. Nobody can feel that such conventions are really compulsory; and consequently nobody can believe in the stage pathos that accepts them as an inexorable fate, or in the reality of the figures who indulge in such pathos. Sitting at such plays we do not believe: we make-believe. And the habit of make-believe becomes at last so rooted, that criticism of the theatre insensibly ceases to be criticism at all, and becomes more and more a chronicle of the fashionable enterprises of the only realities left on the stage: that is, the performers in their own persons. In this phase the playwright who attempts to revive genuine drama produces the disagreeable impression of the pedant who attempts to start a serious discussion at a fashionable at-home. Later on, when he has driven the tea services out and made the people who had come to use the theatre as a drawing-room understand that it is they and not the dramatists who are the intruders, he has to face the accusation that his plays ignore human feeling, an illusion produced by that very resistance of fact and law to human feeling which creates drama. It is the *deus ex machina* who, by suspending that resistance, makes the fall of the curtain an immediate necessity, since drama ends exactly where resistance ends. Yet the introduction of this resistance produces so strong an impression of heartlessness nowadays that a distinguished critic has summed up the impression made on him by Mrs Warren's Profession, by declaring that "the difference between the spirit of Tolstoy and the spirit of Mr Shaw is the difference between the spirit of Christ and the spirit of Euclid." But the epigram would be as good if Tolstoy's name were put in place of mine and [Gabriele] D'Annunzio's[11] in place of Tolstoy's. At the same time I accept the enormous compliment to my reasoning powers with sincere complacency; and I promise my flatterer that when he is sufficiently accustomed to and therefore undazzled by problem on the stage to be able to attend to the familiar factor of humanity in it as well as to the unfamiliar one of a real environment, he will both see and feel that Mrs Warren's Profession is no mere theorem, but a play of instincts and temperaments in conflict with each other and with a flinty social problem that never yields an inch to mere sentiment.

I go further than this. I declare that the real secret of the cynicism and inhumanity of which shallower critics accuse me is the unexpectedness with which my characters behave like human beings, instead of conforming to the romantic logic of the stage. The axioms and postulates of that dreary mimanthropometry[12] are so well known that it is almost impossible for its slaves to write tolerable last acts to their plays, so conventionally do their conclusions follow from their premises. Because I have thrown this logic ruthlessly overboard, I am accused of ignoring, not stage logic, but, of all things, human feeling. People with completely theatrified imaginations tell me that no girl would treat her mother as Vivie Warren does, meaning that no stage heroine would in a popular sentimental play. They say this just as they might say that no two straight lines would enclose a space. They do not see how completely inverted their vision has become even when I throw its preposterousness in their faces, as I repeatedly do in this

11. Italian poet, novelist, dramatist (his *La Gioconda* was performed by Eleanora Duse in London in 1900) and political leader.
12. A portmanteau word combining 'mime' and 'anthropometry', conveying the suggestion of a grotesque theatrical measuring of the human body and its functional capacities.

very play. Praed, the sentimental artist (fool that I was not to make him a theatre critic instead of an architect!), burlesques them by expecting all through the piece that the feelings of the others will be logically deducible from their family relationships and from his "conventionally unconventional" social code. The sarcasm is lost on the critics: they, saturated with the same logic, only think him the sole sensible person on the stage. Thus it comes about that the more completely the dramatist is emancipated from the illusion that men and women are primarily reasonable beings, and the more powerfully he insists on the ruthless indifference of their great dramatic antagonist, the external world, to their whims and emotions, the surer he is to be denounced as blind to the very distinction on which his whole work is built. Far from ignoring idiosyncrasy, will, passion, impulse, whim, as factors in human action, I have placed them so nakedly on the stage that the elderly citizen, accustomed to see them clothed with the veil of manufactured logic about duty, and to disguise even his own impulses from himself in this way, finds the picture as unnatural as Carlyle's suggested painting of parliament sitting without its clothes [*Sartor Resartus*, Chapter 9].

I now come to those critics who, intellectually baffled by the problem in Mrs Warren's Profession, have made a virtue of running away from it on the gentlemanly ground that the theatre is frequented by women as well as by men, and that such problems should not be discussed or even mentioned in the presence of women.[13] With that sort of chivalry I cannot argue: I simply affirm that Mrs Warren's Profession is a play for women; that it was written for women; that it has been performed and produced mainly through the determination of women that it should be performed and produced; that the enthusiasm of women made its first performance excitingly successful; and that not one of these women had any inducement to support it except their belief in the timeliness and the power of the lesson the play teaches. Those who were "surprised to see ladies present" were men; and when they proceeded to explain that the journals they represented could not possibly demoralize the public by describing such a play, their editors cruelly devoted the space saved by their delicacy to reporting at unusual length an exceptionally abominable police case.

My old Independent Theatre manager, Mr Grein, besides that reproach

---

13. J. T. Grein had described the performance as 'an exceedingly uncomfortable one', for 'there was a majority of women to listen to that which could only be understood by a minority of men. Nor was the play fit for women's ears . . . Even men need not know all the ugliness that lies below the surface of everyday life.'

to me for shattering his ideals, complains that Mrs Warren is not wicked enough, and names several romancers who would have clothed her black soul with all the terrors of tragedy. I have no doubt they would; but that is just what I did not want to do. Nothing would please our sanctimonious British public more than to throw the whole guilt of Mrs Warren's profession on Mrs Warren herself. Now the whole aim of my play is to throw that guilt on the British public itself. Mr Grein may remember that when he produced my first play, Widowers' Houses, exactly the same misunderstanding arose. When the virtuous young gentleman rose up in wrath against the slum landlord, the slum landlord very effectually shewed him that slums are the product, not of individual Harpagons, but of the indifference of virtuous young gentlemen to the condition of the city they live in, provided they live at the west end of it on money earned by somebody else's labor. The notion that prostitution is created by the wickedness of Mrs Warren is as silly as the notion—prevalent, nevertheless, to some extent in Temperance circles—that drunkenness is created by the wickedness of the publican. Mrs Warren is not a whit a worse woman than the reputable daughter who cannot endure her. Her indifference to the ultimate social consequence of her means of making money, and her discovery of that means by the ordinary method of taking the line of least resistance to getting it, are too common in English society to call for any special remark. Her vitality, her thrift, her energy, her outspokenness, her wise care of her daughter, and the managing capacity which has enabled her and her sister to climb from the fried fish shop down by the Mint to the establishments of which she boasts, are all high English social virtues. Her defence of herself is so overwhelming that it provokes [Malcolm Watson in] the St James's Gazette to declare that "the tendency of the play is wholly evil" because "it contains one of the boldest and most specious defences of an immoral life for poor women that has ever been penned." Happily the St James's Gazette here speaks in its haste. Mrs Warren's defence of herself is not only bold and specious, but valid and unanswerable. But it is no defence at all of the vice which she organizes. It is no defence of an immoral life to say that the alternative offered by society collectively to poor women is a miserable life, starved, overworked, fetid, ailing, ugly. Though it is quite natural and *right* for Mrs Warren to choose what is, according to her lights, the least immoral alternative, it is none the less infamous of society to offer such alternatives. For the alternatives offered are not morality and immorality, but two sorts of immorality. The man who cannot see that starvation, overwork, dirt, and disease are as anti-social as prostitution—that they are the vices and crimes of a nation, and not merely its misfortunes—is (to put it as politely as possible) a hopelessly Private Person.[14]

The notion that Mrs Warren must be a fiend is only an example of the violence and passion which the slightest reference to sex rouses in undisciplined minds, and which makes it seem natural to our lawgivers to punish silly and negligible indecencies with a ferocity unknown in dealing with, for example, ruinous financial swindling. Had my play been entitled Mr Warren's Profession, and Mr Warren been a bookmaker, nobody would have expected me to make him a villain as well. Yet gambling is a vice, and bookmaking an institution, for which there is absolutely nothing to be said. The moral and economic evil done by trying to get other people's money without working for it (and this is the essence of gambling) is not only enormous but uncompensated. There are no two sides to the question of gambling, no circumstances which force us to tolerate it lest its suppression lead to worse things, no consensus of opinion among responsible classes, such as magistrates and military commanders, that it is a necessity, no Athenian records of gambling made splendid by the talents of its professors, no contention that instead of violating morals it only violates a legal institution which is in many respects oppressive and unnatural, no possible plea that the instinct on which it is founded is a vital one. Prostitution can confuse the issue with all these excuses: gambling has none of them. Consequently, if Mrs Warren must needs be a demon, a bookmaker must be a cacodemon. Well, does anybody who knows the sporting world really believe that bookmakers are worse than their neighbors? On the contrary, they have to be a good deal better; for in that world nearly everybody whose social rank does not exclude such an occupation would be a bookmaker if he could; but the strength of character required for handling large sums of money and for strict settlements and unflinching payment of losses is so rare that successful bookmakers are rare too. It may seem that at least public spirit cannot be one of a bookmaker's virtues; but I can testify from personal experience that excellent public work is done with money subscribed by bookmakers. It is true that there are abysses in bookmaking: for example, welshing. Mr Grein hints that there are abysses in Mrs Warren's profession also. So there are in every profession: the error lies in supposing that every member of them sounds these depths. I sit on a public body which prosecutes Mrs Warren zealously; and I can assure Mr Grein that she is often leniently dealt with because she has conducted her business

14. Shaw apparently had in mind the etymology of 'idiot', from the Greek ἰδιώτης, meaning private person, commoner, plebeian.

"respectably" and held herself above its vilest branches. The degrees in infamy are as numerous and as scrupulously observed as the degrees in the peerage: the moralist's notion that there are depths at which the moral atmosphere ceases is as delusive as the rich man's notion that there are no social jealousies or snobberies among the very poor. No: had I drawn Mrs Warren as a fiend in human form, the very people who now rebuke me for flattering her would probably be the first to deride me for deducing character logically from occupation instead of observing it accurately in society.

One critic is so enslaved by this sort of logic that he calls my portraiture of the Reverend Samuel Gardner an attack on religion. According to this view Subaltern Iago is an attack on the army, Sir John Falstaff an attack on knighthood, and King Claudius an attack on royalty. Here again the clamor for naturalness and human feeling, raised by so many critics when they are confronted by the real thing on the stage, is really a clamor for the most mechanical and superficial sort of logic. The dramatic reason for making the clergyman what Mrs Warren calls "an old stick-in-the-mud," whose son, in spite of much capacity and charm, is a cynically worthless member of society, is to set up a mordant contrast between him and the woman of infamous profession, with her well brought-up, straightforward, hardworking daughter. The critics who have missed the contrast have doubtless observed often enough that many clergymen are in the Church through no genuine calling, but simply because, in circles which can command preferment, it is the refuge of the fool of the family; and that clergymen's sons are often conspicuous reactionists against the restraints imposed on them in childhood by their father's profession. These critics must know, too, from history if not from experience, that women as unscrupulous as Mrs Warren have distinguished themselves as administrators and rulers, both commercially and politically. But both observation and knowledge are left behind when journalists go to the theatre. Once in their stalls, they assume that it is "natural" for clergymen to be saintly, for soldiers to be heroic, for lawyers to be hard-hearted, for sailors to be simple and generous, for doctors to perform miracles with little bottles, and for Mrs Warren to be a beast and a demon. All this is not only not natural, but not dramatic. A man's profession only enters into the drama of his life when it comes into conflict with his nature. The result of this conflict is tragic in Mrs Warren's case, and comic in the clergyman's case (at least we are savage enough to laugh at it); but in both cases it is illogical, and in both cases natural. I repeat, the critics who accuse me of sacrificing nature to logic are so sophisticated by their profession that to them logic is nature, and nature absurdity.

Many friendly critics are too little skilled in social questions and moral discussions to be able to conceive that respectable gentlemen like themselves, who would instantly call the police to remove Mrs Warren if she ventured to canvass them personally, could possibly be in any way responsible for her proceedings. They remonstrate sincerely, asking me what good such painful exposures can possibly do. They might as well ask what good Lord Shaftesbury[15] did by devoting his life to the exposure of evils (by no means yet remedied) compared to which the worst things brought into view or even into surmise in this play are trifles. The good of mentioning them is that you make people so extremely uncomfortable about them that they finally stop blaming "human nature" for them, and begin to support measures for their reform. Can anything be more absurd than the copy of The Echo which contains a notice of the performance of my play? It is edited by a gentleman [S. K. Ratcliffe] who, having devoted his life to work of the Shaftesbury type, exposes social evils and clamors for their reform in every column except one; and that one is occupied by the declaration of the paper's kindly theatre critic, that the performance left him "wondering what useful purpose the play was intended to serve." The balance has to be redressed by the more fashionable papers, which usually combine capable art criticism with West End solecism on politics and sociology. It is very noteworthy, however, on comparing the press explosion produced by Mrs Warren's Profession in 1902 with that produced by Widowers' Houses about ten years earlier, that whereas in 1892 the facts were frantically denied and the persons of the drama flouted as monsters of wickedness, in 1902 the facts are admitted, and the characters recognized, though it is suggested that this is exactly why no gentleman should mention them in public. Only one writer has ventured to imply this time that the poverty mentioned by Mrs Warren has since been quietly relieved, and need not have been dragged back to the footlights. I compliment him on his splendid mendacity, in which he is unsupported, save by a little plea in a theatrical paper which is innocent enough to think that ten guineas a year with board and lodging is an impossibly low wage for a barmaid. It goes on to cite Mr Charles Booth[16] as having testified that there are many laborers' wives who are happy and contented on eighteen shillings a week. But I can

15. Anthony Ashley Cooper, Seventh Earl of Shaftesbury, was a reformist politician, who as a Member of Parliament had supported Catholic Emancipation, repeal of the Corn Laws, factory reform, and the army welfare work of Florence Nightingale.
16. English social reformer, author of *Life and Labour of the People in London* (17 vols., 1891–1903).

go further than that myself. I have seen an Oxford agricultural laborer's wife looking cheerful on eight shillings a week; but that does not console me for the fact that agriculture in England is a ruined industry. If poverty does not matter as long as it is contented, then crime does not matter as long as it is unscrupulous. The truth is that it is only then that it does matter most desperately. Many persons are more comfortable when they are dirty than when they are clean; but that does not recommend dirt as a national policy.

[*The next five paragraphs were deleted in the 1930 revision for the Collected Edition*]

Here I must for the present break off my arduous work of educating the press. We shall resume our studies later on; but just now I am tired of playing the preceptor; and the eager thirst of my pupils for improvement does not console me for the slowness of their progress. Besides, I must reserve space to gratify my own vanity and do justice to the six artists who acted my play, by placing on record the hitherto unchronicled success of the first representation. It is not often that an author, after a couple of hours of those rare alternations of excitement and intensely attentive silence which only occur in the theatre when actors and audience are reacting on one another to the utmost, is able to step on the stage and apply the strong word genius to the representation with the certainty of eliciting an instant and overwhelming assent from the audience. That was my good fortune on the afternoon of Sunday the fifth of January last. I was certainly extremely fortunate in my interpreters in the enterprise, and that not alone in respect of their artistic talent; for had it not been for their superhuman patience, their imperturbable good-humor and good-fellowship, there could have been no performance. The terror of the Censor's power gave us trouble enough to break up any ordinary commercial enterprise. Managers promised and even engaged their theatres to us after the most explicit warnings that the play was unlicensed, and at the last moment suddenly realized that Mr Redford had their livelihoods in the hollow of his hand, and backed out. Over and over again the date and place were fixed and the tickets printed, only to be cancelled, until at last the desperate and overworked manager of the Stage Society could only laugh, as criminals broken on the wheel used to laugh at the second stroke. We rehearsed under great difficulties. Christmas pieces and plays for the New Year were being prepared in all directions; and my six actor colleagues were busy people, with engagements in these pieces in addition to their current professional work every night. On several raw winter days stages for rehearsal were unattainable even by the most distinguished applicants; and we shared corridors and saloons with them whilst the stage was given over to children in training for Boxing night.[17] At last we had to rehearse at an hour at which no actor or actress has been out of bed within the memory of man; and we sardonically congratulated one another every morning on our rosy matutinal looks and the improvement wrought by early rising in our healths and characters. And all this, please observe, for a Society without treasury or commercial prestige, for a play which was being denounced in advance as unmentionable, for an author without influence at the fashionable theatres! I victoriously challenge the West End managers to get as much done for interested motives, if they can.

Three causes made the production the most notable that has fallen to my lot. First, the veto of the Censor, which put the supporters of the play on their mettle. Second, the chivalry of the Stage Society, which, in spite of my urgent advice to the contrary, and my demonstration of the difficulties, dangers, and expenses the enterprise would cost, put my discouragements to shame and resolved to give battle at all costs to the attempt of the Censorship to suppress the play. Third, the artistic spirit of the actors, who made the play their own and carried it through triumphantly in spite of a series of disappointments and annoyances much more trying to the dramatic temperament than mere difficulties.

The acting, too, required courage and character as well as skill and intelligence. The veto of the Censor introduced a quite novel element of moral responsibility into the undertaking. And the characters were very unusual on the English stage. The younger heroine is, like her mother, an Englishwoman to the backbone, and not, like the heroines of our fashionable drama, a prima donna of Italian origin. Consequently she was sure to be denounced as unnatural and undramatic by the critics. The most vicious man in the play is not in the least a stage villain: indeed, he regards his own moral character with the sincere complacency of a hero of melodrama. The amiable devotee of romance and beauty is shown at an age which brings out the futilization which these worships are apt to produce if they are made the staple of life instead of the sauce. The attitude of the clever young people to their elders is faithfully presented as one of pitiless ridicule and

17. Boxing Day in England is the first weekday after Christmas, a legal holiday marked by distribution of gift 'boxes' to servants, errand boys, and postmen. Boxing night was the traditional opening night of the annual theatrical 'Pantomimes', in which hordes of juveniles performed.

unsympathetic criticism, and forms a spectacle incredible to those who, when young, were not cleverer than their nearest elders, and painful to those sentimental parents who shrink from the cruelty of youth, which pardons nothing because it knows nothing. In short, the characters and their relations are of a kind that the routineer critic has not yet learnt to place; so that their misunderstanding was a foregone conclusion. Nevertheless, there was no hesitation behind the curtain. When it went up at last, a stage much too small for the company was revealed to an auditorium much too small for the audience. But the players, though it was impossible for them to forget their own discomfort, at once made the spectators forget theirs. It certainly was a model audience, responsive from the first line to the last; and it got no less than it deserved in return.

I grieve to have to add that the second performance, given for the edification of the London press and of those members of the Stage Society who cannot attend the Sunday performances, was a less inspiriting one than the first. A solid phalanx of theatre-weary journalists in an afternoon humor, most of them committed to irreconcilable disparagement of problem plays, and all of them bound by etiquet to be as undemonstrative as possible, is not exactly the sort of audience that rises at the performers and cures them of the inevitable reaction after an excitingly successful first night. The artist nature is a sensitive and therefore a vindictive one; and masterful players have a way with recalcitrant audiences of rubbing a play into them instead of delighting them with it. I should describe the second performance of Mrs Warren's Profession, especially as to its earlier stages, as decidedly a rubbed-in one. The rubbing was no doubt salutary; but it must have hurt some of the thinner skins. The charm of the lighter passages fled; and the strong scenes, though they again carried everything before them, yet discharged that duty in a grim fashion, doing execution on the enemy rather than moving them to repentance and confession. Still, to those who had not seen the first performance, the effect was sufficiently impressive; and they had the advantage of witnessing a fresh development in Mrs Warren, who, artistically jealous, as I took it, of the overwhelming effect of the end of the second act on the previous day, threw herself into the fourth act in quite a new way, and achieved the apparently impossible feat of surpassing herself. The compliments paid to Miss Fanny Brough by the critics, eulogistic as they are, are the compliments of men three-fourths duped as Partridge was duped by Garrick.[18] By much of her acting they

18. Mr Partridge is a schoolmaster in Fielding's *Tom Jones* (1749), who mistakes David Garrick's stage performance as Hamlet for a real-life occurrence (much like

were so completely taken in that they did not recognize it as acting at all. Indeed, none of the six players quite escaped this consequence of their own thoroughness. There was a distinct tendency among the less experienced critics to complain of their sentiments and behavior. Naturally, the author does not share that grievance.

I have induced Mr Frederick Evans, who is fortunately a member of the Stage Society, to undertake the portraits which commemorate the performance in this little volume.[19] We have done our best not to spoil Mr Evans' work in reproduction; but it has been impossible, without greatly raising the price of the book, either to give full-sized prints from his plates, or to employ the only process capable of preserving the subtler qualities which collectors of his photographs prize. The great majority of readers will no doubt be satisfied with the "likenesses," to which we can do at least partial justice.

PICCARD'S COTTAGE [St Catherine's, Guildford].
January, 1902.

[Portions of the following section of the 1930 text were transferred from the preface to How He Lied to Her Husband, *1907; the balance was newly written]*

In 1905 Arnold Daly produced Mrs Warren's Profession in New York. The press of that city instantly raised a cry that such persons as Mrs Warren are "ordure" and should not be mentioned in the presence of decent people. This hideous repudiation of humanity and social conscience so took possession of the New York journalists that the few among them who kept their feet morally and intellectually could do nothing to check the epidemic of foul language, gross suggestion, and raving obscenity of word and thought that broke out. The writers abandoned all self-restraint under the impression that they were upholding virtue instead of outraging it. They infected each other with their hysteria until they were for all practical purposes indecently mad. They finally forced the police to arrest Daly and his company and led the magistrate to express his loathing of the duty thus forced upon him of reading an unmentionable and abominable play. Of course the convulsion soon exhausted itself. The magistrate, naturally

---

the earlier-mentioned 'simple sailor' at Wapping who shouts warnings to Othello from the gallery).
19. A dozen illustrations of members of the Stage Society cast, photographed at a post-production session by Frederick H. Evans (one of Shaw's favourite photographers), were included in the 1902 edition.

somewhat impatient when he found that what he had to read was a strenuously ethical play forming part of a book which had been in circulation unchallenged for eight years, and had been received without protest by the whole London and New York press, gave the journalists a piece of his mind as to their moral taste in plays. By consent, he passed the case on to a higher court, which declared that the play was not immoral; acquitted Daly; and made an end of the attempt to use the law to declare living women to be "ordure," and thus enforce silence as to the far-reaching fact that you cannot cheapen women in the market for industrial purposes without cheapening them for other purposes as well. I hope Mrs Warren's Profession will be played everywhere, in season and out of season, until Mrs Warren has bitten that fact into the public conscience, and shamed the newspapers which support a tariff to keep up the price of every American commodity except American manhood and womanhood.

Unfortunately, Daly had already suffered the usual fate of those who direct public attention to the profits of the sweater or the pleasures of the voluptuary. He was morally lynched side by side with me. Months elapsed before the decision of the courts vindicated him; and even then, since his vindication implied the condemnation of the press, which was by that time sober again, and ashamed of its orgy, his triumph received a rather sulky and grudging publicity. In the meantime he had hardly been able to approach an American city, including even those cities which had heaped applause on him as the defender of hearth and home when he produced Candida, without having to face articles discussing whether mothers could allow their daughters to attend such plays as You Never Can Tell, written by the infamous author of Mrs Warren's Profession, and acted by the monster who produced it. What made this harder to bear was that though no fact is better established in theatrical business than the financial disastrousness of moral discredit, the journalists who had done all the mischief kept paying vice the homage of assuming that it is enormously popular and lucrative, and that Daly and I, being exploiters of vice, must therefore be making colossal fortunes out of the abuse heaped on us, and had in fact provoked it and welcomed it with that express object. Ignorance of real life could hardly go further.

I was deeply disgusted by this unsavory mobbing. And I have certain sensitive places in my soul: I do not like that word "ordure." Apply it to my work, and I can afford to smile, since the world, on the whole, will smile with me. But to apply it to the woman in the street, whose spirit is of one substance with your own and her body no less holy: to look your women folk in the face afterwards and not go out and hang yourself: that is not on the list of pardonable sins.

Shortly after these events a leading New York newspaper, which was among the most abusively clamorous for the suppression of Mrs Warren's Profession, was fined heavily for deriving part of its revenue from advertisements of Mrs Warren's houses.[20]

Many people have been puzzled by the fact that whilst stage entertainments which are frankly meant to act on the spectators as aphrodisiacs are everywhere tolerated, plays which have an almost horrifying contrary effect are fiercely attacked by persons and papers notoriously indifferent to public morals on all other occasions. The explanation is very simple. The profits of Mrs Warren's profession are shared not only by Mrs Warren and Sir George Crofts, but by the landlords of their houses, the newspapers which advertise them, the restaurants which cater for them, and, in short, all the trades to which they are good customers, not to mention the public officials and representatives whom they silence by complicity, corruption, or blackmail. Add to these the employers who profit by cheap female labor, and the shareholders whose dividends depend on it (you find such people everywhere, even on the judicial bench and in the highest places in Church and State), and you get a large and powerful class with a strong pecuniary incentive to protect Mrs Warren's profession, and a correspondingly strong incentive to conceal, from their own consciences no less than from the world, the real sources of their gain. These are the people who declare that it is feminine vice and not poverty that drives women to the streets, as if vicious women with independent incomes ever went there. These are the people who, indulgent or indifferent to aphrodisiac plays, raise the moral hue and cry against performances of Mrs Warren's Profession, and drag actresses to the police court to be insulted, bullied, and threatened for fulfilling their engagements. For please observe that the judicial decision in New York State in favor of the play did not end the matter. In Kansas City, for instance, the municipality, finding itself restrained by the courts from preventing the performance, fell back on a local bye-law against indecency. It summoned the actress who impersonated Mrs Warren to the police court, and offered her and her colleagues the alternative of leaving the city or being prosecuted under this bye-law.[21]

20. The personal column of the *New York Herald* (which ran to several pages daily) was popularly known for many years as the 'Whores' Daily Guide and Compendium'. Eventually the postal authorities ordered the publishers to cease and desist.
21. The No. 1 touring company of *Mrs Warren's Profession* commenced its tour in Kansas City, Missouri, on Sunday, 31 March 1907. A threat by the Mayor, Henry

Now nothing is more possible than that the city councillors who suddenly displayed such concern for the morals of the theatre were either Mrs Warren's landlords, or employers of women at starvation wages, or restaurant keepers, or newspaper proprietors, or in some other more or less direct way sharers of the profits of her trade. No doubt it is equally possible that they were simply stupid men who thought that indecency consists, not in evil, but in mentioning it. I have, however, been myself a member of a municipal council, and have not found municipal councillors quite so simple and inexperienced as this. At all events I do not propose to give the Kansas councillors the benefit of the doubt. I therefore advise the public at large, which will finally decide the matter, to keep a vigilant eye on gentlemen who will stand anything at the theatre except a performance of Mrs Warren's Profession, and who assert in the same breath that (a) the play is too loathsome to be bearable by civilized people, and (b) that unless its performance is prohibited the whole town will throng to see it. They may be merely excited and foolish; but I am bound to warn the public that it is equally likely that they may be collected and knavish.

At all events, to prohibit the play is to protect the evil which the play exposes; and in view of that fact, I see no reason for assuming that the prohibitionists are disinterested moralists, and that the author, the managers, and the performers, who depend for their livelihood on their personal reputations and not on rents, advertisements, or dividends, are grossly inferior to them in moral sense and public responsibility.

It is true that in Mrs Warren's Profession, Society, and not any individual, is the villain of the piece; but it does not follow that the people who take offence at it are all champions of society. Their credentials cannot be too carefully examined.

POSTSCRIPT (1930) On reading the above after a lapse of 28 years, with the ban on Mrs Warren withdrawn and forgotten, I should have discarded it as an overdone fuss about nothing that now matters were it not for a

---

M. Beardsley, and the Board of Police Commissioners to suppress the four scheduled performances was thwarted by a federal restraining order obtained by the theatre management. At a hearing by a federal circuit judge on 3 April, the jurist declined to lift the injunction against the city before the final performance that night, stating that as a New York court had examined the play and its judges had pronounced the tendencies of the play as not evil, 'I would hate to say, on this casual hearing, that [the New York] court was wrong.' None of the Kansas City newspapers reported the summoning of the actress Rose Coghlan to the police court as alleged by Shaw.

recent incident. Before describing this I must explain that with the invention of the cinematograph a new censorship has come into existence, created, not this time by Act of Parliament, but by the film manufacturers to provide themselves with the certificates of propriety which have proved so useful to the theatre managers. This private censorship has acquired public power through its acceptance by the local authorities, without whose licence the films cannot be exhibited in places of public entertainment.

A lady [Elizabeth Baxter] who has devoted herself to the charitable work of relieving the homeless and penniless people who are to be found every night in London on the Thames Embankment had to deal largely with working men who had come to London from the country under the mistaken impression that there is always employment there for everybody, and with young women, also from the provinces, who had been lured to London by offers of situations which were really traps set for them by the agents of the White Slave traffic. The lady rightly concluded that much the best instrument for warning the men, and making known to the women the addresses of the organization for befriending unprotected girl travellers, is the cinema. She caused a film [*The Night Patrol*] to be made for this purpose. The Film Censor [Ernest Shortt] immediately banned the part of the film which gave the addresses to the girls and shewed them the risks they ran. The lady appealed to me to help her to protest. After convincing myself by witnessing a private exhibition of the film that it was quite innocent I wrote to the Censor, begging him to examine the film personally, and remedy what seemed to be a rule-of-thumb mistake by his examiners. He not only confirmed their veto, but left uncontradicted a report in all the papers that he had given as his reason that the lady had paraded the allurements of vice, and that such parades could not be tolerated by him. The sole allurements were the smart motor car in which the heroine of the film was kidnapped, and the fashionable clothes of the two very repulsive agents who drugged her in it. In every other respect her experiences were as disagreeable as the sternest moralist could desire.

I then made a tour of the picture houses to see what the Film Censor considers allowable. Of the films duly licensed by him two were so nakedly pornographic that their exhibition could hardly have been risked without the Censor's certificate of purity. One of them presented the allurements of a supposedly French brothel so shamelessly that I rose and fled in disgust long before the end, though I am as hardened to vulgar salacity in the theatre as a surgeon is to a dissecting room.

The only logical conclusion apparent is that the White Slave traffickers are in complete control of our picture theatres, and can close them to our

Rescue workers as effectively as they can reserve them for advertisements of their own trade. I spare the Film Censor that conclusion. The conclusion I press upon him and on the public is my old one of twenty-eight years ago: that all the evil effects of such corrupt control are inevitably produced gratuitously by Censors with the best intentions.

POSTSCRIPT 1933. In spite of the suppression of my play for so many years by the censorship the subject broke out into a campaign for the abolition of the White Slave Traffic which still occupies the League of Nations at Geneva.[22] But my demonstration that the root of the evil is economic was ruthlessly ignored by the profiteering press (that is, by the entire press); and when at last parliament proceeded to legislate, its contribution to the question was to ordain that Mrs Warren's male competitors should be flogged instead of fined. This had the double effect of stimulating the perverted sexuality which delights in flogging, and driving the traffic into female hands, leaving Mrs Warren triumphant.

The ban on performances of the play has long since been withdrawn [1925]; and when it is performed the critics hasten to declare that the scandal of underpaid virtue and overpaid vice is a thing of the past. Yet when the war created an urgent demand for women's labor in 1914 the Government proceeded to employ women for twelve hours a day at a wage of five ha'pence an hour. It is amazing how the grossest abuses thrive on their reputation for being old unhappy far-off things in an age of imaginary progress.

22. White slave traffic had long been a major governmental problem in Britain. In December 1912 its Criminal Law Amendment Act (1885) was revised to make procuration a severely penalized misdemeanour, including punishment for procurers by flogging (which Shaw focused on in his 1930 expansion of the preface: see p. 112). The act was further amended in 1922. (See also, in Volume 2, the section 'Under the Whip' in Shaw's 'Parents and Children' preface to *Misalliance*, 1914.) One of the earliest acts of the League of Nations (1921) was to convene a conference in Geneva to give earnest consideration to the problem of international traffic in prostitution.

Epistle Dedicatory to Arthur Bingham Walkley (Man and Superman)

First published in 1903

My dear Walkley[1]

You once asked me why I did not write a Don Juan play. The levity with which you assumed this frightful responsibility has probably by this time enabled you to forget it; but the day of reckoning has arrived: here is your play! I say your play, because *qui facit per alium facit per se* [he who does something through another does it himself]. Its profits, like its labor, belong to me: its morals, its manners, its philosophy, its influence on the young, are for you to justify. You were of mature age when you made the suggestion; and you knew your man. It is hardly fifteen years since, as twin pioneers of the New Journalism of that time, we two, cradled in the same new sheets, began an epoch in the criticism of the theatre and the opera house by making it the pretext for a propaganda of our own views of life. So you cannot plead ignorance of the character of the force you set in motion. You meant me to *épater le bourgeois* [shock the middle class]; and if he protests, I hereby refer him to you as the accountable party.

I warn you that if you attempt to repudiate your responsibility, I shall suspect you of finding the play too decorous for your taste. The fifteen years have made me older and graver. In you I can detect no such becoming change. Your levities and audacities are like the loves and comforts prayed for by Desdemona [*Othello*, II: i]: they increase, even as your days do

---

1. Shaw and Walkley became colleagues and friends on the staff of the *Star* when that Liberal newspaper was founded in 1888, with Shaw as a leader-writer (briefly), then music critic, and Walkley the paper's dramatic critic until he accepted an appointment in March 1900 as dramatic critic of *The Times*. He was by no means a champion of Shaw's work and views, as attested by his review of the published text of *Man and Superman* (*Times Literary Supplement*, 26 May 1905):

> On the one hand [Shaw is] a born dramatist, and the greatest; on the other a man who is no dramatist at all [because of] . . . the masked interdependence of the action–plot and the idea–plot and the curious way in which the one is warped and maimed in being made to serve as the vehicle for the other.

grow. No mere pioneering journal dares meddle with them now: the stately Times itself is alone sufficiently above suspicion to act as your chaperone; and even the Times must sometimes thank its stars that new plays are not produced every day, since after each such event its gravity is compromised, its platitude turned to epigram, its portentousness to wit, its propriety to elegance, and even its decorum into naughtiness by criticisms which the traditions of the paper do not allow you to sign at the end, but which you take care to sign with the most extravagant flourishes between the lines. I am not sure that this is not a portent of Revolution. In XVIII century France the end was at hand when men bought the Encyclopedia and found [its rationalist founder, Denis] Diderot there. When I buy the Times and find you there, my prophetic ear catches a rattle of XX century tumbrils.

However, that is not my present anxiety. The question is, will you not be disappointed with a Don Juan play in which not one of that hero's *mille e tre*[2] adventures is brought upon the stage? To propitiate you, let me explain myself. You will retort that I never do anything else: it is your favorite jibe at me that what I call drama is nothing but explanation. But you must not expect me to adopt your inexplicable, fantastic, petulant, fastidious ways: you must take me as I am, a reasonable, patient, consistent, apologetic, laborious person, with the temperament of a schoolmaster and the pursuits of a vestryman. No doubt that literary knack of mine which happens to amuse the British public distracts attention from my character; but the character is there none the less, solid as bricks. I have a conscience; and conscience is always anxiously explanatory. You, on the contrary, feel that a man who discusses his conscience is much like a woman who discusses her modesty. The only moral force you condescend to parade is the force of your wit: the only demand you make in public is the demand of your artistic temperament for symmetry, elegance, style, grace, refinement, and the cleanliness which comes next to godliness if not before it. But my conscience is the genuine pulpit article: it annoys me to see people comfortable when they ought to be uncomfortable; and I insist on making them think in order to bring them to conviction of sin. If you dont like my preaching you must lump it. I really cannot help it.

In the preface to my Plays for Puritans I explained the predicament of our contemporary English drama, forced to deal almost exclusively with cases of sexual attraction, and yet forbidden to exhibit the incidents of that

2. In Mozart's *Don Giovanni* (1787), Leporello reports the number of sexual conquests his master enjoyed in Spain as one thousand and three.

attraction or even to discuss its nature. Your suggestion that I should write a Don Juan play was virtually a challenge to me to treat this subject myself dramatically. The challenge was difficult enough to be worth accepting, because, when you come to think of it, though we have plenty of dramas with heroes and heroines who are in love and must accordingly marry or perish at the end of the play, or about people whose relations with one another have been complicated by the marriage laws, not to mention the looser sort of plays which trade on the tradition that illicit love affairs are at once vicious and delightful, we have no modern English plays in which the natural attraction of the sexes for one another is made the mainspring of the action. That is why we insist on beauty in our performers, differing herein from the countries [Germany and Norway] our friend William Archer holds up as examples of seriousness to our childish theatres. There the Juliets and Isoldes, the Romeos and Tristans, might be our mothers and fathers. Not so the English actress. The heroine she impersonates is not allowed to discuss the elemental relations of men and women: all her romantic twaddle about novelet-made love, all her purely legal dilemmas as to whether she was married or "betrayed," quite miss our hearts and worry our minds. To console ourselves we must just look at her. We do so; and her beauty feeds our starving emotions. Sometimes we grumble ungallantly at the lady because she does not act as well as she looks. But in a drama which, with all its preoccupation with sex, is really void of sexual interest, good looks are more desired than histrionic skill.

Let me press this point on you, since you are too clever to raise the fool's cry of paradox whenever I take hold of a stick by the right instead of the wrong end. Why are our occasional attempts to deal with the sex problem on the stage so repulsive and dreary that even those who are most determined that sex questions shall be held open and their discussion kept free, cannot pretend to relish these joyless attempts at social sanitation? Is it not because at bottom they are utterly sexless?[3] What is the usual formula for such plays? A woman has, on some past occasion, been brought into conflict with the law which regulates the relations of the sexes. A man, by falling in love with her, or marrying her, is brought into conflict with the social convention which discountenances the woman. Now the conflicts of individuals with law and convention can be dramatized like all other human conflicts; but they are purely judicial; and the fact that we are much more curious about the suppressed relations between the man and the

3. Shaw had in mind plays like Pinero's *The Profligate* and *The Notorious Mrs Ebbsmith* and Henry Arthur Jones's *Michael and His Lost Angel* (1896).

woman than about the relations between both and our courts of law and
private juries of matrons, produces that sensation of evasion, of dissatisfac-
tion, of fundamental irrelevance, of shallowness, of useless disagreeableness,
of total failure to edify and partial failure to interest, which is as familiar to
you in the theatres as it was to me when I, too, frequented those uncomfortable buildings, and found our popular playwrights in the mind to (as they
thought) emulate Ibsen.

I take it that when you asked me for a Don Juan play you did not want
that sort of thing. Nobody does: the successes such plays sometimes obtain
are due to the incidental conventional melodrama with which the
experienced popular author instinctively saves himself from failure. But
what did you want? Owing to your unfortunate habit—you now, I hope,
feel its inconvenience—of not explaining yourself, I have had to discover
this for myself. First, then, I have had to ask myself, what is a Don Juan?
Vulgarly, a libertine. But your dislike of vulgarity is pushed to the length
of a defect (universality of character is impossible without a share of
vulgarity); and even if you could acquire the taste, you would find yourself
overfed from ordinary sources without troubling me. So I took it that you
demanded a Don Juan in the philosophic sense.

Philosophically, Don Juan is a man who, though gifted enough to be
exceptionally capable of distinguishing between good and evil, follows his
own instincts without regard to the common, statute, or canon law; and
therefore, whilst gaining the ardent sympathy of our rebellious instincts
(which are flattered by the brilliancies with which Don Juan associates
them) finds himself in mortal conflict with existing institutions, and defends
himself by fraud and force as unscrupulously as a farmer defends his crops
by the same means against vermin. The prototypic Don Juan, invented
early in the XVI century by a Spanish monk,[4] was presented, according to
the ideas of that time, as the enemy of God, the approach of whose
vengeance is felt throughout the drama, growing in menace from minute to
minute. No anxiety is caused on Don Juan's account by any minor
antagonist: he easily eludes the police, temporal and spiritual; and when an
indignant father seeks private redress with the sword, Don Juan kills him
without an effort. Not until the slain father returns from heaven as the
agent of God, in the form of his own statue, does he prevail against his

---

4. Shaw's dating is faulty. The tale of Don Juan's dissolute life, originating in
popular legend, was first dramatized in 1620 in *El Burlador de Seville* ('The Trickster
of Seville') by the monk Gabriel Tellez, writing under the pseudonym Tirso de
Molina.

slayer and cast him into hell. The moral is a monkish one: repent and reform now; for tomorrow it may be too late. This is really the only point on which Don Juan is sceptical; for he is a devout believer in an ultimate hell, and risks damnation only because, as he is young, it seems so far off that repentance can be postponed until he has amused himself to his heart's content.

But the lesson intended by an author is hardly ever the lesson the world chooses to learn from his book. What attracts and impresses us in El Burlador de Sevilla is not the immediate urgency of repentance, but the heroism of daring to be the enemy of God. From Prometheus to my own Devil's Disciple, such enemies have always been popular. Don Juan became such a pet that the world could not bear his damnation. It reconciled him sentimentally to God in a second version, and clamored for his canonization for a whole century, thus treating him as English journalism has treated that comic foe of the gods, Punch. Molière's Don Juan casts back to the original in point of impenitence; but in piety he falls off greatly. True, he also proposes to repent; but in what terms! *"Oui, ma foi! il faut s'amender. Encore vingt ou trente ans de cette vie-ci, et puis nous songerons à nous."* [Yes, indeed, it's necessary to repent. Still I'll have twenty or thirty years of this life and then I'll think about it.] After Molière comes the artist-enchanter, the master beloved by masters, Mozart, revealing the hero's spirit in magical harmonies, elfin tones, and elate darting rhythms as of summer lightning made audible. Here you have freedom in love and in morality mocking exquisitely at slavery to them, and interesting you, attracting you, tempting you, inexplicably forcing you to range the hero with his enemy the statue on a transcendent plane, leaving the prudish daughter and her priggish lover on a crockery shelf below to live piously ever after.

After these completed works Byron's fragment does not count for much philosophically. Our vagabond libertines are no more interesting from that point of view than the sailor who has a wife in every port; and Byron's hero is, after all, only a vagabond libertine. And he is dumb: he does not discuss himself with a Sganarelle-Leporello[5] or with the fathers or brothers of his mistresses: he does not even, like Casanova, tell his own story. In fact he is not a true Don Juan at all; for he is no more an enemy of God than any romantic and adventurous young sower of wild oats. Had you and I been in his place at his age, who knows whether we might not have done as he did, unless indeed your fastidiousness had saved you from the empress

5. Both are servants, the first of Molière's Don Juan, the second of Mozart's Don Giovanni.

Catherine.[6] Byron was as little of a philosopher as Peter the Great: both were instances of that rare and useful, but unedifying variation, an energetic genius born without the prejudices or superstitions of his contemporaries. The resultant unscrupulous freedom of thought made Byron a bolder poet than Wordsworth just as it made Peter a bolder king than George III; but as it was, after all, only a negative qualification, it did not prevent Peter from being an appalling blackguard and an arrant poltroon, nor did it enable Byron to become a religious force like Shelley. Let us, then, leave Byron's Don Juan out of account. Mozart's is the last of the true Don Juans; for by the time he was of age, his cousin Faust had, in the hands of Goethe, taken his place and carried both his warfare and his reconciliation with the gods far beyond mere lovemaking into politics, high art, schemes for reclaiming new continents from the ocean, and recognition of an eternal womanly principle in the universe. Goethe's Faust and Mozart's Don Juan were the last words of the XVIII century on the subject; and by the time the polite critics of the XIX century, ignoring William Blake as superficially as the XVIII had ignored Hogarth or the XVII Bunyan, had got past the Dickens-Macaulay Dumas-Guizot stage and the Stendhal-Meredith-Turgenieff stage,[7] and were confronted with philosophic fiction by such pens as Ibsen's and Tolstoy's, Don Juan had changed his sex and become Doña Juana, breaking out of the Doll's House and asserting herself as an individual instead of a mere item in a moral pageant.

Now it is all very well for you at the beginning of the XX century to ask me for a Don Juan play; but you will see from the foregoing survey that Don Juan is a full century out of date for you and for me; and if there are millions of less literate people who are still in the XVIII century, have they not Molière and Mozart, upon whose art no human hand can improve? You would laugh at me if at this time of day I dealt in duels and ghosts and "womanly" women. As to mere libertinism, you would be the first to remind me that the Festin de Pierre of Molière is not a play for amorists, and that one bar of the voluptuous sentimentality of Gounod or Bizet would appear as a licentious stain on the score of Don Giovanni. Even the more abstract parts of the Don Juan play are dilapidated past use: for instance, Don Juan's supernatural antagonist hurled those who refuse to

6. One of the Don's adventures in Byron's *Don Juan* (1819-24) is to become 'man-mistress' to the insatiable Russian Empress.
7. All four writers in the first stage reflected the accepted morality of their communities. Those in the second stage were literary rebels, exploring complicated states of conscience and consciousness.

repent into lakes of burning brimstone, there to be tormented by devils with horns and tails. Of that antagonist, and of that conception of repentance, how much is left that could be used in a play by me dedicated to you? On the other hand, those forces of middle class public opinion which hardly existed for a Spanish nobleman in the days of the first Don Juan, are now triumphant everywhere. Civilized society is one huge bourgeoisie: no nobleman dares now shock his greengrocer. The women, "marchesane, principesse, cameriere, cittadine" [marchioness, princess, waitress, citizen] and all, are become equally dangerous: the sex is aggressive, powerful: when women are wronged they do not group themselves pathetically to sing "*Protegga il giusto cielo*" [*Don Giovanni*, I: iv, 'May the just heaven protect . . .']: they grasp formidable legal and social weapons, and retaliate. Political parties are wrecked and public careers undone by a single indiscretion. A man had better have all the statues in London to supper with him, ugly as they are, than be brought to the bar of the Nonconformist Conscience by Donna Elvira. Excommunication has become almost as serious a business as it was in the tenth century.

As a result, Man is no longer, like Don Juan, victor in the duel of sex. Whether he has ever really been may be doubted: at all events the enormous superiority of Woman's natural position in this matter is telling with greater and greater force. As to pulling the Nonconformist Conscience by the beard as Don Juan plucked the beard of the Commandant's statue in the convent of San Francisco, that is out of the question nowadays: prudence and good manners alike forbid it to a hero with any mind. Besides, it is Don Juan's own beard that is in danger of plucking. Far from relapsing into hypocrisy, as Sganarelle feared, he has unexpectedly discovered a moral in his immorality. The growing recognition of his new point of view is heaping responsibility on him. His former jests he has had to take as seriously as I have had to take some of the jests of Mr W. S. Gilbert. His scepticism, once his least tolerated quality, has now triumphed so completely that he can no longer assert himself by witty negations, and must, to save himself from cipherdom, find an affirmative position. His thousand and three affairs of gallantry, after becoming, at most, two immature intrigues leading to sordid and prolonged complications and humiliations, have been discarded altogether as unworthy of his philosophic dignity and compromising to his newly acknowledged position as the founder of a school. Instead of pretending to read Ovid he does actually read Schopenhauer and Nietzsche, studies [Edward] Westermarck,[8] and is

8. Finnish philosopher and anthropologist, author of *The History of Human Marriage* (1891).

concerned for the future of the race instead of for the freedom of his own instincts. Thus his profligacy and his dare-devil airs have gone the way of his sword and mandoline into the rag shop of anachronisms and superstitions. In fact, he is now more Hamlet than Don Juan; for though the lines put into the actor's mouth to indicate to the pit that Hamlet is a philosopher are for the most part mere harmonious platitude which, with a little debasement of the word-music, would be properer to Pecksniff, yet if you separate the real hero, inarticulate and unintelligible to himself except in flashes of inspiration, from the performer who has to talk at any cost through five acts; and if you also do what you must always do in Shakespear's tragedies: that is, dissect out the absurd sensational incidents and physical violences of the borrowed story from the genuine Shakespearian tissue, you will get a true Promethean foe of the gods, whose instinctive attitude towards women much resembles that to which Don Juan is now driven. From this point of view Hamlet was a developed Don Juan whom Shakespear palmed off as a reputable man just as he palmed poor Macbeth off as a murderer. Today the palming off is no longer necessary (at least on your plane and mine) because Don Juanism is no longer misunderstood as mere Casanovism. Don Juan himself is almost ascetic in his desire to avoid that misunderstanding; and so my attempt to bring him up to date by launching him as a modern Englishman into a modern English environment has produced a figure superficially quite unlike the hero of Mozart.

And yet I have not the heart to disappoint you wholly of another glimpse of the Mozartian *dissoluto punito* [dissolute one punished] and his antagonist the statue. I feel sure you would like to know more of that statue—to draw him out when he is off duty, so to speak. To gratify you, I have resorted to the trick of the strolling theatrical manager who advertizes the pantomime of Sinbad the Sailor with a stock of second-hand picture posters designed for Ali Baba. He simply thrusts a few oil jars into the valley of diamonds, and so fulfils the promise held out by the hoardings to the public eye. I have adapted this easy device to our occasion by thrusting into my perfectly modern three-act play a totally extraneous act in which my hero, enchanted by the air of the Sierra, has a dream in which his Mozartian ancestor appears and philosophizes at great length in a Shavio-Socratic dialogue with the lady, the statue, and the devil.

But this pleasantry is not the essence of the play. Over this essence I have no control. You propound a certain social substance, sexual attraction to wit, for dramatic distillation; and I distil it for you. I do not adulterate the product with aphrodisiacs nor dilute it with romance and water; for I am merely executing your commission, not producing a popular play for the market. You must therefore (unless, like most wise men, you read the play first and the preface afterwards) prepare yourself to face a trumpery story of modern London life, a life in which, as you know, the ordinary man's main business is to get means to keep up the position and habits of a gentleman, and the ordinary woman's business is to get married. In 9,999 cases out of 10,000, you can count on their doing nothing, whether noble or base, that conflicts with these ends; and that assurance is what you rely on as their religion, their morality, their principles, their patriotism, their reputation, their honor and so forth.

On the whole, this is a sensible and satisfactory foundation for society. Money means nourishment and marriage means children; and that men should put nourishment first and women children first is, broadly speaking, the law of Nature and not the dictate of personal ambition. The secret of the prosaic man's success, such as it is, is the simplicity with which he pursues these ends: the secret of the artistic man's failure, such as that is, is the versatility with which he strays in all directions after secondary ideals. The artist is either a poet or a scallawag: as poet, he cannot see, as the prosaic man does, that chivalry is at bottom only romantic suicide: as scallawag, he cannot see that it does not pay to spunge and beg and lie and brag and neglect his person. Therefore do not misunderstand my plain statement of the fundamental constitution of London society as an Irishman's reproach to your nation. From the day I first set foot on this foreign soil I knew the value of the prosaic qualities of which Irishmen teach Englishmen to be ashamed as well as I knew the vanity of the poetic qualities of which Englishmen teach Irishmen to be proud. For the Irishman instinctively disparages the quality which makes the Englishman dangerous to him; and the Englishman instinctively flatters the fault that makes the Irishman harmless and amusing to him. What is wrong with the prosaic Englishman is what is wrong with the prosaic men of all countries: stupidity. The vitality which places nourishment and children first, heaven and hell a somewhat remote second, and the health of society as an organic whole nowhere, may muddle successfully through the comparatively tribal stages of gregariousness; but in XIX century nations and XX century commonwealths the resolve of every man to be rich at all costs, and of every woman to be married at all costs, must, without a highly scientific social organization, produce a ruinous development of poverty, celibacy, prostitution, infant mortality, adult degeneracy, and everything that wise men most dread. In short, there is no future for men, however brimming with crude vitality, who are neither intelligent nor politically educated enough to be Socialists. So do not misunderstand me in the other direction either: if I appreciate the vital qualities of the Englishman as I appreciate the vital qualities of the bee, I do not guarantee the Englishman against being, like the bee (or the Canaanite) smoked out and unloaded of his honey by beings inferior to himself in simple acquisitiveness, combativeness, and fecundity, but superior to him in imagination and cunning.[9]

The Don Juan play, however, is to deal with sexual attraction, and not with nutrition, and to deal with it in a society in which the serious business of sex is left by men to women, as the serious business of nutrition is left by women to men. That the men, to protect themselves against a too aggressive prosecution of the women's business, have set up a feeble romantic convention that the initiative in sex business must always come from the man, is true; but the pretence is so shallow that even in the theatre, that last sanctuary of unreality, it imposes only on the inexperienced. In Shakespear's plays the woman always takes the initiative. In his problem plays and his popular plays alike the love interest is the interest of seeing the woman hunt the man down. She may do it by charming him, like Rosalind, or by stratagem, like Mariana; but in every case the relation between the woman and the man is the same: she is the pursuer and contriver, he the pursued and disposed of. When she is baffled, like Ophelia, she goes mad and commits suicide; and the man goes straight from her funeral to a fencing match. No doubt Nature, with very young creatures, may save the woman the trouble of scheming: Prospero knows that he has only to throw Ferdinand and Miranda together and they will mate like a pair of doves; and there is no need for Perdita to capture Florizel as the lady doctor in All's Well That Ends Well (an early Ibsenite heroine) captures Bertram. But the mature cases all illustrate the Shakespearean law. The one apparent exception, Petruchio, is not a real one: he is most carefully characterized as a purely commercial matrimonial adventurer. Once he is assured that Katharine has money, he undertakes to marry her before he has seen her.[10] In real life we find not only Petruchios, but Mantalinis and Dobbins[11] who

9. Sometime after the fifteenth century BC, the Canaanites in Palestine were conquered and absorbed by the Israelites.
10. The Shakespearian characters are Rosalind in *As You Like It*, Mariana in *Measure for Measure*, Ophelia in *Hamlet*, Prospero, Ferdinand and Miranda in *The Tempest*, Perdita and Florizel in *The Winter's Tale*, 'Doctor' Helena and Bertram in *All's Well That Ends Well*, and Petruchio and Katharina in *The Taming of the Shrew*.
11. Alfred Mantalini is an extravagant philanderer in Dickens's *Nicholas Nickleby* (1838–9). Captain William Dobbins finally wins the hand of Amelia Sedley in Thackeray's *Vanity Fair* (1847–8).

pursue women with appeals to their pity or jealousy or vanity, or cling to them in a romantically infatuated way. Such effeminates do not count in the world scheme: even Bunsby dropping like a fascinated bird into the jaws of Mrs MacStinger [in Dickens's *Dombey and Son*] is by comparison a true tragic object of pity and terror. I find in my own plays that Woman, projecting herself dramatically by my hands (a process over which I assure you I have no more real control than I have over my wife), behaves just as Woman did in the plays of Shakespear.

And so your Don Juan has come to birth as a stage projection of the tragi-comic love chase of the man by the woman; and my Don Juan is the quarry instead of the huntsman. Yet he is a true Don Juan, with a sense of reality that disables convention, defying to the last the fate which finally overtakes him. The woman's need of him to enable her to carry on Nature's most urgent work, does not prevail against him until his resistance gathers her energy to a climax at which she dares to throw away her customary exploitations of the conventional affectionate and dutiful poses, and claim him by natural right for a purpose that far transcends their mortal personal purposes.

Among the friends to whom I have read this play in manuscript are some of our own sex who are shocked at the "unscrupulousness," meaning the utter disregard of masculine fastidiousness, with which the woman pursues her purpose. It does not occur to them that if women were as fastidious as men, morally or physically, there would be an end of the race. Is there anything meaner than to throw necessary work upon other people and then disparage it as unworthy and indelicate. We laugh at the haughty American nation because it makes the negro clean its boots and then proves the moral and physical inferiority of the negro by the fact that he is a shoeblack; but we ourselves throw the whole drudgery of creation on one sex, and then imply that no female of any womanliness or delicacy would initiate any effort in that direction. There are no limits to male hypocrisy in this matter. No doubt there are moments when man's sexual immunities are made acutely humiliating to him. When the terrible moment of birth arrives, its supreme importance and its superhuman effort and peril, in which the father has no part, dwarf him into the meanest insignificance: he slinks out of the way of the humblest petticoat, happy if he be poor enough to be pushed out of the house to outface his ignominy by drunken rejoicings. But when the crisis is over he takes his revenge, swaggering as the breadwinner, and speaking of Woman's "sphere" with condescension, even with chivalry, as if the kitchen and the nursery were less important than the office in the city. When his swagger is exhausted he drivels into erotic poetry or sentimental uxoriousness; and the Tennysonian King Arthur posing at Guinevere becomes Don Quixote grovelling before Dulcinea. You must admit that here Nature beats Comedy out of the field: the wildest hominist or feminist farce is insipid after the most commonplace "slice of life." The pretence that women do not take the initiative is part of the farce. Why, the whole world is strewn with snares, traps, gins, and pitfalls for the capture of men by women. Give women the vote, and in five years there will be a crushing tax on bachelors. Men, on the other hand, attach penalties to marriage, depriving women of property, of the franchise, of the free use of their limbs, of that ancient symbol of immortality, the right to make oneself at home in the house of God by taking off the hat, of everything that he can force Woman to dispense with without compelling himself to dispense with her. All in vain. Woman must marry because the race must perish without her travail: if the risk of death and the certainty of pain, danger, and unutterable discomforts cannot deter her, slavery and swaddled ankles will not. And yet we assume that the force that carries women through all these perils and hardships, stops abashed before the primnesses of our behavior for young ladies. It is assumed that the woman must wait, motionless, until she is wooed. Nay, she often does wait motionless. That is how the spider waits for the fly. But the spider spins her web. And if the fly, like my hero, shews a strength that promises to extricate him, how swiftly does she abandon her pretence of passiveness, and openly fling coil after coil about him until he is secured for ever!

If the really impressive books and other art-works of the world were produced by ordinary men, they would express more fear of women's pursuit than love of their illusory beauty. But ordinary men cannot produce really impressive art-works. Those who can are men of genius: that is, men selected by Nature to carry on the work of building up an intellectual consciousness of her own instinctive purpose. Accordingly, we observe in the man of genius all the unscrupulousness and all the "self-sacrifice" (the two things are the same) of Woman. He will risk the stake and the cross; starve, when necessary, in a garret all his life; study women and live on their work and care as Darwin studied worms and lived upon sheep; work his nerves into rags without payment, a sublime altruist in his disregard of himself, an atrocious egotist in his disregard of others. Here Woman meets a purpose as impersonal, as irresistible as her own; and the clash is sometimes tragic. When it is complicated by the genius being a woman, then the game is one for a king of critics: your George Sand becomes a mother to gain experience for the novelist and to develop her, and gobbles up men of genius, Chopins, Mussets and the like, as mere *hors d'œuvres*.

I state the extreme case, of course; but what is true of the great man who incarnates the philosophic consciousness of Life and the woman who incarnates its fecundity, is true in some degree of all geniuses and all women. Hence it is that the world's books get written, its pictures painted, its statues modelled, its symphonies composed, by people who are free from the otherwise universal dominion of the tyranny of sex. Which leads us to the conclusion, astonishing to the vulgar, that art, instead of being before all things the expression of the normal sexual situation, is really the only department in which sex is a superseded and secondary power, with its consciousness so confused and its purpose so perverted, that its ideas are mere fantasy to common men. Whether the artist becomes poet or philosopher, moralist or founder of a religion, his sexual doctrine is nothing but a barren special pleading for pleasure, excitement, and knowledge when he is young, and for contemplative tranquillity when he is old and satiated. Romance and Asceticism, Amorism and Puritanism are equally unreal in the great Philistine world. The world shewn us in books, whether the books be confessed epics or professed gospels, or in codes, or in political orations, or in philosophic systems, is not the main world at all: it is only the self-consciousness of certain abnormal people who have the specific artistic talent and temperament. A serious matter this for you and me, because the man whose consciousness does not correspond to that of the majority is a madman; and the old habit of worshipping madmen is giving way to the new habit of locking them up. And since what we call education and culture is for the most part nothing but the substitution of reading for experience, of literature for life, of the obsolete fictitious for the contemporary real, education, as you no doubt observed at Oxford, destroys, by supplantation, every mind that is not strong enough to see through the imposture and to use the great Masters of Arts as what they really are and no more: that is, patentees of highly questionable methods of thinking, and manufacturers of highly questionable, and for the majority but half valid representations of life. The schoolboy who uses his Homer to throw at his fellow's head makes perhaps the safest and most rational use of him; and I observe with reassurance that you occasionally do the same, in your prime, with your Aristotle.

Fortunately for us, whose minds have been so overwhelmingly sophisticated by literature, what produces all these treatises and poems and scriptures of one sort or another is the struggle of Life to become divinely conscious of itself instead of blindly stumbling hither and thither in the line of least resistance. Hence there is a driving towards truth in all books on matters where the writer, though exceptionally gifted, is normally constituted, and has no private axe to grind. Copernicus had no motive for misleading his fellowmen as to the place of the sun in the solar system: he looked for it as honestly as a shepherd seeks his path in a mist. But Copernicus would not have written love stories scientifically. When it comes to sex relations, the man of genius does not share the common man's danger of capture, nor the woman of genius the common woman's overwhelming specialization. And that is why our scriptures and other art works, when they deal with love, turn from honest attempts at science in physics to romantic nonsense, erotic ecstasy, or the stern asceticism of satiety ("the road of excess leads to the palace of wisdom" said William Blake ['Proverbs of Hell', *The Marriage of Heaven and Hell*, 1790–93]; for "you never know what is enough unless you know what is more than enough").

There is a political aspect of this sex question which is too big for my comedy, and too momentous to be passed over without culpable frivolity. It is impossible to demonstrate that the initiative in sex transactions remains with Woman, and has been confirmed to her, so far, more and more by the suppression of rapine and discouragement of importunity, without being driven to very serious reflections on the fact that this initiative is politically the most important of all the initiatives, because our political experiment of democracy, the last refuge of cheap misgovernment, will ruin us if our citizens are ill bred.

When we two were born, this country was still dominated by a selected class bred by political marriages. The commercial class had not then completed the first twentyfive years of its new share of political power;[12] and it was itself selected by money qualification, and bred, if not by political marriage, at least by a pretty rigorous class marriage. Aristocracy and plutocracy still furnish the figureheads of politics; but they are now dependent on the votes of the promiscuously bred masses. And this, if you please, at the very moment when the political problem, having suddenly ceased to mean a very limited and occasional interference, mostly by way of jobbing public appointments, in the mismanagement of a tight but parochial little island, with occasional meaningless prosecution of dynastic

12. The Reform Act of 1832 advanced the democratic process in England by extending suffrage to many in the middle classes and by providing more equitable distribution of parliamentary seats, thus representing the new industrial centres.

wars, has become the industrial reorganization of Britain, the construction
of a practically international Commonwealth, and the partition of the
whole of Africa and perhaps the whole of Asia by the civilized Powers.
Can you believe that the people whose conceptions of society and conduct,
whose power of attention and scope of interest, are measured by the British
theatre as you know it today, can either handle this colossal task themselves,
or understand and support the sort of mind and character that is (at least
comparatively) capable of handling it? For remember: what our voters are
in the pit and gallery they are also in the polling booth. We are all now
under what [Edmund] Burke called "the hoofs of the swinish multitude"
[*Reflections on the Revolution in France*, 1790]. Burke's language gave great
offence because the implied exceptions to its universal application made it a
class insult; and it certainly was not for the pot to call the kettle black. The
aristocracy he defended, in spite of the political marriages by which it tried
to secure breeding for itself, had its mind undertrained by silly schoolmasters
and governesses, its character corrupted by gratuitous luxury, its self-respect
adulterated to complete spuriousness by flattery and flunkeyism. It is no
better today and never will be any better: our very peasants have something
morally hardier in them that culminates occasionally in a Bunyan, a Burns,
or a Carlyle.[13] But observe, this aristocracy, which was overpowered from
1832 to 1885 by the middle class, has come back to power by the votes of
"the swinish multitude." Tom Paine has triumphed over Edmund Burke;[14]
and the swine are now courted electors. How many of their own class have
these electors sent to parliament? Hardly a dozen out of 670, and these only
under the persuasion of conspicuous personal qualifications and popular
eloquence. The multitude thus pronounces judgment on its own units: it
admits itself unfit to govern, and will vote only for a man morphologically
and generically transfigured by palatial residence and equipage, by transcendent tailoring, by the glamor of aristocratic kinship. Well, we two know
these transfigured persons, these college passmen, these well groomed
monocular Algys and Bobbies, these cricketers to whom age brings golf
instead of wisdom, these plutocratic products of "the nail and sarspan
business as he got his money by."[15] Do you know whether to laugh or cry

13. Bunyan was the son of a tinsmith, Burns of a farmer, Carlyle of a mason.
14. The patrician Edmund Burke, British statesman and parliamentarian, produced
the hostile and denunciatory *Reflections on the Revolution in France*. It was answered
by 'American Citizen' Thomas Paine, former British sailor and exciseman, son of
a Quaker corsetmaker, and author of *Common Sense* (1776), who, in his *Rights of
Man* (1791–2), made a case for the principles of republicanism.
15. In Dickens's *Pickwick Papers* (Chapter 13) a voice in the crowd encourages a

at the notion that they, poor devils! will drive a team of continents as they drive a four-in-hand; turn a jostling anarchy of casual trade and speculation into an ordered productivity; and federate our colonies into a world-Power of the first magnitude? Give these people the most perfect political constitution and the soundest political program that benevolent omniscience can devise for them, and they will interpret it into mere fashionable folly or canting charity as infallibly as a savage converts the philosophical theology of a Scotch missionary into crude African idolatry.

I do not know whether you have any illusions left on the subject of education, progress, and so forth. I have none. Any pamphleteer can shew the way to better things; but when there is no will there is no way. My nurse was fond of remarking that you cannot make a silk purse out of a sow's ear; and the more I see of the efforts of our churches and universities and literary sages to raise the mass above its own level, the more convinced I am that my nurse was right. Progress can do nothing but make the most of us all as we are, and that most would clearly not be enough even if those who are already raised out of the lowest abysses would allow the others a chance. The bubble of Heredity has been pricked: the certainty that acquirements are negligible as elements in practical heredity has demolished the hopes of the educationists as well as the terrors of the degeneracy mongers; and we know now that there is no hereditary "governing class" any more than a hereditary hooliganism. We must either breed political capacity or be ruined by Democracy, which was forced on us by the failure of the older alternatives. Yet if Despotism failed only for want of a capable benevolent despot, what chance has Democracy, which requires a whole population of capable voters: that is, of political critics who, if they cannot govern in person for lack of spare energy or specific talent for administration, can at least recognize and appreciate capacity and benevolence in others, and so govern through capably benevolent representatives? Where are such voters to be found today? Nowhere. Plutocratic inbreeding has produced a weakness of character that is too timid to face the full stringency of a thoroughly competitive struggle for existence and too lazy and petty to organize the commonwealth co-operatively. Being cowards, we defeat natural selection under cover of philanthropy: being sluggards, we neglect artificial selection under cover of delicacy and morality.

Yet we must get an electorate of capable critics or collapse as Rome and Egypt collapsed. At this moment the Roman decadent phase of *panem et*

---

parliamentary candidate: 'Success to the Mayor ... and may he never desert the nail and sarspan business as he got his money by.'

circenses [bread and circuses] is being inaugurated under our eyes. Our newspapers and melodramas are blustering about our imperial destiny; but our eyes and hearts turn eagerly to the American millionaire. As his hand goes down to his pocket, our fingers go up to the brims of our hats by instinct. Our ideal prosperity is not the prosperity of the industrial north, but the prosperity of the Isle of Wight, of Folkestone and Ramsgate, of Nice and Monte Carlo [popular vacation resorts]. That is the only prosperity you see on the stage, where the workers are all footmen, parlormaids, comic lodging-letters [real-estate agents], and fashionable professional men, whilst the heroes and heroines are miraculously provided with unlimited dividends and eat gratuitously, like the knights in Don Quixote's books of chivalry. The city papers prate of the competition of Bombay with Manchester and the like. The real competition is the competition of Regent Street with the Rue de Rivoli [for shopping by wealthy visitors], of Brighton and the south coast with the Riviera, for the spending money of the American Trusts. What is all this growing love of pageantry, this effusive loyalty, this officious rising and uncovering at a wave from a flag or a blast from a brass band? Imperialism? Not a bit of it. Obsequiousness, servility, cupidity roused by the prevailing smell of money. When Mr Carnegie rattled his millions in his pockets all England became one rapacious cringe. Only, when [Cecil] Rhodes[16] (who had probably been reading my Socialism for Millionaires) left word that no idler was to inherit his estate, the bent backs straightened mistrustfully for a moment. Could it be that the Diamond King was no gentleman after all? However, it was easy to ignore a rich man's solecism. The ungentlemanly clause was not mentioned again; and the backs soon bowed themselves back into their natural shape.

But I hear you asking me in alarm whether I have actually put all this tub thumping into a Don Juan comedy. I have not. I have only made my Don Juan a political pamphleteer, and given you his pamphlet in full by way of appendix. You will find it at the end of the book. I am sorry to say that it is a common practice with romancers to announce their hero as a man of extraordinary genius, and then leave his works entirely to the reader's imagination; so that at the end of the book you whisper to yourself ruefully that but for the author's solemn preliminary assurance you should hardly have given the gentleman credit for ordinary good sense. You cannot accuse me of this pitiable barrenness, this feeble evasion. I not only tell you that my hero wrote a revolutionists' handbook: I give you the

16. British colonial and imperial statesman, who dedicated his fortunes, based on diamond mining in South Africa's Kimberley field, to the public service.

handbook at full length for your edification if you care to read it. And in that handbook you will find the politics of the sex question as I conceive Don Juan's descendant to understand them. Not that I disclaim the fullest responsibility for his opinions and for those of all my characters, pleasant and unpleasant. They are all right from their several points of view; and their points of view are, for the dramatic moment, mine also. This may puzzle the people who believe that there is such a thing as an absolutely right point of view, usually their own. It may seem to them that nobody who doubts this can be in a state of grace. However that may be, it is certainly true that nobody who agrees with them can possibly be a dramatist, or indeed anything else that turns upon a knowledge of mankind. Hence it has been pointed out that Shakespear had no conscience. Neither have I, in that sense.

You may, however, remind me that this digression of mine into politics was preceded by a very convincing demonstration that the artist never catches the point of view of the common man on the question of sex, because he is not in the same predicament. I first prove that anything I write on the relation of the sexes is sure to be misleading; and then I proceed to write a Don Juan play. Well, if you insist on asking me why I behave in this absurd way, I can only reply that you asked me to, and that in any case my treatment of the subject may be valid for the artist, amusing to the amateur, and at least intelligible and therefore possibly suggestive to the Philistine. Every man who records his illusions is providing data for the genuinely scientific psychology which the world still waits for. I plank down my view of the existing relations of men to women in the most highly civilized society for what it is worth. It is a view like any other view and no more, neither true nor false, but, I hope, a way of looking at the subject which throws into the familiar order of cause and effect a sufficient body of fact and experience to be interesting to you, if not to the playgoing public of London. I have certainly shewn little consideration for that public in this enterprise; but I know that it has the friendliest disposition towards you and me as far as it has any consciousness of our existence, and quite understands that what I write for you must pass at a considerable height over its simple romantic head. It will take my books as read and my genius for granted, trusting me to put forth work of such quality as shall bear out its verdict. So we may disport ourselves on our own plane to the top of our bent; and if any gentleman points out that neither this epistle dedicatory nor the dream of Don Juan in the third act of the ensuing comedy is suitable for immediate production at a popular theatre we need not contradict him. Napoleon provided Talma with a pit of kings,[17] with what effect on Talma's acting is not recorded. As for me, what I have always wanted is a pit of philosophers; and this is a play for such a pit.

I should make formal acknowledgment to the authors whom I have pillaged in the following pages if I could recollect them all. The theft of the brigand-poetaster from Sir Arthur Conan Doyle is deliberate;[18] and the metamorphosis of Leporello into Enry Straker, motor engineer and New Man, is an intentional dramatic sketch of the contemporary embryo of Mr H. G. Wells's anticipation of the efficient engineering class which will, he hopes, finally sweep the jabberers out of the way of civilization [*Anticipations of the Reaction of Mechanical and Scientific Progress upon Human Life and Thought*, 1902]. Mr Barrie has also, whilst I am correcting my proofs, delighted London with a servant who knows more than his masters [*The Admirable Crichton*, 1902]. The conception of Mendoza Limited I trace back to a certain West Indian colonial secretary,[19] who, at a period when he and I and Mr Sidney Webb were sowing our political wild oats as a sort of Fabian Three Musketeers, without any prevision of the surprising respectability of the crop that followed, recommended Webb, the encyclopedic and inexhaustible, to form himself into a company for the benefit of the shareholders. Octavius I take over unaltered from Mozart; and I hereby authorize any actor who impersonates him, to sing "*Dalla sua pace*" (if he can) at any convenient moment during the representation. Ann was suggested to me by the XV century Dutch morality called Everyman, which Mr William Poel[20] has lately resuscitated so triumphantly. I trust he will work that vein further, and recognize that Elizabethan Renascence fustian is no more bearable after medieval poesy than Scribe after Ibsen. As I sat watching Everyman at the Charterhouse,[21] I said to myself Why not Everywoman? Ann was the result: every woman is not Ann; but Ann is Everywoman.

17. In 1808 Napoleon commanded the French actor-manager François-Joseph Talma to perform Voltaire's *Mort de César* before an audience of crowned heads in Erfurt, Prussia.
18. The brigand El Cuchillo, who finds criticism of his verse unbearable, appears in a story 'How the Brigadier Held the King', in Conan Doyle's *The Exploits of Brigadier Gerard* (1896).
19. Sydney Olivier, secretary of the Fabian Society 1886–90 and member of its Executive Committee 1887–99, was colonial secretary of British Honduras 1890–96 and of Jamaica 1899–1904. He became Governor of Jamaica in 1907.
20. Actor, manager, scholar, and founder of the Elizabethan Stage Society.
21. The Charterhouse, in Smithfield (London), founded in 1371, was one of nine monasteries in England housing the Carthusian order of monks. It later was the site of a chapel, almshouse, and school. Poel staged *Everyman*, for the first time in some four hundred years, in the grounds of the Charterhouse on 13 July 1901.

That the author of Everyman was no mere artist, but an artist-philosopher, and that the artist-philosophers are the only sort of artists I take quite seriously, will be no news to you. Even Plato and Boswell, as the dramatists who invented Socrates and Dr Johnson, impress me more deeply than the romantic playwrights. Ever since, as a boy, I first breathed the air of the transcendental regions at a performance of Mozart's Zauberflöte, I have been proof against the garish splendors and alcoholic excitements of the ordinary stage combinations of Tappertitian[22] romance with the police intelligence. Bunyan, Blake, Hogarth, and Turner (these four apart and above all the English classics), Goethe, Shelley, Schopenhauer, Wagner, Ibsen, Morris, Tolstoy, and Nietzsche are among the writers whose peculiar sense of the world I recognize as more or less akin to my own. Mark the word peculiar. I read Dickens and Shakespear without shame or stint; but their pregnant observations and demonstrations of life are not co-ordinated into any philosophy or religion: on the contrary, Dickens's sentimental assumptions are violently contradicted by his observations; and Shakespear's pessimism is only his wounded humanity. Both have the specific genius of the fictionist and the common sympathies of human feeling and thought in pre-eminent degree. They are often saner and shrewder than the philosophers just as Sancho Panza was often saner and shrewder than Don Quixote. They clear away vast masses of oppressive gravity by their sense of the ridiculous, which is at bottom a combination of sound moral judgment with lighthearted good humor. But they are concerned with the diversities of the world instead of with its unities: they are so irreligious that they exploit popular religion for professional purposes without delicacy or scruple (for example, Sydney Carton [in *A Tale of Two Cities*, 1859] and the ghost in Hamlet!): they are anarchical, and cannot balance their exposures of Angelo [in *Measure for Measure*] and Dogberry [in *Much Ado about Nothing*], Sir Leicester Dedlock [in *Bleak House*, 1852–3] and Mr Tite Barnacle[23] [in *Little Dorrit*, 1855–7], with any portrait of a prophet or a worthy leader: they have no constructive ideas: they regard those who have them as dangerous fanatics: in all their fictions there is no leading thought or inspiration for which any man could conceivably risk the spoiling of his hat in a shower, much less his life. Both are alike forced to borrow motives for the more strenuous actions of their personages from

22. In Dickens's *Barnaby Rudge* (1841), Simon Tappertit is an embodiment of youthful conceit and amorousness.
23. Of the Shakespearian characters, Angelo is hypocritical, Dogberry muddled. Both of the Dickens characters are pompously obstructive.

the common stockpot of melodramatic plots; so that Hamlet has to be stimulated by the prejudices of a policeman and Macbeth by the cupidities of a bushranger. Dickens, without the excuse of having to manufacture motives for Hamlets and Macbeths, superfluously punts his crew down the stream of his monthly parts by mechanical devices which I leave you to describe, my own memory being quite baffled by the simplest question as to Monks in Oliver Twist, or the long lost parentage of Smike, or the relations between the Dorrit and Clennam families so inopportunely discovered by Monsieur Rigaud Blandois.[24] The truth is, the world was to Shakespear a great "stage of fools" [*Lear*, IV: vi] on which he was utterly bewildered. He could see no sort of sense in living at all; and Dickens saved himself from the despair of the dream in The Chimes[25] by taking the world for granted and busying himself with its details. Neither of them could do anything with a serious positive character: they could place a human figure before you with perfect verisimilitude; but when the moment came for making it live and move, they found, unless it made them laugh, that they had a puppet on their hands, and had to invent some artificial external stimulus to make it work. This is what is the matter with Hamlet all through: he has no will except in his bursts of temper. Foolish Bardolaters make a virtue of this after their fashion: they declare that the play is the tragedy of irresolution; but all Shakespear's projections of the deepest humanity he knew have the same defect: their characters and manners are lifelike; but their actions are forced on them from without, and the external force is grotesquely inappropriate except when it is quite conventional, as in the case of Henry V. Falstaff is more vivid than any of these serious reflective characters, because he is self-acting: his motives are his own appetites and instincts and humors. Richard III, too, is delightful as the whimsical comedian who stops a funeral to make love to the corpse's son's widow; but when, in the next act, he is replaced by a stage villain who smothers babies and offs with people's heads, we are revolted at the imposture and repudiate the changeling. Faulconbridge, Coriolanus,

24. Monks is Oliver's half-brother, who tries to deprive him of his inheritance, in Dickens's *Oliver Twist* (1837–9). Smike is the retarded and crippled lad befriended by the eponymous hero of Dickens's *Nicholas Nickleby* (1838–9). Amy Dorrit, dutiful daughter of the imprisoned debtor William Dorrit, in Dickens's *Little Dorrit* (1855–7), finally marries Arthur Clennam, adopted son of the puritanical Mrs Clennam, who through the agency of the villainous Rigaud, alias Blandois, is discovered to have suppressed a codicil in a will that benefited the Dorrit family.
25. *The Chimes* (1844), one of Dickens's Christmas books, in which Toby Veck has a nightmare of awful misfortunes befalling his daughter.

Leontes[26] are admirable descriptions of instinctive temperaments: indeed the play of Coriolanus is the greatest of Shakespear's comedies; but description is not philosophy; and comedy neither compromises the author nor reveals him. He must be judged by those characters into which he puts what he knows of himself, his Hamlets and Macbeths and Lears and Prosperos. If these characters are agonizing in a void about factitious melodramatic murders and revenges and the like, whilst the comic characters walk with their feet on solid ground, vivid and amusing, you know that the author has much to shew and nothing to teach. The comparison between Falstaff and Prospero is like the comparison between Micawber [in Dickens's *David Copperfield*] and David Copperfield. At the end of the book you know Micawber, whereas you only know what has happened to David, and are not interested enough in him to wonder what his politics or religion might be if anything so stupendous as a religious or political idea, or a general idea of any sort, were to occur to him. He is tolerable as a child; but he never becomes a man, and might be left out of his own biography altogether but for his usefulness as a stage confidant, a Horatio or "Charles his friend": what they call on the stage a feeder.

Now you cannot say this of the works of the artist-philosophers. You cannot say it, for instance, of [John Bunyan's] The Pilgrim's Progress [1678]. Put your Shakespearean hero and coward, Henry V and Pistol or Parolles, beside Mr Valiant and Mr Fearing, and you have a sudden revelation of the abyss that lies between the fashionable author who could see nothing in the world but personal aims and the tragedy of their disappointment or the comedy of their incongruity, and the field preacher who achieved virtue and courage by identifying himself with the purpose of the world as he understood it. The contrast is enormous: Bunyan's coward stirs your blood more than Shakespear's hero, who actually leaves you cold and secretly hostile. You suddenly see that Shakespear, with all his flashes and divinations, never understood virtue and courage, never conceived how any man who was not a fool could, like Bunyan's hero, look back from the brink of the river of death over the strife and labor of his pilgrimage, and say "yet do I not repent me"; or, with the panache of a millionaire, bequeath "my sword to him that shall succeed me in my pilgrimage, and my courage and skill to him that can get it" [Part II]. This is the true joy in life, the being used for a purpose recognized by yourself as a mighty one;

26. Shakespearian characters: Philip Faulconbridge is a scheming bastard son in *King John*, Coriolanus the patrician consul in *The Tragedy of Coriolanus*, Leontes the king of Sicilia in *The Winter's Tale*.

the being thoroughly worn out before you are thrown on the scrap heap; the being a force of Nature instead of a feverish selfish little clod of ailments and grievances complaining that the world will not devote itself to making you happy. And also the only real tragedy in life is the being used by personally minded men for purposes which you recognize to be base. All the rest is at worst mere misfortune or mortality: this alone is misery, slavery, hell on earth; and the revolt against it is the only force that offers a man's work to the poor artist, whom our personally minded rich people would so willingly employ as pandar, buffoon, beauty monger, sentimentalizer and the like.

It may seem a long step from Bunyan to Nietzsche; but the difference between their conclusions is merely formal. Bunyan's perception that righteousness is filthy rags, his scorn for Mr Legality in the village of Morality, his defiance of the Church as the supplanter of religion, his insistence on courage as the virtue of virtues, his estimate of the career of the conventionally respectable and sensible Worldly Wiseman as no better at bottom than the life and death of Mr Badman: all this, expressed by Bunyan in the terms of a tinker's theology, is what Nietzsche has expressed in terms of post-Darwin, post-Schopenhauer philosophy; Wagner in terms of polytheistic mythology; and Ibsen in terms of mid-XIX century Parisian dramaturgy. Nothing is new in these matters except their novelties: for instance, it is a novelty to call Justification by Faith "Wille," and Justification by Works "Vorstellung." The sole use of the novelty is that you and I buy and read Schopenhauer's treatise on Will and Representation when we should not dream of buying a set of sermons on Faith versus Works. At bottom the controversy is the same, and the dramatic results are the same. Bunyan makes no attempt to present his pilgrims as more sensible or better conducted than Mr Worldly Wiseman. Mr W. W.'s worst enemies, Mr Embezzler, Mr Never-go-to-Church-on-Sunday, Mr Bad Form, Mr Murderer, Mr Burglar, Mr Co-respondent, Mr Blackmailer, Mr Cad, Mr Drunkard, Mr Labor Agitator and so forth, can read the Pilgrim's Progress without finding a word said against them; whereas the respectable people who snub them and put them in prison, such as Mr W. W. himself and his young friend Civility; Formalist and Hypocrisy; Wildhead, Inconsiderate, and Pragmatick (who were clearly young university men of good family and high feeding); that brisk lad Ignorance, Talkative, By-ends of Fairspeech and his mother-in-law Lady Feigning, and other reputable gentlemen and citizens, catch it very severely. Even Little Faith, though he gets to heaven at last, is given to understand that it served him right to be mobbed by the brothers Faint Heart, Mistrust, and Guilt, all three recognized members of respectable society and veritable pillars of the law. The whole allegory is a consistent attack on morality and respectability, without a word that one can remember against vice and crime. Exactly what is complained of in Nietzsche and Ibsen, is it not? And also exactly what would be complained of in all the literature which is great enough and old enough to have attained canonical rank, officially or unofficially, were it not that books are admitted to the canon by a compact which confesses their greatness in consideration of abrogating their meaning; so that the reverend rector can agree with the prophet Micah as to his inspired style without being committed to any complicity in Micah's furiously Radical opinions. Why, even I, as I force myself, pen in hand, into recognition and civility, find all the force of my onslaught destroyed by a simple policy of non-resistance. In vain do I redouble the violence of the language in which I proclaim my heterodoxies. I rail at the theistic credulity of Voltaire, the amoristic superstition of Shelley, the revival of tribal soothsaying and idolatrous rites which [Thomas] Huxley[27] called Science and mistook for an advance on the Pentateuch, no less than at the welter of ecclesiastical and professional humbug which saves the face of the stupid system of violence and robbery which we call Law and Industry. Even atheists reproach me with infidelity and anarchists with nihilism because I cannot endure their moral tirades. And yet, instead of exclaiming "Send this inconceivable Satanist to the stake," the respectable newspapers pith me [that is, eviscerate my spirit or substance] by announcing "another book by this brilliant and thoughtful writer." And the ordinary citizen, knowing that an author who is well spoken of by a respectable newspaper must be all right, reads me, as he reads Micah, with undisturbed edification from his own point of view. It is narrated that in the eighteenseventies an old lady, a very devout Methodist, moved from Colchester to a house in the neighborhood of the City Road, in London, where, mistaking the Hall of Science for a chapel, she sat at the feet of Charles Bradlaugh[28] for many years, entranced by his eloquence, without questioning his orthodoxy or moulting a feather of her faith. I fear I shall be defrauded of my just martyrdom in the same way.

However, I am digressing, as a man with a grievance always does. And after all, the main thing in determining the artistic quality of a book is not the opinions it propagates, but the fact that the writer has opinions. The

27. A firm believer in Darwinism, as evidenced in such works as *Man's Place in Nature* (1863).
28. Political and social reformer, leader of the National Secularist Society, which met in its Hall of Science.

old lady from Colchester was right to sun her simple soul in the energetic radiance of Bradlaugh's genuine beliefs and disbeliefs rather than in the chill of such mere painting of light and heat as elocution and convention can achieve. My contempt for *belles lettres*, and for amateurs who become the heroes of the fanciers of literary virtuosity, is not founded on any illusion of mine as to the permanence of those forms of thought (call them opinions) by which I strive to communicate my bent to my fellows. To younger men they are already outmoded; for though they have no more lost their logic than an XVIII century pastel has lost its drawing or its color, yet, like the pastel, they grow indefinably shabby, and will grow shabbier until they cease to count at all, when my books will either perish, or, if the world is still poor enough to want them, will have to stand, with Bunyan's, by quite amorphous qualities of temper and energy. With this conviction I cannot be a bellettrist. No doubt I must recognize, as even the Ancient Mariner did, that I must tell my story entertainingly if I am to hold the wedding guest spellbound in spite of the siren sounds of the loud bassoon. But "for art's sake" alone I would not face the toil of writing a single sentence. I know that there are men who, having nothing to say and nothing to write, are nevertheless so in love with oratory and with literature that they delight in repeating as much as they can understand of what others have said or written aforetime. I know that the leisurely tricks which their want of conviction leaves them free to play with the diluted and misapprehended message supply them with a pleasant parlor game which they call style. I can pity their dotage and even sympathize with their fancy. But a true original style is never achieved for its own sake: a man may pay from a shilling to a guinea, according to his means, to see, hear, or read another man's act of genius; but he will not pay with his whole life and soul to become a mere virtuoso in literature, exhibiting an accomplishment which will not even make money for him, like fiddle playing. Effectiveness of assertion is the Alpha and Omega of style. He who has nothing to assert has no style and can have none: he who has something to assert will go as far in power of style as its momentousness and his conviction will carry him. Disprove his assertion after it is made, yet its style remains. Darwin has no more destroyed the style of Job nor of Handel than Martin Luther destroyed the style of Giotto. All the assertions get disproved sooner or later; and so we find the world full of a magnificent débris of artistic fossils, with the matter-of-fact credibility gone clean out of them, but the form still splendid. And that is why the old masters play the deuce with our mere susceptibles. Your Royal Academician thinks he can get the style of Giotto without Giotto's beliefs, and correct his perspective into the bargain. Your man of letters thinks he can get Bunyan's or Shakespear's style without Bunyan's conviction or Shakespear's apprehension, especially if he takes care not to split his infinitives. And so with your Doctors of Music, who, with their collections of discords duly prepared and resolved or retarded or anticipated in the manner of the great composers, think they can learn the art of Palestrina from Cherubini's treatise.[29] All this academic art is far worse than the trade in sham antique furniture; for the man who sells me an oaken chest which he swears was made in the XIII century, though as a matter of fact he made it himself only yesterday, at least does not pretend that there are any modern ideas in it; whereas your academic copier of fossils offers them to you as the latest outpouring of the human spirit, and, worst of all, kidnaps young people as pupils and persuades them that his limitations are rules, his observances dexterities, his timidities good taste, and his emptinesses purities. And when he declares that art should not be didactic, all the people who have nothing to teach and all the people who dont want to learn agree with him emphatically.

I pride myself on not being one of these susceptibles. If you study the electric light with which I supply you in that Bumbledonian[30] public capacity of mine [as a borough councillor] over which you make merry from time to time, you will find that your house contains a great quantity of highly susceptible copper wire which gorges itself with electricity and gives you no light whatever. But here and there occurs a scrap of intensely insusceptible, intensely resistant material; and that stubborn scrap grapples with the current and will not let it through until it has made itself useful to you as those two vital qualities of literature, light and heat. Now if I am to be no mere copper wire amateur but a luminous author, I must also be a most intensely refractory person, liable to go out and to go wrong at inconvenient moments, and with incendiary possibilities. These are the faults of my qualities; and I assure you that I sometimes dislike myself so much that when some irritable reviewer chances at that moment to pitch into me with zest, I feel unspeakably relieved and obliged. But I never dream of reforming, knowing that I must take myself as I am and get what work I can out of myself. All this you will understand; for there is community of material between us: we are both critics of life as well as of art;

---

29. Giovanni Pierluigi da Palestrina was an Italian composer of madrigals and masses. Maria Luigi Cherubini, Italian composer of opera, was the author of a *Treatise on Counterpoint and Fugue* (1835).
30. Derived from Bumble, the pompous beadle in the parish workhouse, where Oliver Twist was born.

and you have perhaps said to yourself when I have passed your windows "There, but for the grace of God, go I."[31] An awful and chastening reflection, which shall be the closing cadence of this immoderately long letter from yours faithfully,

WOKING, 1903.   G. BERNARD SHAW.

POSTSCRIPT.—Amid unprecedented critical cerebration over this book of ours—alas! that your own voice should be dedicated to silence!—I find myself warned to prepare a new edition. I take the opportunity to correct a slip or two. You may have noticed (nobody else has, by the way) that I fitted you with a quotation from Othello, and then unconsciously referred it to A Winter's Tale.[32] I correct this with regret; for half its appropriateness goes with Florizel and Perdita: still, one must not trifle with Shakespear; so I have given Desdemona back her property.

On the whole, the book has done very well. The strong critics are impressed; the weak intimidated; the connoisseurs tickled by my literary bravura (put in to please you): the humorists alone, oddly enough, sermonize me, scared out of their profession into the quaintest tumults of conscience. Not all my reviewers have understood me: like Englishmen in France, confidently uttering their own island diphthongs as good French vowels, many of them offer, as samples of the Shavian philosophy, the likest article from their own stock. Others are the victims of association of ideas: they call me Pessimist because my remarks wound their self-complacency, and Renegade because I would have my mob all Cæsars instead of Toms, Dicks, and Harrys. Worst of all, I have been accused of preaching a Final Ethical Superman: no other, in fact, than our old friend the Just Man made Perfect! [Hebrews 12: 23] This misunderstanding is so galling that I lay down my pen without another word lest I should be tempted to make the postscript longer even than the letter.

POSTSCRIPT 1933. The evolutionary theme of the third act of Man and Superman was resumed by me twenty years later in the preface to Back to Methuselah, where it is developed as the basis of the religion of the near future.

31. Attributed to John Bradford, English Protestant minister, who in 1555 was burned as a heretic, charged with sedition against Queen Mary Tudor.
32. Shaw's gaffe (in the second paragraph of the preface) was amended in the second printing (October 1903), in which this postscript was first published.

The Commonsense of Municipal Trading

First published in 1904

There is a child's schoolbook, which I have never seen, entitled Reading Without Tears.[1] I am half tempted to borrow from its author to the extent of calling this book Municipal Trade[2] Without Figures. At all events, there are no figures in this book; and the reader will soon learn from it that the figures with which he has been so grievously pelted from other quarters do not matter. The question whether municipal trading is sound in principle cannot be settled by the figures of this or that adventure in it, anymore than the soundness of banking or insurance can be settled by the figures of this or that big dividend or disastrous liquidation. Besides, the balance sheet of a city's welfare cannot be stated in figures. Counters of a much more spiritual kind are needed, and some imagination and conscience to add them up, as well.

I hope nobody will be deterred from reading this book by the notion that the subject is a dry one. It is, on the contrary, one of the most succulent in the whole range of literature. If I, a playwright and philosopher by profession and predilection, have found it not only possible but interesting to spend my afternoons for six years in the committee rooms of a suburban Vestry and Borough Council to gain the practical knowledge which is at the back of this little book,[3] the most romantic of my literary customers may very well endure to hear me draw the moral of my experience for four hours.

I purposely send the book out on the eve of the London County Election. That election will turn on two main themes: Municipal Trading and the

---

1. Or, A Pleasant Mode of Learning to Read (1857), by F. L. Bevan.
2. Nationalization on a borough level. Some of the Borough Councils in London had the option of replacing private companies with public services and supplies, as, for example, in furnishing electric power for home lighting.
3. In November 1903 Shaw resigned from the St Pancras Borough Council. He had served on the Public Health, Parliamentary, Electricity, Housing and Drainage Committees.

Education Act.[4] Mr Sidney Webb has just issued a concise book on London Education. I offer this as a complementary treatise on municipal trading. If the elector will carefully study both, and strictly abstain from the newspapers on both subjects until after the election, he will, I venture to hope, vote with his eyes as widely and impartially opened as anything short of practical first hand municipal experience can open them.

LONDON.
February, 1904.   G. B. S.

4. Shaw was running as a Progressive candidate for St Pancras in the London County Council election, to be held on 5 March 1904. He was defeated, in part at least, because of his stand on the two issues he cites here. He advocated municipalization of the drink traffic, thus alienating the temperance societies: though a teetotaller, he wanted to nationalize the traffic and have the state receive the profits while monitoring the effects. He also weakened his election chances by favouring improvement in Church schools, thus antagonizing Nonconformist groups. Shaw insisted that half the nation's children had to choose between the Church school and no school at all, an echo of Sidney Webb's *The Education Act, 1903: How to Make the Best of It* (Fabian Tract No. 117, 1904, which Shaw as editor had revised).

Fabianism and the Fiscal Question

First published in the de luxe edition issued by the Fabian Society, 1904

———

The literary man who places a well-known style at the disposal of the Fabian Society will inevitably be credited with more than his share of the opinions his pen drives home. I therefore hasten to explain that though I am the penman of this Tract its authorship is genuinely collective. The original draft, itself made after much conference with representative members of the Society, has been repeatedly amended in committee before being finally submitted to the whole body of members, and reduced here and expanded there to their greatest common measure.

The result of this process will be evident enough to expert critics. The very important questions of dumping, of sweating in foreign countries, and of the pressure of colonial opinion, have been virtually omitted. There was no room for a treatment of these phenomena sufficiently elaborate and qualified to secure the necessary agreement. In dealing with the actual political controversy now raging, we have had to confine ourselves to description, without more partiality than the occasional liveliness of our language may imply. Even as it is, careless readers will probably overlook the distinction made throughout between [Richard] Cobden's[1] doctrine of Free Trade, which the Society repudiates, and the particular device of taxation of imports. The doctrine of Free Trade is not simply that imports should not be taxed, but that a country's prosperity can be secured automatically by abolishing State interference with commerce, and allowing everyone to buy in the cheapest market and sell in the dearest. Every Factory Act and every Fair Wages Clause is a repudiation of Free Trade: in fact, as Mr Balfour has remarked in one of the few flashes of wit which have enlivened the controversy so far, it may well be asked whether the very existence of a Government is not an infraction of Free Trade. And as the nation listens without confusion to Mr Balfour and

1. English manufacturer and Radical politician. A member of the House of Commons in the 1840s, he became the successful champion of the Anti-Corn-Law League, a group dedicated to Free Trade in grain.

Mr Chamberlain[2] vying with each other in solemn assurances that they are thorough Free Traders in principle, and that this is indeed the very reason why they seek power to impose import duties, perhaps the Fabian Society may be allowed to say that it is thoroughly Protectionist in principle without therefore being in the least committed to approval of import duties.

As for my individual opinions, which I only mention because it is so obviously vain to expect that they will be left out of account by the reviewers, all I can say here is that I quite believe that if the counsels given in the following pages be carried into effect by the nation, we shall not need to trouble about such makeshifts as tariffs. But the counsels are arduous. They will perhaps be popular on that account; for I have noticed a widespread opinion among young Britons lately that the way to become strong is to lift heavy weights. Personally I incline rather to the opinion that the way to lift heavy weights is to become strong. With all proper respect to those of us who have lately taken to describing themselves as "God's Englishmen,"[3] I am inclined to fear that a relapse into tariffs may prove more suited to our strength and sagacity than the Fabian plan, and that perhaps the leave-things-alone-and-muddle-through plan is still more in our line than tariff making. Democracy has given us a power which we have neither been bred to use nor schooled to understand: the vote, flung at us as if it were a talisman that would make magicians of us, is but the latest quack remedy for ailments that only the profoundest political science can treat successfully. In this controversy the number of even our legislators who have shewn any knowledge of its merest ABC can be counted on the fingers of one of the hands of an employee in an American sawmill. Our ignorance is frightful. However, no doubt it will be as easy for a group of determined manufacturers, with the aid of plenty of money and a capable agitator, to force the nation from free imports into taxed ones, as it was for

2. Arthur Balfour, British Conservative statesman and former Chief Secretary for Ireland 1887–92, was Prime Minister 1902–5. Joseph Chamberlain, Unionist Colonial Secretary in the Balfour Cabinet, startled the political world in 1903 by an announcement that he rejected the British policy of Free Trade in favour of Imperial (Colonial) Preference as the means of national salvation, and that he advocated an imposition of tariffs on foreign imports. A battle raged for three years before the fall of the Balfour Government and victory for the Free Traders.
3. It is unclear which Britons took to using this self-descriptive appellation, which had its origin in Milton's *Areopagitica* (1664): 'God is decreeing to begin some new and great period in His Church, even to the reforming of the Reformation itself. What does He then but reveal Himself to His servants, and as His manner is, first to His Englishmen?'

them in the forties to force the nation from taxed corn to free corn. For my own part, therefore, I have hitherto tried to advise the working folk how to make the best of it when they are so forced rather than to offer them alternative methods which we all seem to be morally and intellectually incapable of pursuing. Nobody will be better pleased than I if I have underrated myself and my neighbors.

Finally, may I inform purchasers of this *édition de luxe* (for such it is) that they can obtain as many plain copies as they desire from the Secretary of the Fabian Society, 3 Clement's Inn, London, W.C., at the reasonable rate of a penny each, or ninepence per dozen [Fabian Tract No. 116, 1904]. The present more costly form [one shilling] has been issued with a view to the profit of the bookseller, the dignity of the reviewer, and the luxurious tastes of the plutocratic classes.

G. B. S.

The Irrational Knot

First published (American edition) in 1905; amended 1931

═══

This novel was written in the year 1880; but this preface was not written until 25 years later for an American edition. In 1880 I was twentyfour; and four years had elapsed since I had exported myself from Dublin to London in a condition of extreme rawness and inexperience concerning the specifically English side of the life with which the book pretends to deal. Everybody wrote novels then. It was my second attempt; and it shared the fate of my first. Nobody would publish it, though I tried all the London publishers and some American ones. And I should not greatly blame them if I could feel sure that it was the book's faults and not its qualities that repelled them.

I have narrated elsewhere [see above: pp. 93–4] how in the course of time the rejected MS. became Mrs Annie Besant's excuse for lending me her ever-helping hand by publishing it as a serial in a little propagandist magazine of hers. That was how it got loose beyond all possibility of recapture. It is out of my power now to stand between it and the American public.

At present, of course, I am not the author of The Irrational Knot. Physiologists inform us that the substance of our bodies (and consequently of our souls) is shed and renewed at such a rate that no part of us lasts longer than eight years: I am therefore not now in any atom of me the person who wrote The Irrational Knot in 1880. The last of that author perished in 1888; and two of his successors have since joined the majority. Fourth of his line, I cannot be expected to take any very lively interest in the novels of my literary great-grandfather. Even my personal recollections of him are becoming vague and overlaid with those most misleading of all traditions, the traditions founded on the lies a man tells, and at last comes to believe, about himself *to* himself. Certain things, however, I remember very well. For instance, I am significantly clear as to the price of the paper on which I wrote The Irrational Knot. It was cheap—a white demy[1] of

---

1. Demy writing or printing paper varies in size from 38.5 cm × 50 cm to 45 cm × 57.5 cm ($15\frac{1}{2}''$ × 20″ to 18″ × 23″).

unpretentious quality—so that sixpennorth [six pennies' worth] lasted a long time. My daily allowance of composition was five pages of this demy in quarto; and I held my natural laziness sternly to that task day in, day out, to the end. I remember also that Bizet's Carmen[2] being then new in London, I used it as a safety-valve for my romantic impulses. When I was tired of the sordid realism of Edward Conolly [protagonist of Shaw's novel] (whose name does not rhyme to Polly, as the Irish stress is on the first syllable) I threw down my pen and went to the piano to forget him in the glamorous society of Carmen and her crimson toreador and yellow dragoon. Not that Bizet's music could infatuate me as it infatuated Nietzsche.[3] Nursed on greater masters, I thought less of him than he deserved; but the Carmen music was—in places—exquisite of its kind, and could enchant a young man romantic enough to have come to the end of romance before I began to create in art for myself. I still could enjoy other people's romances.

When I say that *I* did and felt these things, I mean, of course, that the predecessor whose name I bear did and felt them. The I of today is (? am) cool towards Carmen; and Carmen, I regret to say, does not take the slightest interest in him (? me). And now enough of this juggling with past and present Shaws. The grammatical complications of being a first person and several extinct third persons at the same moment are so frightful that I must return to the ordinary misusage, and ask the reader to make the necessary corrections in his or her own mind.

This book is not wholly a compound of intuition and ignorance. Take for example the profession of my hero, an Irish-American electrical engineer. That was by no means a flight of fancy. For you must not suppose, because I am a man of letters, that I never tried to earn an honest living. I began trying to commit that sin against my nature when I was fifteen, and persevered from youthful timidity and diffidence, until I was twentythree.[4] My last attempt was in 1879, when a company was formed in London to exploit an ingenious invention by Mr Thomas Alva Edison: a much too ingenious invention as it proved, being nothing less than a telephone of such stentorian efficiency that it bellowed your most private communications all over the house instead of whispering them with some

2. Georges Bizet's *Carmen* (1875) was first performed in London in 1878.
3. In *Der Fall Wagner* (1888), Nietzsche found *Carmen* to be healthfully Dionysian rather than weakly romantic, as with the music of Wagner.
4. From 1871 to 1876 Shaw rose from office boy to junior clerk to head cashier in the office of the Dublin estate agents C. Uniacke Townshend & Co.

sort of discretion. This was not what the British stockbroker wanted; so the company was soon merged in the National Telephone Company after making a place for itself in the history of literature, quite unintentionally, by providing me with a job. Whilst the Edison Telephone Company lasted, it crowded the basement of a huge pile of offices in Queen Victoria Street with American artificers. These deluded and romantic men gave me a glimpse of the skilled proletariat of the United States. They sang obsolete sentimental songs with genuine emotion; and their language was frightful even to an Irishman. They worked with a ferocious energy which was out of all proportion to the actual result achieved. Indomitably resolved to assert their republican manhood by taking no orders from a tall-hatted Englishman whose stiff politeness covered his conviction that they were, relatively to himself, inferior and common persons, they insisted on being slave-driven with genuine American oaths by a genuine free and equal American foreman. They utterly despised the artfully slow British work-man who did as little for his wages as he possibly could; never hurried himself; and had a deep reverence for any one whose pocket could be tapped by respectful behavior. Need I add that they were contemptuously wondered at by this same British workman as a parcel of outlandish adult boys, who sweated themselves for their employer's benefit instead of look-ing after their own interests? They adored Mr Edison as the greatest man of all time in every possible department of science, art and philosophy, and execrated Mr Graham Bell, the inventor of the rival telephone, as his Satanic adversary; but each of them had (or pretended to have) on the brink of completion, an improvement on the telephone, usually a new transmitter. They were free-souled creatures, excellent company: sensitive, cheerful, and profane; liars, braggarts, and hustlers; with an air of making slow old England hum which never left them even when, as often hap-pened, they were wrestling with difficulties of their own making, or struggling in no-thoroughfares from which they had to be retrieved like strayed sheep by Englishmen without imagination enough to go wrong.

In this environment I remained for some months. As I was interested in physics and had read Tyndall and Helmholtz, besides having learnt something in Ireland through a friendship with one of Mr Graham Bell's cousins who was also a chemist and physicist,[5] I was, I believe, the only person in the entire establishment who knew the current scientific explana-

5. Shaw had known Chichester A. Bell in Dublin and London since 1874. Bell departed for the United States in 1880 to assist Alexander Graham Bell in his laboratory experiments, but in later years returned to England.

tion of telephony; and as I soon struck up a friendship with our official lecturer, a Colchester man whose strong point was pre-scientific agriculture, I often discharged his duties for him in a manner which, I am persuaded, laid the foundation of Mr Edison's London reputation: my sole reward being my boyish delight in the half-concealed incredulity of our visitors (who were convinced by the hoarsely startling utterances of the telephone that the speaker, alleged by me to be twenty miles away, was really using a speaking-trumpet in the next room), and their obvious uncertainty, when the demonstration was over, as to whether they ought to tip me or not: a question they either decided in the negative or never decided at all; for I never got anything.

So much for my electrical engineer! To get him into contact with fashionable society before he became famous was also a problem easily solved. I knew of three English peers who actually preferred physical laboratories to stables, and scientific experts to gamekeepers: in fact, one of the experts was a friend of mine. And I knew from personal experience that if science brings men of all ranks into contact, art, especially music, does the same for men and women. An electrician who can play an accompaniment can go anywhere and know anybody. As far as mere access and acquaintance go there are no class barriers for him. My difficulty was not to get my hero into society, but to give any sort of plausibility to my picture of society when I got him into it. I lacked the touch of the literary diner-out; and I had, as the reader will probably find to his cost, the classical tradition which makes all the persons in a novel, except the comically vernacular ones, or the speakers of phonetically spelt dialect, utter themselves in the formal phrases and studied syntax of XVIII century rhetoric. In short, I wrote in the style of Scott and Dickens; and as fashionable society then spoke and behaved, as it still does, in no style at all, my transcriptions of Oxford and Mayfair may nowadays suggest an unaccountable and ludicrous ignorance of a very superficial and accessible code of manners. I was not, however, so ignorant as might have been inferred at that time from my unpresentable and almost desperate financial condition.

I had, to begin with, a sort of backstairs knowledge; for in my teens I struggled for life in the office of an Irish gentleman who acted as land agent and private banker for many persons of distinction. Now it is possible for a London author to dine out in the highest circles for twenty years without learning as much about the human frailties of his hosts as the family solicitor or (in Ireland) the family land agent learns in twenty days; and some of this knowledge inevitably reaches his clerks, especially the clerk who keeps the cash, which was my particular department. He learns, if capable of the lesson, that the aristocratic profession has as few geniuses as any other profession; so that if you want a peerage of more than, say, half a dozen members, you must fill it up with many common persons, and even with some deplorably mean ones. For "service is no inheritance"[6] either in the kitchen or the House of Lords; and the case presented by Mr [J. M.] Barrie in his play of The Admirable Crichton, where the butler is the man of quality, and his master, the Earl, the man of rank, is no fantasy, but a quite common occurrence, and indeed to some extent an inevitable one, because the English are extremely particular in selecting their butlers, whilst they do not select their barons at all, taking them as the accident of birth sends them. The consequences include much ironic comedy. For instance, we have in England a curious belief in first rate people, meaning all the people we do not know; and this consoles us for the undeniable second-rateness of the people we do know, besides saving the credit of aristocracy as an institution. The unmet aristocrat is devoutly believed in; but he is always round the corner, never at hand. That *the* smart set exists; that there is above and beyond that smart set a class so blue of blood and exquisite in nature that it looks down even on the King with haughty condescension; that scepticism on this nice point is a stigma of plebeian baseness: all these imaginings are so common here that they constitute the real popular sociology of England as much as an unlimited credulity as to vaccination constitutes the real popular science of England. It is, of course, a timid superstition. A British peer or peeress who happens by chance to be genuinely noble is just as isolated at court as Goethe would have been among all the other grandsons of publicans, if they had formed a distinct class in Frankfurt or Weimar. This I knew very well when I wrote my novels; and if, as I suspect, I failed to create a convincingly verisimilar atmosphere of aristocracy, it was not because I had any illusions or ignorances as to the common humanity of the peerage, and not because I gave literary style to its conversation, but because, as I had no money, I had to blind myself to its enormous importance, with the result that I missed the point of view, and with it the whole moral basis, of the class which rightly values money, and plenty of it, as the first condition of a bearable life.

Money is indeed the most important thing in the world; and all sound and successful personal and national morality should have this fact for its basis. Every teacher or twaddler who denies it or suppresses it, is an enemy of life. Money controls morality; and what makes the United States of

6. Jonathan Swift's *Directions to Servants: General Rules* (1745).

America look so foolish even in foolish Europe is that they are always in a state of flurried concern and violent interference with morality, whereas they throw their money into the street to be scrambled for, and presently find that their cash reserves are not in their own hands, but in the pockets of a few millionaires who, bewildered by their luck, and unspeakably incapable of making any truly economic use of it, endeavor to "do good" with it by letting themselves be fleeced by philanthropic committee men, building contractors, librarians and professors, in the name of education, science, art and what not; so that sensible people exhale relievedly when the pious millionaire dies, and his heirs, demoralized by being brought up on his outrageous income, begin the socially beneficent work of scattering his fortune through the channels of the trades that flourish by riotous living.

This, as I have said, I did not then understand; for I knew money only by the want of it. Ireland is a poor country; and my father was a poor man in a poor country. By this I do not mean that he was hungry and homeless, a hewer of wood and a drawer of water. My friend Mr James Huneker, a man of gorgeous imagination and incorrigible romanticism, has described me to the American public as a peasant lad who has raised himself, as all American presidents are assumed to have raised themselves, from the humblest departments of manual labor to the loftiest eminence.[7] James flatters me. Had I been born a peasant, I should now be a tramp. My notion of my father's income is even vaguer than his own was—and that is saying a good deal—but he always had an income of at least three figures (four, if you count in dollars instead of pounds); and what made him poor was that he conceived himself as born to a social position which even in Ireland could have been maintained in dignified comfort only on twice or thrice what he had. And he married on that assumption. Fortunately for me, social opportunity is not always to be measured by income. There is an important economic factor, first analysed by an American economist (General Walker),[8] and called rent of ability. Now this rent, when the ability is of the artistic or political sort, is often paid in kind. For example, a London possessor of such ability may, with barely enough money to maintain a furnished bedroom and a single presentable suit of clothes, see everything worth seeing that a millionaire can see, and know everybody worth knowing that he can know. Long before I reached this point myself,

7. American critic of music, drama and art, whose article in *Success Magazine* (April 1905) was subtitled 'His Rise from an Irish Peasant Lad'.
8. F. A. Walker, Civil War general, educator, economist, author of *The Wages Question* (1876) and *Land and Its Rent* (1883).

a very trifling accomplishment gave me glimpses of the sort of fashionable life a peasant never sees. Thus I remember one evening during the novel-writing period when nobody would pay a farthing for a stroke of my pen, walking along Sloane Street in that blessed shield of literary shabbiness, evening dress. A man accosted me with an eloquent appeal for help, ending with the assurance that he had not a penny in the world. I replied, with exact truth, "Neither have I." He thanked me civilly, and went away, apparently not in the least surprised, leaving me to ask myself why I did not turn beggar too, since I felt sure that a man who did it as well as he, must be in comfortable circumstances.

Another reminiscence. A little past midnight, in the same costume, I was turning from Piccadilly into Bond Street, when a lady of the pavement, out of luck that evening so far, confided to me that the last bus for Brompton had passed, and that she should be grateful to any gentleman who would give her a lift in a hansom. My old-fashioned Irish gallantry had not then been worn off by age and England: besides, as a novelist who could find no publisher, I was touched by the similarity of our trades and predicaments. I excused myself very politely on the ground that my wife (invented for the occasion) was waiting for me at home, and that I felt sure so attractive a lady would have no difficulty in finding another escort. Unfortunately this speech made so favorable an impression on her that she immediately took my arm and declared her willingness to go anywhere with me, on the flattering ground that I was a perfect gentleman. In vain did I try to persuade her that in coming up Bond Street and deserting Piccadilly she was throwing away her last chance of a hansom: she attached herself so devotedly to me that I could not without actual violence shake her off. At last I made a stand at the end of Old Bond Street. I took out my purse; opened it; and held it upside down. Her countenance fell, poor girl! She turned on her heel with a melancholy flirt of her skirt, and vanished.

Now on both these occasions I had been in the company of people who spent at least as much in a week as I did in a year. Why was I, a penniless and unknown young man, admitted there? Simply because, though I was an execrable pianist, and never improved until the happy invention of the pianola made a Paderewski of me, I could play a simple accompaniment at sight more congenially to a singer than most amateurs. It is true that the musical side of London society, with its streak of Bohemianism, and its necessary toleration of foreign ways and professional manners, is far less typically English than the sporting side or the political side or the Philistine side; so much so, indeed, that people may and do pass their lives in it without ever discovering what English plutocracy in the mass is really like: still, if you wander in it nocturnally for a fitful year or so as I did, with empty pockets and an utter impossibility of approaching it by daylight (owing to the too obvious decay of the morning wardrobe), you have something more actual to go on than the hallucinations of a peasant lad setting his foot manfully on the lowest rung of the social ladder. I never climbed any ladder: I have achieved eminence by sheer gravitation; and I hereby warn all peasant lads not to be duped by my pretended example into regarding their present servitude as a practicable first step to a celebrity so dazzling that its subject cannot even suppress his own bad novels.

Conceive me then at the writing of The Irrational Knot as a person neither belonging to the world I describe nor wholly ignorant of it, and on certain points quite incapable of conceiving it intuitively. A whole world of art which did not exist for it lay open to me. I was familiar with the greatest in that world: mighty poets, painters, and musicians were my intimates. I found the world of artificial greatness founded on convention and money so repugnant and contemptible by comparison that I had no sympathetic understanding of it. People are fond of blaming valets because no man is a hero to his valet.[9] But it is equally true that no man is a valet to his hero; and the hero, consequently, is apt to blunder very ludicrously about valets, through judging them from an irrelevant standard of heroism: heroism, remember, having its faults as well as its qualities. I, always on the heroic plane imaginatively, had two disgusting faults which I did not recognize as faults because I could not help them. I was poor and (by day) shabby. I therefore tolerated the gross error that poverty, though an inconvenience and a trial, is not a sin and a disgrace; and I stood for my self-respect on the things I had: probity, ability, knowledge of art, laboriousness, and whatever else came cheaply to me. Because I could walk into Hampton Court Palace and the National Gallery (on free days) and enjoy Mantegna and Michael Angelo whilst millionaires were yawning miserably over inept gluttonies; because I could suffer more by hearing a movement of Beethoven's Ninth Symphony taken at a wrong tempo than a duchess by losing a diamond necklace, I was indifferent to the repulsive fact that if I had fallen in love with the duchess I did not possess a morning suit in which I could reasonably have expected her to touch me with the furthest

9. '*Il n'y a point de héros pour son valet de chambre.*' A letter written in 1728 credits the remark to Mme de Cornuel (d. 1694). See *Lettres de Mlle Aïssé à Mme de Calandrini* (1853). The same observation is made in Samuel Foote's play *The Patron* (1764).

protended pair of tongs; and I did not see that to remedy this I should have been prepared to wade through seas of other people's blood. Indeed it is this perception which constitutes an aristocracy nowadays. It is the secret of all our governing classes, which consist finally of people who, though perfectly prepared to be generous, humane, cultured, philanthropic, public spirited and personally charming in the second instance, are unalterably resolved, in the first, to have money enough for a handsome and delicate life, and will, in pursuit of that money, batter in the doors of their fellow-men, sell them up, sweat them in fetid dens, shoot, stab, hang, imprison, sink, burn and destroy them in the name of law and order. And this shews their fundamental sanity and rightmindedness; for a sufficient income is indispensable to the practice of virtue; and the man who will let any unselfish consideration stand between him and its attainment is a weakling, a dupe and a predestined slave. If I could convince our impecunious mobs of this, the world would be reformed before the end of the week; for the sluggards who are content to be wealthy without working and the dastards who are content to work without being wealthy, together with all the pseudo-moralists and ethicists and cowardice mongers generally, would be exterminated without shrift, to the unutterable enlargement of life and ennoblement of humanity. We might even make some beginnings of civilization under such happy circumstances.

In the days of The Irrational Knot I had not learnt this lesson; consequently I did not understand the British peerage, just as I did not understand that glorious and beautiful phenomenon, the "heartless" rich American woman, who so thoroughly and admirably understands that conscience is a luxury, and should be indulged in only when the vital needs of life have been abundantly satisfied. The instinct which has led the British peerage to fortify itself by American alliances is healthy and well inspired. Thanks to it, we shall still have a few people to maintain the tradition of a handsome, free, proud, costly life, whilst the craven mass of us are keeping up our starveling pretence that it is more important to be good than to be rich, and piously cheating, robbing, and murdering one another by doing our duty as policemen, soldiers, bailiffs, jurymen, turnkeys, hangmen, trades-men, and curates, at the command of those who know that the golden grapes are *not* sour. Why, good heavens! we shall all pretend that this straightforward truth of mine is mere Swiftian satire, because it would require a little courage to take it seriously and either act on it or make me drink the hemlock for uttering it.

There was the less excuse for my blindness because I was at that very moment laying the foundations of my high fortune by the most ruthless disregard of all the quack duties which lead the peasant lad of fiction to the White House, and harness the real peasant boy to the plough until he is finally swept, as rubbish, into the workhouse. I was an ablebodied and ableminded young man in the strength of my youth; and my family, then heavily embarrassed, needed my help urgently. That I should have chosen to be a burden to them instead was, according to all the conventions of peasant lad fiction, monstrous. Well, without a blush I embraced the monstrosity. I did not throw myself into the struggle for life: I threw my mother into it. I was not a staff to my father's old age: I hung on to his coat tails. His reward was to live just long enough to read a review of one of these silly novels written in an obscure journal by a personal friend of my own (now eminent in literature as Mr John Mackinnon Robertson)[10] prefiguring me to some extent as a considerable author. I think, myself, that this was a handsome reward, far better worth having than a nice pension from a dutiful son struggling slavishly for his parent's bread in some sordid trade. Handsome or not, it was the only return he ever had for the little pension [£1 a week] he contrived to export from Ireland for his family. My mother reinforced it by drudging in her elder years at the art of music which she had followed in her prime freely for love. I only helped to spend it. People wondered at my heartlessness: one young and romantic lady had the courage to remonstrate openly and indignantly with me,[11] "for the which," as Pepys [*Diary*, 1893–9 edn.] said of the shipwright's wife who refused his advances, "I did respect her." Callous as [Milton's] Comus to moral babble, I steadily wrote my five pages a day and made a man of myself (at my mother's expense) instead of a slave. And I protest that I will not suffer James Huneker or any romanticist to pass me off as a peasant boy qualifying for a chapter in [Samuel] Smiles's Self Help [1859], or a good son supporting a helpless mother, instead of a stupendously selfish artist leaning with the full weight of his hungry body on an energetic and capable woman. No, James: such lies are not only unnecessary, but fearfully depressing and fundamentally immoral, besides being hardly fair to the supposed peasant lad's parents. My mother worked for my living instead of preaching that it was my duty to work for hers: therefore take off your hat to her, and blush.

It is now open to any one who pleases to read The Irrational Knot. I do

---

10. Journalist, politician and Shakespearian scholar. The review was of *Cashel Byron's Profession*, in *Our Corner* (May 1886).
11. The young lady was a student nurse Alice Lockett, whom Shaw met and became infatuated with in 1881.

not recommend him to; but it is possible that the same mysterious force which drove me through the labor of writing it may have had some purpose which will sustain others through the labor of reading it, and even reward them with some ghastly enjoyment of it. For my own part I cannot stand it. It is to me only one of the heaps of spoiled material that all apprenticeship involves. I consent to its publication because I remember that British colonel who called on Beethoven when the elderly composer was working at his posthumous quartets, and offered him a commission for a work in the style of his jejune septet. Beethoven drove the Colonel out of the house with objurgation. I think that was uncivil. There is a time for the septet, and a time for the posthumous quartets. It is true that if a man called on me now and asked me to write something like The Irrational Knot I should have to exercise great self-control. But there are people who read Man and Superman, and then tell me (actually to my face) that I have never done anything so good as Cashel Byron's Profession. After this, there may be a public for even The Irrational Knot; so let it go.

LONDON.
26 May 1905.

POSTSCRIPT.—Since writing the above I have looked through the proofsheets of this book, and found, with some access of respect for my youth, that it is a fiction of the first order. By this I do not mean that it is a masterpiece in that order, or even a pleasant example of it, but simply that, such as it is, it is one of those fictions in which the morality is original and not readymade. Now this quality is the true diagnostic of the first order in literature, and indeed in all the arts, including the art of life. It is, for example, the distinction that sets Shakespear's Hamlet above his other plays, and that sets Ibsen's work as a whole above Shakespear's work as a whole. Shakespear's morality is a mere reach-me-down; and because Hamlet does not feel comfortable in it and struggles against the misfit, he suggests something better, futile as his struggle is, and incompetent as Shakespear shews himself in his effort to think out the revolt of his feeling against readymade morality. Ibsen's morality is original all through: he knows well that the men in the street have no use for principles, because they can neither understand nor apply them; and that what they can understand and apply are arbitrary rules of conduct, often frightfully destructive and inhuman, but at least definite rules enabling the common stupid man to know where he stands and what he may do and not do without getting into trouble. Now to all writers of the first order, these rules, and the need for them produced by the moral and intellectual incompetence of the ordinary human animal, are no more invariably beneficial and respectable than the sunlight which ripens the wheat in Sussex and leaves the desert deadly in Sahara, making the cheeks of the ploughman's child rosy in the morning and striking the ploughman brain-sick or dead in the afternoon; no more inspired (and no less) than the religion of the Andaman islanders;[12] as much in need of frequent throwing away and replacement as the community's boots. By writers of the second order the readymade morality is accepted as the basis of all moral judgment and criticism of the characters they portray, even when their genius forces them to represent their most attractive heroes and heroines as violating the ready-made code in all directions. Far be it from me to pretend that the first order is more readable than the second! Shakespear, Scott, Dickens, Dumas *père* are not, to say the least, less readable than Euripides and Ibsen. Nor is the first order always more constructive; for Byron, Oscar Wilde, and [François de] Larochefoucauld did not get further in positive philosophy than Ruskin and Carlyle, though they could snuff Ruskin's Seven Lamps [*The Seven Lamps of Architecture*, 1849] with their fingers without flinching. Still, the first order remains the first order and the second the second for all that: no man who shuts his eyes and opens his mouth when religion and morality are offered to him on a long spoon can share the same Parnassian bench with those who make an original contribution to religion and morality, were it only a criticism.

Therefore on coming back to this Irrational Knot as a stranger after twentyfive years, I am proud to find that its morality is not readymade. The drunken prima donna of a bygone type of musical burlesque is not depicted as an immoral person, but as a person with a morality of her own, no worse in its way than the morality of her highly respectable wine merchant in *its* way. The sociology of the successful inventor is his own sociology too; and it is by his originality in this respect that he passes irresistibly through all the readymade prejudices that are set up to bar his promotion. And the heroine, nice, amiable, benevolent, and anxious to please and behave well, but hopelessly secondhand in her morals and nicenesses, and consequently without any real moral force

12. Andaman Islands, in the Bay of Bengal. The inhabitants have a limited brain capacity (about 1300 cc); their languages are unconnected with any known family of speech.

now that the threat of hell has lost its terrors for her, is left destitute among the failures which are so puzzling to thoughtless people. "I cannot understand why she is so unlucky: she is such a nice woman!": that is the formula. As if people with any force in them ever were altogether nice!

And so I claim the first order for this jejune exploit of mine, and invite you to note that the final chapter, so remote from Scott and Dickens and so close to Ibsen, was written years before Ibsen came to my knowledge, thus proving that the revolt of the Life Force against readymade morality in the XIX century was not the work of a Norwegian microbe, but would have worked itself into expression in English literature had Norway never existed. In fact, when Miss Lord's translation of A Doll's House appeared in the eighteeneighties, and so excited some of my Socialist friends that they got up a private reading of it in which I was cast for the part of Krogstad,[13] its novelty as a morally original study of a marriage did not stagger me as it staggered Europe. I had made a morally original study of a marriage myself, and made it, too, without any melodramatic forgeries, spinal diseases, and suicides, though I had to confess to a study of dipsomania. At all events, I chattered and ate caramels in the back drawing-room (our green-room) whilst Eleanor Marx, as Nora, brought Helmer to book at the other side of the folding doors. Indeed I concerned myself very little about Ibsen until, later on, William Archer translated Peer Gynt to me *viva voce*, when the magic of the great poet opened my eyes in a flash to the importance of the social philosopher.[14]

I seriously suggest that The Irrational Knot may be regarded as an early attempt on the part of the Life Force to write A Doll's House in English by the instrumentality of a very immature writer aged 24. And though I say it that should not, the choice was not such a bad shot for a stupid instinctive force that has to work and become conscious of itself by means of human brains. If we could only realize that though the Life Force supplies us with its own purpose it has no other brains to work with than those it has painfully and imperfectly evolved in our heads, the peoples of the earth would learn some pity for their gods; and we should have a religion that

13. Ibsen's *A Doll's House* was first translated into English (1882) as *Nora* by Henrietta Frances Lord. The reading probably occurred in 1885, but is not recorded in Shaw's diary.
14. Shaw subsequently undertook to collaborate with Hans Braekstad, an Anglo-Norse journalist, on a translation of the play, Braekstad to read the play to Shaw in literal English, and Shaw to 'put it into shape' (Diary, 28 August 1888) – in verse! The project soon was abandoned.

would not be contradicted at every turn by the Thing-That-Is giving the lie to the Thing-That-Ought-To-Be.[15]

WELWYN.
Sunday, 25 June 1905.

15. Shaw may have had in mind Swift's *Gulliver's Travels* (1726), in which the Houyhnhnms refer to lying as saying 'the thing which is not'; or a frequently cited passage from Ecclesiastes (1: 9): 'The thing that hath been, it is that which shall be; and that which is done is that which shall be done; and there is no new thing under the sun.'

Alvin Langdon Coburn

Preface to the catalogue of an exhibition of the photographic work of Coburn at the galleries of the Royal Photographic Society of Great Britain, London, 5 February–31 March 1906

═══

Mr Alvin Langdon Coburn[1] is one of the most accomplished and sensitive artist-photographers now living. This seems impossible at his age—twenty-three; but as he began at eight, he has fifteen years' technical experience behind him. Hence, no doubt, his remarkable command of the one really difficult technical process in photography—printing. Technically good negatives are more often the result of the survival of the fittest than of special creation: the photographer is like the cod which produces a million eggs in order that one may reach maturity. The ingenuities of development which are so firmly believed in by old hands who still use slow "ordinary" plates, and develop them in light enough to fog a modern fast color-sensitive plate in half a second, do not seem to produce any better results than the newer timing system which is becoming compulsory now that plates are panchromatic and dark rooms must be really dark. The latitude of modern plates and films, especially those with fast emulsions superimposed on slow ones, may account partly for the way in which workers like Mr Evans get bright windows and dark corners on the same plate without overexposure in the one or underexposure in the other. And as to choosing the picture, that is not a manipulative accomplishment at all: it can be done by a person with the right gift at the first snapshot as well as at the last contribution to The Salon[2] by a veteran. But printing remains the test of the genuine expert.

Very few photographers excel in more than one process. Among our best men, the elder use platinotype[3] almost exclusively for exhibition work. People who cannot see the artistic qualities of Mr Evans's work say that he is "simply" an extraordinarily skilful platinotype printer, and that

1. Young American photographer, whose frontispieces for the 'New York Edition' of Henry James, 1907–9, were highly admired.
2. The annual exhibition of the Photographic Society, London.
3. A permanent print in platinum black obtained by use of a platinum salt in the developer.

anybody's negatives would make artistic pictures if he printed them. The people who say this have never tried (I have); but there is no doubt about the excellence of the printing. Mr Horsley Hinton[4] not only excels in straightforward platinotype printing, but practises dark dexterities of combination printing, putting the Jungfrau [mountain in the Swiss Alps] into your back garden without effort, and being able, in fact, to do anything with his methods except explain them intelligibly to his envious disciples. The younger men are gummists, and are reviled as "splodgers" [splotchers] by the generation which cannot work the gum process.[5]

But Mr Coburn uses and adapts both processes with an instinctive skill and range of effect which makes even expert photographers, after a few wrong guesses, prefer to ascertain how his prints are made by the humble and obvious method of asking him. The device of imposing a gum print on a platinotype—a device which has puzzled many critics, and which was originally proposed as a means of subduing contrast (for which, I am told, it is of no use)—was seized on by Mr Coburn as a means of getting a golden brown tone, quite foreign to pure or chemically toned platinotype, whilst preserving the feathery delicacy of the platinotype image. Lately, having condescended to oil painting as a subsidiary study, he has produced some photographic portraits of remarkable force, solidity, and richness of color, by multiple printing in gum. Yet it is not safe to count on his processes being complicated. Some of his finest prints are simple bromide enlargements, though they do not look in the least like anybody else's enlargements. In short, Mr Coburn gets what he wants one way or another. If he sees a certain quality in a photogravure which conveys what he wants, he naïvely sets to work to make a photogravure exactly as a schoolboy with a Kodak might set to work with a shilling packet of P.O.P.[6] He improvises variations on the three-color process with casual pigments and a single negative taken on an ordinary plate. If he were examined by the City and Guilds Institute,[7] and based his answers on his own practice, he would probably be removed from the classroom to a lunatic asylum. It is his results that place him "hors concours [out of the competition]."

4. English photographer, author of *Platinotype Printing* (1899).
5. A printing process in which the paper is coated with a solution of gum or glue, containing a pigment sensitized with a dichromic acid.
6. Printing Out Papers: ready-to-use sensitive papers that require fixing and toning for permanent image and colour.
7. Technical courses in evening classes were offered under the general direction of the Institute and the Board of Education.

But, after all, the decisive quality in a photographer is the faculty of seeing certain things and being tempted by them. Any man who makes photography the business of his life can acquire technique enough to do anything he really wants to do: where there's a will there's a way. It is Mr Coburn's vision and susceptibility that make him interesting, and make his fingers clever. Look at his portrait of Mr Gilbert Chesterton,[8] for example! "Call that technique? Why, the head is not even on the plate. The delineation is so blunt that the lens must have been the bottom knocked out of a tumbler; and the exposure was too long for a vigorous image." All this is quite true; but just look at Mr Chesterton himself! He is our Quinbus Flestrin,[9] the young Man Mountain, a large, abounding, gigantically cherubic person who is not only large in body and mind beyond all decency, but seems to be growing larger as you look at him—"swellin' wisibly" as Tony Weller puts it [in Dickens's *Pickwick Papers*]. Mr Coburn has represented him as swelling off the plate in the very act of being photographed, and blurring his own outlines in the process. Also, he has caught the Chestertonian resemblance to [Honoré de] Balzac, and unconsciously handled his subject as [Auguste] Rodin handled Balzac.[10] You may call the placing of the head on the plate wrong, the focussing wrong, the exposure wrong, if you like; but Chesterton is right; and a right impression of Chesterton is what Mr Coburn was driving at. If you consider that result merely a lucky blunder, look at the portrait of Mr Bernard Partridge![11] There is no lack of vigor in that image: it is deliberately weighted by comparative underexposure (or its equivalent in underdevelopment), and the result is a powerfully characteristic likeness. Look again at the profile portrait of myself "en penseur" [in thought], a mere strip of my head.[12] Here the exposure is precisely right, and the definition exquisite without the least hardness. These three portraits were all taken with the same lens in the same camera, under similar circumstances. But there is no reduction of three different subjects to a common technical denominator, as there would have been if Franz Hals had painted them. It

---

8. Novelist, essayist, biographer, journalist and one of Shaw's favourite debating opponents.
9. The name the Lilliputians give to Gulliver, meaning in their language 'young man mountain'.
10. Rodin in his sculpture (first exhibited as a maquette in 1898, scandalizing the art world) depicted Balzac as a natural force emerging from shapeless matter.
11. English caricaturist and illustrator, chief cartoonist of *Punch* from 1890.
12. A discreetly nude photograph of Shaw in the attitude of Rodin's *The Thinker*.

is the technique that has been adapted to the subject. With the same batch of films, the same lens, the same camera, the same developer, Mr Coburn can handle you as Bellini handled everybody; as Hals handled everybody; as Gainsborough handled everybody; or as Holbein handled everybody, according to his vision of you.[13] He is free of that clumsy tool—the human hand—which will always go its own single way and no other. And he takes full advantage of his freedom instead of contenting himself, like most photographers, with a formula that becomes almost as tiresome and mechanical as manual work with a brush or crayon.

In landscape he shews the same power. He is not seduced by the picturesque, which is pretty cheap in photography and very tempting: he drives at the poetic, and invariably seizes something that plunges you into a mood, whether it is a mass of cloud brooding over a river, or a great lump of a warehouse in a dirty street. There is nothing morbid in his choices: the mood chosen is often quite a holiday one; only not exactly a Bank Holiday: rather the mood that comes in the day's work of a man who is really a free worker and not a commercial slave. But anyhow, his impulse is always to convey a mood and not to impart local information, or to supply pretty views and striking sunsets. This is done without any impoverishment or artification: you are never worried with that infuriating academicism which already barnacles photography so thickly—selection of planes of sharpness, conventions of composition, suppression of detail, and so on. Mr Coburn goes straight over all that to his mark, and does not make difficulties until he meets them, being, like most joyous souls, in no hurry to bid the devil good morning. And so, good luck to him, and to all artists of his stamp!

G. B. S.

13. The four painters represent four countries, four periods, and four distinct styles: Giovanni Bellini, leader of the Venetian school; Franz Hals, celebrated Dutch portrait painter; Thomas Gainsborough, English landscape and portrait painter; Hans Holbein 'the Younger', German designer and painter.

The Author's Apology

Preface to Dramatic Opinions and Essays, *1906*

In justice to many well-known public persons who are handled rather recklessly in the following pages, I beg my readers not to mistake my journalistic utterances for final estimates of their worth and achievements as dramatic artists and authors. It is not so much that the utterances are unjust; for I have never claimed for myself the divine attribute of justice. But as some of them are hardly even reasonably fair I must honestly warn the reader that what he is about to study is not a series of judgments aiming at impartiality, but a siege laid to the theatre of the XIX century by an author who had to cut his own way into it at the point of the pen, and throw some of its defenders into the moat.

Pray do not conclude from this that the things hereinafter written were not true, or not the deepest and best things I knew how to say. Only, they must be construed in the light of the fact that all through I was accusing my opponents of failure because they were not doing what I wanted, whereas they were often succeeding very brilliantly in doing what they themselves wanted. I postulated as desirable a certain kind of play in which I was destined ten years later to make my mark (as I very well foreknew in the depth of my own unconsciousness); and I brought everybody: authors, actors, managers and all, to the one test: were they coming my way or staying in the old grooves?

Sometimes I made allowances for the difference in aim, especially in the case of personal friends. But as a rule I set up my own standard of what the drama should be and how it should be presented; and I used all my art to make every deviation in aiming at this standard, every recalcitrance in approaching it, every refusal to accept it seem ridiculous and old-fashioned. In this, however, I only did what all critics do who are worth their salt. The critics who attacked Ibsen and defended Shakespear whilst I was defending Ibsen and attacking Shakespear; or who were acclaiming the reign of Irving at the Lyceum Theatre as the Antonine age[1] of the

---

1. The Roman Empire from AD 138 to 180 enjoyed the enlightened and benevolent leadership of the emperors Antoninus Pius and Marcus Aurelius Antoninus.

Shakespearean drama whilst I was battering at it in open preparation for its subsequent downfall, were no more impartial than I. And when my own turn came to be criticized, I also was attacked because I produced what I wanted to produce and not what some of my critics wanted me to produce.

Dismissing, then, the figment of impartiality as attainable only through an indifference which would have prevented me from writing about the theatre at all, or even visiting it, what merit have these essays to justify their republication? Well, they contain something like a body of doctrine, because when I criticized I really did know definitely what I wanted. Very few journalistic critics do. When they attack a new man as Ibsen was attacked, they are for the most part only resisting a change which upsets their habits, the proof being that when they get the sort of play they blame the innovator for not producing, they turn up their noses at it, yawn over it, even recommend the unfortunate author to learn from the newcomer how to open his eyes and use his brains. Weariness of the theatre is the prevailing note of London criticism. Only the ablest critics believe that the theatre is really important: in my time none of them would claim for it, as I claimed for it, that it is as important as the Church was in the Middle Ages and much more important than the Church was in London in the years under review. A theatre to me is a place "where two or three are gathered together" [Matthew 18: 20]. The apostolic succession from Eschylus to myself is as serious and as continuously inspired as that younger institution, the apostolic succession of the Christian Church.

Unfortunately this Christian Church, founded gaily with a pun,[2] has been so largely corrupted by rank Satanism that it has become the Church where you must not laugh; and so it is giving way to that older and greater Church to which I belong: the Church where the oftener you laugh the better, because by laughter only can you destroy evil without malice, and affirm good fellowship without mawkishness. When I wrote, I was well aware of what an unofficial census of Sunday worshippers presently proved: that churchgoing in London has been largely replaced by playgoing. This would be a very good thing if the theatre took itself seriously as a factory of thought, a prompter of conscience, an elucidator of social conduct, an armory against despair and dulness, and a temple of the Ascent of Man.[3] I

2. Jesus conferred upon Simon Bar Jona the name of 'Rock' (Aramaic: *kepa*; Greek: πέτρος, petros), and promised him that He would build His Church upon this 'rock' (Matthew 16: 16–18).
3. A motto of the Darwinians.

took it seriously in that way, and preached about it instead of merely chronicling its news and alternately petting and snubbing it as a licentious but privileged form of public entertainment. This, I believe, is why my sermons gave so little offence, and created so much interest. The artists of the theatre, led by Sir Henry Irving, were winning their struggle to be considered ladies and gentlemen, qualified for official honors. Now for their gentility and knighthoods I cared very little: what lay at the root of my criticism was their deeper claim to be considered, not merely actors and actresses, but men and women, not hired buffoons and posturers, however indulged, but hierophants of a cult as eternal and sacred as any professed religion in the world. And so, consciously or unconsciously, I was forgiven when many of my colleagues, less severe because less in earnest on the subject, gave deadly offence.

1906.

POSTSCRIPT, 1931. The foregoing was prefaced to a reprint of a selection from my [*Saturday Review*] criticisms entitled Dramatic Opinions and Essays [1906], edited in America by the late James Huneker. Let me add now what I should have added then: that a certain correction should be made, especially in reading my onslaught on Shakespear, but also in valuing my vigorous slating of my contemporaries, for the devastating effect produced in the nineties by the impact of Ibsen on the European theatre. Until then Shakespear had been conventionally ranked as a giant among psychologists and philosophers. Ibsen dwarfed him so absurdly in those aspects that it became impossible for the moment to take him seriously as an intellectual force. And if this was Shakespear's fate what could the others expect? The appearance of a genius of the first order is always hard on his competitors. Salieri said of Mozart "If this young man goes on what is to become of us?"[4] and was actually accused of poisoning him. And certainly no one has since been just to Salieri. If my head had not been full of Ibsen and Wagner in the nineties I should have been kinder and more reasonable in my demands. Also, perhaps, less amusing. So forgive; but make the necessary allowances.

G. B. S.

4. Otto Jahn attributes to Salieri, in his *Life of Mozart* (1882), the following reaction to Mozart's death: 'It is a pity to lose so great a genius, but a good thing for us that he is dead. For if he had lived much longer, we should not have earned a crust of bread by our compositions.'

Preface for Politicians
(John Bull's Other Island)

First published in 1907

═══

John Bull's Other Island was written in 1904 at the request of Mr William Butler Yeats, as a patriotic contribution to the repertory of the Irish Literary Theatre.[1] Like most people who have asked me to write plays, Mr Yeats got rather more than he bargained for. The play was at that time beyond the resources of the new Abbey Theatre, which the Irish enterprise owed to the public spirit of Miss A. E. F. Horniman (an Englishwoman, of course), who, twelve years ago, played an important part in the history of the modern English stage as well as in my own personal destiny by providing the necessary capital for that memorable season at the Avenue Theatre[2] which forced my Arms and the Man and Mr Yeats's Land of Heart's Desire on the recalcitrant London playgoer, and gave a third Irish playwright, Dr John Todhunter, an opportunity which the commercial theatres could not have afforded him.

There was another reason for changing the destination of John Bull's Other Island. It was uncongenial to the whole spirit of the neo-Gaelic movement,[3] which is bent on creating a new Ireland after its own ideal, whereas my play is a very uncompromising presentment of the real old Ireland. The next thing that happened was the production of the play in London at the Court Theatre [1 November 1904] by Messrs [John] Vedrenne and [Harley

---

1. In 1897 W. B. Yeats, Lady Gregory, and Edward Martyn drafted a manifesto proposing an Irish Literary Theatre, to be devoted to fostering native, poetic drama, which came into being two years later. In 1904 it was reorganized as the Irish National Theatre Society, performing in Dublin's Abbey Theatre.
2. Miss Horniman underwrote, anonymously, the season of plays presented at the Avenue by Florence Farr. When John Todhunter's *Comedy of Sighs*, with Yeats's *The Land of Heart's Desire* as curtain-raiser, failed to draw audiences, Shaw hastily completed *Arms and the Man* to succeed the Todhunter play on the bill.
3. The Neo-Gaelic movement was set in motion by the Gaelic League, founded in 1893 by Douglas Hyde, later first president of Eire (official name of Ireland) 1938–45.

Granville] Barker,[4] and its immediate and enormous popularity with delighted and flattered English audiences. This constituted it a successful commercial play, and made it unnecessary to resort to the special machinery or tax the special resources of the Irish Literary Theatre for its production.

How Tom Broadbent took it

Now I have a good deal more to say about the relations between the Irish and the English than will be found in my play. Writing the play for an Irish audience, I thought it would be good for them to be shewn very clearly that the loudest laugh they could raise at the expense of the absurdest Englishman was not really a laugh on their side; that he would succeed where they would fail; that he could inspire strong affection and loyalty in an Irishman who knew the world and was moved only to dislike, mistrust, impatience and even exasperation by his own countrymen; that his power of taking himself seriously, and his insensibility to anything funny in danger and destruction, was the first condition of economy and concentration of force, sustained purpose, and rational conduct. But the need for this lesson in Ireland is the measure of its demoralizing superfluousness in England. English audiences very naturally swallowed it eagerly and smacked their lips over it, laughing all the more heartily because they felt that they were taking a caricature of themselves with the most tolerant and large-minded goodhumor. They were perfectly willing to allow me to represent Tom Broadbent as infatuated in politics, hypnotized by his newspaper leader-writers and parliamentary orators into an utter paralysis of his common sense, without moral delicacy or social tact, provided I made him cheerful, robust, goodnatured, free from envy, and above all, a successful muddler-through in business and love. Not only did no English critic allow that the success in business of Messrs English Broadbent and Irish Doyle might possibly have been due to some extent to Doyle, but one writer actually dwelt with much feeling on the pathos of Doyle's failure as an engineer (a circumstance not mentioned nor suggested in my play) in contrast with Broadbent's solid success. No doubt, when the play is performed in Ireland, the Dublin critics will regard it as self-evident that without Doyle Broadbent would have become bankrupt in six months. I

4. Vedrenne and Barker joined forces in 1904 to create Britain's first repertory theatre at the Royal Court, for which Shaw provided a number of new plays as well as several older ones.

should say, myself, that the combination was probably much more effective than either of the partners would have been alone. I am persuaded further—without pretending to know more about it than anyone else—that Broadbent's special contribution was simply the strength, self-satisfaction, social confidence and cheerful bumptiousness that money, comfort, and good feeding bring to all healthy people; and that Doyle's special contribution was the freedom from illusion, the power of facing facts, the nervous industry, the sharpened wits, the sensitive pride of the imaginative man who has fought his way up through social persecution and poverty. I do not say that the confidence of the Englishman in Broadbent is not for the moment justified. The virtues of the English soil are not less real because they consist of coal and iron, not of metaphysical sources of character. The virtues of Broadbent are not less real because they are the virtues of the money that coal and iron have produced. But as the mineral virtues are being discovered and developed in other soils, their derivative virtues are appearing so rapidly in other nations that Broadbent's relative advantage is vanishing. In truth I am afraid (the misgiving is natural to a by-this-time slightly elderly playwright) that Broadbent is out of date. The successful Englishman of today, when he is not a transplanted Scotchman or Irishman, often turns out on investigation to be, if not an American, an Italian, or a Jew, at least to be depending on the brains, the nervous energy, and the freedom from romantic illusions (often called cynicism) of such foreigners for the management of his sources of income. At all events I am persuaded that a modern nation that is satisfied with Broadbent is in a dream. Much as I like him, I object to be governed by him, or entangled in his political destiny. I therefore propose to give him a piece of my mind here, as an Irishman, full of an instinctive pity for those of my fellow-creatures who are only English.

WHAT IS AN IRISHMAN?

When I say that I am an Irishman I mean that I was born in Ireland, and that my native language is the English of Swift and not the unspeakable jargon of the mid-XIX century London newspapers. My extraction is the extraction of most Englishmen: that is, I have no trace in me of the commercially imported North Spanish strain which passes for aboriginal Irish: I am a genuine typical Irishman of the Danish, Norman, Cromwellian, and (of course) Scotch invasions. I am violently and arrogantly Protestant by family tradition; but let no English Government therefore count on my allegiance: I am English enough to be an inveterate Republican and Home

Ruler. It is true that one of my grandfathers was an Orangeman; but then his sister was an abbess; and his uncle, I am proud to say, was hanged as a rebel. When I look round me on the hybrid cosmopolitans, slum poisoned or square pampered, who call themselves Englishmen today, and see them bullied by the Irish Protestant garrison as no Bengalee now lets himself be bullied by an Englishman; when I see the Irishman everywhere standing clearheaded, sane, hardily callous to the boyish sentimentalities, susceptibilities, and credulities that make the Englishman the dupe of every charlatan and the idolater of every numskull, I perceive that Ireland is the only spot on earth which still produces the ideal Englishman of history. Blackguard, bully, drunkard, liar, foulmouth, flatterer, beggar, backbiter, venal functionary, corrupt judge, envious friend, vindictive opponent, unparalleled political traitor: all these your Irishman may easily be, just as he may be a gentleman (a species extinct in England, and nobody a penny the worse); but he is never quite the hysterical, nonsense-crammed, factproof, truth-terrified, unballasted sport of all the bogey panics and all the silly enthusiasms that now calls itself "God's Englishman." England cannot do without its Irish and its Scots today, because it cannot do without at least a little sanity.

THE PROTESTANT GARRISON

The more Protestant an Irishman is—the more English he is, if it flatters you to have it put that way, the more intolerable he finds it to be ruled by English instead of Irish folly. A "loyal" Irishman is an abhorrent phenomenon, because it is an unnatural one. No doubt English rule is vigorously exploited in the interests of the property, power, and promotion of the Irish classes as against the Irish masses. Our delicacy is part of a keen sense of reality which makes us a very practical, and even, on occasion, a very coarse people. The Irish soldier takes the King's shilling and drinks the King's health; and the Irish squire takes the title deeds of the English settlement and rises uncovered to the strains of the English national anthem. But do not mistake this cupboard loyalty for anything deeper. It gains a broad base from the normal attachment of every reasonable man to the established government as long as it is bearable; for we all, after a certain age, prefer peace to revolution and order to chaos, other things being equal. Such considerations produce loyal Irishmen as they produce loyal Poles and Fins, loyal Hindoos, loyal Filipinos, and faithful slaves. But there is nothing more in it than that. If there is an entire lack of gall in the feeling of the Irish gentry towards the English, it is because the Englishman is always gaping admiringly at the Irishman as at some clever child prodigy. He overrates him with a generosity born of a traditional conviction of his own superiority in the deeper aspects of human character. As the Irish gentleman, tracing his pedigree to the conquest or one of the invasions, is equally convinced that if this superiority really exists, he is the genuine true blue heir to it, and as he is easily able to hold his own in all the superficial social accomplishments, he finds English society agreeable, and English houses very comfortable, Irish establishments being generally straitened by an attempt to keep a park and a stable on an income which would not justify an Englishman in venturing upon a wholly detached villa.

OUR TEMPERAMENTS CONTRASTED

But however pleasant the relations between the Protestant garrison and the English gentry may be, they are always essentially of the nature of an *entente cordiale* between foreigners. Personally I like Englishmen much better than Irishmen (no doubt because they make more of me) just as many Englishmen like Frenchmen better than Englishmen, and never go on board a Peninsular and Oriental steamer when one of the ships of the Messageries Maritimes is available. But I never think of an Englishman as my countryman. I should as soon think of applying that term to a German. And the Englishman has the same feeling. When a Frenchman fails to make the distinction, we both feel a certain disparagement involved in the misapprehension. Macaulay, seeing that the Irish had in Swift an author worth stealing, tried to annex him by contending that he must be classed as an Englishman because he was not an aboriginal Celt [*History of England*, 1849–61]. He might as well have refused the name of Briton to [Joseph] Addison because he did not stain himself blue and attach scythes to the poles of his sedan chair. In spite of all such trifling with facts, the actual distinction between the idolatrous Englishman and the fact-facing Irishman, of the same extraction though they be, remains to explode those two hollowest of fictions, the Irish and English "races." There is no Irish race any more than there is an English race or a Yankee race. There *is* an Irish climate, which will stamp an immigrant more deeply and durably in two years, apparently, than the English climate will in two hundred. It is reinforced by an artificial economic climate which does some of the work attributed to the natural geographic one; but the geographic climate is eternal and irresistible, making a mankind and a womankind that Kent, Middlesex, and East Anglia cannot produce and do not want to imitate.

How can I sketch the broad lines of the contrast as they strike me? Roughly I should say that the Englishman is wholly at the mercy of his imagination, having no sense of reality to check it. The Irishman, with a far subtler and more fastidious imagination, has one eye always on things as they are. If you compare [Thomas] Moore's visionary Minstrel Boy [in *Irish Melodies*, 1807–35] with Mr Rudyard Kipling's quasi-realistic Soldiers Three [1888], you may yawn over Moore or gush over him, but you will not suspect him of having had any illusions about the contemporary British private; whilst as to Mr Kipling, you will see that he has not, and unless he settles in Ireland for a few years will always remain constitutionally and congenitally incapable of having, the faintest inkling of the reality which he idolizes as Tommy Atkins [in *Barrack-Room Ballads*, 1892]. Perhaps you have never thought of illustrating the contrast between English and Irish by Moore and Mr Kipling, or even by Parnell and Gladstone. Sir Boyle Roche[5] and Shakespear may seem more to your point. Let me find you a more dramatic instance. Think of the famous meeting between the Duke of Wellington, that intensely Irish Irishman, and Nelson, that intensely English Englishman. Wellington's contemptuous disgust at Nelson's theatricality as a professed hero, patriot, and rhapsode, a theatricality which in an Irishman would have been an insufferably vulgar affectation, was quite natural and inevitable. Wellington's formula for that kind of thing was a well-known Irish one: "Sir: dont be a damned fool." It is the formula of all Irishmen for all Englishmen to this day. It is the formula of Larry Doyle for Tom Broadbent in my play, in spite of Doyle's affection for Tom. Nelson's genius, instead of producing intellectual keenness and scrupulousness, produced mere delirium. He was drunk with glory, exalted by his fervent faith in the sound British patriotism of the Almighty, nerved by the vulgarest anti-foreign prejudice, and apparently unchastened by any reflections on the fact that he had never had to fight a technically capable and properly equipped enemy except on land, where he had never been successful. Compare Wellington, who had to fight Napoleon's armies, Napoleon's marshals, and finally Napoleon himself, without one moment of illusion as to the human material he had to command, without one gush of the "Kiss me, Hardy"[6] emotion which enabled Nelson to idolize his crews and his staff, without forgetting even in his dreams that the normal British officer of that time was an incapable amateur (as he still is) and the

5. Irish MP, who opposed Catholic emancipation and fought for the Union.
6. These were the final words of Nelson to his Flag Captain, Thomas Masterman Hardy, at his death aboard the *Victory* on 21 October 1805.

normal British soldier a never-do-well (he is now a depressed and respectable young man). No wonder Wellington became an accomplished comedian in the art of anti-climax, scandalizing the unfortunate Croker,[7] responding to the demand for glorious sentiments by the most disenchanting touches of realism, and, generally, pricking the English windbag at its most explosive crises of distention. Nelson, intensely nervous and theatrical, made an enormous fuss about victories so cheap that he would have deserved shooting if he had lost them, and, not content with lavishing splendid fighting on helpless adversaries like the heroic [François-Paul] De Brueys or [Pierre de] Villeneuve[8] (who had not even the illusion of heroism when he went like a lamb to the slaughter), got himself killed by his passion for exposing himself to death in that sublime defiance of it which was perhaps the supreme tribute of the exquisite coward to the King of Terrors (for, believe me, you cannot be a hero without being a coward: supersense cuts both ways), the result being a tremendous effect on the gallery. Wellington, most capable of captains, was neither a hero nor a patriot: perhaps not even a coward; and had it not been for the Nelsonic anecdotes invented for him—"Up guards, and at em" and so forth—and the fact that the antagonist with whom he finally closed was such a master of theatrical effect that Wellington could not fight him without getting into his limelight, nor overthrow him (most unfortunately for us all) without drawing the eyes of the whole world to the catastrophe, the Iron Duke would have been almost forgotten by this time. Now that contrast is English against Irish all over, and is the more delicious because the real Irishman in it is the Englishman of tradition, whilst the real Englishman is the traditional theatrical foreigner.

The value of the illustration lies in the fact that Nelson and Wellington were both in the highest degree efficient, and both in the highest degree incompatible with one another on any other footing than one of independence. The government of Nelson by Wellington or of Wellington by Nelson is felt at once to be a dishonorable outrage to the governed and a finally impossible task for the governor.

7. John Wilson Croker, Irish-born British MP 1807–32 and Secretary to the Admiralty 1810–30, was a long-time friend of the Duke of Wellington. Much of our knowledge of Wellington derives from Croker's Boswellian memoirs and diaries published in 1884.

8. De Brueys, French Vice Admiral, lost his undermanned fleet to Nelson in the Battle of the Nile (1798). De Villeneuve, commander of a fleet of ill-trained French and Spanish sailors, was defeated in the Battle of Trafalgar (1805). Before the battle Napoleon accused de Villeneuve of 'excessive pusillanimity'.

I daresay some Englishman will now try to steal Wellington as Macaulay tried to steal Swift. And he may plead with some truth that though it seems impossible that any other country than England could produce a hero so utterly devoid of common sense, intellectual delicacy, and international chivalry as Nelson, it may be contended that Wellington was rather an XVIII century aristocratic type, than a specifically Irish type. George IV and Byron, contrasted with Gladstone, seem Irish in respect of a certain humorous blackguardism, and a power of appreciating art and sentiment without being duped by them into mistaking romantic figments for realities. But faithlessness and the need for carrying off the worthlessness and impotence that accompany it, produce in all nations a gay, sceptical, amusing, blaspheming, witty fashion which suits the flexibility of the Irish mind very well; and the contrast between this fashion and the energetic infatuations that have enabled intellectually ridiculous men, without wit or humor, to go on crusades and make successful revolutions, must not be confused with the contrast between the English and Irish idiosyncrasies. The Irishman makes a distinction which the Englishman is too lazy intellectually (the intellectual laziness and slovenliness of the English is almost beyond belief) to make. The Englishman, impressed with the dissoluteness of the faithless wits of the Restoration and the Regency, and with the victories of the wilful zealots of the patriotic, religious, and revolutionary wars, jumps to the conclusion that wilfulness is the main thing. In this he is right. But he overdoes his jump so far as to conclude also that stupidity and wrongheadedness are better guarantees of efficiency and trustworthiness than intellectual vivacity, which he mistrusts as a common symptom of worthlessness, vice, and instability. Now in this he is most dangerously wrong. Whether the Irishman grasps the truth as firmly as the Englishman may be open to question; but he is certainly comparatively free from the error. That affectionate and admiring love of sentimental stupidity for its own sake, both in men and women, which shines so steadily through the novels of Thackeray would hardly be possible in the works of an Irish novelist. Even Dickens, though too vital a genius and too severely educated in the school of shabby-genteel poverty to have any doubt of the national danger of fatheadedness in high places, evidently assumes rather too hastily the superiority of Mr Meagles to Sir John Chester and Harold Skimpole.[9] On

9. Mr Meagles is a good-natured, retired banker in *Little Dorrit*, who prides himself on being a practical man; Sir John Chester is a smooth villain in *Barnaby Rudge*, a literary portrait of Lord Chesterfield; Harold Skimpole is a selfish sentimentalist in *Bleak House*, genially caricaturing Leigh Hunt.

the other hand, it takes an Irishman years of residence in England to learn to respect and like a blockhead. An Englishman will not respect nor like anyone else. Every English statesman has to maintain his popularity by pretending to be ruder, more ignorant, more sentimental, more superstitious, more stupid than any man who has lived behind the scenes of public life for ten minutes can possibly be. Nobody dares to publish really intimate memoirs of him or really private letters of his until his whole generation has passed away, and his party can no longer be compromised by the discovery that the platitudinizing twaddler and hypocritical opportunist was really a man of some perception as well as of strong constitution, pegaway industry, personal ambition, and party keenness.

ENGLISH STUPIDITY EXCUSED

I do not claim it as a natural superiority in the Irish nation that it dislikes and mistrusts fools, and expects its political leaders to be clever and humbug-proof. It may be that if our resources included the armed force and virtually unlimited money which push the political and military figureheads of England through bungled enterprises to a muddled success, and create an illusion of some miraculous and divine innate English quality that enables a general to become a conqueror with abilities that would not suffice to save a cabman from having his licence marked, and a member of parliament to become Prime Minister with the outlook on life of a sporting country solicitor educated by a private governess, we should lapse into gross intellectual sottishness, and prefer leaders who encouraged our vulgarities by sharing them, and flattered us by associating them with purchased successes, to our betters. But as it is, we cannot afford that sort of encouragement and flattery in Ireland. The odds against which our leaders have to fight would be too heavy for the fourth-rate Englishmen whose leadership consists for the most part in marking time ostentatiously until they are violently shoved, and then stumbling blindly forward (or backward) wherever the shove sends them. We cannot crush England as a Pickford's van [ubiquitous vehicle of a British furniture-removal firm] might crush a perambulator. We are the perambulator and England the Pickford. We must study her and our real weaknesses and real strength; we must practise upon her slow conscience and her quick terrors; we must deal in ideas and political principles since we cannot deal in bayonets; we must outwit, outwork, outstay her; we must embarrass, bully, even conspire and assassinate when nothing else will move her, if we are not all to be driven deeper and deeper into the shame and misery of our servitude. Our leaders must be not only determined enough, but clever enough to do this. We have no illusions as to the existence of any mysterious Irish pluck, Irish honesty, Irish bias on the part of Providence, or sterling Irish solidity of character, that will enable an Irish blockhead to hold his own against England. Blockheads are of no use to us: we were compelled to follow a supercilious, unpopular, tongue-tied, aristocratic Protestant Parnell, although there was no lack among us of fluent imbeciles, with majestic presences and oceans of dignity and sentiment, to promote into his place could they have done his work for us. It is obviously convenient that Mr [John] Redmond[10] should be a better speaker and rhetorician than Parnell; but if he began to use his powers to make himself agreeable instead of making himself reckoned with by the enemy; if he set to work to manufacture and support English shams and hypocrisies instead of exposing and denouncing them; if he constituted himself the permanent apologist of doing nothing, and, when the people insisted on his doing something, only roused himself to discover how to pretend to do it without really changing anything, he would lose his leadership as certainly as an English politician would, by the same course, attain a permanent place on the front bench. In short, our circumstances place a premium on political ability whilst the circumstances of England discount it; and the quality of the supply naturally follows the demand. If you miss in my writings that hero-worship of dotards and duffers which is planting England with statues of disastrous statesmen and absurd generals, the explanation is simply that I am an Irishman and you an Englishman.

Irish Protestantism Really Protestant

When I repeat that I am an Irish Protestant, I come to a part of the relation between England and Ireland that you will never understand unless I insist on explaining it to you with that Irish insistence on intellectual clarity to which my English critics are so intensely recalcitrant.

First, let me tell you that in Ireland Protestantism is really Protestant. It is true that there is an Irish Protestant Church (disestablished some 35 years ago) in spite of the fact that a Protestant Church is, fundamentally, a

10. Irish politician, MP 1891–1918 and leader of the Parnellite group on the death of Parnell in 1891. He became a driving force and organizer in the Home Rule movement.

contradiction in terms. But this means only that the Protestants use the word Church to denote their secular organization, without troubling themselves about the metaphysical sense of Christ's famous pun, "Upon this rock I will build my church." The Church of England, which is a reformed Anglican Catholic Anti-Protestant Church, is quite another affair. An Anglican is acutely conscious that he is not a Wesleyan; and many Anglican clergymen do not hesitate to teach that all Methodists incur damnation. In Ireland all that the member of the Irish Protestant Church knows is that he is not a Roman Catholic. The decorations of even the "lowest" English Church seem to him to be extravagantly Ritualistic and Popish. I myself entered the Irish Church by baptism, a ceremony performed by my uncle [the Reverend William George Carroll] in "his own church" [St Bride's]. But I was sent, with many boys of my own denomination, to a Wesleyan school [Connexional School, 1865–8] where the Wesleyan catechism was taught without the least protest on the part of the parents, although there was so little presumption in favor of any boy there being a Wesleyan that if all the Church boys had been withdrawn at any moment, the school would have become bankrupt. And this was by no means analogous to the case of those working class members of the Church of England in London, who send their daughters to Roman Catholic schools rather than to the public elementary schools. They do so for the definite reason that the nuns teach girls good manners and sweetness of speech, which have no place in the County Council curriculum. But in Ireland the Church parent sends his son to a Wesleyan school (if it is convenient and socially eligible) because he is indifferent to the form of Protestantism, provided it is Protestantism. There is also in Ireland a characteristically Protestant refusal to take ceremonies and even sacraments very seriously except by way of strenuous objection to them when they are conducted with candles or incense. For example, I was never confirmed, although the ceremony was specially needed in my case as the failure of my appointed godfather to appear at my baptism had led to his responsibilities being assumed on the spot, at my uncle's order, by the sexton. And my case was a very common one, even among people quite untouched by modern scepticisms. Apart from the weekly churchgoing, which holds its own as a respectable habit, the initiations are perfunctory, the omissions regarded as negligible. The distinction between churchman and dissenter, which in England is a class distinction, a political distinction, and even occasionally a religious distinction, does not exist. Nobody is surprised in Ireland to find that the squire who is the local pillar of the formerly established Church is also a Plymouth Brother, and, except on certain special or fashionable occasions, attends the Methodist meeting-house. The parson has no priestly character and no priestly influence: the High Church curate of course exists and has his vogue among religious epicures of the other sex; but the general attitude of his congregation towards him is that of Dr Clifford. The clause in the Apostles' creed professing belief in a Catholic Church is a standing puzzle to Protestant children; and when they grow up they dismiss it from their minds more often than they solve it, because they really are not Catholics but Protestants to the extremest practicable degree of individualism. It is true that they talk of church and chapel with all the Anglican contempt for chapel; but in Ireland the chapel means the Roman Catholic church, for which the Irish Protestant reserves all the class rancor, the political hostility, the religious bigotry, and the bad blood generally that in England separates the Establishment from the non-conforming Protestant organizations. When a vulgar Irish Protestant speaks of a "Papist" he feels exactly as a vulgar Anglican vicar does when he speaks of a Dissenter. And when the vicar is Anglican enough to call himself a Catholic priest, wear a cassock, and bless his flock with two fingers, he becomes horrifically incomprehensible to the Irish Protestant Churchman, who, on his part, puzzles the Anglican by regarding a Methodist as tolerantly as an Irishman who likes grog regards an Irishman who prefers punch.

A Fundamental Anomaly

Now nothing can be more anomalous, and at bottom impossible, than a Conservative Protestant party standing for the established order against a revolutionary Catholic party. The Protestant is theoretically an anarchist as far as anarchism is practicable in human society: that is, he is an individualist, a free-thinker, a self-helper, a Whig, a Liberal, a mistruster and vilifier of the State, a rebel. The Catholic is theoretically a Collectivist, a self-abnegator, a Tory, a Conservative, a supporter of Church and State one and undivisible, an obeyer. This would be a statement of fact as well as of theory if men were Protestants and Catholics by temperament and adult choice instead of by family tradition. The peasant who supposed that Wordsworth's son would carry on the business now the old gentleman was gone was not a whit more foolish than we who laugh at his ignorance of the nature of poetry whilst we take it as a matter of course that a son should "carry on" his father's religion. Hence, owing to our family system, the Catholic Churches are recruited daily at the font by temperamental

Protestants, and the Protestant organizations by temperamental Catholics, with consequences most disconcerting to those who expect history to be deducible from the religious professions of the men who make it.

Still, though the Roman Catholic Church may occasionally catch such Tartars as Luther and Voltaire, or the Protestant organizations as [John Cardinal] Newman and [Henry Cardinal] Manning, the general run of mankind takes its impress from the atmosphere in which it is brought up. In Ireland the Roman Catholic peasant cannot escape the religious atmosphere of his Church. Except when he breaks out like a naughty child he is docile; he is reverent; he is content to regard knowledge as something not his business; he is a child before his Church, and accepts it as the highest authority in science and philosophy. He speaks of himself as a son of the Church, calling his priest father instead of brother or Mister. To rebel politically, he must break away from parish tutelage and follow a Protestant leader on national questions. His Church naturally fosters his submissiveness. The British Government and the Vatican may differ very vehemently as to whose subject the Irishman is to be; but they are quite agreed as to the propriety of his being a subject. Of the two, the British Government allows him more liberty, giving him as complete a democratic control of local government as his means will enable him to use, and a voice in the election of a formidable minority in the House of Commons, besides allowing him to read and learn what he likes—except when it makes a tufthunting onslaught on a seditious newspaper. But if he dared to claim a voice in the selection of his parish priest, or a representative at the Vatican, he would be denounced from the altar as an almost inconceivable blasphemer; and his educational opportunities are so restricted by his Church that he is heavily handicapped in every walk of life that requires any literacy. It is the aim of his priest to make him and keep him a submissive Conservative; and nothing but gross economic oppression and religious persecution could have produced the strange phenomenon of a revolutionary movement not only tolerated by the Clericals, but, up to a certain point, even encouraged by them. If there is such a thing as political science, with natural laws like any other science, it is certain that only the most violent external force could effect and maintain this unnatural combination of political revolution with Papal reaction, and of hardy individualism and independence with despotism and subjugation.

That violent external force is the clumsy thumb of English rule. If you would be good enough, ladies and gentlemen of England, to take your thumb away and leave us free to do something else than bite it, the unnaturally combined elements in Irish politics would fly asunder and recombine according to their proper nature with results entirely satisfactory to real Protestantism.

The Nature of Political Hatred

Just reconsider the Home Rule [Irish self-government] question in the light of that very English characteristic of the Irish people, their political hatred of priests. Do not be distracted by the shriek of indignant denial from the Catholic papers and from those who have witnessed the charming relations between the Irish peasantry and their spiritual fathers. I am perfectly aware that the Irish love their priests as devotedly as the French loved them before the Revolution or as the Italians loved them before they imprisoned the Pope in the Vatican. They love their landlords too: many an Irish gentleman has found in his nurse a foster-mother more interested in him than his actual mother. They love the English, as every Englishman who travels in Ireland can testify. Please do not suppose that I speak satirically: the world is full of authentic examples of the concurrence of human kindliness with political rancor. Slaves and schoolboys often love their masters; Napoleon and his soldiers made desperate efforts to save from drowning the Russian soldiers under whom they had broken the ice with their cannon; even the relations between nonconformist peasants and country parsons in England are not invariably unkindly; in the southern States of America planters are often traditionally fond of negroes and kind to them, with substantial returns in humble affection; soldiers and sailors often admire and cheer their officers sincerely and heartily; nowhere is actual personal intercourse found compatible for long with the intolerable friction of hatred and malice. But people who persist in pleading these amiabilities as political factors must be summarily bundled out of the room when questions of State are to be discussed. Just as an Irishman may have English friends whom he may prefer to any Irishman of his acquaintance, and be kind, hospitable, and serviceable in his intercourse with Englishmen, whilst being perfectly prepared to make the Shannon run red with English blood if Irish freedom could be obtained at that price; so an Irish Catholic may like his priest as a man and revere him as a confessor and spiritual pastor whilst being implacably determined to seize the first opportunity of throwing off his yoke. This is political hatred: the only hatred that civilization allows to be mortal hatred.

THE REVOLT AGAINST THE PRIEST

Realize, then, that the popular party in Ireland is seething with rebellion against the tyranny of the Church. Imagine the feelings of an English farmer if the parson refused to marry him for less than £20, and if he had virtually no other way of getting married! Imagine the Church Rates revived in the form of an unofficial Income Tax scientifically adjusted to your taxable capacity by an intimate knowledge of your affairs verified in the confessional! Imagine being one of a peasantry reputed the poorest in the world, under the thumb of a priesthood reputed the richest in the world! Imagine a Catholic middle class continually defeated in the struggle of professional, official, and fashionable life by the superior education of its Protestant competitors, and yet forbidden by its priests to resort to the only efficient universities in the country! Imagine trying to get a modern education in a seminary of priests, where every modern book worth reading is on the index, and the earth is still regarded, not perhaps as absolutely flat, yet as being far from so spherical as Protestants allege! Imagine being forbidden to read this preface because it proclaims your own grievance! And imagine being bound to submit to all this because the popular side must hold together at all costs in the face of the Protestant enemy! That is, roughly, the predicament of Roman Catholic Ireland.

PROTESTANT LOYALTY: A FORECAST

Now let us have a look at Protestant Ireland. I have already said that a "loyal" Irishman is an abhorrent phenomenon, because he is an unnatural one. In Ireland it is not "loyalty" to drink the English king's health and stand uncovered to the English national anthem: it is simply exploitation of English rule in the interests of the property, power, and promotion of the Irish classes as against the Irish masses. From any other point of view it is cowardice and dishonor. I have known a Protestant go to Dublin Castle [headquarters of the British Viceroy to Ireland] to be sworn in as a special constable, quite resolved to take the baton and break the heads of a patriotic faction just then upsetting the peace of the town, yet back out at the last moment because he could not bring himself to swallow the oath of allegiance tendered with the baton. There is no such thing as genuine loyalty in Ireland. There is a separation of the Irish people into two hostile camps: one Protestant, gentlemanly, and oligarchical; the other Roman Catholic, popular, and democratic. The oligarchy governs Ireland as a bureaucracy deriving authority from the king of England. It cannot cast him off without casting off its own ascendancy. Therefore it naturally exploits him sedulously, drinking his health, waving his flag, playing his anthem, and using the foolish word "traitor" freely in its cups. But let the English Government make a step towards the democratic party, and the Protestant garrison revolts at once, not with tears and prayers and anguish of soul and years of trembling reluctance, as the parliamentarians of the XVII century revolted against Charles I, but with acrid promptitude and strident threatenings. When England finally abandons the garrison by yielding to the demand for Home Rule, the Protestants will not go under, nor will they waste much time in sulking over their betrayal, and comparing their fate with that of [Charles] Gordon[11] left by Gladstone to perish on the spears of heathen fanatics. They cannot afford to retire into an Irish Faubourg St Germain.[12] They will take an energetic part in the national government, which will be sorely in need of parliamentary and official forces independent of Rome. They will get not only the Protestant votes, but the votes of Catholics in that spirit of toleration which is everywhere extended to heresies that happen to be politically serviceable to the orthodox. They will not relax their determination to hold every inch of the government of Ireland that they can grasp; but as that government will then be a national Irish government instead of as now an English government, their determination will make them the vanguard of Irish Nationalism and Democracy as against Romanism and Sacerdotalism, leaving English Unionists grieved and shocked at their discovery of the true value of an Irish Protestant's loyalty.

But there will be no open break in the tradition of the party. The Protestants will still be the party of Union, which will then mean, not the Repeal of Home Rule, but the maintenance of the Federal Union of English-speaking commonwealths, now theatrically called the Empire. They will pull down the Union Jack without the smallest scruple; but they know the value of the Channel Fleet, and will cling closer than brothers to that and any other Imperial asset that can be exploited for the protection of Ireland against foreign aggression or the sharing of expenses with the

11. 'Chinese' Gordon was slain in the fall of Khartoum after the British government failed to send troops in time to lift a siege by the Mahdists (1885).
12. A district on the Left Bank of Paris with wide boulevards and aristocratic streets, secluded eighteenth-century mansions of the old aristocracy, and the Palace of the Luxembourg.

British taxpayer. They know that the Irish coast is for the English invasion-scaremonger the heel of Achilles, and that they can use this to make him pay for the boot.

PROTESTANT PUGNACITY

If any Englishman feels incredulous as to this view of Protestantism as an essentially Nationalist force in Ireland, let him ask himself which leader he, if he were an Irishman, would rather have back from the grave to fight England: the Catholic Daniel O'Connell[13] or the Protestant Parnell. O'Connell organized the Nationalist movement only to draw its teeth, to break its determination, and to declare that Repeal of the Union was not worth the shedding of a drop of blood. He died in the bosom of his Church, not in the bosom of his country. The Protestant leaders, from Lord Edward Fitzgerald[14] to Parnell, have never divided their devotion. If any Englishman thinks that they would have been more sparing of blood than the English themselves are, if only so cheap a fluid could have purchased the honor of Ireland, he greatly mistakes the Irish Protestant temper. The notion that Ireland is the only country in the world not worth shedding a drop of blood for is not a Protestant one, and certainly not countenanced by English practice. It was hardly reasonable to ask Parnell to shed blood *quant. suff.* [in sufficient quantity] in Egypt to put an end to the misgovernment of the Khedive [Viceroy of Egypt 1863–79] and replace him by Lord Cromer[15] for the sake of the English bondholders, and then to expect him to become a Tolstoyan or an O'Connellite in regard to his own country. With a wholly Protestant Ireland at his back he might have bullied England into conceding Home Rule; for the insensibility of the English governing classes to philosophical, moral, social considerations—in short, to any considerations which require a little intellectual exertion and sympathetic alertness—is tempered, as we Irish well know, by an absurd susceptibility to intimidation.

For let me halt a moment here to impress on you, O English reader, that

13. Irish nationalist leader and MP (elected 1828) known as the Liberator.
14. MP in the Irish Parliament, who joined the United Irishmen (1796), committed to the establishment of an Irish republic. Seized and mortally wounded by the English as a conspirator after an attempt to negotiate for a French invasion, he died in prison.
15. Evelyn Baring, First Earl of Cromer, had for many years been Agent and Consul General in Egypt. The deposed Khedive was Ismail Pasha. See p. 315.

no fact has been more deeply stamped into us than that we can do nothing with an English Government unless we frighten it, any more than you can yourself. When power and riches are thrown haphazard into children's cradles as they are in England, you get a governing class without industry, character, courage, or real experience; and under such circumstances reforms are produced only by catastrophes followed by panics in which "something must be done." Thus it costs a cholera epidemic [1832 and 1840, in two pandemic waves, each lasting several years] to achieve a Public Health Act [1848], a Crimean War [1854–6] to reform the Civil Service [from 1855], and a gunpowder plot to disestablish the Irish Church.[16] It was by the light, not of reason, but of the moon,[17] that the need for paying serious attention to the Irish land question was seen in England. It cost the American War of Independence and the Irish Volunteer movement[18] to obtain the Irish parliament of 1782, the constitution of which far overshot the nationalist mark of today in the matter of independence.

It is vain to plead that this is human nature and not class weakness. The Japanese have proved that it is possible to conduct social and political changes intelligently and providentially instead of drifting along helplessly until public disasters compel a terrified and inconsiderate rearrangement. Innumerable experiments in local government have shewn that when men are neither too poor to be honest nor too rich to understand and share the needs of the people—as in New Zealand, for example—they can govern much more providently than our little circle of aristocrats and plutocrats.

THE JUST ENGLISHMAN

English Unionists, when asked what they have to say in defence of their rule of subject peoples, often reply that the Englishman is just, leaving us

---

16. Robert Catesby, Guy Fawkes and a few other Roman Catholics were apprehended on 4 November 1605, a day before they planned to blow up the Houses of Parliament while king, lords, and commons were assembled. The plot was in part a protest against the Established (Episcopal) Irish Church, which was finally disestablished by an Act of Parliament in 1869, effective January 1871.
17. The reference is to the Irish terrorist 'Moonlighters', night raiders who assailed those who incurred the hostility of the Land League.
18. The Volunteer movement started in Belfast on 17 March 1778, spreading rapidly to Armagh, King's County, Dublin and Wexford (members actually marched in New York's first St Patrick's Day parade in 1779), in small groups that grew into a national militia of 80,000 by 1781.

divided between our derision of so monstrously inhuman a pretension, and our impatience with so gross a confusion of the mutually exclusive functions of judge and legislator. For there is only one condition on which a man can do justice between two litigants, and that is that he shall have no interest in common with either of them, whereas it is only by having every interest in common with both of them that he can govern them tolerably. The indispensable preliminary to Democracy is the representation of every interest: the indispensable preliminary to justice is the elimination of every interest. When we want an arbitrator or an umpire, we turn to a stranger: when we want a government, a stranger is the one person we will not endure. The Englishman in India, for example, stands, a very statue of justice, between two natives. He says, in effect, "I am impartial in your religious disputes because I believe in neither of your religions. I am impartial in your conflicts of custom and sentiment because your customs and sentiments are different from, and abysmally inferior to, my own. Finally, I am impartial as to your interests because they are both equally opposed to mine, which is to keep you both equally powerless against me in order that I may extract money from you to pay salaries and pensions to myself and my fellow Englishmen as judges and rulers over you. In return for which you get the inestimable benefit of a government that does absolute justice as between Indian and Indian, being wholly preoccupied with the maintenance of absolute injustice as between India and England."

It will be observed that no Englishman, without making himself ridiculous, could pretend to be perfectly just or disinterested in English affairs, or would tolerate a proposal to establish the Indian or Irish system in Great Britain. Yet if the justice of the Englishman is sufficient to ensure the welfare of India or Ireland, it ought to suffice equally for England. But the English are wise enough to refuse to trust to English justice themselves, preferring democracy. They can hardly blame the Irish for taking the same view.

In short, dear English reader, the Irish Protestant stands outside that English Mutual Admiration Society which you call the Union or the Empire. You may buy a common and not ineffective variety of Irish Protestant by delegating your powers to him, and in effect making him the oppressor and you his sorely bullied and bothered catspaw and military maintainer; but if you offer him nothing for his loyalty except the natural superiority of the English character, you will—well, try the experiment, and see what will happen! You would have a ten-times better chance with the Roman Catholic; for he has been saturated from his youth up with the Imperial idea of foreign rule by a spiritually superior international power, and is trained to submission and abnegation of his private judgment. A Roman Catholic garrison would take its orders from England and let her rule Ireland if England were Roman Catholic. The Protestant garrison simply seizes on the English power; uses it for its own purposes; and occasionally orders the English Government to remove an Irish secretary who has dared to apply English ideas to the affairs of the garrison. Whereupon the English Government abjectly removes him, and implores him, as a gentleman and a loyal Englishman, not to reproach it in the face of the Nationalist enemy.

Such incidents naturally do not shake the sturdy conviction of the Irish Protestant that he is more than a match for any English Government in determination and intelligence. Here, no doubt, he flatters himself; for his advantage is not really an advantage of character, but of comparative directness of interest, concentration of force on one narrow issue, simplicity of aim, with freedom from the scruples and responsibilities of world-politics. The business is Irish business, not English; and he is Irish. And his object, which is simply to secure the dominance of his own caste and creed behind the power of England, is simpler and clearer than the confused aims of English Cabinets struggling ineptly with the burdens of empire, and biassed by the pressure of capital anywhere rather than in Ireland. He has no responsibility, no interest, no status outside his own country and his own movement, which means that he has no conscience in dealing with England; whereas England, having a very uneasy conscience, and many hindering and hampering responsibilities and interests in dealing with him, gets bullied and driven by him, and finally learns sympathy with Nationalist aims by her experience of the tyranny of the Orange party.[19]

IRISH CATHOLICISM FORECAST

Let us suppose that the establishment of a national government were to annihilate the oligarchic party by absorbing the Protestant garrison and making it a Protestant National Guard. The Roman Catholic laity, now a cipher, would organize itself; and a revolt against Rome and against the

19. The Orange Order, a Protestant Irish society named after William III of Orange, was formed in 1795 'to maintain the laws and peace of the country and the Protestant Constitution'. The movement waned in the first half of the nineteenth century, but rallied to provide a core of resistance when Gladstone in 1885 declared himself in favour of Irish Home Rule.

priesthood would ensue. The Roman Catholic Church would become the official Irish Church. The Irish parliament would insist on a voice in the promotion of churchmen; fees and contributions would be regulated; blackmail would be resisted; sweating in conventual factories and workshops would be stopped; and the ban would be taken off the universities. In a word, the Roman Catholic Church, against which Dublin Castle is powerless, would meet the one force on earth that can cope with it victoriously. That force is Democracy, a thing far more Catholic than itself. Until that force is let loose against it, the Protestant garrison can do nothing to the priesthood except consolidate it and drive the people to rally round it in defence of their altars against the foreigner and the heretic. When it *is* let loose, the Catholic laity will make as short work of sacerdotal tyranny in Ireland as it has done in France and Italy. And in doing so it will be forced to face the old problem of the relations of Church and State. A Roman Catholic party must submit to Rome: an anti-clerical Catholic party must of necessity become an Irish Catholic party. The Holy Roman Empire, like the other Empires, has no future except as a Federation of national Catholic Churches; for Christianity can no more escape Democracy than Democracy can escape Socialism. It is noteworthy in this connection that the Anglican Catholics have played and are playing a notable part in the Socialist movement in England in opposition to the individualist Secularists of the urban proletariat; but they are quit of the preliminary dead lift that awaits the Irish Catholic. Their Church has thrown off the yoke of Rome, and is safely and permanently Anglicized. But the Catholic Church in Ireland is still Roman. Home Rule will herald the day when the Vatican will go the way of Dublin Castle, and the island of the saints assume the headship of her own Church. It may seem incredible that long after the last Orangeman shall lay down his chalk for ever, the familiar scrawl on every blank wall in the north of Ireland "To hell with the Pope!" may reappear in the south, traced by the hands of Catholics who shall have forgotten the traditional counter legend, "To hell with King William!" (of glorious, pious, and immortal memory); but it may happen so. "The island of the saints" is no idle phrase. Religious genius is one of our national products; and Ireland is no bad rock to build a Church on. Holy and beautiful is the soul of Catholic Ireland: her prayers are lovelier than the teeth and claws of Protestantism, but not so effective in dealing with the English.

English Voltaireanism

Let me familiarize the situation by shewing how closely it reproduces the English situation in its essentials. In England, as in France, the struggle between the priesthood and the laity has produced a vast body of Voltaireans. But the essential identity of the French and English movements has been obscured by the ignorance of the ordinary Englishman, who, instead of knowing the distinctive tenets of his church or sect, vaguely believes them to be the eternal truth as opposed to the damnable error of all the other denominations. He thinks of Voltaire as a French "infidel," instead of as the champion of the laity against the official theocracy of the State Church. The Nonconformist leaders of our Free Churches are all Voltaireans. The warcry of the Passive Resisters is Voltaire's warcry, "Écrasez l'infâme [Erase the infamy]." No account need be taken of the technical difference between Voltaire's "infâme" and Dr Clifford's. One was the unreformed Roman Church of France; the other is the reformed Anglican Church; but in both cases the attack has been on a priestly tyranny and a professional monopoly. Voltaire convinced the Genevan ministers that he was the philosophic champion of their Protestant, Individualistic, Democratic Deism against the State Church of Roman Catholic France; and his heroic energy and beneficence as a philanthropist, which now only makes the list of achievements on his monument at Ferney the most impressive epitaph in Europe, then made the most earnest of the Lutheran ministers glad to claim a common inspiration with him. Unfortunately Voltaire had an irrepressible sense of humor. He joked about Habakkuk [a Hebrew prophet]; and jokes about Habakkuk smelt too strongly of brimstone to be tolerated by Protestants to whom the Bible was not a literature but a fetish and a talisman. And so Voltaire, in spite of the church he "erected to God," became in England the bogey-atheist of three generations of English ignoramuses, instead of the legitimate successor of Martin Luther and John Knox.[20]

Nowadays, however, Voltaire's jokes are either forgotten or else fall flat on a world which no longer venerates Habakkuk; and his true position is becoming apparent. The fact that Voltaire was a Roman Catholic layman, educated at a Jesuit college, is the conclusive reply to the shallow people who imagine that Ireland delivered up to the Irish democracy—that is, to

20. Scottish-born Calvinist minister, author of *History of the Reformation of Religion within the Realm of Scotland* (1586).

the Catholic laity—would be delivered up to the tyranny of the priest-hood.

SUPPOSE!

Suppose, now, that the conquest of France by Henry V of England had endured, and that France in the XVIII century had been governed by an English viceroy through a Huguenot bureaucracy and a judicial bench appointed on the understanding that loyalty for them meant loyalty to England, and patriotism a willingness to die in defence of the English conquest and of the English Church, would not Voltaire in that case have been the meanest of traitors and self-seekers if he had played the game of England by joining in its campaign against his own and his country's Church? The energy he threw into the defence of [Jean] Calas and [Pierre-Paul] Sirven[21] would have been thrown into the defence of the Frenchmen whom the English would have called "rebels"; and he would have been forced to identify the cause of freedom and democracy with the cause of "l'infâme." The French revolution would have been a revolution against England and English rule instead of against aristocracy and ecclesiasticism; and all the intellectual and spiritual forces in France, from [Jacques] Turgot[22] to De Tocqueville, would have been burnt up in mere anti-Anglicism and nationalist dithyrambs instead of contributing to political science and broadening the thought of the world.

What would have happened in France is what has happened in Ireland; and that is why it is only the small-minded Irish, incapable of conceiving what religious freedom means to a country, who do not loathe English rule. For in Ireland England is nothing but the Pope's policeman. She imagines she is holding the Vatican cardinals at bay when she is really strangling the Voltaires, the Foxes and Penns, the Cliffords, Hortons, Campbells, Walters, and Silvester Hornes, who are to be found among the Roman Catholic laity as plentifully as among the Anglican Catholic laity

21. Calas was a Huguenot merchant accused on hearsay evidence of murdering his son (actually a suicide) to prevent him from becoming a Roman Catholic. He was executed, but through the efforts of Voltaire posthumously exonerated. Sirven was a French Protestant who also was defended by Voltaire, but executed.
22. One of the Physiocrats, a school of French political economists who advocated a society that would stress natural and economic laws, and seek harmony between man-made and natural law.

in England.[23] She gets nothing out of Ireland but infinite trouble, infinite confusion and hindrance in her own legislation, a hatred that circulates through the whole world and poisons it against her, a reproach that makes her professions of sympathy with Finland and Macedonia[24] ridiculous and hypocritical, whilst the priest takes all the spoils, in money, in power, in pride, and in popularity.

IRELAND'S REAL GRIEVANCE

But it is not the spoils that matter. It is the waste, the sterilization, the perversion of fruitful brain power into flatulent protest against unnecessary evil, the use of our very entrails to tie our own hands and seal our own lips in the name of our honor and patriotism. As far as money or comfort is concerned, the average Irishman has a more tolerable life—especially now that the population is so scanty—than the average Englishman. It is true that in Ireland the poor man is robbed and starved and oppressed under judicial forms which confer the imposing title of justice on a crude system of bludgeoning and perjury. But so is the Englishman. The Englishman, more docile, less dangerous, too lazy intellectually to use such political and legal power as lies within his reach, suffers more and makes less fuss about it than the Irishman. But at least he has nobody to blame but himself and his fellow countrymen. He does not doubt that if an effective majority of the English people made up their minds to alter the Constitution, as the majority of the Irish people have made up their minds to obtain Home Rule, they could alter it without having to fight an overwhelmingly powerful and rich neighboring nation, and fight, too, with ropes round their necks. He can attack any institution in his country without betraying it to foreign vengeance and foreign oppression. True, his landlord may turn him out of his cottage if he goes to a Methodist chapel instead of to the parish church. His customers may stop their orders if he votes Liberal instead of Conservative. English ladies and gentlemen who would perish sooner than shoot a fox do these things without the smallest sense of

23. This list of Nonconformist religious reformers includes George Fox and William Penn, members of the Society of Friends; Robert Horton, Congregational pastor and prolific writer, author of *Revelation and the Bible* (1892); Reginald Campbell, Fabian and minister of City Temple, London; Ensor Walters, associated with the West London Mission and member of the St Pancras Borough Council; Silvester Horne, a minister who became a Liberal MP.
24. Countries struggling for independence, one from Russia, the other from Turkey.

indecency and dishonor. But they cannot muzzle his intellectual leaders. The English philosopher, the English author, the English orator can attack every abuse and expose every superstition without strengthening the hands of any common enemy. In Ireland every such attack, every such exposure, is a service to England and a stab to Ireland. If you expose the tyranny and rapacity of the Church, it is an argument in favor of Protestant ascendancy. If you denounce the nepotism and jobbery of the new local authorities, you are demonstrating the unfitness of the Irish to govern themselves, and the superiority of the old oligarchical grand juries.

And there is the same pressure on the other side. The Protestant must stand by the garrison at all costs: the Unionist must wink at every bureaucratic abuse, connive at every tyranny, magnify every official blockhead, because their exposure would be a victory for the Nationalist enemy. Every Irishman is in Lancelot's position: his honor rooted in dishonor stands; and faith unfaithful keeps him falsely true.

THE CURSE OF NATIONALISM

It is hardly possible for an Englishman to understand all that this implies. A conquered nation is like a man with cancer: he can think of nothing else, and is forced to place himself, to the exclusion of all better company, in the hands of quacks who profess to treat or cure cancer. The windbags of the two rival platforms are the most insufferable of all windbags. It requires neither knowledge, character, conscience, diligence in public affairs, nor any virtue, private or communal, to thump the Nationalist or Orange tub: nay, it puts a premium on the rancor or callousness that has given rise to the proverb that if you put an Irishman on a spit you can always get another Irishman to baste him. Jingo oratory in England is sickening enough to serious people: indeed one evening's mafficking[25] in London produced a determined call for the police. Well, in Ireland all political oratory is Jingo oratory; and all political demonstrations are maffickings. English rule is such an intolerable abomination that no other subject can reach the people. Nationalism stands between Ireland and the light of the world. Nobody in Ireland of any intelligence likes Nationalism any more than a man with a broken arm likes having it set. A healthy nation is as unconscious of its nationality as a healthy man of his bones. But if you break a nation's

25. Unrestrained celebration, originating in the victory over the Boers at Mafeking, 1900.

nationality it will think of nothing else but getting it set again. It will listen to no reformer, to no philosopher, to no preacher, until the demand of the Nationalist is granted. It will attend to no business, however vital, except the business of unification and liberation.

That is why everything is in abeyance in Ireland pending the achievement of Home Rule. The great movements of the human spirit which sweep in waves over Europe are stopped on the Irish coast by the English guns of the Pigeon House Fort.[26] Only a quaint little offshoot of English pre-Raphaelitism called the Gaelic movement has got a footing by using Nationalism as a stalking-horse, and popularizing itself as an attack on the native language of the Irish people, which is most fortunately also the native language of half the world, including England. Every election is fought on nationalist grounds; every appointment is made on nationalist grounds; every judge is a partisan in the nationalist conflict; every speech is a dreary recapitulation of nationalist twaddle; every lecture is a corruption of history to flatter nationalism or defame it; every school is a recruiting station; every church is a barrack; and every Irishman is unspeakably tired of the whole miserable business, which nevertheless is and perforce must remain his first business until Home Rule makes an end of it, and sweeps the nationalist and the garrison hack together into the dustbin.

There is indeed no greater curse to a nation than a nationalist movement, which is only the agonizing symptom of a suppressed natural function. Conquered nations lose their place in the world's march because they can do nothing but strive to get rid of their nationalist movements by recovering their national liberty. All demonstrations of the virtues of a foreign government, though often conclusive, are as useless as demonstrations of the superiority of artificial teeth, glass eyes, silver windpipes, and patent wooden legs to the natural products. Like Democracy, national self-government is not for the good of the people: it is for the satisfaction of the people. One Antonine [Roman] emperor, one St Louis [King Louis IX of France], one Richelieu,[27] may be worth ten democracies in point of what is called good government; but there is no satisfaction for the people in them. To deprive a dyspeptic of his dinner and hand it over to a man who can digest it better is a highly logical proceeding; but it is not a sensible

26. An early nineteenth-century fortification built by the British to protect Dublin's disused Pigeonhouse Harbour, thus preventing the occupation forces from being cut off from resupply from England. It was closed down in 1897.
27. Under King Louis IX, France successfully negotiated to regain many of her provinces from England. As Chief of the Royal Council under Louis XIII, Richelieu pursued a policy of establishment of royal absolutism.

one. To take the government of Ireland away from the Irish and hand it over to the English on the ground that they can govern better would be a precisely parallel case if the English had managed their own affairs so well as to place their superior faculty for governing beyond question. But as the English are avowed muddlers—rather proud of it, in fact—even the logic of that case against Home Rule is not complete. Read Mr Charles Booth's account of London [*Life and Labour in East London*, 1889], Mr [B. S.] Rowntree's account of York [*Poverty: A Study of Town Life*, 1901], and the latest official report on Dundee; and then pretend, if you can, that Englishmen and Scotchmen have not more cause to hand over their affairs to an Irish parliament than to clamor for another nation's cities to devastate and another people's business to mismanage.

A NATURAL RIGHT

The question is not one of logic at all, but of natural right. English universities have for some time past encouraged an extremely foolish academic exercise which consists in disproving the existence of natural rights on the ground that they cannot be deduced from the principles of any known political system. If they could, they would not be natural rights but acquired ones. Acquired rights are deduced from political constitutions; but political constitutions are deduced from natural rights. When a man insists on certain liberties without the slightest regard to demonstrations that they are not for his own good, nor for the public good, nor moral, nor reasonable, nor decent, nor compatible with the existing constitution of society, then he is said to claim a natural right to that liberty. When, for instance, he insists on living, in spite of the irrefutable demonstrations of many able pessimists, from the author of the book of Ecclesiastes to Schopenhauer, that life is an evil, he is asserting a natural right to live. When he insists on a vote in order that his country may be governed according to his ignorance instead of the wisdom of the Privy Council, he is asserting a natural right to self-government. When he insists on guiding himself at 21 by his own inexperience and folly and immaturity instead of by the experience and sagacity of his father, or the well-stored mind of his grandmother, he is asserting a natural right to independence. Even if Home Rule were as unhealthy as an Englishman's eating, as intemperate as his drinking, as filthy as his smoking, as licentious as his domesticity, as corrupt as his elections, as murderously greedy as his commerce, as cruel as his prisons, and as merciless as his streets, Ireland's claim to self-government would still be as good as England's. King James the First proved[28] so cleverly and conclusively that the satisfaction of natural rights was incompatible with good government that his courtiers called him Solomon. We, more enlightened, call him Fool, solely because we have learnt that nations insist on being governed by their own consent—or, as they put it, by themselves and for themselves—and that they will finally upset a good government which denies them this even if the alternative be a bad government which at least creates and maintains an illusion of democracy. America, as far as one can ascertain, is much worse governed, and has a much more disgraceful political history than England under Charles I; but the American Republic is the stabler government because it starts from a formal concession of natural rights, and keeps up an illusion of safeguarding them by an elaborate machinery of democratic election. And the final reason why Ireland must have Home Rule is that she has a natural right to it.

A WARNING

Finally, some words of warning to both nations. Ireland has been deliberately ruined again and again by England. Unable to compete with us industrially, she has destroyed our industries by the brute force of prohibitive taxation. She was perfectly right. That brute force was a more honorable weapon than the poverty which we used to undersell her. We lived with and as our pigs, and let loose our wares in the Englishman's market at prices which he could compete with only by living like a pig himself. Having the alternative of stopping our industry altogether, he very naturally and properly availed himself of it. We should have done the same in his place. To bear malice against him on that score is to poison our blood and weaken our constitutions with unintelligent rancor. In wrecking all the industries that were based on the poverty of our people England did us an enormous service. In omitting to do the same on her own soil, she did herself a wrong that has rotted her almost to the marrow. I hope that when Home Rule is at last achieved, one of our first legislative acts will be to fortify the subsistence of our people behind the bulwark of a standard

28. King James's *The True Law of Free Monarchies* (1598) and *Basilikon Doron* (1599), detailing his views of the nature of royal authority and its basis in divine right, were written when he ruled Scotland as James VI. He did not ascend the English throne as James I until 1603.

wage, and to impose crushing import duties on every English trade that flourishes in the slum and fattens on the starvation of our unfortunate English neighbors.

DOWN WITH THE SOLDIER!

Now for England's share of warning. Let her look to her Empire; for unless she makes it such a Federation for civil strength and defence that all free peoples will cling to it voluntarily, it will inevitably become a military tyranny to prevent them from abandoning it; and such a tyranny will drain the English taxpayer of his money more effectually than its worst cruelties can ever drain its victims of their liberty. A political scheme that cannot be carried out except by soldiers will not be a permanent one. The soldier is an anachronism of which we must get rid. Among people who are proof against the suggestions of romantic fiction there can no longer be any question of the fact that military service produces moral imbecility, ferocity, and cowardice, and that the defence of nations must be undertaken by the civil enterprise of men enjoying all the rights and liberties of citizenship, and trained by the exacting discipline of democratic freedom and responsibility. For permanent work the soldier is worse than useless: such efficiency as he has is the result of dehumanization and disablement. His whole training tends to make him a weakling. He has the easiest of lives: he has no freedom and no responsibility. He is politically and socially a child, with rations instead of rights, treated like a child, punished like a child, dressed prettily and washed and combed like a child, excused for outbreaks of naughtiness like a child, forbidden to marry like a child, and called Tommy like a child. He has no real work to keep him from going mad except housemaid's work: all the rest is forced exercise, in the form of endless rehearsals for a destructive and terrifying performance which may never come off, and which, when it does come off, is not like the rehearsals. His officer has not even housekeeper's work to keep him sane. The work of organizing and commanding bodies of men, which builds up the character and resource of the large class of civilians who live by it, only demoralizes the military officer, because his orders, however disastrous or offensive, must be obeyed without regard to consequences: for instance, if he calls his men dogs, and perverts a musketry drill order to make them kneel to him as an act of personal humiliation, and thereby provokes a mutiny among men not yet thoroughly broken in to the abjectness of the military condition, he is not, as might be expected, shot, but, at worst, reprimanded, whilst the leader of the mutiny, instead of getting the Victoria Cross and a public testimonial, is condemned to five years' penal servitude by Lynch Law[29] (technically called martial law) administered by a trade union of officers. Compare with this the position of, for instance, our railway managers or our heads of explosive factories. They have to handle large bodies of men whose carelessness or insubordination may cause wholesale destruction of life and property; yet any of these men may insult them, defy them, or assault them without special penalties of any sort. The military commander dares not face these conditions: he lives in perpetual terror of his men, and will undertake their command only when they are stripped of all their civil rights, gagged, and bound hand and foot by a barbarous slave code. Thus the officer learns to punish, but never to rule; and when an emergency like the Indian Mutiny [of the Bengal native army in 1857] comes, he breaks down; and the situation has to be saved by a few untypical officers with character enough to have retained their civilian qualities in spite of the messroom. This, unfortunately, is learnt by the public, not on the spot, but from Lord Roberts fifty years later [Speeches and Letters ... On Imperial Defence, 1906].

Besides the Mutiny we have had the Crimean and South African wars, the Dreyfus affair in France, the incidents of the anti-militarist campaign by the Social-Democrats in Germany, and now the Denshawai affair in the Nile delta, all heaping on us sensational demonstrations of the fact that soldiers pay the penalty of their slavery and outlawry by becoming, relatively to free civilians, destructive, cruel, dishonest, tyrannical, hysterical, mendacious, alarmists at home and terrorists abroad, politically reactionary, and professionally incapable. If it were humanly possible to militarize all the humanity out of a man, there would be absolutely no defence to this indictment. But the military system is so idiotically academic and impossible, and renders its victims so incapable of carrying it out with any thoroughness except when, in an occasional hysterical outburst of terror and violence, that hackneyed comedy of civil life, the weak man putting his foot down, becomes the military tragedy of the armed man burning, flogging, and murdering in a panic, that a body of soldiers and officers is in the main, and under normal circumstances, much like any other body of laborers and gentlemen. Many of us count among our personal friends and relatives officers whose amiable and honorable character seems to contradict

29. During the American Revolution Charles Lynch, Virginia plantation owner and justice of the peace, presided over an extra-legal court to deal with lawlessness. The convicted received summary punishment, giving rise to the term Lynch Law.

everything I have just said about the military character. You have only to describe Lynch courts and acts of terrorism to them as the work of Ribbonmen [in Ireland], Dacoits [in India], Moonlighters [in Ireland], Boxers [in China], or—to use the general term most familiar to them—"natives," and their honest and generous indignation knows no bounds: they feel about them like men, not like soldiers. But the moment you bring the professional side of them uppermost by describing precisely the same proceedings to them as the work of regular armies, they defend them, applaud them, and are ready to take part in them as if their humanity had been blown out like a candle. You find that there is a blind spot on their moral retina, and that this blind spot is the military spot.

The excuse, when any excuse is made, is that discipline is supremely important in war. Now most soldiers have no experience of war; and to assume that those who have are therefore qualified to legislate for it, is as absurd as to assume that a man who has been run over by an omnibus is thereby qualified to draw up wise regulations for the traffic of London. Neither our military novices nor our veterans are clever enough to see that in the field, discipline either keeps itself or goes to pieces; for humanity under fire is a quite different thing from humanity in barracks: when there is danger the difficulty is never to find men who will obey, but men who can command. It is in time of peace, when an army is either a police force (in which case its work can be better done by a civilian constabulary) or an absurdity, that discipline is difficult, because the wasted life of the soldier is unnatural, except to a lazy man, and his servitude galling and senseless, except to a docile one. Still, the soldier is a man, and the officer sometimes a gentleman in the literal sense of the word; and so, what with humanity, laziness, and docility combined, they manage to rub along with only occasional outbursts of mutiny on the one side and class rancor and class cowardice on the other.

They are not even discontented; for the military and naval codes simplify life for them just as it is simplified for children. No soldier is asked to think for himself, to judge for himself, to consult his own honor and manhood, to dread any consequence except the consequence of punishment to his own person. The rules are plain and simple; the ceremonies of respect and submission are as easy and mechanical as a prayer wheel; the orders are always to be obeyed thoughtlessly, however inept or dishonorable they may be. As the late Laureate [Alfred Lord Tennyson] said in the two stinging lines in which he branded the British soldier with the dishonor of Esau, "theirs not to reason why, theirs but to do and die ['The Charge of the Light Brigade', 1854]." To the moral imbecile and political sluggard these conditions are as congenial and attractive as they are abhorrent and intolerable to the William Tell[30] temperament. Just as the most incorrigible criminal is always, we are told, the best behaved convict, so the man with least conscience and initiative makes the best behaved soldier, and that not wholly through mere fear of punishment, but through a genuine fitness for and consequent happiness in the childlike military life. Such men dread freedom and responsibility as a weak man dreads a risk or a heavy burden; and the objection to the military system is that it tends to produce such men by a weakening disuse of the moral muscles. No doubt this weakness is just what the military system aims at, its ideal soldier being, not a complete man, but a docile unit of cannon-fodder which can be trusted to respond promptly and certainly to the external stimulus of a shouted order, and is intimidated to the pitch of being afraid to run away from a battle. It may be doubted whether even in the Prussian heyday of the system, when floggings of hundreds and even thousands of lashes were matters of ordinary routine, this detestable ideal was ever realized; but your courts-martial are not practical enough to take that into account: it is characteristic of the military mind continually to ignore human nature and cry for the moon instead of facing modern social facts and accepting modern democratic conditions. And when I say the military mind, I repeat that I am not forgetting the patent fact that the military mind and the humane mind can exist in the same person; so that an officer who will take all the civilian risks, from city traffic to fox-hunting, without uneasiness, and who will manage all the civil employees on his estate and in his house and stables without the aid of a Mutiny Act, will also, in his military capacity, frantically declare that he dare not walk about in a foreign country unless every crime of violence against an Englishman in uniform is punished by the bombardment and destruction of a whole village, or the wholesale flogging and execution of every native in the neighborhood, and also that unless he and his fellow-officers have power, without the intervention of a jury, to punish the slightest self-assertion or hesitation to obey orders, however grossly insulting or disastrous those orders may be, with sentences which are reserved in civil life for the worst crimes, he cannot secure the obedience and respect of his men, and the country will accordingly lose all its colonies and dependencies, and be helplessly conquered in the German invasion which he confidently expects to occur in the course of a fortnight or so. That is to say, in so far as he is an ordinary gentleman he behaves sensibly

30. In Swiss legend a hero in the fight for independence from Austria; slayer of the tyrant Gessler.

and courageously; and in so far as he is a military man he gives way without shame to the grossest folly, cruelty and poltroonery. If any other profession in the world had been stained by these vices, and by false witness, forgery, swindling, torture, compulsion of men's families to attend their executions, digging up and mutilation of dead enemies, all wantonly added to the devastation proper to its own business, as the military profession has been within recent memory in England, France, and the United States of America (to mention no other countries), it would be very difficult to induce men of capacity and character to enter it. And in England it is, in fact, largely dependent for its recruits on the refuse of industrial life, and for its officers on the aristocratic and plutocratic refuse of political and diplomatic life, who join the army and pay for their positions in the more or less fashionable clubs which the regimental messes provide them with—clubs which, by the way, occasionally figure in ragging scandals as circles of extremely coarse moral character.

Now in countries which are denied Home Rule: that is, in which the government does not rest on the consent of the people, it must rest on military coercion; and the bureaucracy, however civil and legal it may be in form and even in the character of its best officials, must connive at all the atrocities of military rule, and become infected in the end with the chronic panic characteristic of militarism. In recent witness whereof, let me shift the scene from Ireland to Egypt, and tell the story of the Denshawai affair of June 1906 by way of object-lesson.

THE DENSHAWAI HORROR[31]

Denshawai is a little Egyptian village in the Nile delta. Besides the dilapidated huts among the reeds by the roadside, and the palm trees, there are towers of unbaked brick, as unaccountable to an English villager as a Kentish oast-house [kiln for drying hops or malt] to an Egyptian. These towers are pigeon-houses; for the villagers keep pigeons just as an English farmer keeps poultry.

Try to imagine the feelings of an English village if a party of Chinese officers suddenly appeared and began shooting the ducks, the geese, the

31. This section was published (in English, German and French) as a propaganda pamphlet by the German Information Service in 1940, under the title *The Denshawai Horror and Other Colonial Atrocities*, as part of its series *The True Image of Britain*. Copies were distributed throughout North Africa.

hens, and the turkeys, and carried them off, asserting that they were wild birds, as everybody in China knew, and that the pretended indignation of the farmers was a cloak for hatred of the Chinese, and perhaps for a plot to overthrow the religion of Confucius and establish the Church of England in its place! Well, that is the British equivalent of what happened at Denshawai when a party of English officers went pigeon-shooting there the year before last [1905]. The inhabitants complained and memorialized [petitioned]; but they obtained no redress: the law failed them in their hour of need. So one leading family of pigeon farmers, Mahfouz by name, despaired of the law; and its head, Hassan Mahfouz, aged 60, made up his mind not to submit tamely to a repetition of the outrage. Also, British officers were ordered not to shoot pigeons in the villages without the consent of the Omdeh, or headman, though nothing was settled as to what might happen to the Omdeh if he ventured to refuse.

Fancy the feelings of Denshawai when on the 13th of June last [1906] there drove to the village four khaki-clad British officers with guns, one of them being a shooter of the year before, accompanied by one other officer on horseback, and also by a dragoman [guide] and an Ombashi, or police official! The oriental blood of Hassan Mahfouz boiled; and he warned them that they would not be allowed to shoot pigeons; but as they did not understand his language, the warning had no effect. They sent their dragoman to ask the Omdeh's permission to shoot; but the Omdeh was away; and all the interpreter could get from the Omdeh's deputy, who knew better than to dare an absolute refusal, was the pretty obvious reply that they might shoot if they went far enough away from the village. On the strength of this welcome, they went from 100 to 300 yards away from the houses (these distances were afterwards officially averaged at 500 yards), and began shooting the villagers' pigeons. The villagers remonstrated and finally seized the gun of the youngest officer. It went off in the struggle, and wounded three men and the wife of one Abd-el-Nebi, a young man of 25. Now the lady, though, as it turned out, only temporarily disabled by a charge of pigeon shot in the softest part of her person, gave herself up for dead; and the feeling in the village was much as if our imaginary Chinese officers, on being interfered with in their slaughter of turkeys, had killed an English farmer's wife. Abd-el-Nebi, her husband, took the matter to heart, not altogether without reason, we may admit. His threshing-floor also caught fire somehow (the official English theory is that he set it on fire as a signal for revolt to the entire Moslem world); and all the lads and loafers in the place were presently on the spot. The other officers, seeing their friend in trouble, joined him. Abd-el-Nebi hit the supposed murderer of his wife with a stick; Hassan Mahfouz used a stick also; and the lads and loafers began to throw stones and bricks. Five London policemen would have seen that there was nothing to be done but fight their way out, as there is no use arguing with an irritated mob, especially if you do not know its language. Had the shooting party been in the charge of a capable non-commissioned officer, he would perhaps have got it safely off. As it was, the officers tried propitiation, making their overtures in pantomime. They gave up their guns; they offered watches and money to the crowd, crying Baksheesh [alms]; and the senior officer actually collared the junior and pretended to arrest him for the murder of the woman. Naturally they were mobbed worse than before; and what they did not give to the crowd was taken from them, whether as payment for the pigeons, blood money, or simple plunder was not gone into. The officers, two Irishmen and three Englishmen, having made a hopeless mess of it, and being now in serious danger, made for their carriages, but were dragged out of them again, one of the coachmen being knocked senseless. They then "agreed to run," the arrangement being that the Englishmen, being the juniors, should run away to camp and bring help to the Irishmen. They bolted accordingly; but the third, the youngest, seeing the two Irishmen hard put to it, went back and stood by them. Of the two fugitives, one, after a long race in the Egyptian afternoon sun, got to the next village and there dropped, smitten by sunstroke, of which he died. The other ran on and met a patrol, which started to the rescue.

Meanwhile, the other three officers had been taken out of the hands of the lads and the loafers, of Abd-el-Nebi and Hassan Mahfouz, by the elders and watchmen, and saved from further injury, but not before they had been severely knocked about, one of them having one of the bones of his left arm broken near the wrist—simple fracture of the thin end of the ulna. They were also brought to the threshing-floor; shewn the wounded woman; informed by gestures that they deserved to have their throats cut for murdering her; and kicked (with naked feet, fortunately); but at this point the elders and constables stopped the mobbing. Finally the three were sent off to camp in their carriages; and the incident ended for that day.

No English mob, under similar provocation, would have behaved any better; and few would have done as little mischief. It is not many months since an old man—not a foreigner and not an unbeliever—was kicked to death in the streets of London because the action of a park constable in turning him out of a public park exposed him to suspicion of misconduct. At Denshawai, the officers were not on duty. In their private capacity as sportsmen, they committed a serious depredation on a very poor village by slaughtering its stock. In an English village they would have been tolerated because the farmers would have expected compensation for damage, and the villagers coals and blankets and employment in country house, garden and stable, or as beaters, huntsmen and the like, from them. But Denshawai had no such inducements to submit to their thoughtless and selfish aggression. One of them had apparently killed a woman and wounded three men with his gun: in fact his own comrade virtually convicted him of it before the crowd by collaring him as a prisoner. In short, the officers had given outrageous provocation; and they had shewn an amiable but disastrous want of determination and judgment in dealing with the riot they provoked. They should have been severely reprimanded and informed that they had themselves to thank for what happened to them; and the villagers who assaulted them should have been treated with leniency, and assured that pigeon-shooting would not be allowed in future.

That is what should have ensued. Now for what actually did ensue.

Abd-el-Nebi, in consideration of the injury to his wife, was only sentenced to penal servitude for life. And our clemency did not stop there. His wife was not punished at all—not even charged with stealing the shot which was found in her person. And lest Abd-el-Nebi should feel lonely at 25 in beginning penal servitude for the rest of his days, another young man, of 20, was sent to penal servitude for life with him.

No such sentimentality was shewn to Hassan Mahfouz. An Egyptian pigeon farmer who objects to British sport; threatens British officers and gentlemen when they shoot his pigeons; and actually hits those officers with a substantial stick, is clearly a ruffian to be made an example of. Penal servitude was not enough for a man of 60 who looked 70, and might not have lived to suffer five years of it. So Hassan was hanged; but as a special mark of consideration for his family, he was hanged in full view of his own house, with his wives and children and grandchildren enjoying the spectacle from the roof. And lest this privilege should excite jealousy in other households, three other Denshavians were hanged with him. They went through the ceremony with dignity, professing their faith ("Mahometan, I regret to say," Mr Pecksniff would have said [in *Martin Chuzzlewit*]). Hassan, however, "in a loud voice invoked ruin upon the houses of those who had given evidence against him"; and Darweesh [one of the condemned] was impatient and presumed to tell the hangman to be quick. But then Darweesh was a bit of a brigand: he had been imprisoned for bearing false witness; and his resistance to the British invasion is the only officially recorded incident of his life which is entirely to his credit. He and Abd-el-Nebi (who had been imprisoned for theft) were the only disreputable characters among the punished. Ages of the four hanged men respectively, 60, 50, 22 and 20.

Hanging, however, is the least sensational form of public execution: it lacks those elements of blood and torture for which the military and bureaucratic imagination lusts. So, as they had room for only one man on the gallows, and had to leave him hanging half an hour to make sure work and give his family plenty of time to watch him swinging ("slowly turning round and round on himself," as the local papers described it), thus having two hours to kill as well as four men, they kept the entertainment going by flogging eight men with fifty lashes each: eleven more than the utmost permitted by the law of Moses in times which our Army of Occupation no doubt considers barbarous. But then Moses conceived his law as being what he called the law of God, and not simply an instrument for the gratification of his own cruelty and terror. It is unspeakably reassuring to learn from the British official reports laid before parliament that "due dignity was observed in carrying out the executions," that "all possible humanity was shewn in carrying them out," and that "the arrangements were admirable, and reflect great credit on all concerned." As this last testimonial apparently does not refer to the victims, they are evidently officially considered not to have been concerned in the proceedings at all. Finally, Lord Cromer certifies that the Englishman in charge of the proceedings is "a singularly humane man, and is very popular amongst the natives of Egypt by reason of the great sympathy he has always shewn for them." It will be seen that Parliamentary Papers, Nos. 3 and 4, Egypt, 1906, are not lacking in unconscious humor. The official walrus pledges himself in every case for the kindliness of the official carpenter.[32]

One man was actually let off, to the great danger of the British Empire perhaps. Still, as he was an epileptic, and had already had several fits in the court of Judge Lynch, the doctor said Better not; and he escaped. This was very inconvenient; for the number of floggees had been made up solely to fill the time occupied by the hangings at the rate of two floggings per hanging; and the breakdown of the arrangement through Said Suleiman Kheirallah's inconsiderate indisposition [epilepsy] made the execution of Darweesh tedious, as he was hanging for fully quarter of an hour without any flogging to amuse his fellow villagers and the officers and men of the Inniskilling Dragoons, the military mounted police, and the mounted infantry. A few spare sentences of flogging should have been kept in hand to provide against accidents.

32. A play on Lewis Carroll's *Through the Looking-Glass*.

In any case there was not time to flog everybody, nor to flog three of the floggees enough; so these three had a year's hard labor apiece in addition to their floggings. Six others were not flogged at all, but were sent to penal servitude for seven years each. One man got fifteen years. Total for the morning's work: four hanged, two to penal servitude for life, one to fifteen years penal servitude, six to seven years penal servitude, three to imprisonment for a year with hard labor and fifty lashes, and five to fifty lashes.

Lord Cromer certifies that these proceedings were "just and necessary." He also gives his reasons. It appears that the boasted justice introduced into Egypt by the English in 1882 was imaginary, and that the real work of coping with Egyptian disorder was done by Brigandage Commissions, composed of Egyptians. These Commissions, when an offence was reported, descended on the inculpated village; seized everybody concerned; and plied them with tortures, mentionable and unmentionable, until they accused everybody they were expected to accuse. The accused were in turn tortured until they confessed anything and everything they were accused of. They were then killed, flogged, or sent to penal servitude. This was the reality behind the illusion that soothed us after bombarding Alexandria.[33] The bloodless, white-gloved native courts set up to flatter our sense of imperial justice had, apparently, about as much to do with the actual government of the fellaheen [peasant labourer] as the annual court which awards the Dunmow flitch of bacon[34] has to do with our divorce court. Eventually a Belgian judge [Raymond Janssens, not a judge but former Avocat Général in the Brussels court of appeals], who was appointed Procureur Général [1903–11], exposed the true state of affairs.

Then the situation had to be faced. Order had to be maintained somehow; but the regular native courts which saved the face of the British Occupation were useless for the purpose; and the Brigandage Commissions were so abominable and demoralizing that they made more mischief than they prevented. Besides, there was Mr Wilfrid Scawen Blunt[35] on the warpath

33. The British bombardment in 1882 was followed by the British occupation of all of Egypt.
34. A custom begun at Little Dunmow, a market town in Essex, England, in the fourteenth century, of awarding a side of bacon to the man who took an oath that he had not repented of his marriage for a year and a day. The custom continues to be observed, but now at Great Dunmow.
35. Poet, traveller, diarist, and advocate of the Nationalist Party in Egypt, who had recently published a polemic on *Atrocities of Justice under British Rule in Egypt* (1906; revised with new preface, 1907).

against tyranny and torture, threatening to get questions asked in parliament. A new sort of tribunal in the nature of a court-martial had therefore to be invented to replace the Brigandage Commissions; but simple British military courts-martial, though probably the best available form of official Lynch Law, were made impossible by the jealousy of the "loyal" (to England) Egyptians, who, it seems, rule the Occupation and bully England exactly as the "loyal" Irish rule the Garrison and bully the Unionists nearer home. That kind of loyalty, not being a natural product, has to be purchased; and the price is an official job of some sort with a position and a salary attached. Hence we got, in 1895, a tribunal constituted in which three English officials sat with two Egyptian officials, exercising practically unlimited powers of punishment without a jury and without appeal. They represent the best of our judicial and military officialism. And what that best is may be judged by the sentences on the Denshawai villagers.

Lord Cromer's justification of the tribunal is practically that, bad as it is, the Brigandage Commissions were worse. Also (lest we should propose to carry our moral superiority any further) that the Egyptians are so accustomed to associate law and order with floggings, executions, torture and Lynch Law, that they will not respect any tribunal which does not continue these practices. This is a far-reaching argument: for instance, it suggests that Church of England missionaries might do well to adopt the rite of human sacrifice when evangelizing tribes in whose imagination that practice is inseparably bound up with religion. It suggests that the sole reason why the Denshawai tribunal did not resort to torture for the purpose of extorting confessions and evidence was that parliament might not stand it—though really a parliament which stood the executions would, one would think, stand anything. The tribunal had certainly no intention of allowing witnesses to testify against British officers; for, as it happened, the Ombashi who accompanied them on the two shooting expeditions, one Ahmed Hassan Zakzouk, aged 26, was rash enough to insist that after the shot that struck the woman, the officers fired on the mob twice. This appears in the parliamentary paper; but the French newspaper *L'Égypte* is quoted by Mr Wilfrid Scawen Blunt as reporting that Zakzouk, on being asked by one of the English judges whether he was not afraid to say such a thing, replied "Nobody in the world is able to frighten me: the truth is the truth," and was promptly told to stand down. Mr Blunt adds that Zakzouk was then tried for his conduct in connection with the affair before a Court of Discipline, which awarded him two years imprisonment and fifty lashes. Without rudely calling this a use of torture to intimidate anti-British witnesses, I may count on the assent of most reasonable people when I say that Zakzouk probably regards himself as having received a rather strong hint to make his evidence agreeable to the Occupation in future.

Not only was there of course no jury at the trial, but considerably less than no defence. Barristers of sufficient standing to make it very undesirable for them to offend the Occupation were instructed to "defend" the prisoners. Far from defending them, they paid high compliments to the Occupation as one of the choicest benefits rained by Heaven on their country, and appealed for mercy for their miserable clients, whose conduct had "caused the unanimous indignation of all Egyptians." "Clemency," they said, "was above equity." The tribunal in delivering judgment remarked that "the counsel for the defence had a full hearing: nevertheless the defence broke down completely, and all that their counsel could say on behalf of the prisoners practically amounted to an appeal to the mercy of the Court."

Now the proper defence, if put forward, would probably have convinced Lord Cromer that nothing but the burning of the village and the crucifixion of all its inhabitants could preserve the British Empire. That defence was obvious enough: the village was invaded by five armed foreigners who attempted for the second time to slaughter the villagers' farming stock and carry it off; in resisting an attempt to disarm them four villagers had been wounded; the villagers had lost their tempers and knocked the invaders about; and the older men and watchmen had finally rescued the aggressors and sent them back with no worse handling than they would have got anywhere for the like misconduct.

One can imagine what would have happened to the man, prisoner or advocate, who should have dared to tell the truth in this fashion. The prisoners knew better than to attempt it. On the scaffold, Darweesh turned to his house as he stood on the trap, and exclaimed "May God compensate us well for this world of meanness, for this world of injustice, for this world of cruelty." If he had dared in court thus to compare God with the tribunal to the disadvantage of the latter, he would no doubt have had fifty lashes before his hanging, to teach him the greatness of the Empire. As it was, he kept his views to himself until it was too late to do anything worse to him than hang him. In court, he did as all the rest did. They lied; they denied; they set up desperate alibis; they protested they had been in the next village, or tending cattle a mile off, or threshing, or what not. One of them, when identified, said "All men are alike." He had only one eye. Darweesh, who had secured one of the officers' guns, declared that his enemies had come in the night and buried it in his house, where his mother sat on it, like Rachel on Laban's stolen teraphim [small household gods], until she was dragged off. A pitiable business, yet not so pitiable as the virtuous indignation with which Judge Lynch, himself provable by his own judgment to be a prevaricator, hypocrite, tyrant, and coward of the first water, preened himself at its expense. When Lord Cromer, in his official apology for Judge Lynch, says that "the prisoners had a perfectly fair trial"—not, observe, a trial as little unfair as human frailty could make it, which is the most that can be said for any trial on earth, but "a *perfectly fair trial*"—he no doubt believes what he says; but his opinion is interesting mainly as an example of the state of his mind, and of the extent to which, after thirty years of official life in Egypt, one loses the plain sense of English words.

Lord Cromer recalls how, in the eighties, a man threatened with the courbash by a Moudir [district governor] in the presence of Sir Claude MacDonald,[36] said "You dare not flog me now that the British are here." "So bold an answer," says Lord Cromer, "was probably due to the presence of a British officer." What would that man say now? What does Lord Cromer say now? He deprecates "premature endeavors to thrust Western ideas on an Eastern people," by which he means that when you are in Egypt you must do as the Egyptians do: terrorize by the lash and the scaffold. Thus does the East conquer its conquerors. In 1883 Lord Dufferin[37] was abolishing the bastinado [cudgel] as "a horrible and infamous punishment." In 1906 Lord Cromer guarantees ferocious sentences of flogging as "just and necessary," and can see "nothing reprehensible in the manner in which they were carried out." "I have," he adds, "passed nearly thirty years of my life in an earnest endeavor to raise the moral and material condition of the people of Egypt. I have been assisted by a number of very capable officials, all of whom, I may say, have been animated by the same spirit as myself." Egypt may well shudder as she reads those words. If the first thirty years have been crowned by the Denshawai incident, what will Egypt be like at the end of another thirty years of moral elevation "animated by the same spirit"?

It is pleasanter to return to Lord Cromer's first letter on Denshawai, written to Sir Edward Grey[38] the day after the shooting party. It says that "orders will shortly be issued by the General prohibiting officers in the army from shooting pigeons in the future under any circumstances

36. Military attaché to Lord Cromer in Egypt.
37. Frederick Blackwood, First Marquess of Dufferin and Ava, a British diplomat, who, while serving in Egypt 1882–3 as British Commissioner, prepared a report that was the basis for subsequent humane reforms.
38. Secretary of State for Foreign Affairs 1905–16.

whatever." But pray why this prohibition, if, as the tribunal declared, the officers were "guests" – actually *guests!* – "who had done nothing to deserve blame"?

Mr [Charles de Mansfeldt] Findlay[39] is another interesting official correspondent of Sir Edward. Even after the trial, at which it had been impossible to push the medical evidence further than to say that the officer who died of sunstroke had been predisposed to it by the knocking about he had suffered and by his flight under the Egyptian sun, whilst the officers who had remained defenceless in the hands of the villagers were in court, alive and well, Mr Findlay writes that the four hanged men were "convicted of a brutal and premeditated murder," and complains that "the native press disregards the fact" and "is being conducted with such an absolute disregard for truth as to make it evident that large sums of money have been expended." Mr Findlay is also a bit of a philosopher. "The Egyptian, being a fatalist," he says, "does not greatly fear death, and there is therefore much to be said for flogging as a judicial punishment in Egypt." Logically, then, the four hanged men ought to have been flogged instead. But Mr Findlay does not draw that conclusion. Logic is not his strong point: he is a man of feeling, and a very nervous one at that. "I do not believe that this brutal attack on British officers had anything directly to do with political animosity. It is, however, due to the insubordinate spirit which has been sedulously fostered during the last year by unscrupulous and interested agitators." Again, "it is my duty to warn you of the deplorable effect which is being produced in Egypt by the fact that Members of Parliament have seriously called in question the unanimous sentence passed by a legally constituted Court, of which the best English and the best native Judge were members. This fact will, moreover, supply the lever which has, up to the present, been lacking to the venal agitators who are at the head of the so-called patriotic party." I find Mr Findlay irresistible, so exquisitely does he give us the measure and flavor of officialism. "A few days after the Denshawai affray some natives stoned and severely injured an irrigation inspector. Two days ago three natives knocked a soldier off his donkey and kicked him in the stomach: his injuries are serious. In the latter case theft appears to have been the motive. My object in mentioning these instances is to shew the results to be expected if once respect for the law is shaken. Should the present state of things continue, and, still more, should the agitation in this country find support at home, the date is not far distant when the

---

39. Counsellor of the Embassy at Cairo until his transfer in 1907. He later was known as Sir Mansfeldt de Cardonnel Findlay.

necessity will arise for bringing in a press law and for considerably increasing the army of occupation." Just think of it! In a population of nearly ten millions, one irrigation inspector is stoned. The Denshawai executions are then carried out to make the law respected. The result is that three natives knock a soldier off his donkey and rob him. Thereupon Mr Findlay, appalled at the bankruptcy of civilization, sees nothing for it now but suppression of the native newspapers and a considerable increase in the army of occupation! And Lord Cromer writes "All I need say is that I concur generally in Mr Findlay's remarks, and that, had I remained in Egypt, I should in every respect have adopted the same course as that which he pursued."

But I must resolutely shut this rich parliamentary paper. I have extracted enough to paint the picture, and enforce my warning to England that if her Empire means ruling the world as Denshawai has been ruled in 1906—and that, I am afraid, is what the Empire does mean to the main body of our aristocratic-military caste and to our Jingo plutocrats—then there can be no more sacred and urgent political duty on earth than the disruption, defeat, and suppression of the Empire, and, incidentally, the humanization of its supporters by the sternest lessons of that adversity which comes finally to institutions which make themselves abhorred by the aspiring will of humanity towards divinity. As for the Egyptians, any man cradled by the Nile who, after the Denshawai incident, will ever voluntarily submit to British rule, or accept any bond with us except the bond of a Federation of free and equal states, will deserve the worst that Lord Cromer can consider "just and necessary" for him. That is what you get by attempting to prove your supremacy by the excesses of frightened soldiers and denaturalized officials instead of by courageous helpfulness and moral superiority.

In any case let no Englishman who is content to leave Abd-el-Nebi and his twenty-year-old neighbor in penal servitude for life, and to plume himself on the power to do it, pretend to be fit to govern either my country or his own. The responsibility cannot be confined to the tribunal and to the demoralized officials of the Occupation. The House of Commons had twenty-four hours clear notice, with the telegraph under the hand of Sir Edward Grey, to enable it to declare that England was a civilized Power and would not stand these barbarous lashings and vindictive hangings. Yet Mr [John] Dillon,[40] representing the Irish party, which well knows what British Occupations and Findlay "loyalism" mean, protested

40. Irish MP (1880–83, 1885–1918), who succeeded John Redmond as chairman of the Irish Nationalist Party in 1918.

in vain. Sir Edward, on behalf of the new Liberal Government (still simmering with virtuous indignation at the flogging of Chinamen and the military executions in South Africa in the forced presence of the victims' families under the late Imperialist Government),[41] not only permitted and defended the Denshawai executions, but appealed to the House almost passionately not to criticize or repudiate them, on the ground—how incredible it now appears!—that Abd-el-Nebi and Hassan Mahfouz and Darweesh and the rest were the fuglemen of a gigantic Moslem plot to rise against Christendom in the name of the Prophet and sweep Christendom out of Africa and Asia by a colossal second edition of the Indian Mutiny. That this idiotic romance, gross and ridiculous as the lies of Falstaff, should have imposed on any intelligent and politically experienced human being, is strange enough—though the secret shame of revolted humanity will make cabinet ministers snatch at fantastic excuses—but what humanity will not forgive our foreign secretary for is his failure to see that even if such a conspiracy really existed, England should have faced it and fought it bravely by honorable means, instead of wildly lashing and strangling a handful of poor peasants to scare Islam into terrified submission. Were I abject enough to grant to Sir Edward Grey as valid that main asset of "thinking Imperi-

41. In March 1906 Alfred (First Viscount) Milner, High Commissioner for South Africa 1897–1905, was censured by Parliament for approving corporal punishment of Chinese coolies imported to work in the gold-mining industry of South Africa. Major-General John French, Field Commander of the British Forces in South Africa, had cold-bloodedly required relatives and all male residents of the town of Dordrecht to witness the hanging of convicted rebels on 13 and 23 July 1901. When the Secretary of State for War, in reaction to an outcry in the press and great indignation in Parliament, telegraphed the Commander-in-Chief, Lord Kitchener, to account for French behaving 'at variance with British practice', Kitchener responded on 27 July that he had told French 'not to coerce anyone to attend, and to carry out executions as privately as possible. His reason will be no doubt that cases of private execution have occurred which disloyal population subsequently denied and refused to believe' (South African Telegrams, Vol. XI, Ending on the 30th July 1901: Confidential document, Ministry of Defence Library). Despite the protests from London and Kitchener's assurance to the outraged Cape Ministry and the Governor of Cape Colony on 27 July that he had 'already given instructions which will have desired effect' (Journal of the Principal Events connected with South Africa 1st July to 31st August 1901: Secret document, Ministry of Defence Library), Douglas Haig in a letter of 7 September described a further public execution, at Colesburg, on that date, in which three rebels were put to death by firing-squad (Thomas Pakenham, The Boer War, 1979). The practice was still in effect in November, as attested by a question in the House of Commons on 27 January 1902.

ally," the conviction that we are all going to be murdered, I should still suggest to him that we can at least die like gentlemen? Might I even be so personal as to say that the reason for giving him a social position and political opportunities that are denied to his tradesmen is that he is supposed to understand better than they that honor is worth its danger and its cost, and that life is worthless without honor? It is true that Sir John Falstaff did not think so; but Sir John is hardly a model for Sir Edward. Yet even Sir John would have had enough gumption to see that the Denshawai panic was more dangerous to the Empire than the loss of ten pitched battles.

As cowardice is highly infectious, would it not be desirable to supersede officials who, after years of oriental service, have lost the familiar art of concealing their terrors? I am myself a sedentary literary civilian, constitutionally timid; but I find it possible to keep up appearances, and can even face the risk of being run over, or garotted, or burnt out in London without shrieking for martial law, suppression of the newspapers, exemplary flogging and hanging of motor-bus drivers, and compulsory police service. Why are soldiers and officials on foreign service so much more cowardly than citizens? Is it not clearly because the whole Imperial military system of coercion and terrorism is unnatural, and that the truth formulated by William Morris that "no man is good enough to be another man's master"[42] is true also of nations, and very specially true of those plutocrat-ridden Powers which have of late stumbled into an enormous increase of material wealth without having made any intelligent provision for its proper distribution and administration?

However, the economic reform of the Empire is a long business, whereas the release of Abd-el-Nebi and his neighbors is a matter of the stroke of a pen, once public opinion is shamed into activity. I fear I have stated their case very unfairly and inadequately, because I am hampered, as an Irishman, by my implacable hostility to English domination. Mistrusting my own prejudices, I have taken the story from the two parliamentary papers in which our officials have done their utmost to whitewash the tribunals and the pigeon-shooting party, and to blackwash the villagers. Those who wish to have it told to them by an Englishman of unquestionable personal and social credentials, and an intimate knowledge of Egypt and the Egyptians, can find it in Mr Wilfrid Scawen Blunt's pamphlet entitled "Atrocities of British Rule in Egypt." When they have read it they will appreciate my

42. Morris's assertion appears to have had its origin in a speech by Abraham Lincoln, in the Lincoln–Douglas debates, at Peoria on 15 October 1854: 'No man is good enough to govern another man without that other's consent.'

forbearance; and when I add that English rule in Ireland has been "animated by the same spirit" (I thank Lord Cromer for the phrase) as English rule in Egypt, and that this is the inevitable spirit of all coercive military rule, they will perhaps begin to understand why Home Rule is a necessity not only for Ireland, but for all constituents of those Federations of Commonwealths which are now the only permanently practicable form of Empire.

POSTSCRIPT. These sheets had passed through the press when the news came of Lord Cromer's resignation [1907]. As he accuses himself of failing health, he will perhaps forgive me for accusing him of failing judgment, and for suggesting that his retirement from office might well be celebrated in Egypt by the retirement, at his intercession, of Abd-el-Nebi and the rest from penal servitude.

A YEAR LATER [first published in the 1912 Home Rule Edition.] It may be a relief to some of my readers to learn that very shortly after the publication of the above account of the Denshawai atrocity, I received a private assurance that Abd-el-Nebi and his fellow-prisoners would be released on the following New Year's Day [1908], which is the customary occasion in Egypt for such acts of grace and clemency as the Occupation may allow the Khedive to perform, and that in the meantime their detention would not be rigorous. As the hanged men could not be unhanged nor the flogged men unflogged, this was all that could be done. I am bound to add, in justice to the Government, that this was, as far as I could ascertain, an act of pure conscience on the part of the Cabinet; for there was no sign of any serious pressure of public opinion. One or two newspapers seemed to be amused at my calling the Denshawai villagers Denshavians; but they shewed no other interest in the matter: another illustration of how hopeless it is to induce one modern nation, preoccupied as it necessarily is with its own affairs, to take any real interest in the welfare of another, even when it professes to govern that other in a superior manner for its good. Sir Edward Grey's reputation as a great Minister for Foreign Affairs was not shaken in the least: the eulogies which were heaped on him by both parties increased in volume; and an attempt which I made to call attention to the real character of the Anglo-Russian agreement[43] as to Persia, which was held up as a masterpiece of his

43. This agreement, to maintain 'the independence and integrity' of Persia, signed on 31 August, was designed, according to Shaw, for 'the speculators of England and Russia'. See preface to *The White Prophet*, p. 321.

diplomacy (I was apparently the only person who had taken the trouble to read it) had no effect. Not until Sir Edward ventured to threaten a really formidable European Power in 1911, and threatened it successfully from his point of view, did a sudden and violent agitation against him spring up. Until then, men of both parties idolized him without knowing why, just as they had formerly idolized Lord Cromer and Lord Milner without knowing why. They will now very possibly turn on him and rend him, also without knowing why. The one thing they will not do is to blame themselves, which is the only blaming that can be of any profit to them.

TWENTYFOUR YEARS LATER. The sequel to these events confirmed my unheeded warning with a sanguinary completeness of which I had no prevision. At Easter 1916 a handful of Irishmen seized the Dublin Post Office and proclaimed an Irish Republic, with one of their number, a schoolmaster named [Padraic] Pearse, as President. If all Ireland had risen at this gesture it would have been a serious matter for England, then up to her neck in the war against the Central Empires. But there was no response: the gesture was a complete failure. All that was necessary was to blockade the Post Office until its microcosmic republic was starved out and made ridiculous. What actually happened would be incredible if there were not so many living witnesses of it. From a battery planted at Trinity College (the Irish equivalent of Oxford University), and from a warship in the river Liffey, a bombardment was poured on the centre of the city which reduced more than a square mile of it to such a condition that when, in the following year, I was taken through Arras and Ypres to shew me what the German artillery had done to these cities in two and a half years, I laughed and said, "You should see what the British artillery did to my native city in a week." It would not be true to say that not one stone was left upon another; for the marksmanship was so bad that the Post Office itself was left standing amid a waste of rubbish heaps; and enough scraps of wall were left for the British Army, which needed recruits, to cover with appeals to the Irish to remember Belgium lest the fate of Louvain should befall their own hearths and homes.

Having thus worked up a harebrained romantic adventure into a heroic episode in the struggle for Irish freedom, the victorious artillerists proceeded to kill their prisoners of war in a drawn-out string of executions. Those who were executed accordingly became not only national heroes, but the martyrs whose blood was the seed of the present Irish Free State [established 1921]. Among those who escaped was its first President. Nothing more blindly savage, stupid, and terror-mad could have been devised by

England's worst enemies. It was a very characteristic example of the mentality produced by the conventional gentleman-militarist education at Marlborough [a college originally for the sons of clergymen] and Sandhurst [Royal Military Academy] and the conventional gentleman-diplomatist education at Eton and Oxford, Harrow and Cambridge. Is it surprising that the Russian Soviet Government, though fanatically credulous as to the need for popular education, absolutely refused to employ as teachers anyone who had been touched by the equivalent public school and university routine in Russia, and stuck to its resolution even at the cost of carrying on for some years with teachers who were hardly a day ahead of their pupils?

But the Post Office episode was eclipsed by an event which was much more than an episode, as it shattered the whole case for parliamentary government throughout the world. The Irish Nationalists, after thirty years of constitutional procedure in the British Parliament, had carried an Act to establish Irish Home Rule, as it was then called, which duly received the royal assent and became a statute of the realm. Immediately the British officers on service in Ireland mutinied, refusing to enforce the Act or operate against the northern Orangemen who were openly arming themselves to resist it. They were assured of support by their fellow-officers at home. The Act was suspended after prominent English statesmen had taken part in the military manœuvres of the Orangemen. The Prime Minister publicly pledged himself that Belfast, the Orange capital, would not in any case be coerced. In short, the Act was shelved under a threat of civil war; and the Clan na Gael [Irish-American organization], which in America had steadfastly maintained that the constitutional movement was useless, as England would in the last resort repudiate the constitution and hold Ireland against the Irish by physical force, and had been rebuked, lectured, and repudiated by the parliamentary Home Rulers for a whole generation for saying so, was justified. The Catholic Irish accordingly armed themselves and drilled as Volunteers in spite of the hostility of the Government, which meanwhile gave every possible assistance to the parallel preparations of the Orangemen. An Irish parliament (or Dail) sat in Dublin and claimed to be the national government. Irish courts were set up for the administration of Irish justice; Irish order was kept by Irish police; Irish taxes were collected by Irish officials; and British courts were boycotted. Upon this interesting but hopeless attempt to ignore British rule the Government let loose a specially recruited force (known to history as the Black and Tans) with *carte blanche* to kill, burn, and destroy, save only that they must stop short of rapine. They wrecked the Irish courts and produced a state of anarchy. They struck at the Irish through the popular co-operative stores and creameries, which they burnt. The people found a civil leader in Arthur Griffith[44] and a military one in Michael Collins.[45] The Black and Tans had the British Government at their back: Collins had the people at his back. He threatened that for every creamery or co-operative store or cabin or cottage burnt by the Black and Tans he would burn two country houses of the Protestant gentry. The country houses that were not burnt were raided at night and laid under contribution for needed supplies. If the occupants reported the raid, the house was burnt. The Black and Tans and the ordinary constabulary were treated as enemies in uniform; that is, they were shot at sight and their stations burnt; or they were ambushed and killed in petty battles. Those who gave warnings or information of any helpful kind to them were mercilessly executed without privilege of sex or benefit of clergy. Collins, with allies in every street and hamlet, proved able to carry out his threat. He won the crown of the Reign of Terror; and the position of the Protestant gentry became unbearable.

Thus by fire and bullet, murder and torture and devastation, a situation was produced in which the British Government had either to capitulate at the cost of a far more complete concession of self-government to Ireland than that decreed by the repudiated Home Rule Act, or to let loose the military strength of England in a Cromwellian reconquest, massacre, and replantation which it knew that public opinion in England and America would not tolerate; for some of the most conspicuous English champions of Ulster warned the Government that they could stand no more of the Black and Tan terrorism. And so we settled the Irish Question, not as civilized and reasonable men should have settled it, but as dogs settle a dispute over a bone.

Future historians will probably see in these catastrophes a ritual of human sacrifice without which the savages of the XX century could not effect any redistribution of political power or wealth. Nothing was learnt from Denshawai or the Black and Tan terror. In India, which is still struggling for self-government, and obviously must finally have it, a military panic led to the cannonading of a forbidden public meeting at Amritsar, the crowd being dealt with precisely as if it were a body of

44. Leader of the delegation that negotiated the Anglo–Irish treaty (1921) with Lloyd George's government, recognizing the Irish Free State. Griffith was elected as the Free State's first president in 1922.
45. A leader in Sinn Fein and commander-in-chief of the military forces of the Free State, he became head of the Free State Provisional Government after Griffith's death on 12 August 1922. Ten days later he was assassinated in an ambush by the Republicans (Shaw had dined with him three nights earlier).

German shocktroops rushing the British trenches in Flanders. In London the police would have broken a score or two of heads and dragged a handful of ringleaders to the police courts. And there was the usual combination of mean spite with hyperbolical violence. Indians were forced to crawl past official buildings on their hands and knees. The effect was to make British imperial rule ridiculous in Europe, and implacably resented in India.

In Egypt the British domination died of Denshawai; but at its deathbed the British Sirdar [Lt.-Gen. Sir L. O. F. Stack, British Commander-in-Chief of the Egyptian Army] was assassinated [1924], whereupon the British Government, just then rather drunk after a sweeping election victory secured by an anti-Russian scare, announced to an amazed world that it was going to cut off the Nile at its source and destroy Egypt by stopping its water supply. Of course nothing happened but an ignominious climb down; but the incident illustrates my contention that our authority, when it is too far flung (as our patriotic rhapsodists put it), goes stark mad at the periphery if a pin drops. As to what further panics and atrocities will ensue before India is left to govern itself as much as Ireland and Egypt now are I am in the dark until the event enlightens me. But on the folly of allowing military counsels to prevail in political settlements I may point to the frontiers established by the victors after the war of 1914–18. Almost every one of these frontiers has a new war implicit in it, because the soldier recognizes no ethnographical, linguistic, or moral boundaries: he demands a line that he can defend, or rather that Napoleon or Wellington could have defended; for he has not yet learnt to think of offence and defence in terms of airplanes which ignore his Waterloo ridges. And the inevitable nationalist rebellions against these military frontiers, and the atrocities by which they are countered, are in full swing as I write.

Meanwhile, John Bull's Other Island, though its freedom has destroyed all the romantic interest that used to attach to it, has become at last highly interesting to the student of political science as an experiment in political structure. Protestant Ulster, which armed against the rest of Ireland and defied the British Parliament to the cry of "We wont have it," meaning that they would die in the last ditch singing "O God, our help in ages past" [Isaac Watts, *Psalms of David, Imitated* . . ., 1719, as amended by John Wesley] rather than suffer or tolerate Home Rule, is now suffering and indeed hugging Home Rule on a much more homely scale than the Home Rulers ever demanded or dreamt of; for it has a Belfast Home Rule Parliament instead of an Irish one. And it has allowed Catholic Ireland to secure the Irish parliament. Thus, of the two regional parliaments which have been established on a sectarian basis, Protestant Ulster has been left with the smaller. Now it happens that Protestant Ulster is industrial Ireland and Catholic Ireland agricultural Ireland. And throughout the world for a century past the farmer, the peasant, and the Catholic have been the bulwark of the industrial capitalists against the growing political power of the industrial proletariat organized in trade unions, Labor parties, and the ubiquitous sodalities of that new ultra-Catholic Church called Socialism.

From this defensive alliance the Ulster employers, blinded by an obsolete bigotry and snobbery, have deliberately cut themselves off. In my preface of 1906, and again in my 1912 preface to a sixpenny edition of this play called the Home Rule edition, I exhorted the Protestants to take their chance, trust their grit, and play their part in a single parliament ruling an undivided Ireland. They did not take my advice. Probably they did not even read it, being too deeply absorbed in the History of Maria Monk,[46] or the latest demonstration that all the evil in the world is the work of an underground conspiracy entitled by them "the Jesuits." It is a pity they did not begin their political education, as I began mine, by reading Karl Marx. It is true that I had occasion to point out that Marx was not infallible; but he left me with a very strong disposition to back the economic situation to control all the other situations, religious, nationalist, or romantic, in the long run. And so I do not despair of seeing Protestant Ulster seeking the alliance it repudiated. The Northern Parliament will not merge into the Oireachtas [Parliament of the Free State]; for until both of them are superseded by a completely modernized central government, made for action and not for obstruction, they will remain more effective as regional parliaments than they would be as national ones; but they will soon have to take counsel together through conferences which will recur until they become a permanent institution and finally develop into what the Americans call Congress, or Federal Government of the whole island. No doubt this will be received in Belfast (if noticed at all) with shouts of "We wont have it." But I have heard that cry before, and regard it as a very hopeful sign that they will have it gladly enough when they have the luck to get it.

Ayot St Lawrence.
November, 1929.

---

46. Author of a sensational book (1836) falsely 'disclosing' shocking activities in a Montreal convent from which she had supposedly escaped.

How He Lied to Her Husband

First published in 1907

═══

Like many other works of mine, this playlet is a *pièce d'occasion*. In 1904 it happened that the late Arnold Daly, who was then playing the part of Napoleon in The Man of Destiny in New York, found that whilst the play was too long to take a secondary place in the evening's performance, it was too short to suffice by itself. I therefore took advantage of four days continuous rain during a holiday in the north of Scotland to write How He Lied to Her Husband for Daly. In his hands, it served its turn very effectively.[1]

Trifling as it is, I print it as a sample of what can be done with even the most hackneyed stage framework by filling it in with an observed touch of actual humanity instead of with doctrinaire romanticism. Nothing in the theatre is staler than the situation of husband, wife, and lover, or the fun of knockabout farce. I have taken both, and got an original play out of them, as anybody else can if only he will look about him for his material instead of plagiarizing Othello and the thousand plays that have proceeded on Othello's romantic assumptions and false point of honor.

[*The balance of the preface was transferred by Shaw, with omissions, to the preface to* Mrs Warren's Profession *when he revised and enlarged it for the Collected Edition, 1930. See above: pp. 134–7*]

---

1. The young American actor-manager Arnold Daly, who had produced *Candida* in New York in December 1903 with enormous success, first performed *How He Lied to Her Husband* on a double bill with *The Man of Destiny* on 26 September 1904.

Major Barbara

First published in 1907

===

FIRST AID TO CRITICS

Before dealing with the deeper aspects of Major Barbara, let me, for the credit of English literature, make a protest against an unpatriotic habit into which many of my critics have fallen. Whenever my view strikes them as being at all outside the range of, say, an ordinary suburban church-warden, they conclude that I am echoing Schopenhauer, Nietzsche, Ibsen, Strindberg, Tolstoy, or some other heresiarch in northern or eastern Europe.

I confess there is something flattering in this simple faith in my accomplishment as a linguist and my erudition as a philosopher. But I cannot countenance the assumption that life and literature are so poor in these islands that we must go abroad for all dramatic material that is not common and all ideas that are not superficial. I therefore venture to put my critics in possession of certain facts concerning my contact with modern ideas.

About half a century ago, an Irish novelist, Charles Lever, wrote a story entitled A Day's Ride: A Life's Romance. It was published by Charles Dickens in Household Words, and proved so strange to the public taste that Dickens pressed Lever to make short work of it. I read scraps of this novel when I was a child; and it made an enduring impression on me. The hero was a very romantic hero, trying to live bravely, chivalrously, and powerfully by dint of mere romance-fed imagination, without courage, without means, without knowledge, without skill, without anything real except his bodily appetites. Even in my childhood I found in this poor devil's unsuccessful encounters with the facts of life, a poignant quality that romantic fiction lacked. The book, in spite of its first failure, is not dead: I saw its title the other day in the catalogue of [Christian B.] Tauchnitz.[1]

Now why is it that when I also deal in the tragi-comic irony of the

1. German printer and publisher, who began publication in Leipzig (1841) of an English-language 'Tauchnitz Edition' of a *Collection of British and American Authors*. It succeeded beyond anyone's wildest imagination.

conflict between real life and the romantic imagination, critics never affiliate me to my countryman and immediate forerunner, Charles Lever, whilst they confidently derive me from a Norwegian author of whose language I do not know three words, and of whom I knew nothing until years after the Shavian *Anschauung* [intuition] was already unequivocally declared in books full of what came, ten years later, to be perfunctorily labelled Ibsenism? I was not Ibsenist even at second hand; for Lever, though he may have read Henri Beyle, *alias* Stendhal, certainly never read Ibsen. Of the books that made Lever popular, such as Charles O'Malley [1841] and Harry Lorrequer [1839], I know nothing but the names and some of the illustrations. But the story of the day's ride and life's romance of Potts (claiming alliance with Pozzo di Borgo[2]) caught me and fascinated me as something strange and significant, though I already knew all about Alnaschar and Don Quixote and Simon Tappertit[3] and many another romantic hero mocked by reality. From the plays of Aristophanes to the tales of Stevenson that mockery has been made familiar to all who are properly saturated with letters.

Where, then, was the novelty in Lever's tale? Partly, I think, in a new seriousness in dealing with Potts's disease. Formerly, the contrast between madness and sanity was deemed comic: Hogarth shews us [in his series of paintings *A Rake's Progress*] how fashionable people went in parties to Bedlam to laugh at the lunatics. I myself have had a village idiot exhibited to me as something irresistibly funny. On the stage the madman was once a regular comic figure: that was how Hamlet got his opportunity before Shakespear touched him. The originality of Shakespear's version lay in his taking the lunatic sympathetically and seriously, and thereby making an advance towards the eastern consciousness of the fact that lunacy may be inspiration in disguise, since a man who has more brains than his fellows necessarily appears as mad to them as one who has less. But Shakespear did not do for Pistol [in *Henry IV Part II* and *Henry V*] and Parolles [in *All's Well That Ends Well*] what he did for Hamlet. The particular sort of madman they represented, the romantic make-believer, lay outside the pale of sympathy in literature: he was pitilessly despised and ridiculed here as he was in the east under the name of Alnaschar, and was doomed to be, centuries later, under the name of Simon Tappertit. When Cervantes relented over Don Quixote, and Dickens relented over Pickwick, they did

2. Russian diplomat whose name is associated with foreign intrigue involving such personages as Napoleon, Tsar Nicholas, and Wellington.
3. Alnaschar, a beggar in *The Arabian Nights*; Tappertit, an aspiring anarchist in Dickens's *Barnaby Rudge*.

not become impartial: they simply changed sides, and became friends and apologists where they had formerly been mockers.

In Lever's story there is a real change of attitude. There is no relenting towards Potts: he never gains our affections like Don Quixote and Pickwick: he has not even the infatuate courage of Tappertit. But we dare not laugh at him, because, somehow, we recognize ourselves in Potts. We may, some of us, have enough nerve, enough muscle, enough luck, enough tact or skill or address or knowledge to carry things off better than he did; to impose on the people who saw through him; to fascinate Katinka (who cut Potts so ruthlessly at the end of the story); but for all that, we know that Potts plays an enormous part in ourselves and in the world, and that the social problem is not a problem of story-book heroes of the older pattern, but a problem of Pottses, and of how to make men of them. To fall back on my old phrase [in the preface to *Plays Pleasant*], we have the feeling—one that Alnaschar, Pistol, Parolles, and Tappertit never gave us— that Potts is a piece of really scientific natural history as distinguished from funny story telling. His author is not throwing a stone at a creature of another and inferior order, but making a confession, with the effect that the stone hits each of us full in the conscience and causes our self-esteem to smart very sorely. Hence the failure of Lever's book to please the readers of Household Words. That pain in the self-esteem nowadays causes critics to raise a cry of Ibsenism. I therefore assure them that the sensation first came to me from Lever and may have come to him from Beyle, or at least out of the Stendhalian atmosphere. I exclude the hypothesis of complete original- ity on Lever's part, because a man can no more be completely original in that sense than a tree can grow out of air.

Another mistake as to my literary ancestry is made whenever I violate the romantic convention that all women are angels when they are not devils; that they are better looking than men; that their part in courtship is entirely passive; and that the human female form is the most beautiful object in nature. Schopenhauer wrote a splenetic essay which, as it is neither polite nor profound, was probably intended to knock this nonsense violently on the head. A sentence denouncing the idolized form as ugly has been largely quoted.[4] The English critics have read that sentence; and I

4. In his essay 'On Women' in *Parerga und Paralipomena* (1851) the German philosopher Arthur Schopenhauer wrote: 'Only the male intellect, clouded by the sexual impulse, could call the undersized, narrow-shouldered, broad-hipped, and short-legged sex the fair sex' (tr. E. Belfort Bax, in *Selected Essays of Arthur Schopenhauer*, 1891).

must here affirm, with as much gentleness as the implication will bear, that it has yet to be proved that they have dipped any deeper. At all events, whenever an English playwright represents a young and marriageable woman as being anything but a romantic heroine, he is disposed of without further thought as an echo of Schopenhauer. My own case is a specially hard one, because, when I implore the critics who are obsessed with the Schopenhauerian formula to remember that playwrights, like sculptors, study their figures from life, and not from philosophic essays, they reply passionately that I am not a playwright and that my stage figures do not live. But even so, I may and do ask them why, if they must give the credit of my plays to a philosopher, they do not give it to an English philosopher? Long before I ever read a word by Schopenhauer, or even knew whether he was a philosopher or a chemist, the Socialist revival of the eighteen-eighties brought me into contact, both literary and personal, with Ernest Belfort Bax, an English Socialist and philosophic essayist, whose handling of modern feminism would provoke romantic protests from Schopenhauer himself, or even Strindberg. As a matter of fact I hardly noticed Schopenhauer's disparagements of women when they came under my notice later on, so thoroughly had Bax familiarized me with the homoist attitude, and forced me to recognize the extent to which public opinion, and consequently legislation and jurisprudence, is corrupted by feminist sentiment.

Belfort Bax's essays [*Outspoken Essays*, 1897] were not confined to the Feminist question. He was a ruthless critic of current morality. Other writers have gained sympathy for dramatic criminals by eliciting the alleged "soul of goodness in things evil"; but Bax would propound some quite undramatic and apparently shabby violation of our commercial law and morality, and not merely defend it with the most disconcerting ingenuity, but actually prove it to be a positive duty that nothing but the certainty of police persecution should prevent every right-minded man from at once doing on principle. The Socialists were naturally shocked, being for the most part morbidly moral people; but at all events they were saved later on from the delusion that nobody but Nietzsche had ever challenged our mercanto-Christian morality. I first heard the name of Nietzsche from a German mathematician, Miss [Sophie] Borchardt, who had read my Quintessence of Ibsenism, and told me that she saw what I had been reading: namely, Nietzsche's Jenseits von Gut und Böse [*Beyond Good and Evil*]. Which I protest I had never seen, and could not have read with any comfort, for want of the necessary German, if I had seen it.

Nietzsche, like Schopenhauer, is the victim in England of a single much quoted sentence containing the phrase "big blonde beast" [in his *The Genealogy of Morals*, 1887]. On the strength of this alliteration it is assumed that Nietzsche gained his European reputation by a senseless glorification of selfish bullying as the rule of life, just as it is assumed, on the strength of the single word Superman (*Übermensch*) borrowed by me from Nietzsche, that I look for the salvation of society to the despotism of a single Napoleonic Superman, in spite of my careful demonstration of the folly of that outworn infatuation. But even the less recklessly superficial critics seem to believe that the modern objection to Christianity as a pernicious slave-morality was first put forward by Nietzsche. It was familiar to me before I ever heard of Nietzsche. The late Captain [F. J.] Wilson,[5] author of several queer pamphlets, propagandist of a metaphysical system called Comprehensionism, and inventor of the term "Crosstianity" to distinguish the retrograde element in Christendom, was wont thirty years ago, in the discussions of the Dialectical Society, to protest earnestly against the beatitudes of the Sermon on the Mount as excuses for cowardice and servility, as destructive of our will, and consequently of our honor and manhood. Now it is true that Captain Wilson's moral criticism of Christianity was not a historical theory of it, like Nietzsche's; but this objection cannot be made to Stuart-Glennie, the successor of [H. T.] Buckle [author of a celebrated history of English civilization] as a philosophic historian, who devoted his life to the elaboration and propagation of his theory that Christianity is part of an epoch (or rather an aberration, since it began as recently as 6000 B.C. and is already collapsing) produced by the necessity in which the numerically inferior white races found themselves to impose their domination on the colored races by priestcraft, making a virtue and a popular religion of drudgery and submissiveness in this world not only as a means of achieving saintliness of character but of securing a reward in heaven. Here was the slave-morality view formulated by a Scotch philosopher of my acquaintance long before we all began chattering about Nietzsche.

As Stuart-Glennie traced the evolution of society to the conflict of races, his theory made some sensation among Socialists—that is, among the only people who were seriously thinking about historical evolution at all—by its collision with the class-conflict theory of Karl Marx. Nietzsche, as I gather, regarded the slave-morality as having been invented and imposed on the world by slaves making a virtue of necessity and a religion of their servitude.

5. An eccentric member of the Dialectical Society, which Shaw joined in 1881.

Stuart-Glennie regarded the slave-morality as an invention of the superior white race to subjugate the minds of the inferior races whom they wished to exploit, and who would have destroyed them by force of numbers if their minds had not been subjugated. As this process is in operation still, and can be studied at first hand not only in our Church schools and in the struggle between our modern proprietary classes and the proletariat, but in the part played by Christian missionaries in reconciling the black races of Africa to their subjugation by European Capitalism, we can judge for ourselves whether the initiative came from above or below. My object here is not to argue the historical point, but simply to make our theatre critics ashamed of their habit of treating Britain as an intellectual void, and assuming that every philosophical idea, every historic theory, every criticism of our moral, religious and juridical institutions, must necessarily be either a foreign import, or else a fantastic sally (in rather questionable taste) totally unrelated to the existing body of thought. I urge them to remember that this body of thought is the slowest of growths and the rarest of blossomings, and that if there be such a thing on the philosophic plane as a matter of course, it is that no individual can make more than a minute contribution to it. In fact, their conception of clever persons parthenogenetically bringing forth complete original cosmogonies by dint of sheer "brilliancy" is part of that ignorant credulity which is the despair of the honest philosopher, and the opportunity of the religious impostor.

THE GOSPEL OF ST ANDREW UNDERSHAFT

It is this credulity that drives me to help my critics out with Major Barbara by telling them what to say about it. In the millionaire Undershaft I have represented a man who has become intellectually and spiritually as well as practically conscious of the irresistible natural truth which we all abhor and repudiate: to wit, that the greatest of our evils, and the worst of our crimes is poverty, and that our first duty, to which every other consideration should be sacrificed, is not to be poor. "Poor but honest," "the respectable poor," and such phrases are as intolerable and as immoral as "drunken but amiable," "fraudulent but a good after-dinner speaker," "splendidly criminal," or the like. Security, the chief pretence of civilization, cannot exist where the worst of dangers, the danger of poverty, hangs over everyone's head, and where the alleged protection of our persons from violence is only an accidental result of the existence of a police force whose real business is to force the poor man to see his children starve whilst idle people overfeed pet dogs with the money that might feed and clothe them.

It is exceedingly difficult to make people realize that an evil is an evil. For instance, we seize a man and deliberately do him a malicious injury: say, imprison him for years. One would not suppose that it needed any exceptional clearness of wit to recognize in this an act of diabolical cruelty. But in England such a recognition provokes a stare of surprise, followed by an explanation that the outrage is punishment or justice or something else that is all right, or perhaps by a heated attempt to argue that we should all be robbed and murdered in our beds if such stupid villainies as sentences of imprisonment were not commited daily. It is useless to argue that even if this were true, which it is not, the alternative to adding crimes of our own to the crimes from which we suffer is not helpless submission. Chickenpox is an evil; but if I were to declare that we must either submit to it or else repress it sternly by seizing everyone who suffers from it and punishing them by inoculation with smallpox, I should be laughed at; for though nobody could deny that the result would be to prevent chickenpox to some extent by making people avoid it much more carefully, and to effect a further apparent prevention by making them conceal it very anxiously, yet people would have sense enough to see that the deliberate propagation of smallpox was a creation of evil, and must therefore be ruled out in favor of purely humane and hygienic measures. Yet in the precisely parallel case of a man breaking into my house and stealing my wife's diamonds I am expected as a matter of course to steal ten years of his life, torturing him all the time. If he tries to defeat that monstrous retaliation by shooting me, my survivors hang him. The net result suggested by the police statistics is that we inflict atrocious injuries on the burglars we catch in order to make the rest take effectual precautions against detection; so that instead of saving our wives' diamonds from burglary we only greatly decrease our chances of ever getting them back, and increase our chances of being shot by the robber if we are unlucky enough to disturb him at his work.

But the thoughtless wickedness with which we scatter sentences of imprisonment, torture in the solitary cell and on the plank bed, and flogging, on moral invalids and energetic rebels, is as nothing compared to the silly levity with which we tolerate poverty as if it were either a wholesome tonic for lazy people or else a virtue to be embraced as St Francis embraced it. If a man is indolent, let him be poor. If he is drunken, let him be poor. If he is not a gentleman, let him be poor. If he is addicted to the fine arts or to pure science instead of to trade and finance, let him be poor. If he chooses to spend his urban eighteen shillings a week or his agricultural thirteen shillings a week on his beer and his family instead of saving it up for his old age, let him be poor. Let nothing be done for "the undeserving": let him be poor. Serve him right! Also—somewhat inconsistently—blessed are the poor!

Now what does this Let Him Be Poor mean? It means let him be weak. Let him be ignorant. Let him become a nucleus of disease. Let him be a standing exhibition and example of ugliness and dirt. Let him have rickety children. Let him be cheap, and drag his fellows down to his own price by selling himself to do their work. Let his habitations turn our cities into poisonous congeries of slums. Let his daughters infect our young men with the diseases of the streets, and his sons revenge him by turning the nation's manhood into scrofula, cowardice, cruelty, hypocrisy, political imbecility, and all the other fruits of oppression and malnutrition. Let the undeserving become still less deserving; and let the deserving lay up for himself, not treasures in heaven, but horrors in hell upon earth. This being so, is it really wise to let him be poor? Would he not do ten times less harm as a prosperous burglar, incendiary, ravisher or murderer, to the utmost limits of humanity's comparatively negligible impulses in these directions? Suppose we were to abolish all penalties for such activities, and decide that poverty is the one thing we will not tolerate—that every adult with less than, say, £365 a year, shall be painlessly but inexorably killed, and every hungry half naked child forcibly fattened and clothed, would not that be an enormous improvement on our existing system, which has already destroyed so many civilizations, and is visibly destroying ours in the same way?

Is there any radicle of such legislation in our parliamentary system? Well, there are two measures just sprouting in the political soil, which may conceivably grow to something valuable. One is the institution of a Legal Minimum Wage. The other, Old Age Pensions. But there is a better plan than either of these. Some time ago I mentioned the subject of Universal Old Age Pensions to my fellow Socialist [T. J.] Cobden-Sanderson [printer of the Dove's Press], famous as an artist-craftsman in bookbinding and printing. "Why not Universal Pensions for Life?" said Cobden-Sanderson. In saying this, he solved the industrial problem at a stroke. At present we say callously to each citizen "If you want money, earn it" as if his having or not having it were a matter that concerned himself alone. We do not even secure for him the opportunity of earning it: on the contrary, we allow our industry to be organized in open dependence on the maintenance of "a reserve army of unemployed" for the sake of "elasticity." The sensible course would be Cobden-Sanderson's: that is, to give every man enough to live well on, so as to guarantee the community against the possibility of a case of the malignant disease of poverty, and then (necessarily) to see that he earned it.

Undershaft, the hero of Major Barbara, is simply a man who, having grasped the fact that poverty is a crime, knows that when society offered him the alternative of poverty or a lucrative trade in death and destruction, it offered him, not a choice between opulent villainy and humble virtue, but between energetic enterprise and cowardly infamy. His conduct stands the Kantian test,[6] which Peter Shirley's does not. Peter Shirley is what we call the honest poor man. Undershaft is what we call the wicked rich one: Shirley is Lazarus, Undershaft Dives [Luke 16: 19–31]. Well, the misery of the world is due to the fact that the great mass of men act and believe as Peter Shirley acts and believes. If they acted and believed as Undershaft acts and believes, the immediate result would be a revolution of incalculable beneficence. To be wealthy, says Undershaft, is with me a point of honor for which I am prepared to kill at the risk of my own life. This preparedness is, as he says, the final test of sincerity. Like [Jean] Froissart's medieval hero,[7] who saw that "to rob and pill was a good life" he is not the dupe of that public sentiment against killing which is propagated and endowed by people who would otherwise be killed themselves, or of the mouth-honor paid to poverty and obedience by rich and insubordinate do-nothings who want to rob the poor without courage and command them without superiority. Froissart's knight, in placing the achievement of a good life before all the other duties—which indeed are not duties at all when they conflict with it, but plain wickednesses—behaved bravely, admirably, and, in the final analysis, public-spiritedly. Medieval society, on the other hand, behaved very badly indeed in organizing itself so stupidly that a good life could be achieved by robbing and pilling. If the knight's contemporaries had been all as resolute as he, robbing and pilling would have been the shortest way to the gallows, just as, if we were all as resolute and

6. Immanuel Kant's philosophic test is to 'act so as to treat humanity, in thyself or any other, as an end always, and never as a means only' (*Fundamental Principles of the Metaphysic of Ethics*, 1785, tr. T. K. Abbott, 1895).
7. Froissart, French chronicler and raconteur, spent most of his life at the courts of princes. The 'medieval hero' was Aymerigot Marcell, a brigand who was *routier* and captain of one of the most notorious of the free companies of discharged soldiers, plundering at their pleasure in fourteenth-century France. Of him Froissart wrote: 'Then he sayde and imagyned, to pill and to robbe, all thynge considered, was a good lyfe, and so repented him of his good doing' (*Chronicles*, tr. Lord Berners (1902) in Third and Fourth Book, Chapter 166).

clearsighted as Undershaft, an attempt to live by means of what is called "an independent income" would be the shortest way to the lethal chamber. But as, thanks to our political imbecility and personal cowardice (fruits of poverty, both), the best imitation of a good life now procurable is life on an independent income, all sensible people aim at securing such an income, and are, of course, careful to legalize and moralize both it and all the actions and sentiments which lead to it and support it as an institution. What else can they do? They know, of course, that they are rich because others are poor. But they cannot help that: it is for the poor to repudiate poverty when they have had enough of it. The thing can be done easily enough: the demonstrations to the contrary made by the economists, jurists, moralists and sentimentalists hired by the rich to defend them, or even doing the work gratuitously out of sheer folly and abjectness, impose only on those who want to be imposed on.

The reason why the independent income-tax payers are not solid in defence of their position is that since we are not medieval rovers through a sparsely populated country, the poverty of those we rob prevents our having the good life for which we sacrifice them. Rich men or aristocrats with a developed sense of life—men like Ruskin and William Morris and Kropotkin[8]—have enormous social appetites and very fastidious personal ones. They are not content with handsome houses: they want handsome cities. They are not content with bediamonded wives and blooming daughters: they complain because the charwoman is badly dressed, because the laundress smells of gin, because the sempstress is anemic, because every man they meet is not a friend and every woman not a romance. They turn up their noses at their neighbor's drains, and are made ill by the architecture of their neighbor's houses. Trade patterns made to suit vulgar people do not please them (and they can get nothing else): they cannot sleep nor sit at ease upon "slaughtered" cabinet makers' furniture. The very air is not good enough for them: there is too much factory smoke in it. They even demand abstract conditions: justice, honor, a noble moral atmosphere, a mystic nexus to replace the cash nexus. Finally they declare that though to rob and pill with your own hand on horseback and in steel coat may have been a good life, to rob and pill by the hands of the policeman, the bailiff, and the soldier, and to underpay them meanly for doing it, is not a good life, but rather fatal to all possibility of even a tolerable one. They call on the poor to revolt, and, finding the poor shocked at their ungentlemanliness,

8. Russian revolutionist, leader of the anarchist movement in London 1886–1914, and social philosopher.

despairingly revile the proletariat for its "damned wantlessness" (*verdammte Bedürfnislosigkeit*).

So far, however, their attack on society has lacked simplicity. The poor do not share their tastes nor understand their art-criticisms. They do not want the simple life, nor the esthetic life; on the contrary, they want very much to wallow in all the costly vulgarities from which the elect souls among the rich turn away with loathing. It is by surfeit and not by abstinence that they will be cured of their hankering after unwholesome sweets. What they do dislike and despise and are ashamed of is poverty. To ask them to fight for the difference between the Christmas number of the Illustrated London News and the Kelmscott Chaucer[9] is silly: they prefer the News. The difference between a stock-broker's cheap and dirty starched white shirt and collar and the comparatively costly and carefully dyed blue shirt of William Morris is a difference so disgraceful to Morris in their eyes that if they fought on the subject at all, they would fight in defence of the starch. "Cease to be slaves, in order that you may become cranks" is not a very inspiring call to arms; nor is it really improved by substituting saints for cranks. Both terms denote men of genius; and the common man does not want to live the life of a man of genius: he would much rather live the life of a pet collie if that were the only alternative. But he does want more money. Whatever else he may be vague about, he is clear about that. He may or may not prefer Major Barbara to the Drury Lane pantomime; but he always prefers five hundred pounds to five hundred shillings.

Now to deplore this preference as sordid, and teach children that it is sinful to desire money, is to strain towards the extreme possible limit of impudence in lying and corruption in hypocrisy. The universal regard for money is the one hopeful fact in our civilization, the one sound spot in our social conscience. Money is the most important thing in the world. It represents health, strength, honor, generosity and beauty as conspicuously and undeniably as the want of it represents illness, weakness, disgrace, meanness and ugliness. Not the least of its virtues is that it destroys base people as certainly as it fortifies and dignifies noble people. It is only when it is cheapened to worthlessness for some and made impossibly dear to others, that it becomes a curse. In short, it is a curse only in such foolish social conditions that life itself is a curse. For the two things are inseparable: money is the counter that enables life to be distributed socially: it *is* life as truly as sovereigns and bank notes are money. The first duty of every citizen is to insist on having money on reasonable terms; and this demand is

9. Morris's last piece of work, the crowning glory of his printing press, 1896.

not complied with by giving four men three shillings each for ten or twelve hours' drudgery and one man a thousand pounds for nothing. The crying need of the nation is not for better morals, cheaper bread, temperance, liberty, culture, redemption of fallen sisters and erring brothers, nor the grace, love and fellowship of the Trinity, but simply for enough money. And the evil to be attacked is not sin, suffering, greed, priestcraft, kingcraft, demagogy, monopoly, ignorance, drink, war, pestilence, nor any other of the scapegoats which reformers sacrifice, but simply poverty.

Once take your eyes from the ends of the earth and fix them on this truth just under your nose; and Andrew Undershaft's views will not perplex you in the least. Unless indeed his constant sense that he is only the instrument of a Will or Life Force which uses him for purposes wider than his own, may puzzle you. If so, that is because you are walking either in artificial Darwinian darkness, or in mere stupidity. All genuinely religious people have that consciousness. To them Undershaft the Mystic will be quite intelligible, and his perfect comprehension of his daughter the Salvationist and her lover the Euripidean republican natural and inevitable. That, however, is not new, even on the stage. What is new, as far as I know, is that article in Undershaft's religion which recognizes in Money the first need and in poverty the vilest sin of man and society.

This dramatic conception has not, of course, been attained *per saltum* [by a leap]. Nor has it been borrowed from Nietzsche or from any man born beyond the Channel. The late Samuel Butler, in his own department the greatest English writer of the latter half of the XIX century, steadily inculcated the necessity and morality of a conscientious Laodiceanism [that is, indifference] in religion and of an earnest and constant sense of the importance of money. It drives one almost to despair of English literature when one sees so extraordinary a study of English life as Butler's posthumous Way of All Flesh [1903] making so little impression that when, some years later, I produce plays in which Butler's extraordinarily fresh, free and future-piercing suggestions have an obvious share, I am met with nothing but vague cacklings about Ibsen and Nietzsche, and am only too thankful that they are not about Alfred de Musset and George Sand. Really, the English do not deserve to have great men. They allowed Butler to die practically unknown, whilst I, a comparatively insignificant Irish journalist, was leading them by the nose into an advertisement of me which has made my own life a burden. In Sicily there is a Via Samuele Butler. When an English tourist sees it, he either asks "Who the devil was Samuele Butler?" or wonders why the Sicilians should perpetuate the memory of the author of Hudibras [seventeenth-century satirist of the same name].

Well, it cannot be denied that the English are only too anxious to recognize a man of genius if somebody will kindly point him out to them. Having pointed myself out in this manner with some success, I now point out Samuel Butler, and trust that in consequence I shall hear a little less in future of the novelty and foreign origin of the ideas which are now making their way into the English theatre through plays written by Socialists. There are living men whose originality and power are as obvious as Butler's and when they die that fact will be discovered. Meanwhile I recommend them to insist on their own merits as an important part of their own business.

THE SALVATION ARMY

When Major Barbara was produced in London, the second act was reported in an important northern newspaper [the *Clarion*] as a withering attack on the Salvation Army, and the despairing ejaculation of Barbara deplored by a London daily as a tasteless blasphemy. And they were set right, not by the professed critics of the theatre, but by religious and philosophical publicists like Sir Oliver Lodge [in the *Clarion*, 29 December 1905] and Dr Stanton Coit, and strenuous Nonconformist journalists like William Stead [in the *Review of Reviews*, January 1906], who not only understood the act as well as the Salvationists themselves, but also saw it in its relation to the religious life of the nation, a life which seems to lie not only outside the sympathy of many of our theatre critics, but actually outside their knowledge of society. Indeed nothing could be more ironically curious than the confrontation Major Barbara effected of the theatre enthusiasts with the religious enthusiasts.[10] On the one hand was the playgoer, always seeking pleasure, paying exorbitantly for it, suffering unbearable discomforts for it, and hardly ever getting it. On the other hand was the Salvationist, repudiating gaiety and courting effort and sacrifice, yet always in the wildest spirits, laughing, joking, singing, rejoicing, drumming, and tambourining: his life flying by in a flash of excitement, and his death arriving as a climax of triumph. And, if you please, the playgoer despising the Salvationist as a joyless person, shut out from the heaven of the theatre, self-condemned to a life of hideous gloom; and the Salvationist

10. Shaw's use of 'enthusiast' here, and variations elsewhere in the preface, should call to mind its etymology – God within – and its connection with the highly emotional nineteenth-century Wesleyan Methodism.

mourning over the playgoer as over a prodigal with vine leaves in his hair, careering outrageously to hell amid the popping of champagne corks and the ribald laughter of sirens! Could misunderstanding be more complete, or sympathy worse misplaced?

Fortunately, the Salvationists are more accessible to the religious character of the drama than the playgoers to the gay energy and artistic fertility of religion. They can see, when it is pointed out to them, that a theatre, as a place where two or three are gathered together [Matthew 18: 20], takes from that divine presence an inalienable sanctity of which the grossest and profanest farce can no more deprive it than a hypocritical sermon by a snobbish bishop can desecrate Westminster Abbey. But in our professional playgoers this indispensable preliminary conception of sanctity seems wanting. They talk of actors as mimes and mummers, and, I fear, think of dramatic authors as liars and pandars, whose main business is the voluptuous soothing of the tired city speculator when what he calls the serious business of the day is over. Passion, the life of drama, means nothing to them but primitive sexual excitement: such phrases as "impassioned poetry" or "passionate love of truth" have fallen quite out of their vocabulary and been replaced by "passional crime" and the like. They assume, as far as I can gather, that people in whom passion has a larger scope are passionless and therefore uninteresting. Consequently they come to think of religious people as people who are not interesting and not amusing. And so, when Barbara cuts the regular Salvation Army jokes, and snatches a kiss from her lover across his drum, the devotees of the theatre think they ought to appear shocked, and conclude that the whole play is an elaborate mockery of the Army. And then either hypocritically rebuke me for mocking, or foolishly take part in the supposed mockery!

Even the handful of mentally competent critics got into difficulties over my demonstration of the economic deadlock in which the Salvation Army finds itself. Some of them thought that the Army would not have taken money from a distiller and a cannon founder: others thought it should not have taken it: all assumed more or less definitely that it reduced itself to absurdity or hypocrisy by taking it. On the first point the reply of the Army itself was prompt and conclusive. As one of its officers said, they would take money from the devil himself and be only too glad to get it out of his hands and into God's. They gratefully acknowledged that publicans[11] not only give them money but allow

11. In British usage this is a keeper of a public house; here, however, it has biblical overtones of a collector of tolls or tributes.

them to collect it in the bar—sometimes even when there is a Salvation meeting outside preaching teetotalism. In fact, they questioned the verisimilitude of the play, not because Mrs Baines took the money, but because Barbara refused it.

On the point that the Army ought not to take such money, its justification is obvious. It must take the money because it cannot exist without money, and there is no other money to be had. Practically all the spare money in the country consists of a mass of rent, interest, and profit, every penny of which is bound up with crime, drink, prostitution, disease, and all the evil fruits of poverty, as inextricably as with enterprise, wealth, commercial probity, and national prosperity. The notion that you can earmark certain coins as tainted is an unpractical individualist superstition. None the less the fact that all our money is tainted gives a very severe shock to earnest young souls when some dramatic instance of the taint first makes them conscious of it. When an enthusiastic young clergyman of the Established Church first realizes that the Ecclesiastical Commissioners receive the rents of sporting public houses, brothels, and sweating dens; or that the most generous contributor at his last charity sermon was an employer trading in female labor cheapened by prostitution as unscrupulously as a hotel keeper trades in waiters' labor cheapened by tips, or commissionaires' labor cheapened by pensions; or that the only patron who can afford to rebuild his church or his schools or give his boys' brigade a gymnasium or a library is the son-in-law of a Chicago meat king, that young clergyman has, like Barbara, a very bad quarter hour. But he cannot help himself by refusing to accept money from anybody except sweet old ladies with independent incomes and gentle and lovely ways of life. He has only to follow up the income of the sweet ladies to its industrial source; and there he will find Mrs Warren's profession and the poisonous canned meat and all the rest of it. His own stipend has the same root. He must either share the world's guilt or go to another planet. He must save the world's honor if he is to save his own. This is what all the Churches find just as the Salvation Army and Barbara find it in the play. Her discovery that she is her father's accomplice; that the Salvation Army is the accomplice of the distiller and the dynamite maker; that they can no more escape one another than they can escape the air they breathe; that there is no salvation for them through personal righteousness, but only through the redemption of the whole nation from its vicious, lazy, competitive anarchy: this discovery has been made by everyone except the Pharisees and (apparently) the professional playgoers, who still wear their Tom

Hood shirts[12] and underpay their washerwomen without the slightest misgiving as to the elevation of their private characters, the purity of their private atmospheres, and their right to repudiate as foreign to themselves the coarse depravity of the garret and the slum. Not that they mean any harm: they only desire to be, in their little private way, what they call gentlemen. They do not understand Barbara's lesson because they have not, like her, learnt it by taking their part in the larger life of the nation.

BARBARA'S RETURN TO THE COLORS

Barbara's return to the colors may yet provide a subject for the dramatic historian of the future. To go back to the Salvation Army with the knowledge that even the Salvationists themselves are not saved yet; that poverty is not blessed, but a most damnable sin; and that when General Booth chose Blood and Fire for the emblem of Salvation instead of the Cross, he was perhaps better inspired than he knew: such knowledge, for the daughter of Andrew Undershaft, will clearly lead to something hope-fuller than distributing bread and treacle at the expense of Bodger.[13]

It is a very significant thing, this instinctive choice of the military form of organization, this substitution of the drum for the organ, by the Salvation Army. Does it not suggest that the Salvationists divine that they must actually fight the devil instead of merely praying at him? At present, it is true, they have not quite ascertained his correct address. When they do, they may give a very rude shock to that sense of security which he has gained from his experience of the fact that hard words, even when uttered by eloquent essayists and lecturers, or carried unanimously at enthusiastic public meetings on the motion of eminent reformers, break no bones. It has been said that the French Revolution was the work of Voltaire, Rousseau and the Encyclopedists. It seems to me to have been the work of men who had observed that virtuous indignation, caustic criticism, conclusive argument and instructive pamphleteering, even when done by the most earnest and witty literary geniuses, were as useless as praying, things going steadily from bad to worse whilst the Social Contract and the pamphlets of Voltaire were at the height of their vogue. Eventually, as we know, perfectly respectable citizens and earnest philanthropists connived at the September

12. In a poem 'The Song of the Shirt' (1843), Thomas Hood presented the plight of women who work 'in poverty, hunger, and dirt' making shirts for the rich.
13. Sir Horace Bodger (Lord Saxmundham), an important character in *Major Barbara* who never appears, is a millionaire liquor industrialist.

massacres[14] because hard experience had convinced them that if they contented themselves with appeals to humanity and patriotism, the aristocracy, though it would read their appeals with the greatest enjoyment and appreciation, flattering and admiring the writers, would none the less continue to conspire with foreign monarchists to undo the revolution and restore the old system with every circumstance of savage vengeance and ruthless repression of popular liberties.

The XIX century saw the same lesson repeated in England. It had its Utilitarians, its Christian Socialists, its Fabians (still extant): it had Bentham, Mill, Dickens, Ruskin, Carlyle, Butler, Henry George, and Morris. And the end of all their efforts is the Chicago described by Mr Upton Sinclair [in his novel *The Jungle*, 1906], and the London in which the people who pay to be amused by my dramatic representation of Peter Shirley turned out to starve at forty because there are younger slaves to be had for his wages, do not take, and have not the slightest intention of taking, any effective step to organize society in such a way as to make that everyday infamy impossible. I, who have preached and pamphleteered like any Encyclopedist, have to confess that my methods are no use, and would be no use if I were Voltaire, Rousseau, Bentham, Marx, Mill, Dickens, Carlyle, Ruskin, Butler, and Morris all rolled into one, with Euripides, More, Montaigne, Molière, Beaumarchais, Swift, Goethe, Ibsen, Tolstoy, Jesus and the prophets all thrown in (as indeed in some sort I actually am, standing as I do on all their shoulders). The problem being to make heroes out of cowards, we paper apostles and artist-magicians have succeeded only in giving cowards all the sensations of heroes whilst they tolerate every abomination, accept every plunder, and submit to every oppression. Christianity, in making a merit of such submission, has marked only that depth in the abyss at which the very sense of shame is lost. The Christian has been like Dickens' doctor in the debtor's prison [Dr Haggage in *Little Dorrit*], who tells the newcomer of its ineffable peace and security: no duns; no tyrannical collectors of rates, taxes, and rent; no importunate hopes nor exacting duties; nothing but the rest and safety of having no farther to fall.

Yet in the poorest corner of this soul-destroying Christendom vitality suddenly begins to germinate again. Joyousness, a sacred gift long dethroned by the hellish laughter of derision and obscenity, rises like a flood miraculously out of the fetid dust and mud of the slums; rousing marches and impetuous dithyrambs rise to the heavens from people among whom the depressing noise called "sacred music" is a standing joke; a flag with Blood

14. Executions of the Royalists in Paris, carried out from 2 to 6 September 1792.

and Fire on it is unfurled, not in murderous rancor, but because fire is beautiful and blood a vital and splendid red; Fear, which we flatter by calling Self, vanishes; and transfigured men and women carry their gospel through a transfigured world, calling their leader General, themselves captains and brigadiers, and their whole body an Army: praying, but praying only for refreshment, for strength to fight, and for needful MONEY (a notable sign, that) preaching, but not preaching submission; daring ill-usage and abuse, but not putting up with more of it than is inevitable; and practising what the world will let them practise, including soap and water, color and music. There is danger in such activity; and where there is danger there is hope. Our present security is nothing, and can be nothing, but evil made irresistible.

WEAKNESSES OF THE SALVATION ARMY

For the present, however, it is not my business to flatter the Salvation Army. Rather must I point out to it that it has almost as many weaknesses as the Church of England itself. It is building up a business organization which will compel it eventually to see that its present staff of enthusiast-commanders shall be succeeded by a bureaucracy of men of business who will be no better than bishops, and perhaps a good deal more unscrupulous. That has always happened sooner or later to great orders founded by saints; and the order founded by St William Booth is not exempt from the same danger. It is even more dependent than the Church on rich people who would cut off supplies at once if it began to preach that indispensable revolt against poverty which must also be a revolt against riches. It is hampered by a heavy contingent of pious elders who are not really Salvationists at all, but Evangelicals of the old school. It still, as Commissioner Howard affirms,[15] "sticks to Moses," which is flat nonsense at this time of day if the Commissioner means, as I am afraid he does, that the Book of Genesis contains a trustworthy scientific account of the origin of species, and that the god to whom Jephthah sacrificed his daughter is any less obviously a tribal idol than Dagon [Philistine deity] or Chemosh [Moabite deity].

Further, there is still too much other-worldliness about the Army. Like Frederick's grenadier,[16] the Salvationist wants to live for ever (the most

15. Salvation Army commissioner T. Henry Howard became chief of staff of the Army in 1912.
16. 'Ihr Racker', Frederick the Great is reported to have told his guards at Kolin, 18 June 1757, 'wollt ihr ewig leben?' ('Confound you, do you want to live forever?')

monstrous way of crying for the moon); and though it is evident to anyone who has ever heard General Booth and his best officers that they would work as hard for human salvation as they do at present if they believed that death would be the end of them individually, they and their followers have a bad habit of talking as if the Salvationists were heroically enduring a very bad time on earth as an investment which will bring them in dividends later on in the form, not of a better life to come for the whole world, but of an eternity spent by themselves personally in a sort of bliss which would bore any active person to a second death. Surely the truth is that the Salvationists are unusually happy people. And is it not the very diagnostic of true salvation that it shall overcome the fear of death? Now the man who has come to believe that there is no such thing as death, the change so called being merely the transition to an exquisitely happy and utterly careless life, has not overcome the fear of death at all: on the contrary, it has overcome him so completely that he refuses to die on any terms whatever. I do not call a Salvationist really saved until he is ready to lie down cheerfully on the scrap heap, having paid scot and lot and something over, and let his eternal life pass on to renew its youth in the battalions of the future.

Then there is the nasty lying habit called confession, which the Army encourages because it lends itself to dramatic oratory, with plenty of thrilling incident. For my part, when I hear a convert relating the violences and oaths and blasphemies he was guilty of before he was saved, making out that he was a very terrible fellow then and is the most contrite and chastened of Christians now, I believe him no more than I believe the millionaire who says he came up to London or Chicago as a boy with only three halfpence in his pocket. Salvationists have said to me that Barbara in my play would never have been taken in by so transparent a humbug as Snobby Price; and certainly I do not think Snobby could have taken in any experienced Salvationist on a point on which the Salvationist did not wish to be taken in. But on the point of conversion all Salvationists wish to be taken in; for the more obvious the sinner the more obvious the miracle of his conversion. When you advertize a converted burglar or reclaimed drunkard as one of the attractions at an experience meeting, your burglar can hardly have been too burglarious or your drunkard too drunken. As long as such attractions are relied on, you will have your Snobbies claiming to have beaten their mothers when they were as a matter of prosaic fact habitually beaten by them, and your Rummies of the tamest respectability pretending to a past of reckless and dazzling vice. Even when confessions are sincerely autobiographic we should beware of assuming that the impulse to make them was pious or that the interest of the hearers is wholesome. As well might we assume that the poor people who insist on shewing disgusting ulcers to district visitors are convinced hygienists, or that the curiosity which sometimes welcomes such exhibitions is a pleasant and creditable one. One is often tempted to suggest that those who pester our police superintendents with confessions of murder might very wisely be taken at their word and executed, except in the few cases in which a real murderer is seeking to be relieved of his guilt by confession and expiation. For though I am not, I hope, an unmerciful person, I do not think that the inexorability of the deed once done should be disguised by any ritual, whether in the confessional or on the scaffold.

And here my disagreement with the Salvation Army, and with all propagandists of the Cross (which I loathe as I loathe all gibbets) becomes deep indeed. Forgiveness, absolution, atonement, are figments: punishment is only a pretence of cancelling one crime by another; and you can no more have forgiveness without vindictiveness than you can have a cure without a disease. You will never get a high morality from people who conceive that their misdeeds are revocable and pardonable, or in a society where absolution and expiation are officially provided for us all. The demand may be very real; but the supply is spurious. Thus Bill Walker, in my play, having assaulted the Salvation Lass [Jenny Hill], presently finds himself overwhelmed with an intolerable conviction of sin under the skilled treatment of Barbara. Straightway he begins to try to unassault the lass and deruffianize his deed, first by getting punished for it in kind, and, when that relief is denied him, by fining himself a pound to compensate the girl. He is foiled both ways. He finds the Salvation Army as inexorable as fact itself. It will not punish him: it will not take his money. It will not tolerate a redeemed ruffian: it leaves him no means of salvation except ceasing to be a ruffian. In doing this, the Salvation Army instinctively grasps the central truth of Christianity and discards its central superstition: that central truth being the vanity of revenge and punishment, and that central superstition the salvation of the world by the gibbet.

For, be it noted, Bill has assaulted an old and starving woman also; and for this worse offence he feels no remorse whatever, because she makes it clear that her malice is as great as his own. "Let her have the law of me, as she said she would," says Bill: "what I done to her is no more on what you might call my conscience than sticking a pig." This shews a perfectly natural and wholesome state of mind on his part. The old woman, like the law she threatens him with, is perfectly ready to play the game of retaliation with him: to rob him if he steals, to flog him if he strikes, to murder him if he kills. By example and precept the law and public opinion teach him to impose his will on others by anger, violence, and cruelty, and to wipe off the moral score by punishment. That is sound Crosstianity. But this Crosstianity has got entangled with something which Barbara calls Christianity, and which unexpectedly causes her to refuse to play the hangman's game of Satan casting out Satan. She refuses to prosecute a drunken ruffian; she converses on equal terms with a blackguard to whom no lady should be seen speaking in the public street: in short, she imitates Christ. Bill's conscience reacts to this just as naturally as it does to the old woman's threats. He is placed in a position of unbearable moral inferiority, and strives by every means in his power to escape from it, whilst he is still quite ready to meet the abuse of the old woman by attempting to smash a mug on her face. And that is the triumphant justification of Barbara's Christianity as against our system of judicial punishment and the vindictive villain-thrashings and "poetic justice" of the romantic stage.

For the credit of literature it must be pointed out that the situation is only partly novel. Victor Hugo long ago [in *Les Misérables*, 1862] gave us the epic of the convict and the bishop's candlesticks, of the Crosstian policeman annihilated by his encounter with the Christian Valjean. But Bill Walker is not, like Valjean, romantically changed from a demon into an angel. There are millions of Bill Walkers in all classes of society today; and the point which I, as a professor of natural psychology, desire to demonstrate, is that Bill, without any change in his character or circumstances whatsoever, will react one way to one sort of treatment and another way to another.

In proof I might point to the sensational object lesson provided by our commercial millionaires today. They begin as brigands: merciless, unscrupulous, dealing out ruin and death and slavery to their competitors and employees, and facing desperately the worst that their competitors can do to them. The history of the English factories, the American Trusts, the exploitation of African gold, diamonds, ivory and rubber, outdoes in villainy the worst that has ever been imagined of the buccaneers of the Spanish Main. Captain Kidd would have marooned a modern Trust magnate for conduct unworthy of a gentleman of fortune. The law every day seizes on unsuccessful scoundrels of this type and punishes them with a cruelty worse than their own, with the result that they come out of the torture house more dangerous than they went in, and renew their evil doing (nobody will employ them at anything else) until they are again seized, again tormented, and again let loose, with the same result.

But the successful scoundrel is dealt with very differently, and very Christianly. He is not only forgiven: he is idolized, respected, made much of, all but worshipped. Society returns him good for evil in the most extravagant overmeasure. And with what result? He begins to idolize himself, to respect himself, to live up to the treatment he receives. He preaches sermons; he writes books of the most edifying advice to young men, and actually persuades himself that he got on by taking his own advice; he endows educational institutions; he supports charities; he dies finally in the odor of sanctity, leaving a will which is a monument of public spirit and bounty. And all this without any change in his character. The spots of the leopard and the stripes of the tiger are as brilliant as ever; but the conduct of the world towards him has changed; and his conduct has changed accordingly. You have only to reverse your attitude towards him—to lay hands on his property, revile him, assault him, and he will be a brigand again in a moment, as ready to crush you as you are to crush him, and quite as full of pretentious moral reasons for doing it.

In short, when Major Barbara says that there are no scoundrels, she is right: there are no absolute scoundrels, though there are impracticable people of whom I shall treat presently. Every reasonable man (and woman) is a potential scoundrel and a potential good citizen. What a man is depends on his character; but what he does, and what we think of what he does, depends on his circumstances. The characteristics that ruin a man in one class make him eminent in another. The characters that behave differently in different circumstances behave alike in similar circumstances. Take a common English character like that of Bill Walker. We meet Bill everywhere: on the judicial bench, on the episcopal bench, in the Privy Council, at the War Office and Admiralty, as well as in the Old Bailey dock or in the ranks of casual unskilled labor. And the morality of Bill's characteristics varies with these various circumstances. The faults of the burglar are the qualities of the financier: the manners and habits of a duke would cost a city clerk his situation. In short, though character is independent of circumstances, conduct is not; and our moral judgments of character are not: both are circumstantial. Take any condition of life in which the circumstances are for a mass of men practically alike: felony, the House of Lords, the factory, the stables, the gipsy encampment or where you please! In spite of diversity of character and temperament, the conduct and morals of the individuals in each group are as predicable and as alike in the main as if they were a flock of sheep, morals being mostly only social habits and circumstantial necessities. Strong people know this and count upon it. In nothing have the master-minds of the world been distinguished from the ordinary suburban season-ticket holder more than in their straightforward perception of the fact that mankind is practically a single species, and not a menagerie of gentlemen and bounders, villains and heroes, cowards and daredevils, peers and peasants, grocers and aristocrats, artisans and laborers, washerwomen and duchesses, in which all the grades of income and caste represent distinct animals who must not be introduced to one another or intermarry. Napoleon constructing a galaxy of generals and courtiers, and even of monarchs, out of his collection of social nobodies; Julius Cæsar appointing as governor of Egypt the son of a freedman—one who but a short time before would have been legally disqualified for the post even of a private soldier in the Roman army; Louis XI making his barber his privy councillor: all these had in their different ways a firm hold of the scientific fact of human equality, expressed by Barbara in the Christian formula that all men are children of one father. A man who believes that men are naturally divided into upper and lower and middle classes morally is making exactly the same mistake as the man who believes that they are naturally divided in the same way socially. And just as our persistent attempts to found political institutions on a basis of social inequality have always produced long periods of destructive friction relieved from time to time by violent explosions of revolution; so the attempt—will Americans please note—to found moral institutions on a basis of moral inequality can lead to nothing but unnatural Reigns of the Saints relieved by licentious Restorations; to Americans who have made divorce a public institution turning the face of Europe into one huge sardonic smile by refusing to stay in the same hotel with a Russian man of genius [Gorky] who has changed wives without the sanction of South Dakota; to grotesque hypocrisy, cruel persecution, and final utter confusion of conventions and compliances with benevolence and respectability. It is quite useless to declare that all men are born free if you deny that they are born good. Guarantee a man's goodness and his liberty will take care of itself. To guarantee his freedom on condition that you approve of his moral character is formally to abolish all freedom whatsoever, as every man's liberty is at the mercy of a moral indictment which any fool can trump up against everyone who violates custom, whether as a prophet or as a rascal. This is the lesson Democracy has to learn before it can become anything but the most oppressive of all the priesthoods.

Let us now return to Bill Walker and his case of conscience against the Salvation Army. Major Barbara, not being a modern [Johann] Tetzel,[17] or

17. German Dominican monk, vendor of indulgences.

the treasurer of a hospital, refuses to sell absolution to Bill for a sovereign. Unfortunately, what the Army can afford to refuse in the case of Bill Walker, it cannot refuse in the case of Bodger. Bodger is master of the situation because he holds the purse strings. "Strive as you will," says Bodger, in effect: "me you cannot do without. You cannot save Bill Walker without my money." And the Army answers, quite rightly under the circumstances, "We will take money from the devil himself sooner than abandon the work of Salvation." So Bodger pays his conscience-money and gets the absolution that is refused to Bill. In real life Bill would perhaps never know this. But I, the dramatist whose business it is to shew the connexion between things that seem apart and unrelated in the haphazard order of events in real life, have contrived to make it known to Bill, with the result that the Salvation Army loses its hold of him at once.

But Bill may not be lost, for all that. He is still in the grip of the facts and of his own conscience, and may find his taste for blackguardism permanently spoiled. Still, I cannot guarantee that happy ending. Walk through the poorer quarters of our cities on Sunday when the men are not working, but resting and chewing the cud of their reflections. You will find one expression common to every mature face: the expression of cynicism. The discovery made by Bill Walker about the Salvation Army has been made by everyone there. They have found that every man has his price; and they have been foolishly or corruptly taught to mistrust and despise him for that necessary and salutary condition of social existence. When they learn that General Booth, too, has his price, they do not admire him because it is a high one, and admit the need of organizing society so that he shall get it in an honorable way: they conclude that his character is unsound and that all religious men are hypocrites and allies of their sweaters and oppressors. They know that the large subscriptions which help to support the Army are endowments, not of religion, but of the wicked doctrine of docility in poverty and humility under oppression; and they are rent by the most agonizing of all the doubts of the soul, the doubt whether their true salvation must not come from their most abhorrent passions, from murder, envy, greed, stubbornness, rage, and terrorism, rather than from public spirit, reasonableness, humanity, generosity, tenderness, delicacy, pity and kindness. The confirmation of that doubt, at which our newspapers have been working so hard for years past, is the morality of militarism; and the justification of militarism is that circumstances may at any time make it the true morality of the moment. It is by producing such moments that we produce violent and sanguinary revolutions, such as the one now in progress in Russia and the one which Capitalism in England and America is daily and diligently provoking.

At such moments it becomes the duty of the Churches to evoke all the powers of destruction against the existing order. But if they do this, the existing order must forcibly suppress them. Churches are suffered to exist only on condition that they preach submission to the State as at present capitalistically organized. The Church of England itself is compelled to add to the thirtysix articles in which it formulates its religious tenets, three more in which it apologetically protests that the moment any of these articles comes in conflict with the State it is to be entirely renounced, abjured, violated, abrogated and abhorred, the policeman being a much more important person than any of the Persons of the Trinity. And this is why no tolerated Church nor Salvation Army can ever win the entire confidence of the poor. It must be on the side of the police and the military, no matter what it believes or disbelieves; and as the police and the military are the instruments by which the rich rob and oppress the poor (on legal and moral principles made for the purpose), it is not possible to be on the side of the poor and of the police at the same time. Indeed the religious bodies, as the almoners of the rich, become a sort of auxiliary police, taking off the insurrectionary edge of poverty with coals and blankets, bread and treacle, and soothing and cheering the victims with hopes of immense and inexpensive happiness in another world when the process of working them to premature death in the service of the rich is complete in this.

CHRISTIANITY AND ANARCHISM

Such is the false position from which neither the Salvation Army nor the Church of England nor any other religious organization whatever can escape except through a reconstitution of society. Nor can they merely endure the State passively, washing their hands of its sins. The State is constantly forcing the consciences of men by violence and cruelty. Not content with exacting money from us for the maintenance of its soldiers and policemen, its gaolers and executioners, it forces us to take an active personal part in its proceedings on pain of becoming ourselves the victims of its violence. As I write these lines, a sensational example is given to the world. A royal marriage [between King Alphonso XIII of Spain and Princess Victoria of Battenberg] has been celebrated [in Madrid, 31 May 1906], first by sacrament in a cathedral, and then by a bullfight having for its main amusement the spectacle of horses gored and disembowelled by the bull, after which, when the bull is so exhausted as to be no longer dangerous, he is killed by a cautious matador. But the ironic contrast between the bullfight and the sacrament of marriage does not move anyone. Another contrast—that between the splendor, the happiness, the atmosphere of kindly admiration surrounding the young couple, and the price paid for it under our abominable social arrangements in the misery, squalor and degradation of millions of other young couples—is drawn at the same moment by a novelist, Mr Upton Sinclair, who chips a corner of the veneering from the huge meat packing industries of Chicago, and shews it to us as a sample of what is going on all over the world underneath the top layer of prosperous plutocracy. One man is sufficiently moved by that contrast to pay his own life as the price of one terrible blow at the responsible parties. His poverty has left him ignorant enough to be duped by the pretence that the innocent young bride and bridegroom, put forth and crowned by plutocracy as the heads of a State in which they have less personal power than any policeman, and less influence than any Chairman of a Trust, are responsible. At them accordingly he launches his sixpennorth of fulminate, missing his mark, but scattering the bowels of as many horses as any bull in the arena, and slaying twentythree persons, besides wounding ninetynine. And of all these, the horses alone are innocent of the guilt he is avenging: had he blown all Madrid to atoms with every adult person in it, not one could have escaped the charge of being an accessory, before, at, and after the fact, to poverty and prostitution, to such wholesale massacre of infants as Herod never dreamt of, to plague, pestilence and famine, battle, murder and lingering death—perhaps not one who had not helped, through example, precept, connivance, and even clamor, to teach the dynamiter his well-learnt gospel of hatred and vengeance, by approving every day of sentences of years of imprisonment so infernal in their unnatural stupidity and panic-stricken cruelty, that their advocates can disavow neither the dagger nor the bomb without stripping the mask of justice and humanity from themselves also.

Be it noted that at this very moment there appears the biography of one of our dukes [George Campbell, Eighth Duke of Argyll], who, being a Scot, could argue about politics, and therefore stood out as a great brain among our aristocrats. And what, if you please, was his grace's favorite historical episode, which he declared he never read without intense satisfaction? Why, the young General Bonapart's pounding of the Paris mob to pieces in 1795, called in playful approval by our respectable classes "the whiff of grapeshot,"[18]

18. 'Whiff of Grapeshot': the title of the final chapter of Carlyle's *The French Revolution* (1837), in which he describes how Bonaparte with artillery quelled the insurrection against the Convention on 5 October 1795.

though Napoleon, to do him justice, took a deeper view of it, and would fain have had it forgotten. And since the Duke of Argyll was not a demon, but a man of like passions with ourselves, by no means rancorous or cruel as men go, who can doubt that all over the world proletarians of the ducal kidney are now revelling in "the whiff of dynamite" (the flavor of the joke seems to evaporate a little, does it not?) because it was aimed at the class they hate even as our argute duke hated what he called the mob.

In such an atmosphere there can be only one sequel to the Madrid explosion. All Europe burns to emulate it. Vengeance! More blood! Tear "the Anarchist beast" to shreds. Drag him to the scaffold. Imprison him for life. Let all civilized States band together to drive his like off the face of the earth; and if any State refuses to join, make war on it. This time the leading London newspaper, anti-Liberal and therefore anti-Russian in politics, does not say "Serve you right" to the victims, as it did, in effect, when Bobrikoff, and Plehve, and Grand Duke Sergius, were in the same manner unofficially fulminated into fragments.[19] No: fulminate our rivals in Asia by all means, ye brave Russian revolutionaries; but to aim at an English princess! monstrous! hideous! hound down the wretch to his doom; and observe, please, that we are a civilized and merciful people, and, however much we may regret it, must not treat him as Ravaillac and Damiens were treated.[20] And meanwhile, since we have not yet caught him, let us soothe our quivering nerves with the bullfight, and comment in a courtly way on the unfailing tact and good taste of the ladies of our royal houses, who, though presumably of full normal natural tenderness, have been so effectually broken in to fashionable routine that they can be taken to see the horses slaughtered as helplessly as they could no doubt be taken to a gladiator show, if that happened to be the mode just now.

Strangely enough, in the midst of this raging fire of malice, the one man who still has faith in the kindness and intelligence of human nature is the fulminator, now a hunted wretch, with nothing, apparently, to secure his triumph over all the prisons and scaffolds of infuriate Europe except the

---

19. Nicolai I. Bobrikov, Russian general and Governor-General of Finland 1898–1904. Viatcheslof K. Plehve, Russian Minister of the Interior, assassinated on 28 July 1904. Grand Duke Sergius was assassinated in Moscow on 17 February 1905.
20. François Ravaillac assassinated Henry IV of France in 1610. In the course of his trial he was frequently put to torture and then eventually executed on 27 May 1610. Robert Damiens, a Frenchman who attained notoriety by attacking and slightly wounding Louis XV of France, was sentenced to be torn to pieces by horses after torture.

revolver in his pocket and his readiness to discharge it at a moment's notice into his own or any other head. Think of him setting out to find a gentleman and a Christian in the multitude of human wolves howling for his blood. Think also of this: that at the very first essay he finds what he seeks, a veritable grandee of Spain, a noble, high-thinking, unterrified, malice-void soul, in the guise—of all masquerades in the world!—of a modern editor.[21] The Anarchist wolf, flying from the wolves of plutocracy, throws himself on the honor of the man. The man, not being a wolf (nor a London editor), and therefore not having enough sympathy with his exploit to be made bloodthirsty by it, does not throw him back to the pursuing wolves—gives him, instead, what help he can to escape, and sends him off acquainted at last with a force that goes deeper than dynamite, though you cannot buy so much of it for sixpence. That righteous and honorable high human deed is not wasted on Europe, let us hope, though it benefits the fugitive wolf only for a moment. The plutocratic wolves presently smell him out. The fugitive shoots the unlucky wolf whose nose is nearest; shoots himself; and then convinces the world, by his photograph, that he was no monstrous freak of reversion to the tiger, but a good looking young man with nothing abnormal about him except his appalling courage and resolution (that is why the terrified shriek Coward at him): one to whom murdering a happy young couple on their wedding morning would have been an unthinkably unnatural abomination under rational and kindly human circumstances.

Then comes the climax of irony and blind stupidity. The wolves, balked of their meal of fellow-wolf, turn on the man, and proceed to torture him, after their manner, by imprisonment, for refusing to fasten his teeth in the throat of the dynamiter and hold him down until they came to finish him.

Thus, you see, a man may not be a gentleman nowadays even if he wishes to. As to being a Christian, he is allowed some latitude in that matter, because, I repeat, Christianity has two faces. Popular Christianity has for its emblem a gibbet, for its chief sensation a sanguinary execution after torture, for its central mystery an insane vengeance bought off by a trumpery expiation. But there is a nobler and profounder Christianity which affirms the sacred mystery of Equality, and forbids the glaring futility and folly of vengeance, often politely called punishment or justice. The gibbet part of Christianity is tolerated. The other is criminal felony. Connoisseurs in irony are well aware of the fact that the only editor in

21. José Nákens, editor of the radical paper *El Motin* and member of the Republican Party, gave aid to the would-be assassin, Mateo Morral.

England [G. W. Foote] who denounces punishment as radically wrong, also repudiates Christianity; calls his paper The Freethinker; and has been imprisoned for "bad taste" under the law against blasphemy.

SANE CONCLUSIONS

And now I must ask the excited reader not to lose his head on one side or the other, but to draw a sane moral from these grim absurdities. It is not good sense to propose that laws against crime should apply to principals only and not to accessories whose consent, counsel, or silence may secure impunity to the principal. If you institute punishment as part of the law, you must punish people for refusing to punish. If you have a police, part of its duty must be to compel everybody to assist the police. No doubt if your laws are unjust, and your policemen agents of oppression, the result will be an unbearable violation of the private consciences of citizens. But that cannot be helped: the remedy is, not to license everybody to thwart the law if they please, but to make laws that will command the public assent, and not to deal cruelly and stupidly with lawbreakers. Everybody disapproves of burglars; but the modern burglar, when caught and overpowered by a householder, usually appeals, and often, let us hope, with success, to his captor not to deliver him over to the useless horrors of penal servitude. In other cases the lawbreaker escapes because those who could give him up do not consider his breach of the law a guilty action. Sometimes, even, private tribunals are formed in opposition to the official tribunals; and these private tribunals employ assassins as executioners, as was done, for example, by Mahomet[22] before he had established his power officially, and by the Ribbon lodges of Ireland in their long struggle with the landlords.[23] Under such circumstances, the assassin goes free although everybody in the district knows who he is and what he has done. They do not betray him, partly because they justify him exactly as the regular Government justifies its official executioner, and partly because they would themselves be assassinated if they betrayed him: another method learnt from the official government. Given a tribunal, employing a slayer who has no personal

22. A series of assassinations of foes of the Prophet, by his expressed authority, were committed by his followers between AD 624 and 628. See Sir William Muir, *The Life of Mohammad* (1923).
23. Ribbon Lodge, or Ribbon Society, was a Roman Catholic secret league formed in the north and north-west of Ireland early in the nineteenth century to counteract the Protestant influence. It is associated with agrarian disorders.

quarrel with the slain; and there is clearly no moral difference between official and unofficial killing.

In short, all men are anarchists with regard to laws which are against their consciences, either in the preamble or in the penalty. In London our worst anarchists are the magistrates, because many of them are so old and ignorant that when they are called upon to administer any law that is based on ideas or knowledge less than half a century old, they disagree with it, and being mere ordinary homebred private Englishmen without any respect for law in the abstract, naïvely set the example of violating it. In this instance the man lags behind the law; but when the law lags behind the man, he becomes equally an anarchist. When some huge change in social conditions, such as the industrial revolution of the XVIII and XIX centuries, throws our legal and industrial institutions out of date, Anarchism becomes almost a religion. The whole force of the most energetic geniuses of the time in philosophy, economics, and art, concentrates itself on demonstrations and reminders that morality and law are only conventions, fallible and continually obsolescing. Tragedies in which the heroes are bandits, and comedies in which law-abiding and conventionally moral folk are compelled to satirize themselves by outraging the conscience of the spectators every time they do their duty, appear simultaneously with economic treatises entitled "What is Property? Theft!" and with histories of "The Conflict between Religion and Science."

Now this is not a healthy state of things. The advantages of living in society are proportionate, not to the freedom of the individual from a code, but to the complexity and subtlety of the code he is prepared not only to accept but to uphold as a matter of such vital importance that a lawbreaker at large is hardly to be tolerated on any plea. Such an attitude becomes impossible when the only men who can make themselves heard and remembered throughout the world spend all their energy in raising our gorge against current law, current morality, current respectability, and legal property. The ordinary man, uneducated in social theory even when he is schooled in Latin verse, cannot be set against all the laws of his country and yet persuaded to regard law in the abstract as vitally necessary to society. Once he is brought to repudiate the laws and institutions he knows, he will repudiate the very conception of law and the very groundwork of institutions, ridiculing human rights, extolling brainless methods as "historical," and tolerating nothing except pure empiricism in conduct, with dynamite as the basis of politics and vivisection as the basis of science. That is hideous; but what is to be done? Here am I, for instance, by class a respectable man, by common sense a hater of waste and disorder, by intellectual constitution legally minded to the verge of pedantry, and by temperament apprehensive and economically disposed to the limit of old-maidishness; yet I am, and have always been, and shall now always be, a revolutionary writer, because our laws make law impossible; our liberties destroy all freedom; our property is organized robbery; our morality is an impudent hypocrisy; our wisdom is administered by inexperienced or malexperienced dupes, our power wielded by cowards and weaklings, and our honor false in all its points. I am an enemy of the existing order for good reasons; but that does not make my attacks any less encouraging or helpful to people who are its enemies for bad reasons. The existing order may shriek that if I tell the truth about it, some foolish person may drive it to become still worse by trying to assassinate it. I cannot help that, even if I could see what worse it could do than it is already doing. And the disadvantage of that worst even from its own point of view is that society, with all its prisons and bayonets and whips and ostracisms and starvations, is powerless in the face of the Anarchist who is prepared to sacrifice his own life in the battle with it. Our natural safety from the cheap and devastating explosives which every Russian student can make, and every Russian grenadier has learnt to handle in Manchuria [in the Russo-Japanese War, 1904–5], lies in the fact that brave and resolute men, when they are rascals, will not risk their skins for the good of humanity, and, when they are not, are sympathetic enough to care for humanity, abhorring murder, and never committing it until their consciences are outraged beyond endurance. The remedy is, then, simply not to outrage their consciences.

Do not be afraid that they will not make allowances. All men make very large allowances indeed before they stake their own lives in a war to the death with society. Nobody demands or expects the millennium. But there are two things that must be set right, or we shall perish, like Rome, of soul atrophy disguised as empire.

The first is, that the daily ceremony of dividing the wealth of the country among its inhabitants shall be so conducted that no crumb shall, save as a criminal's ration, go to any able-bodied adults who are not producing by their personal exertions not only a full equivalent for what they take, but a surplus sufficient to provide for their superannuation and pay back the debt due for their nurture.

The second is that the deliberate infliction of malicious injuries which now goes on under the name of punishment be abandoned; so that the thief, the ruffian, the gambler, and the beggar, may without inhumanity be handed over to the law, and made to understand that a State which is too humane to punish will also be too thrifty to waste the life of honest men in watching or restraining dishonest ones. That is why we do not imprison dogs. We even take our chance of their first bite. But if a dog delights to bark and bite, it goes to the lethal chamber. That seems to me sensible. To allow the dog to expiate his bite by a period of torment, and then let him loose in a much more savage condition (for the chain makes a dog savage) to bite again and expiate again, having meanwhile spent a great deal of human life and happiness in the task of chaining and feeding and tormenting him, seems to me idiotic and superstitious. Yet that is what we do to men who bark and bite and steal. It would be far more sensible to put up with their vices, as we put up with their illnesses, until they give more trouble than they are worth, at which point we should, with many apologies and expressions of sympathy, and some generosity in complying with their last wishes, place them in the lethal chamber and get rid of them. Under no circumstances should they be allowed to expiate their misdeeds by a manufactured penalty, to subscribe to a charity, or to compensate the victims. If there is to be no punishment there can be no forgiveness. We shall never have real moral responsibility until everyone knows that his deeds are irrevocable, and that his life depends on his usefulness. Hitherto, alas! humanity has never dared face these hard facts. We frantically scatter conscience money and invent systems of conscience banking, with expiatory penalties, atonements, redemptions, salvations, hospital subscription lists and what not, to enable us to contract-out of the moral code. Not content with the old scapegoat and sacrificial lamb, we deify human saviors, and pray to miraculous virgin intercessors. We attribute mercy to the inexorable; soothe our consciences after committing murder by throwing ourselves on the bosom of divine love; and shrink even from our own gallows because we are forced to admit that it, at least, is irrevocable—as if one hour of imprisonment were not as irrevocable as any execution!

If a man cannot look evil in the face without illusion, he will never know what it really is, or combat it effectually. The few men who have been able (relatively) to do this have been called cynics, and have sometimes had an abnormal share of evil in themselves, corresponding to the abnormal strength of their minds; but they have never done mischief unless they intended to do it. That is why great scoundrels have been beneficent rulers whilst amiable and privately harmless monarchs have ruined their countries by trusting to the hocus-pocus of innocence and guilt, reward and punishment, virtuous indignation and pardon, instead of standing up to the facts without either malice or mercy. Major Barbara stands up to Bill Walker in that way, with the result that the ruffian who cannot get hated, has to hate himself. To relieve this agony he tries to get punished; but the Salvationist whom he tries to provoke is as merciless as Barbara, and only prays for him. Then he tries to pay, but can get nobody to take his money. His doom is the doom of Cain, who, failing to find either a savior, a policeman, or an almoner to help him to pretend that his brother's blood no longer cried from the ground, had to live and die a murderer. Cain took care not to commit another murder, unlike our railway shareholders (I am one) who kill and maim shunters by hundreds to save the cost of automatic couplings, and make atonement by annual subscriptions to deserving charities. Had Cain been allowed to pay off his score, he might possibly have killed Adam and Eve for the mere sake of a second luxurious reconciliation with God afterwards. Bodger, you may depend on it, will go on to the end of his life poisoning people with bad whisky, because he can always depend on the Salvation Army or the Church of England to negotiate a redemption for him in consideration of a trifling percentage of his profits.

There is a third condition too, which must be fulfilled before the great teachers of the world will cease to scoff at its religions. Creeds must become intellectually honest. At present there is not a single credible established religion in the world. That is perhaps the most stupendous fact in the whole world-situation. This play of mine, Major Barbara, is, I hope, both true and inspired; but whoever says that it all happened, and that faith in it and understanding of it consist in believing that it is a record of an actual occurrence, is, to speak according to Scripture, a fool and a liar, and is hereby solemnly denounced and cursed as such by me, the author, to all posterity.

LONDON.
June, 1906.

The Perfect Wagnerite

Preface to the first German edition, Ein Wagner Brevier,
tr. Siegfried Trebitsch, 1907; published in English by Brentano's,
New York, 1909

In reading through this German version of my book in the manuscript of my friend Siegfried Trebitsch,[1] I was struck by the inadequacy of the merely negative explanation given by me of the irrelevance of Night Falls on The Gods to the general philosophic scheme of The Ring. That explanation is correct as far as it goes; but, put as I put it, it now seems to me to suggest that the operatic character of Night Falls on The Gods was the result of indifference or forgetfulness produced by the lapse of twentyfive years between the first projection of the work and its completion. Now it is clear that in whatever other ways Wagner may have changed, he never became careless and he never became indifferent. I have therefore inserted a new section in which I shew how the revolutionary history of Western Europe from the Liberal explosion of 1848 to the confused attempt at a socialist, military, and municipal administration in Paris in 1871 (that is to say, from the beginning of The Niblung's Ring by Wagner to the long-delayed completion of Night Falls on The Gods), demonstrated practically that the passing away of the present order was going to be a much more complicated business than it appears in Wagner's Siegfried. I have therefore interpolated a new chapter[2] which will perhaps induce some readers of the original English text to read the book again in German.

For some time to come, indeed, I shall have to refer English readers to this German edition as the most complete in existence.

My obligation to Herr Trebitsch for making me a living German author instead of merely a translated English one is so great that I am bound to point out that he is not responsible for my views or Wagner's, and that it is as an artist and a man of letters, and not as a propagandist, that he is

---

1. Austrian writer and journalist who became Shaw's Central European interpreter and authorized German translator.
2. *'Warum Wagner seinen sinn Geändert hat'* ('Why He Changed His Mind').

conveying to the German speaking peoples political criticisms which occasionally reflect on contemporary authorities with a European reputation for sensitiveness. And as the very sympathy which makes his translations so excellent may be regarded with suspicion, let me hasten to declare I am bound to Germany by the ties that hold my nature most strongly. Not that I like the average German: nobody does, even in his own country. But then the average man is not popular anywhere; and as no German considers himself an average one, each reader will, as an exceptional man, sympathize with my dislike of the common herd. And if I cannot love the typical modern German, I can at least pity and understand him. His worst fault is that he cannot see that it is possible to have too much of a good thing. Being convinced that duty, industry, education, loyalty, patriotism and respectability are good things (and I am magnanimous enough to admit that they are not altogether bad things when taken in strict moderation at the right time and in the right place), he indulges in them on all occasions shamelessly and excessively. He commits hideous crimes when crime is presented to him as part of his duty; his craze for work is more ruinous than the craze for drink; when he can afford secondary education for his sons you find three out of every five of them with their minds lamed for life by examinations which only a thoroughly wooden head could go through with impunity; and if a king is patriotic and respectable (few kings are) he puts up statues to him and exalts him above Charlemagne and Henry the Fowler [King Henry I of Germany, called 'Der Vogel-Fanger']. And when he meets a man of genius, he instinctively insults him, starves him, and, if possible, imprisons and kills him.

Now I do not pretend to be perfect myself. Heaven knows I have to struggle hard enough every day with what the Germans call my higher impulses. I know too well the temptation to be moral, to be self-sacrificing, to be loyal and patriotic, to be respectable and well-spoken of. But I wrestle with it and—as far as human frailty will allow—conquer it, whereas the German abandons himself to it without scruple or reflection, and is actually proud of his pious intemperance and self-indulgence. Nothing will cure him of this mania. It may end in starvation, crushing taxation, suppression of all freedom to try new social experiments and reform obsolete institutions, in snobbery, jobbery, idolatry, and an omnipresent tyranny in which his doctor and his schoolmaster, his lawyer and his priest, coerce him worse than any official or drill sergeant: no matter: it is respectable, says the German, therefore it must be good, and cannot be carried too far; and everybody who rebels against it must be a rascal. Even the Social-Democrats in Germany differ from the rest only in carrying academic orthodoxy

beyond human endurance—beyond even German endurance. I am a Socialist and a Democrat myself, the hero of a hundred platforms, one of the
leaders of the most notable Socialist organizations in England. I am as
conspicuous in English Socialism as [August] Bebel is in German Socialism;
but do you suppose that the German Social-Democrats tolerate me? Not a
bit of it. I have begged again and again to be taken to the bosom of my
German comrades. I have pleaded that the Super-Proletarians of all lands
should unite. I have pointed out that the German Social-Democratic party
has done nothing at its Congresses for the last ten years except the things I
told them to do ten years before, and that its path is white with the bones
of the Socialist superstitions I and my fellow Fabians have slain. Useless.
They do not care a rap whether I am a Socialist or not. All they want to
know is: Am I orthodox? Am I correct in my revolutionary views? Am I
reverent to the revolutionary authorities? Because I am a genuine freethinker they look at me as a policeman looks at a midnight prowler or as a
Berlin bourgeois looks at a suspicious foreigner. They ask "Do you believe
that Marx was omniscient and infallible; that Engels was his prophet; that
Bebel and [Paul] Singer [leaders of the German Social-Democratic Party]
are his inspired apostles; and that Das Kapital is the Bible?" Hastening in
my innocence to clear myself of what I regard as an accusation of credulity
and ignorance, I assure them earnestly that I know ten times as much of
economics and a hundred times as much of practical administration as
Marx did; that I knew Engels personally and rather liked him as a witty
and amiable old 1848 veteran who despised modern Socialism; that I regard
Bebel and Singer as men of like passions with myself, but considerably less
advanced; and that I read Das Kapital in the year 1882 or thereabouts, and
still consider it one of the most important books of the XIX century
because of its power of changing the minds of those who read it, in spite of
its unsound capitalist economics, its parade of quotations from books which
the author had either not read or not understood, its affectation of algebraic
formulas, and its general attempt to disguise a masterpiece of propagandist
journalism and prophetic invective as a drily scientific treatise of the sort
that used to impose on people in 1860, when any book that pretended to
be scientific was accepted as a Bible. In those days Darwin and Helmholtz
were the real fathers of the Church; and nobody would listen to religion,
poetry or rhetoric; so that even Socialism had to call itself "scientific," and
predict the date of the revolution, as if it were a comet, by calculations
founded on "historic laws."

To my amazement these reasonable remarks were received as hideous
blasphemies; none of the party papers were allowed to print any word of

mine; the very Revisionists themselves found that the scandal of my heresy damaged them more than my support aided them; and I found myself an outcast from German Social-Democracy at the moment when, thanks to Trebitsch, the German bourgeoisie and nobility began to smile on me, seduced by the pleasure of playing with fire, and perhaps by Agnes Sorma's acting as Candida [Berlin, 1904].

Thus you may see that when a German, by becoming a Social-Democrat, throws off all the bonds of convention, and stands free from all allegiance to established religion, law, order, patriotism, and learning, he promptly uses his freedom to put on a heavier set of chains; expels anti-militarists with the bloodthirstiest martial anti-foreign ardor; and gives the Kaiser reason to thank heaven that he was born in the comparative freedom and Laodicean tolerance of Kingship, and not in the Calvinistic bigotry and pedantry of Marxism.

Why, then, you may ask, do I say that I am bound to Germany by the ties that hold my nature most strongly? Very simply because I should have perished of despair in my youth but for the world created for me by that great German dynasty which began with Bach and will perhaps not end with Richard Strauss. Do not suppose for a moment that I learnt my art from English men of letters. True, they shewed me how to handle English words; but if I had known no more than that, my works would never have crossed the Channel. My masters were the masters of a universal language: they were, to go from summit to summit, Bach, Handel, Haydn, Mozart, Beethoven and Wagner. Had the Germans understood any of these men, they would have hanged them. Fortunately they did not understand them, and therefore only neglected them until they were dead, after which they learnt to dance to their tunes with an easy conscience. For their sakes Germany stands consecrated as the Holy Land of the capitalist age, just as Italy, for its painters' sakes, is the Holy Land of the early unvulgarized Renascence; France, for its builders' sakes, of the age of Christian chivalry and faith; and Greece, for its sculptors' sakes, of the Periclean age.

These Holy Lands are my fatherlands: in them alone am I truly at home: all my work is but to bring the whole world under this sanctification.

And so, O worthy, respectable, dutiful, patriotic, brave, industrious German reader, you who used to fear only God and your own conscience, and now fear nothing at all, here is my book for you; and—in all sincerity—much good may it do you!

LONDON.
23 October 1907.

The Impossibilities of Anarchism

First published as Fabian Tract No. 45, in 1893. Reprinted, with revisions and an added Foreword, in a volume, Socialism and Individualism, *published by the Fabian Society (Fabian Socialist Series, No. 3), 1908*

———

The following essay was read to a meeting of the Fabian Society on the 16th October 1891. It has circulated ever since as a Fabian Tract, and is reprinted here without any substantial modification of the argument. I have added, perhaps, a dozen sentences, and omitted a dozen more, referring to events which have lost their interest or been forgotten: otherwise it stands as it did. I had hoped to be able to claim that my essay had done its work as far as organized Socialism is concerned, because since 1891 Socialism all over Europe has become definitely constitutional and parliamentary, and is no longer confused with Anarchism by ordinarily well-informed and reasonably honest political journalists. But now that the middle classes are crowding into the Socialist movement, I find that another dose of the antidote to Anarchism is badly needed. The errors of Anarchism are thoroughly popular errors: the middle classes, little as they suspect it and indignantly as they would repudiate it, are saturated with these errors, which they call Individualism, Protestantism, French Revolution principles, and so forth. To them I recommend this reprint.

The word Social-Democrat is used in these pages in its proper sense, to denote a Socialist who is also a Democrat. In England it has come to be used in a narrower sense, to denote doctrinaire Marxism and the characteristic propaganda of the Social-Democratic Federation. Whilst this transient misunderstanding lasts, my readers will have to allow for it by remembering that all Socialists who postulate democracy as the political basis of Socialism, including, of course, the members of the Fabian Society, are entitled to describe themselves as Social-Democrats.

AYOT ST LAWRENCE.
26 December 1907.   G. BERNARD SHAW

The Sanity of Art

*Preface to a revised version (1908) of 'A Degenerate's View of Nordau',
first published in* Liberty, *New York, 1895*

═══════

The re-publication of this open letter to Mr Benjamin Tucker[1] places me,
not for the first time, in the difficulty of the journalist whose work survives
the day on which it was written. What the journalist writes about is what
everybody is thinking about (or ought to be thinking about) at the moment
of writing. To revive his utterances when everybody is thinking about
something else; when the tide of public thought and imagination has
turned; when the front of the stage is filled with new actors; when many
lusty crowers have either survived their vogue or perished with it; when
the little men you patronized have become great, and the great men you
attacked have been sanctified and pardoned by popular sentiment in the
tomb: all these inevitables test the quality of your journalism very severely.
Nevertheless, journalism can claim to be the highest form of literature; for
all the highest literature is journalism. The writer who aims at producing
the platitudes which are "not for an age, but for all time"[2] has his reward
in being unreadable in all ages; whilst Plato and Aristophanes trying to
knock some sense into the Athens of their day, Shakespear peopling that
same Athens with Elizabethan mechanics and Warwickshire hunts, Ibsen
photographing the local doctors and vestrymen of a Norwegian parish,
Carpaccio painting the life of St Ursula exactly as if she were a lady living
in the next street to him, are still alive and at home everywhere among the
dust and ashes of many thousands of academic, punctilious, most archæologic-
ally correct men of letters and art who spent their lives haughtily avoiding
the journalist's vulgar obsession with the ephemeral. I also am a journalist,
proud of it, deliberately cutting out of my works all that is not journalism,
convinced that nothing that is not journalism will live long as literature, or
be of any use whilst it does live. I deal with all periods; but I never study
any period but the present, which I have not yet mastered and never shall;

1. American socialist-anarchist editor and publisher.
2. Ben Jonson, 'To the Memory of Shakespeare' (1623): 'not of an age, but for all
time'.

and as a dramatist I have no clue to any historical or other personage save that part of him which is also myself, and which may be nine tenths of him or ninety-nine hundredths, as the case may be (if, indeed, I do not transcend the creature), but which, anyhow, is all that can ever come within my knowledge of his soul. The man who writes about himself and his own time is the only man who writes about all people and about all time. The other sort of man, who believes that he and his period are so distinct from all other men and periods that it would be immodest and irrelevant to allude to them or assume that they could illustrate anything but his own private circumstances, is the most infatuated of all the egotists, and consequently the most unreadable and negligible of all the authors. And so, let others cultivate what they call literature: journalism for me!

The following remnant of the journalism of 1895 will, I hope, bear out these preliminary remarks, which are none the less valid because they are dragged in here to dismount the critics who ride the high horse of Letters at me. It was undertaken under the following circumstances. In 1893 Doctor Max Nordau,[3] one of those remarkable cosmopolitan Jews who go forth against modern civilization as David went against the Philistines or Charles Martel[4] against the Saracens, smiting it hip and thigh without any sense of common humanity with it, trumped up an indictment of its men of genius as depraved lunatics, and pled it (in German) before the bar of Europe under the title Entartung. It was soon translated for England and America as Degeneration. Like all rigorous and thorough-going sallies of special pleading, it had its value; for the way to get at the merits of a case is not to listen to the fool who imagines himself impartial, but to get it argued with reckless bias for and against. To understand a saint, you must hear the devil's advocate; and the same is true of the artist. Nordau had briefed himself as devil's advocate against the great artistic reputations of the XIX century; and he did his duty as well as it could be done at the price, incidentally saying many more true and important things than most of the counsel on the other side were capable of.

Indeed counsel on the other side mostly threw up their briefs in consternation, and began to protest that they entirely agreed with Dr Nordau, and that though they had perhaps dallied a little with Rossetti, Wagner, Ibsen, Tolstoy, Nietzsche, and the rest of the degenerates before their true

3. German-Jewish author and social critic. His *Entartung* (1892–3) appeared in English translation in 1895.
4. Frankish ruler, grandfather of Charlemagne, who overthrew the Saracens at Tours in AD 732.

character had been exposed, yet they had never really approved of them. Even those who stood to their guns had not sufficient variety of culture to contradict the cosmopolitan doctor on more than one or two points, being often not champions of Art at large, but merely jealous fanciers of some particular artist. Thus the Wagnerians were ready to give up Ibsen; the Ibsenites were equally suspicious of Wagner; the Tolstoyans gave up both; the Nietzscheans were only too glad to see Tolstoy catching it; and the connoisseurs of Impressionism in painting, though fairly impartial in music and literature, could not handle the technics of the case for the defence. Yet Dr Nordau knew so little, and his technical handling of painting and music was so like Captain Lemuel Gulliver's nautical observations, that I, being familiar with all the arts, and as accustomed as any Jew to the revolutionary cosmopolitan climate, looked on at his triumph much as Napoleon looked on at the massacre of the Swiss, thinking how easy it would be to change the rout into the cheapest of victories.[5] However, none of our silly editors had the gumption to offer me the command; so, like Napoleon, I went home and left them to be cut to pieces.

But Destiny will not allow her offers to be completely overlooked. In the Easter of 1895, when Nordau was master of the field, and the newspaper champions of modern Literature and Art were on their knees before him, weeping and protesting their innocence, I was staying in the wooden hotel on Beachy Head, with a select party of Fabians, politicians, and philosophers, diligently trying to ride a bicycle for the first time in my life. My efforts set the coastguards laughing as no audience had ever laughed at my plays. I made myself ridiculous with such success that I felt quite ready to laugh at somebody else. Just then there arrived a proposal from Mr Benjamin Tucker, philosophic Anarchist, and Editor of an American paper called Liberty, which, as it was written valiantly up to its title, was having a desperate struggle for existence in a country where every citizen is free to suppress liberty, and usually does so in such moments as he cares to spare from the pursuit of money. Mr Tucker, seeing that nobody had answered Dr Nordau, and perceiving with the penetration of an unterrified commonsense that a doctor who had written manifest nonsense must be answerable technically by anybody who could handle his weapons, was of opinion

5. 'There is but one step between triumph and failure. I have noticed, in the most important events, that a mere nothing may turn the scale.' (Letter of Napoleon I, 7 October 1797: Arthur Levy, *The Private Life of Napoleon*, 1894: Vol. II, p. 386.) The battle of Rivoli, in which the Swiss were decimated, occurred early in 1797.

that I was the man to do it. Accordingly, said Mr Tucker, I invite you, Shaw, to ascertain the highest price that has ever been paid to any man, even to Gladstone, for a magazine article; and I will pay you that price for a review of Degeneration in the columns of Liberty.

This was really great editing. Mr Tucker got his review, as he deserved, and sent a copy of the number of Liberty containing it (now a collector's treasure), to every paper in the United States. There was a brisk and quick sale of copies in London among the cognoscenti. And Degeneration was never heard of again. It is open to the envious to contend that this was a mere coincidence—that the Degeneration boom was exhausted at that moment; but I naturally prefer to believe that Mr Tucker and I slew it. I may add that the slaughter incidentally ruined Mr Tucker, as a circulation among cognoscenti does not repay the cost of a free distribution to the Philistines; but Mr Tucker was always ruining himself for Liberty and always retrieving the situation by his business ability. I saw him this year in London, as prosperous looking a man as I could desire to dine with, thirsting for fresh struggles with the courts and public departments of the United States.

It may now be asked why, if the work of my essay be done, I need revive it after twelve years of peaceful burial. I should answer: partly because Mr Tucker wishes to reproduce his editorial success in a more permanent form, and is strongly seconded by Messrs Holbrook Jackson and A. R. Orage in England, who have piously preserved a copy of Liberty and desire to make it the beginning of their series of pamphlets in connection with their paper The New Age, and their pet organization The Arts Group of the Fabian Society;[6] partly because on looking through it myself again, I find that as far as it goes it is still readable and likely to be helpful to those who are confused by the eternal strife between the artist-philosophers and the Philistines.

I have left the essay substantially as it first appeared, the main alteration being an expansion of the section dealing with the importance of that mass of law which lies completely outside morals and religion, and is really pure convention: the point being, not that the course prescribed by such law is ethically right, or indeed better in any sense than its direct opposite (as in

6. A. R. Orage and Holbrook Jackson hoped to stimulate Fabian interest in the arts through their group, their journal, and their publishing house The New Age Press, which published the English edition of *The Sanity of Art*. Tucker's American edition was issued the same year.

the rule of the road, for example), but that it is absolutely necessary for economy and smoothness of social action that everybody should do the same thing and be able to count on everybody else doing it. I have appropriated this from Mr Aylmer Maude's[7] criticism of Tolstoyan Anarchism, on which I am unable to improve.

I have also, with the squeamishness of advancing years, softened one or two expressions which now shock me as uncivil to Dr Nordau. In doing so I am not offering him the insult of an attempt to spare his feelings: I am simply trying to mend my own manners.

Finally, let me say that though I think this essay of mine did dispose of Dr Nordau's special pleadings, neither the pleadings nor the criticism dispose of the main question as to how far genius is a morbid symptom. I should rather like Dr Nordau to try again; for I do not see how any observant student of genius from the life can deny that the Arts have their criminals and lunatics as well as their sane and honest men (they are more or less the same men too, just as our ordinary criminals are in the dock by the accident of a single transaction and not by a difference in nature between them and the judge and jury), and that the gratuitous delusion that the great poet and artist can do no wrong is much more mischievous than the necessary convention that the King can do no wrong and that the Pope is infallible.

In my play called The Doctor's Dilemma I have recognized this by dramatizing a rascally genius, with the disquieting result that several highly intelligent and sensitive persons have passionately defended him, on the ground, apparently, that high artistic faculty and an ardent artistic imagination entitle a man to be recklessly dishonest about money and recklessly selfish about women, just as kingship in an African tribe entitles a man to kill whom he pleases on the most trifling provocation. I know no harder practical question than how much selfishness one ought to stand from a gifted person for the sake of his gifts or on the chance of his being right in the long run. The Superman will certainly come like a thief in the night, and be shot at accordingly; but we cannot leave our property wholly undefended on that account. On the other hand, we cannot ask the Superman simply to add a higher set of virtues to current respectable morals; for

7. Member of the Fabian Executive Committee 1907–12, translator of Tolstoy, and author of *The Life of Tolstoy* (1908–10).

he is undoubtedly going to empty a good deal of respectable morality out like so much dirty water, and replace it by new and strange customs, shedding old obligations and accepting new and heavier ones. Every step of his progress must horrify conventional people; and if it were possible for even the most superior man to march ahead all the time, every pioneer of the march towards the Superman would be crucified. Fortunately what actually happens is that your geniuses are for the most part keeping step and marking time with the rest, an occasional stumble forward being the utmost they can accomplish, often visibly against their own notions of propriety. The greatest possible difference in conduct between a genius and his contemporaries is so small that it is always difficult to persuade the people who are in daily contact with the gifted one that he is anybody in particular: all the instances to the contrary (Gorki scandalizing New York,[8] for example) being cases in which the genius is in conflict, not with contemporary feeling in his own class, but with some institution which is far behind the times, like the institution of marriage in Russia (to put it no nearer home). In really contemporary situations, your genius is ever 1 part genius and 99 parts Tory.

Still, especially when we turn from conduct to the expression of opinion—from what the man of genius dares do to what he dares advocate—it is necessary for the welfare of society that genius should be privileged to utter sedition, to blaspheme, to outrage good taste, to corrupt the youthful mind, and, generally, to scandalize one's uncles. But such license is accordable only on the assumption that men of genius are saner, sounder, farther sighted and deeper fathoming than the uncles; and it is idle to demand unlimited toleration of apparently outrageous conduct on the plea that the offender is a genius, even if by the abnormal development of some specific talent he may be highly skilled as an artist. Andrea del Sarto was a better draughtsman and fresco painter than Raphael; but he was a swindler all the same; and no honorable artist would plead on his behalf that misappropriating trust money is one of the superiorities of that very loosely defined diathesis [disease-prone condition] which we call the artistic temperament. If Dr Nordau would make a serious attempt to shew us exactly where we are in this matter by ascertaining the real stigmata of genius; so that we may know whom to crucify, and whom to put above the law, he would place the civilization he attacks under an obligation

8. The United States government had attempted to bar Maxim Gorky's entrance in 1905 because he and his wife were not legally married. See also p. 267.

which would wipe out the marks of all the wounds (mostly thoroughly deserved) he has dealt it.

LONDON.
July, 1907.

The Autobiography of a Super-tramp

Preface to an autobiography by W. H. Davies, 1908

═══

I hasten to protest at the outset that I have no personal knowledge of the incorrigible Supertramp who wrote this amazing book. If he is to be encouraged and approved, then British morality is a mockery, British respectability an imposture, and British industry a vice. Perhaps they are: I have always kept an open mind on the subject; but still one may ask some better ground for pitching them out of window than the caprice of a tramp.

I hope these expressions will not excite unreasonable expectations of a thrilling realistic romance, or a scandalous chronicle, to follow. Mr Davies's[1] autobiography is not a bit sensational: it might be the Post Office Directory for the matter of that. A less simple minded supertramp would not have thought it worth writing at all; for it mentions nothing that might not have happened to any of us. As to scandal, I, though a most respectable author, have never written half so proper a book. These pudent pages are unstained with the frightful language, the debased dialect, of the fictitious proletarians of Mr Rudyard Kipling and other genteel writers. In them the patrons of the casual ward and the dosshouse argue with the decorum of Socrates, and narrate in the style of Tacitus. They have that pleasant combination of childish freshness with scrupulous literary conscientiousness only possible to people for whom speech, spoken or written, but especially written, is still a feat to be admired and shewn off for its own sake. Not for the life of me could I capture that boyish charm and combine it with the *savoir vivre* of an experienced man of the world, much less of an experienced tramp. The innocence of the author's manner and the perfection of his delicacy is such, that you might read his book aloud in an almshouse without shocking the squeamishness of old age. As for the young, nothing shocks the young. The immorality of the matter is stupendous; but it is purely an industrial immorality. As to the sort of immorality that is most dreaded by schoolmistresses and duennas, there is not a word in the book

---

1. Welsh-born poet who trod the English roads as a tramp until 1905, when he chronicled his unconventional life.

The Autobiography of a Super-tramp

Preface to an autobiography by W. H. Davies, 1908

═══

I hasten to protest at the outset that I have no personal knowledge of the incorrigible Supertramp who wrote this amazing book. If he is to be encouraged and approved, then British morality is a mockery, British respectability an imposture, and British industry a vice. Perhaps they are: I have always kept an open mind on the subject; but still one may ask some better ground for pitching them out of window than the caprice of a tramp.

I hope these expressions will not excite unreasonable expectations of a thrilling realistic romance, or a scandalous chronicle, to follow. Mr Davies's[1] autobiography is not a bit sensational: it might be the Post Office Directory for the matter of that. A less simple minded supertramp would not have thought it worth writing at all; for it mentions nothing that might not have happened to any of us. As to scandal, I, though a most respectable author, have never written half so proper a book. These pudent pages are unstained with the frightful language, the debased dialect, of the fictitious proletarians of Mr Rudyard Kipling and other genteel writers. In them the patrons of the casual ward and the dosshouse argue with the decorum of Socrates, and narrate in the style of Tacitus. They have that pleasant combination of childish freshness with scrupulous literary conscientiousness only possible to people for whom speech, spoken or written, but especially written, is still a feat to be admired and shewn off for its own sake. Not for the life of me could I capture that boyish charm and combine it with the *savoir vivre* of an experienced man of the world, much less of an experienced tramp. The innocence of the author's manner and the perfection of his delicacy is such, that you might read his book aloud in an almshouse without shocking the squeamishness of old age. As for the young, nothing shocks the young. The immorality of the matter is stupendous; but it is purely an industrial immorality. As to the sort of immorality that is most dreaded by schoolmistresses and duennas, there is not a word in the book

---

1. Welsh-born poet who trod the English roads as a tramp until 1905, when he chronicled his unconventional life.

which would wipe out the marks of all the wounds (mostly thoroughly deserved) he has dealt it.

LONDON.
July, 1907.

to suggest that tramps know even what it means. On the contrary, I can quite believe that the author would die of shame if he were asked to write such books as [George Eliot's] Adam Bede or David Copperfield.

The manuscript came into my hands under the following circumstances. In the year 1905 I received by post a volume of poems by one William H. Davies, whose address was The Farm House, Kennington S.E. I was surprised to learn that there was still a farmhouse left in Kennington; for I did not then suspect that the Farmhouse, like the Shepherdess Walks and Nightingale Lanes and Whetstone Parks of Bethnal Green and Holborn, is so called nowadays in irony, and is, in fact, a dosshouse, or hostelry where single men can have a night's lodging for, at most, sixpence.

I was not surprised at getting the poems. I get a gift of minor poetry once a week or so; and yet, hardened as I am to it, I still, knowing how much these little books mean to their authors, can seldom throw them aside without a twinge of compunction which I allay by a glance at one of the pages in the faint but inextinguishable hope of finding something valuable there. Sometimes a letter accompanies the book; and then I get a rapid impression, from the handwriting and notepaper as well as from the binding and type in the book, or even from the reputation of the publisher, of the class and type of the author. Thus I guess Cambridge or Oxford or Maida Vale [a district of north-west London] or West Kensington or Exeter or the lakes or the east coast; or a Newdigate[2] prizeman, a romantic Jew, a maiden lady, a shy country parson or whom not, what not, where not. When Mr Davies's book came to hand my imagination failed me. I could not place him. There were no author's compliments, no publisher's compliments, indeed no publisher in the ordinary channel of the trade in minor poetry. The author, as far as I could guess, had walked into a printer's or stationer's shop; handed in his manuscript; and ordered his book as he might have ordered a pair of boots. It was marked "price half a crown." An accompanying letter asked me very civilly if I required a half-crown book of verses; and if so, would I please send the author the half crown: if not, would I return the book. This was attractively simple and sensible. Further, the handwriting was remarkably delicate and individual: the sort of handwriting one might expect from Shelley or George Meredith. I opened the book, and was more puzzled than ever; for before I had read three lines I perceived that the author was a real poet. His work was not in

---

2. Sir Roger Newdigate, English antiquary and MP, founded in 1805 the 'Newdigate Prize' for English verse, a competition open each year to undergraduates of Oxford University.

the least strenuous or modern: there was in it no sign that he had ever read anything later than Cowper or Crabbe, not even Byron, Shelley or Keats, much less Morris, Swinburne, Tennyson, or Henley and Kipling. There was indeed no sign of his ever having read anything otherwise than as a child reads. The result was a freedom from literary vulgarity which was like a draught of clear water in a desert. Here, I saw, was a genuine innocent, writing odds and ends of verse about odds and ends of things, living quite out of the world in which such things are usually done, and knowing no better (or rather no worse) than to get his book made by the appropriate craftsman and hawk it round like any other ware.

Evidently, then, a poor man. It horrified me to think of a poor man spending his savings in printing something that nobody buys: poetry, to wit. I thought of Browning threatening to leave the country when the Surveyor of Taxes fantastically assessed him for an imaginary income derived from his poems. I thought of Morris, who, even after The Earthly Paradise, estimated his income as a poet at a hundred a year. I saw that this man might well be simple enough to suppose that he could go into the verse business and make a living at it as one makes a living by auctioneering or shopkeeping. So instead of throwing the book away as I have thrown so many, I wrote him a letter telling him that he could not live by poetry. Also, I bought some spare copies, and told him to send them to such critics and verse fanciers as he knew of, wondering whether they would recognize a poet when they met one.

And they actually did. I presently saw in a London newspaper an enthusiastic notice of the poems, and an account of an interview with the author, from which I learnt that he was a tramp; that "the farm house" was a dosshouse; and that he was cut off from ordinary industrial pursuits by two circumstances: first, that he had mislaid one of his feet somewhere on his trampings, and now had to make shift as best he could with the other; second, that he was a man of independent means—a *rentier* [a receiver of fixed income]—in short, a gentleman.

The exact amount of his independent income was ten shillings a week. Finding this too much for his needs, he devoted twenty per cent of it to pensioning necessitous friends in his native place; saved a further percentage to print verses with; and lived modestly on the remainder. My purchase of eight copies of the book enabled him, I gathered, to discard all economy for about three months. It also moved him to offer me the privilege (for such I quite sincerely deem it) of reading his autobiography in manuscript. The following pages will enable the world at large to read it in print.

All I have to say by way of recommendation of the book is that I have read it through from beginning to end, and would have read more of it had there been any more to read. It is a placid narrative, unexciting in matter and unvarnished in manner, of the commonplaces of a tramp's life. It is of a very curious quality. Were not the author an approved poet of remarkable sensibility and delicacy I should put down the extraordinary quietness of his narrative to a monstrous callousness. Even as it is, I ask myself with some indignation whether a man should lose a limb with no more to-do than a lobster loses a claw or a lizard his tail, as if he could grow a new one at his next halting place! If such a thing happened to me, I should begin the chapter describing it with "I now come to the event which altered the whole course of my life, and blighted etc. etc." In Mr Davies's pages the thing happens as unexpectedly as it did in real life, and with an effect on the reader as appalling as if he were an actual spectator. Fortunately it only happened once: half a dozen such shocks would make any book unbearable by a sensitive soul.

I do not know whether I should describe our supertramp as a lucky man or an unlucky one. In making him a poet, Fortune gave him her supremest gift; but such high gifts are hardly personal assets: they are often terrible destinies and crushing burdens. Also, he chanced upon an independent income: enough to give him reasonable courage, and not enough to bring him under the hoof of suburban convention, lure him into a premature marriage, or deliver him into the hands of the doctors. Still, not quite enough to keep his teeth in proper repair and his feet dry in all weathers.

Some flat bad luck he has had. I suppose every imaginative boy is a criminal, stealing and destroying for the sake of being great in the sense in which greatness is presented to him in the romance of history. But very few get caught. Mr Davies unfortunately was seized by the police; haled before the magistrate; and made to expiate by stripes the bygone crimes of myself and some millions of other respectable citizens. That was hard luck, certainly. It gives me a feeling of moral superiority to him; for I never fell into the hands of the police—at least they did not go on with the case (one of incendiarism), because the gentleman whose property I burnt had a strong sense of humor and a kindly nature, and let me off when I made him a precocious speech—the first I ever delivered—on the thoughtlessness of youth.[3] It is remarkable what a difference it makes, this matter of the

---

3. When Shaw, aged twelve, set fire to the gorse on Torca Hill, Dalkey, an innocent boy was arrested. Shaw then confessed, because 'it was outside my code of honor to let another bear the burden of my guilt' (Hesketh Pearson, *Bernard Shaw: His Life and Personality*, 1942).

police; though it is obviously quite beside the ethical question. Mr Davies tells us, with his inimitable quiet modesty, that he begged, stole, and drank. Now I have begged and stolen; and if I never drank, that was only an application of the principle of division of labor to the Shaw clan; for several members of it drank enough for ten. But I have always managed to keep out of the casual ward and the police court; and this gives me an ineffable sense of superior respectability when I read the deplorable confessions of Mr Davies, who is a true poet in his disregard for appearances, and is quite at home in tramp wards.

Another effect of this book on me is to make me realize what a slave of convention I have been all my life. When I think of the way I worked tamely for my living during all those years when Mr Davies, a free knight of the highway, lived like a pet bird on titbits, I feel that I have been duped out of my natural liberty. Why had I not the luck, at the outset of my career, to meet that tramp who came to Mr Davies, like Evangelist to Christian [*Pilgrim's Progress*], on the first day of his American pilgrim's progress, and saved him on the very brink of looking for a job, by bidding him to take no thought for the morrow; to ask and it should be given to him; to knock and it should be opened to him; and to free himself from the middle class assumption that only through taking a ticket can one take a train. Let every youth into whose hands this book falls ponder its lesson well, and, when next his parents and guardians attempt to drive him into some inhuman imprisonment and drudgery under the pretext that he should earn his own living, think of the hospitable countrysides of America, with their farm houses overflowing with milk and honey for the tramp, and their offers of adoption for every day laborer with a dash of poetry in him.

And then, how much did I know about hotels until I read this book! I have often wondered how the poor travel; for it is plain that the Ritzes and Metropoles, and even the hotels noted by Baedeker [travel-guide] as "unpretending," are not for them. Where does the man with sixpence in his pocket stay? Mr Davies knows. Read and learn.

It is to be noted that Mr Davies is no propagandist of the illusions of the middle class tramp fancier. You never suspect him of having read Lavengro,[4] or got his notions of nomads from Mr Theodore Watts Dunton.[5] He does not tell you that there is honor among tramps: on the contrary, he makes

4. *Lavengro – the Scholar – the Gypsy – the Priest* (1851) by George Borrow is a semi-autobiographical novel recounting the wanderings of a restless spirit.
5. English literary critic and novelist, in whose work gypsies play important parts.

it clear that only by being too destitute to be worth robbing and murdering can a tramp insure himself against being robbed and murdered by his comrade of the road. The tramp is fastidious and accomplished, audacious and self-possessed; but he is free from divine exploitation: he has no orbit: he has the endless trouble of doing what he likes with himself, and the endless discountenance of being passed by as useless by the Life Force that finds superselfish work for other men. That, I suppose, is why Mr Davies tramps no more, but writes verses and saves money to print them out of eight shillings a week. And this, too, at a moment when the loss of a limb has placed within his reach such success in begging as he had never before dared to dream of!

Mr Davies is now a poet of established reputation. He no longer prints his verses and hawks them: he is regularly published and reviewed. Whether he finds the change a lucrative one I venture to doubt. That the verses in The Soul's Destroyer and in his New Poems will live is beyond question; but whether Mr Davies can live if anything happens to his eight shillings a week (unless he takes to the road again) is another matter. That is perhaps why he has advised himself to write and print his autobiography, and try his luck with it as Man of Letters in a more general sense. Though it is only in verse that he writes exquisitely, yet this book, which is printed as it was written, without any academic corrections from the point of view of the Perfect Commercial Letter Writer, is worth reading by literary experts for its style alone. And since his manner is so quiet, it has been thought well by his friends and his publishers to send a trumpeter before him the more effectually to call attention to him before he begins. I have volunteered for that job for the sake of his poems. Having now done it after my well known manner, I retire and leave the stage to him.

AYOT ST LAWRENCE, 1907.   G. B. S.

The Commonsense of Municipal Trading

Preface to a reissue of the 1904 edition in the Fabian Socialist Series, 1908

When I handed over this work to the Fabian Society to be distributed at a price low enough to make it easy for those most concerned to buy a copy,[1] I did not find it necessary to add any new matter or withdraw any old. The ordinary electioneering opponents of municipal trading had for the most part left my book alone, having neither the economic knowledge, the practical experience of municipal work, nor the literary skill to cope with me. But they still persuade the public that trading municipalities are staggering towards bankruptcy under a burden of ever-increasing debt. The trick is simple: instead of calling the funds of the municipality its capital, you call it "municipal debt," and go on to contend that the success of the municipalities in serving the public at cost price and eliminating idle shareholders, means that they are less capable and businesslike than the commercial concerns which measure their soundness by the excess of their charges over their expenses, and by the resultant magnitude of their dividends.

But the opponents of municipal trading could not, when this book was first published, get over the unanswerable fact that in spite of all their denunciations of our municipalities as bankrupt and mismanaged concerns —denunciations which would have ruined even the soundest private businesses, but against which private businesses have a remedy (witness the enormous damages obtained by "the Soap Trust" against a popular newspaper[2] which can slander municipal trading with complete impunity)— municipal credit, as shewn by the prices of its stock, remained unshaken; and the very people who were declaring it to be worthless were glad to invest their own money in municipal stock at gilt-edged prices. They did,

1. The Fabian Socialist Series, No. 5 (1908): one shilling in cloth and boards, sixpence in paper wrappers.
2. A combine of about a dozen leading English, Scottish, and Irish soap manufacturers originated with Lever Brothers in October 1906, designed to reduce costs of raw materials without increasing retail prices. In July 1907 an action for libel, brought by Lever against the *Daily Mail* and the *Evening News* (London newspapers owned by Associated Newspapers Ltd), was settled by the defendant for £50,000 damages plus costs.

however, point out triumphantly that the price of municipal stock had fallen, and that the London County Council could no longer get as much money as it wanted at 3 per cent. In reply, I could only say that a controversialist desperate enough to claim that this is the result of a loss of confidence in municipal security is desperate enough for anything. The credit of our municipalities stood as high as ever. What really happened was that the value of money had risen after the South African War. Consols had fallen from above par to nearly eighty. The bank rate had touched seven. The Anti-Municipalizers forget that if they wish to claim a fall in the price of municipal stock as evidence that their campaign against English civic activity is producing some effect, they must point, not to a general fall in prices which has hit private enterprises much harder than public enterprises, but to a fall confined to municipal stocks and unaccompanied by a rise in the price of money. It is no use triumphing over the difficulties of the Borough Treasurer when the Chancellor of the Exchequer and the Rothschilds are in the same straits. The argument would not be worth mentioning but that it illustrates the amazing ineptitude and ignorance with which the question is discussed in the daily press.

Perhaps the stupidest cry raised in the Anti-Municipal agitation—which is really an agitation to reserve all public services for the profit of private individuals—is the cry for "a commercial audit." I venture to believe that no honorable and sensible man who will take the trouble to read these pages will ever again disgrace himself by echoing that cry, or by casting a vote for any person capable of such an elementary blunder. Those who did so at the last municipal elections are now sufficiently ashamed of themselves; and we hear nothing more of the gentlemen who think a reduction of the death-rate a commercial mistake because it does not shew a profit of 10 per cent in cash, as it would have to do before a contractor would undertake it. But we must face the fact that honorable, sensible, and ordinarily intelligent people, from thoughtlessness, ignorance, and the tyranny of commercial habit, do make these blunders, and, as voters, become the tools of the moneyed interests which see in every extension of municipal activity the closing to them of some field which has been to them a veritable Tom Tiddler's ground[3] on which they have been picking up gold and silver at the expense of the ratepayers for years past.

It is generally assumed that the result of the municipal elections of

3. 'We're on Tom Tiddler's ground, picking up gold and silver' is the refrain in a children's game chanted when the area marked off by the central player is successfully invaded.

1907[4] was a severe set-back for municipal trading. The causes of that set-back, in so far as they had produced a genuine revolt of the ratepayer against municipal activity, are explained in this book. Before the revolt occurred I pointed out that our system of rating, and the success with which the cost of our social ameliorations was being evaded by the property owners and by the working classes, and thrown on the struggling mass of middle-class ratepayers, was producing intolerable injustice. The remedy proposed—that of putting back the clock—was impracticable. I knew, and everybody who had ever served on a public body knew, that the first hour spent on a committee would knock out of the new representatives most of the nonsense they had been talking at their election meetings, and that the most intelligent and disinterested of them would presently become ardent municipalizers. But it is still true that until municipal finance is radically reformed, and constitutional machinery provided for public enterprises extending over much larger areas than those marked out by our present obsolete and obstructive municipal boundaries, we shall continue to have ratepayers' revolts, and crippled public enterprise.

In London the issue was so confused with the usual political party considerations that hardly anyone noticed that the clean sweep which was supposed to have been made of Municipal Socialists was really a clean sweep of those Liberals who had been the most determined opponents of the Municipal Socialists in the previous Council. It was these Anti-Socialists who were swept away, whilst the professed Fabian Socialists held their seats in the midst of the *débâcle*. I mention this for the sake of its lesson, which is, that the ratepayers must not put their trust in electioneering literature which proceeds on the wildly erroneous assumption that every Liberal is a Socialist and every Conservative an opponent of State or Municipal activity. There is no salvation for the voter except in understanding exactly what the municipalities are doing; and this book is intended to put him in that position as far as a book can supply the need of that actual first-hand experience of the working of municipalities which only very few of us can obtain, and without which I certainly should not have been able, merely as a man of letters, to make my book of any value.

4. In the London County Council election of 2 March 1907 the Progressives, who had dominated the Council, lost 45 of their 83 seats, and the Moderates all but one of their 34 seats, to Municipal Reform candidates. This resulted from ratepayer anger over heavy tax assessments, managerial extravagance, and jobbery by local-government officials, who had, *The Times* proclaimed in a leader, abandoned 'the principles of sound finance and of careful and judicious administration'. All of the Fabian Progressives, however, including Sidney Webb, held their seats.

In conclusion, I again warn the ratepayer who is gasping for breath under the pressure of the propertied class squeezing rents from him from above, and the working class squeezing education, housing, medical attendance, poor relief, and old age pensions from him from below, that his condition will become more and more precarious, no matter whether he votes Moderate or Progressive, until he takes his public business as seriously and unromantically as his private business, and resorts to the simple and obvious means of relieving and protecting himself that may be gathered from these pages.

Two new developments of the opposition to civic enterprise have occurred lately. One is the practice of circulating to the ratepayers statements implying that municipal trading and taxation of unearned incomes involve irreligion and licentiousness. This I need not deal with: it is only too obvious that the irreligion and licentiousness in which we are already steeped are the result of abandoning our people to the unscrupulous rapacity of commercial enterprise, which makes huge profits out of the evils our municipalities strive constantly to suppress. No municipality has yet taken or proposed to take a single step against religion or morals, whereas private enterprise openly and shamelessly exploits poverty, vice, and irreligion for its own profit to the despair of the ratepayer, who has to pay for dealing with all the disease, the crime, and the depravation of character that enriches the sweater, the distiller, and the brothel-keeper.

The other development is the offer of Tariff Reform as a means of relieving the ratepayer without recourse to Municipal Socialism. On this I have only to say that if Tariff Reform succeeds in suppressing manufactured imports and substituting home production (its original object), it will not be a source of revenue at all. If, however, importation continues, and a revenue is derived from taxing imports, the ratepayer has no security that this revenue will be applied to his relief by increasing our present Grants in Aid[5] by the central government to the local authority rather than to reducing the income-tax on unearned incomes, in which case he would be paying more for imported goods only to see the excess pocketed by the very people who already exact so large a share of his earnings as rent. So, as municipal trading is not an evil to be staved off by any possible means, but a highly desirable and beneficial extension of civilization, equally good for Free Trade and Protectionist countries, there is no reason whatever why the most ardent Tariff Reformer should not also be an ardent Municipal Socialist.

5. Subsidies from central public funds to local governments.

Perhaps the most impudent of the recent complaints of municipal trading is that it drives capital out of the country. It is almost the only sure means of keeping it at home. The present system, which sends English capital to develop Bahia Blanca [in Argentina] whilst leaving Birmingham to wallow in its own death-rate, is driving capital abroad as fast as it will go. Municipal trading, if it had nothing more to recommend it than its effect in making home investment compulsory, would be justified by that alone from the patriotic point of view.

AYOT ST LAWRENCE.
15 January 1908.   G. B. S.

Fabian Essays Twenty Years Later

Preface to the 1908 reprint

===

Since 1889 the Socialist movement has been completely transformed throughout Europe; and the result of the transformation may fairly be described as Fabian Socialism. In the eighteen-eighties, when Socialism revived in England for the first time since the suppression of the Paris Commune in 1871,[1] it was not at first realized that what had really been suppressed for good and all was the romantic revolutionary Liberalism and Radicalism of 1848,[2] to which the Socialists had attached themselves as a matter of course, partly because they were themselves romantic and revolutionary, and partly because both Liberals and Socialists had a common object in Democracy.

Besides this common object the two had a common conception of method in revolution. They were both catastrophic. Liberalism had conquered autocracy and bureaucracy by that method in England and France, and then left industry to make what it could of the new political conditions by the unregulated action of competition between individuals. Briefly, the Liberal plan was to cut off the King's head, and leave the rest to Nature, which was supposed to gravitate towards economic harmonies when not restrained by tyrannical governments. The Socialists were very far ahead of the Liberals in their appreciation of the preponderant importance of industry, even going so far as to maintain, with Buckle and Marx, that all social institutions whatever were imposed by economic conditions, and that there was fundamentally only one tyranny: the tyranny of Capital. Yet even the Socialists had so far formed their political habits in the Liberal school that they were quite disposed to believe that if you cut off the head of King Capital, you might expect to see things come right more or less spontaneously.

1. The Paris Commune was proclaimed on 18 March 1871 by French revolutionaries, who declared Paris to be a free city, recognizing no government but that chosen by the people. The French Army brutally suppressed this liberal uprising.
2. Following the collapse of King Louis-Philippe in 1848, French socialists attempted to revive the principles of the 1798 revolution.

No doubt this general statement shews the Revolutionaries of 1848–71 as simpler than they appear on their own records. [Pierre-Joseph] Proudhon[3] was full of proposals: one of them, the minimum wage, turns out to be of the very first importance now that Mr and Mrs Sidney Webb have put the case for it on an invincible basis of industrial fact and economic theory [in *Industrial Democracy*, 1898]. [Ferdinand] Lassalle[4] really knew something of the nature of law, the practice of Government, and the mind of the governing classes. Marx, though certainly a bit of a Liberal fatalist (did he not say that force is the midwife of progress without reminding us that force is equally the midwife of chaos, and chaos the midwife of martial law?), was at all events no believer in *laissez-faire*. Socialism involves the introduction of design, contrivance, and co-ordination, by a nation consciously seeking its own collective welfare, into the present industrial scramble for private gain; and as it is clear that this cannot be a spontaneous result of a violent overthrow of the existing order, and as the Socialists of 1848–71 were not blind, it would be impossible to substantiate a claim for Fabian Essays as the first text-book of Socialism in which catastrophism is repudiated as a method of Socialism.

Therefore we must not say that the Revolutionists and Internationalists of 1848–71 believed in a dramatic overthrow of the capital system in a single convulsion, followed by the establishment of a new heaven, a new earth, and a new humanity. They were visionaries, no doubt; all political idealists are; but they were quite as practical as the Conservatives and Liberals who now believe that the triumph of their party will secure the happiness and peace of the country. All the same, it was almost impossible to induce them to speak or think of the Socialist State of the future in terms of the existing human material for it. They talked of Communes, and, more vaguely and less willingly, of central departments to co-ordinate the activities of the Communes; but if you ventured to point out that these apparently strange and romantic inventions were simply city corporations under the Local Government Board, they vehemently repudiated such a construction, and accused you of reading the conditions of the present system into Socialism. They had all the old Liberal mistrust of governments and bureaucracy and all the old tendency of bourgeois revolutionists to idolize the working class. They had no suspicion of the extent to which the very existence of society depends on the skilled work of administrators and experts, or how much wisdom and strength of

3. French socialist-anarchist and critic of all extant forms of political organization.
4. Founder of Socialist-Democracy in Germany.

character is required for their control by popular representatives. They actually believed that when their efforts throughout Europe had demonstrated the economics of Socialism to the proletariats of the great capitals, the cry "Proletarians of all lands; unite," would be responded to; and that Capitalism would fall before an International Federation of the working classes of Europe, not in the sense in which some future historian will summarize two or three centuries (in which sense they may prove right enough), but as an immediate practical plan of action likely to be carried through in twenty years by Socialist societies holding completely and disdainfully aloof from ordinary politics. In short, they were romantic amateurs, and, as such, were enormously encouraged and flattered when Marx and Engels insisted on the "scientific" character of their movement in contrast to the "Utopian" Socialism of [Robert] Owen, Fourier, St Simon,[5] and the men of the 1820–48 phase. When the events of 1871 in Paris tested them practically, their hopeless public incapacity forced their opponents to exterminate them in the most appalling massacre of modern times—all the more ghastly because it was a massacre of the innocents.

Public opinion in Europe was reconciled to the massacre by the usual process of slandering the victims. Now had Europe been politically educated no slanders would have been necessary; for even had it been humanly possible that all the Federals mown down with *mitrailleuses* [breech-loading machine-guns, first used in 1870] in Paris were incendiaries and assassins, it would still have been questionable whether indiscriminate massacre is the right way to deal with incendiaries and assassins. But there can be no question as to what must be done with totally incompetent governors. The one thing that is politically certain nowadays is that if a body of men upset the existing government of a modern State without sufficient knowledge and capacity to continue the necessary and honest part of its work, and if, being unable to do that work themselves, they will not let anyone else do it either, their extermination becomes a matter of immediate necessity. It will avail them nothing that they aim higher than their fathers did; that their intentions are good, their action personally disinterested, and their opponents selfish and venal routineers who would themselves be equally at a loss if they had to create a new order instead of merely pulling the wires of

5. François-Charles-Marie Fourier advocated a communistic system for the organization of society based on a natural optimism about the innate harmonies of human nature. Claude-Henri Saint-Simon, founder of French socialism, propounded a positivist philosophy subsequently expounded by Auguste Comte.

an old one. Anyone who looks at the portraits of the members of the Paris Commune can see at a glance that they compared very favorably in all the external signs of amiability and refinement with any governing body then or now in power in Europe. But they could not manage the business they took upon themselves; and [Louis-Adolphe] Thiers[6] could. Marx's demonstration that they were heroes and martyrs and that Thiers and his allies were rascals did not help in the least, though it was undeniably the ablest document in the conflict of moral claptrap that obscured the real issues—so able indeed as a piece of literature, that more than thirty years after its publication it struck down the Marquis [Gaston] de Gallifet[7] as if it had appeared in the Temps or Débats of the day before. It was amiable of the Federals to be so much less capable of exterminating Thiers than he was of exterminating them; but sentimental amiability is not by itself a qualification for administering great modern States.

Now the Fabian Society, born in 1884, and reaching the age of discretion in less than two years, had no mind to be exterminated. Martyrdom was described by one of us as "the only way in which a man can become famous without ability."[8] Further, we had no illusions as to the treatment we should receive if, like the Paris Federals, we terrified the property classes before they were disabled by a long series of minor engagements. In Paris in 1871, ordinary sane people hid themselves in their houses for weeks under the impression that the streets were not safe: they did not venture out until they ran a serious risk of being shot at sight by their own partisans in the orgy of murder and cruelty that followed the discovery that the Commune could fight only as a rat fights in a corner. Human nature has not changed since then. In 1906 a Fabian essayist stood one May morning in the Rue de Rivoli, and found himself almost the only soul in the west end of Paris who dared appear there.[9] The cultured inhabitants of that select quarter were hiding in their houses as before, with their larders full of hams and their baths full of live fish to provision them for a siege. There was much less danger of a revolution that day than there is of Primrose Hill [just north of Regent's Park, London] becoming an active volcano at six

6. He crushed the Paris Commune of 1871 and became, in name as well as in fact, president of the republic.
7. French general, who as war minister brutally suppressed the Commune of 1871.
8. Spoken by General Burgoyne in Shaw's *The Devil's Disciple* (1896).
9. The Fabian essayist was Shaw. Having spent Labour Day, 1 May 1906, in the Place de la République, he wrote: 'the only message that occurs to me is that it will presently be well to organize some means of protecting the public against the police and military' (*Labour Leader*, 11 May 1906).

o'clock this evening; and the purpose of the Government and its party newspapers in manufacturing the scare to frighten the bourgeoisie into supporting them at the general election just then beginning was obvious, one would have thought, to the dimmest political perspicacity. In the evening that same essayist, in the Place de la Révolution, saw a crowd of sightseers assembled to witness the promised insurrection, and the troops and the police assembled to save society from it. It was very like Trafalgar Square in 1887,[10] when the same violent farce was enacted in London. Occasionally the troops rode down some of the sightseers and the police arrested some of them. Enough persons lost their temper to make a few feeble attempts at riot, and to supply arrests for the morning papers. Next day Society, saved, came out of its hiding places; sold the fish from its baths and the hams from its larders at a sacrifice (the weather being very hot and the hams in questionable condition); and voted gratefully for the government that had frightened it out of its senses with an imaginary revolution and a ridiculous "complot." England laughed at the Parisians (though plenty of English visitors had left Paris to avoid the threatened Reign of Terror); yet in the very next month our own propertied classes in Cairo, terrified by the Nationalist movement in Egypt, fell into a paroxysm of cowardice and cruelty, and committed the Denshawai atrocity,[11] compared to which the massacre of Glencoe was a trifle.[12] The credulity which allows itself to be persuaded by reiteration of the pious word Progress that we live in a gentler age than our fathers, and that the worst extremities of terror and vengeance are less to be apprehended from our newly enriched automobilist classes than they were from the aristocracies of the older orders, is not a Fabian characteristic. The Fabian knows that property does not hesitate to shoot, and that now, as always, the unsuccessful revolutionist may expect calumny, perjury, cruelty, judicial and military massacre without mercy. And the Fabian does not intend to get thus handled if he can help it. If there is to be any shooting, he intends to be at the State end of the gun. And he knows that it will take him a good many years to get

10. On 'Bloody Sunday', 13 November 1887, political radicals attempted to gather in Trafalgar Square as a protest against the Government's closing of the area to public meetings. A show of police strength quickly dispersed the assembling crowd.
11. See 'The Denshawai Horror' in preface (1907) to *John Bull's Other Island* (p. 225).
12. In 1692 Englishmen aligned with William III in his battle for recognition in Scotland treacherously exterminated nearly forty members of the MacDonald clan at Glencoe as 'technical traitors' because their chief had delayed taking an oath of allegiance to the new regime.

there. Still, he thinks he sees his way—or rather the rest of his way; for he is already well on the road.

It was in 1885 that the Fabian Society, amid the jeers of the catastrophists, turned its back on the barricades and made up its mind to turn heroic defeat into prosaic success. We set ourselves two definite tasks: first, to provide a parliamentary program for a Prime Minister converted to Socialism as Peel was converted to Free Trade; and second, to make it as easy and matter-of-course for the ordinary respectable Englishman to be a Socialist as to be a Liberal or a Conservative.

These tasks we have accomplished, to the great disgust of our more romantic comrades. Nobody now conceives Socialism as a destructive insurrection ending, if successful, in millennial absurdities. Membership of the Fabian Society, though it involves an express avowal of Socialism, excites no more comment than membership of the Society of Friends, or even of the Church of England. Incidentally, Labor has been organized as a separate political interest in the House of Commons, with the result that in the very next Budget it was confessed for the first time that there are unearned as well as earned incomes in the country: an admission which, if not a surrender of the Capitalist citadel to Socialism, is at all events letting down the drawbridge; for Socialism, on its aggressive side, is, and always has been, an attack on idleness. The resolution to make an end of private property is gathering force every day: people are beginning to learn the difference between a man's property in his walking stick, which is strictly limited by the public condition that he shall not use it to break his neighbor's head or extort money with menaces, and those private rights of property which enable the idle to levy an enormous tribute, amounting at present to no less than £630,000,000 a year, on the earnings of the rest of the community. The old attempt to confuse the issue by asserting that the existence of the family, religion, marriage, etc., etc., are inextricably bound up with the toleration of senseless social theft no longer imposes on anyone: after a whole year of unexampled exploitation of this particular variety of obscene vituperation by the most widely read cheap newspapers in London, no Socialist is a penny the worse for it.

The only really effective weapon of the press against Socialism is silence. Even Bishops cannot get reported when they advocate Socialism and tear to pieces the old pretence that political economy, science, and religion are in favor of our existing industrial system. Socialist speakers now find audiences so readily that, even with comparatively high charges for admission, large halls can be filled to hear them without resorting to the usual channels of advertisement. Their speeches are crammed with facts and figures and irresistible appeals to the daily experience and money troubles of the unfortunate ratepayers and rentpayers who are too harassed by money worries to care about official party politics; but not a word of these is allowed to leak through to the public through the ordinary channels of newspaper reporting. However, the conspiracy of silence has its uses to us. We have converted the people who have actually heard us. The others, having no news of our operations, have left us unmolested until our movement has secured its grip of the public. Now that the alarm has at last been given, nobody, it seems, is left in the camp of our enemies except the ignorant, the politically imbecile, the corruptly interested, and the retinue of broken, drunken, reckless mercenaries who are always ready to undertake a campaign of slander against the opponents of any vested interest which has a bountiful secret service fund. This may seem a strong thing to say; but it is impossible not to be struck by the feebleness and baseness of the opposition to Socialism today as compared with the opposition of twenty years ago. In the days when Herbert Spencer's brightest pupils, from Mrs Sidney Webb to Grant Allen,[13] turned from him to the Socialism in which he could see nothing but "the coming slavery," we could respect him whilst confuting him. Today we neither respect our opponents nor confute them. We simply, like Mrs [Charlotte] Stetson Gilman's[14] prejudice slayer, "walk through them as if they were not there."

Still, we do not affect to underrate the huge public danger of a press which is necessarily in the hands of the very people whose idleness and extravagance keep the nation poor and miserable in spite of its immense resources. It costs quarter of a million to start a London daily paper with any chance of success; and every man who writes for it risks his livelihood every time he pens a word that threatens the incomes of the proprietors and their class. The quantity of snobbish and anti-social public opinion thus manufactured is formidable; and a new sort of crime—the incitement by newspapers of mobs to outrage and even murder—hitherto tried only on religious impostors, is beginning to be applied to politics. The result is likely to be another illustration of the impossibility of combining individual freedom with economic slavery. We have had to throw freedom of contract to the winds to save the working classes from extermination as a result of "free" contracts between penniless fathers of starving families and rich

13. Novelist and scientific popularist, a thoughtful exponent of the evolutionary idea in various aspects of biology and anthropology.
14. American author of *In This Our World* (1895), in which appears the poem 'An Obstacle' quoted by Shaw.

employers. Freedom of the press is hardly less illusory when the press belongs to the slave owners of the nation, and not a single journalist is really free. We think it well therefore at this moment to warn our readers not to measure the extent of our operations or our influence, much less the strength of our case, by what they read of us in the papers. The taste for spending one's life in drudgery and never-ending pecuniary anxiety solely in order that certain idle and possibly vicious people may fleece you for their own amusement, is not so widespread as the papers would have us think. Even that timidest of Conservatives, the middle class man with less than £500 a year (sometimes less than £100) is beginning to ask himself why his son should go, half-educated, to a clerks' desk at fifteen, to enable another man's son to go to a university and complete an education of which, as a hereditary idler, he does not intend to make use. To tell him that such self-questioning is a grave symptom of Free Love and Atheism may terrify him; but it does not convince. And the evolution of Socialism from the Red sceptre on the barricade, with community of wives (all *pétroleuses* [incendiarists using paraffin]), and Compulsory Atheism, to the Fabian Society and the Christian Social Union, constitutional, respectable, even official, eminent, and titled, is every day allaying his dread of it and increasing his scepticism as to the inevitability of the ever more and more dreaded knock of the ground landlord's agent and the rate collector.

Now, as everyone knows, the course of evolution, in Socialism or anything else, does not involve the transformation of the earlier forms into the later. The earlier forms persist side by side with the later until they are either deliberately exterminated by them or put out of countenance so completely that they lose the heart to get born. This is what has happened in the evolution of Fabian Socialism. Fabian Socialism has not exterminated the earlier types; and though it has put them so much out of countenance that they no longer breed freely, still there they are still, preaching, collecting subscriptions, and repulsing from Socialism many worthy citizens who are quite prepared to go as far, and farther, than the Fabian Society. Occasionally they manage even to contest a parliamentary seat in the name of Socialism, and to reassure the Capitalist parties by coming out at the foot of the poll with fewer votes than one would have thought possible for any human candidate, were he even a flat-earth-man, in these days when everyone can find a following of some sort. More often, however, they settle down into politically negligible sects, with a place of weekly meeting in which they preach to one another every week, except in the summer months, when they carry the red flag into the open air and denounce society as it passes or loiters to listen. Now far be it from us to repudiate these comrades. If a man has been brought to conviction of sin by the Countess of Huntingdon's Connection,[15] and subsequently enters the Church and becomes an Archbishop, he will always have sufficient tenderness for the Connection to refrain from attacking it, and to remember that many of its members are better Christians and better men than the more worldly-wise pillars of the Church. The principal leaders of the Fabian movement are in the same position with regard to many little societies locally known as "the Socialists." We know that their worship of Marx (of whose works they are for the most part ignorant, and of whose views they are intellectually incapable) and their repetition of shibboleths about the Class War and the socialization of all the means of production, distribution, and exchange have no more application to practical politics than the Calvinistic covenants which so worried Cromwell when he, too, tried to reconcile his sectarian creed with the practical exigencies of government and administration. We know also, and are compelled on occasion to say bluntly out, that these little sects are ignorant and incapable in public affairs; that in many cases their assumption of an extreme position is an excuse for doing nothing under cover of demanding the impossible; and that their inability to initiate any practical action when they do by chance get represented on public bodies often leads to their simply voting steadily for our opponents by way of protest against what they consider the compromising opportunism of the Fabians. There are moments when they become so intolerable a nuisance to the main body of the movement that we are sorely tempted to excommunicate them formally, and warn the public that they represent nobody but their silly selves. But such a declaration, though it would be perfectly true as far as political and administrative action is concerned, would be misleading on the whole. In England, everyone begins by being absurdly ignorant of public life and inept at public action. Just as the Conservative and Liberal Parties are recruited at Primrose League[16] meetings and Liberal and Radical demonstrations at which hardly one word of sense or truth is uttered, but at which nevertheless the novice finds himself in a sympathetic atmosphere, so even the Fabian Society consists largely of Socialists who sowed their wild oats in one or other of these little sects of Impossibilists. Therefore we not only suffer them as gladly as human nature allows, but give them what help and countenance we can when we can do so without specifically endorsing

15. Selina Hastings Huntingdon, English religious leader, founded a sect of Calvinistic Methodists, known as the Countess of Huntingdon's Connection.
16. A Conservative association founded in memory of Benjamin Disraeli.

their blunders. Fortunately the immense additions which have been made to the machinery of democracy in England in the last twenty years, from the County Councils of 1888 to the education authorities of 1902,[17] have acted as schools of public life to thousands of men of small means who in the old days must have remained Impossibilists from want of public experience. One hour on a responsible committee of a local authority which has to provide for some public want and spend some public money, were it but half-a-crown, will cure any sensible man of Impossibilism for the rest of his life. And such cures are taking place every day, and converting futile enthusiasts into useful Fabians.

A word as to this book. It is not a new edition of Fabian Essays. They are reprinted exactly as they appeared in 1889, nothing being changed but the price. No other course was possible. When the essays were written, the Essayists were in their thirties: they are now in their fifties, except the one, William Clarke, who is in his grave. We were then regarded as young desperadoes who had sacrificed their chances in life by committing themselves publicly to Socialism: we are now quoted as illustrations of the new theory that Socialists, like Quakers, prosper in this world. It is a dangerous theory; for Socialism, like all religions and all isms, can turn weak heads as well as inspire and employ strong ones; but we, at all events, have been fortunate enough to have had our claim to public attention admitted in the nineteen years which have elapsed since our youthful escapade as Fabian Essayists.

It goes without saying that in our present position, and with the experience we have gained, we should produce a very different book if the work were to be done anew. We should not waste our time in killing dead horses, however vigorously they were kicking in 1889. We should certainly be much more careful not to give countenance to the notion that the unemployed can be set to work to inaugurate Socialism; though it remains true that the problem of the unemployed, from the moment when we cease to abandon them callously to their misery or soothe our consciences foolishly by buying them off with alms, will force us to organize them, provide for them, and train them; but the very first condition of success in this will be the abandonment of the old idea that the unemployed tailor

17. A Local Government Act in 1888 established a directly elected county council to administer metropolitan London. The council took over the London School Board's duties of administering elementary education. The 1902 Education Act made county councils throughout the nation responsible for a comprehensive system of education for both elementary and secondary levels.

can be set to make clothes for the unemployed bootmaker and the unemployed bootmaker to make boots for the unemployed tailor, the real difficulty being, not a scarcity of clothes and boots, but a stupid misdistribution of the money to buy them. We should also probably lay more stress on human volition and less on economic pressure and historic evolution as making for Socialism. We should, in short, give the dry practice of our solutions of social problems instead of the inspiration and theory of them. But we should also produce a volume which, though it might appeal more than the present one to administrative experts, to bankers, lawyers, and constructive statesmen, would have much less charm for the young, and for the ordinary citizen who is in these matters an amateur.

Besides, the difference between the view of the young and the elderly is not necessarily a difference between wrong and right. The Tennysonian process of making stepping stones of our dead selves to higher things ['Prologue', *In Memoriam*, 1850] is pious in intention, but it sometimes leads downstairs instead of up. When Herbert Spencer in his later days expunged from his Social Statics the irresistible arguments for Land Nationalization by which he anticipated Henry George,[18] we could not admit that the old Spencer had any right to do this violence to the young Spencer, or was less bound either to confute his position or admit it than if the two had been strangers to one another. Having had this lesson, we do not feel free to alter even those passages which no longer represent our latest conclusions. Fortunately, in the main we have nothing to withdraw, nothing to regret, nothing to apologize for, and much to be proud of. So we leave our book as it first came into the world, merely writing "Errors Excepted" as solicitors do: that is, with the firm conviction that the errors, if they exist at all, do not greatly matter.

21 May 1908.   G. BERNARD SHAW.

---

18. American author and political economist, whose *Progress and Poverty* (1879) advocated that all expense of government be met by a single tax upon rent.

The Critics of the White Prophet

Written as a preface for the second edition of Hall Caine's novel, which did not eventuate. Issued instead as a pamphlet by the publisher, William Heinemann, 1909

The fact that The White Prophet is a romance by an honest man is a guarantee of its political importance, because romances are the only documents that are now free to tell the truth and sure to be read.

In the Egyptian question, as in all questions of our Imperial foreign policy, nothing is genuine except the romance. The official reports are seldom sincere: they can be depended on only when the writers, infatuated by their class and color prejudices, their national conceit (which they call patriotism), their official self-importance, and their invincible ignorance of human nature, blurt out and even boast of deeds and views which men of normal outlook and unblunted social conscience would be ashamed to commit or avow.

For example, the officials of the Occupation in Egypt, from Lord Cromer downwards, thought the Denshawai affair rather a fine thing. Under this impression they themselves supplied the evidence that it was the most sensationally revolting villainy that has disgraced English rule in our time. It was not founded on the popular theory that East and West are congenitally unlike, and that the methods that succeed with one will not succeed with the other. On the contrary, the argument was that as the Easterns are born murderers, torturers, perjurers, tyrants, and corrupters of justice, and understand nothing else, we must shew them that we are their masters in all these departments of despotic government, and can out-murder them, out-torture them, out-lie them, out-tyrannize them, out-corrupt them, and, generally, go one worse than they on all points of political conduct. When some of us pointed to the fact that the records of the Egyptian courts shewed a white-gloved absence of crime greatly to the credit of the Egyptians, and that this had been cited as a proof of our success in civilizing Egypt, we were told that the regular courts were a put-up bluff, and that the real work of "civilization" had been done by native lynching raids ("Brigandage Commissions"), in which the raiders tortured the Egyptians until they accused one another of whatever crimes were alleged to have been committed, then tortured the accused until they confessed, and finally dealt with the people thus convicted with such ferocity as the methods employed might have led the victims to expect. These facts were planked down by Lord Cromer the moment the alleged freedom of Egypt from crime was turned against him in argument instead of being held up as the glory of his administration.

But for the most part, the hard facts never reach us. What we get instead is the romance of the thing. The British boy reads with delight the stories of [Ned] Kelly the Bushranger and [Charles] Peace the Burglar. He thinks they were very fine fellows; and the more crimes they commit—especially fighting crimes—the more he admires them. The British adult reads stories of "prancing pro-Consuls,"[1] and the more hanging and flogging and bullying there is in the stories the prouder he feels of being an Englishman.

Then there is the romance of danger and terror. If an Egyptian were conceived as an agricultural laborer, a milkman, a shoemaker, a grocer, or anything ordinary or honest or real, England could no more be persuaded to care about him or read about him than if he were carrying on the same unexciting pursuits in New Cross as a native of Peckham [a section of south London]. But conceive him as a human rattlesnake, a deadly and dangerous enemy of England, a fanatic eager to wade into paradise knee-deep in British blood, a member of a huge anti-Christian conspiracy known as Islam! Then the Briton who flogs and murders him, with or without a sham trial, is transfigured as a man of dauntless nerve and iron will, saving Western civilization from destruction, instead of the silly, mischievous, and panic-stricken grownup schoolboy he actually is. What deluded us into the Denshawai abomination was puerile penny-number romance. Sir Edward Grey, who could have stopped it, is not at all a cruel or unamiable person—quite the contrary; but he belongs to a class in which the men and women never get out of leading-strings [for the support of infants in learning to walk] from their cradles to their graves; and he has a full share of the pleasant boyishness in fair weather and the petulant obstinacy in foul weather which such unremitted tutelage inevitably produces in the human subject. He was credulous enough to believe that there was a frightful conspiracy of Islam against Christendom just ready to explode in a universal St Bartholomew

---

1. Deputy consuls representing Britain in colonies or dependencies; but popularly used to denote any civil servant in colonial service, as in Kipling's 'The Pro-Consuls' (*The Years Between*, 1919): 'They that dig foundations deep,/Fit for realms to rise upon . . .'

massacre,[2] and—more *jejune* still—that the splendid and masterful counterstroke needed to decapitate the hydra at one blow was to seize on the inhabitants of a village in which some British officers had been mobbed for persisting in getting up shooting expeditions to kill the villagers' farm stock (on the ground that pigeons were made to be shot by British sports-men), and, in the presence of their families and under the windows of their houses, hang them, flog them, and send the survivors to prison for life or for long terms of penal servitude. Now if Sir Edward Grey were a Nero, if Lord Cromer were a fiend, this horrible business might at least have grati-fied them and the overfed people who have that specific lust for cruelty which plays an unacknowledged but influential part in modern science and politics. But that they should have been simply Tom Sawyer and Huckleberry Finn, wrecking an Empire to gratify their taste for the sort of romance that is sold in penny volumes by Limehouse [in London's East End] stationers, is really enough to make one clamor for a statutory disqualification of the English country gentleman from any share whatever in affairs of State.

A Bedouin would not look at Denshawai in this way. He would see the finger of God in it. Oriental rulers, being subtler psychologists than English country gentlemen, have always known that the way to impress ignorant and thoughtless people with the greatness of a conqueror, a dynasty, or a religious movement, is to connect it with some horrifying sacrifice of human life. Thus a tribal king buries twenty people alive under the pillars of his hut-palace, and a conquering invader builds himself a monument of cut-off heads. Our pro-Consuls pick up the idea in the East rather too readily. Egyptian Nationalism needed just such a consecration of horror to drive it deep into the imaginations of the Egyptian people. Lord Cromer and Sir Edward Grey made Egypt a present of one which they intended for England's use. They forgot that when you get above the Hottentot [S. African native] or Kalmuck [Mongol tribesman] level the impression made is not on the side of the tyrants, but of the victims. The blood of the martyrs is the seed of the Church. The conscientious atrocities of "Bloody Mary" drove Protestantism into the very bones of the English people for three hundred years. The Crucifixion has been to Christianity what it was intended to be to Pharisaism and Roman Imperialism. Denshawai was the Crucifixion of Egyptian Nationalism. Henceforth, when an Egyptian wavers in his determination to recover Egypt for the Egyptians and drive

2. A massacre of the Huguenots initiated by Catherine de Medici, which began in Paris on St Bartholomew's Day, 24 August 1572. It is estimated that 50,000 Huguenots throughout France were slain.

out the Occupation bag and baggage, the word Denshawai will screw him up to the Nationalist mark like a magic spell.

The apology for Denshawai was as boyishly lighthearted as the crime itself. In the presence of their families we had hanged four men and given eight fifty lashes (the doctor forbidding one flogging of an epileptic). We sent two men to penal servitude for life because one of them struck a British officer who had just shot his wife (unintentionally, but the man did not know that). We sent one man to penal servitude for fifteen years, six men for seven years, and three to a year's hard labor in addition to their floggings. Until the bluebooks[3] appeared, public opinion here was kept quiet by the usual expedient of inducing panic-stricken British gentlemen to preserve the Empire from destruction by lying like horse copers [traders]. But when the murder was out (literally), and Mr Wilfrid Scawen Blunt's protests were substantiated by the official reports, we all behaved charmingly, being good fellows at heart. "Dear me! Was it all a mistake?" we said. And with a delightful sense of behaving handsomely we released all the prisoners without a stain on their characters. And no doubt if the hanged men could have been unhanged and the flogged men unflogged, their cases would have received the kindest consideration. As to Sir Edward Grey, his position was rather improved than otherwise by an event which, in the opinion of the Egyptians, should have made him for ever impossible as Foreign Minister in any civilized country.

As to Lord Cromer, had he not restored the finances of Egypt? We fell back on that whenever our consciences gave us a prick. It is not clear how he could have helped himself. It is absolutely certain that a wooden idol could have done the same. What was the history of that part of the business? Whilst masses of English men, women and children, were rotting in our slums and dying prematurely like flies for want of English capital to be invested in the rebuilding and sanitation of English cities, English capitalists were sending their capital in millions out of the country to pay for the profligacies of Ismail; and Ismail was extorting the interest from the starving Egyptians by the kourbash [whip]. When he had ruined them so that he could extort no more we took the land of Egypt in execution for the debt, and sent Ismail about his business. As Egypt is a fertile land with an industrious population, and as, after Ismail went and Baring (now Lord Cromer) came, the sun shone and the Nile flowed and the people worked without being robbed, matters righted themselves easily enough. But Lord

3. Blue-wrapped parliamentary publications providing facts on controversial issues and verbatim reports of governmental hearings.

Cromer's friends assured us that he was the Sun, and the Nile, and the labor of the Egyptians; and we patriotically and idiotically rejoiced in the superiority of the Englishman to Pharaoh. No doubt an intelligent biographer could shew that Lord Cromer did not get his reputation for nothing, and that there was some solid ability behind his unlucky panics and blunders; but to say that he saved Egypt from ruin in any other sense than that in which every policeman saves the lives of the people in the street he patrols, is justifiable only at public dinners, where it is polite to talk nonsense.

Sooner or later the grosser follies and falsehoods get exposed. As we have seen, the fools and liars convict themselves boastfully out of their own mouths because they conceive their folly as wisdom and patriotism, believe their own lies, and know that their intentions are good. But who is it that detects the exposure, and drives its lesson home to the public? Usually the man of letters. Across the Channel, when the officers and gentlemen who represented the old nobility and the old religion of France had with the most patriotic and pious intentions perjured and forged their way through the Dreyfus affair, it was a novelist, Zola, who smashed their conspiracy up and brought the nation to its senses. In Egypt it was a poet, Mr Wilfrid Scawen Blunt, who released the survivors of Denshawai, and reduced the apologists who had certified it as "just and necessary" to giving equally credulous and well-meant, and equally mistaken certificates to the vivisectors of dogs and rabbits in England. And it is again a man of letters, Hall Caine, who has gone deeper and put his finger on the real reason why our pro-Consuls get stuffed with these silly romances of a murderous conspiracy of Islam against Christendom.

That reason is that the situation of Pontius Pilate and Caiaphas is constantly and inevitably reproduced whenever we seize a foreign territory as Rome seized Judæa. Pontius Pilate becomes the catspaw of Caiaphas exactly as Dublin Castle is the catspaw of the Roman Catholic hierarchy in Ireland, or as, in Hall Caine's romance, the Consul-General becomes the catspaw of the Grand Cadi [judge]. When an original religious genius arises—Jesus, Mahomet, Savonarola, St Francis, or St Clare—his first attack is on the Temple, and whilst the people make him the leader of their eternal revolt against priestly tyranny and corruption, the priests accuse him of political conspiracy, and incite the military authorities to put him down with fire and sword. Thus they make Pontius Pilate crucify Jesus; Mahomet escapes them by the skin of his teeth, and, seeing that he must smash or be smashed, comes back in arms and conquers both priest and soldier; Savonarola is burnt by the cardinals; St Francis dies young, before it becomes expedient to burn him; and St Clare, who survives him, fights the Pope to the last because she wants her Clares to be Poor Clares, and he wants them to be women of property. This situation, with its explanation of the cry of Smash the Mahdi,[4] and of the cock-and-bull story of the conspiracy of Islam which the Egyptian Caiaphases planted on Lord Cromer and Sir Edward Grey, is the one which Hall Caine has presented in the form of a romance. In no other form would our credulous, pleasure-loving, intellectually lazy governing classes read it. Since romance is to carry the day, Hall Caine has used it on the right side, and beaten Caiaphas at his own game.

Hall Caine has also seen what none of our officials and Foreign Office Ministers have ever dreamt of—I mean the coming reconciliation between the best Christians and the best Mahometans. The greatest thing that the Empire has done is to knock out of us all the insular and insolent bigotry that used to assume that our share of inspiration and revelation was the whole, and that other people's prophets were impostors and other people's creeds damnable errors. Whilst Arab children were taught to respect Jesus in the name of Mahomet, English children were taught to despise and slander Mahomet in the name of Jesus. This is a heavy score to the credit of Mahomet. But the same fate finally overtook both prophets: the cults established on their teachings ended by claiming their authority for most of the errors they strove against. Christianity has already undergone one Reformation, and is very badly in want of another. Mahometanism is in the same predicament. Now as the essential religious ideas by which both sects (they are only sects, big as they are) will be reformed are the same, the opportunity for a reconciliation is a golden one, and Hall Caine, in seeing and understanding it, has risen to the height of his profession. I myself tried for years to induce some publisher to reissue [J. M.] Rodwell's translation of the Koran [1861], as I had found [George] Sale's translation [1734] unreadable; and at last, thanks to Mr Ernest Rhys, the editor of Everyman's Library, we have a cheap and dainty edition of it [1909] which every traveller in the East ought to carry with him, if only to convince himself that the average Arab knows even less about it than the average Englishman knows about the Bible. True, he will find there the false doctrine of a material hell which Mahomet was driven to invent for the intimidation of those who could not be weaned from crude idolatry by his intellectual and

4. Mahdi: 'the expected one' (Arabic). Among Muslems the title has been taken by several leaders, notably by Mohammed Ahmed, who overran the Egyptian Sudan in 1885.

spiritual appeal; but it does not lie with us to reproach him with that trick: we have used it too freely ourselves. For the rest, his doctrine rises far above the baser forms of Christianity; and it has, from the point of view of the sceptical educated Englishman of the Darwinian period (that is, of the governing class of today), the advantage that whereas many such Englishmen do not believe that Jesus ever existed, and, of those who do, many despise him because he was not "fit" to survive in the struggle for life, Mahomet's existence is as unquestionable as Henry the Eighth's, and his success was as solid as Mr [Andrew] Carnegie's. Also, when his followers persisted in trying to degrade him from the rank of prophet to that of a vulgar wizard (exactly as in the case of Jesus), he honestly and impatiently told them again and again that he was only a man, and could not perform miracles. Thus he appeals to men who are by temperament anti-Christian, just as he appealed to Napoleon, who said at St Helena that he thought Mahometanism was on the whole the most useful of the religions.

Now as to the definite charges made against Hall Caine for The White Prophet. I leave out of the question the hackneyed literary attack. Hall Caine sells a thousand copies where most other men of letters either sell a hundred or cannot escape from journalism into books at all. We console ourselves by taking advantage of the fact that his style is different from ours to declare publicly that he has no style at all. And when he does a stroke of important public work like The White Prophet, we disloyally join the official hue and cry against him, for which we ought to be shot as traitors to our profession. However, that matters to nobody but our petty selves. The public charges against Hall Caine are the important ones.

First, he is charged with using Lord Cromer as a model for one of his characters. Well, why should he not? He had to present a type of which Lord Cromer has been held up as the ideal representative. He has given his figure a private history that completely detaches it from Lord Cromer as a private man. And he has taken Lord Cromer's public traits at the highest valuation of Lord Cromer's most devoted flatterers. He has certainly not said an unfavorable word for which he has not Lord Cromer's own warrant in published official documents. It is true that the figure he draws is a character in a romance; but are the innumerable newspaper articles that told the tale of the conspiracy of Islam, and the strong, stern Englishmen who stamped it out by hanging and flogging helpless, unarmed, unorganized peasants, any the less romances, and very vile and silly romances too? If we refuse to read bluebooks, and insist on having romances, let us at least have them written by a master hand, with some knowledge and conscience behind it.

The next charge is that Hall Caine's picture of the British Occupation is not in accord with the facts. This is true. Hall Caine has neither the cynicism nor the specific talent for extravagant farce to paint the official Occupation as it really is. When I did it—when I told the story of how the officials demanded the suppression of the Egyptian newspapers and "a considerable increase in the army of occupation" because three thieves knocked a soldier off a donkey [preface to *John Bull's Other Island*, 1907]— everybody laughed, but nobody believed me. I quoted the official letters and gave the official references in vain: the facts were too absurd, too grotesquely comic, to be credible. There are truths too ridiculous to be thinkable except as jokes, just as there are truths too shameful to be mentioned by decent writers. Hall Caine has throughout represented Occupation officialism as public-spirited, high-minded, and earnestly patriotic even when misled and mistaken. There is no evidence that it deserves any such compliment. On its own shewing it is mostly snobbish, uppish, huffish, narrow, ignorant, conceited, and subject to paroxysms of panic in which it is capable of falsehood, cruelty, and injustice. But it is protected from exposure by the idolatry of officialism which has lately taken possession of England. Only the other day Mr Walkley, an upper division civil servant and one of the most brilliant critical essayists in the country,[5] told the Select Committee on stage plays,[6] in effect, that he had no faith in the power of Decency, Honor, Virtue, the grace of God, or the common law to keep the English theatre from debauchery, but that all that these forces could not do could be done infallibly, omnisciently, and omnipotently—in short, divinely—by an official. And the Speaker of the House of Commons endorsed his opinion. Both gentlemen naïvely added that the theatre had become so corrupt under official despotism that they could not take their daughters to see officially licensed plays without careful inquiry beforehand as to their decency. What is to be done in the face of such idolatrous infatuation? Had Hall Caine not generously attributed to the Occupation officials a large supply of his own conscience and public spirit, nobody would have believed him to be sane.

The next charge—a well-worn one—is that The White Prophet has inflamed sedition and provoked riot and insurrection. The curt reply that it hasnt is too trite to be interesting; besides, it is a mere fact, and facts are not

5. A. B. Walkley, dramatic critic of *The Times*, was until 1919 an administrator in the Post Office Department.
6. The Joint Select Committee of the House of Lords and the House of Commons on Stage Plays (Censorship), which met from 29 July to 2 November 1909.

popular in this country. Why does the official world always make this charge? For exactly the same reason that the lion-tamers at the music-halls always put up strong railings and carry terrible whips and iron bars when they enter the den and stand dauntlessly in the midst of twenty lions. If they revealed the fact that the lions have been carefully fed to such an extent that the offer of a nice, plump baby would simply nauseate them— if they reminded the audience that African travellers testify that it takes several days starvation to induce a lion to attack a man—people would not pay to see the performance. But it is more romantic to believe that the performer is facing a frightful danger with iron nerve. Even when the lady (it is more effective when a lady does it) has openly to slash a lion across the eyes with a whip before it can be persuaded even to growl at her, the audience still loves to think that she is taking her life in her hand. Now this is a very favorite official performance in Egypt, except that as our officials go through it with sheep instead of lions, more sensational steps have to be taken to persuade the public that the Egyptian sheep is the most savage of man-eaters. It is lucky for the officials that the English are not logical; for the first half of the official story is that the Egyptians are such abject slaves and cowards that England had to rescue them from the most horrible oppression by Ismail, and could make soldiers of them only by giving them English officers; and the second half is that they are so desperately ferocious, bloody-minded and implacable, that at a word of encouragement from an English novelist they will rise and sweep the Occupation into the Nile after ravishing all the white women and massacring all the white men. But nobody sees the incoherence. As the first half shews the Englishman as magnificently superior, and the second as dauntlessly brave, he does not notice that they flatly contradict one another.

The truth is that if Hall Caine could really make tyranny dangerous he would be the greatest living benefactor of the human race. Men, whether white or red, yellow or black, are not too insurrectionary, but too docile, too sheepish, too cowardly, to keep the world decent. That is why their condition is so miserable and their history so dishonorable. If we could depend on a sanguinary revolution in England once a month until the crooked be made straight and the rough places plain [Isaiah 40: 4], we should presently be a happy and prosperous nation. The real objection to The White Prophet is that it may make the Egyptians too patient and confiding, by persuading them that all Englishmen are as sympathetic and as high-minded as Hall Caine.

Finally, there is the objection that Hall Caine's hero, an Arab, has a "creeping" resemblance to Jesus, though why such a resemblance should give any Christian the creeps is not stated. Worse still, he has, in doing so, suggested that Jesus was a reality instead of a picture by [William] Holman Hunt.[7] Mr Gilbert Chesterton has just said very truly and forcibly [in *George Bernard Shaw*, 1909] that the one thing you must not assume in England is that God is something real, "like a tiger." If we keep a god at all, we keep him as we keep a watchdog: he may bite everybody else—indeed that is what he is for—but he must not bite us. Hall Caine's prophet does not wag his tail at the door of the British Consulate and bark and bite at the door of the mosque. He is a humane and honorable preacher, who appears superhuman in England only because he is neither a snob nor a sensualist. But suppose he *were* a reincarnation of Jesus! Does any Christian who has the faintest notion of what his religion means doubt that the spirit of Jesus is kept alive among us by continual reincarnation, and cannot be kept alive in any other way? What are we coming to when even professional writers are ignorant of this commonplace? The illiteracy which would forbid a man of letters to write an Imitation of Christ [like that of Thomas à Kempis] might be forgiven to the Irish peasant who is afraid to mention the fairies, and tremblingly alludes to them as "themselves" when the terrifying subject is forced on him; but that London journalists should have sunk to such an abyss of tribal ignorance is enough to make us ask, with a gasp, how long it will be before the civilized nations of Europe and Asia will come and conquer us for our own good as Cæsar conquered us in the comparatively enlightened age of Boadicea.[8]

Fortunately Hall Caine represents English feeling far more than the press or the governing class. He is comparatively a free man and can speak out. The press is not free. Its notion of foreign policy is to hold up as masterpieces of diplomacy such contemptible documents as the Anglo-Russian agreement [signed on 31 August 1907], in which the speculators of England and Russia, conspiring to tempt capital out of their own countries into Persia, have made a "Keep off the Grass" compact for dividing the spoils, and have entrapped our Foreign Office into committing England to its enforcement. As far as I can ascertain, I am the only man in these Islands—not, I hope, excepting Sir Edward Grey himself—who has read this much puffed agreement, consequently I am the only man who blushes when it is

7. One of the initiators of the Pre-Raphaelite movement. His famed canvas 'The Light of the World' (1854) represents Jesus knocking at the door of the human soul.
8. A variant for Boudicca, queen of the Iceni in east Britain, who led a revolt against the Romans in AD 60.

mentioned. It is a characteristic product of the British foreign policy that made a deadly enemy of Russia by undertaking to make war on any Power that helped her against Japan, and then assured us that if we were not abjectly polite to the Tsar the tender friendship it had cemented between us and Russia would be shaken to the foundations. When our governing class loses the power of remembering yesterday and foreseeing tomorrow, and spends today in talking manifest folly, it is time for the man of letters to take the instruction of public opinion out of its hands. And it is extremely reassuring to find that there is at least one man of letters who is not shirking that duty. In bravely and disinterestedly shouldering it Hall Caine deserves well of his countrymen, and though it is perhaps too much to hope that they will have the political sagacity to appreciate his public spirit as a citizen, they may have imagination enough to come under his spell as a romancer, as they have done so often before when his books concerned them far less vitally than The White Prophet.

PARKNASILLA.
6 September 1909.   G. BERNARD SHAW.

Socialism and Superior Brains

Preface to a reprint of Shaw's article, 'Mr Mallock's Proposed Trumpet Performance', originally published in the Fortnightly Review, *April 1894; revised for publication in 1909 as Fabian Tract No. 146*

═══

In January 1909, Mr Keir Hardie[1] delivered an address in which he pointed out that the remarkable increase in our national income, of which so much was being said in the controversy then raging between Free Traders and Tariff Reformers,[2] had not been shared by the working classes, who were no better off than before. Immediately Mr W. H. Mallock[3] wrote to The Times accusing Mr Keir Hardie of ignorance of political economy, on the ground that an educated man would have known that as the increase had been produced by the exceptional ability of the employers and inventors, there was no reason to claim any share of it for the employee class. Thereupon I lost patience with Mr Mallock and wrote the following letter to The Times [5 February 1909].

MR MALLOCK'S IDEALS
To the Editor of The Times

Sir—Mr Mallock's controversy with Mr [Leo] Chiozza Money[4] over the figures of Mr Keir Hardie may very well be left to the embarrassed silence in which goodnatured people sit when a person of some distinction

1. Scottish politician, a founder (1893) and long-time leader of the Independent Labour Party and the subsequent Labour Party (1900); first leader of the Labour Party in Parliament (1906–7).
2. Free traders advocated cheap food through tax-free imports; tariff reformers sought some imposition of tariffs on non-colonial imports. See preface to *Fabianism and the Fiscal Question* (1904), p. 169 above.
3. Author of *The New Republic* (1877) and other controversial works defending orthodoxy in religion and advocating conservative principles in politics. His assault on Fabian economics, in which he attacked the validity of *Fabian Essays in Socialism*, had prompted Shaw's response in 1894.
4. Economist, Fabian, and Liberal Member of Parliament.

volunteers an absurd blunder as a contribution to a subject which he has not mastered. The notion that the people who are now spending in week-end hotels, in motor cars, in Switzerland, the Riviera, and Algeria the remarkable increase in unearned incomes noted by Mr Keir Hardie have ever invented anything, ever directed anything, ever even selected their own investments without the aid of a stockbroker or solicitor, ever as much as seen the industries from which their incomes are derived, betrays not only the most rustic ignorance of economic theory, but a practical ignorance of society so incredible in a writer of Mr Mallock's position that I find it exceedingly difficult to persuade my fellow Socialists that he really believes what he teaches. They regard me as a cynic when I tell them that even the cleverest man will believe anything he wishes to believe, in spite of all the facts and all the textbooks in the world.

However, that is not the point that moves me to utterance on this occasion. If Mr Mallock does not know the difference between the rents of land and capital and the "rent of ability"—if he is so ignorant of ordinary business and patent law as not to know that the cleverest inventor cannot possibly extract a farthing more from his invention than his stupidest competitor when it has been communized fourteen years after its registration—he must not expect the Socialists to educate him. My quarrel with him is deeper than the technics of distribution. Mr Mallock is preaching an ideal; and I want every gentleman in England to repudiate that ideal, whether he be Socialist, Individualist, Liberal, Free Fooder, Tariff Reformer, or Home Ruler.

The ideal is, not that the greatest among you shall be servants of all the rest, but that whenever one of us discovers a means of increasing wealth and happiness, steps should be taken to restrict the increase to the discoverer alone, leaving the rest of the community as poor as if the discovery had never been made. If Mr Mallock does not mean this, he means nothing. If he does mean it, what does his University say to him? What does the Church say to him? What does every officer in the Army and Navy say to him? What does every Civil servant say to him, every statesman, every member of the humblest local authority, every professional man, every country gentleman, every man of honor, gentle or simple, who asks no more than a sufficient and dignified subsistence in return for the best service he is capable of giving to his country and to the world? This is not a question of the difference between the Socialist and the anti-Socialist: it is a question of the difference between the gentleman and the cad. Lord Lansdowne is not a Socialist, and Lord Charles Beresford is not a

Socialist;[5] but Lord Lansdowne has not asked for the hundreds of millions he saved Europe by making our treaty with Japan, and Lord Charles Beresford, if the German fleet attacked ours, would not refuse to conduct our naval defence unless the country were to be given to him as prize money when he had saved it. It is true that we have tradesmen—some of them in business on a very large scale both here and in America—impudent enough and base enough to demand for themselves every farthing that their business ability adds to the wealth of their country. If these *canaille* [rabble] were surgeons with a monopoly of a capital operation, they would refuse to save a patient's life until they had extorted his entire fortune as a fee. If they were judges, they would sneer at a judge's modest £5000 a year, and demand the total insurance value of the protection they afforded to society. If they were lifeboat coxswains or firemen, they would bargain for the kit of a drowning sailor or the nighty of a child in a burning house before they would throw a lifebuoy or mount a ladder. They are justly despised by men of Mr Mallock's profession and education; and when Mr Mallock challenges the right of our workmen to a share in the increased product of industry by asking whether their labor "has become more productive in respect of the laborer's own exclusive operations," he not only lays himself open to the obvious counter-question as to whether the "exclusive operations" of our employers could produce anything more than the exclusive operations of our laborers, but, what is far more serious, he seems to be lending the credit of his reputation, his education, and the high social and intellectual prestige of his class to the most abandoned sort of blackguardism that is still outside the criminal law.

It is fortunate for us that few of our tradesmen are so vile or so silly as the commercial theory by which theorists attempt to justify them. The man who has "made" £20,000 a year for himself knows very well that his success does not afford the smallest presumption that his services have been more important than those of a police-constable with 24s. a week. He does not dream of posing as the superior of the captain of a battleship with a modest income of three figures. Mr Carnegie "divides up" his surplus millions, and makes wildly Socialistic proposals, never for a moment suggesting that he is fifty times as clever as Mr Mallock because

5. Henry Fitzmaurice, Fifth Marquess Lansdowne, was foreign secretary 1900–1906, during which time (August 1905) Britain signed the Anglo-Japanese Agreement. Admiral Lord Charles Beresford was Commander-in-Chief of the Channel Fleet 1907–9.

he is fifty times as rich. I am not supposed to be an exceptionally modest man; but I did not advance the fact that I have made more money by a single play than Shakespear did by all his plays put together as a simple proof that I am enormously superior to Shakespear as a playwright. Our millionaires unload—awkwardly and unwisely sometimes, it is true, but still they unload—and do not talk nonsense about being 650 times as clever or as sober or as industrious as a dock-laborer because they have 650 times his income. The man who pretends that the distribution of income in this country reflects the distribution of ability or character is an ignoramus. The man who says that it could by any possible political device be made to do so is an unpractical visionary. But the man who says that it ought to do so is something worse than an ignoramus and more disastrous than a visionary: he is, in the profoundest Scriptural sense of the word, a fool.[6]

In conclusion, may I confess that nothing is so terrifying to the Socialist today as the folly of his opponents? There is nothing to keep the inevitable advance steady, to force the rank and file to keep their best men forward. A paper called The Anti-Socialist[7] is brought out with a flourish of trumpets. I open it, and find *vers de société* and a caricature of myself by a French artist, who depicts me in a French frock-coat, a Grand Old Man collar [as affected by Gladstone], and the countenance of Henri Rochefort.[8] A Belgian navvy [an unskilled labourer] is labelled "Ramsay Macdonald":[9] an American knockabout from the *café chantant* is carefully marked "Keir Hardie." Is it worth while to spend so much money to provide our Socialist debaters with footballs? If the Socialists did not know the difficult-ies of Socialism better than their opponents, and were not therefore far sterner Tories than the tariff reformers and far sounder Liberals than the free-traders; if all decent men were not nine-tenths Socialists to begin with, whether they know it or not; if there were any possibility of controversy as to the fundamental proposition of Socialism that whoever does not by the work of his prime repay the debt of his nurture and education, support him-self in his working days, and provide for his retirement, inflicts on society pre-cisely the same injury as a thief, then indeed the prospect would be black for civilization. As it is, I will continue to back the red flag against the black

6. Scripturally, a fool is not devoid of wits but deliberately closes his eyes to wisdom.
7. Published by the Anti-Socialist Union of Great Britain, founded in 1908.
8. French journalist and politician, known for his anti-establishment positions.
9. Secretary of the Labour Party and former Fabian, who in 1924 became the first Labour Prime Minister.

one; and with that I leave the Anti-Socialist League to sweep up the fragments of Mr Mallock and produce their next champion.—Yours truly,

February 2. G. BERNARD SHAW.

Mr Mallock made two replies to this letter. The first was sent to The Times, the readers of which had had my letter before them. It is practically a surrender without a blow. The second was sent to the other daily papers, the readers of which had not seen my letter. It is an attempt to retreat in fighting order.

The Times letter is as follows:

MR BERNARD SHAW ON MR MALLOCK
TO THE EDITOR OF THE TIMES

SIR—If Mr Bernard Shaw cares to look into the pages of my Critical Examination of Socialism, he will find the opinion or "ideal" which he attributes to me stated with the most minute precision and emphatically repudiated. So far as I myself am concerned, his long letter is absolutely without relevance:—I am your obedient servant,

February 5. W. H. MALLOCK.

The letter to the other papers ran thus:

MR MALLOCK AND G. B. SHAW
TO THE EDITOR OF THE MORNING ADVERTISER

SIR—Mr Shaw, although in his letter to the press, published this morning, he diverges into a variety of details, says that his main object is to criticize an opinion, or an "ideal" which he imputes to myself. The ideal translates itself into the doctrine that whatever increment of wealth is produced by ability as distinct from labor ought to be entirely appropriated by the gifted individual producing it, and that nobody else should receive from it any benefit. I have no right to demand that Mr Shaw should read my writings, but it is reasonable to demand that he should read them before he attempts to criticize my opinions or "ideals." If he had taken the trouble to read my Critical Examination of Socialism, he would have found that the particular ideal or opinion which he imputes to me is described in that book with the utmost precision, but is described only that it may be in precise terms repudiated.

On page 202 he will find the following passages:—"If, therefore, the claims of labor are based on, and limited to, the amount of wealth which is produced by labor itself . . . what labor would receive would be far less, not more, than what it receives today. . . . Is it, then, here contended, many readers will ask, that if matters are determined by ideal justice, or anything like practical wisdom, the remuneration of labor in general ought henceforth to be lessened, or, at all events, precluded from any possibility of increase? . . . If anyone thinks that such is the conclusion which is here suggested, let him suspend his opinion until we return to it, as we shall do, and deal with it in a more comprehensive way." This question is taken up again, page 283, as follows:—"Is it, then, the reader will ask, the object of the present volume to suggest that the true course of social reform in the future . . . would be to bind down the majority to the little maximum they could produce by their own unaided efforts? The object of this volume is the precise opposite. It is not to suggest that they should possess no more than they produce. It is to place their claim to a surplus not produced by themselves on a true instead of a fantastic basis." Mr Shaw may be left to read what follows if he pleases.

With regard to two other definite points, he touches farther on what he calls my opinions, or my "rustic ignorance" of economics. One of these relates to the "rent of ability." If he turns to pages 191–193 of my Critical Examination of Socialism, he will find this question discussed with great minuteness, the truth contained in the doctrine held by himself and other Socialists admitted and endorsed, and an element in the problem, which is yet more important, but to which they are entirely blind, specified. With regard to what Mr Shaw says about conflagrations and "babies' nighties," he will find this precise point anticipated and dealt with on page 122, Critical Examination. I have, let me repeat, no right to claim that Mr Shaw should read a line of anything I have written; but if in attempting to criticize the opinions and "ideals" of a writer, he imputes to him an ignorance or neglect of problems, *e.g.* the rent of ability, which he has discussed far more minutely than has Mr Shaw himself, and attributes to him opinions which he has elaborately repudiated, Mr Shaw will have hardly added to his reputation as a critic either of economic theory or of anything else. Mr Shaw writes about myself very much as a man would write who mistook the Book of Genesis for the Koran.—I am, Sir, yours, etc.

February 5, 1909.   W. H. MALLOCK.

I am usually willing "to build a bridge of silver for a flying foe,"[10] but in this case I cannot let Mr Mallock off without pursuing him to utter extinction. The book to which Mr Mallock refers as shewing that he has dealt with my argument does nothing of the kind: it reaffirms his error as strongly as he knows how to do it. Even if it contained a recantation, I should still have to deal with his unprovoked attack on Mr Keir Hardie, and with his Short Epitome of Eight Lectures on the Principal Fallacies of Socialism, in which he speaks of the Socialist "promise of distributing among the great mass of the population that portion of the annual income *which is at present in the hands of an exceptionally able minority*."

But the Critical Examination of Socialism contains no recantation. What it does contain is a statement that though everything that men enjoy over and above what a savage can wring from nature with his unaided hands is due to the exceptional ability of the few (represented, Mr Mallock implies, by our rich class today), yet it is not expedient to strip them of everything they possess above that level, as otherwise they would have no interest in civilization, and would revolt. Therefore Mr Mallock promises to shew, in a future book, how society can be arranged so as to give us all just enough to bribe us to allow the rich to remain in undisturbed enjoyment of their present position. If anyone doubts the fairness of this description of Mr Mallock's last chapter, the book is easily accessible in the excellent cheap edition published by John Murray in November 1908. In spite of the extravagance of the fundamental proposition of the book, which is that what a man produces is "that amount of wealth which would not have been produced at all had his efforts not been made" (pp. 206–207), thereby making every necessary laborer the producer of the entire wealth of the world, it is well worth reading, because it happens that any prejudice that may still linger against Socialism is almost wholly based on such childish ignorance of existing social conditions, and defended by such absurd arguments, that Mr Mallock is forced by his sense of intellectual honor to begin by making a clean sweep of the blunders of his own supporters. In doing so, he

10. 'For a flying foe / Discreet and provident conquerors build up / A bridge of gold': Philip Massinger, *The Guardian*, I: i (1633).

knocks the bottom out of Unsocialism as effectively as in his religious polemics he has knocked the bottom out of the vulgar sectarianism that passes for religion in this country. His object is to clear the ground for his own peculiar Individualism and Catholicism; but he has cleared it equally for the Fabian Society, which has the same interest as Mr Mallock in dispelling ignorance and confusion of thought. Besides, it is as well that the world should know that just as it seems clear to many laborers that the men who walk about in frock-coats and tall hats, talking and writing letters, are not workers at all, and produce nothing, so these very frock-coated men believe, like Mr Mallock, that the hired laborer is a brainless machine that owes the very fuel and grease that keep it working to the intelligence of the class that exploits it.

However, I need not argue the case with Mr Mallock now. It happens that in 1894 a wave of discussion of Socialism was passing over the press. Mr Mallock was then already ventilating his theory that the distribution of wealth in this country into big fortunes for the few and pittances for the many, corresponds to the natural division of the British race into a handful of geniuses and many millions of mediocrities. His diagrams are still extant to shew the lengths to which he went. Mr Frank Harris[11] was then editing The Fortnightly Review. He asked me could I answer Mr Mallock. I replied boyishly that any Socialist over the age of six could knock Mr Mallock into a cocked hat. He invited me to try my hand; and the result was the following essay, which appeared in the Review in April 1894. I emphasize the date to shew that Mr Mallock has had plenty of time to consider my case and answer it. When he put forth his Critical Examination of Socialism and accused Mr Keir Hardie of illiterate ignorance, he forgot that his own Unsocialism had been critically examined, and that Mr Keir Hardie had all the classic economists, from Adam Smith to [John E.] Cairnes,[12] at his back. Mr Keir Hardie is, in fact, on this subject, demonstrably a better read and better informed authority than Mr Mallock.

I reprint my arguments as they appeared in 1894. During the fifteen years since, Oblivion has made a few topical allusions unintelligible, and Death has changed some present tenses into past ones. I have dealt with these by a few inessential alterations, and omitted some chaff and some literary digressions; but the case against Mr Mallock stands as it did.

11. American-born editor and writer, who gained fame when he acquired the *Saturday Review* in 1894. He also gained the lifelong friendship of Shaw, who was his dramatic critic 1895–8.
12. Irish-born, mid-Victorian political economist, considered by many to be the last classical economist.

What I Owe to German Culture

Preface to the first volume of Dramatische Werke, *1911. Original English text first published in* Adam International Review, *Spring 1970*

=====

As I take up my pen to acknowledge my debt to German culture, I am reminded that in England some of my most impatient public utterances have been denials of this very debt. In my preface to Major Barbara in particular, I had to express my exasperation at the parrot cries of Schopenhauer and Nietzsche with which the theatre critics of London hailed every passage in my plays which struck them as having an intellectual air. I vehemently reproved them, not for their appalling ignorance of English literature (no one in England expects a theatre critic to be acquainted with literature: in fact his emoluments seldom justify his employers in demanding so expensive a qualification) but for the want of national self-respect which led them to assume that intellect is not a natural product of the English climate, and must therefore be a foreign importation. I pointed out that even if they were right in regarding intellect as unpleasant and unmannerly, they could not deny that many English authors had been guilty of it, and that it was clear to any competent student that it was quite as much from these authors as from those of Germany and Scandinavia, that I had inherited the themes I have attempted to elaborate before handing them on to the next generation.

Nevertheless my culture is very largely a German culture. It is true that of German literary culture I know disgracefully little; indeed, but for Goethe and Schiller I should have read nothing except the works of a few of my own contemporaries and the prose works of Richard Wagner. In some mysterious way I am in possession of some of the views of Kant, Schopenhauer, Fichte, Feuerbach, Hegel, Lessing, Ferdinand Lassalle, Helmholtz and Weismann; but I cannot honestly say that I have ever read them, though no doubt I have read scraps of them, as I have read scraps of everything. Also I could name several German authors: Klopstock, Herder, Kotzebue, etc., etc., etc.; but on my honor I do not know whether Herder wrote plays or novels or sermons or treatises on chemistry or philosophy. As to Klopstock [etymologically 'beating rod'] I conceive him as a sort of flaxen haired

Struwwelpeter[1]-Messiah, just because the name Klopstock suggested a mop to my childish imagination, though where the Messiah notion came from I do not know. Then there was a fashion among English Socialists twenty-five years ago of pretending to have read Karl Marx and Friedrich Engels (the fashion still lingers in Germany among the older Social-Democrats, I am told); and I actually did read the famous first volume of Das Kapital, only to discover that nobody else had read it and that it contained not a word on the subject of Socialism. But I do not count Marx as a German author, nor indeed as an author of any nationality. He belongs to the Anti-Bourgeoisie; and his cry was "Anti-Bourgeois of all lands: assemble and quarrel." Which they still do, every three years. The world owes Marx a great debt for his exposure of the selfishness and stupidity of that respectable middle class which Germany and England adore; and Das Kapital is one of the books which changes men's minds when they can be persuaded to read it; yet it is the book of a man who took no part in normal German or English society, and wrote of Capitalists and Workmen like a Class War Correspondent and not like a fellow creature. I have included Lassalle because, though he too was a Socialist and a Jew (and I beg you to remember that Jew is not in England a Schimpfwort [term of abuse] and that I am myself a Socialist), he seems to me to have been one of the inventors of modern Germany.

Also—now that I come to think of it—I read in my childhood a story by one Jean Paul Richter [prolific writer of novels and romances], and also Grimm's Fairy Tales. I still think Grimm the most entertaining of German authors. I was early taught to regard Germany as a very serious place because I was a little Irish Protestant and knew that Martin Luther was a German. I therefore concluded that all Germans went to heaven, an opinion which I no longer hold with any conviction.

I think this will give the reader a very fair notion of the sort of mess my mind is in on the subject of German literature generally. I should add that my acquaintance with the German language is of the most precarious kind. When I speak of reading German authors I must not be understood as having read them in the original. I fully intend to learn German some day. Everybody should. But I am not yet fiftyfive; and there is plenty of time still. Meanwhile, when I receive a visit from a German who does not speak English, I find it a good plan to listen to him with an air of keen interest and, when he pauses for breath, to exclaim enthusiastically "Ausgezeichnet!" ['First-rate!'] I do not know exactly what *Ausgezeichnet*

1. 'Shock-headed Peter' (a colloquialism) is a popular figure in German juvenile literature, created in 1847 by Heinrich Hoffmann, who also illustrated the work.

means; but it always pleases the German and leaves him under the impression that I both speak and understand his language perfectly. But if I presume on this success and endeavor to impart my views to the German in his own language, the result is always the same. I bewilder him, and send his wife into uncontrollable fits of laughter. In short, dear reader, my knowledge of German is probably very like your knowledge of English. As to reading, I have a theory that if it is absolutely necessary, I can with great labor and the help of a dictionary, read a German book; but I carefully abstain from putting the theory to the test of practice. If you write me a letter in German and use the Latin script, I will not say that I may not contrive to gather your meaning; but it would be wiser of you to write in English or French.

But there is a language which is European, if not universal; and that is the language of music. That language is a mother tongue to me. I may know nothing about Klopstock or Herder; but about Bach, Haydn, Mozart, Beethoven, Wagner and Richard Strauss I probably know more than most Germans. I know their works far better than I know English dramatic literature. I know that music has superseded words for many dramatic purposes. When I find my colleagues trying to write sentimental love scenes I ask them whether they have ever heard Tristan und Isolde, and whether they seriously think people will listen to mere word-music after tone poetry—whether they think they can even touch Verdi and Gounod with their lame verbal descriptions of the indescribable, much less Wagner. Certainly I cannot. I knew quite well when I began writing for the stage that I must become either a composer or a librettist unless I could enlarge the spoken drama by a new sort of love scene.

Perhaps the reason I looked this necessity so boldly in the face was that I had a new sort of love scene ready, and was quite done with Romeo and Juliet. My love scene really went back to Hamlet and Ophelia; and I must leave the German critics to follow up that hint as best they can; for I have no room here for any explanatory treatise. But I must say a word as to the general situation with regard to love scenes as it stood when I began to write for the theatre, and as it remains today. We had two sorts of material: the moral romance which we all recommended to our daughters, and the immoral romance which we kept on the top shelf for ourselves. The moral romance was much the more agreeable of the two: it made quite pleasant reading and playgoing when it was readable or bearable at all, because it entertained us without making us think. The immoral romance was painful, unwholesome, discouraging, and often fearfully tedious; but it satisfied our curiosity about matters that were forbidden to moral romance; and it fed our minds as well as our imaginations.

As all drama represents conflict of some kind, both moral and immoral romance had their stock conflicts. In moral romance the lovers struggled against the plots laid to separate them by jealous villains, against hardhearted parents, misadventure by sea or land, innocent misunderstandings, and even hardships of duty, provided duty was always allowed first place and was reconciled with happiness before the curtain fell. In the immoral play the conflict was always with morality. The hero was in love with someone else's wife, or she with someone else's husband. The children appealed to you on the ground that they were illegitimate. The two sorts of romance were equally hypocritical, because immoral romance was always striving to convince you that immorality is really the highest ideal morality. It was more the romance of the unmentionable than of the genuinely human. In Germany, I am told, its quest of the unmentionable was so resolute that when it had mentioned all the unmentionable things that were nevertheless natural, and, by dint of mentioning them, made them at last mentionable, there was nothing left for it but the unmentionable things that are not natural, at which point it became nauseous to normal people and ridiculous to everybody. But long before immoral romance reached this stage, moral romance had gone to the dogs much more hopelessly. Moral romance had never defied morality; but, like most moral people, it had practised a good deal of furtive naughtiness. It did not ask you to sympathize with immoral people: on the contrary, it killed them or sent them to prison in the last chapter or the last act; but before that edifying conclusion was reached it had dwelt on their immoralities with a licence which the immoral romancers dared not claim. Also it had left out all the painful and troublesome facts of life, and thereby done much more than the immoralists to encourage the notion that the romantic life is careless about money (that is to say, dishonest), careless about clothes and cleanliness, careless about law and order, contemptuous of public affairs and learning as dry subjects, and responsive to no stimulus but that of concupiscence. In short, it had become Bohemian.

Now a child brought up in a Bohemian household, if it has character enough to perceive manifest evils and react against them, grows up with a strong appreciation of the value of money, health, public spirit, and high social organization, and with a hearty loathing of the sound of a piano before dinner and the sight of complimentary tickets for theatres and concerts. And as it was mostly in Bohemian households that an early knowledge of art was obtainable, we at last found ourselves face to face with a generation of writers who were in contemptuous revolt against the old Bohemianism.

Just consider what this meant. Moral romance had dropped one by one all the convictions and responsibilities that bound it to respectable society. Whilst immoral romance had been enlarging the list of mentionable subjects, moral romance was enlarging the list of unmentionable ones. First it had ruled out religion as unromantic and therefore dry and unpleasant. With religion went philosophy, politics, law, business, until very soon there was absolutely nothing that a moral romancer could mention except sex and its operations. Imagine then what moral romance became when it consisted of stories about sex told by Bohemians: that is, by dishonest, dirty, lazy, selfish anarchic people, detached by their habits from all the organic part of society. Imagine this Bohemian Alsatia, when its moral sense was perishing through atrophy, discovering that the efforts of the immoralists had produced a lucrative market for immoral romance and that there was no longer any need to make even a pretence of conventional propriety! Is it surprising that moral romance went headlong to the devil, and became the most corrupting artistic force in modern society?

Nobody will ever understand the present situation until they have not only unravelled this confusion of the moral with the immoral romancers in their common disregard of conventional decency, but realize that the newest comers are in conflict, not with the old moralists, whom they have long left for dead on the field, but with the old immoralists who imagine themselves still pioneers. Nothing bothers the "advanced" German who makes my acquaintance more than the fact that I am a respectable man; that I am legally married to the lady I live with; that I do all my literary work between breakfast and lunch and am always in bed before midnight; that I work so hard at municipal administration that I was invited to become a burgomaster; that the world in which men spend their evenings at suppers drinking champagne with actresses and artists' models and dancers is so unknown to me that I gravely doubt whether it has any real existence and wonder how, if it does exist, its unfortunate victims can endure it (all the actresses and dancers I know are hardworking respectable women); that Bohemianism disgusts me and vice bores me; and that, in short, I might retire from literature and become a respectable cheese merchant tomorrow without altering my domestic habits in any respect. To a romantic German this is incredible: to a romantic Frenchman it is worse than incredible: it is scandalous. I see elderly Frenchmen of genius laboriously undertaking gallantries because public opinion expects it of them, and inducing impossible countesses and baronesses and princesses to travel about with them because a French romancer without a mistress is like a marquis without a valet: nobody believes his rank is genuine. I do not know whether such sacrifices are made to Bohemianism in Germany. I hear scraps of gossip about pianists which seem to indicate that when they are respectable men (and they probably all are or they could not work so hard) they are expected in common decency to conceal it. I sometimes think that artists hire mistresses as beggars hire babies, merely to touch the sympathies of the public, their relations being really blameless. I do not say that the hiring consideration is anything so vulgar as money: the reputation of being an artist's mistress is delightful to some women and gets them into interesting society, especially if they are thoroughly respectable by nature (your really improper person always marries a bourgeois and covets a reputation for marble virtue). Whether this be so or not, the fact remains that the present generation of men of genius—I will not say I belong to it; for perhaps I am a little too old; but for which at all events I helped to break the path—is distinguished by a strong civic spirit, a hatred of waste and disorder, and an intense rebellion against the tyranny of sex. And this at once brings it into open conflict with the vice which has become the common theme of both moralists and immoralists, and into sympathy with the bourgeois virtues.

But now observe the consequences of this. The moment the artists adopted the bourgeois virtues, they discovered that the bourgeoisie did not really possess them or understand them. It is true that our bourgeois do to a certain extent compel one another to practise these virtues, or, at worst, to conceal their vices; but they still speak and think of their virtues as self-sacrifices and painful mortifications of their own nature. The bourgeois never pretends to be Saint Francis nor Sir Galahad: he always poses as Casanova tamed and broken-in to monogamous respectability. No doubt he takes this romantic view of himself mainly because he has never tried the dissoluteness he secretly adores. A month of such a life as Casanova led (or said he led) would send him back to his fireside for ever. But still he is conscious that he is under a moral tyranny which is at many points so inhuman that it would break down if there were not clandestine arrangements by which virtue can be tempered by vice until it becomes bearable. Add to this that marriage, the very citadel of his morality, is unboundedly licentious and yet legally regulated and socially recognized. The romantic immoralist may laugh scornfully when marriage is called not only voluptuous, but safe, comfortable, and free. No doubt there is always the risk that any given marriage may turn out a misery and slavery, especially where the divorce laws are as monstrous as they are in England, for instance. But compare our marriages with the so-called free unions which the romantic immoralists form when they go beyond the talking stage! Marriage is both freer and happier. The freedom of the free union is illusory: a man may divorce or leave his lawful wife on reasonable provocation, and can always demand a certain standard of conduct from her; but who can get rid of a mistress except by what everyone will call a callous act of base desertion; and what claims can he make on her for good domestic conduct when he has not made her his wife? If you wish to see the bondage of marriage intensified tenfold, complicated by ostracism and blackmail, embittered by despair of escape, and without any of the compensation and securities that marriage offers, you will find it in the households of the few immoralists who practise what they preach.

Thus immoralism and amorism are even greater frauds than Morality and Respectability. Every exposure of the unreality of moral romance leads rebellious spirits to immoral romance only to find that it is much worse. Inevitably then, a school of writers arises which has observed this, and which, whilst it still chastises the moralists with whips, chastises the immoralists with scorpions. As an example I will cite neither a German nor an English author, but a French one: [Eugène] Brieux.[2] The attack on bourgeois marriage can hardly be carried further than in Les Trois Filles de M. Dupont and Maternité. All the old-fashioned critics who learnt their business when there were only two sorts of theatre poets: the moralists and the immoralists, and both were Bohemians, immediately classed Brieux as an immoralist with vine leaves in his hair. But presently Brieux wrote Les Hannetons, an exposure of the illicit, so-called free *ménage*, which would scare the boldest libertine into marriage. The critics are bewildered: they ask is Saul then among the prophets? Whilst they are disputing, Brieux is made a member of the [French] Academy; and the immoralists cry: "We told you he was no artist: he is at last convicted of being a respectable man."

Take another example from England and Germany. Read [George] Du Maurier's Trilby, with its amiable, sentimental glorification of Bohemian life in the Quartier Latin, and its sympathetic heroine who was a saint as well as an artist's model. Millions of English and American readers found it the nicest story they had ever read. Then read The Song of Songs by Hermann Sudermann. No Puritan ever penned such an attack on Bohemianism. Sudermann's doctrine is, in effect, "Respectability may be hypocrisy, but Bohemianism is damnation."

That our social institutions are unreasonable and out of date; that some of the conditions of marriage are inhuman and others abominable; that

2. French journalist who, under the influence of Ibsen, employed the stage for airing controversial views on contemporary social problems.

capitalistic private property has worse results than private war; that there is no more justification either in logic or in practical necessity for the practice of releasing a rich man from civil or industrial service than from military; that our established religions are all so loaded with incredible and savage superstitions that their profession is only possible to people who are either stupid and ignorant or willing to profess what they do not believe; that poverty is so widespread and mischievous that the only hope of civilization lies in changes that seemed revolutionary to our fathers: all this, and a good deal more to the same effect, does not make immorality and illegality one whit more or less uncomfortable, degrading and undesirable, or Bohemian-ism less disreputable than they would be under the most perfect conceivable institutions. Yet literature is kind to Bohemia, because it is so often the lot of the literary man at the beginning, when he is still struggling to gain a footing among the few who live by their pens, to be thrust down by his poverty into Bohemia. There he can find a sort of artistic society which is at least better than no society at all. Many a lonely wretch has been saved from despair by a few evenings spent in circles where a little brains, a little wit, a little youthful good looks, a little skill as a musician, a little reputation in the theatres, a little post on a newspaper staff, are the only qualifications for presentation and welcome. And he has carried through the rest of his life a grateful recollection of these evenings, and, like Du Maurier, has defended the Bohemians against the scorn of the bourgeoisie. But this indulgence, this sentimentality, is the cruelest of mercies. It makes the artist the spoilt child of the community. And when such a profound conception of the importance of art as that which was popularized by Richard Wagner once takes hold of the rising generation, they perceive that the artist is just the one child of the community who must not be spoilt. The country in which to be a Junker is to be a trained and disciplined man with principles and a place in society, even though the training be only that of the drill sergeant and the principles obsolete prejudice, whilst to be an artist is to have no training, no discipline, no principles, and no place in society, but only enough individual technical skill (not always even that) to make him petulant and conceited, is a lost country; for nowadays people learn from nothing except art: the churches are empty except when the musician and orator fills them; and unless our artists are prophets or at least priests, nothing can save us from social putrefaction but the coarse virilities of Junkerdom. And how much of even this virility will be left when it is diluted with a few more billions of American dollars, may be left to the imagination.

Hence the new generation of artists has as its social task, not the barren repetition of supercilious ironies at the expense of the bourgeoisie, and the sentimental glorification of *dames aux camélias* and the like, but the redemption of art from Bohemianism and outlawry. How to make the German a good artist without making him either a narrowminded hypocritical bourgeois or a stupid domineering Junker: that is our job. If you have grasped this, you will understand why in these plays of mine, anti-bourgeois as they are, I have shewn some respect for the bishop and the judge and even for the slum landlord and the businesslike procuress; whilst to the Bohemian artist—to "the man of genius who is not also a man of honor"[3]—I have been pitiless.

Now not even Richard Strauss himself can give this new turn to the drama by music. Before ideas blossom into emotions they have to be cultivated for many years. They begin as jokes, epigrams, apparent paradoxes: they end as political and religious constitutions. Not until men have lived and died for them do they cease to sound like eccentric discords and go straight to our hearts as simple harmonies. Besides, much as I have learnt from music, and frankly as I abandon romance to the musician, there is a music of words as well as of tones. There are many masterpieces of such music in the English language. Neither Shakespear nor Milton has now any intellectual message for modern Europe; and as to the Bible, I do not know how it stands in Germany, but in the British Empire when an attempt is made to put its precepts into practice by Doukhobors, Tolstoyans, Peculiar People[4] and the like, we put them in prison. Yet Shakespear, Milton and the Bible still cast the spell of their word music on us. I also profess to be a word musician; but as this sort of music cannot be translated, and must be replaced by an independent and original German word music, I must leave the German honors of that to my friend Trebitsch, and speak only of what I owe to German music. Well, I owe to Mozart the discovery that the march of the human spirit need not be a funeral procession—that one can throw away all the ponderous insignia and dull affectations and solemn mirthless grimaces of our official, academic, and sacerdotal idols,

3. Sir Colenso Ridgeon in Act IV of Shaw's *The Doctor's Dilemma* (1906) opines: 'The most tragic thing in the world is a man of genius who is not also a man of honor.'
4. The Doukhobors are a religious community of Nonconformists, first arising among Russian peasants in the eighteenth century and now perpetuated in Canada, who believe essentially that the Church is where two or three are gathered together. The word means 'spirit-fighter'. The Peculiar People are a small sect of Christian faith-healers, who accept a literal interpretation of James 5: 15, that 'the prayer of faith shall save the sick'. See also preface to *The Doctor's Dilemma*, p. 348.

and attain all the heights and sound all the depths of the soul in the most impetuous gaiety of spirit and the most exquisite tenderness of feeling. From that time I held all the pomps of art to be blemishes—sometimes to the great hindrance of my credit; for the English will not believe that a doctrine is serious unless it bores them or terrifies them. From Beethoven and his successors I learnt to construct plays by the development of themes, and to throw over the mechanical tracks of Scribe and his school as Wagner threw over the mechanical dance patterns of decorative music.

I might cite many other specific points; but to avoid being tedious I may sum the whole matter up by saying that my pretension to be an educated man and the heir of a high culture, is founded, not on ancient Greek and Roman literature, nor on any systematic study of modern literature, but on that extraordinary body of German art which began with Johann Sebastian Bach and is still alive in the hands of Richard Strauss. I am not forgetting my debt to Italian music and painting: indeed the moment I attempt to define my obligations I find that I have creditors everywhere, and that German science and philosophy, French literature, politics, medieval architecture, Greek art and Roman history, are all in the cairn on which I have laid my pebble; but my knowledge of them is desultory compared to my grasp of modern German music from its birth to its maturity. By its struggles with stupidity and its dallyings with romance I have been able to interpret all the other arts including my own. Even a German *régisseur* [director] could learn something from music as to the execution of my plays. It is not for nothing that the most distinguished of my English colleagues, Harley Granville Barker, when he finds a puzzled actor rehearsing a part in one of my plays under the impression that the Shaw drama, being ultra-intellectual, demands a thoughtfulness and restraint which conveys nothing to the audience but paralyzed bewilderment, he exclaims "For heaven's sake remember that this is not a play but an opera and deliver every speech as if you expected an encore."

I must now come to my debt to the German theatre; and the debt is so great that it seems ungracious to say, as I must, that I value this edition of my dramatic works partly because I am not content to be judged by German theatrical performances of them even in places where such performances are within reach of everybody. In England we laud the German theatre to the skies. No writer on the theatre is listened to here unless he begins by picturing the English theatre as a place fit only for parlormaids and office boys, and the German theatre as a rendezvous for artists and philosophers. We clamor for repertory theatres because Germany has repertory theatres. Repertory theatres, we say, mean Shakespear, Goethe, Ibsen,

Euripides and Aristophanes every night. English theatres, engaged for the run of a single play, mean—well, perhaps I had better not mention names.

Though I employ these eulogies in England without scruple as sticks to beat the English theatre, I am not altogether duped by them. There are advantages in the London system, and disadvantages in the German. These German disadvantages, though they do not on the whole outweigh the English advantages, nevertheless produce grotesque results in plays like mine, which do not deal in established stage types and situations. Let me describe an experience which illustrates this.

At a hotel in a German town [Munich, 1908] which shall be nameless here, I saw in the hall an *affiche* announcing that Candida, by Bernard Shaw, was to be performed that evening at the Residenz-Theater. As I had never seen one of the famous German performances of my plays, I immediately instructed the hall porter to procure tickets for me. He promptly tried to dissuade me from such an act of folly. He explained carefully that the play, though an English play, would be performed in German and that therefore I should not understand it. When I convinced him that I knew this, he only redoubled his dissuasions. The play, he said, was nothing: nobody went to see it: I should not only be disappointed in the quality of the piece, but would make myself publicly ridiculous by attending a performance shunned by all travellers with any sort of *savoir vivre*. In vain did I beg him to allow me to incur this disgrace: he flatly and positively refused to compromise his reputation as a hotel porter by buying tickets for Candida; and in the end I had to spare his dignity and pay at the doors of the theatre.

The moment the curtain rose, I all but burst into a shriek of laughter. For there, instead of a well-groomed British clergyman, smart, close-cropped, and cleanshaven, was a sort of colossal Gigerl-Aaron,[5] caricatured from the illustrations in a family Bible. A thick valance of hair covered the back of his neck and rested on his shoulders; his beard would have sufficed for a whole Sanhedrin [highest court and council of the ancient Jewish nation]; his eyebrows were like arched sausages; his lower lip was the white, thick, broad lip of a Marabout [Muhammadan hermit]; and his coat was a gabardine descending to his heels. He was, in short, a German stage pastor. Now if he had been in the least like a real German pastor, I should have forgiven the *régisseur* for disregarding my plain directions. But I had just travelled from one end of Germany to the other in a motor car,

5. As 'Gigerl' means a dandy, this would be a foppish treatment of the Biblical patriarch.

through town and village, observing all sorts and conditions of German men; and not one figure like this outrageous pastor had I seen anywhere.

The actor was a good actor. His representation of a German stage pastor with a German stage trouble in his German stage household and a deeply wounded German stage heart could not have been improved on. And since the conventions of the German stage have some root, however remote, in human nature, there were some points of contact between his performance and my play, which is also human. But never for a moment was he the Reverend James Mavor Morell, or even the Reverend Pastor Hans Schulz.

Yet I forgot how absurd he was when the poet entered. The poet is very carefully described in my play as an English stripling of the upper class, dressed with the carelessness of a boy and a poet's disregard of convention. But the Erster Liebhaber [juvenile lead in a stock company, usually a lover or hero] of this German theatre knew nothing of such strange realities. His business was to play Erster Liebhaber, to marry unmarried heroines and seduce married ones. And he knew only one way of doing it or dressing it; and that was the seductive way. He was clad like a German clerk on an English bank holiday, with pink striped collar, cutaway coat, and brilliant patent leather shoes. He had a little moustache—a seducer's moustache. And he was painfully puzzled and uneasy, not because the character he was representing is supposed to be nervous before strangers, but because the words he had to speak were not the accustomed words. He spoke them bravely as if they were the accustomed words; but he felt that they were all wrong, and doubtless cursed the foreign author who did not know how to write an Erster Liebhaber's part properly.

The rest were more plausible. The heroine, a clever Jewess (once more I beg you to remember that this is not in England a Schimpfwort [a term of abuse]), not only acted well, but was quite credible. Her stage father was accustomed to be a Colonel, or at least a banker in plays where he stood in that relation to the heroine; but by telling myself that Candida's father really kept a curiosity shop and picture gallery in Frankfort, I enjoyed his performance.

Now in England I could not have secured for a provincial performance a company with half the skill and practice of this German company; but I could easily have secured a much better performance. My Erster Liebhaber would not have known how to act an Erster Liebhaber, or perhaps anything else; but for that very reason he would have accepted the part just as it was written and tried to make the best of it. And as I should have selected and engaged him, for my play alone, not because he was Erster Liebhaber in the theatre and was therefore entitled to all the *jeune premier* parts, but solely for his personal suitability to the character, he would not have had to begin by disguising himself or doing violence to his own temperament. The English system has its disadvantages; for so much stress is laid on the suitability of an actor's personality that London plays are written to suit the favorite London actors just as their clothes are made to fit them by their tailors; but in any case an English actor is generally found playing a part suited to him, and always playing that part and not substituting one of the conventions of the repertory system. I speak of this with knowledge; for in my childhood the German system survived in my native town; and I saw the *Gastspieler* [touring star] going round with all sorts of plays, from Shakespear to Sardou, and casting them from the permanent local company, who had lost all habit and power of imagining themselves human beings or studying anything in a part except the words. There were leading juveniles, leading ladies, "heavies" (male and female), first and second old men and women, first and second low comedians, singing chambermaids (soubrettes), walking gentlemen and "utilities"; but there were no actors in the present London sense of the term. All this has become so much a thing of the past in England that I never dreamt of seeing the poet and the clergyman in Candida played by a leading juvenile and a heavy, as it would have been in Dublin in my boyhood. But I did see it so played at last, in Germany; and I hope I may never see it again.

Now I do not suggest for a moment that the performance of my plays in Berlin or at the Burgtheater in Vienna [is] to be classed with that which I have described above. I am informed that these performances exceed in excellence anything that a London author can dream of. But the whole German speaking world does not live in Berlin and Vienna. Much of it lives out of reach of any theatre. Some of it lives in such cities as that in which I saw Candida performed (wild horses shall not drag its name from me, yet it was no obscure third-rate townlet, but a famous German art centre). Therefore it is as well that the Germans should be able to read my plays as well as see them in the theatre; so that they may be able to judge how far what they have seen really represents what I have written.

As to my friend the translator, I can only offer him my sympathy. He has expiated the crime of having discovered my works and made them successful in Germany by suffering all the insults and misunderstandings which afflict an original author complicated by the disparagements which fall on the head of the translator. I am not now alluding to the complaints which are the common lot of all translators. My plays have the effect of persuading every German who knows English that he could make a better version than Herr Trebitsch. I am accustomed to that in all countries. But

Germans go further than this. They begin by denying the translator's knowledge of English. They go on to deny his knowledge of German. They then go on to deny my knowledge of German; and when I confess my deficiencies they tell me to my face that I do not know English enough to understand my own meaning, and therefore cannot judge whether Herr Trebitsch has grasped it or not. They then proceed to wild inventions of a personal character; and when I mildly assure them that I have actually seen and spoken to Herr Trebitsch; that he is, in fact, an intimate friend in my household, and that therefore I find it difficult to believe that he is (for instance) a Pole, a Bulgarian, a Tartar, an American, an Esquimaux, a French Swiss, with all sorts of absurd histories attached to each confidential biography of him, I am told that I am either a very bad judge of men or that I am not telling the truth. I therefore take this opportunity of asking his German critics[6] as a personal favor, to give me up as hopeless on the subject of Herr Trebitsch. It is clear to me that if his translations are not translations at all, but audacious forgeries made by a man ignorant of my language, then he must be a highly talented dramatist to achieve such success in the theatre, and a quite diabolically clever man to converse and correspond with me in a language he does not know. Also, his generosity in sharing with me the *tantièmes* [royalties] earned by plays in which it appears I have had no share, entitles him to my eternal gratitude. Therefore, with all due respect to Herr Trebitsch's correctors and biographers, I must inform them, in the English phrase, that "if they dont like him, they must lump him"; for there is no man in Europe to whom I am more deeply indebted or with whom I feel happier in all our relations, whether of business, or art, or of personal honor and friendship. And I conclude this long preface by my best bow to the German nation, and a very cordial shakehands with Siegfried Trebitsch.

LONDON.
21 December 1910.

---

6. Of these the two most virulently condemnatory were Leon Kellner and Max Meyerfeld (translator of Wilde and Galsworthy).

Preface on Doctors

Preface to The Doctor's Dilemma, 1911

=====

It is not the fault of our doctors that the medical service of the community, as at present provided for, is a murderous absurdity. That any sane nation, having observed that you could provide for the supply of bread by giving bakers a pecuniary interest in baking for you, should go on to give a surgeon a pecuniary interest in cutting off your leg, is enough to make one despair of political humanity. But that is precisely what we have done. And the more appalling the mutilation, the more the mutilator is paid. He who corrects the ingrowing toe-nail receives a few shillings: he who cuts your inside out receives hundreds of guineas, except when he does it to a poor person for practice.

Scandalized voices murmur that these operations are necessary. They may be. It may also be necessary to hang a man or pull down a house. But we take good care not to make the hangman and the housebreaker the judges of that. If we did, no man's neck would be safe and no man's house stable. But we do make the doctor the judge, and fine him anything from sixpence to several hundred guineas if he decides in our favor. I cannot knock my shins severely without forcing on some surgeon the difficult question, "Could I not make a better use of a pocketful of guineas than this man is making of his leg? Could he not write as well—or even better—on one leg than on two? And the guineas would make all the difference in the world to me just now. My wife—my pretty ones—the leg may mortify—it is always safer to operate—he will be well in a fortnight—artificial legs are now so well made that they are really better than natural ones—evolution is towards motors and leglessness, &c., &c., &c."

Now there is no calculation that an engineer can make as to the behavior of a girder under a strain, or an astronomer as to the recurrence of a comet, more certain than the calculation that under such circumstances we shall be dismembered unnecessarily in all directions by surgeons who believe the operations to be necessary solely because they want to perform them. The process metaphorically called bleeding the rich man is performed not only metaphorically but literally every day by surgeons who are quite as honest as most of us. After all, what harm is there in it? The surgeon need not take off the rich man's (or woman's) leg or arm: he can remove the appendix or the uvula, and leave the patient none the worse after a fortnight or so in bed, whilst the nurse, the general practitioner, the apothecary, and the surgeon will be the better.

DOUBTFUL CHARACTER BORNE BY THE MEDICAL PROFESSION

Again I hear the voices indignantly muttering old phrases about the high character of a noble profession and the honor and conscience of its members. I must reply that the medical profession has not a high character; it has an infamous character. I do not know a single thoughtful and well-informed person who does not feel that the tragedy of illness at present is that it delivers you helplessly into the hands of a profession which you deeply mistrust, because it not only advocates and practises the most revolting cruelties in the pursuit of knowledge, and justifies them on grounds which would equally justify practising the same cruelties on yourself or your children, or burning down London to test a patent fire extinguisher, but, when it has shocked the public, tries to reassure it with lies of breath-bereaving brazenness. That is the character the medical profession has got just now. It may be deserved or it may not: there it is at all events: and the doctors who have not realized this are living in a fool's paradise. As to the honor and conscience of doctors, they have as much as any other class of men, no more and no less. And what other men dare pretend to be impartial where they have a strong pecuniary interest on one side? Nobody supposes that doctors are less virtuous than judges; but a judge whose salary and reputation depended on whether the verdict was for plaintiff or defendant, prosecutor or prisoner, would be as little trusted as a general in the pay of the enemy. To offer me a doctor as my judge, and then weight his decision with a bribe of a large sum of money and a virtual guarantee that if he makes a mistake it can never be proved against him, is to go wildly beyond the ascertained strain which human nature will bear. It is simply unscientific to allege or believe that doctors do not under existing circumstances perform unnecessary operations and manufacture and prolong lucrative illnesses. The only ones who can claim to be above suspicion are those who are so much sought after that their cured patients are immediately replaced by fresh ones. And there is this curious psychological fact to be remembered: a serious illness or a death advertizes the doctor exactly as a hanging advertizes the barrister who defended the person hanged. Suppose, for example, a royal personage gets something wrong with his throat, or has a pain in his inside. If a doctor effects some trumpery cure with a wet compress or a peppermint lozenge nobody takes the least notice of him. But if he operates on the throat and kills the patient, or extirpates an internal organ and keeps the whole nation palpitating for days whilst the patient hovers in pain and fever between life and death, his fortune is made: every rich man who omits to call him in when the same symptoms appear in his household is held not to have done his utmost duty to the patient. The wonder is that there is a king or queen left alive in Europe.

DOCTORS' CONSCIENCES

There is another difficulty in trusting to the honor and conscience of a doctor. Doctors are just like other Englishmen: most of them have no honor and no conscience: what they commonly mistake for these is sentimentality and an intense dread of doing anything that everybody else does not do, or omitting to do anything that everybody else does. This of course does amount to a sort of working or rule-of-thumb conscience; but it means that you will do anything, good or bad, provided you get enough people to keep you in countenance by doing it also. It is the sort of conscience that makes it possible to keep order on a pirate ship, or in a troop of brigands. It may be said that in the last analysis there is no other sort of honor or conscience in existence—that the assent of the majority is the only sanction known to ethics. No doubt this holds good in political practice. If mankind knew the facts, and agreed with the doctors, then the doctors would be in the right; and any person who thought otherwise would be a lunatic. But mankind does not agree, and does not know the facts. All that can be said for medical popularity is that until there is a practicable alternative to blind trust in the doctor, the truth about the doctor is so terrible that we dare not face it. Molière saw through the doctors [as in *Le Malade imaginaire*, 1673]; but he had to call them in just the same. Napoleon had no illusions about them; but he had to die under their treatment just as much as the most credulous ignoramus that ever paid sixpence for a bottle of strong medicine. In this predicament most people, to save themselves from unbearable mistrust and misery, or from being driven by their conscience into actual conflict with the law, fall back on the old rule that if you cannot have what you believe in you must believe in what you have. When your child is ill or your wife dying, and you happen to be very fond of them, or even when, if you are not fond of them, you are human enough to forget every personal grudge before the spectacle of a fellow creature in pain or peril, what you want is comfort, reassurance, something to clutch at, were it but a straw. This the doctor brings you. You have a wildly urgent feeling that something must be done; and the doctor does something. Sometimes what he does kills the patient; but you do not know that; and the doctor assures you that all that human skill could do has been done. And nobody has the brutality to say to the newly bereft father, mother, husband, wife, brother, or sister, "You have killed your lost darling by your credulity."

THE PECULIAR PEOPLE

Besides, the calling in of the doctor is now compulsory except in cases where the patient is an adult and not too ill to decide the steps to be taken. We are subject to prosecution for manslaughter or for criminal neglect if the patient dies without the consolations of the medical profession. This menace is kept before the public by the Peculiar People. The Peculiars, as they are called, have gained their name by believing that the Bible is infallible, and taking their belief quite seriously. The Bible is very clear as to the treatment of illness. The Epistle of James, chapter v., contains the following explicit directions:—

14. Is any sick among you? let him call for the elders of the Church; and let them pray over him, anointing him with oil in the name of the Lord:

15. And the prayer of faith shall save the sick, and the Lord shall raise him up; and if he have committed sins, they shall be forgiven him.

The Peculiars obey these instructions and dispense with doctors. They are therefore prosecuted for manslaughter when their children die.

When I was a young man, the Peculiars were usually acquitted. The prosecution broke down when the doctor in the witness box was asked whether, if the child had had medical attendance, it would have lived. It was, of course, impossible for any man of sense and honor to assume divine omniscience by answering this in the affirmative, or indeed pretending to be able to answer it at all. And on this the judge had to instruct the jury that they must acquit the prisoner. Thus a judge with a keen sense of law (a very rare phenomenon on the Bench, by the way) was spared the possibility of having to sentence one prisoner (under the Blasphemy Laws) for questioning the authority of Scripture, and another for ignorantly and superstitiously accepting it as a guide to conduct. Today all this is changed. The doctor never hesitates to claim divine omniscience, nor to clamor for laws to punish any scepticism on the part of laymen. A modern doctor thinks nothing of signing the death certificate of one of his own diphtheria patients, and then going into the witness box and swearing a Peculiar into prison for six months by assuring the jury, on oath, that if the prisoner's child, dead of diphtheria, had been placed under his treatment instead of that of St James, it would not have died. And he does so not only with impunity, but with public applause, though the logical course would be to prosecute him either for the murder of his own patient, or for perjury in the case of St James. Yet no barrister, apparently, dreams of asking for the statistics of the relative case-mortality in diphtheria among the Peculiars and among the believers in doctors, on which alone any valid opinion could be founded. The barrister is as superstitious as the doctor is infatuated; and the Peculiar goes unpitied to his cell, though nothing whatever has been proved except that his child died without the interference of a doctor as effectually as any of the hundreds of children who die every day of the same diseases in the doctor's care.

RECOIL OF THE DOGMA OF MEDICAL INFALLIBILITY ON THE DOCTOR

On the other hand, when the doctor is in the dock, or is the defendant in an action for malpractice, he has to struggle against the inevitable result of his former pretences to infinite knowledge and unerring skill. He has taught the jury and the judge, and even his own counsel, to believe that every doctor can, with a glance at the tongue, a touch on the pulse, and a reading of the clinical thermometer, diagnose with absolute certainty a patient's complaint, also that on dissecting a dead body he can infallibly put his finger on the cause of death, and, in cases where poisoning is suspected, the nature of the poison used. Now all this supposed exactness and infallibility is imaginary; and to treat a doctor as if his mistakes were necessarily malicious or corrupt malpractices (an inevitable deduction from the postulate that the doctor, being omniscient, cannot make mistakes) is as unjust as to blame the nearest apothecary for not being prepared to supply you with sixpenny-worth of the elixir of life, or the nearest motor garage for not having perpetual motion on sale in gallon tins. But if apothecaries and motor car makers habitually advertized elixir of life and perpetual motion, and succeeded in creating a strong general belief that they could supply it, they would find themselves in an awkward position if they were indicted for allowing a customer to die, or for burning a chauffeur by putting petrol into his car. That is the predicament the doctor finds himself in when he has to defend himself against a charge of malpractice by a plea of ignorance and fallibility. His plea is received with flat incredulity; and he gets little sympathy, even from laymen who know, because he has brought the incredulity on himself. If he escapes, he can only do so by opening the eyes of the jury to the facts that medical science is as yet very imperfectly differentiated from common curemongering witchcraft; that diagnosis, though it means in many instances (including even the identification of pathogenic bacilli under the microscope) only a choice among terms so loose that they would not be accepted as definitions in any really exact science, is, even at that, an uncertain and difficult matter on which doctors often differ; and that the very best medical opinion and treatment varies widely from doctor to doctor, one practitioner prescribing six or seven scheduled poisons for so familiar a disease as enteric [typhoid] fever where another will not tolerate drugs at all; one starving a patient whom another would stuff; one urging an operation which another would regard as unnecessary and dangerous; one giving alcohol and meat which another would sternly forbid, &c., &c., &c.: all these discrepancies arising not between the opinion of good doctors and bad ones (the medical contention is, of course, that a bad doctor is an impossibility), but between practitioners of equal eminence and authority. Usually it is impossible to persuade the jury that these facts are facts. Juries seldom notice facts; and they have been taught to regard any doubts of the omniscience and omnipotence of doctors as blasphemy. Even the fact that doctors themselves die of the very diseases they profess to cure passes unnoticed. We do not shoot out our lips and shake our heads, saying, "They save others: themselves they cannot save" [paraphrase of Luke 23: 35]: their reputation stands, like an African king's palace, on a foundation of dead bodies; and the result is that the verdict goes against the defendant when the defendant is a doctor accused of malpractice.

Fortunately for the doctors, they very seldom find themselves in this position, because it is so difficult to prove anything against them. The only evidence that can decide a case of malpractice is expert evidence: that is, the evidence of other doctors; and every doctor will allow a colleague to decimate a whole countryside sooner than violate the bond of professional etiquet by giving him away. It is the nurse who gives the doctor away in private, because every nurse has some particular doctor whom she likes; and she usually assures her patients that all the others are disastrous noodles, and soothes the tedium of the sick-bed by gossip about their blunders. She will even give a doctor away for the sake of making the patient believe that she knows more than the doctor. But she dare not, for her livelihood, give the doctor away in public. And the doctors stand by one another at all costs. Now and then some doctor in an unassailable position, like the late Sir William Gull,[1] will go into the witness box and say what he really thinks about the way a patient has been treated; but such behavior is considered little short of infamous by his colleagues.

WHY DOCTORS DO NOT DIFFER

The truth is, there would never be any public agreement among doctors if they did not agree to agree on the main point of the doctor being always in the right. Yet the two guinea man never thinks that the five shilling man is right: if he did, he would be understood as confessing to an overcharge of £1:17s.; and on the same ground the five shilling man cannot encourage the notion that the owner of the sixpenny surgery round the corner is quite up to his mark. Thus even the layman has to be taught that infallibility is not quite infallible, because there are two qualities of it to be had at two prices.

But there is no agreement even in the same rank at the same price. During the first great epidemic of influenza towards the end of the XIX century [1889–90 and for several subsequent years] a London evening paper sent round a journalist-patient to all the great consultants of that day, and published their advice and prescriptions: a proceeding passionately denounced by the medical papers as a breach of confidence of these eminent physicians. The case was the same; but the prescriptions were different, and so was the advice. Now a doctor cannot think his own treatment right and at the same time think his colleague right in prescribing a different treatment when the patient is the same. Anyone who has ever known doctors well enough to hear medical shop talked without reserve knows that they are full of stories about each other's blunders and errors, and that the theory of their omniscience and omnipotence no more holds good among themselves than it did with Molière and Napoleon. But for this very reason no doctor dare accuse another of malpractice. He is not sure enough of his own opinion to ruin another man by it. He knows that if such conduct were tolerated in his profession no doctor's livelihood or reputation would be worth a year's purchase. I do not blame him: I should

1. Court physician, who attended the Prince of Wales for typhoid in 1871.

do the same myself. But the effect of this state of things is to make the medical profession a conspiracy to hide its own shortcomings. No doubt the same may be said of all professions. They are all conspiracies against the laity; and I do not suggest that the medical conspiracy is either better or worse than the military conspiracy, the legal conspiracy, the sacerdotal conspiracy, the pedagogic conspiracy, the royal and aristocratic conspiracy, the literary and artistic conspiracy, and the innumerable industrial, commercial, and financial conspiracies, from the trade unions to the great exchanges, which make up the huge conflict which we call society. But it is less suspected. The Radicals who used to advocate, as an indispensable preliminary to social reform, the strangling of the last king with the entrails of the last priest, substituted compulsory vaccination for compulsory baptism without a murmur.

THE CRAZE FOR OPERATIONS

Thus everything is on the side of the doctor. When men die of disease they are said to die from natural causes. When they recover (and they mostly do) the doctor gets the credit of curing them. In surgery all operations are recorded as successful if the patient can be got out of the hospital or nursing home alive, though the subsequent history of the case may be such as would make an honest surgeon vow never to recommend or perform the operation again. The large range of operations which consist of amputating limbs and extirpating organs admits of no direct verification of their necessity. There is a fashion in operations as there is in sleeves and skirts: the triumph of some surgeon who has at last found out how to make a once desperate operation fairly safe is usually followed by a rage for that operation not only among the doctors, but actually among their patients. There are men and women whom the operating table seems to fascinate: half-alive people who through vanity, or hypochondria, or a craving to be the constant objects of anxious attention or what not, lose such feeble sense as they ever had of the value of their own organs and limbs. They seem to care as little for mutilation as lobsters or lizards, which at least have the excuse that they grow new claws and new tails if they lose the old ones. Whilst this book was being prepared for the press a case was tried in the Courts, of a man who sued a railway company for damages because a train had run over him and amputated both his legs. He lost his case because it was proved that he had deliberately contrived the occurrence himself for the sake of getting an idler's pension at the expense of the railway company, being too dull to realize how much more he had to lose than to gain by the bargain even if he had won his case and received damages above his utmost hopes.

This amazing case makes it possible to say, with some prospect of being believed, that there is in the classes who can afford to pay for fashionable operations a sprinkling of persons so incapable of appreciating the relative importance of preserving their bodily integrity (including the capacity for parentage) and the pleasure of talking about themselves and hearing themselves talked about as the heroes and heroines of sensational operations, that they tempt surgeons to operate on them not only with huge fees, but with personal solicitation. Now it cannot be too often repeated that when an operation is once performed, nobody can ever prove that it was unnecessary. If I refuse to allow my leg to be amputated, its mortification and my death may prove that I was wrong; but if I let the leg go, nobody can ever prove that it would not have mortified had I been obstinate. Operation is therefore the safe side for the surgeon as well as the lucrative side. The result is that we hear of "conservative surgeons" as a distinct class of practitioners who make it a rule not to operate if they can possibly help it, and who are sought after by the people who have vitality enough to regard an operation as a last resort. But no surgeon is bound to take the conservative view. If he believes that an organ is at best a useless survival, and that if he extirpates it the patient will be well and none the worse in a fortnight, whereas to await the natural cure would mean a month's illness, then he is clearly justified in recommending the operation even if the cure without operation is as certain as anything of the kind ever can be. Thus the conservative surgeon and the radical or extirpatory surgeon may both be right as far as the ultimate cure is concerned; so that their consciences do not help them out of their differences.

CREDULITY AND CHLOROFORM

There is no harder scientific fact in the world than the fact that belief can be produced in practically unlimited quantity and intensity, without observation or reasoning, and even in defiance of both, by the simple desire to believe founded on a strong interest in believing. Everybody recognizes this in the case of the amatory infatuations of the adolescents who see angels and heroes in obviously (to others) commonplace and even objectionable maidens and youths. But it holds good over the entire field of human activity. The hardest-headed materialist will become a consulter of table-rappers and slate-writers if he loses a child or a wife so beloved that the desire to revive and communicate with them becomes irresistible. The cobbler believes that there is nothing like leather. The Imperialist who regards the conquest of England by a foreign power as the worst of political misfortunes believes that the conquest of a foreign power by England would be a boon to the conquered. Doctors are no more proof against such illusions than other men. Can anyone then doubt that under existing conditions a great deal of unnecessary and mischievous operating is bound to go on, and that patients are encouraged to imagine that modern surgery and anesthesia have made operations much less serious matters than they really are? When doctors write or speak to the public about operations, they imply, and often say in so many words, that chloroform has made surgery painless. People who have been operated on know better. The patient does not feel the knife, and the operation is therefore enormously facilitated for the surgeon; but the patient pays for the anesthesia with hours of wretched sickness; and when that is over there is the pain of the wound made by the surgeon, which has to heal like any other wound. This is why operating surgeons, who are usually out of the house with their fee in their pockets before the patient has recovered consciousness, and who therefore see nothing of the suffering witnessed by the general practitioner and the nurse, occasionally talk of operations very much as the hangman in [Dickens's] Barnaby Rudge talked of executions, as if being operated on were a luxury in sensation as well as in price.

MEDICAL POVERTY

To make matters worse, doctors are hideously poor. The Irish gentleman doctor of my boyhood, who took nothing less than a guinea, though he might pay you four visits for it, seems to have no equivalent nowadays in English society. Better be a railway porter than an ordinary English general practitioner. A railway porter has from eighteen to twenty-three shillings a week from the Company merely as a retainer; and his additional fees from the public, if we leave the third-class twopenny tip out of account (and I am by no means sure that even this reservation need be made), are equivalent to doctor's fees in the case of second-class passengers, and double doctor's fees in the case of first. Any class of educated men thus treated tends to become a brigand class, and doctors are no exception to the rule. They are offered disgraceful prices for advice and medicine. Their patients are for the most part so poor and so ignorant that good advice would be resented as impracticable and wounding. When you are so poor that you cannot afford to refuse eighteenpence from a man who is too poor to pay you any more, it is useless to tell him that what he or his sick child needs is not medicine, but more leisure, better clothes, better food, and a better drained and ventilated house. It is kinder to give him a bottle of something almost as cheap as water, and tell him to come again with another eighteenpence if it does not cure him. When you have done that over and over again every day for a week, how much scientific conscience have you left? If you are weak-minded enough to cling desperately to your eighteenpence as denoting a certain social superiority to the sixpenny doctor, you will be miserably poor all your life; whilst the sixpenny doctor, with his low prices and quick turnover of patients, visibly makes much more than you do and kills no more people.

A doctor's character can no more stand out against such conditions than the lungs of his patients can stand out against bad ventilation. The only way in which he can preserve his self-respect is by forgetting all he ever learnt of science, and clinging to such help as he can give without cost merely by being less ignorant and more accustomed to sick-beds than his patients. Finally, he acquires a certain skill at nursing cases under poverty-stricken domestic conditions, just as women who have been trained as domestic servants in some huge institution with lifts, vacuum cleaners, electric lighting, steam heating, and machinery that turns the kitchen into a laboratory and engine house combined, manage, when they are sent out into the world to drudge as general servants, to pick up their business in a new way, learning the slatternly habits and wretched makeshifts of homes where even bundles of kindling wood are luxuries to be anxiously economized.

THE SUCCESSFUL DOCTOR

The doctor whose success blinds public opinion to medical poverty is almost as completely demoralized. His promotion means that his practice becomes more and more confined to the idle rich. The proper advice for most of their ailments is typified in Abernethy's "Live on sixpence a day and earn it."[2] But here, as at the other end of the scale, the right advice is neither agreeable nor practicable. And every hypochondriacal rich lady or

2. The surgeon John Abernethy, author of *The Abernethian Code of Health and Longevity* (1830), which ran to many editions.

gentleman who can be persuaded that he or she is a lifelong invalid means anything from fifty to five hundred pounds a year for the doctor. Operations enable a surgeon to earn similar sums in a couple of hours; and if the surgeon also keeps a nursing home, he may make considerable profits at the same time by running what is the most expensive kind of hotel. These gains are so great that they undo much of the moral advantage which the absence of grinding pecuniary anxiety gives the rich doctor over the poor one. It is true that the temptation to prescribe a sham treatment because the real treatment is too dear for either patient or doctor does not exist for the rich doctor. He always has plenty of genuine cases which can afford genuine treatment; and these provide him with enough sincere scientific professional work to save him from the ignorance, obsolescence, and atrophy of scientific conscience into which his poorer colleagues sink. But on the other hand his expenses are enormous. Even as a bachelor, he must, at London west end rates, make over a thousand a year before he can afford even to insure his life. His house, his servants, and his equipage (or autopage) must be on the scale to which his patients are accustomed, though a couple of rooms with a camp bed in one of them might satisfy his own requirements. Above all, the income which provides for these outgoings stops the moment he himself stops working. Unlike the man of business, whose managers, clerks, warehousemen and laborers keep his business going whilst he is in bed or in his club, the doctor cannot earn a farthing by deputy. Though he is exceptionally exposed to infection, and has to face all weathers at all hours of the night and day, often not enjoying a complete night's rest for a week, the money stops coming in the moment he stops going out; and therefore illness has special terrors for him, and success no certain permanence. He dare not stop making hay while the sun shines; for it may set at any time. Men do not resist pressure of this intensity. When they come under it as doctors they pay unnecessary visits; they write prescriptions that are as absurd as the rub of chalk with which an Irish tailor once charmed away a wart from my father's finger; they conspire with surgeons to promote operations; they nurse the delusions of the *malade imaginaire* (who is always really ill because, as there is no such thing as perfect health, nobody is ever really well); they exploit human folly, vanity, and fear of death as ruthlessly as their own health, strength, and patience are exploited by selfish hypochondriacs. They must do all these things or else run pecuniary risks that no man can fairly be asked to run. And the healthier the world becomes, the more they are compelled to live by imposture and the less by that really helpful activity of which all doctors get enough to preserve them from utter corruption. For even the most hardened humbug who ever prescribed ether tonics to ladies whose need for tonics is of precisely the same character as the need of poorer women for a glass of gin, has to help a mother through child-bearing often enough to feel that he is not living wholly in vain.

THE PSYCHOLOGY OF SELF-RESPECT IN SURGEONS

The surgeon, though often more unscrupulous than the general practitioner, retains his self-respect more easily. The human conscience can subsist on very questionable food. No man who is occupied in doing a very difficult thing, and doing it very well, ever loses his self-respect. The shirk, the duffer, the malingerer, the coward, the weakling, may be put out of countenance by his own failures and frauds; but the man who does evil skilfully, energetically, masterfully, grows prouder and bolder at every crime. The common man may have to found his self-respect on sobriety, honesty and industry; but a Napoleon needs no such props for his sense of dignity. If Nelson's conscience whispered to him at all in the silent watches of the night, you may depend on it it whispered about the Baltic and the Nile and Cape St Vincent, and not about his unfaithfulness to his wife. A man who robs little children when no one is looking can hardly have much self-respect or even self-esteem; but an accomplished burglar must be proud of himself. In the play to which I am at present preluding I have represented an artist who is so entirely satisfied with his artistic conscience, even to the point of dying like a saint with its support, that he is utterly selfish and unscrupulous in every other relation without feeling at the smallest disadvantage. The same thing may be observed in women who have a genius for personal attractiveness: they expend more thought, labor, skill, inventiveness, taste and endurance on making themselves lovely than would suffice to keep a dozen ugly women honest; and this enables them to maintain a high opinion of themselves, and an angry contempt for unattractive and personally careless women, whilst they lie and cheat and slander and sell themselves without a blush. The truth is, hardly any of us have ethical energy enough for more than one really inflexible point of honor. Andrea del Sarto, like Louis Dubedat in my play, must have expended on the attainment of his great mastery of design and his originality in fresco painting more conscientiousness and industry than go to the making of the reputations of a dozen ordinary mayors and churchwardens; but (if [Giorgio] Vasari is to be believed [in *Lives of the Painters*, 1550]) when the King of France entrusted him with money to buy pictures for him, he stole it to spend on his wife. Such cases are not confined to eminent artists. Unsuccessful, unskilful men are often much more scrupulous than successful ones. In the ranks of ordinary skilled labor many men are to be found who earn good wages and are never out of a job because they are strong, indefatigable, and skilful, and who therefore are bold in a high opinion of themselves; but they are selfish and tyrannical, gluttonous and drunken, as their wives and children know to their cost.

Not only do these talented energetic people retain their self-respect through shameful misconduct: they do not even lose the respect of others, because their talents benefit and interest everybody, whilst their vices affect only a few. An actor, a painter, a composer, an author, may be as selfish as he likes without reproach from the public if only his art is superb; and he cannot fulfil this condition without sufficient effort and sacrifice to make him feel noble and martyred in spite of his selfishness. It may even happen that the selfishness of an artist may be a benefit to the public by enabling him to concentrate himself on their gratification with a recklessness of every other consideration that makes him highly dangerous to those about him. In sacrificing others to himself he is sacrificing them to the public he gratifies; and the public is quite content with that arrangement. The public actually has an interest in the artist's vices.

It has no such interest in the surgeon's vices. The surgeon's art is exercised at its expense, not for its gratification. We do not go to the operating table as we go to the theatre, to the picture gallery, to the concert room, to be entertained and delighted: we go to be tormented and maimed lest a worse thing should befall us. It is of the most extreme importance to us that the experts on whose assurance we face this horror and suffer this mutilation should have no interests but our own to think of; should judge our cases scientifically; and should feel about them kindly. Let us see what guarantees we have: first for the science, and then for the kindness.

Are Doctors Men of Science?

I presume nobody will question the existence of a widely spread popular delusion that every doctor is a man of science. It is escaped only in the very small class which understands by science something more than conjuring with retorts and spirit lamps, magnets and microscopes, and discovering magical cures for disease. To a sufficiently ignorant man every captain of a trading schooner is a Galileo, every organ-grinder a Beethoven, every piano-tuner a Helmholtz, every Old Bailey barrister a Solon, every Seven

Dials[3] pigeon-dealer a Darwin, every scrivener a Shakespear, every loco-
motive engine a miracle, and its driver no less wonderful than George
Stephenson.[4] As a matter of fact, the rank and file of doctors are no more
scientific than their tailors; or, if you prefer to put it the reverse way, their
tailors are no less scientific than they. Doctoring is an art, not a science: any
layman who is interested in science sufficiently to take in one of the
scientific journals and follow the literature of the scientific movement,
knows more about it than those doctors (probably a large majority) who
are not interested in it, and practise only to earn their bread. Doctoring is
not even the art of keeping people in health (no doctor seems able to advise
you what to eat any better than his grandmother or the nearest quack): it is
the art of curing illnesses. It does happen exceptionally that a practising
doctor makes a contribution to science (my play describes a very notable
one); but it happens much oftener that he draws disastrous conclusions
from his clinical experience because he has no conception of scientific
method, and believes, like any rustic, that the handling of evidence and
statistics needs no expertness. The distinction between a quack doctor and a
qualified one is mainly that only the qualified one is authorized to sign
death certificates, for which both sorts seem to have about equal occasion.
Unqualified practitioners now make large incomes as hygienists, and are
resorted to as frequently by cultivated amateur scientists who understand
quite well what they are doing as by ignorant people who are simply
dupes. Bone-setters make fortunes under the very noses of our greatest
surgeons from educated and wealthy patients; and some of the most successful doctors on the register use quite heretical methods of treating disease,
and have qualified themselves solely for convenience. Leaving out of account the village witches who prescribe spells and sell charms, the humblest
professional healers in this country are the herbalists. These men wander
through the fields on Sunday seeking for herbs with magic properties of
curing disease, preventing childbirth, and the like. Each of them believes
that he is on the verge of a great discovery, in which Virginia Snake Root[5]
will be an ingredient, heaven knows why! Virginia Snake Root fascinates
the imagination of the herbalist as mercury used to fascinate the alchemists.
On week days he keeps a shop in which he sells packets of pennyroyal,

3. A junction of seven roads in the West End of London, formerly a notorious
warren of disreputable characters.
4. English inventor, who developed the use of steam-engines on British railways.
5. The creeping stem of a plant, *Liatris spicata* (Button Snake Root), used in North
America for snake bites because of its diuretic action.

dandelion, &c., labelled with little lists of the diseases they are supposed to cure, and apparently do cure to the satisfaction of the people who keep on buying them. I have never been able to perceive any distinction between the science of the herbalist and that of the duly registered doctor. A relative of mine [Shaw's mother] recently consulted a doctor about some of the ordinary symptoms which indicate the need for a holiday and a change. The doctor satisfied himself that the patient's heart was a little depressed. Digitalis being a drug labelled as a heart specific by the profession, he promptly administered a stiff dose. Fortunately the patient was a hardy old lady who was not easily killed. She recovered with no worse result than her conversion to Christian Science, which owes its vogue quite as much to public despair of doctors as to superstition. I am not, observe, here concerned with the question as to whether the dose of digitalis was judicious or not: the point is, that a farm laborer consulting a herbalist would have been treated in exactly the same way.

BACTERIOLOGY AS A SUPERSTITION

The smattering of science that all—even doctors—pick up from the ordinary newspapers nowadays only makes the doctor more dangerous than he used to be. Wise men used to take care to consult doctors qualified before 1860, who were usually contemptuous of or indifferent to the germ theory and bacteriological therapeutics; but now that these veterans have mostly retired or died, we are left in the hands of the generations which, having heard of microbes much as St Thomas Aquinas heard of angels, suddenly concluded that the whole art of healing could be summed up in the formula: Find the microbe and kill it. And even that they did not know how to do. The simplest way to kill most microbes is to throw them into an open street or river and let the sun shine on them, which explains the fact that when great cities have recklessly thrown all their sewage into the open river the water has sometimes been cleaner twenty miles below the city than thirty miles above it. But doctors instinctively avoid all facts that are reassuring, and eagerly swallow those that make it a marvel that anyone could possibly survive three days in an atmosphere consisting mainly of countless pathogenic germs. They conceive microbes as immortal until slain by a germicide administered by a duly qualified medical man. All through Europe people are adjured, by public notices and even under legal penalties, not to throw their microbes into the sunshine, but to collect them carefully in a handkerchief; shield the handkerchief from the sun in the darkness and warmth of the pocket; and send it to a laundry to be mixed up with everybody else's handkerchiefs, with results only too familiar to local health authorities.

In the first frenzy of microbe killing, surgical instruments were dipped in carbolic oil, which was a great improvement on not dipping them in anything at all and simply using them dirty; but as microbes are so fond of carbolic oil that they swarm in it, it was not a success from the anti-microbe point of view. Formalin [formaldehyde] was squirted into the circulation of consumptives until it was discovered that formalin nourishes the tubercle bacillus handsomely and kills men. The popular theory of disease is the common medical theory: namely, that every disease had its microbe duly created in the garden of Eden, and has been steadily propagating itself and producing widening circles of malignant disease ever since. It was plain from the first that if this had been even approximately true, the whole human race would have been wiped out by the plague long ago, and that every epidemic, instead of fading out as mysteriously as it rushed in, would spread over the whole world. It was also evident that the characteristic microbe of a disease might be a symptom instead of a cause. An unpunctual man is always in a hurry; but it does not follow that hurry is the cause of unpunctuality: on the contrary, what is the matter with the patient is sloth. When Florence Nightingale said bluntly that if you overcrowded your soldiers in dirty quarters there would be an outbreak of smallpox among them, she was snubbed as an ignorant female who did not know that smallpox can be produced only by the importation of its specific microbe.

If this was the line taken about smallpox, the microbe of which has never yet been run down and exposed under the microscope by the bacteriologist, what must have been the ardor of conviction as to tuberculosis, tetanus, enteric fever, Maltese fever,[6] diphtheria, and the rest of the diseases in which the characteristic bacillus had been identified! When there was no bacillus it was assumed that, since no disease could exist without a bacillus, it was simply eluding observation. When the bacillus was found, as it frequently was, in persons who were not suffering from the disease, the theory was saved by simply calling the bacillus an impostor, or pseudo-bacillus. The same boundless credulity which the public exhibit as to a doctor's power of diagnosis was shewn by the doctors themselves as to the analytic microbe hunters. These witch finders would give you a

6. A bacterial disease common in humans and cattle, also referred to as Mediterranean fever, classified as brucellosis.

certificate of the ultimate constitution of anything from a sample of the water from your well to a scrap of your lungs, for seven-and-sixpence. I do not suggest that the analysts were dishonest. No doubt they carried the analysis as far as they could afford to carry it for the money. No doubt also they could afford to carry it far enough to be of some use. But the fact remains that just as doctors perform for half-a-crown, without the least misgiving, operations which could not be thoroughly and safely performed with due scientific rigor and the requisite apparatus by an unaided private practitioner for less than some thousands of pounds, so did they proceed on the assumption that they could get the last word of science as to the constituents of their pathological samples for a two-hours cab fare.

ECONOMIC DIFFICULTIES OF IMMUNIZATION

I have heard doctors affirm and deny almost every possible proposition as to disease and treatment. I can remember the time when doctors no more dreamt of consumption and pneumonia being infectious than they now dream of sea-sickness being infectious, or than so great a clinical observer as [Thomas] Sydenham[7] dreamt of smallpox being infectious. I have heard doctors deny that there is such a thing as infection. I have heard them deny the existence of hydrophobia as a specific disease differing from tetanus. I have heard them defend prophylactic measures and prophylactic legislation as the sole and certain salvation of mankind from zymotic [infectious] disease; and I have heard them denounce both as malignant spreaders of cancer and lunacy. But the one objection I have never heard from a doctor is the objection that prophylaxis by the inoculatory methods most in vogue is an economic impossibility under our private practice system. They buy some stuff from somebody for a shilling, and inject a pennyworth of it under their patient's skin for half-a-crown, concluding that, since this primitive rite pays the somebody and pays them, the problem of prophylaxis has been satisfactorily solved. The results are sometimes no worse than the ordinary results of dirt getting into cuts; but neither the doctor nor the patient is quite satisfied unless the inoculation "takes": that is, unless it produces perceptible illness and disablement. Sometimes both doctor and patient get more value in this direction than they bargain for. The results of ordinary private-practice-inoculation at their worst are bad

7. Sometimes referred to as the father of English medicine; a seventeenth-century physician who pioneered in clinical medicine and epidemiology.

enough to be indistinguishable from those of the most discreditable and dreaded disease known; and doctors, to save the credit of the inoculation, have been driven to accuse their patient or their patient's parents of having contracted this disease independently of the inoculation, an excuse which naturally does not make the family any more resigned, and leads to public recriminations in which the doctors, forgetting everything but the immediate quarrel, naïvely excuse themselves by admitting, and even claiming as a point in their favor, that it is often impossible to distinguish the disease produced by their inoculation and the disease they have accused the patient of contracting. And both parties assume that what is at issue is the scientific soundness of the prophylaxis. It never occurs to them that the particular pathogenic germ which they intended to introduce into the patient's system may be quite innocent of the catastrophe, and that the casual dirt introduced with it may be at fault. When, as in the case of smallpox or cowpox, the germ has not yet been detected, what you inoculate is simply undefined matter that has been scraped off an anything but chemically clean calf suffering from the disease in question. You take your chance of the germ being in the scrapings, and, lest you should kill it, you take no precautions against other germs being in it as well. Anything may happen as the result of such an inoculation. Yet this is the only stuff of the kind which is prepared and supplied even in State establishments: that is, in the only establishments free from the commercial temptation to adulterate materials and scamp precautionary processes.

Even if the germ were identified, complete precautions would hardly pay. It is true that microbe farming is not expensive. The cost of breeding and housing two head of cattle would provide for the breeding and housing of enough microbes to inoculate the entire population of the globe since human life first appeared on it. But the precautions necessary to insure that the inoculation shall consist of nothing else but the required germ in the proper state of attenuation are a very different matter from the precautions necessary in the distribution and consumption of beefsteaks. Yet people expect to find vaccines and anti-toxins and the like retailed at "popular prices" in private enterprise shops just as they expect to find ounces of tobacco and papers of pins.

THE PERILS OF INOCULATION

The trouble does not end with the matter to be inoculated. There is the question of the condition of the patient. The discoveries of Sir Almroth

Wright[8] have shewn that the appalling results which led to the hasty dropping in 1894 of [Robert] Koch's[9] tuberculin were not accidents, but perfectly orderly and inevitable phenomena following the injection of dangerously strong "vaccines" at the wrong moment, and reinforcing the disease instead of stimulating the resistance to it. To ascertain the right moment a laboratory and a staff of experts are needed. The general practitioner, having no such laboratory and no such experience, has always chanced it, and insisted, when he was unlucky, that the results were not due to the inoculation, but to some other cause: a favorite and not very tactful one being the drunkenness or licentiousness of the patient. But though a few doctors have now learnt the danger of inoculating without any reference to the patient's "opsonic index" at the moment of inoculation, and though those other doctors who are denouncing the danger as imaginary and opsonin as a craze or a fad, obviously do so because it involves an operation which they have neither the means nor the knowledge to perform, there is still no grasp of the economic change in the situation. They have never been warned that the practicability of any method of extirpating disease depends not only on its efficacy, but on its cost. For example, just at present the world has run raving mad on the subject of radium, which has excited our credulity precisely as the apparitions at Lourdes excited the credulity of Roman Catholics. Suppose it were ascertained that every child in the world could be rendered absolutely immune from all disease during its entire life by taking half an ounce of radium to every pint of its milk. The world would be none the healthier, because not even a Crown Prince—no, not even the son of a Chicago Meat King, could afford the treatment. Yet it is doubtful whether doctors would refrain from prescribing it on that ground. The recklessness with which they now recommend wintering in Egypt or at Davos [Davos-Platz, Switzerland] to people who cannot afford to go to Cornwall, and the orders given for champagne jelly and old port in households where such luxuries must obviously be acquired at the cost of stinting necessaries, often make one wonder whether it is possible for a man to go through a medical training and retain a spark of common sense.

This sort of inconsiderateness gets cured only in the classes where poverty,

8. Irish-born bacteriologist, discoverer of opsonin, a constituent of blood serum whose prevalence or absence (opsonin index) renders bacteria more or less susceptible to destruction by phagocytes (white cells) after injection of tuberculin. A long-time friend of Shaw who inspired his play and its protagonist Ridgeon.
9. Nobel-prize-winning (1905) German bacteriologist, who discovered the bacillus of tuberculosis.

pretentious as it is even at its worst, cannot pitch its pretences high enough to make it possible for the doctor (himself often no better off than the patient) to assume that the average income of an English family is about £2000 a year, and that it is quite easy to break up a home, sell an old family seat at a sacrifice, and retire into a foreign sanatorium devoted to some "treatment" that did not exist two years ago and probably will not exist (except as a pretext for keeping an ordinary hotel) two years hence. In a poor practice the doctor must find cheap treatments for cheap people, or humiliate and lose his patients either by prescribing beyond their means or sending them to the public hospitals. When it comes to prophylactic inoculation, the alternative lies between the complete scientific process, which can only be brought down to a reasonable cost by being very highly organized as a public service in a public institution, and such cheap, nasty, dangerous and scientifically spurious imitations as ordinary vaccination, which will probably be ended, like its equally vaunted forerunner, XVIII century inoculation, by a purely reactionary law making all sorts of vaccination, scientific or not, criminal offences. Naturally, the poor doctor (that is, the average doctor) defends ordinary vaccination frantically, as it means to him the bread of his children. To secure the vehement and practically unanimous support of the rank and file of the medical profession for any sort of treatment or operation, all that is necessary is that it can be easily practised by a rather shabbily dressed man in a surgically dirty room in a surgically dirty house without any assistance, and that the materials for it shall cost, say, a penny, and the charge for it to a patient with £100 a year be half-a-crown. And, on the other hand, a hygienic measure has only to be one of such refinement, difficulty, precision and costliness as to be quite beyond the resources of private practice, to be ignored or angrily denounced as a fad.

TRADE UNIONISM AND SCIENCE

Here we have the explanation of the savage rancor that so amazes people who imagine that the controversy concerning vaccination is a scientific one. It has really nothing to do with science. The medical profession, consisting for the most part of very poor men struggling to keep up appearances beyond their means, find themselves threatened with the extinction of a considerable part of their incomes: a part, too, that is easily and regularly earned, since it is independent of disease, and brings every person born into the nation, healthy or not, to the doctors. To boot, there is the occasional windfall of an epidemic, with its panic and rush for revaccination. Under such circumstances, vaccination would be defended desperately were it twice as dirty, dangerous, and unscientific in method as it actually is. The note of fury in the defence, the feeling that the anti-vaccinator is doing a cruel, ruinous, inconsiderate thing in a mood of malignant folly: all this, so puzzling to the observer who knows nothing of the economic side of the question, and only sees that the anti-vaccinator, having nothing whatever to gain and a good deal to lose by placing himself in opposition to the law and to the outcry that adds private persecution to legal penalties, can have no interest in the matter except the interest of a reformer in abolishing a corrupt and mischievous superstition, becomes intelligible the moment the tragedy of medical poverty and the lucrativeness of cheap vaccination is taken into account.

In the face of such economic pressure as this, it is silly to expect that medical teaching, any more than medical practice, can possibly be scientific. The test to which all methods of treatment are finally brought is whether they are lucrative to doctors or not. It would be difficult to cite any proposition less obnoxious to science than that advanced by [C. F. S.] Hahnemann:[10] to wit, that drugs which in large doses produce certain symptoms, counteract them in very small doses, just as in more modern practice it is found that a sufficiently small inoculation with typhoid rallies our powers to resist the disease instead of prostrating us with it. But Hahnemann and his followers were frantically persecuted for a century by generations of apothecary-doctors whose incomes depended on the quantity of drugs they could induce their patients to swallow. These two cases of ordinary vaccination and homeopathy are typical of all the rest. Just as the object of a trade union under existing conditions must finally be, not to improve the technical quality of the work done by its members, but to secure a living wage for them, so the object of the medical profession today is to secure an income for the private doctor; and to this consideration all concern for science and public health must give way when the two come into conflict. Fortunately they are not always in conflict. Up to a certain point doctors, like carpenters and masons, must earn their living by doing the work that the public wants from them; and as it is not in the nature of things possible that such public want should be based on unmixed disutility,

10. German physician, founder of homœopathy, which held – contrary to the 'allopathy' of orthodox therapeutics – that the cure of disease is affected by drugs capable of producing in a healthy individual symptoms similar to those of the disease to be treated.

it may be admitted that doctors have their uses, real as well as imaginary. But just as the best carpenter or mason will resist the introduction of a machine that is likely to throw him out of work, or the public technical education of unskilled laborers' sons to compete with him, so the doctor will resist with all his powers of persecution every advance of science that threatens his income. And as the advance of scientific hygiene tends to make the private doctor's visits rarer, and the public inspector's frequenter, whilst the advance of scientific therapeutics is in the direction of treatments that involve highly organized laboratories, hospitals, and public institutions generally, it unluckily happens that the organization of private practitioners which we call the medical profession is coming more and more to represent, not science, but desperate and embittered anti-science: a state of things which is likely to get worse until the average doctor either depends upon or hopes for an appointment in the public health service for his livelihood.

So much for our guarantees as to medical science. Let us now deal with the more painful subject of medical kindness.

DOCTORS AND VIVISECTION

The importance to our doctors of a reputation for the tenderest humanity is so obvious, and the quantity of benevolent work actually done by them for nothing (a great deal of it from sheer good nature) so large, that at first sight it seems unaccountable that they should not only throw all their credit away, but deliberately choose to band themselves publicly with outlaws and scoundrels by claiming that in the pursuit of their professional knowledge they should be free from the restraints of law, of honor, of pity, of remorse, of everything that distinguishes an orderly citizen from a South Sea buccaneer, or a philosopher from an inquisitor. For here we look in vain for either an economic or a sentimental motive. In every generation fools and blackguards have made this claim; and honest and reasonable men, led by the strongest contemporary minds, have repudiated it and exposed its crude rascality. From Shakespear and Dr Johnson to Ruskin and Mark Twain, the natural abhorrence of sane mankind for the vivisector's cruelty, and the contempt of able thinkers for his imbecile casuistry, have been expressed by the most popular spokesmen of humanity. If the medical profession were to outdo the Anti-Vivisection Societies in a general professional protest against the practice and principles of the vivisectors, every doctor in the kingdom would gain substantially by the immense relief and reconciliation which would follow such a reassurance of the humanity of the doctor. Not one doctor in a thousand is a vivisector, or has any interest in vivisection, either pecuniary or intellectual, or would treat his dog cruelly or allow anyone else to do it. It is true that the doctor complies with the professional fashion of defending vivisection, and assuring you that people like Shakespear and Dr Johnson and Ruskin and Mark Twain are ignorant sentimentalists, just as he complies with any other silly fashion: the mystery is, how it became the fashion in spite of its being so injurious to those who follow it. Making all possible allowance for the effect of the brazen lying of the few men who bring a rush of despairing patients to their doors by professing in letters to the newspapers to have learnt from vivisection how to cure certain diseases, and the assurances of the sayers of smooth things that the practice is quite painless under the law, it is still difficult to find any civilized motive for an attitude by which the medical profession has everything to lose and nothing to gain.

The Primitive Savage Motive

I say civilized motive advisedly; for primitive tribal motives are easy enough to find. Every savage chief who is not a Mahomet learns that if he wishes to strike the imagination of his tribe—and without doing that he cannot rule them—he must terrify or revolt them from time to time by acts of hideous cruelty or disgusting unnaturalness. We are far from being as superior to such tribes as we imagine. It is very doubtful indeed whether Peter the Great could have effected the changes he made in Russia if he had not fascinated and intimidated his people by his monstrous cruelties and grotesque escapades. Had he been a XIX century king of England, he would have had to wait for some huge accidental calamity: a cholera epidemic, a war, or an insurrection, before waking us up sufficiently to get anything done. Vivisection helps the doctor to rule us as Peter ruled the Russians. The notion that the man who does dreadful things is superhuman, and that therefore he can also do wonderful things either as ruler, avenger, healer, or what not, is by no means confined to barbarians. Just as the manifold wickednesses and stupidities of our criminal code are supported, not by any general comprehension of law or study of jurisprudence, not even by simple vindictiveness, but by the superstition that a calamity of any sort must be expiated by a human sacrifice; so the wickednesses and stupidities of our medicine men are rooted in superstitions that have no more to do with science than the traditional ceremony of christening an ironclad has to do with the effectiveness of its armament. We have only to turn to Macaulay's description of the treatment of Charles II in his last illness to see how strongly his physicians felt that their only chance of cheating death was by outraging nature in tormenting and disgusting their unfortunate patient.[11] True, this was more than two centuries ago; but I have heard my own XIX century grandfather describe the cupping and firing and nauseous medicines of his time with perfect credulity as to their beneficial effects; and some more modern treatments appear to me quite as barbarous. It is in this way that vivisection pays the doctor. It appeals to the fear and credulity of the savage in us; and without fear and credulity half the private doctor's occupation and seven-eighths of his influence would be gone.

THE HIGHER MOTIVE. THE TREE OF KNOWLEDGE

But the greatest force of all on the side of vivisection is the mighty and indeed divine force of curiosity. Here we have no decaying tribal instinct which men strive to root out of themselves as they strive to root out the tiger's lust for blood. On the contrary, the curiosity of the ape, or of the child who pulls out the legs and wings of a fly to see what it will do without them, or who, on being told that a cat dropped out of the window will always fall on its legs, immediately tries the experiment on the nearest cat from the highest window in the house (I protest I did it myself from the first floor only), is as nothing compared to the thirst for knowledge of the philosopher, the poet, the biologist, and the naturalist. I have always despised Adam because he had to be tempted by the woman, as she was by the serpent, before he could be induced to pluck the apple from the tree of knowledge. I should have swallowed every apple on the tree the moment the owner's back was turned. When [Thomas] Gray said "Where ignorance is bliss, 'tis folly to be wise" ['On a Distant Prospect of Eton College'], he forgot that it is godlike to be wise; and since nobody wants bliss particularly, or could stand more than a very brief taste of it if it were attainable, and since everybody, by the deepest law of the Life Force, desires to be godlike, it is stupid, and indeed blasphemous and despairing, to hope that the thirst for knowledge will either diminish or consent to be subordinated to any other end whatsoever. We shall see later on that the

11. *Critical and Historical Essays* (1866), in a review of Lord Manon's *History of the War of the Succession in Spain*; first published in the *Edinburgh Review*, January 1833.

claim that has arisen in this way for the unconditioned pursuit of knowledge is as idle as all dreams of unconditioned activity; but none the less the right to knowledge must be regarded as a fundamental human right. The fact that men of science have had to fight so hard to secure its recognition, and are still so vigorously persecuted when they discover anything that is not quite palatable to vulgar people, makes them sorely jealous for that right; and when they hear a popular outcry for the suppression of a method of research which has an air of being scientific, their first instinct is to rally to the defence of that method without further consideration, with the result that they sometimes, as in the case of vivisection, presently find themselves fighting on a false issue.

THE FLAW IN THE ARGUMENT

I may as well pause here to explain their error. The right to know is like the right to live. It is fundamental and unconditional in its assumption that knowledge, like life, is a desirable thing, though any fool can prove that ignorance is bliss, and that "a little knowledge is a dangerous thing" [Alexander Pope's 'Essay on Criticism'] (a little being the most that any of us can attain), as easily as that the pains of life are more numerous and constant than its pleasures, and that therefore we should all be better dead. The logic is unimpeachable; but its only effect is to make us say that if these are the conclusions logic leads to, so much the worse for logic, after which curt dismissal of Folly, we continue living and learning by instinct: that is, as of right. We legislate on the assumption that no man may be killed on the strength of a demonstration that he would be happier in his grave, not even if he is dying slowly of cancer and begs the doctor to despatch him quickly and mercifully. To get killed lawfully he must violate somebody else's right to live by committing murder. But he is by no means free to live unconditionally. In society he can exercise his right to live only under very stiff conditions. In countries where there is compulsory military service he may even have to throw away his individual life to save the life of the community.

It is just so in the case of the right to knowledge. It is a right that is as yet very imperfectly recognized in practice. But in theory it is admitted that an adult person in pursuit of knowledge must not be refused it on the ground that he would be better or happier without it. Parents and priests may forbid knowledge to those who accept their authority; and social taboo may be made effective by acts of legal persecution under cover of repressing blasphemy, obscenity, and sedition; but no government now openly forbids its subjects to pursue knowledge on the ground that knowledge is in itself a bad thing, or that it is possible for any of us to have too much of it.

LIMITATIONS OF THE RIGHT TO KNOWLEDGE

But neither does any government exempt the pursuit of knowledge, any more than the pursuit of life, liberty, and happiness (as the American Constitution puts it), from all social conditions. No man is allowed to put his mother into the stove because he desires to know how long an adult woman will survive at a temperature of 500° Fahrenheit, no matter how important or interesting that particular addition to the store of human knowledge may be. A man who did so would have short work made not only of his right to knowledge, but of his right to live and all his other rights at the same time. The right to knowledge is not the only right; and its exercise must be limited by respect for other rights, and for its own exercise by others. When a man says to Society, "May I torture my mother in pursuit of knowledge?" Society replies "No." If he pleads, "What! Not even if I have a chance of finding out how to cure cancer by doing it?" Society still says, "Not even then." If the scientist, making the best of his disappointment, goes on to ask may he torture a dog, the stupid and callous people who do not realize that a dog is a fellow-creature, and sometimes a good friend, may say Yes, though Shakespear, Dr Johnson, and their like may say No. But even those who say "You may torture *a* dog" never say "You may torture *my* dog." And nobody says, "Yes, because in the pursuit of knowledge you may do as you please." Just as even the stupidest people say, in effect, "If you cannot attain to knowledge without burning your mother you must do without knowledge," so the wisest people say, "If you cannot attain to knowledge without torturing a dog, you must do without knowledge."

A FALSE ALTERNATIVE

But in practice you cannot persuade any wise man that this alternative can ever be forced on anyone but a fool, or that a fool can be trusted to learn anything from any experiment, cruel or humane. The Chinaman who burnt down his house to roast his pig [as in Charles Lamb's 'A Dissertation upon Roast Pig'] was no doubt honestly unable to conceive any less disastrous way of cooking his dinner; and the roast must have been spoiled after all (a perfect type of the average vivisectionist experiment); but this did not prove that the Chinaman was right: it only proved that the Chinaman was an incapable cook and, fundamentally, a fool.

Take another celebrated experiment: one in sanitary reform. In the days of Nero Rome was in the same predicament as London today. If someone would burn down London, and it were rebuilt, as it would now have to be, subject to the sanitary by-laws and Building Act provisions enforced by the London County Council, it would be enormously improved; and the average lifetime of Londoners would be considerably prolonged. Nero argued in the same way about Rome. He employed incendiaries to set it on fire; and he played the harp in scientific raptures whilst it was burning. I am so far of Nero's way of thinking that I have often said, when consulted by despairing sanitary reformers, that what London needs to make her healthy is an earthquake. Why, then, it may be asked, do not I, as a public-spirited man, employ incendiaries to set it on fire, with a heroic disregard of the consequences to myself and others? Any vivisector would, if he had the courage of his opinions. The reasonable answer is that London can be made healthy without burning her down; and that as we have not enough civic virtue to make her healthy in a humane and economical way, we should not have enough to rebuild her in that way. In the old Hebrew legend, God lost patience with the world as Nero did with Rome, and drowned everybody except a single family. But the result was that the progeny of that family reproduced all the vices of their predecessors so exactly that the misery caused by the flood might just as well have been spared: things went on just as they did before. In the same way, the list of diseases which vivisection claims to have cured is long; but the returns of the Registrar-General shew that people still persist in dying of them as if vivisection had never been heard of. Any fool can burn down a city or cut an animal open; and an exceptionally foolish fool is quite likely to promise enormous benefits to the race as the result of such activities. But when the constructive, benevolent part of the business comes to be done, the same want of imagination, the same stupidity and cruelty, the same laziness and want of perseverance that prevented Nero or the vivisector from devising or pushing through humane methods, prevents him from bringing order out of the chaos and happiness out of the misery he has made. At one time it seemed reasonable enough to declare that it was impossible to find whether or not there was a stone inside a man's body except by exploring it with a knife, or to find out what the sun is made of without visiting it in a balloon. Both these impossibilities have been achieved, but not by vivisectors. The Röntgen rays [X-rays] need not hurt the patient; and spectrum analysis involves no destruction. After such triumphs of humane experiment and reasoning, it is useless to assure us that there is no other key to knowledge except cruelty. When the vivisector offers us that assurance, we reply simply and contemptuously, "You mean that you are not clever or humane or energetic enough to find one."

CRUELTY FOR ITS OWN SAKE

It will now, I hope, be clear why the attack on vivisection is not an attack on the right to knowledge: why, indeed, those who have the deepest conviction of the sacredness of that right are the leaders of the attack. No knowledge is finally impossible of human attainment; for even though it may be beyond our present capacity, the needed capacity is not unattainable. Consequently no method of investigation is the only method; and no law forbidding any particular method can cut us off from the knowledge we hope to gain by it. The only knowledge we lose by forbidding cruelty is knowledge at first hand of cruelty itself, which is precisely the knowledge humane people wish to be spared.

But the question remains: Do we all really wish to be spared that knowledge? Are humane methods really to be preferred to cruel ones? Even if the experiments come to nothing, may not their cruelty be enjoyed for its own sake, as a sensational luxury? Let us face these questions boldly, not shrinking from the fact that cruelty is one of the primitive pleasures of mankind, and that the detection of its Protean disguises as law, education, medicine, discipline, sport and so forth, is one of the most difficult of the unending tasks of the legislator.

OUR OWN CRUELTIES

At first blush it may seem not only unnecessary, but even indecent, to discuss such a proposition as the elevation of cruelty to the rank of a human right. Unnecessary, because no vivisector confesses to a love of cruelty for its own sake or claims any general fundamental right to be cruel. Indecent, because there is an accepted convention to repudiate cruelty; and vivisection is only tolerated by the law on condition that, like judicial torture, it shall be done as mercifully as the nature of the practice allows. But the moment the controversy becomes embittered, the recriminations bandied between the opposed parties bring us face-to-face with some very ugly truths. On one occasion [22 May 1900] I was invited to speak at a large Anti-Vivisection meeting in the Queen's Hall in London. I found myself on the platform with fox hunters, tame stag hunters, men and women whose calendar was divided, not by pay days and quarter days, but by seasons for killing animals for sport: the fox, the hare, the otter, the partridge and the rest having each its appointed date for slaughter. The ladies among us wore hats and cloaks and head-dresses obtained by wholesale massacres, ruthless trappings, callous extermination of our fellow creatures. We insisted on our butchers supplying us with white veal, and were large and constant consumers of *pâté de foie gras*: both comestibles being obtained by revolting methods. We sent our sons to public schools where indecent flogging is a recognized method of taming the young human animal. Yet we were all in hysterics of indignation at the cruelties of the vivisectors. These, if any were present, must have smiled sardonically at such inhuman humanitarians, whose daily habits and fashionable amusements cause more suffering in England in a week than all the vivisectors of Europe do in a year. I made a very effective speech, not exclusively against vivisection, but against cruelty; and I have never been asked to speak since by that Society, nor do I expect to be, as I should probably give such offence to its most affluent subscribers that its attempts to suppress vivisection would be seriously hindered. But that does not prevent the vivisectors from freely using the "youre another" retort, and using it with justice.

We must therefore give ourselves no airs of superiority when denouncing the cruelties of vivisection. We all do just as horrible things, with even less excuse. But in making that admission we are also making short work of the virtuous airs with which we are sometimes referred to the humanity of the medical profession as a guarantee that vivisection is not abused—much as if our burglars should assure us that they are too honest to abuse the practice of burgling. We are, as a matter of fact, a cruel nation; and our habit of disguising our vices by giving polite names to the offences we are determined to commit, does not, unfortunately for my own comfort, impose on me. Vivisectors can hardly pretend to be better than the classes from which they are drawn, or those above them; and if these classes are capable of sacrificing animals in various cruel ways under cover of sport, fashion, education, discipline, and even, when the cruel sacrifices are human sacrifices, of political economy, it is idle for the vivisector to pretend that he is incapable of practising cruelty for pleasure or profit or both under the cloak of science. We are all tarred with the same brush; and the vivisectors are not slow to remind us of it, and to protest vehemently against being branded as exceptionally cruel and as devisers of horrible instruments of torture by people whose main notion of enjoyment is cruel sport, and whose requirements in the way of villainously cruel traps occupy pages of the catalogue of the Army and Navy Stores.

THE SCIENTIFIC INVESTIGATION OF CRUELTY

There is in man a specific lust for cruelty which infects even his passion of pity and makes it savage. Simple disgust at cruelty is very rare. The people who turn sick and faint and those who gloat are often alike in the pains they take to witness executions, floggings, operations or any other exhibitions of suffering, especially those involving bloodshed, blows, and laceration. A craze for cruelty can be developed just as a craze for drink can; and nobody who attempts to ignore cruelty as a possible factor in the attraction of vivisection and even of anti-vivisection, or in the credulity with which we accept its excuses, can be regarded as a scientific investigator of it. Those who accuse vivisectors of indulging the well-known passion of cruelty under the cloak of research are therefore putting forward a strictly scientific psychological hypothesis, which is also simple, human, obvious, and probable. It may be as wounding to the personal vanity of the vivisector as Darwin's Origin of Species [1859] was to the people who could not bear to think that they were cousins to the monkeys (remember Goldsmith's anger when he was told that he could not move his upper jaw);[12] but science has to consider only the truth of the hypothesis, and not whether conceited people will like it or not. In vain do the sentimental champions of vivisection declare themselves the most humane of men, inflicting suffering only to relieve it, scrupulous in the use of anesthetics, and void of all passion except the passion of pity for a disease-ridden world. The really scientific investigator answers that the question cannot be settled by hysterical protestations, and that if the vivisectionist rejects deductive reasoning, he had better clear his character by his own favorite method of experiment.

12. Lord Macaulay's essay on Goldsmith, for the eighth edition of the *Encyclopaedia Britannica* (1853–60).

Suggested Laboratory Tests of the Vivisector's Emotions

Take the hackneyed case of the Italian who tortured mice, ostensibly to find out about the effects of pain rather less than the nearest dentist could have told him, and who boasted of the ecstatic sensations (he actually used the word love) with which he carried out his experiments. Or the gentleman who starved sixty dogs to death to establish the fact that a dog deprived of food gets progressively lighter and weaker, becoming remarkably emaciated, and finally dying: an undoubted truth, but ascertainable without laboratory experiments by a simple inquiry addressed to the nearest policeman, or, failing him, to any sane person in Europe. The Italian is diagnosed as a cruel voluptuary: the dog-starver is passed over as such a hopeless fool that it is impossible to take any interest in him. Why not test the diagnosis scientifically? Why not perform a careful series of experiments on persons under the influence of voluptuous ecstasy, so as to ascertain its physiological symptoms? Then perform a second series on persons engaged in mathematical work or machine designing, so as to ascertain the symptoms of cold scientific activity? Then note the symptoms of a vivisector performing a cruel experiment; and compare them with the voluptuary symptoms and the mathematical symptoms? Such experiments would be quite as interesting and important as any yet undertaken by the vivisectors. They might open a line of investigation which would finally make, for instance, the ascertainment of the guilt or innocence of an accused person a much exacter process than the very fallible methods of our criminal courts. But instead of proposing such an investigation, our vivisectors offer us all the pious protestations and all the huffy recriminations that any common unscientific mortal offers when he is accused of unworthy conduct.

Routine

Yet most vivisectors would probably come triumphant out of such a series of experiments, because vivisection is now a routine, like butchering or hanging or flogging; and many of the men who practise it do so only because it has been established as part of the profession they have adopted. Far from enjoying it, they have simply overcome their natural repugnance and become indifferent to it, as men inevitably become indifferent to anything they do often enough. It is this dangerous power of custom that makes it so difficult to convince the common sense of mankind that any established commercial or professional practice has its root in passion. Let a routine once spring from passion, and you will presently find thousands of routineers following it passionlessly for a livelihood. Thus it always seems strained to speak of the religious convictions of a clergyman, because nine out of ten clergymen have no religious convictions: they are ordinary officials carrying on a routine of baptizing, marrying, and churching; praying, reciting, and preaching; and, like solicitors or doctors, getting away from their duties with relief to hunt, to garden, to keep bees, to go into society, and the like. In the same way many people do cruel and vile things without being in the least cruel or vile, because the routine to which they have been brought up is superstitiously cruel and vile. To say that every man who beats his children and every schoolmaster who flogs a pupil is a conscious debauchee is absurd: thousands of dull, conscientious people beat their children conscientiously, because they were beaten themselves and think children ought to be beaten. The ill-tempered vulgarity that instinctively strikes at and hurts a thing that annoys it (and all children are annoying), and the simple stupidity that requires from a child perfection beyond the reach of the wisest and best adults (perfect truthfulness coupled with perfect obedience is quite a common condition of leaving a child unwhipped), produce a good deal of flagellation among people who not only do not lust after it, but who hit the harder because they are angry at having to perform an uncomfortable duty. These people will beat merely to assert their authority, or to carry out what they conceive to be a divine order on the strength of the precept of Solomon recorded in the Bible [1 Kings 2: 1–9], which carefully adds that Solomon completely spoilt his own son and turned away from the god of his fathers to the sensuous idolatry in which he ended his days.

In the same way we find men and women practising vivisection as senselessly as a humane butcher, who adores his fox terrier, will cut a calf's throat and hang it up by its heels to bleed slowly to death because it is the custom to eat veal and insist on its being white; or as a German purveyor nails a goose to a board and stuffs it with food because fashionable people eat *pâté de foie gras*; or as the crew of a whaler breaks in on a colony of seals and clubs them to death in wholesale massacre because ladies want sealskin jackets; or as fanciers blind singing birds with hot needles, and mutilate the ears and tails of dogs and horses. Let cruelty or kindness or anything else once become customary and it will be practised by people to whom it is not at all natural, but whose rule of life is simply to do only what everybody else does, and who would lose their employment and starve if they indulged in any peculiarity. A respectable man will lie daily, in speech and in print, about the qualities of the article he lives by selling, because it is customary to do so. He will flog his boy for telling a lie, because it is customary to do so. He will also flog him for not telling a lie if the boy tells inconvenient or disrespectful truths, because it is customary to do so. He will give the same boy a present on his birthday, and buy him a spade and bucket at the seaside, because it is customary to do so, being all the time neither particularly mendacious, nor particularly cruel, nor particularly generous, but simply incapable of ethical judgment or independent action.

Just so do we find a crowd of petty vivisectionists daily committing atrocities and stupidities, because it is the custom to do so. Vivisection is customary as part of the routine of preparing lectures in medical schools. For instance, there are two ways of making the action of the heart visible to students. One, a barbarous, ignorant, and thoughtless way, is to stick little flags into a rabbit's heart and let the students see the flags jump. The other, an elegant, ingenious, well-informed, and instructive way, is to put a sphygmograph on the student's wrist and let him see a record of his heart's action traced by a needle on a slip of smoked paper. But it has become the custom for lecturers to teach from the rabbit; and the lecturers are not original enough to get out of their groove. Then there are the demonstrations which are made by cutting up frogs with scissors. The most humane man, however repugnant the operation may be to him at first, cannot do it at lecture after lecture for months without finally—and that very soon—feeling no more for the frog than if he were cutting up pieces of paper. Such clumsy and lazy ways of teaching are based on the cheapness of frogs and rabbits. If machines were as cheap as frogs, engineers would not only be taught the anatomy of machines and the functions of their parts: they would also have machines misused and wrecked before them so that they might learn as much as possible by using their eyes, and as little as possible by using their brains and imaginations. Thus we have, as part of the routine of teaching, a routine of vivisection which soon produces complete indifference to it on the part even of those who are naturally humane. If they pass on from the routine of lecture preparation, not into general practice, but into research work, they carry this acquired indifference with them into the laboratory, where any atrocity is possible, because all atrocities satisfy curiosity. The routine man is in the majority in his profession always: consequently the moment his practice is tracked down to its source in human passion there is a great and quite sincere poohpoohing from himself, from the mass of the profession, and from the mass of the public, which sees that the average doctor is much too commonplace and decent a person to be capable of passionate wickedness of any kind.

Here, then, we have in vivisection, as in all the other tolerated and instituted cruelties, this anti-climax: that only a negligible percentage of those who practise and consequently defend it get any satisfaction out of it. As in Mr [John] Galsworthy's play Justice the useless and detestable torture of solitary imprisonment is shewn at its worst without the introduction of a single cruel person into the drama, so it would be possible to represent all the torments of vivisection dramatically without introducing a single vivisector who had not felt sick at his first experience in the laboratory. Not that this can exonerate any vivisector from suspicion of enjoying his work (or *her* work: a good deal of the vivisection in medical schools is done by women). In every autobiography which records a real experience of school or prison life, we find that here and there among the routineers there is to be found the genuine amateur, the orgiastic flogging schoolmaster or the nagging warder, who has sought out a cruel profession for the sake of its cruelty. But it is the genuine routineer who is the bulwark of the practice, because, though you can excite public fury against a Sade, a Bluebeard, or a Nero, you cannot rouse any feeling against dull Mr Smith doing his duty: that is, doing the usual thing. He is so obviously no better and no worse than anyone else that it is difficult to conceive that the things he does are abominable. If you would see public dislike surging up in a moment against an individual, you must watch one who does something unusual, no matter how sensible it may be. The name of Jonas Hanway [eighteenth-century British philanthropist] lives as that of a brave man because he was the first who dared to appear in the streets of this rainy island with an umbrella.

THE OLD LINE BETWEEN MAN AND BEAST

But there is still a distinction to be clung to by those who dare not tell themselves the truth about the medical profession because they are so helplessly dependent on it when death threatens the household. That distinction is the line that separates the brute from the man in the old classification. Granted, they will plead, that we are all cruel; yet the tame stag hunter does not hunt men; and the sportsman who lets a leash of greyhounds loose on a hare would be horrified at the thought of letting them loose on a human child. The lady who gets her cloak by flaying a sable does not flay a negro; nor does it ever occur to her that her veal cutlet might be improved on by a slice of tender baby.

Now there was a time when some trust could be placed in this distinction. The Roman Catholic Church still maintains, with what it must permit me to call a stupid obstinacy, and in spite of St Francis and St Anthony, that animals have no souls and no rights; so that you cannot sin against an animal, or against God by anything you may choose to do to an animal. Resisting the temptation to enter on an argument as to whether you may not sin against your own soul if you are unjust or cruel to the least of those whom St Francis called his little brothers, I have only to point out here that nothing could be more despicably superstitious in the opinion of a vivisector than the notion that science recognizes any such step in evolution as the step from a physical organism to an immortal soul. That conceit has been taken out of all our men of science, and out of all our doctors, by the evolutionists; and when it is considered how completely obsessed biological science has become in our days, not by the full scope of evolution, but by that particular method of it which has neither sense nor purpose nor life nor anything human, much less godlike, in it: by the method, that is, of so-called Natural Selection (meaning no selection at all, but mere dead accident and luck), the folly of trusting to vivisectors to hold the human animal any more sacred than the other animals becomes so clear that it would be waste of time to insist further on it. As a matter of fact the man who once concedes to the vivisector the right to put a dog outside the laws of honor and fellowship, concedes to him also the right to put himself outside them; for he is nothing to the vivisector but a more highly developed, and consequently more interesting-to-experiment-on vertebrate than the dog.

VIVISECTING THE HUMAN SUBJECT

I have in my hand a printed and published account by a doctor of how he tested his remedy for pulmonary tuberculosis, which was, to inject a powerful germicide directly into the circulation by stabbing a vein with a syringe [Robert Koch, *An Etiology of Tuberculosis*, 1882; Eng. tr. 1890]. He was one of those doctors who are able to command public sympathy by saying, quite truly, that when they discovered that the proposed treatment was dangerous, they experimented thenceforth on themselves. In this case the doctor was devoted enough to carry his experiments to the point of running serious risks, and actually making himself very uncomfortable. But he did not begin with himself. His first experiment was on two hospital patients. On receiving a message from the hospital to the effect that these two martyrs to therapeutic science had all but expired in convulsions, he experimented on a rabbit, which instantly dropped dead. It was then, and

not until then, that he began to experiment on himself, with the germicide modified in the direction indicated by the experiments made on the
two patients and the rabbit. As a good many people countenance vivisection because they fear that if the experiments are not made on rabbits
they will be made on themselves, it is worth noting that in this case, where
both rabbits and men were equally available, the men, being of course
enormously more instructive and costing nothing, were experimented on
first. Once grant the ethics of the vivisectionists and you not only sanction
the experiment on the human subject, but make it the first duty of the
vivisector. If a guinea pig may be sacrificed for the sake of the very little
that can be learnt from it, shall not a man be sacrificed for the sake of the
great deal that can be learnt from him? At all events, he *is* sacrificed, as this
typical case shows. I may add (not that it touches the argument) that the
doctor, the patients, and the rabbit all suffered in vain, as far as the hoped-
for rescue of the race from pulmonary consumption is concerned.

"THE LIE IS A EUROPEAN POWER" [13]

Now at the very time when the lectures describing these experiments
were being circulated in print and discussed eagerly by the medical profession, the customary denials that patients are experimented on were as loud,
as indignant, as high-minded as ever, in spite of the few intelligent doctors
who point out rightly that all treatments are experiments on the patient.
And this brings us to an obvious but mostly overlooked weakness in the
vivisector's position: that is, his inevitable forfeiture of all claim to have his
word believed. It is hardly to be expected that a man who does not hesitate
to vivisect for the sake of science will hesitate to lie about it afterwards to
protect it from what he deems the ignorant sentimentality of the laity.
When the public conscience stirs uneasily and threatens suppression, there is
never wanting some doctor of eminent position and high character who
will sacrifice himself devotedly to the cause of science by coming forward
to assure the public on his honor that all experiments on animals are
completely painless; although he must know that the very experiments
which first provoked the anti-vivisection movement by their atrocity were
experiments to ascertain the physiological effects of the sensation of extreme

13. In a lecture 'The New Politics' in 1889 (published in *The Road to Equality*,
1971) Shaw identifies 'The lie is one of the European powers' as an epigram by
Ferdinand Lassalle.

pain (the much more interesting physiology of pleasure remains uninvestigated) and that all experiments in which sensation is a factor are voided by its suppression. Besides, vivisection may be painless in cases where the experiments are very cruel. If a person scratches me with a poisoned dagger so gently that I do not feel the scratch, he has achieved a painless vivisection; but if I presently die in torment I am not likely to consider that his humanity is amply vindicated by his gentleness. A cobra's bite hurts so little that the creature is almost, legally speaking, a vivisector who inflicts no pain. By giving his victims chloroform before biting them he could comply with the law completely.

Here, then, is a pretty deadlock. Public support of vivisection is founded almost wholly on the assurances of the vivisectors that great public benefits may be expected from the practice. Not for a moment do I suggest that such a defence would be valid even if proved. But when the witnesses begin by alleging that in the cause of science all the customary ethical obligations (which include the obligation to tell the truth) are suspended, what weight can any reasonable person give to their testimony? I would rather swear fifty lies than take an animal which had licked my hand in good fellowship and torture it. If I did torture the dog, I should certainly not have the face to turn round and ask how any person dare suspect an honorable man like myself of telling lies. Most sensible and humane people would, I hope, reply flatly that honorable men do not behave dishonorably even to dogs. The murderer who, when asked by the chaplain whether he had any other crimes to confess, replied indignantly "What do you take me for?" reminds us very strongly of the vivisectors who are so deeply hurt when their evidence is set aside as worthless.

AN ARGUMENT WHICH WOULD DEFEND ANY CRIME

The Achilles heel of vivisection, however, is not to be found in the pain it causes, but in the line of argument by which it is justified. The medical code regarding it is simply criminal anarchism at its very worst. Indeed, no criminal has yet had the impudence to argue as every vivisector argues. No burglar contends that as it is admittedly important to have money to spend, and as the object of burglary is to provide the burglar with money to spend, and as in many instances it has achieved this object, therefore the burglar is a public benefactor and the police are ignorant sentimentalists. No highway robber has yet harrowed us with denunciations of the puling moralist who allows his child to suffer all the evils of poverty because

certain faddists think it dishonest to garotte an alderman. Thieves and
assassins understand quite well that there are paths of acquisition, even of
the best things, that are barred to all men of honor. Again, has the silliest
burglar ever pretended that to put a stop to burglary is to put a stop to
industry? All the vivisections that have been performed since the world
began have produced nothing so important as the innocent and honorable
discovery of radiography; and one of the reasons why radiography was not
discovered sooner was that the men whose business it was to discover new
clinical methods were coarsening and stupefying themselves with the sensual
villainies and cutthroat's casuistries of vivisection. The law of the conser-
vation of energy holds good in physiology as in other things: every vivisector
is a deserter from the army of honorable investigators. But the vivisector
does not see this. He not only calls his methods scientific: he contends that
there are no other scientific methods. When you express your natural
loathing for his cruelty and your natural contempt for his stupidity, he
imagines that you are attacking science. Yet he has no inkling of the
method and temper of science. The point at issue being plainly whether he
is a rascal or not, he not only insists that the real point is whether some
hot-headed anti-vivisectionist is a liar (which he proves by ridiculously
unscientific assumptions as to the degree of accuracy attainable in human
statement), but never dreams of offering any scientific evidence by his own
methods.

There are many paths to knowledge already discovered; and no enlightened man doubts that there are many more waiting to be discovered. Indeed,
all paths lead to knowledge; because even the vilest and stupidest action
teaches us something about vileness and stupidity, and may accidentally
teach us a good deal more: for instance, a cutthroat learns (and perhaps
teaches) the anatomy of the carotid artery and jugular vein; and there can
be no question that the burning of St Joan of Arc must have been a most
instructive and interesting experiment to a good observer, and could have
been made more so if it had been carried out by skilled physiologists under
laboratory conditions. The earthquake in San Francisco proved invaluable
as an experiment in the stability of giant steel buildings; and the ramming
of the Victoria by the Camperdown[14] settled doubtful points of the greatest
importance in naval warfare. According to vivisectionist logic our builders
would be justified in producing artificial earthquakes with dynamite, and
our admirals in contriving catastrophes at naval manœuvres, in order to
follow up the line of research thus accidentally discovered.

14. English dreadnoughts, on manoeuvres in the Mediterranean in 1893.

The truth is, if the acquisition of knowledge justifies every sort of conduct, it justifies any sort of conduct, from the illumination of Nero's feasts by burning human beings alive (another interesting experiment) to the simplest act of kindness. And in the light of that truth it is clear that the exemption of the pursuit of knowledge from the laws of honor is the most hideous conceivable enlargement of anarchy; worse, by far, than an exemption of the pursuit of money or political power, since these can hardly be attained without some regard for at least the appearances of human welfare, whereas a curious devil might destroy the whole race in torment, acquiring knowledge all the time from his highly interesting experiment. There is more danger in one respectable scientist countenancing such a monstrous claim than in fifty assassins or dynamitards. The man who makes it is ethically imbecile; and whoever imagines that it is a scientific claim has not the faintest conception of what science means. The paths to knowledge are countless. One of these paths is a path through darkness, secrecy, and cruelty. When a man deliberately turns from all other paths and goes down that one, it is scientific to infer that what attracts him is not knowledge, since there are other paths to that, but cruelty. With so strong and scientific a case against him, it is childish for him to stand on his honor and reputation and high character and the credit of a noble profession and so forth: he must clear himself either by reason or by experiment, unless he boldly contends that evolution has retained a passion of cruelty in man just because it is indispensable to the fulness of his knowledge.

THOU ART THE MAN [2 SAMUEL 12: 7]

I shall not be at all surprised if what I have written above has induced in sympathetic readers a transport of virtuous indignation at the expense of the medical profession. I shall not damp so creditable and salutary a sentiment; but I must point out that the guilt is shared by all of us. It is not in his capacity of healer and man of science that the doctor vivisects or defends vivisection, but in his entirely vulgar lay capacity. He is made of the same clay as the ignorant, shallow, credulous, half-miseducated, pecuniarily anxious people who call him in when they have tried in vain every bottle and every pill the advertizing druggist can persuade them to buy. The real remedy for vivisection is the remedy for all the mischief that the medical profession and all the other professions are doing: namely, more knowledge. The juries which send the poor Peculiars to prison, and give vivisectionists heavy damages against humane persons who accuse them of cruelty; the editors and councillors and student-led mobs who are striving to make Vivisection one of the watchwords of our civilization, are not doctors: they are the British public, all so afraid to die that they will cling frantically to any idol which promises to cure all their diseases, and crucify anyone who tells them that they must not only die when their time comes, but die like gentlemen. In their paroxysms of cowardice and selfishness they force the doctors to humor their folly and ignorance. How complete and inconsiderate their ignorance is can only be realized by those who have some knowledge of vital statistics, and of the illusions which beset Public Health legislation.

WHAT THE PUBLIC WANTS AND WILL NOT GET

The demands of this poor public are not reasonable, but they are quite simple. It dreads disease and desires to be protected against it. But it is poor and wants to be protected cheaply. Scientific measures are too hard to understand, too costly, too clearly tending towards a rise in the rates and more public interference with the insanitary, because insufficiently financed, private house. What the public wants, therefore, is a cheap magic charm to prevent, and a cheap pill or potion to cure all disease. It forces all such charms on the doctors.

THE VACCINATION CRAZE

Thus it was really the public and not the medical profession that took up vaccination with irresistible faith, sweeping the invention out of [Edward] Jenner's hands and establishing it in a form which he himself repudiated. Jenner was not a man of science; but he was not a fool; and when he found that people who had suffered from cowpox either by contagion in the milking shed or by vaccination, were not, as he had supposed, immune from smallpox, he ascribed the cases of immunity which had formerly misled him to a disease of the horse, which, perhaps because we do not drink its milk and eat its flesh, is kept at a greater distance in our imagination than our foster mother the cow. At all events, the public, which had been boundlessly credulous about the cow, would not have the horse on any terms; and to this day the law which prescribes Jennerian vaccination is carried out with an anti-Jennerian inoculation because the public would have it so in spite of Jenner. All the grossest lies and superstitions which have disgraced the vaccination craze were taught to the doctors by the public. It was not the doctors who first began to declare that all our old men remember the time when almost every face they saw in the street was horribly pitted with smallpox, and that all this disfigurement has vanished since the introduction of vaccination. Jenner himself alluded to this imaginary phenomenon before the introduction of vaccination, and attributed it to the older practice of smallpox inoculation, by which Voltaire, Catherine II and Lady Mary Wortley Montagu[15] so confidently expected to see the disease made harmless. It was not Jenner who set people declaring that smallpox, if not abolished by vaccination, had at least been made much milder: on the contrary, he recorded a pre-vaccination epidemic in which none of the persons attacked went to bed or considered themselves as seriously ill. Neither Jenner, nor any other doctor ever, as far as I know, inculcated the popular notion that everybody got smallpox as a matter of course before vaccination was invented. That doctors get infected with these delusions, and are in their unprofessional capacity as members of the public subject to them like other men, is true; but if we had to decide whether vaccination was first forced on the public by the doctors or on the doctors by the public, we should have to decide against the public.

STATISTICAL ILLUSIONS

Public ignorance of the laws of evidence and of statistics can hardly be exaggerated. There may be a doctor here and there who in dealing with the statistics of disease has taken at least the first step towards sanity by grasping the fact that as an attack of even the commonest disease is an exceptional event, apparently overwhelming statistical evidence in favor of any prophylactic can be produced by persuading the public that everybody caught the disease formerly. Thus if a disease is one which normally attacks fifteen per cent of the population, and if the effect of a prophylactic is actually to increase the proportion to twenty per cent, the publication of this figure of twenty per cent will convince the public that the prophylactic has reduced the percentage by eighty per cent instead of increasing it by five, because the public, left to itself and to the old gentlemen who are always ready to remember, on every possible subject, that things used to be much worse than they are now (such old gentlemen greatly outnumber the

15. English society leader remembered for her letter-writing, who introduced into England inoculation for smallpox after observing its use in Turkey.

laudatores tempori acti [praisers of the past]), will assume that the former percentage was about 100. The vogue of the [Louis] Pasteur[16] treatment of hydrophobia, for instance, was due to the assumption by the public that every person bitten by a rabid dog necessarily got hydrophobia. I myself heard hydrophobia discussed in my youth by doctors in Dublin before a Pasteur Institute existed, the subject having been brought forward there by the scepticism of an eminent surgeon as to whether hydrophobia is really a specific disease or only ordinary tetanus induced (as tetanus was then supposed to be induced) by a lacerated wound. There were no statistics available as to the proportion of dog bites that ended in hydrophobia; but nobody ever guessed that the cases could be more than two or three per cent of the bites. On me, therefore, the results published by the Pasteur Institute produced no such effect as they did on the ordinary man who thinks that the bite of a mad dog means certain hydrophobia. It seemed to me that the proportion of deaths among the cases treated at the Institute was rather higher, if anything, than might have been expected had there been no Institute in existence. But to the public every Pasteur patient who did not die was miraculously saved from an agonizing death by the beneficent white magic of that most trusty of all wizards, the man of science.

Even trained statisticians often fail to appreciate the extent to which statistics are vitiated by the unrecorded assumptions of their interpreters. Their attention is too much occupied with the cruder tricks of those who make a corrupt use of statistics for advertizing purposes. There is, for example, the percentage dodge. In some hamlet, barely large enough to have a name, two people are attacked during a smallpox epidemic. One dies: the other recovers. One has vaccination marks: the other has none. Immediately either the vaccinists or the anti-vaccinists publish the triumphant news that at such and such a place not a single vaccinated person died of smallpox whilst 100 per cent of the unvaccinated perished miserably; or, as the case may be, that 100 per cent of the unvaccinated recovered whilst the vaccinated succumbed to the last man. Or, to take another common instance, comparisons which are really comparisons between two social classes with different standards of nutrition and education are palmed off as comparisons between the results of a certain medical treatment and its neglect. Thus it is easy to prove that the wearing of tall hats and the carrying of umbrellas enlarges the chest, prolongs life, and confers comparative immunity from disease; for the statistics shew that the

16. Founded the Pasteur Institute (Paris) in 1888 for study of hydrophobia.

classes which use these articles are bigger, healthier, and live longer than the class which never dreams of possessing such things. It does not take much perspicacity to see that what really makes this difference is not the tall hat and the umbrella, but the wealth and nourishment of which they are evidence, and that a gold watch or membership of a club in Pall Mall might be proved in the same way to have the like sovereign virtues. A university degree, a daily bath, the owning of thirty pairs of trousers, a knowledge of Wagner's music, a pew in church, anything, in short, that implies more means and better nurture than the mass of laborers enjoy, can be statistically palmed off as a magic-spell conferring all sorts of privileges.

In the case of a prophylactic enforced by law, this illusion is intensified grotesquely, because only vagrants can evade it. Now vagrants have little power of resisting any disease: their death-rate and their case-mortality rate is always high relatively to that of respectable folk. Nothing is easier, therefore, than to prove that compliance with any public regulation produces the most gratifying results. It would be equally easy even if the regulation actually raised the death-rate, provided it did not raise it sufficiently to make the average householder, who cannot evade regulations, die as early as the average vagrant who can.

The Surprises of Attention and Neglect

There is another statistical illusion which is independent of class differences. A common complaint of houseowners is that the Public Health Authorities frequently compel them to instal costly sanitary appliances which are condemned a few years later as dangerous to health, and forbidden under penalties. Yet these discarded mistakes are always made in the first instance on the strength of a demonstration that their introduction has reduced the death-rate. The explanation is simple. Suppose a law were made that every child in the nation should be compelled to drink a pint of brandy per month, but that the brandy must be administered only when the child was in good health, with its digestion and so forth working normally, and its teeth either naturally or artificially sound. Probably the result would be an immediate and startling reduction in child mortality, leading to further legislation increasing the quantity of brandy to a gallon. Not until the brandy craze had been carried to a point at which the direct harm done by it would outweigh the incidental good, would an anti-brandy party be listened to. That incidental good would be the substitution of attention to the general health of children for the neglect which is now the rule so long as the child is not actually too sick to run about and play as usual. Even if this attention were confined to the children's teeth, there would be an improvement which it would take a good deal of brandy to cancel.

This imaginary case explains the actual case of the sanitary appliances which our local sanitary authorities prescribe today and condemn tomorrow. No sanitary contrivance which the mind of even the very worst plumber can devize could be as disastrous as that total neglect for long periods which gets avenged by pestilences that sweep through whole continents, like the black death and the cholera. If it were proposed at this time of day to discharge all the sewage of London crude and untreated into the Thames, instead of carrying it, after elaborate treatment, far out into the North Sea, there would be a shriek of horror from all our experts. Yet if [Oliver] Cromwell had done that instead of doing nothing, there would probably have been no Great Plague of London [1665]. When the Local Health Authority forces every householder to have his sanitary arrangements thought about and attended to by somebody whose special business it is to attend to such things, then it matters not how erroneous or even directly mischievous may be the specific measures taken: the net result at first is sure to be an improvement. Not until attention has been effectually substituted for neglect as the general rule, will the statistics begin to shew the merits of the particular methods of attention adopted. And as we are far from having arrived at this stage, being as to health legislation only at the beginning of things, we have practically no evidence yet as to the value of methods. Simple and obvious as this is, nobody seems as yet to discount the effect of substituting attention for neglect in drawing conclusions from health statistics. Everything is put to the credit of the particular method employed, although it may quite possibly be raising the death-rate by five per thousand whilst the attention incidental to it is reducing the death-rate fifteen per thousand. The net gain of ten per thousand is credited to the method, and made the excuse for enforcing more of it.

STEALING CREDIT FROM CIVILIZATION

There is yet another way in which specifics which have no merits at all, either direct or incidental, may be brought into high repute by statistics. For a century past civilization has been cleaning away the conditions which favor bacterial fevers. Typhus, once rife, has vanished: plague and cholera have been stopped at our frontiers by a sanitary blockade. We still have epidemics of smallpox and typhoid; and diphtheria and scarlet fever are endemic in the slums. Measles, which in my childhood was not regarded as a dangerous disease, has now become so mortal that notices are posted publicly urging parents to take it seriously. But even in these cases the contrast between the death and recovery rates in the rich districts and in the poor ones has led to the general conviction among experts that bacterial diseases are preventible; and they already are to a large extent prevented. The dangers of infection and the way to avoid it are better understood than they used to be. It is barely twenty years since people exposed themselves recklessly to the infection of consumption and pneumonia in the belief that these diseases were not "catching." Nowadays the troubles of consumptive patients are greatly increased by the growing disposition to treat them as lepers. No doubt there is a good deal of ignorant exaggeration and cowardly refusal to face a human and necessary share of the risk. That has always been the case. We now know that the medieval horror of leprosy was out of all proportion to the danger of infection, and was accompanied by apparent blindness to the infectiousness of smallpox, which has since been worked up by our disease terrorists into the position formerly held by leprosy. But the scare of infection, though it sets even doctors talking as if the only really scientific thing to do with a fever patient is to throw him into the nearest ditch and pump carbolic acid on him from a safe distance until he is ready to be cremated on the spot, has led to much greater care and cleanliness. And the net result has been a series of victories over disease.

Now let us suppose that in the early XIX century somebody had come forward with a theory that typhus fever always begins at the top joint of the little finger; and that if this joint be amputated immediately after birth, typhus fever will disappear. Had such a suggestion been adopted, the theory would have been triumphantly confirmed; for as a matter of fact, typhus fever *has* disappeared. On the other hand cancer and madness have increased (statistically) to an appalling extent. The opponents of the little finger theory would therefore be pretty sure to allege that the amputations were spreading cancer and lunacy. The vaccination controversy is full of such contentions. So is the controversy as to the docking of horses' tails and the cropping of dogs' ears. So is the less widely known controversy as to circumcision and the declaring certain kinds of flesh unclean by the Jews. To advertize any remedy or operation, you have only to pick out all the most reassuring advances made by civilization, and boldly present the two in the relation of cause and effect: the public will swallow the fallacy without a wry face. It has no idea of the need for what is called a control experiment. In Shakespear's time and for long after it, mummy was a favorite medicament. You took a pinch of the dust of a dead Egyptian in a pint of the hottest water you could bear to drink; and it did you a great deal of good. This, you thought, proved what a sovereign healer mummy was. But if you had tried the control experiment of taking the hot water without the mummy, you might have found the effect exactly the same, and that any hot drink would have done as well.

BIOMETRIKA[17]

Another difficulty about statistics is the technical difficulty of calculation. Before you can even make a mistake in drawing your conclusion from the correlations established by your statistics you must ascertain the correlations. When I turn over the pages of Biometrika, a quarterly journal in which is recorded the work done in the field of biological statistics by Professor Karl Pearson[18] and his colleagues, I am out of my depth at the first line, because mathematics are to me only a concept: I never used a logarithm in my life, and could not undertake to extract the square root of four without misgiving. I am therefore unable to deny that the statistical ascertainment of the correlations between one thing and another must be a very complicated and difficult technical business, not to be tackled successfully except by high mathematicians; and I cannot resist Professor Karl Pearson's immense contempt for, and indignant sense of grave social danger in, the unskilled guesses of the ordinary sociologist.

Now the man in the street knows nothing of Biometrika: all he knows is that "you can prove anything by figures," though he forgets this the moment figures are used to prove anything he wants to believe. If he did take in Biometrika he would probably become abjectly credulous as to all the conclusions drawn in it from the correlations so learnedly worked out; though the mathematician whose correlations would fill a Newton with admiration, may, in collecting and accepting data and drawing conclusions from them, fall into quite crude errors by just such popular oversights as I have been describing.

17. Biometry: the science of statistics applied to biological observations.
18. Metaphysician and statistician who, extending David Hume's theories, held that all science is description and not explanation; author of *The Grammar of Science* (1892).

PATIENT-MADE THERAPEUTICS

To all these blunders and ignorances doctors are no less subject than the rest of us. They are not trained in the use of evidence, nor in biometrics, nor in the psychology of human credulity, nor in the incidence of economic pressure. Further, they must believe, on the whole, what their patients believe, just as they must wear the sort of hat their patients wear. The doctor may lay down the law despotically enough to the patient at points where the patient's mind is simply blank; but when the patient has a prejudice the doctor must either keep it in countenance or lose his patient. If people are persuaded that night air is dangerous to health and that fresh air makes them catch cold, it will not be possible for a doctor to make his living in private practice if he prescribes ventilation. We have to go back no further than the days of the Pickwick Papers [1836–7] to find ourselves in a world where people slept in four-post beds with curtains drawn closely round to exclude as much air as possible. Had Mr Pickwick's doctor told him that he would be much healthier if he slept on a camp bed by an open window, Mr Pickwick would have regarded him as a crank and called in another doctor. Had he gone on to forbid Mr Pickwick to drink brandy and water whenever he felt chilly, and assured him that if he were deprived of meat or salt for a whole year, he would not only not die, but would be none the worse, Mr Pickwick would have fled from his presence as from that of a dangerous madman. And in these matters the doctor cannot cheat his patient. If he has no faith in drugs or vaccination, and the patient has, he can cheat him with colored water and pass his lancet through the flame of a spirit lamp before scratching his arm. But he cannot make him change his daily habits without knowing it.

THE REFORMS ALSO COME FROM THE LAITY

In the main, then, the doctor learns that if he gets ahead of the superstitions of his patients he is a ruined man; and the result is that he instinctively takes care not to get ahead of them. That is why all the changes come from the laity. It was not until an agitation had been conducted for many years by laymen, including quacks and faddists of all kinds, that the public was sufficiently impressed to make it possible for the doctors to open their minds and their mouths on the subject of fresh air, cold water, temperance, and the rest of the new fashions in hygiene. At present the tables have been turned on many old prejudices. Plenty of our most popular elderly doctors believe that cold tubs in the morning are unnatural, exhausting, and rheumatic; that fresh air is a fad, and that everybody is the better for a glass or two of port wine every day; but they no longer dare say as much until they know exactly where they are; for many very desirable patients in country houses have lately been persuaded that their first duty is to get up at six in the morning and begin the day by taking a walk barefoot through the dewy grass. He who shews the least scepticism as to this practice is at once suspected of being "an old-fashioned doctor," and dismissed to make room for a younger man.

In short, private medical practice is governed not by science but by supply and demand; and however scientific a treatment may be, it cannot hold its place in the market if there is no demand for it; nor can the grossest quackery be kept off the market if there is a demand for it.

FASHIONS AND EPIDEMICS

A demand, however, can be inculcated. This is thoroughly understood by fashionable tradesmen, who find no difficulty in persuading their customers to renew articles that are not worn out and to buy things they do not want. By making doctors tradesmen, we compel them to learn the tricks of trade; consequently we find that the fashions of the year include treatments, operations, and particular drugs, as well as hats, sleeves, ballads, and games. Tonsils, vermiform appendices, uvulas, even ovaries are sacrificed because it is the fashion to get them cut out, and because the operations are highly profitable. The psychology of fashion becomes a pathology; for the cases have every air of being genuine: fashions, after all, are only induced epidemics, proving that epidemics can be induced by tradesmen, and therefore by doctors.

THE DOCTOR'S VIRTUES

It will be admitted that this is a pretty bad state of things. And the melodramatic instinct of the public, always demanding that every wrong shall have, not its remedy, but its villain to be hissed, will blame, not its own apathy, superstition, and ignorance, but the depravity of the doctors. Nothing could be more unjust or mischievous. Doctors, if no better than other men, are certainly no worse. I was reproached during the performances of The Doctor's Dilemma at the Court Theatre in 1907 [first presented on 20 November 1906] because I made the artist a rascal, the journalist an illiterate incapable, and all the doctors "angels." But I did not go beyond the warrant of my own experience. It has been my luck to have doctors among my friends for nearly forty years past (all perfectly aware of my freedom from the usual credulity as to the miraculous powers and knowledge attributed to them); and though I know that there are medical blackguards as well as military, legal, and clerical blackguards (one soon finds that out when one is privileged to hear doctors talking shop among themselves), the fact that I was no more at a loss for private medical advice and attendance when I had not a penny in my pocket than I was later on when I could afford fees on the highest scale, has made it impossible for me to share that hostility to the doctor as a man which exists and is growing as an inevitable result of the present condition of medical practice. Not that the interest in disease and aberrations which turns some men and women to medicine and surgery is not sometimes as morbid as the interest in misery and vice which turns some others to philanthropy and "rescue work." But the true doctor is inspired by a hatred of ill-health, and a divine impatience of any waste of vital forces. Unless a man is led to medicine or surgery through a very exceptional technical aptitude, or because doctoring is a family tradition, or because he regards it unintelligently as a lucrative and gentlemanly profession, his motives in choosing the career of a healer are clearly generous. However actual practice may disillusion and corrupt him, his selection in the first instance is not a selection of a base character.

THE DOCTOR'S HARDSHIPS

A review of the counts in the indictment I have brought against private medical practice will shew that they arise out of the doctor's position as a competitive private tradesman: that is, out of his poverty and dependence. And it should be borne in mind that doctors are expected to treat other people specially well whilst themselves submitting to specially inconsiderate treatment. The butcher and baker are not expected to feed the hungry unless the hungry can pay; but a doctor who allows a fellow-creature to suffer or perish without aid is regarded as a monster. Even if we must dismiss hospital service as really venal, the fact remains that most doctors do a good deal of gratuitous work in private practice all through their careers. And in his paid work the doctor is on a different footing to the tradesman. Although the articles he sells, advice and treatment, are the same for all classes, his fees have to be graduated like the income tax. The successful fashionable doctor may weed his poorer patients out from time to time, and finally use the College of Physicians to place it out of his own power to accept low fees; but the ordinary general practitioner never makes out his bills without considering the taxable capacity of his patients.

Then there is the disregard of his own health and comfort which results from the fact that he is, by the nature of his work, an emergency man. We are polite and considerate to the doctor when there is nothing the matter, and we meet him as a friend or entertain him as a guest; but when the baby is suffering from croup, or its mother has a temperature of 104°, or its grandfather has broken his leg, nobody thinks of the doctor except as a healer and savior. He may be hungry, weary, sleepy, run down by several successive nights disturbed by that instrument of torture, the night bell; but who ever thinks of this in the face of sudden sickness or accident? We think no more of the condition of a doctor attending a case than of the condition of a fireman at a fire. In other occupations night-work is specially recognized and provided for. The worker sleeps all day; has his breakfast in the evening; his lunch or dinner at midnight; his dinner or supper before going to bed in the morning; and he changes to day-work if he cannot stand night-work. But a doctor is expected to work day and night. In practices which consist largely of workmen's clubs, and in which the patients are therefore taken on wholesale terms and very numerous, the unfortunate assistant, or the principal if he has no assistant, often does not undress, knowing that he will be called up before he has snatched an hour's sleep. To the strain of such inhuman conditions must be added the constant risk of infection. One wonders why the impatient doctors do not become savage and unmanageable, and the patient ones imbecile. Perhaps they do, to some extent. And the pay is wretched, and so uncertain that refusal to attend without payment in advance becomes often a necessary measure of self-defence, whilst the County Court has long ago put an end to the tradition that the doctor's fee is an honorarium. Even the most eminent physicians, as such biographies as those of [Sir James] Paget[19] shew, are sometimes miserably, inhumanly poor until they are past their prime.

In short, the doctor needs our help for the moment much more than we often need his. The ridicule of Molière, the death of a well-informed and clever writer like the late Harold Frederic[20] in the hands of Christian Scientists (a sort of sealing with his blood of the contemptuous disbelief in

19. British surgeon, one of the founders of modern pathology.
20. American novelist, resident in London, who died in 1898, aged forty-two.

and dislike of doctors he had bitterly expressed in his books), the scathing and quite justifiable exposure of medical practice in the novel by Mr Maarten Maartens entitled The New Religion [1907]: all these trouble the doctor very little, and are in any case well set off by the popularity of Sir Luke Fildes' famous picture [*The Doctor*, 1892], and by the verdicts in which juries from time to time express their conviction that the doctor can do no wrong. The real woes of the doctor are the shabby coat, the wolf at the door, the tyranny of ignorant patients, the work-day of 24 hours, and the uselessness of honestly prescribing what most of the patients really need: that is, not medicine, but money.

THE PUBLIC DOCTOR

What then is to be done?

Fortunately we have not to begin absolutely from the beginning: we already have, in the Medical Officer of Health, a sort of doctor who is free from the worst hardships, and consequently from the worst vices, of the private practitioner. His position depends, not on the number of people who are ill, and whom he can keep ill, but on the number of people who are well. He is judged, as all doctors and treatments should be judged, by the vital statistics of his district. When the death-rate goes up his credit goes down. As every increase in his salary depends on the issue of a public debate as to the health of the constituency under his charge, he has every inducement to strive towards the ideal of a clean bill of health. He has a safe, dignified, responsible, independent position based wholly on the public health; whereas the private practitioner has a precarious, shabby-genteel, irresponsible, servile position, based wholly on the prevalence of illness.

It is true, there are grave scandals in the public medical service. The public doctor may be also a private practitioner eking out his earnings by giving a little time to public work for a mean payment. There are cases in which the position is one which no successful practitioner will accept, and where, therefore, incapables or drunkards get automatically selected for the post, *faute de mieux* [for want of better]; but even in these cases the doctor is less disastrous in his public capacity than in his private one: besides, the conditions which produce these bad cases are doomed, as the evil is now recognized and understood. A popular but unstable remedy is to enable local authorities, when they are too small to require the undivided time of such men as the Medical Officers of our great municipalities, to combine for public health purposes so that each may share the services of a highly paid official of the best class; but the right remedy is a larger area as the sanitary unit.

MEDICAL ORGANIZATION

Another advantage of public medical work is that it admits of organization, and consequently of the distribution of the work in such a manner as to avoid wasting the time of highly qualified experts on trivial jobs. The individualism of private practice leads to an appalling waste of time on trifles. Men whose dexterity as operators or almost divinatory skill in diagnosis are constantly needed for difficult cases, are poulticing whitlows [infections on pedal extremities], vaccinating, changing unimportant dressings, prescribing ether drams for ladies with timid leanings towards dipsomania, and generally wasting their time in the pursuit of private fees. In no other profession is the practitioner expected to do all the work involved in it from the first day of his professional career to the last as the doctor is. The judge passes sentence of death; but he is not expected to hang the criminal with his own hands, as he would be if the legal profession were as unorganized as the medical. The bishop is not expected to blow the organ or wash the baby he baptizes. The general is not asked to plan a campaign or conduct a battle at half-past twelve and to play the drum at half-past two. Even if they were, things would still not be as bad as in the medical profession; for in it not only is the first-class man set to do third-class work, but, what is much more terrifying, the third-class man is expected to do first-class work. Every general practitioner is supposed to be capable of the whole range of medical and surgical work at a moment's notice; and the country doctor, who has not a specialist nor a crack consultant at the end of his telephone, often has to tackle without hesitation cases which no sane practitioner in a town would take in hand without assistance. No doubt this develops the resourcefulness of the country doctor, and makes him a more capable man than his suburban colleague; but it cannot develop the second-class man into a first-class one. If the practice of law not only led to a judge having to hang, but the hangman to judge, or if in the army matters were so arranged that it would be possible for the drummer boy to be in command at Waterloo whilst the Duke of Wellington was playing the drum in Brussels, we should not be consoled by the reflection that our hangmen were thereby made a little more judicial-minded, and our drummers more responsible, than in foreign countries where the legal and military professions recognized the advantages of division of labor.

Under such conditions no statistics as to the graduation of professional ability among doctors are available. Assuming that doctors are normal men and not magicians (and it is unfortunately very hard to persuade people to admit so much and thereby destroy the romance of doctoring) we may guess that the medical profession, like the other professions, consists of a small percentage of highly gifted persons at one end, and a small percentage of altogether disastrous duffers at the other. Between these extremes comes the main body of doctors (also, of course, with a weak and a strong end) who can be trusted to work under regulations with more or less aid from above according to the gravity of the case. Or, to put it in terms of the cases, there are cases that present no difficulties, and can be dealt with by a nurse or student at one end of the scale, and cases that require watching and handling by the very highest existing skill at the other; whilst between come the great mass of cases which need visits from the doctor of ordinary ability and from the chiefs of the profession in the proportion of, say, seven to none, seven to one, three to one, one to one, or, for a day or two, none to one. Such a service is organized at present only in hospitals; though in large towns the practice of calling in the consultant acts, to some extent, as a substitute for it. But in the latter case it is quite unregulated except by professional etiquet, which, as we have seen, has for its object, not the health of the patient or of the community at large, but the protection of the doctor's livelihood and the concealment of his errors. And as the consultant is an expensive luxury, he is a last resource rather than, as he should be, a matter of course in all cases where the general practitioner is not equal to the occasion: a predicament in which a very capable man may find himself at any time through the cropping up of a case of which he has had no clinical experience.

THE SOCIAL SOLUTION OF THE MEDICAL PROBLEM

The social solution of the medical problem, then, depends on that large, slowly advancing, pettishly resisted integration of society called generally Socialism. Until the medical profession becomes a body of men trained and paid by the country to keep the country in health it will remain what it is at present: a conspiracy to exploit popular credulity and human suffering. Already our M.O.H.s (Medical Officers of Health) are in the new position: what is lacking is appreciation of the change, not only by the public but by the private doctors. For, as we have seen, when one of the first-rate posts becomes vacant in one of the great cities, and all the leading M.O.H.s compete for it, they must appeal to the good health of the cities of which they have been in charge, and not to the size of the incomes the local private doctors are making out of the ill-health of their patients. If a competitor can prove that he has utterly ruined every sort of medical private practice in a large city except obstetric practice and the surgery of accidents, his claims are irresistible; and this is the ideal at which every M.O.H. should aim. But the profession at large should none the less welcome him and set its house in order for the social change which will finally be its own salvation. For the M.O.H. as we know him is only the beginning of that army of Public Hygiene which will presently take the place in general interest and honor now occupied by our military and naval forces. It is silly that an Englishman should be more afraid of a German soldier than of a British disease germ, and should clamor for more barracks in the same newspapers that protest against more school clinics, and cry out that if the State fights disease for us it makes us paupers, though they never say that if the State fights the Germans for us it makes us cowards. Fortunately, when a habit of thought is silly it only needs steady treatment by ridicule from sensible and witty people to be put out of countenance and perish. Every year sees an increase in the number of persons employed in the Public Health Service, who would formerly have been mere adventurers in the Private Illness Service. To put it another way, a host of men and women who have now a strong incentive to be mischievous and even murderous rogues will have a much stronger, because a much honester, incentive to be not only good citizens but active benefactors to the community. And they will have no anxiety whatever about their incomes.

THE FUTURE OF PRIVATE PRACTICE

It must not be hastily concluded that this involves the extinction of the private practitioner. What it will really mean for him is release from his present degrading and scientifically corrupting slavery to his patients. As I have already shewn, the doctor who has to live by pleasing his patients in competition with everybody who has walked the hospitals, scraped through the examinations, and bought a brass plate, soon finds himself prescribing water to teetotallers and brandy or champagne jelly to drunkards; beefsteaks and stout in one house, and "uric acid free" vegetarian diet over the way; shut windows, big fires, and heavy overcoats to old Colonels, and open air and as much nakedness as is compatible with decency to young faddists, never once daring to say either "I dont know," or "I dont agree." For the strength of the doctor's, as of every other man's position when the evolution of social organization at last reaches his profession, will be that he will always have open to him the alternative of public employment when the private employer becomes too tyrannous. And let no one suppose that the words doctor and patient can disguise from the parties the fact that they are employer and employee. No doubt doctors who in great demand can be as high-handed and independent as employees are in all classes when a dearth in their labor market makes them indispensable; but the average doctor is not in this position: he is struggling for life in an overcrowded profession, and knows well that "a good bedside manner" will carry him to solvency through a morass of illness, whilst the least attempt at plain dealing with people who are eating too much or drinking too much, or frowsting [hot-housing] too much (to go no further in the list of intemperances that make up so much of family life) would soon land him in the Bankruptcy Court.

Private practice, thus protected, would itself protect individuals, as far as such protection is possible, against the errors and superstitions of State medicine, which are at worst no worse than the errors and superstitions of private practice, being, indeed, all derived from it. Such monstrosities as vaccination are, as we have seen, founded, not on science, but on half-crowns. If the Vaccination Acts, instead of being wholly repealed as they are already half repealed,[21] were strengthened by compelling every parent to have his child vaccinated by a public officer whose salary was completely independent of the number of vaccinations performed by him, and for whom there was plenty of alternative public health work waiting, vaccination would be dead in two years, as the vaccinator would not only not gain by it, but would lose credit through the depressing effects on the vital statistics of his district of the illness and deaths it causes, whilst it would take from him all the credit of that freedom from smallpox which is the result of good sanitary administration and vigilant prevention of infection. Such absurd panic scandals as that of the last London epidemic, where a fee of half-a-crown per re-vaccination produced raids on houses during the absence of parents, and the forcible seizure and re-vaccination of children left to answer the door, can be prevented simply by abolishing the half-crown and all similar follies, paying, not for this or that ceremony of

21. Under the Vaccination Act and Order (1898), modifying the acts of 1867 and 1871, parents were relieved of penalty for failure to conform to the law if they afforded proof that they conscientiously believed vaccination harmful to their children.

witchcraft, but for immunity from disease, and paying, too, in a rational way. The officer with a fixed salary saves himself trouble by doing his business with the least possible interference with the private citizen. The man paid by the job loses money by not forcing his job on the public as often as possible without reference to its results.

The Technical Problem

As to any technical medical problem specially involved, there is none. If there were, I should not be competent to deal with it, as I am not a technical expert in medicine: I deal with the subject as an economist, a politician, and a citizen exercising my common sense. Everything that I have said applies equally to all the medical techniques, and will hold good whether public hygiene be based on the poetic fancies of Christian Science, the tribal superstitions of the druggist and the vivisector, or the best we can make of our real knowledge. But I may remind those who confusedly imagine that the medical problem is also the scientific problem, that all problems are finally scientific problems. The notion that therapeutics or hygiene or surgery is any more or less scientific than making or cleaning boots is entertained only by people to whom a man of science is still a magician who can cure diseases, transmute metals, and enable us to live for ever. It may still be necessary for some time to come to practise on popular credulity, popular love and dread of the marvellous, and popular idolatry, to induce the poor to comply with the sanitary regulations they are too ignorant to understand. As I have elsewhere confessed,[22] I have myself been responsible for ridiculous incantations with burning sulphur, experimentally proved to be quite useless, because poor people are convinced, by the mystical air of the burning and the horrible smell, that it exorcises the demons of smallpox and scarlet fever and makes it safe for them to return to their houses. To assure them that the real secret is sunshine and soap is only to convince them that you do not care whether they live or die, and wish to save money at their expense. So you perform the incantation; and back they go to their houses, satisfied. A religious ceremony—a poetic blessing of the threshold, for instance—would be much better; but unfortunately our religion is weak on the sanitary side. One of the worst misfortunes of Christendom was that reaction against the

22. Shaw as a borough councillor served on the Health Committee, making him quite knowledgeable in the area of municipal health conditions.

voluptuous bathing of the imperial Romans which made dirty habits a part of Christian piety, and in some unlucky places (the Sandwich Islands [later Hawaii], for example) made the introduction of Christianity also the introduction of disease, because the formulators of the superseded native religion, like Mahomet, had been enlightened enough to introduce as religious duties such sanitary measures as ablution and the most careful and reverent treatment of everything cast off by the human body, even to nail clippings and hairs; and our missionaries thoughtlessly discredited this godly doctrine without supplying its place, which was promptly taken by laziness and neglect. If the priests of Ireland could only be persuaded to teach their flocks that it is a deadly insult to the Blessed Virgin to place her image in a cottage that is not kept up to that high standard of Sunday cleanliness to which all her worshippers must believe she is accustomed, and to represent her as being especially particular about stables because her son was born in one, they might do more in one year than all the Sanitary Inspectors in Ireland could do in twenty; and they could hardly doubt that Our Lady would be delighted. Perhaps they do nowadays; for Ireland is certainly a transfigured country since my youth as far as clean faces and pinafores can transfigure it. In England, where so many of the inhabitants are too gross to believe in poetic faiths, too respectable to tolerate the notion that the stable at Bethlehem was a common peasant farmer's stable instead of a first-rate racing one, and too savage to believe that anything can really cast out the devil of disease unless it be some terrifying hoodoo of tortures and stinks, the M.O.H. will no doubt for a long time to come have to preach to fools according to their folly, promising miracles, and threatening hideous personal consequences of neglect of by-laws and the like; therefore it will be important that every M.O.H. shall have, with his (or her) other qualifications, a sense of humor, lest he (or she) should come at last to believe all the nonsense that must needs be talked. But he must, in his capacity of an expert advising the authorities, keep the government itself free of superstition. If Italian peasants are so ignorant that the Church can get no hold of them except by miracles, why, miracles there must be. The blood of St Januarius must liquefy whether the Saint is in the humor or not. To trick a heathen into being a dutiful Christian is no worse than to trick a whitewasher into trusting himself in a room where a smallpox patient has lain, by pretending to exorcise the disease with burning sulphur. But woe to the Church if in deceiving the peasant it also deceives itself; for then the Church is lost, and the peasant too, unless he revolt against it. Unless the Church works the pretended miracle painfully against the grain, and is continually urged by its dislike of the imposture to strive to make the peasant susceptible to the true reasons for behaving well, the Church will become an instrument of his corruption and an exploiter of his ignorance, and will find itself launched upon that persecution of scientific truth of which all priesthoods are accused—and none with more justice than the scientific priesthood.

And here we come to the danger that terrifies so many of us: the danger of having a hygienic orthodoxy imposed on us. But we must face that: in such crowded and poverty ridden civilizations as ours any orthodoxy is better than *laisser-faire*. If our population ever comes to consist exclusively of well-to-do, highly cultivated, and thoroughly instructed free persons in a position to take care of themselves, no doubt they will make short work of a good deal of official regulation that is now of life-and-death necessity to us; but under existing circumstances, I repeat, almost any sort of attention that democracy will stand is better than neglect. Attention and activity lead to mistakes as well as to successes; but a life spent in making mistakes is not only more honorable but more useful than a life spent doing nothing. The one lesson that comes out of all our theorizing and experimenting is that there is only one really scientific progressive method; and that is the method of trial and error. If you come to that, what is *laisser-faire* but an orthodoxy? the most tyrannous and disastrous of all the orthodoxies, since it forbids you even to learn.

THE LATEST THEORIES

Medical theories are so much a matter of fashion, and the most fertile of them are modified so rapidly by medical practice and biological research, which are international activities, that the play which furnishes the pretext for this preface is already slightly outmoded, though I believe it may be taken as a faithful record for the year (1906) in which it was begun. I must not expose any professional man to ruin by connecting his name with the entire freedom of criticism which I, as a layman, enjoy; but it will be evident to all experts that my play could not have been written but for the work done by Sir Almroth Wright in the theory and practice of securing immunization from bacterial diseases by the inoculation of "vaccines" made of their own bacteria: a practice incorrectly called vaccinetherapy (there is nothing vaccine about it) apparently because it is what vaccination ought to be and is not. Until Sir Almroth Wright, following up one of [Elie] Metchnikoff's most suggestive biological romances,[23] discovered that the white corpuscles or phagocytes which attack and devour disease germs for us do their work only when we butter the disease germs appetizingly for them with a natural sauce which Sir Almroth named opsonin, and that our production of this condiment continually rises and falls rhythmically from negligibility to the highest efficiency, nobody had been able even to conjecture why the various serums that were from time to time introduced as having effected marvellous cures, presently made such direful havoc of some unfortunate patient that they had to be dropped hastily. The quantity of sturdy lying that was necessary to save the credit of inoculation in those days was prodigious; and had it not been for the devotion shewn by the military authorities throughout Europe, who would order the entire disappearance of some disease from their armies, and bring it about by the simple plan of changing the name under which the cases were reported, or for our own Metropolitan Asylums Board, which carefully suppressed all the medical reports that revealed the sometimes quite appalling effects of epidemics of revaccination, there is no saying what popular reaction might not have taken place against the whole immunization movement in therapeutics.

The situation was saved when Sir Almroth Wright pointed out that if you inoculated a patient with pathogenic germs at a moment when his powers of cooking them for consumption by the phagocytes was receding to its lowest point, you would certainly make him a good deal worse and perhaps kill him, whereas if you made precisely the same inoculation when the cooking power was rising to one of its periodical climaxes, you would stimulate it to still further exertions and produce just the opposite result. And he invented a technique for ascertaining in which phase the patient happened to be at any given moment. The dramatic possibilities of this discovery and invention will be found in my play. But it is one thing to invent a technique: it is quite another to persuade the medical profession to acquire it. Our general practitioners, I gather, simply declined to acquire it, being mostly unable to afford either the acquisition or the practice of it when acquired. Something simple, cheap, and ready at all times for all comers, is, as I have shewn, the only thing that is economically possible in general practice, whatever may be the case in Sir Almroth's famous laboratory in St Mary's Hospital. It would have become necessary to denounce opsonin in the trade papers as a fad and Sir Almroth as a dangerous man if his practice in the laboratory had not led him to the conclusion that the

23. Russian zoologist and bacteriologist, whose theory of the nature of immunity is that phagocytes can paralyse, kill and digest micro-organisms.

customary inoculations were very much too powerful, and that a comparatively infinitesimal dose would not precipitate a negative phase of cooking activity, and might induce a positive one. And thus it happens that the refusal of our general practitioners to acquire the new technique is no longer quite so dangerous in practice as it was when The Doctor's Dilemma was written: nay, that Sir Ralph Bloomfield Bonington's way of administering inoculations as if they were spoonfuls of squills [a herbal patent medication] may sometimes work fairly well. For all that, I find Sir Almroth Wright, on the 23rd May 1910, warning the Royal Society of Medicine that "the clinician has not yet been prevailed upon to reconsider his position," which means that the general practitioner ("the doctor," as he is called in our homes) is going on just as he did before, and could not afford to learn or practise a new technique even if he had ever heard of it. To the patient who does not know about it he will say nothing. To the patient who does, he will ridicule it, and disparage Sir Almroth. What else can he do, except confess his ignorance and starve?

But now please observe how "the whirligig of time brings its revenges" [Shakespeare's *Twelfth Night*, slightly misquoted]. This latest discovery of the remedial virtue of a very very tiny hair of the dog that bit you reminds us, not only of [Prof. Rudolph] Arndt's law of protoplasmic reaction to stimuli, according to which weak and strong stimuli provoke opposite reactions, but of Hahnemann's homeopathy, which was founded on the fact alleged by Hahnemann that drugs which produce certain symptoms when taken in ordinary perceptible quantities, will, when taken in infinitesimally small quantities, provoke just the opposite symptoms; so that the drug that gives you a headache will also cure a headache if you take little enough of it. I have already explained that the savage opposition which homeopathy encountered from the medical profession was not a scientific opposition; for nobody seems to deny that some drugs act in the alleged manner. It was opposed simply because doctors and apothecaries lived by selling bottles and boxes of doctor's stuff to be taken in spoonfuls or in pellets as large as peas; and people would not pay as much for drops and globules no bigger than pins' heads. Nowadays, however, the more cultivated folk are beginning to be so suspicious of drugs, and the incorrigibly superstitious people so profusely supplied with patent medicines (the medical advice to take them being wrapped round the bottle and thrown in for nothing) that homeopathy has become a way of rehabilitating the trade of prescription compounding, and is consequently coming into professional credit. At which point the theory of opsonins comes very opportunely to shake hands with it.

Add to the newly triumphant homeopathist and the opsonist that other remarkable innovator, the Swedish masseur, who does not theorize about you, but probes you all over with his powerful thumbs until he finds out your sore spots and rubs them away, besides cheating you into a little wholesome exercise; and you have nearly everything in medical practice today that is not flat witchcraft or pure commercial exploitation of human credulity and fear of death. Add to them a good deal of vegetarian and teetotal controversy raging round a clamor for scientific eating and drinking, and resulting in little so far except calling digestion Metabolism and dividing the public between the eminent doctor who tells us that we do not eat enough fish, and his equally eminent colleague who warns us that a fish diet must end in leprosy, and you have all that opposes with any sort of countenance the rise of Christian Science with its cathedrals and congregations and zealots and miracles and cures: all very silly, no doubt, but sane and sensible, poetic and hopeful, compared to the pseudo science of the commercial general practitioner, who foolishly clamors for the prosecution and even the execution of the Christian Scientists when their patients die, forgetting the long deathroll of his own patients.

By the time this preface is in print the kaleidoscope may have had another shake; and opsonin may have gone the way of phlogiston[24] at the hands of its own restless discoverer. I will not say that Hahnemann may have gone the way of Diafoirus [a quack physician in Molière's *Le Malade imaginaire*]; for Diafoirus we have always with us. But we shall still pick up all our knowledge in pursuit of some Will o' the Wisp or other. What is called science has always pursued the Elixir of Life and the Philosopher's Stone, and is just as busy after them today as ever it was in the days of Paracelsus. We call them by different names: Immunization or radiotherapy or what not; but the dreams which lure us into the adventures from which we learn are always at bottom the same. Science becomes dangerous only when it imagines that it has reached its goal. What is wrong with priests and popes is that instead of being apostles and saints, they are nothing but empirics who say "I know" instead of "I am learning," and pray for credulity and inertia as wise men pray for scepticism and activity. Such abominations as the Inquisition and the Vaccination Acts are possible only in the famine years of the soul, when the great vital dogmas of honor, liberty, courage, the kinship of all life, faith that the unknown is greater than the known and is only the As Yet Unknown, and resolution to find a manly highway to it, have been forgotten in a paroxysm of littleness and

24. An imaginary element, the hypothetical principle of fire, replaced by Lavoisier's theory, which regards ordinary combustion as a combining with oxygen.

terror in which nothing is active except concupiscence and the fear of death, playing on which any trader can filch a fortune, any blackguard gratify his cruelty, and any tyrant make us his slaves.

Lest this should seem too rhetorical a conclusion for our professional men of science, who are mostly trained not to believe anything unless it is worded in the jargon of those writers who, because they never really understand what they are trying to say, cannot find familiar words for it, and are therefore compelled to invent a new language of nonsense for every book they write, let me sum up my conclusions as dryly as is consistent with accurate thought and live conviction.

1. Nothing is more dangerous than a poor doctor: not even a poor employer or a poor landlord.

2. Of all the anti-social vested interests the worst is the vested interest in ill-health.

3. Remember that an illness is a misdemeanor; and treat the doctor as an accessory unless he notifies every case to the Public Health Authority.

4. Treat every death as a possible and, under our present system, a probable murder, by making it the subject of a reasonably conducted inquest; and execute the doctor, if necessary, *as* a doctor, by striking him off the register.

5. Make up your mind how many doctors the community needs to keep it well. Do not register more or less than this number; and let registration constitute the doctor a civil servant with a dignified living wage paid out of public funds.

6. Municipalize Harley Street [fashionable centre for London medicine].

7. Treat the private operator exactly as you would treat a private executioner.

8. Treat persons who profess to be able to cure disease as you treat fortune tellers.

9. Keep the public carefully informed, by special statistics and announcements of individual cases, of all illnesses of doctors or in their families.

10. Make it compulsory for a doctor using a brass plate to have inscribed on it, in addition to the letters indicating his qualifications, the words "Remember that I too am mortal."

11. In legislation and social organization, proceed on the principle that invalids, meaning persons who cannot keep themselves alive by their own activities, cannot, beyond reason, expect to be kept alive by the activity of others. There is a point at which the most energetic policeman or doctor, when called upon to deal with an apparently drowned person, gives up artificial respiration, although it is never possible to declare with certainty,

at any point short of decomposition, that another five minutes of the exercise would not effect resuscitation. The theory that every individual alive is of infinite value is legislatively impracticable. No doubt the higher the life we secure to the individual by wise social organization, the greater his value is to the community, and the more pains we shall take to pull him through any temporary danger or disablement. But the man who costs more than he is worth is doomed by sound hygiene as inexorably as by sound economics.

12. Do not try to live for ever. You will not succeed.

13. Use your health, even to the point of wearing it out. That is what it is for. Spend all you have before you die; and do not outlive yourself.

14. Take the utmost care to get well born and well brought up. This means that your mother must have a good doctor. Be careful to go to a school where there is what they call a school clinic, where your nutrition and teeth and eyesight and other matters of importance to you will be attended to. Be particularly careful to have all this done at the expense of the nation, as otherwise it will not be done at all, the chances being about forty to one against your being able to pay for it directly yourself, even if you know how to set about it. Otherwise you will be what most people are at present: an unsound citizen of an unsound nation, without sense enough to be ashamed or unhappy about it.

1911.

POSTSCRIPT, 1930. During the years which have elapsed since the foregoing preface was penned, the need for bringing the medical profession under responsible and effective public control has become constantly more pressing as the inevitable collisions between the march of discovery in therapeutic science and the reactionary obsolescence of the General Medical Council[25] have become more frequent and sensational. A later volume [*Doctor's Delusions: Crude Criminology: Sham Education*, 1931] in the present edition of my works deals with this development.

G. B. S.

---

25. Established in 1858 'to enable persons requiring medical aid to distinguish qualified from unqualified practitioners'.

MARRIAGE NEVERTHELESS INEVITABLE

Now most laws are, and all laws ought to be, stronger than the strongest individual. Certainly the marriage law is. The only people who successfully evade it are those who actually avail themselves of its shelter by pretending to be married when they are not, and by Bohemians who have no position to lose and no career to be closed. In every other case open violation of the marriage laws means either downright ruin or such inconvenience and disablement as a prudent man or woman would get married ten times over rather than face. And these disablements and inconveniences are not even the price of freedom; for, as Brieux has shewn so convincingly in Les Hannetons [*The Incubus*], an avowedly illicit union is often found in practice to be as tyrannical and as hard to escape from as the worst legal one.

We may take it then that when a joint domestic establishment, involving questions of children or property, is contemplated, marriage is in effect compulsory upon all normal people; and until the law is altered there is nothing for us but to make the best of it as it stands. Even when no such establishment is desired, clandestine irregularities are negligible as an alternative to marriage. How common they are nobody knows; for in spite of the powerful protection afforded to the parties by the law of libel, and the readiness of society on various other grounds to be hoodwinked by the keeping up of the very thinnest appearances, most of them are probably never suspected. But they are neither dignified nor safe and comfortable, which at once rules them out for normal decent people. Marriage remains practically inevitable; and the sooner we acknowledge this, the sooner we shall set to work to make it decent and reasonable.

WHAT DOES THE WORD MARRIAGE MEAN?

However much we may all suffer through marriage, most of us think so little about it that we regard it as a fixed part of the order of nature, like gravitation. Except for this error, which may be regarded as constant, we use the word with reckless looseness, meaning a dozen different things by it, and yet always assuming that to a respectable man it can have only one meaning. The pious citizen, suspecting the Socialist (for example) of unmentionable things, and asking him heatedly whether he wishes to abolish marriage, is infuriated by a sense of unanswerable quibbling when the Socialist asks him what particular variety of marriage he means: English

Getting Married

First published in 1911

―――――

THE REVOLT AGAINST MARRIAGE

There is no subject on which more dangerous nonsense is talked and thought than marriage. If the mischief stopped at talking and thinking it would be bad enough; but it goes further, into disastrous anarchical action. Because our marriage law is inhuman and unreasonable to the point of downright abomination, the bolder and more rebellious spirits form illicit unions, defiantly sending cards round to their friends announcing what they have done. Young women come to me and ask me whether I think they ought to consent to marry the man they have decided to live with; and they are perplexed and astonished when I, who am supposed (heaven knows why!) to have the most advanced views attainable on the subject, urge them on no account to compromise themselves without the security of an authentic wedding ring. They cite the example of George Eliot, who formed an illicit union with [George Henry] Lewes. They quote a saying attributed to Nietzsche, that a married philosopher is ridiculous, though the men of their choice are not philosophers. When they finally give up the idea of reforming our marriage institutions by private enterprise and personal righteousness, and consent to be led to the Registry or even to the altar, they insist on first arriving at an explicit understanding that both parties are to be perfectly free to sip every flower and change every hour, as their fancy may dictate, in spite of the legal bond. I do not observe that their unions prove less monogamic than other people's: rather the contrary, in fact; consequently, I do not know whether they make less fuss than ordinary people when either party claims the benefit of the treaty; but the existence of the treaty shews the same anarchical notion that the law can be set aside by any two private persons by the simple process of promising one another to ignore it.

at any point short of decomposition, that another five minutes of the exercise would not effect resuscitation. The theory that every individual alive is of infinite value is legislatively impracticable. No doubt the higher the life we secure to the individual by wise social organization, the greater his value is to the community, and the more pains we shall take to pull him through any temporary danger or disablement. But the man who costs more than he is worth is doomed by sound hygiene as inexorably as by sound economics.

12. Do not try to live for ever. You will not succeed.

13. Use your health, even to the point of wearing it out. That is what it is for. Spend all you have before you die; and do not outlive yourself.

14. Take the utmost care to get well born and well brought up. This means that your mother must have a good doctor. Be careful to go to a school where there is what they call a school clinic, where your nutrition and teeth and eyesight and other matters of importance to you will be attended to. Be particularly careful to have all this done at the expense of the nation, as otherwise it will not be done at all, the chances being about forty to one against your being able to pay for it directly yourself, even if you know how to set about it. Otherwise you will be what most people are at present: an unsound citizen of an unsound nation, without sense enough to be ashamed or unhappy about it.

1911.

POSTSCRIPT, 1930. During the years which have elapsed since the foregoing preface was penned, the need for bringing the medical profession under responsible and effective public control has become constantly more pressing as the inevitable collisions between the march of discovery in therapeutic science and the reactionary obsolescence of the General Medical Council[25] have become more frequent and sensational. A later volume [*Doctor's Delusions: Crude Criminology: Sham Education*, 1931] in the present edition of my works deals with this development.

G. B. S.

25. Established in 1858 'to enable persons requiring medical aid to distinguish qualified from unqualified practitioners'.

terror in which nothing is active except concupiscence and the fear of death, playing on which any trader can filch a fortune, any blackguard gratify his cruelty, and any tyrant make us his slaves.

Lest this should seem too rhetorical a conclusion for our professional men of science, who are mostly trained not to believe anything unless it is worded in the jargon of those writers who, because they never really understand what they are trying to say, cannot find familiar words for it, and are therefore compelled to invent a new language of nonsense for every book they write, let me sum up my conclusions as dryly as is consistent with accurate thought and live conviction.

1. Nothing is more dangerous than a poor doctor: not even a poor employer or a poor landlord.

2. Of all the anti-social vested interests the worst is the vested interest in ill-health.

3. Remember that an illness is a misdemeanor; and treat the doctor as an accessory unless he notifies every case to the Public Health Authority.

4. Treat every death as a possible and, under our present system, a probable murder, by making it the subject of a reasonably conducted inquest; and execute the doctor, if necessary, *as* a doctor, by striking him off the register.

5. Make up your mind how many doctors the community needs to keep it well. Do not register more or less than this number; and let registration constitute the doctor a civil servant with a dignified living wage paid out of public funds.

6. Municipalize Harley Street [fashionable centre for London medicine].

7. Treat the private operator exactly as you would treat a private executioner.

8. Treat persons who profess to be able to cure disease as you treat fortune tellers.

9. Keep the public carefully informed, by special statistics and announcements of individual cases, of all illnesses of doctors or in their families.

10. Make it compulsory for a doctor using a brass plate to have inscribed on it, in addition to the letters indicating his qualifications, the words "Remember that I too am mortal."

11. In legislation and social organization, proceed on the principle that invalids, meaning persons who cannot keep themselves alive by their own activities, cannot, beyond reason, expect to be kept alive by the activity of others. There is a point at which the most energetic policeman or doctor, when called upon to deal with an apparently drowned person, gives up artificial respiration, although it is never possible to declare with certainty,

civil marriage, sacramental marriage, indissoluble Roman Catholic marriage, marriage of divorced persons, Scotch marriage, Irish marriage, French, German, Turkish, or South Dakotan marriage. In Sweden, one of the most highly civilized countries in the world, a marriage is dissolved if both parties wish it, without any question of conduct. That is what marriage means in Sweden. In Clapham [south London] that is what they call by the senseless name of Free Love. In the British Empire we have unlimited Kulin[1] polygamy, Muslim polygamy limited to four wives, child marriages, and, nearer home, marriages of first cousins: all of them abominations in the eyes of many worthy persons. Not only may the respectable British champion of marriage mean any of these widely different institutions; sometimes he does not mean marriage at all. He means monogamy, chastity, temperance, respectability, morality, Christianity, anti-socialism, and a dozen other things that have no necessary connection with marriage. He often means something that he dare not avow: ownership of the person of another human being, for instance. And he never tells the truth about his own marriage either to himself or anyone else.

With those individualists who in the XIX century dreamt of doing away with marriage altogether on the ground that it is a private concern between the two parties with which society has nothing to do, there is now no need to deal. The vogue of "the self-regarding action" has passed; and it may be assumed without argument that unions for the purpose of establishing a family will continue to be registered and regulated by the State. Such registration is marriage, and will continue to be called marriage long after the conditions of the registration have changed so much that no citizen now living would recognize them as marriage conditions at all if he revisited the earth. There is therefore no question of abolishing marriage; but there is a very pressing question of improving its conditions. I have never met anybody really in favor of maintaining marriage as it exists in England today. A Roman Catholic may obey his Church by assenting verbally to the doctrine of indissoluble marriage. But nobody worth counting believes directly, frankly, and instinctively that when a person commits a murder and is put into prison for twenty years for it, the free and innocent husband or wife of that murderer should remain bound by the marriage. To put it briefly, a contract for better for worse is a contract that should not be tolerated. As a matter of fact it is not tolerated fully even by the Roman Catholic Church; for Roman Catholic marriages can be

1. The Kulin was an aristocratic religious sect in Bengal, among whom polygamy was a widespread practice.

dissolved, if not by the temporal Courts, by the Pope. Indissoluble marriage is an academic figment, advocated only by celibates and by comfortably married people who imagine that if other couples are uncomfortable it must be their own fault, just as rich people are apt to imagine that if other people are poor it serves them right. There is always some means of dissolution. The conditions of dissolution may vary widely, from those on which Henry VIII procured his divorce from Katharine of Aragon to the pleas on which American wives obtain divorces (for instance, "mental anguish" caused by the husband's neglect to cut his toe-nails); but there is always some point at which the theory of the inviolable better-for-worse marriage breaks down in practice. South Carolina has indeed passed what is called a freak law declaring that a marriage shall not be dissolved under any circumstances;[2] but such an absurdity will probably be repealed or amended by sheer force of circumstances before these words are in print. The only question to be considered is, What shall the conditions of the dissolution be?

SURVIVALS OF SEX SLAVERY

If we adopt the common romantic assumption that the object of marriage is bliss, then the very strongest reason for dissolving a marriage is that it shall be disagreeable to one or other or both of the parties. If we accept the view that the object of marriage is to provide for the production and rearing of children, then childlessness should be a conclusive reason for dissolution. As neither of these causes entitles married persons to divorce it is at once clear that our marriage law is not founded on either assumption. What it is really founded on is the morality of the tenth commandment, which Englishwomen will one day succeed in obliterating from the walls of our churches by refusing to enter any building where they are publicly classed with a man's house, his ox, and his ass, as his purchased chattels. In this morality female adultery is malversation by the woman and theft by the man, whilst male adultery with an unmarried woman is not an offence at all. But though this is not only the theory of our marriage laws, but the practical morality of many of us, it is no longer an avowed morality, nor does its persistence depend on marriage; for the abolition of marriage would, other things remaining unchanged, leave women more effectually

2. The Constitution of 1895 of the State of South Carolina (Article XVII, Section 3) provided that 'Divorce from the bonds of matrimony shall not be allowed in this State.'

enslaved than they now are. We shall come to the question of the economic dependence of women on men later on; but at present we had better confine ourselves to the theories of marriage which we are not ashamed to acknowledge and defend, and upon which, therefore, marriage reformers will be obliged to proceed.

We may, I think, dismiss from the field of practical politics the extreme sacerdotal view of marriage as a sacred and indissoluble covenant, because, though reinforced by unhappy marriages as all fanaticisms are reinforced by human sacrifices, it has been reduced to a private and socially inoperative eccentricity by the introduction of civil marriage and divorce. Theoretically, our civilly married couples are to a Catholic as unmarried couples are: that is, they are living in open sin. Practically, civilly married couples are received in society, by Catholics and everyone else, precisely as sacramentally married couples are; and so are people who have divorced their wives or husbands and married again. And yet marriage is enforced by public opinion with such ferocity that the least suggestion of laxity in its support is fatal to even the highest and strongest reputations, although laxity of conduct is winked at with grinning indulgence; so that we find the austere Shelley denounced as a fiend in human form, whilst Nelson, who openly left his wife and formed a *ménage à trois* with Sir William and [Emma] Lady Hamilton, was idolized. Shelley might have had an illegitimate child in every county in England if he had done so frankly as a sinner. His unpardonable offence was that he attacked marriage as an institution. We feel a strange anguish of terror and hatred against him, as against one who threatens us with a mortal injury. What is the element in his proposals that produces this effect?

The answer of the specialists is the one already alluded to: that the attack on marriage is an attack on property; so that Shelley was something more hateful to a husband than a horse thief: to wit, a wife thief, and something more hateful to a wife than a burglar: namely, one who would steal her husband's house from over her head, and leave her destitute and nameless on the streets. Now, no doubt this accounts for a good deal of anti-Shelleyan prejudice: a prejudice so deeply rooted in our habits that, as I have shewn in my play, men who are bolder freethinkers than Shelley himself can no more bring themselves to commit adultery than to commit any common theft, whilst women who loathe sex slavery more fiercely than Mary Wollstonecraft[3] are unable to face the insecurity and discredit of the

3. Mary Wollstonecraft Godwin, mother of Shelley's wife Mary, was the author of *A Vindication of the Rights of Woman* (1792).

vagabondage which is the masterless woman's only alternative to celibacy. But in spite of all this there is a revolt against marriage which has spread so rapidly within my recollection that though we all still assume the existence of a huge and dangerous majority which regards the least hint of scepticism as to the beauty and holiness of marriage as infamous and abhorrent, I sometimes wonder why it is so difficult to find an authentic living member of this dreaded army of convention outside the ranks of the people who never think about public questions at all, and who, for all their numerical weight and apparently invincible prejudices, accept social changes today as tamely as their forefathers accepted the Reformation under Henry [VIII] and Edward [VI], the Restoration under Mary [Tudor], and, after Mary's death, the shandygaff [oddly mixed drink] which Elizabeth compounded from both doctrines and called the Articles of the Church of England. If matters were left to these simple folk, there would never be any changes at all; and society would perish like a snake that could not cast its skins. Nevertheless the snake does change its skin in spite of them; and there are signs that our marriage-law skin is causing discomfort to thoughtful people and will presently be cast whether the others are satisfied with it or not. The question therefore arises: What is there in marriage that makes the thoughtful people so uncomfortable?

THE NEW ATTACK ON MARRIAGE

The answer to this question is an answer which everybody knows and nobody likes to give. What is driving our ministers of religion and statesmen to blurt it out at last is the plain fact that marriage is now beginning to depopulate the country with such alarming rapidity that we are forced to throw aside our modesty like people who, awakened by an alarm of fire, rush into the streets in their nightdresses or in no dresses at all. The fictitious Free Lover, who was supposed to attack marriage because it thwarted his inordinate affections and prevented him from making life a carnival, has vanished and given place to the very real, very strong, very austere avenger of outraged decency who declares that the licentiousness of marriage, now that it no longer recruits the race, is destroying it.

As usual, this change of front has not yet been noticed by our newspaper controversialists and by the suburban season-ticket holders whose minds the newspapers make. They still defend the citadel on the side on which nobody is attacking it, and leave its weakest front undefended.

The religious revolt against marriage is a very old one. Christianity

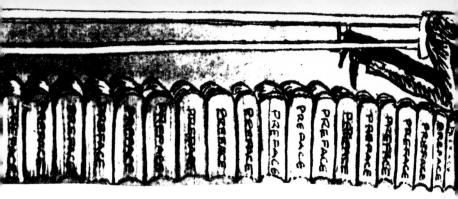

COMPLETE PREFACES

VOLUME 1: 1889–1913

EDITED BY DAN H. LAURENCE
AND DANIEL J. LEARY

Poverty, nationalism, health care, family values--topics as timely as this morning's newspaper--were themes that inspired

Allen Lane
THE PENGUIN PRESS

Penguin USA   Viking Penguin   375 Hudson Street   New York, New York 10014   Telephone 212-366-2000

NEWS

"I have never aimed at style in my life: style is a sort of melody that comes into my sentences by itself. If a writer says what he has to say as accurately and effectively as he can, his style will take care of itself, if he has a style."

(Preface to *Immaturity*, 1930)

BERNARD SHAW

began with a fierce attack on marriage; and to this day the celibacy of the Roman Catholic priesthood is a standing protest against its compatibility with the higher life. St Paul's reluctant sanction of marriage; his personal protest that he countenanced it of necessity and against his own conviction; his contemptuous "better to marry than to burn" [1 Corinthians 7: 9] is only out of date in respect of his belief that the end of the world was at hand and that there was therefore no longer any population question. His instinctive recoil from its worst aspect as a slavery to pleasure which induces two people to accept slavery to one another has remained an active force in the world to this day, and is now stirring more uneasily than ever. We have more and more Pauline celibates whose objection to marriage is the intolerable indignity of being supposed to desire or live the married life as ordinarily conceived. Every thoughtful and observant minister of religion is troubled by the determination of his flock to regard marriage as a sanctuary for pleasure, seeing as he does that the known libertines of his parish are visibly suffering much less from intemperance than many of the married people who stigmatize them as monsters of vice.

A Forgotten Conference of Married Men

The late Hugh Price Hughes [founder of the West London Mission], an eminent Methodist divine, once organized in London a conference of respectable men to consider the subject. Nothing came of it (nor indeed could have come of it in the absence of women); but it had its value as giving the young sociologists present, of whom I was one, an authentic notion of what a picked audience of respectable men understood by married life. It was certainly a staggering revelation. Peter the Great would have been shocked; Byron would have been horrified; Don Juan would have fled from the conference into a monastery. The respectable men all regarded the marriage ceremony as a rite which absolved them from the laws of health and temperance; inaugurated a life-long honeymoon; and placed their pleasures on exactly the same footing as their prayers. It seemed entirely proper and natural to them that out of every twenty-four hours of their lives they should pass eight shut up in one room with their wives alone, and this, not birdlike, for the mating season, but all the year round and every year. How they settled even such minor questions as to which party should decide whether and how much the window should be open and how many blankets should be on the bed, and at what hour they should go to bed and get up so as to avoid disturbing one another's sleep, seemed insoluble questions to me. But the members of the conference did not seem to mind. They were content to have the whole national housing problem treated on a basis of one room for two people. That was the essence of marriage for them.

Please remember, too, that there was nothing in their circumstances to check intemperance. They were men of business; that is, men for the most part engaged in routine work which exercized neither their minds nor their bodies to the full pitch of their capacities. Compared with statesmen, first-rate professional men, artists, and even with laborers and artisans as far as muscular exertion goes, they were underworked, and could spare the fine edge of their faculties and the last few inches of their chests without being any the less fit for their daily routine. If I had adopted their habits, a startling deterioration would have appeared in my writing before the end of a fortnight, and frightened me back to what they would have considered an impossible asceticism. But they paid no penalty of which they were conscious. They had as much health as they wanted: that is, they did not feel the need of a doctor. They enjoyed their smokes, their meals, their respectable clothes, their affectionate games with their children, their prospects of larger profits or higher salaries, their Saturday half holidays and Sunday walks, and the rest of it. They did less than two hours work a day and took from seven to nine office hours to do it in. And they were no good for any mortal purpose except to go on doing it. They were respectable only by the standard they themselves had set. Considered seriously as electors governing an empire through their votes, and choosing and maintaining its religious and moral institutions by their powers of social persecution, they were a black-coated army of calamity. They were incapable of comprehending the industries they were engaged in, the laws under which they lived, or the relation of their country to other countries. They lived the lives of old men contentedly. They were timidly conservative at the age at which every healthy human being ought to be obstreperously revolutionary. And their wives went through the routine of the kitchen, nursery, and drawing room just as they went through the routine of the office. They had all, as they called it, settled down, like balloons that had lost their lifting margin of gas; and it was evident that the process of settling down would go on until they settled into their graves. They read old-fashioned newspapers with effort, and were just taking with avidity to a new sort of paper, costing a halfpenny, which they believed to be extraordinarily bright and attractive, and which never really succeeded until it became extremely dull, discarding all serious news and replacing it by vapid tittle-tattle, and substituting for political articles informed by at least some pretence of knowledge of economics, history, and constitutional law, such paltry follies and sentimentalities, snobberies and partisaneries, as ignorance can understand and irresponsibility relish.

What they called patriotism was a conviction that because they were born in Tooting or Camberwell [districts of London], they were the natural superiors of Beethoven, of Rodin, of Ibsen, of Tolstoy and all other benighted foreigners. Those of them who did not think it wrong to go to the theatre liked above everything a play in which the hero was called Dick; was continually fingering a briar pipe; and, after being overwhelmed with admiration and affection through three acts, was finally rewarded with the legal possession of a pretty heroine's person on the strength of a staggering lack of virtue. Indeed their only conception of the meaning of the word virtue was abstention from stealing other men's wives or from refusing to marry their daughters.

As to law, religion, ethics, and constitutional government, any counterfeit could impose on them. Any atheist could pass himself off on them as a bishop, any anarchist as a judge, any despot as a Whig, any sentimental socialist as a Tory, any philtre-monger or witch-finder as a man of science, any phrase-maker as a statesman. Those who did not believe the story of Jonah and the great fish were all the readier to believe that metals can be transmuted and all diseases cured by radium, and that men can live for two hundred years by drinking sour milk. Even these credulities involved too severe an intellectual effort for many of them: it was easier to grin and believe nothing. They maintained their respect for themselves by "playing the game" (that is, doing what everybody else did), and by being good judges of hats, ties, dogs, pipes, cricket, gardens, flowers, and the like. They were capable of discussing each other's solvency and respectability with some shrewdness, and could carry out quite complicated systems of paying visits and "knowing" one another. They felt a little vulgar when they spent a day at Margate, and quite distinguished and travelled when they spent it at Boulogne. They were, except as to their clothes, "not particular": that is, they could put up with ugly sights and sounds, unhealthy smells, and inconvenient houses, with inhuman apathy and callousness. They had, as to adults, a theory that human nature is so poor that it is useless to try to make the world any better, whilst as to children they believed that if they were only sufficiently lectured and whipped, they could be brought to a state of moral perfection such as no fanatic has ever ascribed to his deity. Though they were not intentionally malicious, they practised the most appalling cruelties from mere thoughtlessness, thinking nothing of imprisoning men and women for periods up to twenty years for breaking into their houses; of treating their children as wild beasts to be tamed by a system of blows and imprisonment which they called education; and of keeping pianos in their houses, not for musical purposes, but to torment their daughters with a senseless stupidity that would have revolted an inquisitor.

In short, dear reader, they were very like you and me. I could fill a hundred pages with the tale of our imbecilities and still leave much untold; but what I have set down here haphazard is enough to condemn the system that produced us. The corner-stone of that system was the family and the institution of marriage as we have it today in England.

HEARTH AND HOME

There is no shirking it: if marriage cannot be made to produce something better than we are, marriage will have to go, or else the nation will have to go. It is no use talking of honor, virtue, purity, and wholesome, sweet, clean English home lives when what is meant is simply the habits I have described. The flat fact is that English home life today is neither honorable, virtuous, wholesome, sweet, clean, nor in any creditable way distinctively English. It is in many respects conspicuously the reverse; and the result of withdrawing children from it completely at an early age, and sending them to a public school and then to a university, does, in spite of the fact that these institutions are class warped and in some respects quite abominably corrupt, produce sociabler men. Women, too, are improved by the escape from home provided by women's colleges; but as very few of them are fortunate enough to enjoy this advantage, most women are so thoroughly home-bred as to be unfit for human society. So little is expected of them that in Sheridan's School for Scandal we hardly notice that the heroine is a female cad, as detestable and dishonorable in her repentance as she is vulgar and silly in her naughtiness. It was left to an abnormal critic like George Gissing[4] to point out the glaring fact that in the collection of life studies of Victorian women to be found in the novels of Dickens, the most convincingly real ones are either vilely unamiable or comically contemptible; whilst his attempts to manufacture admirable heroines by idealizations of home-bred womanhood are not only absurd but not even pleasantly absurd: one has no patience with them.

As all this is corrigible by reducing home life and domestic sentiment to

4. Realist writer, author of *Charles Dickens: A Critical Study* (1898).

something like reasonable proportions in the life of the individual, the danger of it does not lie in human nature. Home life as we understand it is no more natural to us than a cage is natural to a cockatoo. Its grave danger to the nation lies in its narrow views, its unnaturally sustained and spitefully jealous concupiscences, its petty tyrannies, its false social pretences, its endless grudges and squabbles, its sacrifice of the boy's future by setting him to earn money to help the family when he should be in training for his adult life (remember the boy Dickens and the blacking factory), and of the girl's chances by making her a slave to sick or selfish parents, its unnatural packing into little brick boxes of little parcels of humanity of ill-assorted ages, with the old scolding or beating the young for behaving like young people, and the young hating and thwarting the old for behaving like old people, and all the other ills, mentionable and unmentionable, that arise from excessive segregation. It sets these evils up as benefits and blessings representing the highest attainable degree of honor and virtue, whilst any criticism of or revolt against them is savagely persecuted as the extremity of vice. The revolt, driven under ground and exacerbated, produces debauchery veiled by hypocrisy, an overwhelming demand for licentious theatrical entertainments which no censorship can stem, and, worst of all, a confusion of virtue with the mere morality that steals its name until the real thing is loathed because the imposture is loathsome. Literary traditions spring up in which the libertine and profligate—Tom Jones and Charles Surface—are the heroes, and decorous, law-abiding persons—Blifil and Joseph Surface[5]—are the villains and butts. People like to believe that Nell Gwynne has every amiable quality and the Bishop's wife every odious one. Poor Mr Pecksniff, who is generally no worse than a humbug with a turn for pompous talking, is represented as a criminal instead of as a very typical English paterfamilias keeping a roof over the head of himself and his daughters by inducing people to pay him more for his services than they are worth. In the extreme instances of reaction against convention, female murderers get sheaves of offers of marriage; and when Nature throws up that rare phenomenon, an unscrupulous libertine, his success among "well brought-up" girls is so easy, and the devotion he inspires so extravagant, that it is impossible not to see that the revolt against conventional respectability has transfigured a commonplace rascal into a sort of Anarchist Savior. As to the respectable voluptuary, who joins Omar Khayyam [dining] clubs and vibrates to Swinburne's invocation of Dolores to "come down and redeem us from virtue," he is to be found in every suburb.

5. The first and third appear in Fielding's novel *Tom Jones* (1749); the second and fourth are brothers in Sheridan's play *The School for Scandal* (1777).

TOO MUCH OF A GOOD THING

We must be reasonable in our domestic ideals. I do not think that life at a public school is altogether good for a boy any more than barrack life is altogether good for a soldier. But neither is home life altogether good. Such good as it does, I should say, is due to its freedom from the very atmosphere it professes to supply. That atmosphere is usually described as an atmosphere of love; and this definition should be sufficient to put any sane person on guard against it. The people who talk and write as if the highest attainable state is that of a family stewing in love continuously from the cradle to the grave, can hardly have given five minutes serious consideration to so outrageous a proposition. They cannot have even made up their minds as to what they mean by love; for when they expatiate on their thesis they are sometimes talking about kindness, and sometimes about mere appetite. In either sense they are equally far from the realities of life. No healthy man or animal is occupied with love in any sense for more than a very small fraction indeed of the time he devotes to business and to recreations wholly unconnected with love. A wife entirely preoccupied with her affection for her husband, a mother entirely preoccupied with her affection for her children, may be all very well in a book (for people who like that kind of book); but in actual life she is a nuisance. Husbands may escape from her when their business compels them to be away from home all day; but young children may be, and quite often are, killed by her cuddling and coddling and doctoring and preaching: above all, by her continuous attempts to excite precocious sentimentality, a practice as objectionable, and possibly as mischievous, as the worst tricks of the worst nursemaids.

LARGE AND SMALL FAMILIES

In most healthy families there is a revolt against this tendency. The exchanging of presents on birthdays and the like is barred by general consent, and the relations of the parties are placed by express treaty on an unsentimental footing.

Unfortunately this mitigation of family sentimentality is much more characteristic of large families than small ones. It used to be said that members of large families get on in the world; and it is certainly true that for purposes of social training a household of twenty surpasses a household of five as an Oxford College surpasses an eight-roomed house in a cheap street. Ten children, with the necessary adults, make a community in which an excess of sentimentality is impossible. Two children make a doll's house, in which both parents and children become morbid if they keep to themselves. What is more, when large families were the fashion, they were organized as tyrannies much more than as "atmospheres of love." Francis Place[6] tells us that he kept out of his father's way because his father never passed a child within his reach without striking it; and though the case was an extreme one, it was an extreme that illustrated a tendency. Sir Walter Scott's father, when his son incautiously expressed some relish for his porridge, dashed a handful of salt into it with an instinctive sense that it was his duty as a father to prevent his son enjoying himself. [John] Ruskin's mother gratified the sensual side of her maternal passion, not by cuddling her son, but by whipping him when he fell downstairs or was slack in learning the Bible off by heart; and this grotesque safety-valve for voluptuousness, mischievous as it was in many ways, had at least the advantage that the child did not enjoy it and was not debauched by it, as he would have been by transports of sentimentality.

But nowadays we cannot depend on these safeguards, such as they were. We no longer have large families: all the families are too small to give the children the necessary social training. The Roman father is out of fashion; and the whip and the cane are becoming discredited, not so much by the old arguments against corporal punishment (sound as these were) as by the gradual wearing away of the veil from the fact that flogging is a form of debauchery. The advocate of flogging as a punishment is now exposed to very disagreeable suspicions; and ever since Rousseau rose to the effort of making a certain very ridiculous confession on the subject, there has been a growing perception that child whipping, even for the children themselves, is not always the innocent and highminded practice it professes to be. At all events there is no getting away from the facts that families are smaller than they used to be, and that passions which formerly took effect in tyranny have been largely diverted into sentimentality. And though a little sentimentality may be a very good thing, chronic sentimentality is a horror, more dangerous, because more possible, than the erotomania which we all condemn when we are not thoughtlessly glorifying it as the ideal married state.

6. Trade unionist working man, instrumental in the passage of the 1832 trade bill.

THE GOSPEL OF LAODICEA

Let us try to get at the root error of these false domestic doctrines. Why was it that the late Samuel Butler, with a conviction that increased with his experience of life, preached the gospel of Laodicea, urging people to be temperate in what they called goodness as in everything else? Why is it that I, when I hear some well-meaning person exhort young people to make it a rule to do at least one kind action every day, feel very much as I should if I heard them persuade children to get drunk at least once every day? Apart from the initial absurdity of accepting as permanent a state of things in which there would be in this country misery enough to supply occasion for several thousand million kind actions per annum, the effect on the character of the doers of the actions would be so appalling, that one month of any serious attempt to carry out such counsels would probably bring about more stringent legislation against actions going beyond the strict letter of the law in the way of kindness than we have now against excess in the opposite direction.

There is no more dangerous mistake than the mistake of supposing that we cannot have too much of a good thing. The truth is, an immoderately good man is very much more dangerous than an immoderately bad man: that is why Savonarola was burnt and John of Leyden[7] torn to pieces with red-hot pincers whilst multitudes of unredeemed rascals were being let off with clipped ears, burnt palms, a flogging, or a few years in the galleys. That is why Christianity never got any grip of the world until it virtually reduced its claims on the ordinary citizen's attention to a couple of hours every seventh day, and let him alone on week-days. If the fanatics who are preoccupied day in and day out with their salvation were healthy, virtuous, and wise, the Laodiceanism of the ordinary man might be regarded as a deplorable shortcoming; but, as a matter of fact, no more frightful misfortune could threaten us than a general spread of fanaticism. What people call goodness has to be kept in check just as carefully as what they call badness; for the human constitution will not stand very much of either without serious psychological mischief, ending in insanity or crime. The fact that the insanity may be privileged, as Savonarola's was up to the point of wrecking the social life of Florence, does not alter the case. We always hesitate to treat a dangerously good man as a lunatic because he may turn

7. Dutch Anabaptist fanatic, executed after leading a rebellion in Münster and proclaiming himself king.

out to be a prophet in the true sense: that is, a man of exceptional sanity who is in the right when we are in the wrong. However necessary it may have been to get rid of Savonarola, it was foolish to poison Socrates and burn St Joan of Arc. But it is none the less necessary to take a firm stand against the monstrous proposition that because certain attitudes and sentiments may be heroic and admirable at some momentous crisis, they should or can be maintained at the same pitch continuously through life. A life spent in prayer and almsgiving is really as insane as a life spent in cursing and picking pockets: the effect of everybody doing it would be equally disastrous. The superstitious tolerance so long accorded to monks and nuns is inevitably giving way to a very general and very natural practice of confiscating their retreats and expelling them from their country, with the result that they come to England and Ireland, where they are partly unnoticed and partly encouraged because they conduct technical schools and teach our girls softer speech and gentler manners than our comparatively ruffianly elementary teachers. But they are still full of the notion that because it is possible for men to attain the summit of Mont Blanc and stay there for an hour, it is possible for them to live there. Children are punished and scolded for not living there; and adults take serious offence if it is not assumed that they live there.

As a matter of fact, ethical strain is just as bad for us as physical strain. It is desirable that the normal pitch of conduct at which men are not conscious of being particularly virtuous, although they feel mean when they fall below it, should be raised as high as possible; but it is not desirable that they should attempt to live above this pitch any more than that they should habitually walk at the rate of five miles an hour or carry a hundredweight continually on their backs. Their normal condition should be in nowise difficult or remarkable; and it is a perfectly sound instinct that leads us to mistrust the good man as much as the bad man, and to object to the clergyman who is pious extra-professionally as much as to the professional pugilist who is quarrelsome and violent in private life. We do not want good men and bad men any more than we want giants and dwarfs. What we do want is a high quality for our normal: that is, people who can be much better than what we now call respectable without self-sacrifice. Conscious goodness, like conscious muscular effort, may be of use in emergencies; but for everyday national use it is negligible; and its effect on the character of the individual may easily be disastrous.

For Better for Worse

It would be hard to find any document in practical daily use in which these obvious truths seem so stupidly overlooked as they are in the marriage service. As we have seen, the stupidity is only apparent: the service was really only an honest attempt to make the best of a commercial contract of property and slavery by subjecting it to some religious restraint and elevating it by some touch of poetry. But the actual result is that when two people are under the influence of the most violent, most insane, most delusive, and most transient of passions, they are required to swear that they will remain in that excited, abnormal, and exhausting condition continuously until death do them part. And though of course nobody expects them to do anything so impossible and so unwholesome, yet the law that regulates their relations, and the public opinion that regulates that law, is actually founded on the assumption that the marriage vow is not only feasible but beautiful and holy, and that if they are false to it, they deserve no sympathy and no relief. If all married people really lived together, no doubt the mere force of facts would make an end to this inhuman nonsense in a month, if not sooner; but it is very seldom brought to that test. The typical British husband sees much less of his wife than he does of his business partner, his fellow clerk, or whoever works beside him day by day. Man and wife do not, as a rule, live together: they only breakfast together, dine together, and sleep in the same room. In most cases the woman knows nothing of the man's working life and he knows nothing of her working life (he calls it her home life). It is remarkable that the very people who romance most absurdly about the closeness and sacredness of the marriage tie are also those who are most convinced that the man's sphere and the woman's sphere are so entirely separate that only in their leisure moments can they ever be together. A man as intimate with his own wife as a magistrate is with his clerk, or a Prime Minister with the leader of the Opposition, is a man in ten thousand. The majority of married couples never get to know one another at all: they only get accustomed to having the same house, the same children, and the same income, which is quite a different matter. The comparatively few men who work at home—writers, artists, and to some extent clergymen—have to effect some sort of segregation within the house or else run a heavy risk of overstraining their domestic relations. When the pair is so poor that it can afford only a single room, the strain is intolerable: violent quarrelling is the result. Very few couples can live in a single-roomed tenement without exchanging blows quite frequently. In the leisured classes there is often no real family life at all. The boys are at a public school; the girls are in the schoolroom in charge of a governess; the husband is at his club or in a set which is not his wife's; and the institution of marriage enjoys the credit of a domestic peace which is hardly more intimate than the relations of prisoners in the same gaol or guests at the same garden party. Taking these two cases of the single room and the unearned income as the extremes, we might perhaps locate at a guess whereabout on the scale between them any particular family stands. But it is clear enough that the one-roomed end, though its conditions enable the marriage vow to be carried out with the utmost attainable exactitude, is far less endurable in practice, and far more mischievous in its effect on the parties concerned, and through them on the community, than the other end. Thus we see that the revolt against marriage is by no means only a revolt against its sordidness as a survival of sex slavery. It may even plausibly be maintained that this is precisely the part of it that works most smoothly in practice. The revolt is also against its sentimentality, its romance, its Amorism, even against its enervating happiness.

Wanted: an Immoral Statesman

We now see that the statesman who undertakes to deal with marriage will have to face an amazingly complicated public opinion. In fact, he will have to leave opinion as far as possible out of the question, and deal with human nature instead. For even if there could be any real public opinion in a society like ours, which is a mere mob of classes, each with its own habits and prejudices, it would be at best a jumble of superstitions and interests, taboos and hypocrisies, which could not be reconciled in any coherent enactment. It would probably proclaim passionately that it does not matter in the least what sort of children we have, or how few or how many, provided the children are legitimate. Also that it does not matter in the least what sort of adults we have, provided they are married. No statesman worth the name can possibly act on these views. He is bound to prefer one healthy illegitimate child to ten rickety legitimate ones, and one energetic and capable unmarried couple to a dozen inferior apathetic husbands and wives. If it could be proved that illicit unions produce three children each and marriages only one and a half, he would be bound to encourage illicit unions and discourage and even penalize marriage. The common notion that the existing forms of marriage are not political contrivances, but sacred ethical obligations to which everything, even the very existence of the human race, must be sacrificed if necessary (and this is what the vulgar morality we mostly profess on the subject comes to) is one on which no sane Government could act for a moment; and yet it influences, or is believed to influence, so many votes, that no Government will touch the marriage question if it can possibly help it, even when there is a demand for the extension of marriage, as in the case of the recent long-delayed Act legalizing marriage with a deceased wife's sister. When a reform in the other direction is needed (for example, an extension of divorce), not even the existence of the most unbearable hardships will induce our statesmen to move so long as the victims submit sheepishly, though when they take the remedy into their own hands an inquiry is soon begun. But what is now making some action in the matter imperative is neither the sufferings of those who are tied for life to criminals, drunkards, physically unsound and dangerous mates, and worthless and unamiable people generally, nor the immorality of the couples condemned to celibacy by separation orders which do not annul their marriages, but the fall in the birth-rate. Public opinion will not help us out of this difficulty: on the contrary, it will, if it be allowed, punish anybody who mentions it. When Zola tried to repopulate France by writing a novel in praise of parentage [*Fécondité*, 1899], the only comment made here was that the book could not possibly be translated into English, as its subject was too improper.

THE LIMITS OF DEMOCRACY

Now if England had been governed in the past by statesmen willing to be ruled by such public opinion as that, she would have been wiped off the political map long ago. The modern notion that democracy means governing a country according to the ignorance of its majorities is never more disastrous than when there is some question of sexual morals to be dealt with. The business of a democratic statesman is not, as some of us seem to think, to convince the voters that he knows no better than they as to the methods of attaining their common ends, but on the contrary to convince them that he knows much better than they do, and therefore differs from them on every possible question of method. The voter's duty is to take care that the Government consists of men whom he can trust to devize or support institutions making for the common welfare. This is highly skilled work; and to be governed by people who set about it as the man in the street would set about it is to make straight for "red ruin and the breaking up of laws" [Tennyson, 'Guinevere', *Idylls of the King*, 1859–85]. Voltaire said that Mr Everybody is wiser than anybody; and whether he is or not, it is his will that must prevail; but the will and the way are two very different things. For example, it is the will of the people on a hot day that the means of relief from the effects of the heat should be within the reach of everybody. Nothing could be more innocent, more hygienic, more important to the social welfare. But the way of the people on such occasions is mostly to drink large quantities of beer, or, among the more luxurious classes, iced claret cup, lemon squashes, and the like. To take a moral illustration, the will to suppress misconduct and secure efficiency in work is general and salutary; but the notion that the best and only effective way is by complaining, scolding, punishing, and revenging is equally general. When Mrs Squeers [in Dickens's *Nicholas Nickleby*] opened an abscess on her pupil's head with an inky penknife, her object was entirely laudable: her heart was in the right place: a statesman interfering with her on the ground that he did not want the boy cured would have deserved impeachment for gross tyranny. But a statesman tolerating amateur surgical practice with inky penknives in school would be a very bad Minister of Education. It is on the question of method that your expert comes in; and though I am democrat enough to insist that he must first convince a representative body of amateurs that his way is the right way and Mrs Squeers's way the wrong way, yet I would not have them assume that Mrs Squeers's amateur way is likely to be the right way because she belongs to the democracy and the Minister to the bureaucracy, or that any other test is to be applied to it except the test of its effect on human welfare.

THE SCIENCE AND ART OF POLITICS

Political Science means nothing else than the devizing of the best ways of fulfilling the will of the world; and, I repeat, it is skilled work. Once the way is discovered, the methods laid down, and the machinery provided, the work of the statesman is done, and that of the official begins. To illustrate, there is no need for the police officer who governs the street traffic to be or to know any better than the people who obey the wave of his hand. All concerted action involves subordination and the appointment of directors at whose signal the others will act. There is no more need for them to be superior to the rest than for the keystone of an arch to be of harder stone than the coping. But when it comes to devizing the directions which are to be obeyed: that is, to making new institutions and scrapping old ones, then you need aristocracy in the sense of government by the best. A military state organized so as to carry out exactly the impulses of the average soldier would not last a year. The result of trying to make the Church of England reflect the notions of the average churchgoer has reduced it to a cipher except for the purposes of a petulantly irreligious social and political club. Democracy as to the thing to be done may be inevitable (hence the vital need for a democracy of supermen); but democracy as to the way to do it is like letting the passengers drive the train: it can only end in collision and wreck. As a matter of fact, we obtain reforms (such as they are), not by allowing the electorate to draft statutes, but by persuading it that a certain minister and his cabinet are gifted with sufficient political sagacity to find out how to produce the desired result. And the usual penalty of taking advantage of this power to reform our institutions is defeat by a vehement "swing of the pendulum" at the next election. Therein lies the peril and the glory of democratic statesmanship. A statesman who confines himself to popular legislation—or, for the matter of that, a playwright who confines himself to popular plays—is like a blind man's dog who goes wherever the blind man pulls him, on the ground that both of them want to go to the same place.

WHY STATESMEN SHIRK THE MARRIAGE QUESTION

The reform of marriage, then, will be a very splendid and very hazardous adventure for the Prime Minister who takes it in hand. He will be posted on every hoarding and denounced in every Opposition paper, especially in the sporting papers, as the destroyer of the home, the family, of decency, of morality, of chastity and what not. All the commonplaces of the modern anti-Socialist Noodle's Oration will be hurled at him. And he will have to proceed without the slightest concession to it, giving the noodles nothing but their due in the assurance "I know how to attain our ends better than you," and staking his political life on the conviction carried by that assurance, which conviction will depend a good deal on the certainty with which it is made, which again can be attained only by studying the facts of marriage and understanding the needs of the nation. And, after all, he will find that the pious commonplaces on which he and the electorate are agreed conceal an utter difference in the real ends in view: his being public, far-sighted, and impersonal, and those of multitudes of the electorate narrow, personal, jealous, and corrupt. Under such circumstances, it is not to be wondered at that the mere mention of the marriage question makes a

British Cabinet shiver with apprehension and hastily pass on to safer business. Nevertheless the reform of marriage cannot be put off for ever. When its hour comes, what are the points the Cabinet will have to take up?

THE QUESTION OF POPULATION

First, it will have to make up its mind as to how many people we want in the country. If we want less than at present, we must ascertain how many less; and if we allow the reduction to be made by the continued operation of the present sterilization of marriage, we must settle how the process is to be stopped when it has gone far enough. But if we desire to maintain the population at its present figure, or to increase it, we must take immediate steps to induce people of moderate means to marry earlier and to have more children. There is less urgency in the case of the very poor and the very rich. They breed recklessly: the rich because they can afford it, and the poor because they cannot afford the precautions by which the artisans and the middle classes avoid big families. Nevertheless the population declines, because the high birth-rate of the very poor is counterbalanced by a huge infantile-mortality in the slums, whilst the very rich are also the very few, and are becoming sterilized by the spreading revolt of their women against excessive childbearing—sometimes against any childbearing.

This last cause is important. It cannot be removed by any economic readjustment. If every family were provided with £10,000 a year tomorrow, women would still refuse more and more to continue bearing children until they are exhausted whilst numbers of others are bearing no children at all. Even if every woman bearing and rearing a valuable child received a handsome series of payments, thereby making motherhood a real profession as it ought to be, the number of women able or willing to give more of their lives to gestation and nursing than three or four children would cost them might not be very large if the advance in social organization and conscience indicated by such payments involved also the opening up of other means of livelihood to women. And it must be remembered that urban civilization itself, insofar as it is a method of evolution (and when it is not this, it is simply a nuisance), is a sterilizing process as far as numbers go. It is harder to keep up the supply of elephants than of sparrows and rabbits; and for the same reason it will be harder to keep up the supply of highly cultivated men and women than it now is of agricultural laborers. Bees get out of this difficulty by a special system of feeding which enables a queen bee to produce 4000 eggs a day whilst the other females lose their sex altogether and become workers supporting the males in luxury and idleness until the queen has found her mate, when the queen kills him and the quondam females kill all the rest (such at least are the accounts given by romantic naturalists of the matter).

The Right to Motherhood

This system certainly shews a much higher development of social intelligence than our marriage system; but if it were physically possible to introduce it into human society it would be wrecked by an opposite and not less important revolt of women: that is, the revolt against compulsory barrenness. In this two classes of women are concerned: those who, though they have no desire for the presence or care of children, nevertheless feel that motherhood is an experience necessary to their complete psychical development and understanding of themselves and others, and those who, though unable to find or unwilling to entertain a husband, would like to occupy themselves with the rearing of children. My own experience of discussing this question leads me to believe that the one point on which all women are in furious secret rebellion against the existing law is the saddling of the right to a child with the obligation to become the servant of a man. Adoption, or the begging or buying or stealing of another woman's child, is no remedy: it does not provide the supreme experience of bearing the child. No political constitution will ever succeed or deserve to succeed unless it includes the recognition of an absolute right to sexual experience, and is untainted by the Pauline or romantic view of such experience as sinful in itself. And since this experience in its fullest sense must be carried in the case of women to the point of childbearing, it can only be reconciled with the acceptance of marriage with the child's father by legalizing polygyny, because there are more adult women in the country than men. Now though polygyny prevails throughout the greater part of the British Empire, and is as practicable here as in India, there is a good deal to be said against it, and still more to be felt. However, let us put our feelings aside for a moment, and consider the question politically.

Monogamy, Polygyny, and Polyandry

The number of wives permitted to a single husband or of husbands to a single wife under a marriage system, is not an ethical problem: it depends solely on the proportion of the sexes in the population. If in consequence of a great war three-quarters of the men in this country were killed, it would be absolutely necessary to adopt the Mohammedan allowance of four wives to each man in order to recruit the population. The fundamental reason for not allowing women to risk their lives in battle and for giving them the first chance of escape in all dangerous emergencies: in short, for treating their lives as more valuable than male lives, is not in the least a chivalrous reason, though men may consent to it under the illusion of chivalry. It is a simple matter of necessity; for if a large proportion of women were killed or disabled, no possible readjustment of our marriage law could avert the depopulation and consequent political ruin of the country, because a woman with several husbands bears fewer children than a woman with one, whereas a man can produce as many families as he has wives. The natural foundation of the institution of monogamy is not any inherent viciousness in polygyny or polyandry, but the hard fact that men and women are born in about equal numbers. Unfortunately, we kill so many of our male children in infancy that we are left with a surplus of adult women which is sufficiently large to claim attention, and yet not large enough to enable every man to have two wives. Even if it were, we should be met by an economic difficulty. A Kaffir [a member of any of the Bantu-speaking tribes of SE Africa] is rich in proportion to the number of his wives, because the women are the breadwinners. But in our civilization women are not paid for their social work in the bearing and rearing of children and the ordering of households: they are quartered on the wages of their husbands. At least four out of five of our men could not afford two wives unless their wages were nearly doubled. Would it not then be well to try unlimited polygyny; so that the remaining fifth could have as many wives apiece as they could afford? Let us see how this would work.

THE MALE REVOLT AGAINST POLYGYNY

Experience shews that women do not object to polygyny when it is customary: on the contrary, they are its most ardent supporters. The reason is obvious. The question, as it presents itself in practice to a woman, is whether it is better to have, say, a whole share in a tenth-rate man or a tenth share in a first-rate man. Substitute the word Income for the word Man, and you will have the question as it presents itself economically to the dependent woman. The woman whose instincts are maternal, who desires superior children more than anything else, never hesitates. She would take a thousandth share, if necessary, in a husband who was a man in a thousand, rather than have some comparatively weedy weakling all to herself. It is the comparatively weedy weakling, left mateless by polygyny, who objects. Thus, it was not the women of Salt Lake City nor even of America who attacked Mormon polygyny. It was the men. And very naturally. On the other hand, women object to polyandry, because polyandry enables the best women to monopolize all the men, just as polygyny enables the best men to monopolize all the women. That is why all our ordinary men and women are unanimous in defence of monogamy, the men because it excludes polygyny, and the women because it excludes polyandry. The women, left to themselves, would tolerate polygyny. The men, left to themselves, would tolerate polyandry. But polygyny would condemn a great many men, and polyandry a great many women, to the celibacy of neglect. Hence the resistance any attempt to establish unlimited polygyny always provokes, not from the best people, but from the mediocrities and the inferiors. If we could get rid of our inferiors and screw up our average quality until mediocrity ceased to be a reproach, thus making every man reasonably eligible as a father and every woman reasonably desirable as a mother, polygyny and polyandry would immediately fall into sincere disrepute, because monogamy is so much more convenient and economical that nobody would want to share a husband or wife if he (or she) could have a sufficiently good one all to himself (or herself). Thus it appears that it is the scarcity of husbands or wives of high quality that leads women to polygyny and men to polyandry, and that if this scarcity were cured, monogamy, in the sense of having only one husband or wife at a time (facilities for changing are another matter), would be found satisfactory.

DIFFERENCE BETWEEN ORIENTAL AND OCCIDENTAL POLYGYNY

It may now be asked why the polygynist nations have not gravitated to monogamy, like the latter-day saints of Salt Lake City. The answer is not far to seek: their polygyny is limited. By the Mohammedan law a man cannot marry more than four wives; and by the unwritten law of necessity no man can keep more wives than he can afford; so that a man with four wives must be quite as exceptional in Asia as a man with a carriage-and-pair or a motor car is in Europe, where, nevertheless, we may all have as many carriages and motors as we can afford to pay for. Kulin polygyny, though unlimited, is not really a popular institution: if you are a person of high caste you pay another person of very august caste indeed to make your daughter momentarily one of his sixty or seventy momentary wives for the sake of ennobling your grandchildren; but this fashion of a small and intensely snobbish class is negligible as a general precedent. In any case, men and women in the East do not marry anyone they fancy, as in England and America. Women are secluded and marriages are arranged. In Salt Lake City the free unsecluded woman could see and meet the ablest man of the community, and tempt him to make her his tenth wife by all the arts peculiar to women in English-speaking countries. No Eastern woman can do anything of the sort. The man alone has any initiative; but he has no access to the woman; besides, as we have seen, the difficulty created by male licence is not polygyny but polyandry, which is not allowed.

Consequently, if we are to make polygyny a success, we must limit it. If we have two women to every one man, we must allow each man only two wives. That is simple; but unfortunately our own actual proportion is, roughly, something like $1\frac{1}{11}$ women to 1 man. Now you cannot enact that each man shall be allowed $1\frac{1}{11}$ wives, or that each woman who cannot get a husband all to herself shall divide herself between eleven already married husbands. Thus there is no way out for us through polygyny. There is no way at all out of the present system of condemning the superfluous women to barrenness, except by legitimizing the children of women who are not married to the fathers.

THE OLD MAID'S RIGHT TO MOTHERHOOD

Now the right to bear children without taking a husband could not be confined to women who are superfluous in the monogamic reckoning. There is the practical difficulty that although in our population there are about a million monogamically superfluous women, yet it is quite impossible to say of any given unmarried woman that she is one of the superfluous. And there is the difficulty of principle. The right to bear a child, perhaps the most sacred of all women's rights, is not one that should have any conditions attached to it except in the interests of race welfare. There are many women of admirable character, strong, capable, independent, who dislike the domestic habits of men; have no natural turn for mothering and coddling them; and find the concession of conjugal rights to any person under any conditions intolerable by their self-respect. Yet the general sense of the community recognizes in these very women the fittest people to have charge of children, and trusts them, as schoolmistresses and matrons of institutions, more than women of any other type when it is possible to procure them for such work. Why should the taking of a husband be imposed on these women as the price of their right to maternity? I am quite unable to answer that question. I see a good deal of first-rate maternal ability and sagacity spending itself on bees and poultry and village schools and cottage hospitals; and I find myself repeatedly asking myself why this valuable strain in the national breed should be sterilized. Unfortunately, the very women whom we should tempt to become mothers for the good of the race are the very last people to press their services on their country in that way. Plato long ago pointed out the importance of being governed by men with sufficient sense of responsibility and comprehension of public duties to be very reluctant to undertake the work of governing; and yet we have taken his instruction so little to heart that we are at present suffering acutely from government by gentlemen who will stoop to all the mean shifts of electioneering and incur all its heavy expenses for the sake of a seat in Parliament. But what our sentimentalists have not yet been told is that exactly the same thing applies to maternity as to government. The best mothers are not those who are so enslaved by their primitive instincts that they will bear children no matter how hard the conditions are, but precisely those who place a very high price on their services, and are quite prepared to become old maids if the price is refused, and even to feel relieved at their escape. Our democratic and matrimonial institutions may have their merits: at all events they are mostly reforms of something worse; but they put a premium on want of self-respect in certain very important matters; and the consequence is that we are very badly governed and are, on the whole, an ugly, mean, ill-bred race.

IBSEN'S CHAIN STITCH

Let us not forget, however, in our sympathy for the superfluous women, that their children must have fathers as well as mothers. Who are the fathers to be? All monogamists and married women will reply hastily: either bachelors or widowers; and this solution will serve as well as another; for it would be hypocritical to pretend that the difficulty is a practical one. None the less, the monogamists, after due reflection, will point out that if there are widowers enough the superfluous women are not really superfluous, and therefore there is no reason why the parties should not marry respectably like other people. And they might in that case be right if the reasons were purely numerical: that is, if every woman were willing to take a husband if one could be found for her, and every man willing to take a wife on the same terms; also, please remember, if widows would remain celibate to give the unmarried woman a chance. These ifs will not work. We must recognize two classes of old maids: one, the really superfluous women, and the other, the women who refuse to accept maternity on the (to them) unbearable condition of taking a husband. From both classes may, perhaps, be subtracted for the present the large proportion of women who could not afford the extra expense of one or more children. I say "perhaps," because it is by no means sure that within reasonable limits mothers do not make a better fight for subsistence, and have not, on the whole, a better time than single women. In any case, we have two distinct cases to deal with: the superfluous and the voluntary; and it is the voluntary whose grit we are most concerned to fertilize. But here, again, we cannot put our finger on any particular case and pick out Miss Robinson's as superfluous, and Miss Wilkinson's as voluntary. Whether we legitimize the child of the unmarried woman as a duty to the superfluous or as a bribe to the voluntary, the practical result must be the same: to wit, that the condition of marriage now attached to legitimate parentage will be withdrawn from all women, and fertile unions outside marriage recognized by society. Now clearly the consequences would not stop there. The strong-minded ladies who are resolved to be mistresses in their own houses would not be the only ones to take advantage of the new law. Even women to whom a home without a man in it would be no home at all, and who fully intended, if the man turned out to be the right one, to live with him exactly as married couples live, would, if they were possessed of independent means, have every inducement to adopt the new conditions instead of the old ones. Only the women whose sole means of livelihood was wifehood would insist on marriage: hence a tendency would set in to make marriage more and more one of the customs imposed by necessity on the poor, whilst the freer form of union, regulated, no doubt, by settlements and private contracts of various kinds, would become the practice of the rich: that is, would become the fashion. At which point nothing but the achievement of economic independence by women, which is already seen clearly ahead of us, would be needed to make marriage disappear altogether, not by formal abolition, but by simple disuse. The private contract stage of this process was reached in ancient Rome. The only practicable alternative to it seems to be such an extension of divorce as will reduce the risks and obligations of marriage to a degree at which they will be no worse than those of the alternatives to marriage. As we shall see, this is the solution to which all the arguments tend. Meanwhile, note how much reason a statesman has to pause before meddling with an institution which, unendurable as its drawbacks are, threatens to come to pieces in all directions if a single thread of it be cut. Ibsen's similitude [in *Ghosts*] of the machine-made chain stitch, which unravels the whole seam at the first pull when a single stitch is ripped, is very applicable to the knot of marriage.

REMOTENESS OF THE FACTS FROM THE IDEAL

But before we allow this to deter us from touching the sacred fabric, we must find out whether it is not already coming to pieces in all directions by the continuous strain of circumstances. No doubt, if it were all that it pretends to be, and human nature were working smoothly within its limits, there would be nothing more to be said: it would be let alone as it always is let alone during the cruder stages of civilization. But the moment we refer to the facts, we discover that the ideal matrimony and domesticity which our bigots implore us to preserve as the corner-stone of our society is a figment: what we have really got is something very different, questionable at its best, and abominable at its worst. The word pure, so commonly applied to it by thoughtless people, is absurd; because if they do not mean celibate by it, they mean nothing; and if they do mean celibate, then marriage is legalized impurity, a conclusion which is offensive and inhuman. Marriage as a fact is not in the least like marriage as an ideal. If it were, the sudden changes which have been made on the Continent from indissoluble Roman Catholic marriage to marriage that can be dissolved by a box on the ear as in France, by an epithet as in Germany, or simply at the wish of both parties as in Sweden, not to mention the experiments made by some of the American States, would have shaken society to its foundations. Yet they have produced so little effect that Englishmen open their eyes in surprise when told of their existence.

DIFFICULTY OF OBTAINING EVIDENCE

As to what actual marriage is, one would like evidence instead of guesses; but as all departures from the ideal are regarded as disgraceful, evidence cannot be obtained; for when the whole community is indicted, nobody will go into the witness-box for the prosecution. Some guesses we can make with some confidence. For example, if it be objected to any change that our bachelors and widowers would no longer be Galahads, we may without extravagance or cynicism reply that many of them are not Galahads now, and that the only change would be that hypocrisy would no longer be compulsory. Indeed, this can hardly be called guessing: the evidence is in the streets. But when we attempt to find out the truth about our marriages, we cannot even guess with any confidence. Speaking for myself, I can say that I know the inside history of perhaps half a dozen marriages. Any family solicitor knows more than this; but even a family solicitor, however large his practice, knows nothing of the million households which have no solicitors, and which nevertheless make marriage what it really is. And all he can say comes to no more than I can say: to wit, that no marriage of which I have any knowledge is in the least like the ideal marriage. I do not mean that it is worse: I mean simply that it is different. Also, far from society being organized in a defence of its ideal so jealous and implacable that the least step from the straight path means exposure and ruin, it is almost impossible by any extravagance of misconduct to provoke society to relax its steady pretence of blindness, unless you do one or both of two fatal things. One is to get into the newspapers; and the other is to confess. If you confess misconduct to respectable men or women, they must either disown you or become virtually your accomplices: that is why they are so angry with you for confessing. If you get into the papers, the pretence of not knowing becomes impossible. But it is hardly too much to say that if you avoid these two perils, you can do anything you like, as far as your neighbors are concerned. And since we can hardly flatter ourselves that this is the effect of charity, it is difficult not to suspect that our extraordinary forbearance in the matter of stone throwing is that suggested in the well-known parable of the woman taken in adultery which some early freethinker slipped into the Gospel of St John: namely, that we all live in glass houses [John 8: 3]. We may take it, then, that the ideal husband and the ideal wife are no more real human beings than the cherubim. Possibly the great majority keeps its marriage vows in the technical divorce court sense. No husband or wife yet born keeps them or ever can keep them in the ideal sense.

MARRIAGE AS A MAGIC SPELL

The truth which people seem to overlook in this matter is that the marriage ceremony is quite useless as a magic spell for changing in an instant the nature of the relations of two human beings to one another. If a man marries a woman after three weeks acquaintance, and the day after meets a woman he has known for twenty years, he finds, sometimes to his own irrational surprise and his wife's equally irrational indignation, that his wife is a stranger to him, and the other woman an old friend. Also, there is no hocus pocus that can possibly be devized with rings and veils and vows and benedictions that can fix either a man's or woman's affection for twenty minutes, much less twenty years. Even the most affectionate couples must have moments during which they are far more conscious of one another's faults than of one another's attractions. There are couples who dislike one another furiously for several hours at a time; there are couples who dislike one another permanently; and there are couples who never dislike one another; but these last are people who are incapable of disliking anybody. If they do not quarrel, it is not because they are married, but because they are not quarrelsome. The people who are quarrelsome quarrel with their husbands and wives just as easily as with their servants and relatives and acquaintances: marriage makes no difference. Those who talk and write and legislate as if all this could be prevented by making solemn vows that it shall not happen, are either insincere, insane, or hopelessly stupid. There is some sense in a contract to perform or abstain from actions that are reasonably within voluntary control; but such contracts are only needed to provide against the possibility of either party being no longer desirous of the specified performance or abstention. A person proposing or accepting a contract not only to do something but to like doing it would be certified as mad. Yet popular superstition credits the wedding rite with the power of fixing our fancies or affections for life even under the most unnatural conditions.

THE IMPERSONALITY OF SEX

It is necessary to lay some stress on these points, because few realize the extent to which we proceed on the assumption that marriage is a short cut to perfect and permanent intimacy and affection. But there is a still more unworkable assumption which must be discarded before discussions of marriage can get into any sort of touch with the facts of life. That assumption is that the specific relation which marriage authorizes between the parties is the most intimate and personal of human relations, and embraces all the other high human relations. Now this is violently untrue. Every adult knows that the relation in question can and does exist between entire strangers, different in language, color, tastes, class, civilization, morals, religion, character: in everything, in short, except their bodily homology and the reproductive appetite common to all living organisms. Even hatred, cruelty, and contempt are not incompatible with it; and jealousy and murder are as near to it as affectionate friendship. It is true that it is a relation beset with wildly extravagant illusions for inexperienced people, and that even the most experienced people have not always sufficient analytic faculty to disentangle it from the sentiments, sympathetic or abhorrent, which may spring up through the other relations which are compulsorily attached to it by our laws, or sentimentally associated with it in romance. But the fact remains that the most disastrous marriages are those founded exclusively on it, and the most successful those in which it has been least considered, and in which the decisive considerations have had nothing to do with sex, such as liking, money, congeniality of tastes, similarity of habits, suitability of class, &c., &c.

It is no doubt necessary under existing circumstances for a woman without property to be sexually attractive, because she must get married to secure a livelihood; and the illusions of sexual attraction will cause the imagination of young men to endow her with every accomplishment and virtue that can make a wife a treasure. The attraction being thus constantly and ruthlessly used as a bait, both by individuals and by society, any discussion tending to strip it of its illusions and get at its real natural history is nervously discouraged. But nothing can well be more unwholesome for everybody than the exaggeration and glorification of an instinctive function which clouds the reason and upsets the judgment more than all the other instincts put together. The process may be pleasant and romantic; but the consequences are not. It would be far better for everyone, as well as far honester, if young people were taught that what they call love is an appetite which, like all other appetites, is destroyed for the moment by its gratification; that no profession, promise, or proposal made under its influence should bind anybody; and that its great natural purpose so completely transcends the personal interests of any individual or even of any ten generations of individuals that it should be held to be an act of prostitution and even a sort of blasphemy to attempt to turn it to account by exacting a personal return for its gratification, whether by process of law or not. By all means let it be the subject of contracts with society as to its consequences; but to make marriage an open trade in it as at present, with money, board and lodging, personal slavery, vows of eternal exclusive personal sentimentalities and the rest of it as the price, is neither virtuous, dignified, nor decent. No husband ever secured his domestic happiness and honor, nor has any wife ever secured hers, by relying on it. No private claims of any sort should be founded on it: the real point of honor is to take no corrupt advantage of it. When we hear of young women being led astray and the like, we find that what has led them astray is a sedulously inculcated false notion that the relation they are tempted to contract is so intensely personal, and the vows made under the influence of its transient infatuation so sacred and enduring, that only an atrociously wicked man could make light of or forget them. What is more, as the same fantastic errors are inculcated in men, and the conscientious ones therefore feel bound in honor to stand by what they have promised, one of the surest methods to obtain a husband is to practise on his susceptibilities until he is either carried away into a promise of marriage to which he can be legally held, or else into an indiscretion which he must repair by marriage on pain of having to regard himself as a scoundrel and a seducer, besides facing the utmost damage the lady's relatives can do him.

Such a transaction is not an entrance into a "holy state of matrimony": it is as often as not the inauguration of a lifelong squabble, a corroding grudge, that causes more misery and degradation of character than a dozen entirely natural "desertions" and "betrayals." Yet the number of marriages effected more or less in this way must be enormous. When people say that love should be free, their words, taken literally, may be foolish; but they are only expressing inaccurately a very real need for the disentanglement of sexual relations from a mass of exorbitant and irrelevant conditions imposed on them on false pretences to enable needy parents to get their daughters "off their hands" and to keep those who are already married effectually enslaved by one another.

THE ECONOMIC SLAVERY OF WOMEN

One of the consequences of basing marriage on the considerations stated with cold abhorrence by Saint Paul in the seventh chapter of his epistle to the Corinthians, as being made necessary by the unlikeness of most men to himself, is that the sex slavery involved has become complicated by economic slavery; so that whilst the man defends marriage because he is really defending his pleasures, the woman is even more vehement on the same side because she is defending her only means of livelihood. To a woman without property or marketable talent a husband is more necessary than a master to a dog. There is nothing more wounding to our sense of human dignity than the husband hunting that begins in every family when the daughters become marriageable; but it is inevitable under existing circumstances; and the parents who refuse to engage in it are bad parents, though they may be superior individuals. The cubs of a humane tigress would starve; and the daughters of women who cannot bring themselves to devote several years of their lives to the pursuit of sons-in-law often have to expiate their mother's squeamishness by lifelong celibacy and indigence. To ask a young man his intentions when you know he has no intentions, but is unable to deny that he has paid attentions; to threaten an action for breach of promise of marriage; to pretend that your daughter is a musician when she has with the greatest difficulty been coached into playing three pianoforte pieces which she loathes; to use your own mature charms to attract men to the house when your daughters have no aptitude for that department of sport; to coach them, when they have, in the arts by which men can be led to compromise themselves; and to keep all the skeletons carefully locked up in the family cupboard until the prey is duly hunted down and bagged; all this is a mother's duty today; and a very revolting duty it is: one that disposes of the conventional assumption that it is in the faithful discharge of her home duties that a woman finds her self-respect. The truth is that family life will never be decent, much less ennobling, until this central horror of the dependence of women on men is done away with. At present it reduces the difference between marriage and prostitution to the difference between Trade Unionism and unorganized casual labor: a huge difference, no doubt, as to order and comfort, but not a difference in kind.

However, it is not by any reform of the marriage laws that this can be dealt with. It is in the general movement for the prevention of destitution that the means for making women independent of the compulsory sale of their persons, in marriage or otherwise, will be found; but meanwhile those who deal specifically with the marriage laws should never allow themselves for a moment to forget this abomination that "plucks the rose from the fair forehead of an innocent love, and sets a blister there" [*Hamlet*, III: iv], and then calmly calls itself purity, home, motherhood, respectability, honor, decency, and any other fine name that happens to be convenient, not to mention the foul epithets it hurls freely at those who are ashamed of it.

UNPOPULARITY OF IMPERSONAL VIEWS

Unfortunately it is very hard to make an average citizen take impersonal views of any sort in matters affecting personal comfort or conduct. We may be enthusiastic Liberals or Conservatives without any hope of seats in

Parliament, knighthoods, or posts in the Government, because party politics do not make the slightest difference in our daily lives and therefore cost us nothing. But to take a vital process in which we are keenly interested personal instruments and ask us to regard it, and feel about it, and legislate on it, wholly as if it were an impersonal one, is to make a higher demand than most people seem capable of responding to. We all have personal interests in marriage which we are not prepared to sink. It is not only the women who want to get married: the men do too, sometimes on sentimental grounds, sometimes on the more sordid calculation that bachelor life is less comfortable and more expensive, since a wife pays for her status with domestic service as well as with the other services expected of her. Now that children are avoidable, this calculation is becoming more common and conscious than it was: a result which is regarded as "a steady improvement in general morality."

IMPERSONALITY IS NOT PROMISCUITY

There is, too, a really appalling prevalence of the superstition that the sexual instinct in men is utterly promiscuous and that the least relaxation of law and custom must produce a wild outbreak of licentiousness. As far as our moralists can grasp the proposition that we should deal with the sexual relation as impersonal, it seems to them to mean that we should encourage it to be promiscuous: hence their recoil from it. But promiscuity and impersonality are not the same thing. No man ever yet fell in love with the entire female sex, nor any woman with the entire male sex. We often do not fall in love at all; and when we do we fall in love with one person, and remain indifferent to thousands of others who pass before our eyes every day. Selection, carried even to such fastidiousness as to induce people to say quite commonly that there is only one man or woman in the world for them, is the rule in nature. If anyone doubts this, let him open a shop for the sale of picture post-cards, and, when an enamoured lady customer demands a portrait of her favorite actor or a gentleman of his favorite actress, try to substitute some other portrait on the ground that since the sexual instinct is promiscuous, one portrait is as pleasing as another. I suppose no shopkeeper has ever been foolish enough to do such a thing; and yet all our shopkeepers, the moment a discussion arises on marriage, will passionately argue against all reform on the ground that nothing but the most severe coercion can save their wives and daughters from quite indiscriminate rapine.

DOMESTIC CHANGE OF AIR

Our relief at the morality of the reassurance that man is not promiscuous in his fancies must not blind us to the fact that he is (to use the word coined by certain American writers to describe themselves) something of a Varietist. Even those who say there is only one man or woman in the world for them, find that it is not always the same man or woman. It happens that our law permits us to study this phenomenon among entirely law-abiding people. I know one lady who has been married five times. She is, as might be expected, a wise, attractive, and interesting woman. The question is, Is she wise, attractive, and interesting because she has been married five times, or has she been married five times because she is wise, attractive, and interesting? Probably some of the truth lies both ways. I also know of a household consisting of three families, A having married first B, and then C, who afterwards married D. All three unions were fruitful; so that the children had a change both of fathers and mothers. Now I cannot honestly say that these and similar cases have convinced me that people are the worse for a change. The lady who has married and managed five husbands must be much more expert at it than most monogamic ladies; and as a companion and counsellor she probably leaves them nowhere. Mr Kipling's question

> What can they know of England that only England know? [Kipling, 'The English Flag', *Barrack Room Ballads*, 1892; slightly misquoted]

disposes not only of the patriots who are so patriotic that they never leave their own country to look at another, but of the citizens who are so domestic that they have never married again and never loved anyone except their own husbands and wives. The domestic doctrinaires are also the dull people. The impersonal relation of sex may be judicially reserved for one person; but any such reservation of friendship, affection, admiration, sympathy and so forth is only possible to a wretchedly narrow and jealous nature; and neither history nor contemporary society shews us a single amiable and respectable character capable of it. This has always been recognized in cultivated society: that is why poor people accuse cultivated society of profligacy, poor people being often so ignorant and uncultivated that they have nothing to offer each other but the sex relationship, and cannot conceive why men and women should associate for any other purpose.

As to the children of the triple household, they were not only on excellent terms with one another, and never thought of any distinction between their full and their half brothers and sisters; but they had the superior sociability which distinguishes people who live in communities from those who live in small families.

The inference is that changes of partners are not in themselves injurious or undesirable. People are not demoralized by them when they are effected according to law. Therefore we need not hesitate to alter the law merely because the alteration would make such changes easier.

HOME MANNERS ARE BAD MANNERS

On the other hand, we have all seen the bonds of marriage vilely abused by people who are never classed with shrews and wife-beaters: they are indeed sometimes held up as models of domesticity because they do not drink nor gamble nor neglect their children nor tolerate dirt and untidiness, and because they are not amiable enough to have what are called amiable weaknesses. These terrors conceive marriage as a dispensation from all the common civilities and delicacies which they have to observe among strangers, or, as they put it, "before company." And here the effects of indissoluble marriage-for-better-for-worse are very plainly and disagreeably seen. If such people took their domestic manners into general society, they would very soon find themselves without a friend or even an acquaintance in the world. There are women who, through total disuse, have lost the power of kindly human speech and can only scold and complain: there are men who grumble and nag from inveterate habit even when they are comfortable. But their unfortunate spouses and children cannot escape from them.

SPURIOUS "NATURAL" AFFECTION

What is more, they are protected from even such discomfort as the dislike of his prisoners may cause to a gaoler by the hypnotism of the convention that the natural relation between husband and wife and parent and child is one of intense affection, and that to feel any other sentiment towards a member of one's family is to be a monster. Under the influence of the emotion thus manufactured the most detestable people are spoilt with entirely undeserved deference, obedience, and even affection whilst they live, and mourned when they die by those whose lives they wantonly or maliciously made miserable. And this is what we call natural conduct. Nothing could well be less natural. That such a convention should have been established shews that the indissolubility of marriage creates such intolerable situations that only by beglamoring the human imagination with a hypnotic suggestion of wholly unnatural feelings can it be made to keep up appearances.

If the sentimental theory of family relationship encourages bad manners and personal slovenliness and uncleanness in the home, it also, in the case of sentimental people, encourages the practice of rousing and playing on the affections of children prematurely and far too frequently. The lady who says that as her religion is love, her children shall be brought up in an atmosphere of love, and institutes a system of sedulous endearments and exchanges of presents and conscious and studied acts of artificial kindness, may be defeated in a large family by the healthy derision and rebellion of children who have acquired hardihood and common sense in their conflicts with one another. But the small families, which are the rule just now, succumb more easily; and in the case of a single sensitive child the effect of being forced in a hothouse atmosphere of unnatural affection may be disastrous.

In short, whichever way you take it, the convention that marriage and family relationship produce special feelings which alter the nature of human intercourse is a mischievous one. The whole difficulty of bringing up a family well is the difficulty of making its members behave as considerately at home as on a visit in a strange house, and as frankly, kindly, and easily in a strange house as at home. In the middle classes, where the segregation of the artificially limited family in its little brick box is horribly complete, bad manners, ugly dresses, awkwardness, cowardice, peevishness, and all the petty vices of unsociability flourish like mushrooms in a cellar. In the upper class, where families are not limited for money reasons; where at least two houses and sometimes three or four are the rule (not to mention the clubs); where there is travelling and hotel life; and where the men are brought up, not in the family, but in public schools, universities, and the naval and military services, besides being constantly in social training in other people's houses, the result is to produce a set that, in comparison with the middle class, counts as a different and much more sociable species. And in the very poorest class, where people have no homes, only sleeping places crowded with lodgers, and consequently live practically in the streets, sociability again appears, leaving the middle class despised and disliked for its helpless and offensive unsociability as much by those below it as those above it, and yet ignorant enough to be proud of it, and to hold itself up as a model for the reform of the (as it considers) elegantly vicious rich and profligate poor alike.

CARRYING THE WAR INTO THE ENEMY'S COUNTRY

Without pretending to exhaust the subject, I have said enough to make it clear that the moment we lose the desire to defend our present matrimonial and family arrangements, there will be no difficulty in making out an overwhelming case against them. No doubt until then we shall continue to hold up the British home as the Holy of Holies in the temple of honorable motherhood, innocent childhood, manly virtue, and sweet and wholesome national life. But with a clever turn of the hand this holy of holies can be exposed as an Augean stable, so filthy that it would seem more hopeful to burn it down than to attempt to sweep it out. And this latter view will perhaps prevail if the idolaters of marriage persist in refusing all proposals for reform and treating those who advocate it as infamous delinquents. Neither view is of any use except as a poisoned arrow in a fierce fight between two parties determined to discredit each other with a view to obtaining powers of legal coercion over one another.

SHELLEY AND QUEEN VICTORIA

The best way to avert such a struggle is to open the eyes of the thoughtlessly conventional people to the weakness of their position in a mere contest of recrimination. Hitherto they have assumed that they have the advantage of coming into the field without a stain on their characters to combat libertines who have no character at all. They conceive it to be their duty to throw mud; and they feel that even if the enemy can find any mud to throw, none of it will stick. They are mistaken. There will be plenty of that sort of ammunition in the other camp; and most of it will stick very hard indeed. The moral is, do not throw any. If we can imagine Shelley and Queen Victoria arguing out their differences in another world, we may be sure that the Queen has long ago found out that she cannot settle the question by classing Shelley with George IV as a bad man; and Shelley is not likely to have called her vile names on the general ground that as the economic dependence of women makes marriage a money bargain in which the man is the purchaser and the woman the purchased, there is no essential difference between a married woman and the woman of the streets. Unfortunately, all the people whose methods of controversy are represented by our popular newspapers are not Queen Victorias and Shelleys. A great mass of them, when their prejudices are challenged, have no other impulse than to call the challenger names, and, when the crowd seems to be on their side, to maltreat him personally or hand him over to the law, if he is vulnerable to it. Therefore I cannot say that I have any certainty that the marriage question will be dealt with decently and tolerantly. But dealt with it will be, decently or indecently; for the present state of things in England is too strained and mischievous to last. Europe and America have left us a century behind in this matter.

A PROBABLE EFFECT OF GIVING WOMEN THE VOTE

The political emancipation of women is likely to lead to a comparatively stringent enforcement by law of sexual morality (that is why so many of us dread it); and this will soon compel us to consider what our sexual morality shall be. At present a ridiculous distinction is made between vice and crime, in order that men may be vicious with impunity. Adultery, for instance, though it is sometimes fiercely punished by giving an injured husband crushing damages in a divorce suit (injured wives are not considered in this way), is not now directly prosecuted; and this impunity extends to illicit relations between unmarried persons who have reached what is called the age of consent. There are other matters, such as notification of contagious disease and solicitation, in which the hand of the law has been brought down on one sex only. Outrages which were capital offences within the memory of persons still living when committed on women outside marriage, can still be inflicted by men on their wives without legal remedy. At all such points the code will be screwed up by the operation of Votes for Women, if there be any virtue in the franchise at all. The result will be that men will find the more ascetic side of our sexual morality taken seriously by the law. It is easy to foresee the consequences. No man will take much trouble to alter laws which he can evade, or which are either not enforced or enforced on women only. But when these laws take him by the collar and thrust him into prison, he suddenly becomes keenly critical of them, and of the arguments by which they are supported. Now we have seen that our marriage laws will not stand criticism, and that they have held out so far only because they are so worked as to fit roughly our state of society, in which women are neither politically nor personally free, in which indeed women are called womanly only when they regard themselves as existing solely for the use of men. When Liberalism enfranchises them politically, and Socialism emancipates them economically, they will no longer allow the law to take immorality so easily. Both men and women will be forced to behave morally in sex matters; and when they find that this is inevitable they will raise the question of what behavior really should be established as moral. If they decide in favor of our present professed morality, they will have to make a revolutionary change in their habits by becoming in fact what they only pretend to be at present. If, on the other hand, they find that this would be an unbearable tyranny, without even the excuse of justice or sound eugenics, they will reconsider their morality and remodel the law.

THE PERSONAL SENTIMENTAL BASIS OF MONOGAMY

Monogamy has a sentimental basis which is quite distinct from the political one of equal numbers of the sexes. Equal numbers in the sexes are quite compatible with a change of partners every day or every hour. Physically there is nothing to distinguish human society from the farm-yard except that children are more troublesome and costly than chickens and calves, and that men and women are not so completely enslaved as farm stock. Accordingly, the people whose conception of marriage is a farm-yard or slave-quarter conception are always more or less in a panic lest the slightest relaxation of the marriage laws should utterly demoralize society; whilst those to whom marriage is a matter of more highly evolved sentiments and needs (sometimes said to be distinctively human, though birds and animals in a state of freedom evince them quite as touchingly as we) are much more liberal, knowing as they do that monogamy will take care of itself provided the parties are free enough, and that promiscuity is a product of slavery and not of liberty.

The solid foundation of their confidence is the fact that the relationship set up by a comfortable marriage is so intimate and so pervasive of the whole life of the parties to it, that nobody has room in his or her life for more than one such relationship at a time. What is called a household of three is never really of three except in the sense that every household becomes a household of three when a child is born, and may in the same way become a household of four or fourteen if the union be fertile enough. Now no doubt the marriage tie means so little to some people that the addition to the household of half a dozen more wives or husbands would be as possible as the addition of half a dozen governesses or tutors or visitors or servants. A Sultan may have fifty wives as easily as he may have fifty dishes on his table, because in the English sense he has no wives at all; nor have his wives any husband: in short, he is not what we call a married man. And there are sultans and sultanas and seraglios existing in England under English forms. But when you come to the real modern marriage of sentiment, a relation is created which has never to my knowledge been shared by three persons except when all three have been extraordinarily fond of one another. Take for example the famous case of Nelson and Sir William and Lady Hamilton. The secret of this household of three was not only that both the husband and Nelson were devoted to Lady Hamilton, but that they were also apparently devoted to one another. When Hamilton died both Nelson and Emma seem to have been equally heartbroken. When there is a successful household of one man and two women the same unusual condition is fulfilled: the two women not only cannot live happily without the man but cannot live happily without each other. In every other case known to me, either from observation or record, the experiment is a hopeless failure: one of the two rivals for the really intimate affection of the third inevitably drives out the other. The driven-out party may accept the situation and remain in the house as a friend to save appearances, or for the sake of the children, or for economic reasons; but such an arrangement can subsist only when the forfeited relation is no longer really valued; and this indifference, like the triple bond of affection which carried Sir William Hamilton through, is so rare as to be practicably negligible in the establishment of a conventional morality of marriage. Therefore sensible and experienced people always assume that when a declaration of love is made to an already married person, the declaration binds the parties in honor never to see one another again unless they contemplate divorce and remarriage. And this is a sound convention, even for unconventional people. Let me illustrate by reference to a fictitious case: the one imagined in my own play Candida will do as well as another. Here a young man who had been received as a friend into the house of a clergyman falls in love with the clergyman's wife, and, being young and inexperienced, declares his feelings, and claims that he, and not the clergyman, is the more suitable mate for the lady. The clergyman, who has a temper, is first tempted to hurl the youth into the street by bodily violence: an impulse natural, perhaps, but vulgar and improper, and not open, on consideration, to decent men. Even coarse and inconsiderate men are restrained from it by the fact that the sympathy of the woman turns naturally to the victim of physical brutality and against the bully, the Thackerayan notion to the contrary being one of the illusions of literary masculinity. Besides, the husband is not necessarily the stronger man: and appeal to force has resulted in the ignominious defeat of the husband quite as often as in poetic justice as conceived in the conventional novelet. What an honorable and sensible man does when his household is invaded is what the Reverend James Mavor Morell does in my play. He recognizes that just as there is not room for two women in that sacredly intimate relation of sentimental domesticity which is what marriage means to him, so there is no room for two men in that relation with his wife; and he accordingly tells her firmly that she must choose which man will occupy the place that is large enough for one only. He is so far shrewdly unconventional as to recognize that if she chooses the other man, he must give way, legal tie or no legal tie; but he knows that either one or the other must go. And a sensible wife would act in the same way. If a romantic young lady came into her house and proposed to adore her husband on a tolerated footing, she would say "My husband has not room in his life for two wives: either you go out of the house or I go out of it." The situation is not at all unlikely: I had almost said not at all unusual. Young ladies and gentlemen in the greensickly condition which is called calf-love, associating with married couples at dangerous periods of mature life, quite often find themselves in it; and the extreme reluctance of proud and sensitive people to make any assertion of matrimonial rights, or to condescend to jealousy, sometimes make[s] the threatened husband or wife hesitate to take prompt steps and do the apparently conventional thing. But whether they hesitate or act the result is always the same. In a real marriage of sentiment the wife or husband cannot be supplanted by halves; and such a marriage will break very soon under the strain of polygyny or polyandry. What we want at present is a sufficiently clear teaching of this fact to ensure that prompt and decisive action shall always be taken in such cases without any false shame of seeming conventional (a shame to which people capable of such real marriage are specially susceptible), and a rational divorce law to enable the marriage to be dissolved and the parties honorably resorted and recoupled without disgrace and scandal if that should prove the proper solution.

It must be repeated here that no law, however stringent, can prevent polygamy among groups of people who choose to live loosely and be monogamous only in appearance. But such cases are not now under consideration. Also, affectionate husbands like Samuel Pepys, and affectionate wives of the corresponding temperament, may, it appears, engage in transient casual adventures out of doors without breaking up their home life. But within doors that home life may be regarded as naturally monogamous. It does not need to be protected against polygamy; it protects itself.

DIVORCE

All this has an important bearing on the question of divorce. Divorce reformers are so much preoccupied with the injustice of forbidding a woman to divorce her husband for unfaithfulness to his marriage vow, whilst allowing him that power over her, that they are apt to overlook the pressing need for admitting other and far more important grounds for divorce. If we take a document like Pepys' Diary, we learn that a woman may have an incorrigibly unfaithful husband, and yet be much better off than if she had an ill-tempered, peevish, maliciously sarcastic one, or was chained for life to a criminal, a drunkard, a lunatic, an idle vagrant, or a person whose religious faith was contrary to her own. Imagine being married to a liar, a borrower, a mischief maker, a teaser or tormentor of children and animals, or even simply to a bore! Conceive yourself tied for life to one of the perfectly "faithful" husbands who are sentenced to a month's imprisonment occasionally for idly leaving their wives in childbirth without food, fire, or attendance? What woman would not rather marry ten Pepyses? what man a dozen Nell Gwynnes? Adultery, far from being the first and only ground for divorce, might more reasonably be made the last, or wholly excluded. The present law is perfectly logical only if you once admit (as no decent person ever does) its fundamental assumption that there can be no companionship between men and women because the woman has a "sphere" of her own, that of housekeeping, in which the man must not meddle, whilst he has all the rest of human activity for his sphere: the only point at which the two spheres touch being that of replenishing the population. On this assumption the man naturally asks for a guarantee that the children shall be his because he has to find the money to support them. The power of divorcing a woman for adultery is this guarantee, a guarantee that she does not need to protect her[self] against a similar imposture on his part, because he cannot bear children. No doubt he can spend the money that ought to be spent on her children on another woman and her children; but this is desertion, which is a separate matter. The fact for us to seize is that in the eye of the law, adultery without consequences is merely a sentimental grievance, whereas the planting on one man of another man's offspring is a substantial one. And so, no doubt, it is; but the day has gone by for basing laws on the assumption that a woman is less to a man than his dog, and thereby encouraging and accepting the standards of the husbands who buy meat for their bull-pups and leave their wives and children hungry. That basis is the penalty we pay for having borrowed our religion from the East, instead of building up a religion of our own out of our western inspiration and western sentiment. The result is that we all believe that our religion is on its last legs, whereas the truth is that it is not yet born, though the age walks visibly pregnant with it. Meanwhile, as women are dragged down by their oriental servitude to our men, and as, further, women drag down those who degrade them quite as effectually as men do, there are moments when it is difficult to see anything in our sex institutions except a *police des mœurs* [vice squad] keeping the field for a competition as to which sex shall corrupt the other most.

IMPORTANCE OF SENTIMENTAL GRIEVANCES

Any tolerable western divorce law must put the sentimental grievances first, and should carefully avoid singling out any ground of divorce in such a way as to create a convention that persons having that ground are bound in honor to avail themselves of it. It is generally admitted that people should not be encouraged to petition for a divorce in a fit of petulance. What is not so clearly seen is that neither should they be encouraged to petition in a fit of jealousy, which is certainly the most detestable and mischievous of all the passions that enjoy public credit. Still less should people who are not jealous be urged to behave as if they were jealous, and to enter upon duels and divorce suits in which they have no desire to be successful. There should be no publication of the grounds on which a divorce is sought or granted; and as this would abolish the only means the public now has of ascertaining that every possible effort has been made to keep the couple united against their wills, such privacy will only be tolerated when we at last admit that the sole and sufficient reason why people should be granted a divorce is that they want one. Then there will be no more reports of divorce cases, no more letters read in court with an indelicacy that makes every sensitive person shudder and recoil as from a profanation, no more washing of household linen, dirty or clean, in public. We must learn in these matters to mind our own business and not impose our individual notions of propriety on one another, even if it carries us to the length of openly admitting what we are now compelled to assume silently, that every human being has a right to sexual experience, and that the law is concerned only with parentage, which is now a separate matter.

DIVORCE WITHOUT ASKING WHY

The one question that should never be put to a petitioner for divorce is "Why?" When a man appeals to a magistrate for protection from someone who threatens to kill him, on the simple ground that he desires to live, the magistrate might quite reasonably ask him why he desires to live, and why the person who wishes to kill him should not be gratified. Also whether he can prove that his life is a pleasure to himself or a benefit to anyone else, and whether it is good for him to be encouraged to exaggerate the importance of his short span in this vale of tears rather than to keep himself constantly ready to meet his God.

The only reason for not raising these very weighty points is that we find society unworkable except on the assumption that every man has a natural right to live. Nothing short of his own refusal to respect that right in others can reconcile the community to killing him. From this fundamental right many others are derived. The American Constitution [1789], one of the few modern political documents drawn up by men who were forced by the sternest circumstances to think out what they really had to face instead of chopping logic in a university class-room, specifies "liberty and the pursuit of happiness" as natural rights. The terms are too vague to be of much practical use; for the supreme right to life, extended as it now must be to the life of the race, and to the quality of life as well as to the mere fact of breathing, is making short work of many ancient liberties, and exposing the pursuit of happiness as perhaps the most miserable of human occupations. Nevertheless, the American Constitution roughly expresses the conditions to which modern democracy commits us. To impose marriage on two unmarried people who do not desire to marry one another would be admittedly an act of enslavement. But it is no worse than to impose a continuation of marriage on people who have ceased to desire to be married. It will be said that the parties may not agree on that; that one may desire to maintain the marriage the other wishes to dissolve. But the same hardship arises whenever a man in love proposes marriage to a woman and is refused. The refusal is so painful to him that he often threatens to kill himself and sometimes even does it. Yet we expect him to face his ill luck, and never dream of forcing the woman to accept him. His case is the same as that of the husband whose wife tells him she no longer cares for him, and desires the marriage to be dissolved. You will say, perhaps, if you are superstitious, that it is not the same—that marriage makes a difference. You are wrong: there is no magic in marriage. If there were, married couples would never desire to separate. But they do. And when they do, it is simple slavery to compel them to remain together.

ECONOMIC SLAVERY AGAIN THE ROOT DIFFICULTY

The husband, then, is to be allowed to discard his wife when he is tired of her, and the wife the husband when another man strikes her fancy? One must reply unhesitatingly in the affirmative; for if we are to deny every proposition that can be stated in offensive terms by its opponents, we shall never be able to affirm anything at all. But the question reminds us that until the economic independence of women is achieved, we shall have to remain impaled on the other horn of the dilemma and maintain marriage as a slavery. And here let me ask the Government of the day (1910) a question with regard to the Labor Exchanges it has very wisely established throughout the country. What do these Exchanges do when a woman enters and states that her occupation is that of a wife and mother; that she is out of a job; and that she wants an employer? If the Exchanges refuse to entertain her application, they are clearly excluding nearly the whole female sex from the benefit of the Act. If not, they must become matrimonial agencies, unless, indeed, they are prepared to become something worse by putting the woman down as a housekeeper and introducing her to an employer without making marriage a condition of the hiring.

LABOR EXCHANGES AND THE WHITE SLAVERY

Suppose, again, a woman presents herself at the Labor Exchange, and states her trade as that of a White Slave, meaning the unmentionable trade pursued by many thousands of women in all civilized cities. Will the Labor Exchange find employers for her? If not, what will it do with her? If it throws her back destitute and unhelped on the streets to starve, it might as well not exist as far as she is concerned; and the problem of unemployment remains unsolved at its most painful point. Yet if it finds honest employment for her and for all the unemployed wives and mothers, it must find new places in the world for women; and in so doing it must achieve for them economic independence of men. And when this is done, can we feel sure that any woman will consent to be a wife and mother (not to mention the less respectable alternative) unless her position is made as eligible as that of the women for whom the Labor Exchanges are finding independent work? Will not many women now engaged in domestic work under circumstances which make it repugnant to them, abandon it and seek employment under other circumstances? As unhappiness in marriage is almost the only discomfort sufficiently irksome to induce a woman to break up her home, and economic dependence the only compulsion sufficiently stringent to force her to endure such unhappiness, the solution of the problem of finding independent employment for women may cause a great number of childless unhappy marriages to break up spontaneously, whether the marriage laws are altered or not. And here we must extend the term childless marriages to cover households in which the children have grown up and gone their own way, leaving the parents alone together: a point at which many worthy couples discover for the first time that they have long since lost interest in one another, and have been united only by a common interest in their children. We may expect, then, that marriages which are maintained by economic pressure alone will dissolve when that pressure is removed; and as all the parties to them will certainly not accept a celibate life, the law must sanction the dissolution in order to prevent a recurrence of the scandal which has moved the Government to appoint the Commission now sitting to investigate the marriage question: the scandal, that is, of a great number of persons, condemned to celibacy by magisterial separation orders, and, of course, refusing to submit to the condemnation, forming illicit connections to an extent which threatens to familiarize the working classes with an open disuse of marriage. In short, once set women free from their economic slavery, and you will find that unless divorce is made as easy as the dissolution of a business partnership, the practice of dispensing with marriage will presently become so common that conventional couples will be ashamed to get married.

DIVORCE FAVORABLE TO MARRIAGE

Divorce, in fact, is not the destruction of marriage, but the first condition of its maintenance. A thousand indissoluble marriages mean a thousand marriages and no more. A thousand divorces may mean two thousand marriages; for the couples may marry again. Divorce only re-assorts the couples: a very desirable thing when they are ill-assorted. Also, it makes people much more willing to marry, especially prudent people and proud people with a high sense of self-respect. Further, the fact that a divorce is possible often prevents its being petitioned for, not only because it puts married couples on their good behavior towards one another, but because, as no room feels like a prison if the door is left open, the removal of the sense of bondage would at once make marriage much happier than it is now. Also, if the door were always open, there would be no need to rush through it as there is now when it opens for one moment in a lifetime, and may never open again.

From this point of view England has the worst civil marriage law in the world, with the exception of silly South Carolina. In every other reasonably civilized country the grounds on which divorce can be granted admit of so wide an interpretation that all unhappy marriages can be dissolved without resorting to the shameful shifts imposed by our law. Yet the figures just given to the Royal Commission shew that in the State of Washington, where there are eleven different grounds of divorce, and where, in fact, divorce can be had for the asking at a negligible cost, the divorce rate is only 184 per 100,000 of the population, which, if we assume that the 100,000 people represent 20,000 families, means less than one per cent of domestic failures. In Japan the rate is 215, which is said to be the highest on record. This is not very alarming: what is quite hideous is that the rate in England is only 2, a figure which, if we assume that human nature is much the same in Walworth as in Washington, must represent a frightful quantity of useless unhappiness and clandestine polygamy. I am not forgetting my own demonstration that the rate is kept down in Washington by the economic slavery of women; but I must point out that this is at its worst in the middle classes only, because a woman of the working class can turn to and support herself, however poorly; and a woman of the upper classes usually has some property. And in all classes we may guess that the object of many divorces is not the resumption of a single life, but a change of partners. As this change can be effected easily under the existing law in the State of Washington it is not certain that the economic emancipation of women would alter the rate there to any startling extent. What is certain is that it could not conceivably raise it to a figure at which even the most panicky alarmist could persuade sensible people that the whole social fabric was tumbling to pieces. When journalists and bishops and American Presidents and other simple people describe this Washington result as alarming, they are speaking as a peasant speaks of a motor car or an aeroplane when he sees one for the first time. All he means is that he is not used to it and therefore fears that it may injure him. Every advance in civilization frightens these honest folk. This is a pity; but if we were to spare their feelings we should never improve the world at all. To let them frighten us, and then pretend that their stupid timidity is virtue and purity and so forth, is simply moral cowardice.

MALE ECONOMIC SLAVERY AND THE RIGHTS OF BACHELORS

It must not be forgotten that the refusal to accept the indignities, risks, hardships, softships, and divided duties of marriage is not confined to our voluntary old maids. There are men of the mould of Beethoven and Samuel Butler, whom one can hardly conceive as married men. There are the great ecclesiastics, who will not own two loyalties: one to the Church and one to the hearth. There are men like Goethe, who marry late and reluctantly solely because they feel that they cannot in honest friendship refuse the status of marriage to any woman of whose attachment to them they have taken any compromising advantage, either in fact or in appearance. No sensible man can, under existing circumstances, advise a woman to keep house with a man without insisting on his marrying her, unless she is independent of conventional society (a state of things which can occur only very exceptionally); and a man of honor cannot advise a woman to do for his sake what he would not advise her to do for anyone else's. The result is that our Beethovens and Butlers—of whom, in their ordinary human aspect, there are a good many—become barren old bachelors, and rather savage ones at that.

Another difficulty which we always think of in connection with women, but which is by no means without its application to men, is the economic one. The number of men who cannot afford to marry is large enough to produce very serious social results; and the higher the work the man is doing, the more likely he is to find himself in this class until he has reached or passed middle age. The higher departments of science, law, philosophy, poetry, and the fine arts are notoriously starved in youth and early manhood: the marriageable age there, economically speaking, is nearer fifty than twenty. Even in business the leading spirits seldom reach a position of security until they are far beyond the age at which celibacy is tolerable. Account must also be taken of the younger sons of the propertied classes, brought up in households in which the rate of expenditure, though ten times that possible on a younger son's portion, yet represents the only habit of life he has learnt.

Taking all these cases as representing a bachelor class, and bearing in mind that though a man who marries at forty is not called a bachelor, yet he has for twenty years of his adult life been one, and therefore produced all the social problems that arise out of the existence of unmarried men, we must not shrink from asking whether all these gentlemen are celibates, even though we know that the question must be answered very emphatically in the negative. Some of them marry women of property, thereby reproducing the economic dependence of women on men with the sexes reversed. But there are so few women of property available for this purpose in comparison with the number of bachelors who cannot afford to marry, that this resource does not solve the problem of the bachelor who cannot afford a wife. If there were no other resources available, bachelors would make love to the wives and daughters of their friends. This being morally inadmissible, a demand arises for a cheap temporary substitute for marriage. A class of women must be found to protect the wives and daughters of the married by keeping company with the bachelors for hire for as long or as short a time as the bachelor can afford, on the understanding that no claim is to be made on him after the hiring is ended. And such an institution, as we know, exists among us. It is commonly spoken of and thought of as an offence against our marriage morality; but all the experts who write scientific treatises on marriage seem to be agreed that it is, on the contrary, a necessary part of that morality, and must stand and fall with it.

I do not myself think that this view will bear examination. In my play, Mrs Warren's Profession, I have shewn that the institution in question is an economic phenomenon, produced by our underpayment and ill-treatment of women who try to earn an honest living. I am aware that for some reason scientific writers are perversely impatient of this view, and, to discredit it, quote police lists of the reasons given by the victims for adopting their trade, and insist on the fact that poverty is not often alleged. But this means only that the actual word is seldom used. If a prisonful of thieves were asked what induced them to take to thieving, and some replied Poverty, and others Hunger, and others Desire for Excitement, no one would deny that the three answers were really one answer—that poverty means hunger, an intolerable lack of variety and pleasure, and, in short, all sorts of privations. When a girl, similarly interrogated, says she wanted fine clothes, or more fun, or the like, she is really saying that she lacked what no woman with plenty of money need lack. The fact that, according to the testimony of men who profess experience in such matters, you may search Europe in vain for a woman in this trade who has the table manners of a lady, shews that prostitution is not a vocation but a slavery to which women are driven by the miseries of honest poverty. When every young woman has an honorable and comfortable livelihood open to her on reasonable terms, the streets will make no more recruits. When every young man can afford to marry, and marriage reform makes it easy to dissolve unions contracted by young and inexperienced people in the event of their turning out badly, or of one of the pair achieving a position neither comfortable nor suitable for the other, both prostitution and bachelordom will die a natural death. Until then, all talk of "purification" is idle. It is for that reason that I lay little stress on prostitution here, and refer readers who are curious about the psychopathy of bachelordom and spinsterhood to the monumental work of my friend Havelock Ellis.

THE PATHOLOGY OF MARRIAGE

I shall also say as little as possible of the pathology of marriage and its kerbstone breakwater. Only, as there seems to be no bottom to the abyss of public ignorance on the subject, I am compelled to warn my readers that marriage has a pathology and even a criminology. But they are both so frightful that they have been dealt with not only in such treatises as those of [Henry] Havelock Ellis [*Studies in the Psychology of Sex*, Vol. 1, 1897], [Alfred] Fournier [*The Treatment of Syphilis*, 1906], [Pierre-Émile] Duclaux [*L'Hygiène sociale*, 1902], and many German writers, but in such comparatively popular works as The Heavenly Twins by Sarah Grand, and several of the plays of Brieux: notably Les Avariés, Les Trois Filles de M. Dupont, and Maternité. I purposely pass them by quickly, not only because attention has already been called to them by these devoted writers, but because my mission is not to deal with obvious horrors, but to open the eyes of normal respectable men to evils which are escaping their consideration.

As to the evils of disease and contagion, our consciences are sound enough: what is wrong with us is ignorance of the facts. No doubt this is a very formidable ignorance in a country where the first cry of the soul is "Dont tell me: I dont want to know," and where frantic denials and furious suppressions indicate everywhere the cowardice and want of faith which conceives life as something too terrible to be faced. In this particular case "I dont want to know" takes a righteous air, and becomes "I dont want to know anything about the diseases which are the just punishment of wretches who should not be mentioned in my presence or in any book that is intended for family reading." Wicked and foolish as the spirit of this attitude is, the practice of it is so easy and lazy and uppish that it is very common. But its cry is drowned by a louder and more sincere one. We who do not want to know also do not want to go blind, to go mad, to be disfigured, to be barren, to become pestiferous, or to see such things happening to our children. We learn, at last, that the majority of the victims are not the people of whom we so glibly say "Serve them right," but quite innocent children and innocent parents, smitten by a contagion which, no matter in what vice it may or may not have originated, contaminates the innocent and the guilty alike once it is launched exactly as any other contagious disease does; that indeed it often hits the innocent and misses the guilty because the guilty know the danger and take elaborate precautions against it, whilst the innocent, who have been either carefully kept from any knowledge of their danger, or erroneously led to believe that contagion is possible through misconduct only, run into danger blindfold. Once knock this fact into people's minds, and their self-righteous indifference and intolerance soon change into lively concern for themselves and their families.

THE CRIMINOLOGY OF MARRIAGE

The pathology of marriage involves the possibility of the most horrible crime imaginable: that of the person who, when suffering from contagious disease, forces the contagion on another person by an act of violence. Such an act occurring between unmarried people would, within the memory of persons now living, have exposed the aggressor to the penalty of death; and it is still punished unmercifully by an extreme term of penal servitude when it occurs, as it sometimes does, through the hideous countryside superstition that it effects a cure when the victim is a virgin. Marriage makes this outrage absolutely legal. You may with impunity do to the person to whom you are married what you may not do to the most despised outcast of the streets. And this is only the extreme instance of the outlawry which our marriage laws effect. In our anxiety to provide for ourselves a little private Alsatia in which we can indulge ourselves as we please without reproach or interference from law, religion, or even conscience (and this is what marriage has come to mean to many of us), we have forgotten that we cannot escape restraints without foregoing rights; that all the laws that are needed to compel strangers to respect us are equally if not more necessary to compel our husbands and wives to respect us; and that society without law, whether between two or two million persons, means tyranny and slavery.

If the incorrigible sentimentalists here raise their little pipe of "Not if they love one another," I tell them, with such patience as is possible, that if they had ever had five minutes experience of love they would know that love is itself a tyranny requiring special safeguards; that people will perpetrate "for the sake of" those they love, exactions and submissions that they would never dream of proposing to or suffering from those they dislike or regard with indifference; that healthy marriages are partnerships of companionable and affectionate friendship; that cases of chronic lifelong love, whether sentimental or sensual, ought to be sent to the doctor if not to the executioner; and that honorable men and women, when their circumstances permit it, are so far from desiring to be placed helplessly at one another's mercy that they employ every device the law now admits of, from the most stringent marriage settlements to the employment of separate legal advisers, to neutralize the Alsatian evils of the marriage law.

DOES IT MATTER?

A less obviously silly evasion, and one which has a greater air of common sense, is "After all, seeing that most couples get on very well together, does it matter so much?" The same reply might be made by a lazy magistrate when asked for a warrant to arrest a burglar, or by a sleepy fireman wakened by a midnight call for his fire-escape. "After all, very few people have their houses broken into; and fewer still have them burnt. Does it matter?" But tell the magistrate or fireman that it is *his* house that has been broken into, or *his* house that has been burnt; and you will be startled by the change in his attitude. Because a mass of people have shaken down into comfort enough to satisfy them, or at least to cause them no more discomfort than they are prepared to put up with for the sake of a quiet life, less lucky and more sensitive and conscientious people should not be condemned to expose themselves to intolerable wrongs. Besides, people ought not to be content with the marriage law as it is merely because it is not often unbearably uncomfortable. Slaves are very often much more comfortable both in body and mind than fully responsible free men. That does not excuse anybody for embracing slavery. It is no doubt a great pity, from many points of view, that we were not conquered by Napoleon, or even by Bismarck and [Helmuth Karl von] Moltke.[8] None the less we should have been rightly despised if we had not been prepared to fight them for the right to misgovern ourselves.

But, as I have said, I am content, in this matter of the evils of our marriage law, to take care of the pence and let the pounds take care of themselves. The crimes and diseases of marriage will force themselves on

8. Chief of the Prussian general staff; reorganized the Prussian army (1858–63) with Bismarck's support.

public attention by their own virulence. I mention them here only because they reveal certain habits of thought and feeling with regard to marriage of which we must rid ourselves if we are to act sensibly when we take the necessary reforms in hand.

CHRISTIAN MARRIAGE

First among these is the habit of allowing ourselves to be bound not only by the truths of the Christian religion but by the excesses and extravagances which the Christian movement acquired in its earlier days as a violent reaction against what it still calls paganism. By far the most dangerous of these, because it is a blasphemy against life, and, to put it in Christian terms, an accusation of indecency against God, is the notion that sex, with all its operations, is in itself absolutely an obscene thing, and that an immaculate conception is a miracle. So unwholesome an absurdity could only have gained ground under two conditions: one, a reaction against a society in which sensual luxury had been carried to revolting extremes, and, two, a belief that the world was coming to an end, and that therefore sex was no longer a necessity. Christianity, because it began under these conditions, made sexlessness and Communism the two main practical articles of its propaganda; and it has never quite lost its original bias in these directions. In spite of the putting off of the Second Coming from the lifetime of the apostles to the millennium, and of the great disappointment of the year 1000 A.D., in which multitudes of Christians seriously prepared for the end of the world, the prophet who announces that the end is at hand is still popular. Many of the people who ridicule his demonstrations that the fantastic monsters of the book of Revelation are among us in the persons of our own political contemporaries, and who proceed sanely in all their affairs on the assumption that the world is going to last, really do believe that there will be a Judgment Day, and that it *might* even be in their own time. A thunderstorm, an eclipse, or any very unusual weather will make them apprehensive and uncomfortable.

This explains why, for a long time, the Christian Church refused to have anything to do with marriage. The result was, not the abolition of sex, but its excommunication. And, of course, the consequences of persuading people that matrimony was an unholy state were so grossly carnal, that the Church had to execute a complete right-about-face, and try to make people understand that it was a holy state: so holy indeed that it could not be validly inaugurated without the blessing of the Church. And by this teaching it did something to atone for its earlier blasphemy. But the mischief of chopping and changing your doctrine to meet this or that practical emergency instead of keeping it adjusted to the whole scheme of life, is that you end by having half-a-dozen contradictory doctrines to suit half-a-dozen different emergencies. The Church solemnized and sanctified marriage without ever giving up its original Pauline doctrine on the subject. And it soon fell into another confusion. At the point at which it took up marriage and endeavored to make it holy, marriage was, as it still is, largely a survival of the custom of selling women to men. Now in all trades a marked difference is made in price between a new article and a second-hand one. The moment we meet with this difference in value between human beings, we may know that we are in the slave-market, where the conception of our relations to the persons sold is neither religious nor natural nor human nor superhuman, but simply commercial. The Church, when it finally gave its blessing to marriage, did not, in its innocence, fathom these commercial traditions. Consequently it tried to sanctify them too, with grotesque results. The slave-dealer having always asked more money for virginity, the Church, instead of detecting the money-changer and driving him out of the temple, took him for a sentimental and chivalrous lover, and, helped by its only half-discarded doctrine of celibacy, gave virginity a heavenly value to ennoble its commercial pretensions. In short, Mammon, always mighty, put the Church in his pocket, where he keeps it to this day, in spite of the occasional saints and martyrs who contrive from time to time to get their heads and souls free to testify against him.

DIVORCE A SACRAMENTAL DUTY

But Mammon overreached himself when he tried to impose his doctrine of inalienable property on the Church under the guise of indissoluble marriage. For the Church tried to shelter this inhuman doctrine and flat contradiction of the gospel by claiming, and rightly claiming, that marriage is a sacrament. So it is; but that is exactly what makes divorce a duty when the marriage has lost the inward and spiritual grace of which the marriage ceremony is the outward and visible sign. In vain do bishops stoop to pick up the discarded arguments of the atheists of fifty years ago by pleading that the words of Jesus were in an obscure Aramaic dialect, and were probably misunderstood, as Jesus, they think, could not have said anything a bishop would disapprove of. Unless they are prepared to add that the

The Complete Prefaces: Volume 1

statement that those who take the sacrament with their lips but not with their hearts eat and drink their own damnation is also a mistranslation from the Aramaic, they are most solemnly bound to shield marriage from profanation, not merely by permitting divorce, but by making it compulsory in certain cases as the Chinese do.

When spiritual revolt broke out in the XVI century, and the Church was reformed in several countries, the Reformation was so largely a rebellion against sacerdotalism that marriage was very nearly excommunicated again: our modern civil marriage, round which so many fierce controversies and political conflicts have raged, would have been thoroughly approved of by Calvin, and hailed with relief by Luther. But the instinctive doctrine that there is something holy and mystic in sex, a doctrine which many of us now easily dissociate from any priestly ceremony, but which in those days seemed to all who felt it to need a ritual affirmation, could not be thrown on the scrap-heap with the sale of Indulgences and the like; and so the Reformation left marriage where it was: a curious mixture of commercial sex slavery, early Christian sex abhorrence, and later Christian sex sanctification.

OTHELLO AND DESDEMONA

How strong was the feeling that a husband or a wife is an article of property, greatly depreciated in value at second-hand, and not to be used or touched by any person but the proprietor, may be learnt from Shakespear. His most infatuated and passionate lovers are Antony and Othello; yet both of them betray the commercial and proprietary instinct the moment they lose their tempers. "I found you," says Antony, reproaching Cleopatra, "as a morsel cold upon dead Cæsar's trencher [III: xiii]." Othello's worst agony is the thought of "keeping a corner in the thing he loves for others' uses [III: iii: 'than keep a corner in the thing I love']." But this is not what a man feels about the thing he loves, but about the thing he owns. I never understood the full significance of Othello's outburst until I one day heard a lady, in the course of a private discussion as to the feasibility of "group marriage," say with cold disgust that she would as soon think of lending her toothbrush to another woman as her husband. The sense of outraged manhood with which I felt myself and all other husbands thus reduced to the rank of a toilet appliance gave me a very unpleasant taste of what Desdemona might have felt had she overheard Othello's outburst. I was so dumbfounded that I had not the presence of mind to ask the lady whether she insisted on having a doctor, a nurse, a dentist, and even a priest and solicitor all to herself as well. But I had too often heard men speak of women as if they were mere personal conveniences to feel surprised that exactly the same view is held, only more fastidiously, by women.

All these views must be got rid of before we can have any healthy public opinion (on which depends our having a healthy population) on the subject of sex, and consequently of marriage. Whilst the subject is considered shameful and sinful we shall have no systematic instruction in sexual hygiene, because such lectures as are given in Germany, France, and even prudish America (where the great Miltonic tradition in this matter still lives) will be considered a corruption of that youthful innocence which now subsists on nasty stories and whispered traditions handed down from generation to generation of school children: stories and traditions which conceal nothing of sex but its dignity, its honor, its sacredness, its rank as the first necessity of society and the deepest concern of the nation. We shall continue to maintain the White Slave Trade and protect its exploiters by, on the one hand, tolerating the white slave as the necessary breakwater of marriage; and, on the other, trampling on her and degrading her until she has nothing to hope from our Courts; and so, with policemen at every corner, and law triumphant all over Europe, she will still be smuggled and cattle-driven from one end of the civilized world to the other, cheated, beaten, bullied, and hunted into the streets to disgusting overwork, without daring to utter the cry for help that brings, not rescue, but exposure and infamy, yet revenging herself terribly in the end by scattering blindness and sterility, pain and disfigurement, insanity and death among us with the certainty that we are much too pious and genteel to allow such things to be mentioned with a view to saving either her or ourselves from them. And all the time we shall keep enthusiastically investing her trade with every allurement that the art of the novelist, the playwright, the dancer, the milliner, the painter, the limelight man, and the sentimental poet can devize, after which we shall continue to be very much shocked and surprised when the cry of the youth, of the young wife, of the mother, of the infected nurse, and of all the other victims, direct and indirect, arises with its invariable refrain: "Why did nobody warn me?"

WHAT IS TO BECOME OF THE CHILDREN?

I must not reply flippantly, Make them all Wards in Chancery [court guardianship]; yet that would be enough to put any sensible person on the track of the reply. One would think, to hear the way in which people sometimes ask the question, that not only does marriage prevent the difficulty from ever arising, but that nothing except divorce can ever raise it. It is true that if you divorce the parents, the children have to be disposed of. But if you hang the parents, or imprison the parents, or take the children out of the custody of the parents because they hold Shelley's opinions, or if the parents die, the same difficulty arises. And as these things have happened again and again, and as we have had plenty of experience of divorce decrees and separation orders, the attempt to use children as an obstacle to divorce is hardly worth arguing with. We shall deal with the children just as we should deal with them if their homes were broken up by any other cause. There is a sense in which children are a real obstacle to divorce: they give parents a common interest which keeps together many a couple who, if childless, would separate. The marriage law is superfluous in such cases. This is shewn by the fact that the proportion of childless divorces is much larger than the proportion of divorces from all causes. But it must not be forgotten that the interest of the children forms one of the most powerful arguments for divorce. An unhappy household is a bad nursery. There is something to be said for the polygynous or polyandrous household as a school for children: children really do suffer from having too few parents: this is why uncles and aunts and tutors and governesses are often so good for children. But it is just the polygamous household which our marriage law allows to be broken up, and which, as we have seen, is not possible as a typical institution in a democratic country where the numbers of the sexes are about equal. Therefore polygyny and polyandry as a means of educating children fall to the ground, and with them, I think, must go the opinion which has been expressed by Gladstone and others, that an extension of divorce, whilst admitting many new grounds for it, might exclude the ground of adultery. There are, however, clearly many things that make some of our domestic interiors little private hells for children (especially when the children are quite content in them) which would justify any intelligent State in breaking up the home and giving the custody of the children either to the parent whose conscience had revolted against the corruption of the children, or to neither.

Which brings me to the point that divorce should no longer be confined to cases in which one of the parties petitions for it. If, for instance, you have a thoroughly rascally couple making a living by infamous means and bringing up their children to their trade, the king's proctor, instead of pursuing his present purely mischievous function of preventing couples from being divorced by proving that they both desire it, might very well intervene and divorce these children from their parents. At present, if the Queen herself were to rescue some unfortunate child from degradation and misery and place her in a respectable home, and some unmentionable pair of blackguards claimed the child and proved that they were its father and mother, the child would be given to them in the name of the sanctity of the home and the holiness of parentage, after perpetrating which crime the law would calmly send an education officer to take the child out of the parents' hands several hours a day in the still more sacred name of compulsory education. (Of course what would really happen would be that the couple would blackmail the Queen for their consent to the salvation of the child, unless, indeed, a hint from a police inspector convinced them that bad characters cannot always rely on pedantically constitutional treatment when they come into conflict with persons in high station.)

The truth is, not only must the bond between man and wife be made subject to a reasonable consideration of the welfare of the parties concerned and of the community, but the whole family bond as well. The theory that the wife is the property of the husband or the husband of the wife is not a whit less abhorrent and mischievous than the theory that the child is the property of the parent. Parental bondage will go the way of conjugal bondage: indeed the order of reform should rather be put the other way about; for the helplessness of children has already compelled the State to intervene between parent and child more than between husband and wife. If you pay less than £40 a year rent, you will sometimes feel tempted to say to the vaccination officer, the school attendance officer, and the sanitary inspector: "Is this child mine or yours?" The answer is that as the child is a vital part of the nation, the nation cannot afford to leave it at the irresponsible disposal of any individual or couple of individuals as a mere small parcel of private property. The only solid ground that the parent can take is that as the State, in spite of its imposing name, can, when all is said, do nothing with the child except place it in the charge of some human being or another, the parent is no worse a custodian than a stranger. And though this proposition may seem highly questionable at first sight to those who imagine that only parents spoil children, yet those who realize that children are as often spoilt by severity and coldness as by indulgence, and that the notion that natural parents are any worse than adopted parents is probably as complete an illusion as the notion that they are any better, see no serious likelihood that State action will detach children from their parents more than it does at present: nay, it is even likely that the present system of taking the children out of the parents' hands and having the parental duty performed by officials, will, as poverty and ignorance become the exception instead of the rule, give way to the system of simply requiring certain results, beginning with the baby's weight and ending perhaps with some sort of practical arts degree, but leaving parents and children to achieve the results as they best may. Such freedom is, of course, impossible in our present poverty-stricken circumstances. As long as the masses of our people are too poor to be good parents or good anything else except beasts of burden, it is no use requiring much more from them but hewing of wood and drawing of water: whatever is to be done must be done *for* them, mostly, alas! by people whose superiority is merely technical. Until we abolish poverty it is impossible to push rational measures of any kind very far: the wolf at the door will compel us to live in a state of siege and to do everything by a bureaucratic martial law that would be quite unnecessary and indeed intolerable in a prosperous community. But, however we settle the question, we must make the parent justify his custody of the child exactly as we should make a stranger justify it. If a family is not achieving the purposes of a family it should be dissolved just as a marriage should when it, too, is not achieving the purposes of marriage. The notion that there is or ever can be anything magical and inviolable in the legal relations of domesticity, and the curious confusion of ideas which makes some of our bishops imagine that in the phrase "Whom God hath joined," the word God means the district registrar or the Reverend John Smith or William Jones, must be got rid of. Means of breaking up undesirable families are as necessary to the preservation of the family as means of dissolving undesirable marriages are to the preservation of marriage. If our domestic laws are kept so inhuman that they at last provoke a furious general insurrection against them as they already provoke many private ones, we shall in a very literal sense empty the baby out with the bath by abolishing an institution which needs nothing more than a little obvious and easy rationalizing to make it not only harmless but comfortable, honorable, and useful.

THE COST OF DIVORCE

But please do not imagine that the evils of indissoluble marriage can be cured by divorce laws administered on our present plan. The very cheapest undefended divorce, even when conducted by a solicitor for its own sake and that of humanity, costs at least £30 out-of-pocket expenses. To a client on business terms it costs about three times as much. Until divorce is as cheap as marriage, marriage will remain indissoluble for all except the handful of people to whom £100 is a procurable sum. For the enormous majority of us there is no difference in this respect between a hundred and a quadrillion. Divorce is the one thing you may not sue for *in forma pauperis* [in the guise of a pauper: one exempted from liability for costs of a legal action].

Let me, then, recommend as follows:

1. Make divorce as easy, as cheap, and as private as marriage.

2. Grant divorce at the request of either party, whether the other consents or not; and admit no other ground than the request, which should be made without stating any reasons.

3. Confine the power of dissolving marriage for misconduct to the State acting on the petition of the king's proctor or other suitable functionary, who may, however, be moved by either party to intervene in ordinary request cases, not to prevent the divorce taking place, but to enforce alimony if it be refused and the case is one which needs it.

4. Make it impossible for marriage to be used as a punishment as it is at present. Send the husband and wife to penal servitude if you disapprove of their conduct and want to punish them; but do not send them back to perpetual wedlock.

5. If, on the other hand, you think a couple perfectly innocent and well conducted, do not condemn them also to perpetual wedlock against their wills, thereby making the treatment of what you consider innocence on both sides the same as the treatment of what you consider guilt on both sides.

6. Place the work of a wife and mother on the same footing as other work: that is, on the footing of labor worthy of its hire; and provide for unemployment in it exactly as for unemployment in shipbuilding or any other recognized bread-winning trade.

7. And take and deal with all the consequences of these acts of justice instead of letting yourself be frightened out of reason and good sense by fear of consequences. We must finally adapt our institutions to human nature. In the long run our present plan of trying to force human nature into a mould of existing abuses, superstitions, and corrupt interests, produces the explosive forces that wreck civilization.

8. Never forget that if you leave your law to judges and your religion to bishops you will presently find yourself without either law or religion. If you doubt this, ask any decent judge or bishop. Do *not* ask somebody who does not know what a judge is, or what a bishop is, or what the law is, or what religion is. In other words, do not ask your newspaper. Journalists are too poorly paid in this country to know anything that is fit for publication.

CONCLUSIONS

To sum up, we have to depend on the solution of the problem of unemployment, probably on the principles laid down in the Minority Report of the Royal Commission on the Poor Law [1909; written by Beatrice and Sidney Webb], to make the sexual relations between men and women decent and honorable by making women economically independent of men, and (in the younger son section of the upper classes) men economically independent of women. We also have to bring ourselves into line with the rest of Protestant civilization by providing means for dissolving all unhappy, improper, and inconvenient marriages. And, as it is our cautious custom to lag behind the rest of the world to see how their experiments in reform turn out before venturing ourselves, and then take advantage of their experience to get ahead of them, we should recognize that the ancient system of specifying grounds for divorce, such as adultery, cruelty, drunkenness, felony, insanity, vagrancy, neglect to provide for wife and children, desertion, public defamation, violent temper, religious heterodoxy, contagious disease, outrages, indignities, personal abuse, "mental anguish," conduct rendering life burdensome and so forth (all these are examples from some code actually in force at present), is a mistake, because the only effect of compelling people to plead and prove misconduct is that cases are manufactured and clean linen purposely smirched and washed in public, to the great distress and disgrace of innocent children and relatives, whilst the grounds have at the same time to be made so general that any sort of human conduct may be brought within them by a little special pleading and a little mental reservation on the part of witnesses examined on oath. When it comes to "conduct rendering life burdensome," it is clear that no marriage is any longer indissoluble; and the sensible thing to do then is to grant divorce whenever it is desired, without asking why.

The Shewing-up of Blanco Posnet

*First published in 1911, incorporating 'Statement of the Evidence in Chief of
George Bernard Shaw before the Joint-Committee on Stage Plays (Censorship
and Theatre Licensing)', 1909*

═══

THE CENSORSHIP

This little play is really a religious tract in dramatic form. If our silly
censorship would permit its performance, it might possibly help to set
right-side-up the perverted conscience and re-invigorate the starved self-
respect of our considerable class of loose-lived playgoers whose point of
honor is to deride all official and conventional sermons. As it is, it only
gives me an opportunity of telling the story of the Select Committee of
both Houses of Parliament which sat last year to inquire into the working
of the censorship, against which it was alleged by myself and others that as
its imbecility and mischievousness could not be fully illustrated within the
limits of decorum imposed on the press, it could only be dealt with by a
parliamentary body subject to no such limits.

A READABLE BLUEBOOK

Few books of the year 1909 can have been cheaper and more entertaining
than the report of this Committee. Its full title is REPORT FROM THE
JOINT SELECT COMMITTEE OF THE HOUSE OF LORDS AND THE
HOUSE OF COMMONS ON THE STAGE PLAYS (CENSORSHIP) TO-
GETHER WITH THE PROCEEDINGS OF THE COMMITTEE, MINUTES OF
EVIDENCE, AND APPENDICES. What the phrase "the Stage Plays" means
in this title I do not know; nor does anyone else. The number of the
Bluebook is 214. How interesting it is may be judged from the fact that it
contains verbatim reports of long and animated interviews between the
Committee and such witnesses as Mr William Archer, Mr Granville Barker,
Mr J. M. Barrie, Mr Forbes Robertson, Mr Cecil Raleigh, Mr John
Galsworthy, Mr Laurence Housman, Sir Herbert Beerbohm Tree, Mr W.
L. Courtney, Sir William Gilbert, Mr A. B. Walkley, Miss Lena Ashwell,

Professor Gilbert Murray, Mr George Alexander, Mr George Edwardes, Mr Comyns Carr, the Speaker of the House of Commons [James Lowther, First Viscount Ullswater], the Bishop of Southwark [Rt. Revd Edward Talbot, later Bishop of Winchester 1911–23], Mr Hall Caine, Mr Israel Zangwill, Sir Squire Bancroft, Sir Arthur Pinero, and Mr Gilbert Chesterton,[1] not to mention myself and a number of gentlemen less well known to the general public, but important in the world of the theatre. The publication of a book by so many famous contributors would be beyond the means of any commercial publishing firm. His Majesty's Stationery Office sells it to all comers by weight at the very reasonable price of three-and-threepence a copy.

How Not To Do It

It was pointed out by Charles Dickens in Little Dorrit, which remains the most accurate and penetrating study of the genteel littleness of our class governments in the English language, that whenever an abuse becomes oppressive enough to persuade our party parliamentarians that something must be done, they immediately set to work to face the situation and discover How Not To Do It. Since Dickens's day the exposures effected by the Socialists have so shattered the self-satisfaction of modern commercial civilization that it is no longer difficult to convince our governments that something must be done, even to the extent of attempts at a reconstruction of civilization on a thoroughly uncommercial basis. Consequently, the first part of the process described by Dickens: that in which the reformers were snubbed by front bench demonstrations that the administrative departments were consuming miles of red tape in the correctest forms of activity, and that everything was for the best in the best of all possible worlds, is out of fashion; and we are in that other phase, familiarized by the history of the French Revolution, in which the primary assumption is that the country is in danger, and that the first duty of all parties, politicians, and governments is to save it. But as the effect of this is to give governments a great many more things to do, it also gives a powerful stimulus to the art of How Not To Do Them: that is to say, the art of contriving methods of reform which will leave matters exactly as they are.

1. Those named who may require identification are: Raleigh, Housman, and Courtney, playwrights; Zangwill, a novelist and playwright; Edwardes, a theatre manager; Alexander, Ashwell and Bancroft, actor-managers.

The report of the Joint Select Committee is a capital illustration of this tendency. The case against the censorship was overwhelming; and the defence was more damaging to it than no defence at all could have been. Even had this not been so, the mere caprice of opinion had turned against the institution; and a reform was expected, evidence or no evidence. Therefore the Committee was unanimous as to the necessity of reforming the censorship; only, unfortunately, the majority attached to this unanimity the usual condition that nothing should be done to disturb the existing state of things. How this was effected may be gathered from the recommendations finally agreed on, which are as follows.

1. The drama is to be set entirely free by the abolition of the existing obligation to procure a licence from the Censor before performing a play; but every theatre lease is in future to be construed as if it contained a clause giving the landlord power to break it and evict the lessee if he produces a play without first obtaining the usual licence from the Lord Chamberlain.

2. Some of the plays licensed by the Lord Chamberlain are so vicious that their present practical immunity from prosecution must be put an end to; but no manager who procures the Lord Chamberlain's licence for a play can be punished in any way for producing it, though a special tribunal may order him to discontinue the performance; and even this order must not be recorded to his disadvantage on the licence of his theatre, nor may it be given as a judicial reason for cancelling that licence.

3. Authors and managers producing plays without first obtaining the usual licence from the Lord Chamberlain shall be perfectly free to do so, and shall be at no disadvantage compared to those who follow the existing practice, except that they may be punished, have the licences of their theatres endorsed and cancelled, and have the performance stopped pending the proceedings without compensation in the event of the proceedings ending in their acquittal.

4. Authors are to be rescued from their present subjection to an irresponsible secret tribunal which can condemn their plays without giving reasons, by the substitution for that tribunal of a Committee of the Privy Council, which is to be the final authority on the fitness of a play for representation; and this Committee is to sit *in camera* if and when it pleases.

5. The power to impose a veto on the production of plays is to be abolished because it may hinder the growth of a great national drama; but the Office of Examiner of Plays shall be continued; and the Lord Chamberlain shall retain his present powers to license plays, but shall be made responsible to Parliament to the extent of making it possible to ask questions there concerning his proceedings, especially now that members have discovered a method of doing this indirectly.

And so on, and so forth. The thing is to be done; and it is not to be done. Everything is to be changed and nothing is to be changed. The problem is to be faced and the solution to be shirked. And the word of Dickens is to be justified.

THE STORY OF THE JOINT SELECT COMMITTEE

Let me now tell the story of the Committee in greater detail, partly as a contribution to history; partly because, like most true stories, it is more amusing than the official story.

All commissions of public enquiry are more or less intimidated both by the interests on which they have to sit in judgment and, when their members are party politicians, by the votes at the back of those interests; but this unfortunate Committee sat under a quite exceptional cross fire. First, there was the king. The Censor is a member of his household retinue; and as a king's retinue has to be jealously guarded to avoid curtailment of the royal state no matter what may be the function of the particular retainer threatened, nothing but an express royal intimation to the contrary, which is a constitutional impossibility, could have relieved the Committee from the fear of displeasing the king by any proposal to abolish the censorship of the Lord Chamberlain. Now all the lords on the Committee and some of the commoners could have been wiped out of society (in their sense of the word) by the slightest intimation that the king would prefer not to meet them; and this was a heavy risk to run on the chance of "a great and serious national drama" ensuing on the removal of the Lord Chamberlain's veto on Mrs Warren's Profession. Second, there was the Nonconformist conscience, holding the Liberal Government responsible for the Committee it had appointed, and holding also, to the extent of votes enough to turn the scale in some constituencies, that the theatre is the gate of hell, to be tolerated, as vice is tolerated, only because the power to suppress it could not be given to any public body without too serious an interference with certain Liberal traditions of liberty which are still useful to Nonconformists in other directions. Third, there was the commercial interest of the theatrical managers and their syndicates of backers in the City [the commercial centre of London], to whom, as I shall shew later on, the censorship affords a cheap insurance of enormous value. Fourth, there was the powerful interest of the trade in intoxicating liquors, fiercely determined to resist any extension of the authority of teetotaller-led local governing bodies over theatres. Fifth, there were the playwrights, without political power, but with a very close natural monopoly of a talent not only for playwriting but for satirical polemics. And since every interest has its opposition, all these influences had created hostile bodies by the operation of the mere impulse to contradict them, always strong in English human nature.

Why the Managers Love the Censorship

The only one of these influences which seems to be generally misunderstood is that of the managers. It has been assumed repeatedly that managers and authors are affected in the same way by the censorship. When a prominent author protests against the censorship, his opinion is supposed to be balanced by that of some prominent manager who declares that the censorship is the mainstay of the theatre, and his relations with the Lord Chamberlain and the Examiner of Plays a cherished privilege and an inexhaustible joy. This error was not removed by the evidence given before the Joint Select Committee. The managers did not make their case clear there, partly because they did not understand it, and partly because their most eminent witnesses were not personally affected by it, and would not condescend to plead it, feeling themselves, on the contrary, compelled by their self-respect to admit and even emphasize the fact that the Lord Chamberlain in the exercise of his duties as licenser had done those things which he ought not to have done, and left undone those things which he ought to have done. Mr Forbes Robertson and Sir Herbert Tree, for instance, had never felt the real disadvantage of which managers have to complain. This disadvantage was not put directly to the Committee; and though the managers are against me on the question of the censorship, I will now put their case for them as they should have put it themselves, and as it can be read between the lines of their evidence when once the reader has the clue.

The manager of a theatre is a man of business. He is not an expert in politics, religion, art, literature, philosophy, or law. He calls in a playwright just as he calls in a doctor, or consults a lawyer, or engages an architect, depending on the playwright's reputation and past achievements for a satisfactory result. A play by an unknown man may attract him sufficiently to induce him to give that unknown man a trial; but this does not occur often enough to be taken into account: his normal course is to resort to a well-known author and take (mostly with misgiving) what he gets from him. Now this does not cause any anxiety to Mr Forbes Robertson and Sir

Herbert Tree, because they are only incidentally managers and men of business: primarily they are highly cultivated artists, quite capable of judging for themselves anything that the most abstruse playwright is likely to put before them. But the plain-sailing tradesman who must be taken as the typical manager (for the west end of London is not the whole theatrical world) is by no means equally qualified to judge whether a play is safe from prosecution or not. He may not understand it, may not like it, may not know what the author is driving at, may have no knowledge of the ethical, political, and sectarian controversies which may form the intellectual fabric of the play, and may honestly see nothing but an ordinary "character part" in a stage figure which may be a libellous and unmistakeable caricature of some eminent living person of whom he has never heard. Yet if he produces the play he is legally responsible just as if he had written it himself. Without protection he may find himself in the dock answering a charge of blasphemous libel, seditious libel, obscene libel, or all three together, not to mention the possibility of a private action for defamatory libel. His sole refuge is the opinion of the Examiner of Plays, his sole protection the licence of the Lord Chamberlain. A refusal to license does not hurt him, because he can produce another play: it is the author who suffers. The granting of the licence practically places him above the law; for though it may be legally possible to prosecute a licensed play, nobody ever dreams of doing it. The really responsible person, the Lord Chamberlain, could not be put into the dock; and the manager could not decently be convicted when he could produce in his defence a certificate from the chief officer of the King's Household that the play was a proper one.

A TWO GUINEA INSURANCE POLICY

The censorship, then, provides the manager, at the negligible premium of two guineas per play, with an effective insurance against the author getting him into trouble, and a complete relief from all conscientious responsibility for the character of the entertainment at his theatre. Under such circumstances, managers would be more than human if they did not regard the censorship as their most valuable privilege. This is the simple explanation of the rally of the managers and their Associations to the defence of the censorship, of their reiterated resolutions of confidence in the Lord Chamberlain, of their presentations of plate, and, generally, of their enthusiastic contentment with the present system, all in such startling contrast to the denunciations of the censorship by the authors. It also explains why the managerial witnesses who had least to fear from the Censor were the most reluctant in his defence, whilst those whose practice it is to strain his indulgence to the utmost were almost rapturous in his praise. There would be absolute unanimity among the managers in favor of the censorship if they were all simply tradesmen. Even those actor-managers who made no secret before the Committee of their contempt for the present operation of the censorship, and their indignation at being handed over to a domestic official as casual servants of a specially disorderly kind, demanded, not the abolition of the institution, but such a reform as might make it consistent with their dignity and unobstructive to their higher artistic aims. Feeling no personal need for protection against the author, they perhaps forgot the plight of many a manager to whom the modern advanced drama is so much Greek; but they did feel very strongly the need of being protected against Vigilance Societies and Municipalities and common informers in a country where a large section of the community still believes that art of all kinds is inherently sinful.

WHY THE GOVERNMENT INTERFERED

It may now be asked how a Liberal government had been persuaded to meddle at all with a question in which so many conflicting interests were involved, and which had probably no electoral value whatever. Many simple souls believed that it was because certain severely virtuous plays by Ibsen, by M. Brieux, by Mr Granville Barker, and by me, were suppressed by the censorship, whilst plays of a scandalous character were licensed without demur. No doubt this influenced public opinion; but those who imagine that it could influence British governments little know how remote from public opinion and how full of their own little family and party affairs British governments, both Liberal and Unionist, still are. The censorship scandal had existed for years without any parliamentary action being taken in the matter, and might have existed for as many more had it not happened in 1906 that Mr Robert Vernon Harcourt[2] entered parliament as a member of the Liberal Party, of which his father had been one of the leaders during the Gladstone era. Mr Harcourt was thus a young man

2. Playwright and Liberal MP. His comedy *A Question of Age* was presented by Vedrenne and Barker at the Royal Court on 6 February 1906 for six scheduled matinées, but was withdrawn after the second performance.

marked out for office both by his parentage and his unquestionable social position as one of the governing class. Also, and this was much less usual, he was brilliantly clever, and was the author of a couple of plays of remarkable promise. Mr Harcourt informed his leaders that he was going to take up the subject of the censorship. The leaders, recognizing his hereditary right to a parliamentary canter of some sort as a prelude to his public career, and finding that all the clever people seemed to be agreed that the censorship was an anti-Liberal institution and an abominable nuisance to boot, indulged him by appointing a Select Committee of both Houses to investigate the subject. The then Chancellor of the Duchy of Lancaster, Mr Herbert Samuel[3] (now Postmaster-General), who had made his way into the Cabinet twenty years ahead of the usual age, was made Chairman. Mr Robert Harcourt himself was of course a member. With him, representing the Commons, were Mr Alfred Mason,[4] a man of letters who had won a seat in parliament as offhandedly as he has since discarded it, or as he once appeared on the stage [as the Russian officer in Act I] to help me out of a difficulty in casting Arms and the Man when that piece was the newest thing in the advanced drama. There was Mr Hugh Law, an Irish member, son of an Irish Chancellor, presenting a keen and joyous front to English intellectual sloth. Above all, there was Colonel [A.M.R.] Lockwood[5] to represent at one stroke the Opposition and the average popular man. This he did by standing up gallantly for the Censor, to whose support the Opposition was in no way committed, and by visibly defying the most cherished conventions of the average man with a bunch of carnations in his buttonhole as large as a dinnerplate, which would have made a Bunthorne [an aesthete in Gilbert and Sullivan's *Patience*] blench, and which very nearly did make Mr Granville Barker (who has an antipathy to the scent of carnations) faint.

THE PEERS ON THE JOINT SELECT COMMITTEE

The House of Lords then proceeded to its selection. As fashionable drama in Paris and London concerns itself almost exclusively with adultery,

3. A Liberal MP, who later was leader of the Liberal Party, Home Secretary, and first High Commissioner for Palestine; created a Viscount in 1937.
4. Novelist (notably of *The Four Feathers*, 1902) and occasional dramatist.
5. Conservative MP and country squire, who took very little part in politics and never held office.

the first choice fell on Lord Gorell [Sir John Gorell Barnes], who had for many years presided over the Divorce Court. Lord Plymouth [Robert Windsor-Clive], who had been Chairman to the Shakespear Memorial project (now merged in the Shakespear Memorial National Theatre), was obviously marked out for selection; and it was generally expected that the Lords [Victor, Second Earl of] Lytton and [Reginald Brett, Second Viscount] Esher, who had taken a prominent part in the same movement, would have been added. This expectation was not fulfilled. Instead, Lord Willoughby de Broke [Nineteenth Baron], who had distinguished himself as an amateur actor, was selected along with [Thomas W. Legh] Lord Newton [Second Baron], whose special qualifications for the Committee, if he had any, were unknown to the public. Finally [Thomas Lister] Lord Ribblesdale [Fourth Baron], the argute [shrewd in small matters] son of a Scotch mother, was thrown in to make up for any shortcoming in intellectual subtlety that might arise in the case of his younger colleagues; and this completed the two teams.

THE COMMITTEE'S ATTITUDE TOWARDS THE THEATRE

In England, thanks chiefly to the censorship, the theatre is not respected. It is indulged and despised as a department of what is politely called gaiety. It is therefore not surprising that the majority of the Committee began by taking its work uppishly and carelessly. When it discovered that the contemporary drama, licensed by the Lord Chamberlain, included plays which could be described only behind closed doors, and in the discomfort which attends discussions of very nasty subjects between men of widely different ages, it calmly put its own convenience before its public duty by ruling that there should be no discussion of particular plays, much as if a committee on temperance were to rule that drunkenness was not a proper subject of conversation among gentlemen.

A BAD BEGINNING

This was a bad beginning. Everybody knew that in England the censorship would not be crushed by the weight of the constitutional argument against it, heavy as that was, unless it were also brought home to the Committee and to the public that it had sanctioned and protected the very worst practicable examples of the kind of play it professed to extirpate. For it must be remembered that the other half of the practical side of the case, dealing with the merits of the plays it had suppressed, could never secure a unanimous assent. If the Censor had suppressed Hamlet, as he most certainly would have done had it been submitted to him as a new play, he would have been supported by a large body of people to whom incest is a tabooed subject which must not be mentioned on the stage or anywhere else outside a criminal court. Hamlet, Oedipus, and [Shelley's] The Cenci, Mrs Warren's Profession, Brieux's Maternité, and Les Avariés, Maeterlinck's Monna Vanna and Mr Granville Barker's Waste may or may not be great poems, or edifying sermons, or important documents, or charming romances: our tribal citizens know nothing about that and do not want to know anything: all that they do know is that incest, prostitution, abortion, contagious diseases, and nudity are improper, and that all conversations, or books, or plays in which they are discussed are improper conversations, improper books, improper plays, and should not be allowed. The Censor may prohibit all such plays with complete certainty that there will be a chorus of "Quite right too" sufficient to drown the protests of the few who know better. The Achilles heel of the censorship is therefore not the fine plays it has suppressed, but the abominable plays it has licensed: plays which the Committee itself had to turn the public out of the room and close the doors before it could discuss, and which I myself have found it impossible to expose in the press because no editor of a paper or magazine intended for general family reading could admit into his columns the baldest narration of the stories which the Censor has not only tolerated but expressly certified as fitting for presentation on the stage. When the Committee ruled out this part of the case it shook the confidence of the authors in its impartiality and its seriousness. Of course it was not able to enforce its ruling thoroughly. Plays which were merely lightminded and irresponsible in their viciousness were repeatedly mentioned by Mr Harcourt and others. But the really detestable plays, which would have damned the censorship beyond all apology or salvation, were never referred to; and the moment Mr Harcourt or anyone else made the Committee uncomfortable by a move in their direction, the ruling was appealed to at once, and the censorship saved.

A COMIC INTERLUDE

It was part of this nervous dislike of the unpleasant part of its business that led to the comic incident of the Committee's sudden discovery that I had insulted it, and its suspension of its investigation for the purpose of elaborately insulting me back again. Comic to the lookers-on, that is; for the majority of the Committee made no attempt to conceal the fact that they were wildly angry with me; and I, though my public experience and skill in acting enabled me to maintain an appearance of imperturbable good-humor, was equally furious. The friction began as follows.

The precedents for the conduct of the Committee were to be found in the proceedings of the Committee of 1892. That Committee, no doubt recognizing the absurdity of calling on distinguished artists to give their views before it, and then refusing to allow them to state their views except in nervous replies to such questions as it might suit members to put to them, allowed Sir Henry Irving and Sir John Hare to prepare and read written statements, and formally invited them to read them to the Committee before being questioned. I accordingly prepared such a statement. For the greater convenience of the Committee, I offered to have this statement printed at my own expense, and to supply the members with copies. The offer was accepted; and the copies supplied. I also offered to provide the Committee with copies of those plays of mine which had been refused a licence by the Lord Chamberlain. That offer also was accepted; and the books duly supplied.

AN ANTI-SHAVIAN PANIC

As far as I can guess, the next thing that happened was that some timid or unawakened member of the Committee read my statement and was frightened or scandalized out of his wits by it. At all events it is certain that the majority of the Committee allowed themselves to be persuaded to refuse to allow any statement to be read; but to avoid the appearance of pointing this expressly at me, the form adopted was a resolution to adhere strictly to precedent, the Committee being then unaware that the precedents were on my side. Accordingly, when I appeared before the Committee, and proposed to read my statement "according to precedent," the Committee was visibly taken aback. The Chairman was bound by the letter of the decision arrived at to allow me to read my statement, since that course was according to precedent; but as this was exactly what the decision was meant to prevent, the majority of the Committee would have regarded this hoisting of them with their own petard as a breach of faith on the part of the Chairman, who, I infer, was not in agreement with the suppressive majority. There was nothing for it, after a somewhat awkward pause, but to clear me and the public out of the room and reconsider the situation *in camera*. When the doors were opened again I was informed simply that the Committee would not hear my statement. But as the Committee could not very decently refuse my evidence altogether, the Chairman, with a printed copy of my statement in his hand as "proof," was able to come to the rescue to some extent by putting to me a series of questions to which no doubt I might have replied by taking another copy out of my pocket, and quoting my statement paragraph by paragraph, as some of the later witnesses did. But as in offering the Committee my statement for burial in their bluebook I had made a considerable sacrifice, being able to secure greater publicity for it by independent publication on my own account; and as, further, the circumstances of the refusal made it offensive enough to take all heart out of the scrupulous consideration with which I had so far treated the Committee, I was not disposed to give its majority a second chance, or to lose the opportunity offered me by the questions to fire an additional broadside into the censorship. I pocketed my statement, and answered the questions *viva voce*. At the conclusion of this, my examination-in-chief, the Committee adjourned, asking me to present myself again for (virtually) cross-examination. But this cross-examination never came off, as the sequel will shew.

A Rare and Curious First Edition

The refusal of the Committee to admit my statement had not unnaturally created the impression that it must be a scandalous document; and a lively demand for copies at once set in. And among the very first applicants were members of the majority which had carried the decision to exclude the document. They had given so little attention to the business that they did not know, or had forgotten, that they had already been supplied with copies at their own request. At all events, they came to me publicly and cleaned me out of the handful of copies I had provided for distribution to the press.[6] And after the sitting it was intimated to me that yet more copies were desired for the use of the Committee: a demand, under the circumstances, of breath-bereaving coolness. At the same time, a brisk demand arose outside the Committee, not only among people who were anxious to read what I had to say on the subject, but among victims of the craze for collecting first editions, copies of privately circulated pamphlets,

6. Only 250 copies of the paper-wrappered statement were printed.

and other real or imaginary rarities. Such maniacs will cheerfully pay five guineas for any piece of discarded old rubbish of mine when they will not pay as many shillings for a clean new copy of it, because everyone else can get it for the same price too.

The Times to the Rescue

The day after the refusal of the Committee to face my statement, I transferred the scene of action to the columns of The Times, which did yeoman's service to the public on this, as on many other occasions, by treating the question as a public one without the least regard to the supposed susceptibilities of the Court on the one side, or the avowed prejudices of the Free Churches or the interests of the managers or theatrical speculators on the other. The Times published the summarized conclusions of my statement, and gave me an opportunity of saying as much as it was then advisable to say of what had occurred.[7] For it must be remembered that, however impatient and contemptuous I might feel of the intellectual cowardice shewn by the majority of the Committee face to face with myself, it was none the less necessary to keep up its prestige in every possible way, not only for the sake of the dignity and importance of the matter with which it had to deal, and in the hope that the treatment of subsequent witnesses and the final report might make amends for a feeble beginning, but also out of respect and consideration for the minority. For it is fair to say that the majority was never more than a bare majority, and that the worst thing the Committee did—the exclusion of references to particular plays—was perpetrated in the absence of the Chairman.

I, therefore, had to treat the Committee in The Times very much better than its majority deserved, an injustice for which I now apologize. I did not, however, resist the temptation to hint, quite good-humoredly, that my politeness to the Committee had cost me quite enough already, and that I was not prepared to supply the members of the Committee, or anyone else, with extra copies merely as collectors' curiosities.

7. Shaw's letters, captioned 'The Select Committee on the Censorship' and 'The Dramatic Censorship', were published on 2 and 6 August 1909.

The Council of Ten

Then the fat was in the fire. The majority, chaffed for its eagerness to obtain copies of scarce pamphlets retailable at five guineas, went dancing mad. When I presented myself, as requested, for cross-examination, I found the doors of the Committee room shut, and the corridors of the House of Lords filled by a wondering crowd, to whom it had somehow leaked out that something terrible was happening inside. It could not be another licensed play too scandalous to be discussed in public, because the Committee had decided to discuss no more of these examples of the Censor's notions of purifying the stage; and what else the Committee might have to discuss that might not be heard by all the world was not easily guessable.

Without suggesting that the confidence of the Committee was in any way violated by any of its members further than was absolutely necessary to clear them from suspicion of complicity in the scene which followed, I think I may venture to conjecture what was happening. It was felt by the majority, first, that it must be cleared at all costs of the imputation of having procured more than one copy each of my statement, and that one not from any interest in an undesirable document by an irreverent author, but in the reluctant discharge of its solemn public duty; second, that a terrible example must be made of me by the most crushing public snub in the power of the Committee to administer. To throw my wretched little pamphlet at my head and to kick me out of the room was the passionate impulse which prevailed in spite of all the remonstrances of the Commoners, seasoned to the give-and-take of public life, and of the single peer who kept his head. The others, for the moment, had no heads to keep. And the fashion in which they proposed to wreak their vengeance was as follows.

The Sentence

I was to be admitted, as a lamb to the slaughter, and allowed to take my place as if for further examination. The Chairman was then to inform me coldly that the Committee did not desire to have anything more to say to me. The members were thereupon solemnly to hand me back the copies of my statement as so much waste paper, and I was to be suffered to slink away with what countenance I could maintain in such disgrace.

But this plan required the active co-operation of every member of the Committee; and whilst the majority regarded it as an august and impressive vindication of the majesty of parliament, the minority regarded it with equal conviction as a puerile tomfoolery, and declined altogether to act their allotted parts in it. Besides, they did not all want to part with the books. For instance, Mr Hugh Law, being an Irishman, with an Irishman's sense of how to behave like a gallant gentleman on occasion, was determined to be able to assure me that nothing should induce him to give up my statement or prevent him from obtaining and cherishing as many copies as possible. (I quote this as an example to the House of Lords of the right thing to say in such emergencies.) So the program had to be modified. The minority could not prevent the enraged majority from refusing to examine me further; nor could the Chairman refuse to communicate that decision to me. Neither could the minority object to the secretary handing me back such copies as he could collect from the majority. And at that the matter was left. The doors were opened; the audience trooped in; I was called to my place in the dock (so to speak); and all was ready for the sacrifice.

THE EXECUTION

Alas! the majority reckoned without Colonel Lockwood. That hardy and undaunted veteran refused to shirk his share in the scene merely because the minority was recalcitrant and the majority perhaps subject to stage fright. When Mr Samuel had informed me that the Committee had no further questions to ask me with an urbanity which gave the public no clue as to the temper of the majority; when I had jumped up with the proper air of relief and gratitude; when the secretary had handed me his little packet of books with an affability which effectually concealed his dramatic function as executioner; when the audience was simply disappointed at being baulked of the entertainment of hearing Mr Robert Harcourt cross-examine me; in short, when the situation was all but saved by the tact of the Chairman and secretary, Colonel Lockwood rose, with all his carnations blazing, and gave away the whole case by handing me, with impressive simplicity and courtesy, his *two* copies of the precious statement. And I believe that if he had succeeded in securing ten, he would have handed them all back to me with the most sincere conviction that every one of the ten must prove a crushing addition to the weight of my discomfiture. I still cherish that second copy, a little blue-bound pamphlet, methodically autographed "Lockwood B" among my most valued literary trophies.

An innocent lady told me afterwards that she never knew that I could smile so beautifully, and that she thought it shewed very good taste on my part. I was not conscious of smiling; but I should have embraced the Colonel had I dared. As it was, I turned expectantly to his colleagues, mutely inviting them to follow his example. But there was only one Colonel Lockwood on that Committee. No eye met mine except minority eyes, dancing with mischief. There was nothing more to be said. I went home to my morning's work, and returned in the afternoon to receive the apologies of the minority for the conduct of the majority, and to see Mr Granville Barker, overwhelmed by the conscience-stricken politeness of the now almost abject Committee, and by a powerful smell of carnations, heading the long list of playwrights who came there to testify against the censorship, and whose treatment, I am happy to say, was everything they could have desired.

After all, ridiculous as the scene was, Colonel Lockwood's simplicity and courage were much more serviceable to his colleagues than their own inept *coup de théâtre* [theatrical touch] would have been if he had not spoiled it. It was plain to everyone that he had acted in entire good faith, without a thought as to these apparently insignificant little books being of any importance or having caused me or anybody else any trouble, and that he was wounded in his most sensitive spot by the construction my Times letter had put on his action. And in Colonel Lockwood's case one saw the case of his party on the Committee. They had simply been thoughtless in the matter.

I hope nobody will suppose that this in any way exonerates them. When people accept public service for one of the most vital duties that can arise in our society, they have no right to be thoughtless. In spite of the fun of the scene on the surface, my public sense was, and still is, very deeply offended by it. It made an end for me of the claim of the majority to be taken seriously. When the Government comes to deal with the question, as it presumably will before long, I invite it to be guided by the Chairman, the minority, and by the witnesses according to their weight, and to pay no attention whatever to those recommendations which were obviously inserted solely to conciliate the majority and get the report through and the Committee done with.

My evidence will be found in the Bluebook, pp. 46–53. And here is the terrible statement which the Committee went through so much to suppress.

THE REJECTED STATEMENT—PART I

THE WITNESS'S QUALIFICATIONS

I am by profession a playwright. I have been in practice since 1892. I am a member of the Managing Committee of the Society of Authors and of the Dramatic Sub-Committee of that body. I have written nineteen plays, some of which have been translated and performed in all European countries except Turkey, Greece, and Portugal. They have been performed extensively in America. Three of them have been refused licences by the Lord Chamberlain. In one case [*Press Cuttings*] a licence has since been granted. The other two [*Mrs Warren's Profession* and *The Shewing-up of Blanco Posnet*] are still unlicensed. I have suffered both in pocket and reputation by the action of the Lord Chamberlain. In other countries I have not come into conflict with the censorship except in Austria, where the production of a comedy of mine [*Arms and the Man*] was postponed for a year because it alluded to the part taken by Austria in the Servo-Bulgarian war. This comedy was not one of the plays suppressed in England by the Lord Chamberlain. One of the plays so suppressed [*Mrs Warren's Profession*] was prosecuted in America by the police in consequence of an immense crowd of disorderly persons having been attracted to the first performance by the Lord Chamberlain's condemnation of it; but on appeal to a higher court it was decided that the representation was lawful and the intention innocent, since when it has been repeatedly performed.

I am not an ordinary playwright in general practice. I am a specialist in immoral and heretical plays. My reputation has been gained by my persistent struggle to force the public to reconsider its morals. In particular, I regard much current morality as to economic and sexual relations as disastrously wrong; and I regard certain doctrines of the Christian religion as understood in England today with abhorrence. I write plays with the deliberate object of converting the nation to my opinions in these matters. I have no other effectual incentive to write plays, as I am not dependent on the theatre for my livelihood. If I were prevented from producing immoral and heretical plays, I should cease to write for the theatre, and propagate my views from the platform and through books. I mention these facts to shew that I have a special interest in the achievement by my profession of those rights of liberty of speech and conscience which are matters of course in other professions. I object to censorship not merely because the existing form of it grievously injures and hinders me individually, but on public grounds.

THE DEFINITION OF IMMORALITY

In dealing with the question of the censorship, everything depends on the correct use of the word immorality, and a careful discrimination between the powers of a magistrate or judge to administer a code, and those of a censor to please himself.

Whatever is contrary to established manners and customs is immoral. An immoral act or doctrine is not necessarily a sinful one: on the contrary, every advance in thought and conduct is by definition immoral until it has converted the majority. For this reason it is of the most enormous importance that immorality should be protected jealously against the attacks of those who have no standard except the standard of custom, and who regard any attack on custom—that is, on morals—as an attack on society, on religion, and on virtue.

A censor is never intentionally a protector of immorality. He always aims at the protection of morality. Now morality is extremely valuable to society. It imposes conventional conduct on the great mass of persons who are incapable of original ethical judgment, and who would be quite lost if they were not in leading-strings devized by lawgivers, philosophers, prophets, and poets for their guidance. But morality is not dependent on censorship for protection. It is already powerfully fortified by the magistracy and the whole body of law. Blasphemy, indecency, libel, treason, sedition, obscenity, profanity, and all the other evils which a censorship is supposed to avert, are punishable by the civil magistrate with all the severity of vehement prejudice. Morality has not only every engine that lawgivers can devize in full operation for its protection, but also that enormous weight of public opinion enforced by social ostracism which is stronger than all the statutes. A censor pretending to protect morality is like a child pushing the cushions of a railway carriage to give itself the sensation of making the train travel at sixty miles an hour. It is immorality, not morality, that needs protection: it is morality, not immorality, that needs restraint; for morality, with all the dead weight of human inertia and superstition to hang on the back of the pioneer, and all the malice of vulgarity and prejudice to threaten him, is responsible for many persecutions and many martyrdoms.

Persecutions and martyrdoms, however, are trifles compared to the mischief done by censorships in delaying the general march of enlightenment. This can be brought home to us by imagining what would have been the effect of applying to all literature the censorship we still apply to the stage. The works of Linnaeus and the evolutionists of 1790–1830, of Darwin, [Alfred Russel] Wallace, Huxley, Helmholtz, Tyndall, Spencer, Carlyle, Ruskin, and Samuel Butler, would not have been published, as they were all immoral and heretical in the very highest degree, and gave pain to many worthy and pious people. They are at present condemned by the Greek and Roman Catholic censorships as unfit for general reading. A censorship of conduct would have been equally disastrous. The disloyalty of [John] Hampden[8] and of [George] Washington; the revolting immorality of Luther in not only marrying when he was a priest, but actually marrying a nun; the heterodoxy of Galileo; the shocking blasphemies and sacrileges of Mahomet against the idols whom he dethroned to make way for his conception of one god; the still more startling blasphemy of Jesus when He declared God to be the son of man and Himself to be the son of God, are all examples of shocking immoralities (every immorality shocks somebody), the suppression and extinction of which would have been more disastrous than the utmost mischief that can be conceived as ensuing from the toleration of vice.

These facts, glaring as they are, are disguised by the promotion of immoralities into moralities which is constantly going on. Christianity and Mahometanism, once thought of and dealt with exactly as Anarchism is thought of and dealt with today, have become established religions; and fresh immoralities are persecuted in their name. The truth is that the vast majority of persons professing these religions have never been anything but simple moralists. The respectable Englishman who is a Christian because he was born in Clapham would be a Mahometan for the cognate reason if he had been born in Constantinople. He has never willingly tolerated immorality. He did not adopt any innovation until it had become moral; and then he adopted it, not on its merits, but solely because it had become moral. In doing so he never realized that it had ever been immoral: consequently its early struggles taught him no lesson; and he has opposed the next step in human progress as indignantly as if neither manners, customs, nor thought had ever changed since the beginning of the world. Toleration must be imposed on him as a mystic and painful duty by his spiritual and political

8. Member of Parliament who led the opposition to the demands of Charles I for subsidies; impeached but escaped arrest.

leaders, or he will condemn the world to stagnation, which is the penalty of an inflexible morality.

WHAT TOLERATION MEANS

This must be done all the more arbitrarily because it is not possible to make the ordinary moral man understand what toleration and liberty really mean. He will accept them verbally with alacrity, even with enthusiasm, because the word toleration has been moralized by eminent Whigs; but what he means by toleration is toleration of doctrines that he considers enlightened, and, by liberty, liberty to do what he considers right: that is, he does not mean toleration or liberty at all; for there is no need to tolerate what appears enlightened or to claim liberty to do what most people consider right. Toleration and liberty have no sense or use except as toleration of opinions that are considered damnable, and liberty to do what seems wrong. Setting Englishmen free to marry their deceased wife's sisters is not tolerated by the people who approve of it, but by the people who regard it as incestuous. Catholic Emancipation and the admission of Jews to parliament needed no toleration from Catholics and Jews: the toleration they needed was that of the people who regarded the one measure as a facilitation of idolatry, and the other as a condonation of the crucifixion. Clearly such toleration is not clamored for by the multitude or by the press which reflects its prejudices. It is essentially one of those abnegations of passion and prejudice which the common man submits to because uncommon men whom he respects as wiser than himself assure him that it must be so, or the higher affairs of human destiny will suffer.

Such submission is the more difficult because the arguments against tolerating immorality are the same as the arguments against tolerating murder and theft; and this is why the Censor seems to the inconsiderate as obviously desirable a functionary as the police magistrate. But there is this simple and tremendous difference between the cases: that whereas no evil can conceivably result from the total suppression of murder and theft, and all communities prosper in direct proportion to such suppression, the total suppression of immorality, especially in matters of religion and sex, would stop enlightenment, and produce what used to be called a Chinese civilization until the Chinese lately took to immoral courses by permitting railway contractors to desecrate the graves of their ancestors, and their soldiers to wear clothes which indecently revealed the fact that they had legs and waists and even posteriors. At about the same moment a few bold Englishwomen ventured on the immorality of riding astride their horses, a practice that has since established itself so successfully that before another generation has passed away there may not be a new side-saddle in England, or a woman who could use it if there was.

THE CASE FOR TOLERATION

Accordingly, there has risen among wise and far-sighted men a perception of the need for setting certain departments of human activity entirely free from legal interference. This has nothing to do with any sympathy these liberators may themselves have with immoral views. A man with the strongest conviction of the Divine ordering of the universe and of the superiority of monarchy to all forms of government may nevertheless quite consistently and conscientiously be ready to lay down his life for the right of every man to advocate Atheism or Republicanism if he believes in them. An attack on morals may turn out to be the salvation of the race. A hundred years ago nobody foresaw that Tom Paine's centenary would be the subject of a laudatory special article in The Times; and only a few understood that the persecution of his works and the transportation of men for the felony of reading them was a mischievous mistake. Even less, perhaps, could they have guessed that Proudhon, who became notorious by his essay entitled "What is Property? It is Theft," would have received, on the like occasion and in the same paper, a respectful consideration which nobody would now dream of according to [Robert Banks Jenkinson] Lord [Second Earl of] Liverpool[9] or [Henry Peter Brougham] Lord [First Baron] Brougham.[10] Nevertheless there was a mass of evidence to shew that such a development was not only possible but fairly probable, and that the risks of suppressing liberty of propaganda were far graver than the risk of Paine's or Proudhon's writings wrecking civilization. Now there was no such evidence in favor of tolerating the cutting of throats and the robbing of tills. No case whatever can be made out for the statement that a nation cannot do without common thieves and homicidal ruffians. But an overwhelming case can be made out for the statement that no nation can prosper or even continue to

9. Prime Minister 1812–27, conducting what was described as a largely sound but unimaginative administration.
10. British jurist and politician, who was Lord Chancellor 1830–34. As a Member of Parliament he carried the measure making slavery a felony and prepared the measure for freedom of the press. Sponsor of the Public Education Bill and a founder (1828) of London University.

exist without heretics and advocates of shockingly immoral doctrines. The Inquisition and the Star Chamber, which were nothing but censorships, made ruthless war on impiety and immorality. The result was once familiar to Englishmen, though of late years it seems to have been forgotten. It cost England a revolution to get rid of the Star Chamber. Spain did not get rid of the Inquisition, and paid for that omission by becoming a barely third-rate power politically, and intellectually no power at all, in the Europe she had once dominated as the mightiest of the Christian empires.

The Limits to Toleration

But the large toleration these considerations dictate has limits. For example, though we tolerate, and rightly tolerate, the propaganda of Anarchism as a political theory which embraces all that is valuable in the doctrine of *Laisser-Faire* and the method of Free Trade as well as all that is shocking in the views of [Mikhail] Bakounine,[11] we clearly cannot, or at all events will not, tolerate assassination of rulers on the ground that it is "propaganda by deed" or sociological experiment. A play inciting to such an assassination cannot claim the privileges of heresy or immorality, because no case can be made out in support of assassination as an indispensable instrument of progress. Now it happens that we have in the Julius Cæsar of Shakespear a play which the Tsar of Russia or the Governor-General of India would hardly care to see performed in their capitals just now. It is an artistic treasure; but it glorifies a murder which Goethe described as the silliest crime ever committed. It may quite possibly have helped the regicides of 1649 to see themselves, as it certainly helped generations of Whig statesmen to see them, in a heroic light; and it unquestionably vindicates and ennobles a conspirator who assassinated the head of the Roman State not because he abused his position but solely because he occupied it, thus affirming the extreme republican principle that all kings, good or bad, should be killed because kingship and freedom cannot live together. Under certain circumstances this vindication and ennoblement might act as an incitement to an actual assassination as well as to Plutarchian republicanism; for it is one thing to advocate republicanism or royalism: it is quite another to make a hero of Brutus or [François] Ravaillac,[12] or a heroine of Charlotte

11. Nineteenth-century Russian anarchist leader, considered one of the most dangerous men in Europe.
12. French assassin of Henry IV of France (1610).

Corday.[13] Assassination is the extreme form of censorship; and it seems hard to justify an incitement to it on anti-censorial principles. The very people who would have scouted the notion of prohibiting the performances of Julius Cæsar at His Majesty's Theatre in London last year, might now entertain very seriously a proposal to exclude Indians from them, and to suppress the play completely in Calcutta and Dublin; for if the assassin of Cæsar was a hero, why not the assassins of Lord Frederick Cavendish,[14] Presidents Lincoln and McKinley, and Sir Curzon Wyllie?[15] Here is a strong case for some constitutional means of preventing the performance of a play. True, it is an equally strong case for preventing the circulation of the Bible, which was always in the hands of our regicides; but as the Roman Catholic Church does not hesitate to accept that consequence of the censorial principle, it does not invalidate the argument.

Take another actual case. A modern comedy, Arms and the Man, though not a comedy of politics, is nevertheless so far historical that it reveals the unacknowledged fact that as the Servo-Bulgarian War of 1885 was much more than a struggle between the Servians and Bulgarians, the troops engaged were officered by two European Powers of the first magnitude. In consequence, the performance of the play was for some time forbidden in Vienna, and more recently it gave offence in Rome at a moment when popular feeling was excited as to the relations of Austria with the Balkan States. Now if a comedy so remote from political passion as Arms and the Man can, merely because it refers to political facts, become so inconvenient and inopportune that Foreign Offices take the trouble to have its production postponed, what may not be the effect of what is called a patriotic drama produced at a moment when the balance is quivering between peace and war? Is there not something to be said for a political censorship, if not for a moral one? May not those continental governments who leave the stage practically free in every other respect, but muzzle it politically, be justified by the practical exigencies of the situation?

13. Assassin of Jean-Paul Marat (1793).
14. Chief secretary for Ireland, murdered by the Irish 'Invincibles' in 1882.
15. British officer and Indian administrator, assassinated by a Punjabi, Madho Lal Dhingra, at the Imperial Institute, London, in 1909.

The Difference between Law and Censorship

The answer is that a pamphlet, a newspaper article, or a resolution moved at a political meeting can do all the mischief that a play can, and often more; yet we do not set up a permanent censorship of the press or of political meetings. Any journalist may publish an article, any demagogue may deliver a speech without giving notice to the government or obtaining its licence. The risk of such freedom is great; but as it is the price of our political liberty, we think it worth paying. We may abrogate it in emergencies by a Coercion Act, a suspension of the Habeas Corpus Act, or a proclamation of martial law, just as we stop the traffic in a street during a fire, or shoot thieves at sight if they loot after an earthquake. But when the emergency is past, liberty is restored everywhere except in the theatre. The Act of 1843 is a permanent Coercion Act for the theatre, a permanent suspension of the Habeas Corpus Act as far as plays are concerned, a permanent proclamation of martial law with a single official substituted for a court martial. It is, in fact, assumed that actors, playwrights, and theatre managers are dangerous and dissolute characters whose existence creates a chronic state of emergency, and who must be treated as earthquake looters are treated. It is not necessary now to discredit this assumption. It was broken down by the late Sir Henry Irving when he finally shamed the Government into extending to his profession the official recognition enjoyed by the other branches of fine art. Today we have on the roll of knighthood actors, authors, and managers. The rogue and vagabond theory of the depravity of the theatre is as dead officially as it is in general society; and with it has perished the sole excuse for the Act of 1843 and for the denial to the theatre of the liberties secured, at far greater social risk, to the press and the platform.

There is no question here of giving the theatre any larger liberties than the press and the platform, or of claiming larger powers for Shakespear to eulogize Brutus than Lord Rosebery has to eulogize Cromwell. The abolition of the censorship does not involve the abolition of the magistrate and of the whole civil and criminal code. On the contrary, it would make the theatre more effectually subject to them than it is at present; for once a play now runs the gauntlet of the censorship, it is practically placed above the law. It is almost humiliating to have to demonstrate the essential difference between a censor and a magistrate or a sanitary inspector; but it is impossible to ignore the carelessness with which even distinguished critics of the theatre assume that all the arguments proper to the support of a magistracy and body of jurisprudence apply equally to a censorship.

A magistrate has laws to administer: a censor has nothing but his own opinion. A judge leaves the question of guilt to the jury: the Censor is jury and judge as well as lawgiver. A magistrate may be strongly prejudiced against an atheist or an anti-vaccinator, just as a sanitary inspector may have formed a careful opinion that drains are less healthy than cesspools; but the magistrate must allow the atheist to affirm instead of to swear, and must grant the anti-vaccinator an exemption certificate, when their demands are lawfully made; and in cities the inspector must compel the builder to make drains and must prosecute him if he makes cesspools. The law may be only the intolerance of the community; but it is a defined and limited intolerance. The limitation is sometimes carried so far that a judge cannot inflict the penalty for housebreaking on a burglar who can prove that he found the door open and therefore made only an unlawful entry. On the other hand, it is sometimes so vague, as for example in the case of the American law against obscenity, that it makes the magistrate virtually a censor. But in the main a citizen can ascertain what he may do and what he may not do; and, though no one knows better than a magistrate that a single ill-conducted family may demoralize a whole street, no magistrate can imprison or otherwise restrain its members on the ground that their immorality may corrupt their neighbors. He can prevent any citizen from carrying certain specified weapons, but not from handling pokers, table-knives, bricks or bottles of corrosive fluid, on the ground that he might use them to commit murder or inflict malicious injury. He has no general power to prevent citizens from selling unhealthy or poisonous substances, or judging for themselves what substances are unhealthy and what wholesome, what poisonous and what innocuous: what he *can* do is to prevent anybody who has not a specific qualification from selling certain specified poisons of which a schedule is kept. Nobody is forbidden to sell minerals without a licence; but everybody is forbidden to sell silver without a licence. When the law has forgotten some atrocious sin—for instance, contracting marriage whilst suffering from contagious disease—the magistrate cannot arrest or punish the wrongdoer, however he may abhor his wickedness. In short, no man is lawfully at the mercy of the magistrate's personal caprice, prejudice, ignorance, superstition, temper, stupidity, resentment, timidity, ambition, or private conviction. But a playwright's livelihood, his reputation, and his inspiration and mission are at the personal mercy of the Censor. The two do not stand, as the criminal and the judge stand, in the presence of a law that binds them both equally, and was made by neither of them, but by the deliberate collective wisdom of the community. The only law that affects them is the Act of 1843, which empowers one of them to do absolutely and finally what he likes with the other's work. And when it is remembered that the slave in this case is the man whose profession is that of Eschylus and Euripides, of Shakespear and Goethe, of Tolstoy and Ibsen, and the master the holder of a party appointment which by the nature of its duties practically excludes the possibility of its acceptance by a serious statesman or great lawyer, it will be seen that the playwrights are justified in reproaching the framers of that Act for having failed not only to appreciate the immense importance of the theatre as a most powerful instrument for teaching the nation how and what to think and feel, but even to conceive that those who make their living by the theatre are normal human beings with the common rights of English citizens. In this extremity of inconsiderateness it is not surprising that they also did not trouble themselves to study the difference between a censor and a magistrate. And it will be found that almost all the people who disinterestedly defend the censorship today are defending him on the assumption that there is no constitutional difference between him and any other functionary whose duty it is to restrain crime and disorder.

One further difference remains to be noted. As a magistrate grows old his mind may change or decay; but the law remains the same. The censorship of the theatre fluctuates with every change in the views and character of the man who exercises it. And what this implies can only be appreciated by those who can imagine what the effect on the mind must be of the duty of reading through every play that is produced in the kingdom year in, year out.

WHY THE LORD CHAMBERLAIN?

What may be called the high political case against censorship as a principle is now complete. The pleadings are those which have already freed books and pulpits and political platforms in England from censorship, if not from occasional legal persecution. The stage alone remains under a censorship of a grotesquely unsuitable kind. No play can be performed if the Lord Chamberlain happens to disapprove of it. And the Lord Chamberlain's functions have no sort of relationship to dramatic literature. A great judge of literature, a far-seeing statesman, a born champion of liberty of conscience and intellectual integrity—say a Milton, a Chesterfield, a Bentham—would be a very bad Lord Chamberlain: so bad, in fact, that his exclusion from such a post may be regarded as decreed by natural law. On the other hand, a good Lord Chamberlain would be a stickler for morals in the narrowest sense, a busy-body, a man to whom a matter of two inches in the length of a gentleman's sword or the absence of a feather from a lady's head-dress would be a graver matter than the Habeas Corpus Act. The Lord Chamberlain, as Censor of the theatre, is a direct descendant of the King's Master of the Revels, appointed in 1544 by Henry VIII to keep order among the players and musicians of that day when they performed at Court. This first appearance of the theatrical censor in politics as the whipper-in of the player, with its conception of the player as a rich man's servant hired to amuse him, and, outside his professional duties, as a gay, disorderly, anarchic spoilt child, half privileged, half outlawed, probably as much vagabond as actor, is the real foundation of the subjection of the whole profession, actors, managers, authors and all, to the despotic authority of an officer whose business it is to preserve decorum among menials. It must be remembered that it was not until a hundred years later, in the reaction against the Puritans, that a woman could appear on the English stage without being pelted off as the Italian actresses were. The theatrical profession was regarded as a shameless one; and it is only of late years that actresses have at last succeeded in living down the assumption that actress and prostitute are synonymous terms, and made good their position in respectable society. This makes the survival of the old ostracism in the Act of 1843 intolerably galling; and though it explains the apparently unaccountable absurdity of choosing as Censor of dramatic literature an official whose functions and qualifications have nothing whatever to do with literature, it also explains why the present arrangement is not only criticized as an institution, but resented as an insult.

THE DIPLOMATIC OBJECTION TO THE LORD CHAMBERLAIN

There is another reason, quite unconnected with the susceptibilities of authors, which makes it undesirable that a member of the King's Household should be responsible for the character and tendency of plays. The drama, dealing with all departments of human life, is necessarily political. Recent events have shewn—what indeed needed no demonstration—that it is impossible to prevent inferences being made, both at home and abroad, from the action of the Lord Chamberlain. The most talked-about play of the present year (1909), An Englishman's Home,[16] has for its main interest an invasion of England by a fictitious power which is understood, as it is

16. Billed as by 'A Patriot', its author was Major Guy Du Maurier.

meant to be understood, to represent Germany. The lesson taught by the play is the danger of invasion and the need for every English citizen to be a soldier. The Lord Chamberlain licensed this play, but refused to license a parody of it. Shortly afterwards he refused to license another play [Shaw's *Press Cuttings*] in which the fear of a German invasion was ridiculed. The German press drew the inevitable inference that the Lord Chamberlain was an anti-German alarmist, and that his opinions were a reflection of those prevailing in St James's Palace. Immediately after this, the Lord Chamberlain licensed the play. Whether the inference, as far as the Lord Chamberlain was concerned, was justified, is of no consequence. What is important is that it was sure to be made, justly or unjustly, and extended from the Lord Chamberlain to the Throne.

The Objection of Court Etiquet

There is another objection to the Lord Chamberlain's censorship which affects the author's choice of subject. Formerly very little heed was given in England to the susceptibilities of foreign courts. For instance, the notion that the Mikado of Japan should be as sacred to the English playwright as he is to the Japanese Lord Chamberlain would have seemed grotesque a generation ago. Now that the maintenance of *entente cordiale* between nations is one of the most prominent and most useful functions of the crown, the freedom of authors to deal with political subjects, even historically, is seriously threatened by the way in which the censorship makes the King responsible for the contents of every play. One author—the writer of these lines, in fact—has long desired to dramatize the life of Mahomet. But the possibility of a protest from the Turkish Ambassador—or the fear of it—causing the Lord Chamberlain to refuse to license such a play has prevented the play from being written. Now, if the censorship were abolished, nobody but the author could be held responsible for the play. The Turkish Ambassador does not now protest against the publication of Carlyle's essay on the prophet, or of the English translations of the Koran in the prefaces to which Mahomet is criticized as an impostor, or of the older books in which he is reviled as Mahound and classed with the devil himself. But if these publications had to be licensed by the Lord Chamberlain it would be impossible for the King to allow the licence to be issued, as he would thereby be made responsible for the opinions expressed. This restriction of the historical drama is an unmixed evil. Great religious leaders are more interesting and more important subjects for the dramatist than great conquerors. It is a misfortune that public opinion would not tolerate a dramatization of Mahomet in Constantinople. But to prohibit it here, where public opinion would tolerate it, is an absurdity which, if applied in all directions, would make it impossible for the Queen to receive a Turkish ambassador without veiling herself, or the Dean and Chapter of St Paul's to display a cross on the summit of their Cathedral in a city occupied largely and influentially by Jews. Court etiquet is no doubt an excellent thing for court ceremonies; but to attempt to impose it on the drama is about as sensible as an attempt to make everybody in London wear court dress.

WHY NOT AN ENLIGHTENED CENSORSHIP?

In the above cases the general question of censorship is separable from the question of the present form of it. Everyone who condemns the principle of censorship must also condemn the Lord Chamberlain's control of the drama; but those who approve of the principle do not necessarily approve of the Lord Chamberlain being the Censor *ex officio*. They may, however, be entirely opposed to popular liberties, and may conclude from what has been said, not that the stage should be made as free as the church, press, or platform, but that these institutions should be censored as strictly as the stage. It will seem obvious to them that nothing is needed to remove all objections to a censorship except the placing of its powers in better hands.

Now though the transfer of the censorship to, say, the Lord Chancellor, or the Primate, or a Cabinet Minister, would be much less humiliating to the persons immediately concerned, the inherent vices of the institution would not be appreciably less disastrous. They would even be aggravated, for reasons which do not appear on the surface, and therefore need to be followed with some attention.

It is often said that the public is the real censor. That this is to some extent true is proved by the fact that plays which are licensed and produced in London have to be expurgated for the provinces. This does not mean that the provinces are more straitlaced, but simply that in many provincial towns there is only one theatre for all classes and all tastes, whereas in London there are separate theatres for separate sections of playgoers: so that, for example, Sir Herbert Beerbohm Tree can conduct His Majesty's Theatre without the slightest regard to the tastes of the frequenters of the Gaiety Theatre; and Mr George Edwardes can conduct the Gaiety Theatre without catering in any way for lovers of Shakespear. Thus the farcical comedy which has scandalized the critics in London by the libertinage of its jests is played to the respectable dress circle of Northampton with these same jests slurred over so as to be imperceptible by even the most prurient spectator. The public, in short, takes care that nobody shall outrage it.

But the public also takes care that nobody shall starve it, or regulate its dramatic diet as a schoolmistress regulates the reading of her pupils. Even when it wishes to be debauched, no censor can—or at least no censor does—stand out against it. If a play is irresistibly amusing, it gets licensed no matter what its moral aspect may be. A brilliant instance is the Divorçons [1880] of the late Victorien Sardou [and E. de Najac], which may not have been the naughtiest play of the XIX century, but was certainly the very naughtiest that any English manager in his senses would have ventured to produce.[17] Nevertheless, being a very amusing play, it passed the licenser with the exception of a reference to impotence as a ground for divorce which no English actress would have ventured on in any case. Within the last few months a very amusing comedy[18] with a strongly polygamous moral was found irresistible by the Lord Chamberlain. Plenty of fun and a happy ending will get anything licensed, because the public will have it so, and the Examiner of Plays, as the holder of the office [E. F. S. Pigott] testified before the Commission of 1892, feels with the public, and knows that his office could not survive a widespread unpopularity. In short, the support of the mob—that is, of the unreasoning, unorganized, uninstructed mass of popular sentiment—is indispensable to the censorship as it exists today in England. This is the explanation of the toleration by the Lord Chamberlain of coarse and vicious plays. It is not long since a judge before whom a licensed play came in the course of a lawsuit expressed his scandalized astonishment at the licensing of such a work. Eminent churchmen have made similar protests. In some plays the simulation of criminal assaults on the stage has been carried to a point at which a step further would have involved the interference of the police. Provided the treatment of the theme is gaily or hypocritically popular, and the ending happy, the indulgence of the Lord Chamberlain can be counted on. On the other hand, anything unpleasing and unpopular is rigorously censored. Adultery and prostitution are tolerated and even encouraged to such an extent that

17. A translation by Herman Merivale, as *The Queen's Proctor*, was reviewed by Shaw in the *Saturday Review*, 6 June 1896.
18. H. Hamilton Fyfe's *A Modern Aspasia*, presented by the Stage Society on 7 June.

plays which do not deal with them are commonly said not to be plays at all. But if any of the unpleasing consequences of adultery and prostitution—for instance, an *unsuccessful* illegal operation (successful ones are tolerated) or venereal disease—are mentioned, the play is prohibited. This principle of shielding the playgoer from unpleasant reflections is carried so far that when a play was submitted for licence in which the relations of a prostitute with all the male characters in the piece was described as "immoral," the Examiner of Plays objected to that passage, though he made no objection to the relations themselves. The Lord Chamberlain dare not, in short, attempt to exclude from the stage the tragedies of murder and lust, or the farces of mendacity, adultery, and dissolute gaiety in which vulgar people delight. But when these same vulgar people are threatened with an unpopular play in which dissoluteness is shewn to be no laughing matter, it is prohibited at once amid the vulgar applause, the net result being that vice is made delightful and virtue banned by the very institution which is supported on the understanding that it produces exactly the opposite result.

The Weakness of the Lord Chamberlain's Department

Now comes the question, Why is our censorship, armed as it is with apparently autocratic powers, so scandalously timid in the face of the mob? Why is it not as autocratic in dealing with playwrights below the average as with those above it? The answer is that its position is really a very weak one. It has no direct coercive forces, no funds to institute prosecutions and recover the legal penalties of defying it, no powers of arrest or imprisonment, in short, none of the guarantees of autocracy. What it can do is to refuse to renew the licence of a theatre at which its orders are disobeyed. When it happens that a theatre is about to be demolished, as was the case recently with the Imperial Theatre after it had passed into the hands of the Wesleyan Methodists, unlicensed plays can be performed, technically in private, but really in full publicity, without risk. The prohibited plays of Brieux and Ibsen have been performed in London in this way with complete impunity. But the impunity is not confined to condemned theatres. Not long ago a West End manager allowed a prohibited play to be performed at his theatre, taking his chance of losing his licence in consequence. The event proved that the manager was justified in regarding the risk as negligible; for the Lord Chamberlain's remedy—the closing of a popular and well-conducted theatre—was far too extreme to be practicable. Unless the play had so outraged public opinion as to make the manager odious and provoke a clamor for his exemplary punishment, the Lord Chamberlain could only have had his revenge at the risk of having his powers abolished as unsupportably tyrannical.

The Lord Chamberlain then has his powers so adjusted that he is tyrannical just where it is important that he should be tolerant, and tolerant just where he could screw up the standard a little by being tyrannical. His plea that there are unmentionable depths to which managers and authors would descend if he did not prevent them is disproved by the plain fact that his indulgence goes as far as the police, and sometimes further than the public, will let it. If our judges had so little power there would be no law in England. If our churches had so much, there would be no theatre, no literature, no science, no art, possibly no England. The institution is at once absurdly despotic and abjectly weak.

An Enlightened Censorship still worse than the Lord Chamberlain's

Clearly a censorship of judges, bishops, or statesmen would not be in this abject condition. It would no doubt make short work of the coarse and vicious pieces which now enjoy the protection of the Lord Chamberlain, or at least of those of them in which the vulgarity and vice are discoverable by merely reading the prompt copy. But it would certainly disappoint the main hope of its advocates: the hope that it would protect and foster the higher drama. It would do nothing of the sort. On the contrary, it would inevitably suppress it more completely than the Lord Chamberlain does, because it would understand it better. The one play of Ibsen's which is prohibited on the English stage, Ghosts, is far less subversive than A Doll's House. But the Lord Chamberlain does not meddle with such far-reaching matters as the tendency of a play. He refuses to license Ghosts exactly as he would refuse to license Hamlet if it were submitted to him as a new play. He would license even Hamlet if certain alterations were made in it. He would disallow the incestuous relationship between the King and Queen. He would probably insist on the substitution of some fictitious country for Denmark in deference to the near relations of our reigning house with that realm. He would certainly make it an absolute condition that the closet scene, in which a son, in an agony of shame and revulsion, reproaches his mother for her relations with his uncle, should be struck out as unbearably horrifying and improper. But compliance with these conditions would satisfy him. He would raise no speculative objections to the tendency of the play.

This indifference to the larger issues of a theatrical performance could not be safely predicated of an enlightened censorship. Such a censorship might be more liberal in its toleration of matters which are only objected to on the ground that they are not usually discussed in general social conversation or in the presence of children; but it would presumably have a far deeper insight to and concern for the real ethical tendency of the play. For instance, had it been in existence during the last quarter of a century, it would have perceived that those plays of Ibsen's which have been licensed without question are fundamentally immoral to an altogether extraordinary degree. Every one of them is a deliberate act of war on society as at present constituted. Religion, marriage, ordinary respectability, are subjected to a destructive exposure and criticism which seems to mere moralists—that is, to persons of no more than average depth of mind—to be diabolical. It is no exaggeration to say that Ibsen gained his overwhelming reputation by undertaking a task of no less magnitude than changing the mind of Europe with the view of changing its morals. Now you cannot license work of that sort without making yourself responsible for it. The Lord Chamberlain accepted the responsibility because he did not understand it or concern himself about it. But what really enlightened and conscientious official dare take such a responsibility? The strength of character and range of vision which made Ibsen capable of it are not to be expected from any official, however eminent. It is true that an enlightened censor might, whilst shrinking even with horror from Ibsen's views, perceive that any nation which suppressed Ibsen would presently find itself falling behind the nations which tolerated him just as Spain fell behind England; but the proper action to take on such a conviction is the abdication of censorship, not the practice of it. As long as a censor is a censor, he cannot endorse by his licence opinions which seem to him dangerously heretical.

We may, therefore, conclude that the more enlightened a censorship is, the worse it would serve us. The Lord Chamberlain, an obviously unenlightened Censor, prohibits Ghosts and licenses all the rest of Ibsen's plays. An enlightened censorship would possibly license Ghosts; but it would certainly suppress many of the other plays. It would suppress subversiveness as well as what is called bad taste. The Lord Chamberlain prohibits one play by Sophocles because, like Hamlet, it mentions the subject of incest; but an enlightened censorship might suppress all the plays of Euripides because Euripides, like Ibsen, was a revolutionary Freethinker. Under the Lord Chamberlain, we can smuggle a good deal of immoral drama and almost as much coarsely vulgar and furtively lascivious drama as we like. Under a college of cardinals, or bishops, or judges, or any other conceivable form of experts in morals, philosophy, religion, or politics, we should get little except stagnant mediocrity.

THE PRACTICAL IMPOSSIBILITIES OF CENSORSHIP

There is, besides, a crushing material difficulty in the way of an enlightened censorship. It is not too much to say that the work involved would drive a man of any intellectual rank mad. Consider, for example, the Christmas pantomimes. Imagine a judge of the High Court, or an archbishop, or a Cabinet Minister, or an eminent man of letters, earning his living by reading through the mass of trivial doggerel represented by all the pantomimes which are put into rehearsal simultaneously at the end of every year. The proposal to put such mind-destroying drudgery upon an official of the class implied by the demand for an enlightened censorship falls through the moment we realize what it implies in practice.

Another material difficulty is that no play can be judged by merely reading the dialogue. To be fully effective a censor should witness the performance. The *mise-en-scène* [staging] of a play is as much a part of it as the words spoken on the stage. No censor could possibly object to such a speech as "Might I speak to you for a moment, miss?" yet that apparently innocent phrase has often been made offensively improper on the stage by popular low comedians, with the effect of changing the whole character and meaning of the play as understood by the official Examiner. In one of the plays of the present season, the dialogue was that of a crude melodrama dealing in the most conventionally correct manner with the fortunes of a good-hearted and virtuous girl. Its morality was that of the Sunday school. But the principal actress, between two speeches which contained no reference to her action, changed her underclothing on the stage.[19] It is true that in this case the actress was so much better than her part that she succeeded in turning what was meant as an impropriety into an inoffensive stroke of realism; yet it is none the less clear that stage business of this character, on which there can be no check except the actual presence of a censor in the theatre, might convert any dialogue, however innocent, into just the sort

19. *The Chorus Lady* by James Forbes, centring amid a group of chorus girls in a New York theatre dressing-room, was performed by an American company headed by Rose Stahl. The *Times* critic (A. B. Walkley), who highly praised the play, noted that the actresses 'go through the details of their stage toilet like the heroine of [David] Belasco's *Zaza*, and contrive to reveal many secrets of feminine attire without any real offence'.

of entertainment against which the Censor is supposed to protect the public.

It was this practical impossibility that prevented the London County Council from attempting to apply a censorship of the Lord Chamberlain's pattern to the London music halls. A proposal to examine all entertainments before permitting their performance was actually made; and it was abandoned, not in the least as contrary to the liberty of the stage, but because the executive problem of how to do it at once reduced the proposal to absurdity. Even if the Council devoted all its time to witnessing rehearsals of variety performances, and putting each item to the vote, possibly after a prolonged discussion followed by a division, the work would still fall into arrear. No committee could be induced to undertake such a task. The attachment of an inspector of morals to each music hall would have meant an appreciable addition to the ratepayers' burden. In the face of such difficulties the proposal melted away. Had it been pushed through, and the inspectors appointed, each of them would have become a censor, and the whole body of inspectors would have become a *police des mœurs* [watchdog of manners]. Those who know the history of such police forces on the Continent will understand how impossible it would be to procure inspectors whose characters would stand the strain of their opportunities of corruption, both pecuniary and personal, at such salaries as a local authority could be persuaded to offer.

It has been suggested that the present censorship should be supplemented by a board of experts, who should deal, not with the whole mass of plays sent up for licence, but only those which the Examiner of Plays refuses to pass. As the number of plays which the Examiner refuses to pass is never great enough to occupy a Board in permanent session with regular salaries, and as casual employment is not compatible with public responsibility, this proposal would work out in practice as an addition to the duties of some existing functionary. A Secretary of State would be objectionable as likely to be biased politically. An ecclesiastical referee might be biased against the theatre altogether. A judge in chambers would be the proper authority. This plan would combine the inevitable intolerance of an enlightened censorship with the popular laxity of the Lord Chamberlain. The judge would suppress the pioneers, whilst the Examiner of Plays issued two guinea certificates for the vulgar and vicious plays. For this reason the plan would no doubt be popular; but it would be very much as a relaxation of the administration of the Public Health Acts accompanied by the cheapening of gin would be popular.

The Arbitration Proposal

On the occasion of a recent deputation of playwrights to the Prime Minister[20] it was suggested that if a censorship be inevitable, provision should be made for an appeal from the Lord Chamberlain in cases of refusal of licence. The authors of this suggestion propose that the Lord Chamberlain shall choose one umpire and the author another. The two umpires shall then elect a referee, whose decision shall be final.

This proposal is not likely to be entertained by constitutional lawyers. It is a naïve offer to accept the method of arbitration in what is essentially a matter, not between one private individual or body and another, but between a public offender and the State. It will presumably be ruled out as a proposal to refer a case of manslaughter to arbitration would be ruled out. But even if it were constitutionally sound, it bears all the marks of that practical inexperience which leads men to believe that arbitration either costs nothing or is at least cheaper than law. Who is to pay for the time of the three arbitrators, presumably men of high professional standing? The author may not be able: the manager may not be willing: neither of them should be called upon to pay for a public service otherwise than by their contributions to the revenue. Clearly the State should pay. But even so, the difficulties are only beginning. A licence is seldom refused except on grounds which are controversial. The two arbitrators selected by the opposed parties to the controversy are to agree to leave the decision to a third party unanimously chosen by themselves. That is very far from being a simple solution. An attempt to shorten and simplify the passing of the Finance Bill by referring it to an arbitrator chosen unanimously by Mr [Herbert Henry] Asquith and Mr Balfour[21] might not improbably cost more and last longer than a civil war. And why should the chosen referee—if he ever succeeded in getting chosen—be assumed to be a safer authority than the Examiner of Plays? He would certainly be a less responsible one: in fact, being (however eminent) a casual person called in to settle a single case, he would be virtually irresponsible. Worse still, he would take all responsibility away from the Lord Chamberlain, who is at

20. This was a delegation of playwright-members of the Society of Authors in 1907. Due to the illness of the Prime Minister, Sir Henry Campbell-Bannerman, the delegation (with Shaw tactfully absent) was received by his deputy.
21. Balfour, former Prime Minister, was at this time leader of the Opposition. Asquith, Liberal MP, was the present Prime Minister (1908–16).

least an official of the King's Household and a nominee of the Government. The Lord Chamberlain, with all his shortcomings, thinks twice before he refuses a licence, knowing that his refusal is final and may promptly be made public. But if he could transfer his responsibility to an arbitrator, he would naturally do so whenever he felt the slightest misgiving, or whenever, for diplomatic reasons, the licence would come more gracefully from an authority unconnected with the court. These considerations, added to the general objection to the principle of censorship, seem sufficient to put the arbitration expedient quite out of the question.

THE REJECTED STATEMENT—PART II

The Licensing of Theatres

The Distinction between Licensing and Censorship

It must not be concluded that the uncompromising abolition of all censorship involves the abandonment of all control and regulation of theatres. Factories are regulated in the public interest; but there is no censorship of factories. For example, many persons are sincerely convinced that cotton clothing is unhealthy; that alcoholic drinks are demoralizing; and that playing-cards are the devil's picture-books. But though the factories in which cotton, whiskey, and cards are manufactured are stringently regulated under the factory code and the Public Health and Building Acts, the inspectors appointed to carry out these Acts never go to a manufacturer and inform him that unless he manufactures woollens instead of cottons, ginger-beer instead of whiskey, Bibles instead of playing-cards, he will be forbidden to place his products on the market. In the case of premises licensed for the sale of spirits the authorities go a step further. A public-house differs from a factory in the essential particular that whereas disorder in a factory is promptly and voluntarily suppressed, because every moment of its duration involves a measurable pecuniary loss to the proprietor, disorder in a public-house may be a source of profit to the proprietor by its attraction for disorderly customers. Consequently a publican is compelled to obtain a licence to pursue his trade; and this licence lasts only a year, and need not be renewed if his house has been conducted in a disorderly manner in the meantime.

PROSTITUTION AND DRINK IN THEATRES

The theatre presents the same problem as the public-house in respect to disorder. To begin with, a theatre is actually a place licensed for the sale of spirits. The bars at a London theatre can be let without difficulty for £30 a week and upwards. And though it is clear that nobody will pay from a shilling to half a guinea for access to a theatre bar when he can obtain access to an ordinary public-house for nothing, there is no law to prevent the theatre proprietor from issuing free passes broadcast and recouping himself by the profit on the sale of drink. Besides, there may be some other attraction than the sale of drink. When this attraction is that of the play no objection need be made. But it happens that the auditorium of a theatre, with its brilliant lighting and luxurious decorations, makes a very effective shelter and background for the display of fine dresses and pretty faces. Consequently theatres have been used for centuries in England as markets by prostitutes. From the Restoration to the days of [William] Macready[22] all theatres were made use of in this way as a matter of course; and to this, far more than to any prejudice against dramatic art, we owe the Puritan formula that the theatre door is the gate of hell. Macready had a hard struggle to drive the prostitutes from his theatre; and since his time the London theatres controlled by the Lord Chamberlain have become respectable and even socially pretentious. But some of the variety theatres still derive a revenue by selling admissions to women who do not look at the performance, and men who go to purchase or admire the women. And in the provinces this state of things is by no means confined to the variety theatres. The real attraction is sometimes not the performance at all. The theatre is not really a theatre: it is a drink shop and a prostitution market; and the last shred of its disguise is stripped by the virtually indiscriminate issue of free tickets to the men. Access to the stage is also easily obtained; and the plays preferred by the management are those in which the stage is filled with young women who are not in any serious technical sense of the word actresses at all. Considering that all this is now possible at any theatre, and actually occurs at some theatres, the fact that our best theatres are as respectable as they are is much to their credit; but it is still an intolerable evil that respectable managers should have to fight against the free tickets and disorderly housekeeping of unscrupulous competitors. The dramatic

22. English tragedian, manager of Covent Garden 1837–9 and of Drury Lane 1841–3.

author is equally injured. He finds that unless he writes plays which make suitable sideshows for drinking-bars and brothels, he may be excluded from towns where there is not room for two theatres, and where the one existing theatre is exploiting drunkenness and prostitution instead of carrying on a legitimate dramatic business. Indeed everybody connected with the theatrical profession suffers in reputation from the detestable tradition of such places, against which the censorship has proved quite useless.

Here we have a strong case for applying either the licensing system or whatever better means may be devized for securing the orderly conduct of houses of public entertainment, dramatic or other. Liberty must, no doubt, be respected in so far that no manager should have the right to refuse admission to decently dressed, sober, and well-conducted persons, whether they are prostitutes, soldiers in uniform, gentlemen not in evening dress, Indians, or what not; but when disorder is stopped, disorderly persons will either cease to come or else reform their manners. It is, however, quite arguable that the indiscriminate issue of free admissions, though an apparently innocent and good-natured, and certainly a highly popular proceeding, should expose the proprietor of the theatre to the risk of a refusal to renew his licence.

Why the Managers dread Local Control

All this points to the transfer of the control of theatres from the Lord Chamberlain to the municipality. And this step is opposed by the long-run managers, partly because they take it for granted that municipal control must involve municipal censorship of plays, so that plays might be licensed in one town and prohibited in the next, and partly because, as they have no desire to produce plays which are in advance of public opinion, and as the Lord Chamberlain in every other respect gives more scandal by his laxity than trouble by his severity, they find in the present system a cheap and easy means of procuring a certificate which relieves them of all social responsibility, and provides them with so strong a weapon of defence in case of a prosecution that it acts in practice as a bar to any such proceedings. Above all, they know that the Examiner of Plays is free from the pressure of that large body of English public opinion already alluded to, which regards the theatre as the Prohibitionist Teetotaller regards the public-house: that is, as an abomination to be stamped out unconditionally. The managers rightly dread this pressure more than anything else; and they believe that it is so strong in local governments as to be a characteristic bias of municipal authority. In this they are no doubt mistaken. There is not a municipal authority of any importance in the country in which a proposal to stamp out the theatre, or even to treat it illiberally, would have a chance of adoption. Municipal control of the variety theatres (formerly called music halls) has been very far from illiberal, except in the one particular in which the Lord Chamberlain is equally illiberal. That particular is the assumption that a draped figure is decent and an undraped one indecent. It is useless to point to actual experience, which proves abundantly that naked or apparently naked figures, whether exhibited as living pictures, animated statuary, or in a dance, are at their best not only innocent, but refining in their effect, whereas those actresses and skirt dancers who have brought the peculiar aphrodisiac effect which is objected to to the highest pitch of efficiency wear twice as many petticoats as an ordinary lady does, and seldom exhibit more than their ankles. Unfortunately, municipal councillors persist in confusing decency with drapery; and both in London and the provinces certain positively edifying performances have been forbidden or withdrawn under pressure, and replaced by coarse and vicious ones. There is not the slightest reason to suppose that the Lord Chamberlain would have been any more tolerant; but this does not alter the fact that the municipal licensing authorities have actually used their powers to set up a censorship which is open to all the objections to censorship in general, and which, in addition, sets up the objection from which central control is free: namely, the impossibility of planning theatrical tours without the serious commercial risk of having the performance forbidden in some of the towns booked. How can this be prevented?

DESIRABLE LIMITATIONS OF LOCAL CONTROL

The problem is not a difficult one. The municipality can be limited just as the monarchy is limited. The Act transferring theatres to local control can be a charter of the liberties of the stage as well as an Act to reform administration. The power to refuse to grant or renew a licence to a theatre need not be an arbitrary one. The municipality may be required to state the ground of refusal; and certain grounds can be expressly declared as unlawful; so that it shall be possible for the manager to resort to the courts for a mandamus to compel the authority to grant a licence. It can be declared unlawful for a licensing authority to demand from the manager any disclosure of the nature of any entertainment he proposes to give, or to prevent its performance, or to refuse to renew his licence on the ground that the tendency of his entertainments is contrary to religion and morals, or that the theatre is an undesirable institution, or that there are already as many theatres as are needed, or that the theatre draws people away from the churches, chapels, mission halls, and the like in its neighborhood. The assumption should be that every citizen has a right to open and conduct a theatre, and therefore has a right to a licence unless he has forfeited that right by allowing his theatre to become a disorderly house, or failing to provide a building which complies with the regulations concerning sanitation and egress in case of fire, or being convicted of an offence against public decency. Also, the licensing powers of the authority should not be delegated to any official or committee; and the manager or lessee of the theatre should have a right to appear in person or by counsel to plead against any motion to refuse to grant or renew his licence. With these safeguards the licensing power could not be stretched to censorship. The manager would enjoy liberty of conscience as far as the local authority is concerned; but on the least attempt on his part to keep a disorderly house under cover of opening a theatre he would risk his licence.

But the managers will not and should not be satisfied with these limits to the municipal power. If they are deprived of the protection of the Lord Chamberlain's licence, and at the same time efficiently protected against every attempt at censorship by the licensing authority, the enemies of the theatre will resort to the ordinary law, and try to get from the prejudices of a jury what they are debarred from getting from the prejudices of a County Council or City Corporation. Moral Reform Societies, "Purity" Societies, Vigilance Societies, exist in England and America for the purpose of enforcing the existing laws against obscenity, blasphemy, Sabbath-breaking, the debauchery of children, prostitution, and so forth. The paid officials of these societies, in their anxiety to produce plenty of evidence of their activity in the annual reports which go out to the subscribers, do not always discriminate between an obscene postcard and an artistic one, or to put it more exactly, between a naked figure and an indecent one. They often combine a narrow but terribly sincere sectarian bigotry with a complete ignorance of art and history. Even when they have some culture, their livelihood is at the mercy of subscribers and committee men who have none. If these officials had any power of distinguishing between art and blackguardism, between morality and virtue, between immorality and vice, between conscientious heresy and mere baseness of mind and foulness of mouth, they might be trusted by theatrical managers not to abuse the powers of the common informer. As it is, it has been found necessary, in order to enable good music to be performed on Sunday, to take away these powers in that particular, and vest them solely in the Attorney-General. This disqualification of the common informer should be extended to the initiation of all proceedings of a censorial character against theatres. Few people are aware of the monstrous laws against blasphemy which still disgrace our statute book. If any serious attempt were made to carry them out, prison accommodation would have to be provided for almost every educated person in the country, beginning with the Archbishop of Canterbury. Until some government with courage and character enough to repeal them comes into power, it is not too much to ask that such infamous powers of oppression should be kept in responsible hands and not left at the disposal of every bigot ignorant enough to be unaware of the social dangers of persecution. Besides, the common informer is not always a sincere bigot who believes he is performing an action of signal merit in silencing and ruining a heretic. He is unfortunately just as often a blackmailer, who has studied his powers as a common informer in order that he may extort money for refraining from exercising them. If the manager is to be responsible he should be made responsible to a responsible functionary. To be responsible to every fanatical ignoramus who chooses to prosecute him for exhibiting a cast of the Hermes of Praxiteles in his vestibule, or giving a performance of Measure for Measure, is mere slavery. It is made bearable at present by the protection of the Lord Chamberlain's certificate. But when that is no longer available, the common informer must be disarmed if the manager is to enjoy security.

SUMMARY

The general case against censorship as a principle, and the particular case against the existing English censorship and against its replacement by a more enlightened one, is now complete. The following is a recapitulation of the propositions and conclusions contended for.

1. The question of censorship or no censorship is a question of high political principle and not of petty policy.

2. The toleration of heresy and shocks to morality on the stage, and even their protection against the prejudices and superstitions which necessarily enter largely into morality and public opinion, are essential to the welfare of the nation.

3. The existing censorship of the Lord Chamberlain does not only

intentionally suppress heresy and challenges to morality in their serious and avowed forms, but unintentionally gives the special protection of its official licence to the most extreme impropriety that the lowest section of London playgoers will tolerate in theatres especially devoted to their entertainment, licensing everything that is popular and forbidding any attempt to change public opinion or morals.

4. The Lord Chamberlain's censorship is open to the special objection that its application to political plays is taken to indicate the attitude of the Crown on questions of domestic and foreign policy, and that it imposes the limits of etiquet on the historical drama.

5. A censorship of a more enlightened and independent kind, exercised by the most eminent available authorities, would prove in practice more disastrous than the censorship of the Lord Chamberlain, because the more eminent its members were the less possible would it be for them to accept the responsibility for heresy or immorality by licensing them, and because the many heretical and immoral plays which now pass the Lord Chamberlain because he does not understand them, would be understood and suppressed by a more highly enlightened censorship.

6. A reconstructed and enlightened censorship would be armed with summary and effective powers which would stop the evasions by which heretical and immoral plays are now performed in spite of the Lord Chamberlain; and such powers would constitute a tyranny which would ruin the theatre spiritually by driving all independent thinkers from the drama into the uncensored forms of art.

7. The work of critically examining all stage plays in their written form, and of witnessing their performance in order to see that the sense is not altered by the stage business, would, even if it were divided among so many officials as to be physically possible, be mentally impossible to persons of taste and enlightenment.

8. Regulation of theatres is an entirely different matter from censorship, inasmuch as a theatre, being not only a stage, but a place licensed for the sale of spirits, and a public resort capable of being put to disorderly use, and needing special provision for the safety of audiences in cases of fire, etc., cannot be abandoned wholly to private control, and may therefore reasonably be made subject to an annual licence like those now required before allowing premises to be used publicly for music and dancing.

9. In order to prevent the powers of the licensing authority being abused so as to constitute a virtual censorship, any Act transferring the theatres to the control of a licensing authority should be made also a charter of the rights of dramatic authors and managers by the following provisions:

A. The public prosecutor (the Attorney-General) alone should have the right to set the law in operation against the manager of a theatre or the author of a play in respect of the character of the play or entertainment.

B. No disclosure of the particulars of a theatrical entertainment shall be required before performance.

C. Licences shall not be withheld on the ground that the existence of theatres is dangerous to religion and morals, or on the ground that any entertainment given or contemplated is heretical or immoral.

D. The licensing area shall be no less than that of a County Council or City Corporation, which shall not delegate its licensing powers to any minor local authority or to any official or committee; it shall decide all questions affecting the existence of a theatrical licence by vote of the entire body; managers, lessees, and proprietors of theatres shall have the right to plead, in person or by counsel, against a proposal to withhold a licence; and the licence shall not be withheld except for stated reasons, the validity of which shall be subject to the judgment of the high courts.

E. The annual licence, once granted, shall not be cancelled or suspended unless the manager has been convicted by public prosecution of an offence against the ordinary laws against disorderly housekeeping, indecency, blasphemy, etc., except in cases where some structural or sanitary defect in the building necessitates immediate action for the protection of the public against physical injury.

F. No licence shall be refused on the ground that the proximity of the theatre to a church, mission hall, school, or other place of worship, edification, instruction, or entertainment (including another theatre) would draw the public away from such places into its own doors.

PREFACE RESUMED

Mr George Alexander's Protest

On the facts mentioned in the foregoing statement, and in my evidence before the Joint Select Committee, no controversy arose except on one point. Mr George Alexander protested vigorously and indignantly against my admission that theatres, like public-houses, need special control on the ground that they can profit by disorder, and are sometimes conducted with that end in view. Now, Mr Alexander is a famous actor-manager; and it is very difficult to persuade the public that the more famous an actor-manager is the less he is likely to know about any theatre except his own. When the Committee of 1892 reported, I was considered guilty of a perverse paradox when I said that the witness who knew least about the theatre was Henry Irving. Yet a moment's consideration would have shewn that the paradox was a platitude. For about quarter of a century Irving was confined night after night to his own theatre and his own dressingroom, never seeing a play even there because he was himself part of the play; producing the works of long departed authors; and, to the extent to which his talent was extraordinary, necessarily making his theatre unlike any other theatre. When he went to the provinces or to America, the theatres to which he went were swept and garnished for him, and their staffs replaced—as far as he came in contact with them—by his own lieutenants. In the end, there was hardly a first-nighter in his gallery who did not know more about the London theatres and the progress of dramatic art than he; and as to the provinces, if any chief constable had told him the real history and character of many provincial theatres, he would have denounced that chief constable as an ignorant libeller of a noble profession. But the constable would have been right for all that. Now if this was true of Sir Henry Irving, who did not become a London manager until he had roughed it for years in the provinces, how much more true must it be of, say, Mr George Alexander, whose successful march through his profession has passed as far from the purlieus of our theatrical world as the king's naval career from the Isle of Dogs [an area in East London on the north bank of the Thames]? The moment we come to that necessary part of the censorship question which deals with the control of theatres from the point of view of those who know how much money can be made out of them by managers who seek to make the auditorium attractive rather than the stage, you find the managers divided into two sections. The first section consists of honorable and successful managers like Mr Alexander, who know nothing of such abuses, and deny, with perfect sincerity and indignant vehemence, that they exist except, perhaps, in certain notorious variety theatres. The other is the silent section which knows better, but is very well content to be publicly defended and privately amused by Mr Alexander's innocence. To accept a West End manager as an expert in theatres because he is an actor is much as if we were to accept the organist of St Paul's Cathedral as an expert on music halls because he is a musician. The real experts are all in the conspiracy to keep the police out of the theatre. And they are so successful that even the police do not know as much as they should.

The police should have been examined by the Committee, and the whole question of the extent to which theatres are disorderly houses in disguise sifted to the bottom. For it is on this point that we discover behind the phantoms of the corrupt dramatists who are restrained by the censorship from debauching the stage, the reality of the corrupt managers and theatre proprietors who actually do debauch it without let or hindrance from the censorship. The whole case for giving control over theatres to local authorities rests on this reality.

ELIZA AND HER BATH

The persistent notion that a theatre is an Alsatia[23] where the king's writ does not run, and where any wickedness is possible in the absence of a special tribunal and a special police, was brought out by an innocent remark made by Sir William Gilbert, who, when giving evidence before the Committee, was asked by Colonel Lockwood whether a law sufficient to restrain impropriety in books would also restrain impropriety in plays. Sir William replied: "I should say there is a very wide distinction between what is read and what is seen. In a novel one may read that 'Eliza stripped off her dressing-gown and stepped into her bath' without any harm; but I think if that were presented on the stage it would be shocking." All the stupid and inconsiderate people seized eagerly on this illustration as if it were a successful attempt to prove that without a censorship we should be unable to prevent actresses from appearing naked on the stage. As a matter of fact, if an actress could be persuaded to do such a thing (and it would be about as easy to persuade a bishop's wife to appear in church in the same condition) the police would simply arrest her on a charge of indecent exposure. The extent to which this obvious safeguard was overlooked may be taken as a measure of the thoughtlessness and frivolity of the excuses made for the censorship. It should be added that the artistic representation of a bath, with every suggestion of nakedness that the law as to decency allows, is one of the most familiar subjects of scenic art. From the Rhine maidens in Wagner's Trilogy, and the bathers in the second act of

23. A locality, whose name first occurs in the plays of Thomas Shadwell, in the White Friars section of London between Fleet Street and the Thames. As arrest in the locality was possible only under a writ of the Lord Chief Justice, Alsatia became a popular haunt of criminals resisting arrest, until an Act in 1697 put an end to the alleged privileges.

[Meyerbeer's] Les Huguenots, to the ballets of water nymphs in our Christmas pantomimes and at our variety theatres, the sound hygienic propaganda of the bath, and the charm of the undraped human figure, are exploited without offence on the stage to an extent never dreamt of by any novelist.

A KING'S PROCTOR

Another hare was started by Professor Gilbert Murray and Mr Laurence Housman, who, in pure kindness to the managers, asked whether it would not be possible to establish for their assistance a sort of King's Proctor to whom plays might be referred for an official legal opinion as to their compliance with the law before production. There are several objections to this proposal; and they may as well be stated in case the proposal should be revived. In the first place, no lawyer with the most elementary knowledge of the law of libel in its various applications to sedition, obscenity, and blasphemy, could answer for the consequences of producing any play whatsoever as to which the smallest question could arise in the mind of any sane person. I have been a critic and an author in active service for thirty years; and though nothing I have written has ever been prosecuted in England or made the subject of legal proceedings, yet I have never published in my life an article, a play, or a book, as to which, if I had taken legal advice, an expert could have assured me that I was proof against prosecution or against an action for damages by the persons criticized. No doubt a sensible solicitor might have advised me that the risk was no greater than all men have to take in dangerous trades; but such an opinion, though it may encourage a client, does not protect him. For example, if a publisher asks his solicitor whether he may venture on an edition of Sterne's Sentimental Journey, or a manager whether he may produce King Lear without risk of prosecution, the solicitor will advise him to go ahead. But if the solicitor or counsel consulted by him were asked for a guarantee that neither of these works was a libel, he would have to reply that he could give no such guarantee; that, on the contrary, it was his duty to warn his client that both of them are obscene libels; that King Lear, containing as it does perhaps the most appalling blasphemy that despair ever uttered,[24] is a blasphemous libel, and that it is doubtful whether it could not be construed

24. Presumably the passage is: 'As flies to wanton boys, are we to th' gods, / They kill us for their sport' (*Lear*, IV: i).

as a seditious libel as well. As to Ibsen's Brand (the play which made him popular with the most earnestly religious people) no sane solicitor would advise his client even to chance it except in a broadly cultivated and tolerant (or indifferent) modern city. The lighter plays would be no better off. What lawyer could accept any responsibility for the production of Sardou's Divorçons or Clyde Fitch's The Woman in the Case?[25] Put the proposed King's Proctor in operation tomorrow; and what will be the result? The managers will find that instead of insuring them as the Lord Chamberlain does, he will warn them that every play they submit to him is vulnerable to the law, and that they must produce it not only on the ordinary risk of acting on their own responsibility, but at the very grave additional risk of doing so in the teeth of an official warning. Under such circumstances, what manager would resort a second time to the Proctor; and how would the Proctor live without fees, unless indeed the Government gave him a salary for doing nothing? The institution would not last a year, except as a job for somebody.

Counsel's Opinion

The proposal is still less plausible when it is considered that at present, without any new legislation at all, any manager who is doubtful about a play can obtain the advice of his solicitor, or Counsel's opinion, if he thinks it will be of any service to him. The verdict of the proposed King's Proctor would be nothing but Counsel's opinion without the liberty of choice of Counsel, possibly cheapened, but sure to be adverse; for an official cannot give practical advice as a friend and a man of the world; he must stick to the letter of the law and take no chances. And as far as the law is concerned, journalism, literature, and the drama exist only by custom or sufferance.

Wanted: A New Magna Charta

This leads us to a very vital question. Is it not possible to amend the law so as to make it possible for a lawyer to advise his client that he may publish the works of Blake, Zola, and Swinburne, or produce the plays of

25. American playwright specializing in society drama. *The Woman in the Case* had just been produced in London, 2 June 1909.

Ibsen and Mr Granville Barker, or print an ordinary criticism in his newspaper, without the possibility of finding himself in prison, or mulcted in damages and costs in consequence? No doubt it is; but only by a declaration of constitutional right to blaspheme, rebel, and deal with tabooed subjects. Such a declaration is not just now within the scope of practical politics, although we are compelled to act to a great extent as if it was actually part of the constitution. All that can be done is to take my advice and limit the necessary public control of the theatres in such a manner as to prevent its being abused as a censorship. We have ready to our hand the machinery of licensing as applied to public-houses. A licensed victualler can now be assured confidently by his lawyer that a magistrate cannot refuse to renew his licence on the ground that he (the magistrate) is a teetotaller and has seen too much of the evil of drink to sanction its sale. The magistrate must give a judicial reason for his refusal, meaning really a constitutional reason; and his teetotalism is not such a reason. In the same way you can protect a theatrical manager by ruling out certain reasons as unconstitutional, as suggested in my statement. Combine this with the abolition of the common informer's power to initiate proceedings; and you will have gone as far as seems possible at present. You will have local control of the theatres for police purposes and sanitary purposes without censorship; and I do not see what more is possible until we get a formal Magna Charta declaring all the categories of libel and the blasphemy laws contrary to public liberty, and repealing and defining accordingly.

Proposed: A New Star Chamber

Yet we cannot mention Magna Charta without recalling how useless such documents are to a nation which has no more political comprehension nor political virtue than King John. When Henry VII calmly proceeded to tear up Magna Charta by establishing the Star Chamber (a criminal court consisting of a committee of the Privy Council without a jury) nobody objected until, about a century and a half later, the Star Chamber began cutting off the ears of eminent Nonconformist divines and standing them in the pillory; and then the Nonconformists, and nobody else, abolished the Star Chamber. And if anyone doubts that we are quite ready to establish the Star Chamber again, let him read the Report of the Joint Select Committee, on which I now venture to offer a few criticisms.

The report of the Committee, which will be found in the bluebook, should be read with attention and respect as far as page x, up to which point it is an able and well-written statement of the case. From page x onward, when it goes on from diagnosing the disease to prescribing the treatment, it should be read with even greater attention but with no respect whatever, as the main object of the treatment is to conciliate the How Not To Do It majority. It contains, however, one very notable proposal, the same being nothing more nor less than to revive the Star Chamber for the purpose of dealing with heretical or seditious plays and their authors, and indeed with all charges against theatrical entertainments except common police cases of indecency. The reason given is that for which the Star Chamber was created by Henry VII: that is, the inadequacy of the ordinary law. "We consider," says the report, "that the law which prevents or punishes indecency, blasphemy and libel in printed publications" (it does not, by the way, except in the crudest police cases) "would not be adequate for the control of the drama." Therefor a committee of the Privy Council is to be empowered to suppress plays and punish managers and authors at its pleasure, on the motion of the Attorney-General, without a jury. The members of the Committee will, of course, be men of high standing and character: otherwise they would not be on the Privy Council. That is to say, they will have all the qualifications of Archbishop Laud.[26]

Now I have no guarantee that any member of the majority of the Joint Select Committee ever heard of the Star Chamber or of Archbishop Laud. One of them did not know that politics meant anything more than party electioneering. Nothing is more alarming than the ignorance of our public men of the commonplaces of our history, and their consequent readiness to repeat experiments which have in the past produced national catastrophes. At all events, whether they knew what they were doing or not, there can be no question as to what they did. They proposed virtually that the Act of the Long Parliament in 1641 shall be repealed, and the Star Chamber re-established, in order that playwrights and managers may be punished for unspecified offences unknown to the law. When I say unspecified, I should say specified as follows (see page xi of the report) in the case of a play:—

(*a*) To be indecent.

(*b*) To contain offensive personalities.

(*c*) To represent on the stage in an invidious manner a living person, or any person recently dead.

(*d*) To do violence to the sentiment of religious reverence.

26. William Laud, who became Archbishop of Canterbury in 1633, dedicated to absolutism in Church and State, was a resolute opponent of Puritanism and sought to extirpate Calvinism in England and Presbyterianism in Scotland.

(*e*) To be calculated to conduce to vice or crime.

(*f*) To be calculated to impair friendly relations with any foreign power.

(*g*) To be calculated to cause a breach of the peace.

Now it is clear that there is no play yet written, or possible to be written, in this world, that might not be condemned under one or other of these heads. How any sane man, not being a professed enemy of public liberty, could put his hand to so monstrous a catalogue passes my understanding. Had a comparatively definite and innocent clause been added forbidding the affirmation or denial of the doctrine of Transubstantiation, the country would have been up in arms at once. Lord Ribblesdale made an effort to reduce the seven categories to the old formula "not to be fitting for the preservation of good manners, decorum, or the public peace"; but this proposal was not carried; whilst on Lord Gorell's motion a final widening of the net was achieved by adding the phrase "to be calculated to"; so that even if a play does not produce any of the results feared, the author can still be punished on the ground that his play is "calculated" to produce them. I have no hesitation in saying that a committee capable of such an outrageous display of thoughtlessness and historical ignorance as this paragraph of its report implies deserves to be haled before the tribunal it has itself proposed, and dealt with under a general clause levelled at conduct "calculated to" overthrow the liberties of England.

POSSIBILITIES OF THE PROPOSAL

Still, though I am certainly not willing to give Lord Gorell the chance of seeing me in the pillory with my ears cut off if I can help it, I daresay many authors would rather take their chance with a Star Chamber than with a jury, just as some soldiers would rather take their chance with a court-martial than at Quarter Sessions.[27] For that matter, some of them would rather take their chance with the Lord Chamberlain than with either. And though this is no reason for depriving the whole body of authors of the benefit of Magna Charta, still, if the right of the proprietor of a play to refuse the good offices of the Privy Council and to perform the play until his accusers had indicted him at law, and obtained the verdict of a jury against him, were sufficiently guarded, the proposed Committee might be set up and used for certain purposes. For instance, it might be made a condition of the intervention of the Attorney-General or the Director of

27. A local court with limited jurisdiction, which sits quarterly.

Public Prosecutions that he should refer an accused play to the Committee, and obtain their sanction before taking action, offering the proprietor of the play, if the Committee thought fit, an opportunity of voluntarily accepting trial by the Committee as an alternative to prosecution in the ordinary course of law. But the Committee should have no powers of punishment beyond the power (formidable enough) of suspending performances of the play. If it thought that additional punishment was called for, it could order a prosecution without allowing the proprietor or author of the play the alternative of a trial by itself. The author of the play should be made a party to all proceedings of the Committee, and have the right to defend himself in person or by counsel. This would provide a check on the Attorney-General (who might be as bigoted as any of the municipal aldermen who are so much dreaded by the actor-managers) without enabling the Committee to abuse its powers for party, class, or sectarian ends beyond that irreducible minimum of abuse which a popular jury would endorse, for which minimum there is no remedy.

But when everything is said for the Star Chamber that can be said, and every precaution taken to secure to those whom it pursues the alternative of trial by jury, the expedient still remains a very questionable one, to be endured for the sake of its protective rather than its repressive powers. It should abolish the present quaint toleration of rioting in theatres. For example, if it is to be an offence to perform a play which the proposed new Committee shall condemn, it should also be made an offence to disturb a performance which the Committee has not condemned. "Brawling" at a theatre should be dealt with as severely as brawling in church if the censorship is to be taken out of the hands of the public. At present Jenny Geddes[28] may throw her stool at the head of a playwright who preaches unpalatable doctrine to her, or rather, since her stool is a fixture, she may hiss and hoot and make it impossible to proceed with the performance, even although nobody has compelled her to come to the theatre or suspended her liberty to stay away, and although she has no claim on an unendowed theatre for her spiritual necessities, as she has on her parish church. If mob censorship cannot be trusted to keep naughty playwrights in order, still less can it be trusted to keep the pioneers of thought in countenance; and I submit that anyone hissing a play permitted by the new censorship should be guilty of contempt of court.

28. Reputed to have originated an Edinburgh riot (1637) by throwing her folding stool at the officiating bishop in St Giles's Church as a protest against the introduction of English liturgy into Scotland.

STAR CHAMBER SENTIMENTALITY

But what is most to be dreaded in a Star Chamber is not its sternness but its sentimentality. There is no worse censorship than one which considers only the feelings of the spectators, except perhaps one which considers the feelings of people who do not even witness the performance. Take the case of the Passion Play at Oberammergau. The offence given by a representation of the Crucifixion on the stage is not bounded by frontiers: further, it is an offence of which the voluntary spectators are guilty no less than the actors. If it is to be tolerated at all: if we are not to make war on the German Empire for permitting it, nor punish the English people who go to Bavaria to see it and thereby endow it with English money, we may as well tolerate it in London, where nobody need go to see it except those who are not offended by it. When Wagner's Parsifal becomes available for representation in London,[29] many people will be sincerely horrified when the miracle of the Mass is simulated on the stage of Covent Garden, and the Holy Ghost descends in the form of a dove. But if the Committee of the Privy Council, or the Lord Chamberlain, or anyone else, were to attempt to keep Parsifal from us to spare the feelings of these people, it would not be long before even the most thoughtless champions of the censorship would see that the principle of doing nothing that could shock anybody had reduced itself to absurdity. No quarter whatever should be given to the bigotry of people so unfit for social life as to insist not only that their own prejudices and superstitions should have the fullest toleration but that everybody else should be compelled to think and act as they do. Every service in St Paul's Cathedral is an outrage to the opinions of the congregation of the Roman Catholic Cathedral of Westminster. Every Liberal meeting is a defiance and a challenge to the most cherished opinions of the Unionists. A law to compel the Roman Catholics to attend service at St Paul's, or the Liberals to attend the meetings of the Primrose League would be resented as an insufferable tyranny. But a law to shut up both St Paul's and the Westminster Cathedral, and to put down political meetings and associations because of the offence given by them to many worthy and excellent people, would be a far worse tyranny, because it would kill the

---

29. It was at this time proscribed by the British censorship as a blasphemous representation of a sacred subject. The opera was, however, licensed a few years later, when Shaw (as indicated in his pocket diary) apparently attended performances of it on 4 and 12 February and on 4 March 1914.

religious and political life of the country outright, whereas to compel people to attend the services and meetings of their opponents would greatly enlarge their minds, and would actually be a good thing if it were enforced all round. I should not object to a law to compel everybody to read two newspapers, each violently opposed to the other in politics; but to forbid us to read newspapers at all would be to maim us mentally and cashier our country in the ranks of civilization. I deny that anybody has the right to demand more from me, over and above lawful conduct in a general sense, than liberty to stay away from the theatre in which my plays are represented. If he is unfortunate enough to have a religion so petty that it can be insulted (any man is as welcome to insult my religion, if he can, as he is to insult the universe) I claim the right to insult it to my heart's content, if I choose, provided I do not compel him to come and hear me. If I think this country ought to make war on any other country, then, so long as war remains lawful, I claim full liberty to write and perform a play inciting the country to that war without interference from the ambassadors of the menaced country. I may "give pain to many worthy people, and pleasure to none," as the Censor's pet phrase puts it: I may even make Europe a cockpit and Asia a shambles: no matter: if preachers and politicians, statesmen and soldiers, may do these things—if it is right that such things should be done, then I claim my share in the right to do them. If the proposed Committee is meant to prevent me from doing these things whilst men of other professions are permitted to do them, then I protest with all my might against the formation of such a Committee. If it is to protect me, on the contrary, against the attacks that bigots and corrupt pornographers may make on me by appealing to the ignorance and prejudices of common jurors, then I welcome it; but is that really the object of its proposers? And if it is, what guarantee have I that the new tribunal will not presently resolve into a mere committee to avoid unpleasantness and keep the stage "in good taste"? It is no more possible for me to do my work honestly as a playwright without giving pain than it is for a dentist. The nation's morals are like its teeth: the more decayed they are the more it hurts to touch them. Prevent dentists and dramatists from giving pain, and not only will our morals become as carious as our teeth, but toothache and the plagues that follow neglected morality will presently cause more agony than all the dentists and dramatists at their worst have caused since the world began.

ANYTHING FOR A QUIET LIFE

Another doubt: would a Committee of the Privy Council really face the risks that must be taken by all communities as the price of our freedom to evolve? Would it not rather take the popular English view that freedom and virtue generally are sweet and desirable only when they cost nothing? Nothing worth having is to be had without risk. A mother risks her child's life every time she lets it ramble through the countryside, or cross the street, or clamber over the rocks on the shore by itself. A father risks his son's morals when he gives him a latchkey. The members of the Joint Select Committee risked my producing a revolver and shooting them when they admitted me to the room without having me handcuffed. And these risks are no unreal ones. Every day some child is maimed or drowned and some young man infected with disease; and political assassinations have been appallingly frequent of late years. Railway travelling has its risks; motoring has its risks; aeroplaning has its risks; every advance we make costs us a risk of some sort. And though these are only risks to the individual, to the community they are certainties. It is not certain that I will be killed this year in a railway accident; but it is certain that somebody will. The invention of printing and the freedom of the press have brought upon us, not merely risks of their abuse, but the establishment as part of our social routine of some of the worst evils a community can suffer from. People who realize these evils shriek for the suppression of motor cars, the virtual imprisonment and enslavement of the young, the passing of Press Laws (especially in Egypt, India, and Ireland), exactly as they shriek for a censorship of the stage. The freedom of the stage will be abused just as certainly as the complaisance and innocence of the censorship is abused at present. It will also be used by writers like myself for raising very difficult and disturbing questions, social, political, and religious, at moments which may be extremely inconvenient to the government. Is it certain that a Committee of the Privy Council would stand up to all this as the price of liberty? I doubt it. If I am to be at the mercy of a nice amiable Committee of elderly gentlemen (I know all about elderly gentlemen, being one myself) whose motto is the highly popular one, "Anything for a quiet life," and who will make the inevitable abuses of freedom by our blackguards an excuse for interfering with any disquieting use of it by myself, then I shall be worse off than I am with the Lord Chamberlain, whose mind is not broad enough to obstruct the whole range of thought. If it were, he would be given a more difficult post.

Shall the Examiner of Plays Starve?

And here I may be reminded that if I prefer the Lord Chamberlain I can go to the Lord Chamberlain, who is to retain all his present functions for the benefit of those who prefer to be judged by him. But I am not so sure that the Lord Chamberlain will be able to exercise those functions for long if resort to him is to be optional. Let me be kinder to him than he has been to me, and uncover for him the pitfalls which the Joint Select Committee have dug (and concealed) in his path. Consider how the voluntary system must inevitably work. The Joint Select Committee expressly urges that the Lord Chamberlain's licence must not be a bar to a prosecution. Granted that in spite of this reservation the licence would prove in future as powerful a defence as it has been in the past, yet the voluntary clause nevertheless places the manager at the mercy of any author who makes it a condition of his contract that his play shall not be submitted for licence. I should probably take that course without opposition from the manager. For the manager, knowing that three of my plays have been refused a licence, and that it would be far safer to produce a play for which no licence had been asked than one for which it had been asked and refused, would agree that it was more prudent, in my case, to avail himself of the power of dispensing with the Lord Chamberlain's licence. But now mark the consequences. The manager, having thus discovered that his best policy was to dispense with the licence in the few doubtful cases, would presently ask himself why he should spend two guineas each on licences for the many plays as to which no question could conceivably arise. What risk does any manager run in producing such works as [Pinero's] Sweet Lavender, Peter Pan, [H. A. Jones's and Henry Herman's melodrama] The Silver King, or any of the 99 per cent of plays that are equally neutral on controversial questions. Does anyone seriously believe that the managers would continue to pay the Lord Chamberlain two guineas a play out of mere love and loyalty, only to create an additional risk in the case of controversial plays, and to guard against risks that do not exist in the case of the great bulk of other productions? Only those would remain faithful to him who produce such plays as the Select Committee began by discussing *in camera*, and ended by refusing to discuss at all because they were too nasty. These people would still try to get a licence, and would still no doubt succeed as they do today. But could the King's Reader of Plays live on his fees from these plays alone; and if he could how long would his post survive the discredit of licensing only pornographic plays? It is clear to me that the Examiner would be starved out of existence, and the censorship perish of desuetude. Perhaps that is exactly what the Select Committee contemplated. If so, I have nothing more to say, except that I think sudden death would be more merciful.

LORD GORELL'S AWAKENING

In the meantime, conceive the situation which would arise if a licensed play were prosecuted. To make it clearer, let us imagine any other offender—say a company promoter with a fraudulent prospectus—pleading in Court that he had induced the Lord Chamberlain to issue a certificate that the prospectus contained nothing objectionable, and that on the strength of that certificate he issued it; also, that by law the Court could do nothing to him except order him to wind up his company. Some such vision as this must have come to Lord Gorell when he at last grappled seriously with the problem. Mr Harcourt seized the opportunity to make a last rally. He seconded Lord Gorell's proposal that the Committee should admit that its scheme of an optional censorship was an elaborate absurdity, and report that all censorship before production was out of the question. But it was too late: the *volte face* [about face] was too sudden and complete. It was Lord Gorell whose vote had turned the close division which took place on the question of receiving my statement. It was Lord Gorell without whose countenance and authority the farce of the books could never have been performed. Yet here was Lord Gorell, after assenting to all the provisions for the optional censorship paragraph by paragraph, suddenly informing his colleagues that they had been wrong all through and that I had been right all through, and inviting them to scrap half their work and adopt my conclusion. No wonder Lord Gorell got only one vote: that of Mr Harcourt. But the incident is not the less significant. Lord Gorell carried more weight than any other member of the Committee on the legal and constitutional aspect of the question. Had he begun where he left off—had he at the outset put down his foot on the notion that an optional penal law could ever be anything but a gross contradiction in terms, that part of the Committee's proposals would never have come into existence.

JUDGES: THEIR PROFESSIONAL LIMITATIONS

I do not, however, appeal to Lord Gorell's judgment on all points. It is inevitable that a judge should be deeply impressed by his professional experience with a sense of the impotence of judges and laws and courts to deal satisfactorily with evils which are so Protean and elusive as to defy definition, and which yet seem to present quite simple problems to the common sense of men of the world. You have only to imagine the Privy Council as consisting of men of the world highly endowed with common sense, to persuade yourself that the supplementing of the law by the common sense of the Privy Council would settle the whole difficulty. But no man knows what he means by common sense, though every man can tell you that it is very uncommon, even in Privy Councils. And since every ploughman is a man of the world, it is evident that even the phrase itself does not mean what it says. As a matter of fact, it means in ordinary use simply a man who will not make himself disagreeable for the sake of a principle: just the sort of man who should never be allowed to meddle with political rights. Now to a judge a political right, that is, a dogma which is above our laws and conditions our laws, instead of being subject to them, is anarchic and abhorrent. That is why I trust Lord Gorell when he is defending the integrity of the law against the proposal to make it in any sense optional, whilst I very strongly mistrust him, as I mistrust all professional judges, when political rights are in danger.

CONCLUSION

I must conclude by recommending the Government to take my advice wherever it conflicts with that of the Joint Select Committee. It is, I think, obviously more deeply considered and better informed, though I say it that should not. At all events, I have given my reasons; and at that I must leave it. As the tradition which makes Malvolio [in *Twelfth Night*] not only Master of the Revels but Master of the Mind of England, and which has come down to us from Henry VIII, is manifestly doomed to the dustbin, the sooner it goes there the better; for the democratic control which naturally succeeds it can easily be limited so as to prevent it becoming either a censorship or a tyranny. The Examiner of Plays should receive a generous pension, and be set free to practise privately as an expert adviser of theatrical managers. There is no reason why they should be deprived of the counsel they so highly value.

It only remains to say that public performances of The Shewing-up of Blanco Posnet are still prohibited in Great Britain by the Lord Chamberlain. An attempt was made to prevent even its performance in Ireland by some indiscreet Castle officials in the absence of the Lord Lieutenant. This attempt gave extraordinary publicity to the production of the play; and every possible effort was made to persuade the Irish public that the performance would be an outrage to their religion, and to provoke a repetition of the rioting that attended the first performances of Synge's Playboy of the Western World before the most sensitive and, on provocation, the most turbulent audience in the kingdom. The directors of the Irish National [Abbey] Theatre, Lady Gregory and Mr William Butler Yeats, rose to the occasion with inspiriting courage. I am a conciliatory person, and was willing, as I always am, to make every concession in return for having my own way. But Lady Gregory and Mr Yeats not only would not yield an inch, but insisted, within the due limits of gallant warfare, on taking the field with every circumstance of defiance, and winning the battle with every trophy of victory. Their triumph was as complete as they could have desired. The performance [25 August 1909] exhausted the possibilities of success, and provoked no murmur, though it inspired several approving sermons. Later on, Lady Gregory and Mr Yeats brought the play to London and performed it under the Lord Chamberlain's nose, through the instrumentality of the Stage Society.[30]

After this, the play was again submitted to the Lord Chamberlain. But, though beaten, he, too, understands the art of How Not To Do It. He licensed the play, but endorsed on his licence the condition that all the passages which implicated God in the history of Blanco Posnet must be omitted in representation. All the coarseness, the profligacy, the prostitution, the violence, the drinking-bar humor into which the light shines in the play are licensed, but the light itself is extinguished. I need hardly say that I have not availed myself of this licence, and do not intend to.[31] There is enough licensed darkness in our theatres today without my adding to it.

AYOT ST LAWRENCE.
14 July 1910.

POSTSCRIPT.—Since the above was written the Lord Chamberlain has made an attempt to evade his responsibility and perhaps to postpone his doom by appointing [in October 1910] an advisory committee, unknown

---

30. The Irish Players (Abbey Theatre Company) were later to give four public performances in 1916 in Liverpool, this being, paradoxically, outside the jurisdiction of the Lord Chamberlain.
31. The play was not licensed for public performance in London in its unexpurgated state until 1924.

to the law, on which he will presumably throw any odium that may attach to refusals of licences in the future. This strange and lawless body will hardly reassure our moralists, who object much more to the plays he licenses than to those he suppresses, and are therefore unmoved by his plea that his refusals are few and far between. It consists of two eminent actors (one retired), an Oxford professor of literature, and two eminent barristers.[32] As their assembly is neither created by statute nor sanctioned by custom, it is difficult to know what to call it until it advises the Lord Chamberlain to deprive some author of his means of livelihood, when it will, I presume, become a conspiracy, and be indictable accordingly; unless, indeed, it can persuade the Courts to recognize it as a new Estate of the Realm, created by the Lord Chamberlain. This constitutional position is so questionable that I strongly advise the members to resign promptly before the Lord Chamberlain gets them into trouble.

32. The actors were Sir Squire Bancroft (retired 1885) and Sir John Hare. The Oxford don was the critic and essayist Professor Walter Raleigh. The barristers were Sir Edward Carson, KC, MP, and Stanley Buckmaster, KC, MP (future Solicitor-General and Lord Chancellor).

Three Plays by Brieux

Preface to a collection of Brieux's plays (in English translation), 1911

=====

From Molière to Brieux

After the death of Ibsen, Brieux confronted Europe as the most important dramatist west of Russia. In that kind of comedy which is so true to life that we have to call it tragi-comedy, and which is not only an entertainment but a history and a criticism of contemporary morals, he is incomparably the greatest writer France has produced since Molière. The French critics who take it for granted that no contemporary of theirs could possibly be greater than Beaumarchais are really too modest. They have never read Beaumarchais, and therefore do not know how very little of him there is to read, and how, out of the two variations he wrote on his once famous theme [*The Barber of Seville*, 1770, and *The Marriage of Figaro*, 1780], the second is only a petition in artistic and intellectual bankruptcy. Had the French theatre been capable of offering a field to Balzac, my proposition might have to be modified. But as it was no more able to do that than the English theatre was to enlist the genius of Dickens, I may say confidently that in that great comedy which Balzac called "the comedy of humanity,"[1] to be played for the amusement of the gods rather than for that of the French public, there is no summit in the barren plain that stretches from Mount Molière to our own times until we reach Brieux.

How the XIX Century found itself out

It is reserved for some great critic to give us a study of the psychology of the nineteenth century. Those of us who as adults saw it face to face in that last moiety of its days when one fierce hand after another—Marx's, Zola's, Ibsen's, Strindberg's, Turgenieff's, Tolstoy's—stripped its masks off and revealed it as, on the whole, perhaps the most villainous page of recorded human history, can also recall the strange confidence with which it regarded

1. Balzac's series of interrelated novels and stories is titled *La Comédie humaine*.

itself as the very summit of civilization, and talked of the past as a cruel gloom that had been dispelled for ever by the railway and the electric telegraph. But centuries, like men, begin to find themselves out in middle age. The youthful conceit of the XIX had a splendid exponent in Macaulay, and, for a time, a gloriously jolly one during the nonage of Dickens. There was certainly nothing morbid in the air then: Dickens and Macaulay are as free from morbidity as Dumas *père* and [François] Guizot.[2] Even Stendhal [Henri Beyle] and Prosper Mérimée, though by no means burgess optimists, are quite sane. When you come to Zola and Maupassant, Flaubert and the Goncourts,[3] to Ibsen and Strindberg, to Aubrey Beardsley and George Moore, to D'Annunzio and [Spanish dramatist José] Echegaray, you are in a new and morbid atmosphere. French literature up to the middle of the XIX century was still all of one piece with Rabelais, Montaigne and Molière. Zola breaks that tradition completely: he is as different as Karl Marx from Turgot or Darwin from [Georges] Cuvier.[4]

In this new phase we see the bourgeoisie, after a century and a half of complacent vaunting of its own probity and modest happiness (begun by Daniel Defoe in Robinson Crusoe's praises of "the middle station of life"), suddenly turning bitterly on itself with accusations of hideous sexual and commercial corruption. Thackeray's campaign against snobbery and Dickens's against hypocrisy were directed against the vices of respectable men; but now even the respectability was passionately denied: the bourgeois was depicted as a thief, a tyrant, a sweater, a selfish voluptuary whose marriages were simple legalizations of unbridled licentiousness. Sexual irregularities began to be attributed to the sympathetic characters in fiction not as the blackest spots in their portraits, but positively as redeeming humanities in them.

JACK THE RIPPER

I am by no means going here either to revive the old outcry against this school of iconoclasts and disillusioners, or to join the new reaction against it. It told the world many truths: it brought romance back to its senses. Its

2. French politician and historian, author of *Mémoires pour servir à l'histoire de mon temps* (1858–67).
3. Edmond Goncourt and his brother Jules wrote collaborative fiction.
4. French naturalist, considered to be the founder of comparative anatomy and of paleontology.

very repudiation of the graces and enchantments of fine art was necessary; for the artistic morbidezza of Byron and Victor Hugo was too imaginative to allow the Victorian bourgeoisie to accept them as chroniclers of real facts and real people. The justification of Zola's comparative coarseness is that his work could not have been done in any other way. If Zola had had a sense of humor, or a great artist's delight in playing with his ideas, his materials, and his readers, he would have become either as unreadable to the very people he came to wake up as Anatole France is, or as incredible as Victor Hugo was. He would also have incurred the mistrust and hatred of the majority of Frenchmen, who, like the majority of men of all nations, are not merely incapable of fine art, but resent it furiously. A wit is to them a man who is laughing at them: an artist is a man of loose character who lives by telling lying stories and pandering to the voluptuous passions. What they like to read is the police intelligence, especially the murder cases and divorce cases. The invented murders and divorces of the novelists and playwrights do not satisfy them, because they cannot believe in them; and belief that the horror or scandal actually occurred, that real people are shedding real blood and real tears, is indispensable to their enjoyment. To produce this belief by works of fiction, the writer must disguise and even discard the arts of the man of letters and assume the style of the descriptive reporter of the criminal courts. As an example of how to cater for such readers, we may take Zola's Bête Humaine. It is in all its essentials a simple and touching story, like [Abbé] Prévost's Manon Lescaut. But into it Zola has violently thrust the greatest police sensation of the XIX century: the episode of Jack the Ripper.[5] Jack's hideous neurosis is no more a part of human nature than Cæsar's epilepsy or Gladstone's missing finger. One is tempted to accuse Zola of having borrowed it from the newspapers to please his customers just as Shakespear used to borrow stories of murder and jealousy from the tales and chronicles of his time, and heap them on the head of convivial humorists like Iago and Richard III, or gentle poets like Macbeth and Hamlet. Without such allurements, Shakespear could not have lived by his plays. And if he had been rich enough to disregard this consideration, he would still have had to provide sensation enough to induce people to listen to what he was inspired to say. It is only the man who has no message who is too fastidious to beat the drum at the door of his booth.

5. Unidentified perpetrator of several gruesome murders of women in the Whitechapel (East End) district of London, August–November 1888.

RISE OF THE SCIENTIFIC SPIRIT

Still, the Shakespearean murders were romantic murders: the Zolaesque ones were police reports. The old mad heroines, the Ophelias and Lucies of Lammermoor, were rhapsodists with flowers in their hands: the new ones were clinical studies of mental disease. The new note was as conspicuous in the sensational chapters as in the dull chapters, of which there were many. This was the punishment of the middle class for hypocrisy. It had carried the conspiracy of silence which we call decorum to such lengths that when young men discovered the suppressed truths, they felt bound to shout them in the streets. I well remember how when I was a youth in my teens I happened to obtain access to the papers of an Irish crown solicitor through a colleague who had some clerical work to do upon them. The county concerned was not one of the crimeless counties: there was a large camp in it; and the soldier of that day was not the respectable, rather pious, and very low-spirited youth who now makes the King's uniform what the curate's black coat was then. There were not only cases which were tried and not reported: there were cases which could not even be tried, the offenders having secured impunity by pushing their follies to lengths too grotesque to be bearable even in a criminal court—also because of the silly ferocity of the law, which punished the negligible indecencies of drunken young soldiers as atrocious crimes. The effect produced by these revelations on my raw youth was a sense of heavy responsibility for conniving at their concealment. I felt that if camp and barrack life involved these things, they ought to be known. I had been caught by the great wave of scientific enthusiasm which was then passing over Europe as a result of the discovery of Natural Selection by Darwin, and of the blow it dealt to the vulgar Bible worship and redemption mongering which had hitherto passed among us for religion. I wanted to get at the facts. I was prepared for the facts being unflattering: had I not already faced the fact that instead of being a fallen angel I was first cousin to a monkey? Long afterwards, when I was a well-known writer, I said [preface to *Plays Pleasant*] that what we wanted as the basis of our plays and novels was not romance, but a really scientific natural history. Scientific natural history is not compatible with taboo; and as everything connected with sex was tabooed, I felt the need for mentioning the forbidden subjects, not only because of their own importance, but for the sake of destroying taboo by giving it the most violent possible shocks. The same impulse is unmistakably active in Zola and his contemporaries. He also wanted, not works of literary art, but stories he could believe in as records of things that really happen. He imposed Jack the Ripper on his idyll of the railwayman's wife to make it scientific. To all artists and Platonists he made it thereby very unreal; for to the Platonist all accidents are unreal and negligible; but to the people he wanted to get at—the anti-artistic people—he made it readable.

The scientific spirit was unintelligible to the Philistines and repulsive to the dilettanti, who said to Zola: "If you must tell us stories about agricultural laborers, why tell us dirty ones?" But Zola did not want, like the old romancers, to tell a story. He wanted to tell the world the scientific truth about itself. His view was that if you were going to legislate for agricultural laborers, or deal with them or their business in any way, you had better know what they are really like; and in supplying you with the necessary information he did not tell you what you already knew, which included pretty nearly all that could be decorously mentioned, but what you did not know, which was that part of the truth that was tabooed. For the same reason, when he found a generation whose literary notions of Parisian cocotterie were founded on Marguerite Gauthier [*La Dame aux Camélias*], he felt it to be a duty to show them Nana [in *La Terre*, 1887, and *Nana*, 1880]. And it was a very necessary thing to do. If some Irish writer of the seventies had got himself banished from all decent society, and perhaps convicted of obscene libel, by writing a novel shewing the side of camp life that was never mentioned except in the papers of the Crown Solicitor, we should be nearer to a rational military system than we are today.

ZOLAISM AS A SUPERSTITION

It is, unfortunately, much easier to throw the forces of art into a reaction than to recall them when the reaction has gone far enough. A case which came under my own notice years ago illustrates the difficulty. The wife of an eminent surgeon had some talent for drawing. Her husband wrote a treatise on cancer; and she drew the illustrations. It was the first time she had used her gift for a serious purpose; and she worked hard enough at it to acquire considerable skill in depicting cancerous proliferation. The book being finished and published, she resumed her ordinary practice of sketching for pleasure. But all her work now had an uncanny look. When she drew a landscape, it was like a cancer that accidentally looked like a landscape. She had acquired a cancerous technique; and she could not get rid of it.

This happens as easily in literature as in the other arts. The men who trained themselves as writers by dragging the unmentionable to light, presently found that they could do that so much better than anything else that they gave up dealing with the other subjects. Even their quite mentionable episodes had an unmentionable air. Their imitators assumed that unmentionability was an end in itself—that to be decent was to be out of the movement. Zola and Ibsen could not, of course, be confined to mere reaction against taboo. Ibsen was to the last fascinating and full of a strange moving beauty; and Zola often broke into sentimental romance. But neither Ibsen nor Zola, after they once took in hand the work of unmasking the idols of the bourgeoisie, ever again wrote a happy or pleasant play or novel. Ibsen's suicides and catastrophes at last produced the cry of "People dont do such things," which he ridiculed through Judge Brack in Hedda Gabler. This was easy enough: Brack was so far wrong that people do do such things occasionally. But on the whole Brack was right. The tragedy of Hedda in real life is not that she commits suicide but that she continues to live. If such acts of violent rebellion as those of Hedda and Nora and Rebecca and the rest were the inevitable or even the probable consequences of their unfitness to be wives and mothers, or of their contracting repugnant marriages to avoid being left on the shelf, social reform would be very rapid; and we should hear less nonsense as to women like Nora and Hedda being mere figments of Ibsen's imagination. Our real difficulty is the almost boundless docility and submission to social convention which is characteristic of the human race. What balks the social reformer everywhere is that the victims of social evils do not complain, and even strongly resent being treated as victims. The more a dog suffers from being chained the more dangerous it is to release him: he bites savagely at the hand that dares touch his collar. Our Rougon-Macquart[6] families are usually enormously proud of themselves; and though they have to put up with their share of drunkards and madmen, they do not proliferate into Jack-the-Rippers. Nothing that is admittedly and unmistakably horrible matters very much, because it frightens people into seeking a remedy: the serious horrors are those which seem entirely respectable and normal to respectable and normal men. Now the formula of tragedy had come down to the XIX century from days in which this was not recognized, and when life was so thoroughly accepted as a divine institution that in order to make it seem tragic, something dreadful had to happen and somebody had to die. But the tragedy of modern life is that nothing happens, and that the resultant

6. *Les Rougon-Macquart*, a series of twenty novels (1871–93), is described by its author, Émile Zola, as the 'Natural and social history of a family under the Second Empire'.

dulness does not kill. Maupassant's Une Vie is infinitely more tragic than the death of Juliet.

In Ibsen's works we find the old traditions and the new conditions struggling in the same play, like a gudgeon half swallowed by a pike. Almost all the sorrow and the weariness which makes his plays so poignant are the sorrow and weariness of the mean dull life in which nothing happens; but none the less he provides a final catastrophe of the approved fifth-act-blank-verse type. Hedwig and Hedda shoot themselves: Rosmer and Rebecca throw themselves into the mill-race: Solness and Rubeck are dashed to pieces: Borkman dies of acute stage tragedy without discoverable lesions.[7] I will not again say, as I have said before, that these catastrophes are forced, because a fortunate performance often makes them seem inevitable; but I do submit that the omission of them would leave the play sadder and more convincing.

The Passing of the Tragic Catastrophe and the Happy Ending

Not only is the tradition of the catastrophe unsuitable to modern studies of life: the tradition of an ending, happy or the reverse, is equally unworkable. The moment the dramatist gives up accidents and catastrophes, and takes "slices of life" as his material, he finds himself committed to plays that have no endings. The curtain no longer comes down on a hero slain or married: it comes down when the audience has seen enough of the life presented to it to draw the moral, and must either leave the theatre or miss its last train.

The man who faced France with a drama fulfilling all these conditions was Brieux. He was as scientific, as conscientious, as unflinching as Zola without being in the least morbid. He was no more dependent on horrors than Molière, and as sane in his temper. He threw over the traditional forced catastrophe uncompromisingly. You do not go away from a Brieux play with the feeling that the affair is finished or the problem solved for you by the dramatist. Still less do you go away in "that happy, easy, ironically indulgent frame of mind that is the true test of comedy," as Mr Walkley put it in The Times of the 1st October, 1909 [unsigned review of W. Somerset Maugham's comedy *Smith*]. You come away with a very disquieting sense that you are involved in the affair, and must find the way

---

7. Characters in, respectively, *The Wild Duck* and *Hedda Gabler*; *Rosmersholm*; *The Master Builder* and *When We Dead Awaken*; and *John Gabriel Borkman*.

out of it for yourself and everybody else if civilization is to be tolerable to your sense of honor.

THE DIFFERENCE BETWEEN BRIEUX AND MOLIÈRE OR SHAKESPEAR

Brieux's task is thus larger than Molière's. Molière destroyed the prestige of those conspiracies against society which we call the professions, and which thrive by the exploitation of idolatry. He unmasked the doctor, the philosopher, the fencing master, the priest. He ridiculed their dupes: the hypochondriac, the academician, the devotee, the gentleman in search of accomplishments. He exposed the snob: he shewed the gentleman as the butt and creature of his valet, emphasizing thus the inevitable relation between the man who lives by unearned money and the man who lives by weight of service. Beyond bringing this latter point up to a later date Beaumarchais did nothing. But Molière never indicted society. [Edmund] Burke said that you cannot bring an indictment against a nation [*Second Speech on Conciliation with America*, 22 March 1775]; yet within a generation from that utterance men began to draw indictments against whole epochs, especially against the capitalistic epoch. It is true that Molière, like Shakespear, indicted human nature, which would seem to be a broader attack; but such attacks only make thoughtful men melancholy and hopeless, and practical men cynical or murderous. Le Misanthrope, which seems to me, as a foreigner perhaps, to be Molière's dullest and worst play, is like Hamlet in two respects. The first, which is that it would have been much better if it had been written in prose, is merely technical and need not detain us. The second is that the author does not clearly know what he is driving at. Le Festin de Pierre, Molière's best philosophic play, is as brilliant and arresting as Le Misanthrope is neither the one nor the other; but here again there is no positive side: the statue is a hollow creature with nothing to say for himself; and Don Juan makes no attempt to take advantage of his weakness. The reason why Shakespear and Molière are always well spoken of and recommended to the young is that their quarrel is really a quarrel with God for not making men better. If they had quarrelled with a specified class of persons with incomes of four figures for not doing their work better, or for doing no work at all, they would be denounced as seditious, impious, and profligate corruptors of morality.

Brieux wastes neither ink nor indignation on Providence. The idle despair that shakes its fist impotently at the skies, uttering sublime blasphemies, such as

As flies to wanton boys are we to the gods:
They kill us for their sport,

does not amuse Brieux. His fisticuffs are not aimed heavenward: they fall on human noses for the good of human souls. When he sees human nature in conflict with a political abuse he does not blame human nature, knowing that such blame is the favorite trick of those who wish to perpetuate the abuse without being able to defend it. He does not even blame the abuse: he exposes it, and then leaves human nature to tackle it with its eyes open. And his method of exposure is the dramatic method. He is a born dramatist, differing from the ordinary dramatists only in that he has a large mind and a scientific habit of using it. As a dramatist he must take for his theme a conflict of some sort. As a dramatist of large mind he cannot be satisfied with the trumpery conflicts of the Divorce Court and the Criminal Court: of the husband with the seducer, of the policeman with the murderer. Having the scientific conscience in a higher degree than Zola (he has a better head), he cannot be interested in imaginary conflicts which he himself would have to invent like a child at play. The conflict which inspires his dramatic genius must be a big one and a real one. To ask an audience to spend three hours hanging on the question of which particular man some particular woman shall mate with does not strike him as a reasonable proceeding; and if the audience does not agree with him, why, it can go to some fashionable dramatist of the boulevard who does agree with it.

BRIEUX AND THE BOULEVARD

This involves Brieux in furious conflict with the boulevard.[8] Up to quite recent times it was impossible for an Englishman to mention Brieux to a Parisian as the only French playwright who really counted in Europe, without being met with astonished assurances that Brieux is not a playwright at all; that his plays are not plays; that he is not (in [dramatic critic Francisque] Sarcey's sense of the phrase) "*du théâtre*"; that he is a mere pamphleteer without even literary style. And when you expressed your natural gratification at learning that the general body of Parisian dramatists were so highly gifted that Brieux counted for nothing in Paris—when you respectfully asked for the names of a few of the most prominent of the

8. 'Boulevard' drama in Paris in the latter half of the nineteenth century denoted plays that were conventional, fashionable and, generally, commercial successes.

geniuses who had eclipsed him, you were given three or four of which you had never heard, and one or two known to you as those of cynically commercial manipulators of the *ménage à trois*, the innocent wife discovered at the villain's rooms at midnight (to beg him to spare the virtue of a sister, the character of a son, or the life of a father), the compromising letter, the duel, and all the rest of the claptraps out of which dramatic playthings can be manufactured for the amusement of grown-up children. Not until the Académie Française[9] elected Brieux did it occur to the boulevardiers that the enormous difference between him and their pet authors was a difference in which the superiority lay with Brieux.

THE PEDANTRY OF PARIS

Indeed it is difficult for the Englishman to understand how bigotedly the Parisians cling to the claptrap theatre.

The English do not care enough about the theatre to cling to its traditions or persecute anyone for their sake; but the French do. Besides, in fine art, France is a nation of born pedants. The vulgar English painter paints vulgar pictures, and generally sells them. But the vulgar French painter paints classical ones, though whether he sells them or not I do not know: I hope not. The corresponding infatuation in the theatre is for dramas in alexandrines; and alexandrines are far worse than English blank verse, which is saying a good deal. Racine and Corneille, who established the alexandrine tradition, deliberately aimed at classicism, taking the Greek drama as their model. Even a foreigner can hear the music of their verse. Corneille wrote alexandrines as Dryden wrote heroic couplets,—in a virile, stately, handsome and withal human way; and Racine had tenderness and beauty as well. This drama of Racine and Corneille, with the music of Gluck, gave the French in the XVII and XVIII centuries a body of art which was very beautiful, very refined, very delightful for cultivated people, and very tedious for the ignorant. When, through the spread of elementary education, the ignorant invaded the theatre in overwhelming numbers, this exquisite body of art became a dead body, and was practised by nobody except the amateurs—the people who love what has been already done in art and loathe the real life out of which living art must continually grow

9. The French Academy was founded by Cardinal Richelieu in 1634 to provide standards and authority in French language and drama. Membership is limited to forty.

afresh. In their hands it passed from being a commercial failure to being an obsolete nuisance.

Commercially, the classic play was supplanted by a nuisance which was not a failure: to wit, the "well made play" of Scribe and his school. The manufacture of well made plays is not an art: it is an industry. It is not at all hard for a literary mechanic to acquire it: the only difficulty is to find a literary mechanic who is not by nature too much of an artist for the job; for nothing spoils a well made play more infallibly than the least alloy of high art or the least qualm of conscience on the part of the writer. "Art for art's sake" is the formula of the well made play, meaning in practice "Success for money's sake." Now great art is never produced for its own sake. It is too difficult to be worth the effort. All the great artists enter into a terrible struggle with the public, often involving bitter poverty and personal humiliation, and always involving calumny and persecution, because they believe they are apostles doing what used to be called the Will of God, and is now called by many prosaic names, of which "public work" is the least controversial. And when these artists have travailed and brought forth, and at last forced the public to associate keen pleasure and deep interest with their methods and morals, a crowd of smaller men—art confectioners, we may call them—hasten to make pretty entertainments out of scraps and crumbs from the masterpieces. Offenbach laid hands on Beethoven's Seventh Symphony and produced *J'aime les militaires* [*La Grande-Duchesse de Gérolstein*], to the disgust of Schumann, who was nevertheless doing precisely the same thing in a more pretentious way. And these confectioners are by no means mere plagiarists. They bring all sorts of engaging qualities to their work: love of beauty, desire to give pleasure, tenderness, humor, everything except the high republican conscience, the identification of the artist's purpose with the purpose of the universe, which alone makes an artist great.

But the well made play was not confectionery: it had not even the derived virtue of being borrowed from the great playwrights. Its formula grew up in the days when the spread of elementary schooling produced a huge mass of playgoers sufficiently educated to want plays instead of dog-fights, but not educated enough to enjoy or understand the masterpieces of dramatic art. Besides, education or no education, one cannot live on masterpieces alone, not only because there are not enough of them, but because new plays as well as great plays are needed, and there are not enough Molières and Shakespears in the world to keep the demand for novelty satisfied. Hence it has always been necessary to have some formula by which men of mediocre talent and no conscience can turn out plays for the theatrical market. Such men have written melodramas since the theatre existed. It was in the XIX century that the demand for manufactured plays was extended to drawing room plays in which the Forest of Bondy and the Auberge des Adrets, the Red Barn and the Cave at Midnight,[10] had to be replaced by Lord Blank's flat in Whitehall Court and the Great Hall, Chevy Chace.[11] Playgoers, being by that time mostiy poor playgoers, wanted to see how the rich live; wanted to see them actually drinking champagne and wearing real fashionable dresses and trousers with a neatly ironed crease down the knee.

How to Write a Popular Play

The formula for the well made play is so easy that I give it for the benefit of any reader who feels tempted to try his hand at making the fortune that awaits all successful manufacturers in this line. First, you "have an idea" for a dramatic situation. If it strikes you as a splendidly original idea, whilst it is in fact as old as the hills, so much the better. For instance, the situation of an innocent person convicted by circumstances of a crime may always be depended on. If the person is a woman, she must be convicted of adultery. If a young officer, he must be convicted of selling information to the enemy, though it is really a fascinating female spy who has ensnared him and stolen the incriminating document. If the innocent wife, banished from her home, suffers agonies through her separation from her children, and, when one of them is dying (of any disease the dramatist chooses to inflict), disguises herself as a nurse and attends it through its dying convulsion until the doctor, who should be a serio-comic character, and if possible a faithful old admirer of the lady's, simultaneously announces the recovery of the child and the discovery of the wife's innocence, the success of the play may be regarded as assured if the writer has any sort of knack for his work. Comedy is more difficult, because it requires a sense of humor and a good deal of vivacity; but the process is essentially the same: it is the manufacture of a misunderstanding. Having manufactured it, you

10. All were popular melodramas: *The Dog of Montargis, or The Forest of Bondy* (1814) ascribed to T. J. Dibdin; *L'Auberge des Adrets* (1823) by Benjamin Antier, Paulyanthe (Alexandre Chapponier), and Saint-Amante (J. A. Lacoste); *Maria Marten, or The Murder in the Red Barn* (*c.* 1830), author unknown. *The Cave at Midnight* is unidentified; conceivably it is a subtitle.
11. Chevy Chace: an unenclosed game preserve in northern England, scene of a famous Scottish border skirmish celebrated in a folk ballad.

place its culmination at the end of the last act but one, which is the point at which the manufacture of the play begins. Then you make your first act out of the necessary introduction of the characters to the audience, after elaborate explanations, mostly conducted by servants, solicitors, and other low life personages (the principals must all be dukes and colonels and millionaires), of how the misunderstanding is going to come about. Your last act consists, of course, of clearing up the misunderstanding, and generally getting the audience out of the theatre as best you can.

Now please do not misunderstand me as pretending that this process is so mechanical that it offers no opportunity for the exercise of talent. On the contrary, it is so mechanical that without very conspicuous talent nobody can make much reputation by doing it, though some can and do make a living at it. And this often leads the cultivated classes to suppose that all plays are written by authors of talent. As a matter of fact the majority of those who in France and England make a living by writing plays are unknown and, as to education, all but illiterate. Their names are not worth putting on the playbill, because their audiences neither know nor care who the author is, and often believe that the actors improvize the whole piece, just as they in fact do sometimes improvize the dialogue. To rise out of this obscurity you must be a Scribe or a Sardou, doing essentially the same thing, it is true, but doing it wittily and ingeniously, at moments almost poetically, and giving the persons of the drama some touches of real observed character.

WHY THE CRITICS ARE ALWAYS WRONG

Now it is these strokes of talent that set the critics wrong. For the talent, being all expended on the formula, at least consecrates the formula in the eyes of the critics. Nay, they become so accustomed to the formula that at last they cannot relish or understand a play that has grown naturally, just as they cannot admire the Venus of Milo because she has neither a corset nor high heeled shoes. They are like the peasants who are so accustomed to food reeking with garlic that when food is served to them without it they declare that it has no taste and is not food at all.

This is the explanation of the refusal of the critics of all nations to accept great original dramatists like Ibsen and Brieux as real dramatists, or their plays as real plays. No writer of the first order needs the formula any more than a sound man needs a crutch. In his simplest mood, when he is only seeking to amuse, he does not manufacture a plot: he tells a story. He finds no difficulty in setting people on the stage to talk and act in an amusing, exciting or touching way. His characters have adventures and ideas which are interesting in themselves, and need not be fitted into the Chinese puzzle of a plot.

THE INTERPRETER OF LIFE

But the great dramatist has something better to do than to amuse either himself or his audience. He has to interpret life. This sounds a mere pious phrase of literary criticism; but a moment's consideration will discover its meaning and its exactitude. Life as it appears to us in our daily experience is an unintelligible chaos of happenings. You pass Othello in the bazaar in Aleppo, Iago on the jetty in Cyprus, and Desdemona in the nave of St Mark's in Venice without the slightest clue to their relations to one another. The man you see stepping into a chemist's shop to buy the means of committing murder or suicide, may, for all you know, want nothing but a liver pill or a toothbrush. The statesman who has no other object than to make you vote for his party at the next election, may be starting you on an incline at the foot of which lies war, or revolution, or a smallpox epidemic, or five years off your lifetime. The horrible murder of a whole family by the father who finishes by killing himself, or the driving of a young girl on to the streets, may be the result of your discharging an employee in a fit of temper a month before. To attempt to understand life from merely looking on at it as it happens in the streets is as hopeless as trying to understand public questions by studying snapshots of public demonstrations. If we possessed a series of cinematographs of all the executions during the Reign of Terror, they might be exhibited a thousand times without enlightening the audiences in the least as to the meaning of the Revolution: Robespierre would perish as "un monsieur" and Marie Antoinette as "une femme." Life as it occurs is senseless: a policeman may watch it and work in it for thirty years in the streets and courts of Paris without learning as much of it or from it as a child or a nun may learn from a single play by Brieux. For it is the business of Brieux to pick out the significant incidents from the chaos of daily happenings, and arrange them so that their relation to one another becomes significant, thus changing us from bewildered spectators of a monstrous confusion to men intelligently conscious of the world and its destinies. This is the highest function that man can perform—the greatest work he can set his hand to; and this is why the great dramatists of the world, from Euripides and Aristophanes to Shakespear and Molière, and from them to Ibsen and Brieux, take that majestic, and pontifical rank which seems so strangely above all the reasonable pretensions of mere strolling actors and theatrical authors.

How the Great Dramatists torture the Public

Now if the critics are wrong in supposing that the formula of the well made play is not only an indispensable factor in playwriting, but is actually the essence of the play itself—if their delusion is rebuked and confuted by the practice of every great dramatist, even when he is only amusing himself by story telling, what must happen to their poor formula when it impertinently offers its services to a playwright who has taken on his supreme function as the Interpreter of Life? Not only has he no use for it, but he must attack and destroy it; for one of the very first lessons he has to teach to a play-ridden public is that the romantic conventions on which the formula proceeds are all false, and are doing incalculable harm in these days when everybody reads romances and goes to the theatre. Just as the historian can teach no real history until he has cured his readers of the romantic delusion that the greatness of a queen consists in her being a pretty woman and having her head cut off, so the playwright of the first order can do nothing with his audiences until he has cured them of looking at the stage through the keyhole, and sniffing round the theatre as prurient people sniff round the divorce court. The cure is not a popular one. The public suffers from it exactly as a drunkard or a snuff taker suffers from an attempt to conquer the habit. The critics especially, who are forced by their profession to indulge immoderately in plays adulterated with falsehood and vice, suffer so acutely when deprived of them for a whole evening that they hurl disparagements and even abuse and insult at the merciless dramatist who is torturing them. To a bad play of the kind they are accustomed to they can be cruel through superciliousness, irony, impatience, contempt, or even a Rochefoucauldian pleasure in a friend's misfortune.[12] But the hatred provoked by deliberately inflicted pain, the frantic denials as of a prisoner at the bar accused of a disgraceful crime, the clamor for vengeance thinly disguised as artistic justice, the suspicion that the dramatist is using private information and making a personal attack: all these are to be found only when the playwright is no mere *marchand de plaisir*, but, like Brieux, a ruthless revealer of hidden truth and a mighty destroyer of idols.

12. One of Rochefoucauld's maxims reads: 'In the misfortune of our best friends we invariably find something that does not displease us.'

Brieux's Conquest of London

So well does Brieux know this that he has written a play, La Foi, shewing how truth is terrible to men, and how false religions (theatrical romance, by the way, is the falsest and most fantastically held of all the false religions) are a necessity to them. With this play he achieved, for the first time on record, the feat of winning a success in a fashionable London theatre with a cold-blooded thesis play. Those who witnessed the performance of False Gods [*La Foi*] at His Majesty's Theatre this year [1909] were astonished to see that exceptionally large theatre filled with strangely attentive ordinary playgoers, to whose customary requirements and weaknesses no concession was made for a moment by the playwright. They were getting a lesson and nothing else. The same famous acting, the same sumptuous *mise en scène*, had not always saved other plays from failure. There was no enthusiasm: one might almost say there was no enjoyment. The audience for once had something better to do than to amuse themselves. The old playgoers and the critics, who, on the first night, had politely regretted an inevitable failure after waiting, like the maturer ladies at the sack of Ismail in Byron's poem [*Don Juan*, Canto VIII], for the adultery to begin, asked one another incredulously whether there could really be money in this sort of thing. Such feats had been performed before at coterie theatres where the expenses were low and where the plays were seasoned with a good deal of ordinary amusing comedy; but in this play there was not a jest from beginning to end; and the size of the theatre and the expenses of production were on a princely scale. Yet La Foi held its own. The feat was quite unprecedented; and that it should have been achieved for the first time by a Frenchman is about a million times more remarkable than that the first man [Louis Blériot] to fly across the channel [25 July 1909] (the two events were almost simultaneous) should also have been a Frenchman.

Parisian Stupidity

And here I must digress for a moment to remark that though Paris is easily the most prejudiced, old-fashioned, obsolete-minded city in the west of Europe, yet when she produces great men she certainly does not do it by halves. Unfortunately, there is nothing she hates more than a Frenchman of genius. When an Englishman says that you have to go back to Michael Angelo to find a sculptor who can be mentioned in the same breath as Rodin without manifest absurdity, the Parisians indignantly exclaim that only an ignorant foreigner could imagine that a man who was not a pupil at the Beaux Arts could possibly be a sculptor at all. And I have already described how they talk about Brieux, the only French dramatist whose fame crosses frontiers and channels, and fills the continent. To be quite frank, I cannot to this day understand why they made him an Academician instead of starving him to death and then giving him a statue. Can it be that in his early days, before he could gain his living by the theatre, he wrote a spelling book, or delivered a course of lectures on the use of pure line in Greek design? To suppose that they did it because he is a great man is to imply that they know a great Frenchman when they see him, which is contrary to all experience. They never know until the English tell them.

BRIEUX AND THE ENGLISH THEATRE

In England our knowledge of Brieux has been delayed by the childishness of our theatre. This childishness is by no means to be deplored: it means that the theatre is occupied with the elementary education of the masses instead of with the higher education of the classes. Those who desire dramatic performances of the higher sort have procured them only by forming clubs, hiring theatres, engaging performers, and selecting plays for themselves. After 1889, when Ibsen first became known in London through A Doll's House, a succession of these clubs kept what may be called the serious adult drama fitfully alive until 1904, when Messrs. Vedrenne and Barker took the field with a regular theatrical enterprise devoted to this class of work, and maintained it until the National Theatre project was set on foot, and provisional repertory schemes were announced by established commercial managements. It was through one of these clubs, the Stage Society, that Brieux reached the English stage with his Bienfaiteurs [*The Philanthropists*, 1904]. Then the first two plays in this volume [*Maternity*, 1906, and *The Three Daughters of M. Dupont*, 1905] were performed, and, later on, Les Hannetons [1907]. These performances settled for English connoisseurs the question of Brieux's rank among modern playwrights. Later on his Robe Rouge[13] introduced the ordinary playgoers to him; and

13. Shaw errs here in his chronology. *La Robe rouge* (adapted by Bernard Miall as *The Arm of the Law*) was seen in London in February 1904.

he is now no longer one of the curiosities of the coterie theatre, as even Ibsen to some extent still is, but one of the conquerors of the general British public.

THE CENSORSHIP IN FRANCE AND ENGLAND

Unfortunately, he has not yet been able to conquer our detestable, discredited, but still all-powerful censorship. In France he was attacked by the censorship just as in England; but in France the censorship broke itself against him and perished. The same thing would probably have occurred here but for the fact that our Censor, by a grotesque accident of history—to be precise, because Henry VIII began the censorship of the theatre by appointing an officer of his own household [Master of the Revels] to do the work—remains part of the King's retinue; and his abolition involves the curtailment of that retinue and therefore the reduction of the King's State, always a very difficult and delicate matter in a monarchical country. In France the censorship was exercised by the Minister of Fine Arts (a portfolio that does not exist in our Cabinet), and was in the hands of two or three examiners of plays, who necessarily behaved exactly like our Mr Redford; for, as I have so often pointed out, the evils of censorship are made compulsory by the nature of the office, and are not really the fault of the individual censor. These gentlemen, then, prohibited the performance of Brieux's best and most useful plays, just as Mr Redford did here. But as the French Parliament, having nobody to consider but themselves and the interests of the nation, presently refused to vote the salaries of the Censors, the institution died a natural death. We have no such summary remedy here. Our Censor's salary is part of the King's civil list, and is therefore sacred. Years ago, our Playgoers' Club asked me how the censorship could be abolished. I replied [3 December 1899], to the great scandal of that loyal body,— You must begin by abolishing the monarchy.

BRIEUX AND THE ENGLISH CENSORSHIP

Nevertheless, Brieux has left his mark even on the English censorship. This year (1909) the prohibition of his plays was one of the strongest items in the long list of grievances by which the English playwrights compelled the Government to appoint a Select Committee of both houses of Parliament to enquire into the working of the censorship. The report of that Committee admits the charge brought against the Censor of systematically suppressing plays dealing seriously with social problems whilst allowing frivolous and even pornographic plays to pass unchallenged. It advises that the submission of plays to the Censor shall in future be optional, though it does not dare to omit the customary sycophantic recommendation that the Lord Chamberlain shall still retain his privilege of licensing plays; and it proposes that the authors and managers of plays so licensed, though not exempt from prosecution, shall enjoy certain immunities denied in the case of unlicensed plays. There are many other conditions which need not be gone into here; but to a Frenchman the main fact that stands out is that the accident which has made the Censor an officer of the King's Household has prevented a parliamentary committee from recommending the abolition of his control over the theatre in a report which not only has not a word to say in his defence, but expressly declares that his licence affords the public no guarantee that the plays he approves are decent, and that authors of serious plays need protection against his unenlightened despotism.

TABOO

We may therefore take it on the authority of the Select Committee that the prohibition by the English censorship of the public performances of the three plays in this book does not afford the smallest reasonable ground for condemning them as improper—rather the contrary. As a matter of fact, most men, if asked to guess the passages to which the Censor took exception, would guess wrongly. Certainly a Frenchman would. The reason is that though in England as in France what is called decency is not a reasoned discrimination between what needs to be said and what ought not to be said, but simply the observance of a set of taboos, these taboos are not the same in England as in France. A Frenchman of scrupulously correct behavior will sometimes quite innocently make an English lady blush by mentioning something that is unmentionable in polite society in England though quite mentionable in France. To take a simple illustration,—an Englishman, when he first visits France, is always embarrassed, and sometimes shocked, on finding that the person in charge of a public lavatory for men is a woman. I cannot give reciprocal instances of the ways in which Englishmen shock the French nation, because I am happily unconscious of all the *cochonneries* [improprieties] of which I am no doubt guilty when I am in

France. But that I do occasionally shock the brave French bourgeois to the very marrow of his bones by my indelicacy, I have not the smallest doubt. There is only one epithet in universal use for foreigners. That epithet is "dirty."

THE ATTITUDE OF THE PEOPLE TO THE LITERARY ARTS

These differences between nation and nation also exist between class and class and between town and country. I will not here go into the vexed question of whether the peasant's way of blowing his nose or the squire's is the more cleanly and hygienic, though my experience as a municipal councillor of the way in which epidemics are spread by laundries makes me incline to the side of the peasant. What is beyond all question is that each seems disgusting to the other. And when we come from physical facts to moral views and ethical opinions we find the same antagonisms. To a great section—perhaps the largest section—of the people of England and France, all novels, plays, and songs are licentious; and the habit of enjoying them is a mark of a worthless character. To these people the distinctions made by the literary classes between books fit for young girls to read and improper books—between [J. H. Bernardin de St Pierre's] Paul and Virginia and [Théophile Gautier's] Mademoiselle de Maupin or [Guy de Maupassant's] Une Vie, between Mrs Humphry Ward and Ouida—have no meaning: all writers of love stories and all readers of them are alike shameless. Cultivated Paris, cultivated London, are apt to overlook people who, as they seldom read and never write, have no means of making themselves heard. But such simple people heavily outnumber the cultivated; and if they could also outwit them, literature would perish. Yet their intolerance of fiction is as nothing to their intolerance of fact. I lately heard an English gentleman state a very simple fact in these terms: "I never could get on with my mother: she did not like me, and I did not like her: my brother was her pet." To an immense number of living English and French people this speech would suggest that its utterer ought to be burned alive, though the substitution of stepmother for mother and of half-brother for brother would suffice to make it seem quite probable and natural. And this, observe, not in the least because all these horrified people adore and are adored by their mothers, but simply because they have a fixed convention that the proper name of the relation between mother and son is love. However bitter and hostile it may in fact be in some cases, to call it by any other name is a breach of convention; and by the instinctive logic of timidity they infer that a man to whom convention is not sacred is a dangerous man. To them the ten commandments are nothing but arbitrary conventions; and the man who says today that he does not love his mother, may, they conclude, tomorrow steal, rob, murder, commit adultery, and bear false witness against his neighbor.

THE DREAD OF THE ORIGINAL THINKER

This is the real secret of the terror inspired by an original thinker. In repudiating convention he is repudiating that on which his neighbors are relying for their sense of security. But he is usually also doing something even more unpopular. He is proposing new obligations to add to the already heavy burden of duty. When the boy Shelley elaborately and solemnly cursed his father for the entertainment of his friends, he only shocked us. But when the man Shelley told us that we should feed, clothe and educate all the children in the country as carefully as if they were our immediate own, we lost our tempers with him and deprived him of the custody of his own children.

It is useless to complain that the conventional masses are unintelligent. To begin with, they are not unintelligent except in the sense in which all men are unintelligent in matters in which they are not experts. I object to be called unintelligent merely because I do not know enough about mechanical construction to be able to judge whether a motor car of new design is an improvement or not, and therefore prefer to buy one of the old type to which I am accustomed. The brave bourgeois whom Brieux scandalizes must not be dismissed with ridicule by the man of letters because, not being an expert in morals, he prefers the old ways and mistrusts the new. His position is a very reasonable one. He says, in effect, "If I am to enjoy any sense of security, I must be able to reckon on other people behaving in a certain ascertained way. Never mind whether it is the ideally right way or the ideally wrong way: it will suit me well enough if only it is convenient and, above all, unmistakable. Lay it down if you like that people are not to pay debts and are to murder one another whenever they get a chance. In that case I can refuse to give credit, and can carry weapons and learn to use them to defend myself. On the other hand, if you settle that debts are to be enforced and the peace kept by the police, I will give credit and renounce the practice of arms. But the one thing that I cannot stand is not knowing what the social contract is."

THE JUSTIFICATION OF CONVENTIONALITY

It is a cherished tradition in English politics that at a meeting of Lord Melbourne's Cabinet in the early days of Queen Victoria, the Prime Minister, when the meeting threatened to break up in confusion, put his back to the door and said, in the cynically profane manner then fashionable: "Gentlemen: we can tell the House the truth or we can tell it a lie: I do not care a damn which. All I insist on is that we shall all tell the same lie; and you shall not leave the room until you have settled what it is to be."[14] Just so does the bourgeois perceive that the essential thing is not whether a convention is right or wrong, but that everybody shall know what it is and observe it. His cry is always: "I want to know where I stand." Tell him what he may do and what he may not do; and make him feel that he may depend on other people doing or not doing the same; and he feels secure, knowing where he stands and where other people stand. His dread and hatred of revolutions and heresies and men with original ideas is his dread of disorientation and insecurity. Those who have felt earthquakes assure us that there is no terror like the terror of the earth swaying under the feet that have always depended on it as the one immovable thing in the world. That is just how the ordinary respectable man feels when some man of genius rocks the moral ground beneath him by denying the validity of a convention. The popular phrases by which such innovators are described are always of the same kind. The early Christians were called men who wished to turn the world upside down. The modern critics of morals are reproached for "standing on their heads." There is no pretence of argument, or of any understanding of the proposals of the reformers: there is simply panic and a demand for suppression at all costs. The reformer is not forbidden to advance this or that definite opinion, because his assailants are too frightened to know or care what his opinions are: he is forbidden simply to speak in an unusual way about morals and religion, or to mention any subject that is not usually mentioned in public.

This is the terror which the English censorship, like all other censorships, gives effect to. It explains what puzzles most observers of the censorship so much: namely, its scandalous laxity towards and positive encouragement of the familiar and customary pornographic side of theatrical art simultaneously with its intolerance of the higher drama, which is always

14. Much-embroidered version of remarks made by the Prime Minister following a Cabinet meeting (1841), as recorded in the *Dictionary of National Biography*.

unconventional and super-bourgeois in its ethics. To illustrate, let me cite the point on which the English censorship came into conflict with Brieux, when Les Hannetons was first performed by the Stage Society.

WHY LES HANNETONS WAS CENSORED

Les Hannetons is a very powerful and convincing demonstration of the delusiveness of that sort of freedom which men try to secure by refusing to marry, and living with a mistress instead. The play is a comedy: the audience laughs throughout; but the most dissolute man present leaves the theatre convinced that the unfortunate hero had better have been married ten times over than fallen into such bondage as his liaison has landed him in. To witness a performance might very wisely be made part of the curriculum of every university college and polytechnic in the country.

Now those who do not know the ways of the censorship may jump to the conclusion that the objection of the Censor was to the exhibition on the stage of two persons living together in immoral relations. They would be greatly mistaken. The Censor made no difficulty whatever about that. Even the funny but ruthless scene where the woman cajoles the man by kissing him on a certain susceptible spot on his neck—a scene from which our shamed conscience shrinks as from a branding iron—was licensed without a word of remonstrance. But there is a searching passage in the play where the woman confesses to a girl friend that one of the lies by which she induced the man to enter into relations with her was that he was not her first lover. The friend is simple enough to express surprise, thinking that this, far from being an inducement, would have roused jealousy and disgust. The woman replies that, on the contrary, no man likes to face the responsibility of tempting a girl to her first step from the beaten path, and that girls take care accordingly not to let them know it.

This is one of those terrible stripping strokes by which a master of realism suddenly exposes a social sore which has been plastered over with sentimental nonsense about erring Magdalens, vicious nonsense about gaiety, or simply prudish silence. No young man or young woman hearing it, however anarchical their opinions may be as to sexual conduct, can possibly imagine afterwards that the relation between "les hannetons" is honest, charming, sentimentally interesting, or pardonable by the self-respect of either. It is felt instinctively to have something fundamentally dishonorable in it, in spite of the innocence of the natural affection of the pair for one other. Yet this is precisely the passage that the Censor refused to pass. All the rest was duly licensed. The exhibition of the pretty, scheming, lying, sensual girl fixing herself with triumphant success on the meanly prudent sensual man, and having what many women would consider rather a good time of it, was allowed and encouraged by the court certificate of propriety. But the deadly touch that made it impossible for even the most thoughtless pair in the audience to go and do likewise without loathing themselves, was forbidden.

MISADVENTURE OF A FRENCHMAN IN WESTMINSTER ABBEY

In short, the censorship did what it always does: it left the poison on the table and carefully locked up the antidote. And it did this, not from a fiendish design to destroy the souls of the people, but solely because the passage involved a reference by a girl to her virginity, which is unusual and therefore tabooed. The Censor never troubled himself as to the meaning or effect of the passage. It represented the woman as doing an unusual thing: therefore a dangerous, possibly subversive thing. In England, when we are scandalized and can give no direct reason why, we exclaim "What next?" That is the continual cry of the Censor's soul. If a girl may refer to her virginity on the stage, what may she not refer to? This instinctive regard to consequences was once impressed painfully on a pious Frenchman who, in Westminster Abbey, knelt down to pray. The verger, who had never seen such a thing happen before, promptly handed him over to the police and charged him with "brawling." Fortunately, the magistrate had compassion on the foreigner's ignorance; and even went the length of asking why he should not be allowed to pray in church. The reply of the verger was simple and obvious. "If we allowed that," he said, "we should have people praying all over the place." And to this day the rule in Westminster Abbey is that you may stroll about and look at the monuments, but you must not on any account pray. Similarly, on the stage you may represent murder, gluttony, sexual vice, and all the crimes in the calendar and out of it, but you must not say anything unusual about them.

MARRIAGE AND MALTHUS

If Brieux found himself blocked by the censorship when he was exposing the vice of illicit unions, it will surprise no one to learn that his far more urgently needed exposures of the intemperance and corruption of marriage itself [were] fiercely banned. The vulgar, and consequently the official, view of marriage is that it hallows all the sexual relations of the parties to it. That it may mask all the vices of the coarsest libertinage with added elements of slavery and cruelty has always been true to some extent; but during the last forty years it has become so serious a matter that conscientious dramatists have to vivisect legal unions as ruthlessly as illegal ones. For it happens that just about forty years ago the propaganda of Neo-Malthusianism[15] changed the bearing of children from an involuntary condition of marriage to a voluntary one. From the moment this momentous discovery was made, childless marriage became available to male voluptuaries as the cheapest way of keeping a mistress, and to female ones as the most convenient and respectable way of being kept in idle luxury by a man. The effects of this have already been startling, and will yet be revolutionary as far as marriage is concerned, both in law and custom. The work of keeping the populations of Europe replenished received a sudden check, amounting in France and England to a threat of actual retrogression. The appointment of a Royal Commission to enquire into the decline of the birthrate in the very sections of the population which most need to be maintained, is probably not very far off: the more far-seeing of those who know the facts have prophesied such a step for a long time past. The expectation of the Neo-Malthusians that the regulation of births in our families would give the fewer children born a better chance of survival in greater numbers and in fuller health and efficiency than the children of the old unrestricted families, and of the mother exhausted by excessive childbearing, has no doubt been fulfilled in some cases; but, on the whole, artificial sterility seems to be beating natural fertility; for as far as can be judged by certain sectional but typical private censuses, the average number of children produced is being dragged down to one and a half per family by the large proportion of intentionally childless marriages, and the heavy pressure of the cost of private childbearing on the scanty incomes of the masses.

That this will force us to a liberal State endowment of parentage, direct or indirect, is not now doubted by people who understand the problem: in fact, as I write, the first open step has already been taken by the Government's proposal to exempt parents from the full burden of taxation borne by the childless. There has also begun a change in public opinion as to the open abuse of marriage as a mere means by which any pair can procure a

15. Malthusians, influenced by the theories of Thomas Malthus on checks and balances in population, advocated restrictions on marriage and family growth.

certificate of respectability by paying for it, which may quite possibly end in the disuse of the ceremony for all except fertile unions. From the point of view of the Church, it is a manifest profanation that couples whose only aim is a comfortable domesticity should obtain for it the sacrament of religious marriage on pretence of unselfish and publicly important purposes which they have not the smallest intention of carrying out. From the secular point of view, there is no reason why couples who do not intend to have children should be allowed to enslave one another by all the complicated legal restrictions of their liberty and property which are attached to marriage solely to secure the responsibility of parents to the State for their children.

BRIEUX AND THE RESPECTABLE MARRIED MAN

All these by no means remote prospects, familiar though they are to the statesman and sociologist, are amazing to the bourgeois even when he is personally implicated in the change of practice that is creating the necessity for a change in law and in opinion. He has changed his practice privately, without talking about it except in secret, or in passages of unprintable Rabelaisian jocosity with his friends; and he is not only unable to see why anyone else should talk publicly about the change, but terrified lest what he is doing furtively and hypocritically should be suddenly dragged into the light, and his own case recorded, perhaps, in public statistics in support of innovations which vaguely suggest to him the destruction of morals and the break-up of the family. But both his pruderies and his terrors must give way before the absolute necessity for re-examining the foundations of our social structure after the shock they have received from the discovery of artificial sterilization, and their readjustment to the new strains they have to bear as a consequence of that discovery.

Tolstoy, with his Kreutzer Sonata [1889], was the first to carry the war into the enemy's country by showing that marriage intensified instead of eliminating every element of evil in sexual relations; but Brieux was the first dramatist to see not only the hard facts of the situation, but its political importance. He has seen in particular that a new issue has arisen in that eternal conflict of the sexes which is created by the huge difference between the transient pleasure of the man and the prolonged suffering of the woman in maintaining the population. Malthusianism, when it passed from being the speculation of an economist to being the ardent faith of a devoted band of propagandists, touched our feelings mainly as a protest against the burden of excessive childbearing imposed on married women. It was not then foreseen that the triumph of the propaganda might impose a still worse burden on them—the burden of enforced sterility. Before Malthus was born, cases were familiar enough in which wives who had borne two or three children as an inevitable consequence of their conjugal relations had thereupon rebelled against further travail, and discontinued the relations by such a resolute assertion of selfishness as is not easy to an amiable woman and practically not possible to a loving or a jealous wife. But the case of a man refusing to fulfil his parental function and thereby denying the right of his wife to motherhood was unknown. Yet it immediately and inevitably arose the moment men became possessed of the means of doing this without self-denial. A wife could thus be put in a position intolerable to a woman of honor as distinguished from a frank voluptuary. She could be condemned to barren bodily slavery without remedy. To keep silence about so monstrous a wrong as this merely because the subject is a tabooed one was not possible to Brieux. Censorship or no censorship, it had to be said, and indeed shouted from the housetops, if nothing else would make people attend, that this infamy existed and must be remedied. And Brieux touched the evil at its worst spot—in that section of the middle class in which the need for pecuniary prudence has almost swallowed up every more human feeling. In this most wretched of all classes there is no employment for women except the employment of wife and mother, and no provision for women without employment. The fathers are too poor to provide. The daughter must marry whom she can get: if the first chance, which she dares not refuse, is not that of a man whom she positively dislikes, she may consider herself fortunate. Her real hope of affection and self-respect lies in her children. And yet she above all women is subject to the danger that the dread of poverty, which is the ruling factor in her husband's world, may induce him to deny her right and frustrate her function of motherhood, using her simply as a housekeeper and a mistress without paying her the market price of such luxuries or forfeiting his respectability. To make us understand what this horror means, Brieux wrote Les Trois Filles de Monsieur Dupont, or, in equivalent English, The Three Daughters of Mr Smith. Mr Smith, in the person of the Censor, immediately shrieked "You must not mention such things." Mr Smith was wrong: they are just the things that must be mentioned, and mentioned again and yet again, until they are set right. Surely, of all the anomalies of our marriage law, there is none more mischievously absurd than that a woman can have her marriage annulled for her husband's involuntary, but not for his voluntary sterility. And the man is in the same predicament, though his wife now has the same power as he of frustrating the public purpose of all marriages.

Brieux shows the Other Side

But Brieux is not, as the ordinary man mostly is, a mere reactionist against the latest oversights and mistakes, becoming an atheist at every flaw discovered in popular theology, and recoiling into the grossest superstition when some Jesuit who happens by exception to be a clever and subtle man (about the last thing, by the way, that a real live Jesuit ever is) shews him that popular atheism is only theology without mind or purpose. The ordinary man, when Brieux makes him aware of the fact that Malthusianism has produced an unexpected and revolting situation, instantly conceives a violent prejudice against it, pointing to the declining population as evidence that it is bringing ruin on the human race, and clamoring for the return of the conjugal morality of his grandmother, as Theodore Roosevelt did when he was President of the United States of America. It therefore became necessary for Brieux to head him off in his frantic flight by writing another play, Maternity, to remind him of the case for Malthusianism, and to warn him—if he is capable of the warning—that progress is not achieved by panic-stricken rushes back and forward between one folly and another, but by sifting all movements and adding what survives the sifting to the fabric of our morality. For the fact that Malthusianism has made new crimes possible should not discredit it, and cannot stop it, because every step gained by man in his continuous effort to control Nature necessarily does the same. Flying, for instance, which has become practical as a general human art for the first time this year, is capable of such alarming abuse that we are on the eve of a clamor for its restriction,[16] and even for its prohibition, that will speedily make the present clamor against motor cars as completely forgotten as the clamor against bicycles was when motor cars appeared. But the motor car cannot be suppressed: it is improving our roads, improving the manners and screwing up the capacity and conduct of all who use them, improving our regulation of traffic, improving both locomotion and character as every victory over Nature finally improves the world and the race. Malthusianism is no exception to the rule: its obvious abuses, and the new need for protecting marriage from being made a mere charter of libertinage and slavery by its means, must be dealt

16. Blériot's successful flight across the Channel, combined with the world's first air meeting at Reims in August 1909, had alarmed governments throughout Europe into a frightening realization of this new machine's devastating potential as a weapon.

with by improvements in conduct and law, and not by a hopeless attempt to drive us all back to the time of Mrs Gamp. The tyranny which denies to the wife the right to become a mother has become possible through the discovery of the means of escape from the no less unbearable tyranny which compelled her to set another child at the table round which those she had already borne were starving because there was not enough food for them. When the French Government, like Colonel Roosevelt, could think of no better cure for the new tyranny than a revival of the old, Brieux added a play on the old tyranny to his play on the new tyranny.

This is the explanation of what stupid people call the inconsistencies of those modern dramatists who, like Ibsen and Brieux, are prophets as well as playwrights. Ibsen did not write The Wild Duck to ridicule the lesson he had already taught in Pillars of Society and An Enemy of the People: he did it to head off his disciples when, in their stampede from idealism, they forgot the need of ideals and illusions to men not strong enough to bear the truth. Brieux's La Foi has virtually the same theme. It is not an ultramontane tract to defend the Church against the sceptic. It is a solemn warning that you have not, as so many modern sceptics assume, disposed of the doctrine when you have proved that it is false. The miracle of St Januarius [the liquefaction, at Naples, of the dried blood of the saint at certain times of the year] is worked, not by men who believe in it, but by men who know it to be a trick, but know also that men cannot be governed by the truth unless they are capable of the truth, and yet must be governed somehow, truth or no truth. Maternity and The Three Daughters of Mr Smith are not contradictory: they are complementary, like An Enemy of the People and The Wild Duck. I myself have had to introduce into one of my plays [*The Doctor's Dilemma*] a scene in which a young man [Louis Dubedat] defends his vices on the ground that he is one of my disciples. I did so because the incident had actually occurred in a criminal court, where a young prisoner gave the same reason and was sentenced to six months' imprisonment, less, I fear, for the offence than for the attempt to justify it.[17]

The Most Unmentionable of All Subjects

Finally, Brieux attacked the most unmentionable subject of all—the subject of the diseases that are supposed to be the punishment of profligate

17. George Rankin, 26, was prosecuted in London's Central Criminal Courts in May 1906 for writing and publishing a libel concerning his schoolmaster father.

men and worthless women. Here the taboo acquires double force. Not only must not the improper thing be mentioned, but the evil must not be remedied, because it is a just retribution and a wholesome deterrent. The last point may be dismissed by simply inquiring how a disease can possibly act as a deterrent when people are kept in ignorance of its existence. But the punishment theory is a hideous mistake. It might as well be contended that fires should not be put out because they are the just punishment of the incendiary. Most of the victims of these diseases are entirely innocent persons: children who do not know what vice means, and women to whom it is impossible to explain what is the matter with them. Nor are their fathers and husbands necessarily to blame. Even if they were, it would be wicked to leave them unwarned when the consequences can spread so widely beyond themselves; for there are dozens of indirect ways in which this contagion can take place exactly as any other contagion can. The presence of one infected person in a house may lead to the infection of everybody else in it, even if they have never seen one another. In fact it is impossible to prove in any given case that the sufferer is in any way culpable: every profligate excuses himself or herself to the doctor on this ground; and though the excuse may not be believed, its truth is generally possible. Add to the chances of contagion the hereditary transmission of the disease, and the fact that an innocent person receiving it from a guilty partner without other grounds for divorce has no legal redress; and it becomes at once apparent that every guilty case may produce several innocent ones. Under such circumstances, even if it were possible in a civilized community to leave misconduct to be checked by its natural or accidental consequences, or by private vengeance instead of by carefully considered legal measures, such an anarchical solution must be ruled out in the present case, as the disease strikes blindly at everyone whom it reaches, and there are as many innocent paths for its venom as guilty ones. The taboo actually discriminates heavily against the innocent, because, as taboos are not respected in profligate society, systematic profligates learn the danger in their loose conversations, and take precautions, whereas the innocent expose themselves recklessly in complete ignorance, handling possibly contaminated articles and entering possibly infected places without the least suspicion that any such danger exists. In Brieux's play the husband alone is culpable; but his misconduct presently involves his wife, his child, and his child's [wet] nurse. It requires very little imagination to see that this by no means exhausts the possibilities. The nurse, wholly guiltless of the original sin, is likely to spread its consequences far more widely than the original sinner. A grotesque result of this is that there is always a demand, especially in France, for infected nurses, because the doctor, when he knows the child to be infected, feels that he is committing a crime in not warning the nurse; and the only way out of the difficulty is to find a nurse who is already infected and has nothing more to fear. How little the conscience of the family is to be depended on when the interests of a beloved child are in the scale against a mere cold duty to a domestic servant, has been well shown by Brieux in the second act of his play. But indeed anyone who will take the trouble to read the treatise of Fournier, or the lectures of Duclaux, or, in English, the chapters in which Havelock Ellis has dealt with this subject, will need no further instruction to convince him that no play ever written was more needed than Les Avariés.

It must be added that a startling change in the urgency of the question has been produced by recent advances in pathology. Briefly stated, the facts of the change are as follows. In the boyhood of those of us who are now of middle age, the diseases in question were known as mainly of two kinds. One [gonorrhoea], admittedly very common, was considered transient, easily curable, harmless to future generations, and, to everyone but the sufferer, dismissible as a ludicrous incident. The other [syphilis] was known to be one of the most formidable scourges of mankind, capable at its worst of hideous disfigurement and ruinous hereditary transmission, but not at all so common as the more trifling ailment, and alleged by some authorities to be dying out like typhus or plague. That is the belief still entertained by the elderly section of the medical profession and those whom it has instructed.

This easy-going estimate of the situation was alarmingly upset in 1879 by [Albert] Neisser's investigation of the supposedly trivial disease, which he associated with a malignant micro-organism called the gonococcus. The physicians who still ridicule its gravity are now confronted by an agitation led by medical women and professional nurses, who cite a formidable array of authorities for their statements that it is the commonest cause of blindness, and that it is transmitted from father to mother, from mother to child, from child to nurse, producing evils from which the individual attacked never gets securely free. If half the scientific evidence be true, a marriage contracted by a person actively affected in either way is perhaps the worst crime that can be committed with legal impunity in a civilized community. The danger of becoming the victim of such a crime is the worst danger that lurks in marriage for men and women, and in domestic service for nurses.

Stupid people who are forced by these facts to admit that the simple taboo which forbids the subject to be mentioned at all is ruinous, still fall back on the plea that though the public ought to be warned, the theatre is not the proper place for the warning. When asked "What, then *is* the proper place?" they plead that the proper place is out of hearing of the general public: that is, not in a school, not in a church, not in a newspaper, not in a public meeting, but in medical text-books which are read only by medical students. This, of course, is the taboo over again, only sufficiently ashamed of itself to resort to subterfuge. The commonsense of the matter is that a public danger needs a public warning, and the more public the place the more effective the warning.

Why the Unmentionable must be Mentioned on the Stage

But beyond this general consideration there is a special need for the warning in the theatre. The best friends of the theatre cannot deny, and need not seek to deny, that a considerable proportion of our theatrical entertainments stimulate the sexual instincts of the spectators. Indeed this is so commonly the case that a play which contains no sexual appeal is quite openly and commonly written of, even by professional critics of high standing, as being "undramatic," or "not a play at all." This is the basis of the prejudice against the theatre shewn by that section of English society in which sex is regarded as original sin, and the theatre, consequently, as the gate of hell. The prejudice is thoughtless: sex is a necessary and healthy instinct; and its nurture and education is one of the most important uses of all art; and, for the present at all events, the chief use of the theatre.

Now it may be an open question whether the theatre has proved itself worthy of being entrusted with so serious a function. I can conceive a community passing a law forbidding dramatic authors to deal with sex as a motive at all. Although such a law would consign the great bulk of existing dramatic literature to the wastepaper basket, it would neither destroy it wholly nor paralyze all future playwrights. The bowdlerization of Molière and Shakespear on the basis of such a law would leave a surprising quantity of their work intact. The novels of Dickens and his contemporaries are before us to prove how independent the imaginative writer is of the theme so often assumed to be indispensable in fiction. The works in which it is dragged in by the ears on this false assumption are far more numerous than the tales and plays—Manon Lescaut is an example—of which it forms the entire substance. Just as the European dramatist is able to write plays without introducing an accouchement, which is regarded as indispensable in all sympathetic Chinese plays, he can, if he is put to it, dispense with any theme that law or custom could conceivably forbid, and still find himself rich in dramatic material. Let us grant therefore that love might be ruled out by a written law as effectually as cholera is ruled out by an unwritten one without utterly ruining the theatre.

Still, it is none the less beyond all question by any reasonable and thoughtful person that if we tolerate any subject on the stage we must not tolerate it by halves. It may be questioned whether we should allow war on the stage; but it cannot sanely be questioned that, if we do, we must allow its horrors to be represented as well as its glories. Destruction and murder, pestilence and famine, demoralization and cruelty, robbery and jobbery, must be allowed to contend with patriotism and military heroism on the boards as they do in actual war: otherwise the stage might inflame national hatreds and lead to their gratification with a recklessness that would make a cockpit of Europe. Again, if unscrupulous authors are to be allowed to make the stage a parade of champagne bottles, syphons, and tantaluses, scrupulous ones must be allowed to write such plays as L'Assommoir,[18] which has, as a matter of simple fact, effectively deterred many young men from drunkenness. Nobody disputes the reasonableness of this freedom to present both sides. But when we come to sex, the taboo steps in, with the result that all the allurements of sex may be exhibited on the stage heightened by every artifice that the imagination of the voluptuary can devize, but not one of its dangers and penalties. You may exhibit seduction on the stage, but you must not even mention illegitimate conception and criminal abortion. We may, and do, parade prostitution to the point of intoxicating every young person in the theatre; yet no young person may hear a word as to the diseases that follow prostitution and avenge the prostitute to the third and fourth generation of them that buy her. Our shops and business offices are full of young men living in lonely lodgings, whose only artistic recreation is the theatre. In the theatre we practise upon them every art that can make their loneliness intolerable and heighten the charm of the bait in the snares of the street as they go home. But when a dramatist is enlightened enough to understand the danger, and sympathetic enough to come to the rescue with a play to expose the snare and warn the victim, we forbid the manager to perform it on pain of ruin, and denounce the author as a corrupter of morals. One hardly knows whether to laugh or cry at such perverse stupidity.

18. More than half a dozen dramatizations of Émile Zola's novel *L'Assommoir* (*The Liquor Shop*) were performed in England within a year of its publication (1879), notably Charles Reade's *Drink*.

BRIEUX AND VOLTAIRE

It is a noteworthy fact that when Brieux wrote Les Avariés (Damaged Goods) his experience with it recalled in one particular that of Voltaire.

It will be remembered that Voltaire, whose religious opinions were almost exactly those of most English Nonconformists today, took refuge from the Established Church of France near Geneva, the city of Calvin, where he established himself as the first and the greatest of modern Nonconformist philanthropists. The Genevese ministers found his theology so much to their taste that they were prevented from becoming open Voltaireans only by the scandal he gave by his ridicule of the current Genevese idolatry of the Bible, from which he was as free as any of our prominent Baptists and Congregationalists. In the same way, when Brieux, having had his Les Avariés condemned by the now extinct French censorship, paid a visit to Switzerland, he was invited by a Swiss minister to read the play from the pulpit; and though the reading actually took place in a secular building, it was at the invitation and under the auspices of the minister. The minister knew what the Censor did not know: that what Brieux says in Les Avariés needs saying. The minister believed that when a thing needs saying, a man is in due course inspired to say it, and that such inspiration gives him a divine right to be heard. And this appears to be the simple truth of the matter in terms of the minister's divinity. For most certainly Brieux had every worldly inducement to refrain from writing this play, and no motive for disregarding these inducements except the motive that made Luther tear up the Pope's Bull, and Mahomet tell the idolatrous Arabs of Mecca that they were worshipping stones.

The reader will now understand why these three great plays have forced themselves upon us in England as they forced themselves upon Brieux's own countrymen. Just as Brieux had to write them, cost what it might, so we have had to translate them and perform them and finally publish them for those to read who are out of reach of the theatre. The evils they deal with are as rampant in England and America as they are in France. The gonococcus is not an exclusively French microbe: the possibility of sterilizing marriage is not bounded by the Channel, the Rhine, or the Alps. The furious revolt of poor women against bringing into the world more mouths to eat the bread that is already insufficient for their first born, rages with us exactly as it does in the final scene of Maternity. Therefore these three plays are given to the English speaking peoples first. There are others to follow of like importance to us. And there are some, like La Française, which we may read more lightheartedly when we have learnt the lesson of the rest. In La Française an American (who might just as well be an Englishman) has acquired his ideas of France and French life, not from the plays of Brieux, but from the conventional plays and romances which have only one theme—adultery. Visiting France, he is received as a friend in an ordinary respectable French household, where he conceives himself obliged, as a gallant man of the world, to invite his hostess to commit with him the adultery which he imagines to be a matter of course in every French *ménage*. The ignominious failure of his enterprise makes it much better comedy than his success would have made it in an ordinary fashionable play.

As Good Fish in the Sea

The total number of plays produced by Brieux up to the date on which I write these lines is fifteen.[19] The earliest dates as far back as 1890. It is therefore high time for us to begin to read him, as we have already begun to act him. The most pitiful sort of ignorance is ignorance of the few great men who are men of our own time. Most of us die without having heard of those contemporaries of ours, for our opportunities of seeing and applauding whom posterity will envy us. Imagine meeting the ghost of an Elizabethan cockney in heaven, and, on asking him eagerly what Shakespear was like, being told either that the cockney had never heard of Shakespear, or knew of him vaguely as an objectionable writer of plays full of regrettable errors of taste. To save our own ghosts from disgracing themselves in this manner when they are asked about Brieux, is one of the secondary uses of this first instalment of his works in English.

PARKNASILLA AND AYOT ST LAWRENCE, 1909.   G. B. S.

---

19. Actually Brieux had written about two dozen plays since 1890, not including two early (1879–80) one-act collaborations.

Irish Mountains

[*In response to an appeal by the American photographer Alvin Langdon Coburn to supply a preface to a catalogue of an exhibition of Coburn's Irish photographs, Shaw attempted a draft while visiting Niesenkulm, in the Swiss Alps, at the beginning of August 1911. Unable to produce more than a few uninspired and disjointed travel sketches, he abandoned the effort. Three paragraphs (the fourth, fifth, and sixth) were published, as Part II of 'Touring in Ireland', in Shaw's* The Matter with Ireland *(1962), edited by Dan H. Laurence and David H. Greene. The balance of the uncompleted draft is reproduced from the shorthand manuscript in the Harry Ransom Humanities Research Center of the University of Texas at Austin.*]

———

Of set purpose I approach this subject sitting on the summit of a Swiss mountain 9000 feet high, in view of the snowclad giants of the Bernese Oberland and with a dazzling view of Mont Blanc fresh in my memory. Under no other circumstances dare I say deliberately that Irish mountains, the tallest of which would appear the merest pimple from my present elevation, are among the most imposing in the world. If Primrose Hill [north of Regent's Park, London] were in Kerry it would look mysterious, dangerous, romantic: if Hindhead [in Surrey] were in Wicklow it would assume a Pyrenean distinction.

No doubt there is a prosaic explanation of this impressiveness, which may be claimed for Welsh and Scotch mountains also. The truth is, people are much more reasonable about horizontal distances than about vertical ones. No man claims that the further you get away from London the better you see it. He knows that though you can get a very good view of it from Hampstead Heath [in north-central London] on a clear day, it does not follow that you will see it better from Harrow [northwest of London, in Middlesex]. Yet many people imagine that a view of London from a balloon nine thousand feet up would be finer than from a balloon nine hundred feet up. They could not make a greater mistake. I have seen it from a balloon at both heights;[1]

---

1. Shaw had made a two-and-a-half-hour balloon ascent of 9000 feet on 3 July 1906, in company with Harley Granville Barker, the actor Robert Loraine, and Shaw's sister-in-law Mary Cholmondeley.

and I can assure the reader, if he, on reflection, requires any assurance, that nothing on earth is large enough to be impressive as seen from above or below at greater distances than the Irish mountains attain. Horizontal distances are much more effective. A huge cathedral rising from a plain and dwarfing a hundred houses and dwarfing the surrounding houses into mere crab shells, looks stupendous even when several miles away. An amphitheatre at El Djem,[2] in Tunisia, when you first see it across the steppes of that region, looks like a mountain. But from a bird's eye view a cathedral or an amphitheatre is hardly more impressive than a manhole.

This, I suppose, is why you may drive over the Stelvio Pass [in the Adige valley, between Italy and Switzerland], 9000 feet high without any very special imaginative perturbation, whereas when you drive through the pass of Ballaghbeama [through the mountains known as Macgillycuddy's Reeks] in Kerry, you feel as if you were discovering the North West Passage at the risk of your life and even of your soul. No doubt that difference is partly to the credit of the Stelvio engineers.

Those who desire to conciliate the Irish, and be popular in a district, must change their manners if they have come from a busy country where people have to go into action of any sort with their minds made up. In London, in Paris, and in all the crowded and swiftly moving centres where the value of time is high, nobody is so unpopular as the man who does not know what he wants or where he is going to. The English porter, for example, wants a definite order and wants it quickly. It never occurs to him that such definiteness and quickness is uncivil or wounding. He would rather at any time put up with a too peremptory man than be delayed by a too polite one. Consequently the citizen of such centres, when he is the giver of orders, as a tourist mostly is, has a sort of goodhumored, entirely friendly curtness which wastes no time and leaves no questions open; and, when he is a receiver of orders, is on the alert for precisely this kind of expeditious treatment.

In Ireland, as in all places where time is of relatively little value, and where men have leisure to fall into habits of dreaming and preoccupying themselves with their dignity, such manners are much less popular. They are really a mark of superior social training; and they affect the less trained

2. The amphitheatre at El Djem (a modern city on the site of the ancient city of Thysdrus) is considered to be the finest Roman monument in north Africa. It is second in size only to the Colosseum in Rome.

man as if they were an assertion of personal superiority to himself. Once, when driving a motor car to the town of Sneem in Kerry on a market day, I met a drove of pigs. The drovers who had just purchased them, and who, unaccustomed to automobiles, expected nothing less than the cutting to pieces of the whole flock if I came on, lost their heads and bawled at me frantically to stop. It became necessary for me to dictate the correct habits with considerable decision of manner. Thereupon a young farmer gathered all the bitterness of his soul into a single objurgation as I steered past him. "You bloody Englishman" he yelled. This is the secret of the unpopularity of Englishmen and Germans in Ireland. They assume that the good manners of London and Berlin are good manners in Cork and Kerry. They assume that the Irish laborer is on the alert for their orders and wants them short and clear and crisp. But the Irish laborer is not in the highly trained and timesaving attitude at all. He is by no means convinced that it is his destiny or even his business to take orders from anyone. He may be dreaming of being a king, crowned or uncrowned. He may be preoccupied with the subject of Home Rule, or the Church in Ireland, or with dramatic private affairs. Therefore, if you are sufficiently master of the finer shades of manner, you had better convey by your tone an apology for disturbing him. If you are unequal to this, look as if you wanted a porter (or whatever he may be) and, being too bashful to apply to him, are on the point of employing somebody else. He will then proffer his services quite anxiously.

But the Irish, except in the city slums, where humanity is degraded everywhere, practically never misunderstand really good manners, and respond to them with remarkable dignity. Only, it must be understood that by good manners I do not mean an obvious determination to be polite to one's inferiors. Treat an Irishman as if he were a duke, and you another; and he will treat you as if you were a king. Patronize him; and he can be surprisingly offensive. The worst of all ways to treat him is to read oldfashioned Irish novels, and to treat him as a joke. There was a time when it was part of an Irishman's servility to play up to this impertinence. Possibly Wicklow car drivers may still play the stage Irishman for the benefit of English tourists of the less considerate sort. The performance is seldom a good one. But in general you may take it that Ireland is in full reaction against both servility and the stage Irishman. It is a point of honor with the modern Irishman to have no sense of humor.

Irish hotels are not so good as they might be; but they are very far from being as bad as one fears. Ireland is the paradise of fishermen; and the fishing hotels are to the interior what the seaside hotels are to the coast:

they provide quite tolerable refuges in places where in England one would have to make the best of a cold welcome in an inadequate public house. As to food, an unlimited toleration of bacon and eggs, chops and steaks, and salmon, will never starve. What is to be dreaded is the pretentious hotel with a chef, who is generally an Italian whose inveterate carelessness and slovenliness have made life impossible for him in any country sophisticated enough to know the difference between a chef and a sea cook.

The English hotels whose proprietors are foolish enough to offer "French cookery" without knowing anything about it, instead of sticking to the English meals they understand, are bad enough in all conscience; but they at least know the difference between a clean kitchen and a dirty one, and will often insist on a clean one. They imagine that old rinds of cheese are good enough for cooking (the one infallible test of a good restaurant is to order a Welsh Rabbit and taste whether it is made with Leix [an Irish county, in Leinster] cheese or with discarded scraps from the Coffee Room cheese plates); but they at least spare you that most revolting of all culinary flavors: the flavor of dirty water in a dirty saucepan on a plate wiped by a dirty cloth. I have encountered this flavor in an Irish hotel with an Italian chef over whom the managers had no control, and who had probably left his own country to escape the control of the police. But such hotels are usually mere incidents in some feeble and halfhearted attempt on the part of the railway company, or some other more or less academic body, to work up a neglected neighborhood into a beauty spot for tourists. The really successful tourist hotels and railway hotels are exceptionally good; for mediocrity is not a note of Ireland in hotels or anything else: the good hotels are decidedly good: the bad ones are absurdly bad. In the wilds of Kerry there are excellent hotels (under German management, by the way) and a first rate railway hotel at Killarney. In the wilds of Donegal there is the Rosapenna golfing hotel, at which you must engage rooms months beforehand. You must of course beware of imitators. The success of these hotels occasionally leads a London speculator to take an old and quite inadequate house on the coast, with perhaps two good bedrooms in it, and to issue dithyrambic prospectuses with photographs of the Atlantic and of the grandfather's clock in the hall, the result being that rich and exacting travellers arrive in high power motor cars, very angry at having had to risk their tyres over miles of unrolled stone, but buoyed up with hopes of a splendid hotel and a smart dinner at the end of their journey. When they find a secondrate seaside lodging house in charge of a severely "tied" publican,[3] with only "servants bedrooms" available, and nothing to eat but a not very high tea in the parlor, they are apt to bring up an evil report of the land. It is rather easy to circulate delusive prospectuses of hotels and "beauties of nature" nowadays through the wildly unscrupulous and irresponsible bodies called Tourist Development Agencies.

The experienced traveler will gather from the above that Ireland is, in the matter of hotels, much like other countries. As to roads, it is still in the phase in which the inhabitants tell you with pride that such and such a road is "steam-rolled." Kerry to the north of Killarney has got as far as a tarred road in 1910. The mountain and coast roads of Kerry have got a bad reputation which is not deserved. When they were first tried by heavy motor *chars à banc* [open sightseeing omnibuses with crosswise seats facing forward], the results were startling. The roads in many cases proved to be merely thin skins of surface over holes and pits and hollows of all sorts, the subsoil having been washed away by the copious rains for which the country is famous. The cars went through in all directions. Then the county authorities sent a monstrous stone-breaking machine, drawn by a mammoth traction engine, to repair the damage. The result may be imagined. The stone breaker disappeared into the bowels of the earth every twenty yards or so. Its adventures on the road from Parknasilla to Sneem will long be abroad. But the road came out of these trials as gold from the furnace. The holes had to be filled in and the surface very thoroughly made up before this devastating monster could be got out of the way; and the last state of the roads, though much worse than the first in point of reputation, is much better in point of fact. No motorist need now hesitate to land [by ferry] in Waterford [in the south of Ireland] and make straight for the coast of the Kenmare River via Killarney [in the west] without the least fear of finding worse going than in Derbyshire [central England]. Only, one must allow for the Irish magic. Nobody could possibly be terrified by Buxton and Matlock [in Derbyshire], though their roads are often, to say the least, bothersome. But the pass through the Macgillicuddy Reeks, which presents no real difficulty, will impress you as a desperate adventure, and make you feel at every corner that it would perhaps be wiser to turn back before it is too late.

The Irish bog has also to be reckoned with.

★

3. A 'tied' public house is one that has been leased, usually from a major brewery, which exercises control over its operation and requires exclusive sale of its liquor products.

The tourist developers will shamelessly call a dip a glen, a sink a waterfall, a wet boulder a lover's leap, a plank a devil's bridge, and an impracticable stepping stone a *saut de bourrique* [Jenny jump]. They will actually put up sign posts at corners of footpaths directing you to these impostures, and [produce] bad guidebooks with descriptions of them which induce people to walk weary miles to see nothing. And I need hardly add that their descriptions of hotels have about the same relation to facts as [do] their descriptions of nature. Now I do not allege that this sort of humbug has yet gone as far in Ireland as it has in France; but the Irish have a good deal of literary descriptive talent; and

[Text ends here]

John Bull's Other Island

Preface to the Home Rule Edition, 1912, with a headnote added for the
Collected Edition, 1930

=====

(*I reprint this interim preface after much hesitation. It is based on two confident
political assumptions that have since been not merely disproved but catastrophically
shattered.*

*The first was that Parliament in 1912 was still what it had been in the heyday
of Gladstonian Liberalism, when it was utterly inconceivable that an Act of
constitutional reform which had been duly passed and assented-to by the Crown
could be dropped into the waste paper basket because a handful of ladies and
gentlemen objected to it, and the army officers' messes blustered mutinously against
it.*

*The second assumption was that Ireland was politically one and indivisible,
and, consequently, that when Home Rule came, as it was evident it must come, the
Protestants of Ireland must stand together and make the best of it. The possibility
of a Partition by which Belfast Protestantism should accept Home Rule for itself in
a concentration camp and thus abandon its co-religionists outside the camp to what
must then inevitably become a Roman Catholic Home Rule Government of the
rest of Ireland, was undreamt of.*

*How both these things nevertheless happened I have described in a postscript to
the original preface which will be found on a later page [p. 239 in the present
edition]. Readers who skip to that preface will lose nothing by missing this one
except a possibly instructive example of how our eternal march into the future must
always be a blindfold march. I guessed ahead, and guessed wrongly, whilst stupider
and more ignorant fellow-pilgrims guessed rightly.*)

John Bull's Other Island was written when a Unionist Government [anti-
Home Rule party] was in power, and had been in power with one brief
interval for twenty years. The reason for this apparent eclipse of Home
Rule was that the Liberal Party had during that period persisted in assuring
the English people anxiously that it had no intention of doing anything for
England (its object being to shew its abhorrence of Socialism) and that it
cared for nothing but Home Rule in Ireland. Now as the English electors,
being mostly worse off than the Irish, were anxious to have something

done to alleviate their own wretched condition, they steadily voted for the Unionist Party (not because it was Unionist, but because it cared more for England than for Ireland), except on one occasion in 1893, when the Liberals put all their Home Rule tracts in the fire, and fought on a program of English Social Reform, known as the Newcastle Program, drawn up by my friend and Fabian colleague, Mr Sidney Webb, and ingeniously foisted on the Liberals by myself and other Fabians disguised as artless Gladstonian members of certain little local caucuses which called themselves Liberal and Radical Associations, and were open to any passer-by who might astonish them by seeming to take an interest in their routine of bleeding candidates for registration expenses and local subscriptions. The program won the election for the Home Rulers. It was a close thing; but it won it. The Liberals then dropped it; and Lord Rosebery[1] made his famous discovery that programs are a mistake, a view which, though supported with deep conviction by his Party, which still had no desire to do or mean or understand anything that could conceivably benefit anyone in England, had the immediate effect of extinguishing its noble author politically, and sending his party back into opposition for another ten years, at the end of which the Unionists, quite as ignorant of what the people of England were thinking about as Lord Rosebery, entered upon an impassioned defence of the employment of Chinese labor in South Africa without considering the fact that every one of their arguments was equally valid for the introduction of Chinese labor into Lancashire. And as the people of Lancashire were concerned about Lancashire and not at all about South Africa, the Unionist Party followed Lord Rosebery into the shades.

One consequence of this political swing of the pendulum was that John Bull's Other Island, which had up to that moment been a topical play, immediately became a historical one. Broadbent is no longer up-to-date. His *bête noir*, Mr Joseph Chamberlain, has retired from public life. The controversies about Tariff Reform, the Education [London Education Act, 1902–3] and [Liquor] Licensing Bills [1904; 1910], and the South African war, have given way to the far more vital questions raised by Mr [David] Lloyd George's[2] first unskilful essays in Collectivism, and to the agitation for Votes for Women. Broadbent is still strong on the question of Persia:

1. Archibald Primrose, Fifth Earl Rosebery, was Foreign Secretary under Gladstone (1886, 1892–4) and Liberal Prime Minister (1894–5).
2. Chancellor of the Exchequer 1908–15. He became Prime Minister in 1916.

stronger than he was on that of Armenia (probably because Persia is further off); but there is little left of the subjects that excited him in 1904 except Home Rule. And Home Rule is to be disposed of this year.

The Government will no doubt be glad to get rid of it. The English people, with prices up and wages down, care less, if possible, than they ever did about it. Even the governing classes are feeling the pressure of the Home Rule agitations in Egypt and India more than in Ireland; for the Irish, now confident that their battle is won, are keeping comparatively quiet, whilst in the East the question is in the acute stage in which the Government has to explain that really very few people have had confessions extorted by torture in the police stations, and that if the natives would only be reasonable and recognize the advantages of British rule, and their own utter unfitness for self-government, there would be no need to imprison nationalists either in India or Egypt; so that, in effect, the natives have themselves to thank for whatever unpleasantness may happen to them.

The only considerable body of Englishmen really concerned about Home Rule except as a Party question, are those members of the Free Churches, vulgarly called Dissenters or Nonconformists, who believe that the effect of Home Rule would be to deliver Ireland into the hands of the Roman Catholic Church, which they regard as The Scarlet Woman. It is clearly not a very deeply considered apprehension, because there is not a country in the world, not even Spain, where the people are so completely in the hands of the Roman Catholic Church as they are in Ireland under English rule and because of English rule. In the non-Protestant Christian countries which are politically independent, the clericals are struggling, not to regain their lost supremacy (that survives only in Ireland), but for their houses, their property, their right to live in the country they were born in, and to have the political weight due to their merits; for they have merits: the priest is not so black as he is painted in all free countries nowadays. But our Free Churchmen are too much afraid of the Pope, and of the confessional, and of the priest in the house, to see how weak these forces are in the face of democracy. Also, they are not all well off enough to buy plays in six-shilling, or even in eighteenpenny volumes.[3] Therefore, I think it opportune to issue this cheap edition [Constable Sixpenny Series] of John Bull's Other Island this Home Rule Year, because its preface was written by an

---

3. Six shillings was the standard price for a hardcover edition of Shaw's plays, like that containing *John Bull's Other Island*, *How He Lied to Her Husband*, and *Major Barbara* (1907). Most of his plays were also issued individually, in paper wrappers, for eighteenpence.

Irishman of Protestant family and Protestant prejudices, and shews that the one way in which the power of the priest can be kept within its proper limits in Ireland is by setting the Irish people free to take it in hand themselves without seeming to be treacherously taking the side of England against their own country.

Still more needed is this cheap edition in Ireland, where nobody can well afford to pay more than sixpence for anything, since, if I may put it elliptically, the only people in Ireland who can afford more than sixpence are those who live in England. I should like to call the attention of my nervous fellow Protestants in Ireland to the fact that in Italy, the centre of Roman Catholicism, the Pope is in a position closely resembling what that of Louis XVI would have been during the first years of the French Revolution if he, like the Pope, had had no wife to bring him to the scaffold by tempting him to betray his country to a foreign foe. Also that in France, in spite of the revocation of the Edict of Nantes[4] by the Roman Catholic Church at the height of its power, the Huguenots have always wielded, and still wield today, a power that is out of all proportion to their comparative numbers, and even, I am afraid I must add, to their merits. The Huguenot of Ulster is a coward only when he breaks his own backbone by taking the part of a foreign country against his own. Shut him up in Derry with an English King besieging him, and he does not shriek for the Germans to come and help him as if the thumbscrews of the Spanish Armada were already on his hands: he chalks up No Surrender merrily, and puts up one of the famous fights of history. After all, what is the use of protesting that you will not be governed from Rome if the alternative is to be governed from London? The great Protestant Irishmen have been all the more powerful because they loved Ireland better, not only than Rome, but than England. Why was it that the priests had no power to impose a Roman Catholic Leader on the Home Rule movement instead of Parnell? Simply because Parnell was so proud of his Irish birthright that he would rather have been one of even a persecuted minority in an Irish parliament than the Premier of an English Cabinet. He was not afraid of his countrymen: he knew that Protestantism could hold its own only too well in a free Ireland; and even if he had not known it he would have taken his chance rather than sell his birthright and his country. It is the essential dishonor of acting as a foreign garrison in a land where they are not foreigners that makes the position of the Orangemen so impossible, and breaks in them

4. The 1598 measure by Henry IV of France securing religious liberty for Protestants (Huguenots).

the spirit that animates every man in Europe who is fighting for a minority; and what man of any dignity today is not one of a minority that cries in the wilderness against one or other of the manifold iniquities and falsehoods of our civilization? I think if I as a Home Ruler (and many other less orthodox things) can live in England and hold my own in a minority which on some very sensitive points reaches the odds of about 1 to 48,000,000, an Ulster Orangeman should be able to face Home Rule without his knees knocking shamefully in the face of a contemptuous England which despises him none the less because his cowardice seems to serve her own turn.

There are, I know, men and women who are political perverts by nature. The supreme misfortune of being born with one's natural instincts turned against nature by a freak of nature is a phenomenon that occurs politically as well as physiologically. There are Poles who are devoted with all their soul to Russia and the maintenance of Russian rule in Poland, Persians who are risking their lives to introduce it in Persia, Indians and Egyptians who are ready to sacrifice all they possess for England and English rule. And it is not to be denied that among these are persons of high character and remarkable ability, comparing very favorably with the dregs of the nationalist movements, which, just because they are national and normal, are made up of all sorts, and consequently have dregs: pretty nasty ones too. For that matter, if ever a Book of Spies be written, it will include examples of courage, conviction, perseverance, and ability, that will almost persuade shallow people that spies are the real heroes of military history. Even in more personal relations, natural passion cannot pretend to inspire more intense devotion than perverted passion. But when all is said, the pervert, however magnificently he may conduct his campaign against nature, remains abhorrent. When Napoleon, though he boasted of having made peers and marshals of peasants and ostlers, drew the line at promoting a spy, he followed a universal instinct and a sound one. When the Irish Catholic who, feeling bitterly that the domination of the priest is making his own lot hopeless, nevertheless stands shoulder to shoulder with the priest for Home Rule against Dublin Castle, he is behaving naturally and rightly. When the Orangeman sacrifices his nationality to his hatred of the priest, and fights against his own country for its conqueror, he is doing something for which, no matter how bravely he fights, history and humanity will never forgive him: English history and humanity, to their credit be it said, least of all.

Please do not suppose for a moment that I propose that the Irish Protestant should submit to the Irish Roman Catholic. I reproach the Irish

Roman Catholic for his submission to Rome exactly as I reproach the Orangeman for his submission to England. If Catholicism is to be limited in Ireland by any geographical expression (in which case it ceases to be Catholic) let it be Irish Catholicism, not Italian Catholicism. Let us maintain our partnership with Rome as carefully as our partnership with England; but let it be, in the one case as in the other, a free partnership. But the Irish Catholics are not Italian in their politics. They do not oppose Home Rule; and that gives them the right to the support of every Irish Protestant until Home Rule is achieved. After that, let us by all means begin a civil war next day if we are fools enough. A war for an idea may be a folly; but it is not a dishonor. Both parties would be fighting for Ireland; and though the slaying of an Irishman by an Irishman for Ireland may be a tragedy—may be even a crime to those who think that all war is crime—at least it is not unnatural crime, like the slaying of an Irishman by an Irishman for England's sake. There will, of course, be no war of religion: I have shewn in this book that the Protestant under Home Rule will be far safer and stronger than he is today; but even if there were, that is the way to look at it.

The question is still more important for England than for Ireland, in spite of England's indifference to it. In Ireland we are still sane: we do not sneer at our country as "Little Ireland," and cheer for a doubtful commercial speculation called The Empire which we could not point out accurately on the map, and which is populated by such an overwhelming majority of what an Irish peasant would call "black heathens," that they force us to punish our own missionaries for asking them to buy and read The Bible, and compel the Protestant Passive Resisters, who will be sold up rather than pay a rate to maintain a Church school, to pay without a murmur for the establishment of the Roman Catholic Church in Malta. Formerly "Little England,"[5] the "right little, tight little Island [from T. Dibdin's 'The Snug Little Island', 1802]," despised Spain for her imperial policy, and saw her lose her place, not only among the empires, but even among the nations, with self-satisfied superiority. Today England is letting herself be dragged into the path of Spain. She dreams of nothing but the old beginning: an Invincible Armada. Spain reckoned without the Lord of Hosts, who scattered that Invincible Armada for Little England. The modern Imperialist does not believe in the Lord of Hosts; but the Armada was defeated for all that, though England's fleet was far more inferior to it than

5. 'Little Englanders' was a locution used pejoratively at the turn of the century to denote anti-imperialists.

the German fleet will ever again be to the English fleet. The Lord of Hosts may not be quite the sort of power that Philip of Spain conceived it to be: many of us are dropping the personal pronoun, as I have just dropped it lest I should be prosecuted for superstition by the Society for the Encouragement of Cruelty to Animals; but it can still send bigger fleets to the bottom than England can build, and exalt smaller nations than England ever was above drifting congeries of derelict regions held desperately together by terrified soldiers trying to wave half a dozen flags all at once in the name of Empire: a name that every man who has ever felt the sacredness of his own native soil to him, and thus learnt to regard that feeling in other men as something holy and inviolable, spits out of his mouth with enormous contempt.

Not that I have any delusions about Drake and his Elizabethan comrades: they were pirates and slave-traders, not a whit better than the Algerine corsairs who shared with them what modern idiots call "the command of the sea" (much the sea cares about their command!); but it is better to be a pirate trading in slaves out of sheer natural wickedness than a bankrupt in a cocked hat, doing the same things, and worse, against your own conscience, because you are paid for it and are afraid to do anything else. Drake thought nothing of burning a Spanish city; but he was not such a fool as to suppose that if he told off some of his crew to stay and govern that Spanish city by force when it was rebuilt, all the reasonable inhabitants of that town would recognize the arrangement as an enormous improvement, and be very much obliged to him, which is the modern Imperial idea. To singe the King of Spain's beard; pick his pocket; and run away, was, in the absence of any international police, a profitable bit of sport, if a rascally one; but if Drake had put a chain round the King's neck and led him round a prisoner for the rest of his life, he would have suffered as much by such a folly as the King, and probably died sooner of worry, anxiety, expense, and loss through the neglect of his own proper affairs, than the King would have died of captivity. Bermondsey [a London borough south of the Thames] goes to the dogs whilst those whose business it is to govern it are sitting on Bengal; and the more Bengal kicks, the more Bermondsey is neglected, except by the tax collector. The notion that the way to prosper is to insist on managing everybody else's affairs is, on the face of it, a fool's notion. It is at bottom the folly of the ignorant simpletons who long to be kings and chiefs because they imagine that a king or a chief is an idle voluptuary with lots of money, leisure, and power over others, to use irresponsibly for his own amusement.

In short, then, the future is not to the empires, but to federations of self-governing nations, exactly as, within these nations, the future is not to Capitalist Oligarchies, but to Collectivist organizations of free and equal citizens. In short, to Commonwealths.

In expressing this irresistible sentiment of nationality with all the rhetoric to which it lends itself, I am not forgetting that there are international rights as well as national ones. We are not only natives within our own frontiers but inheritors of the earth. England has rights in Ireland as Ireland has rights in England. I demand of every nation right of ingress and egress, roads, police, an efficient post office, and, in reason, freedom of conscience. I am prepared to steam-roller Tibet if Tibet persist in refusing me my international rights. If the Moors and Arabs cannot or will not secure these common human conditions for me in North Africa, I am quite prepared to co-operate with the French, the Italians, and the Spaniards in Morocco, Algeria, Tunisia, and Tripoli, with the Russians in Siberia, with all three and the English and Germans as well in Africa, or with the Americans in the hunting grounds of the red man, to civilize these places; though I know as well as anyone that there are many detestable features in our civilization, many virtues in village and tribal communities, and a very large alloy indeed of brigandage in our explorations and colonizations.

I know also that what compels us to push our frontiers farther and farther into regions we call barbarous is the necessity of policing, not the barbarians, but the European dregs and riffraff who set up little hells of anarchy and infamy just beyond the border, and thus compel us to advance and rope them in, step by step, no matter how much we are adding to that "white man's burden [title of a poem by Kipling, 1899]," which is none the less a real thing because it is not specially a white man's burden any more than it is specially an Englishman's burden, as most of Mr Kipling's readers seem to interpret it. Tribes must make themselves into nations before they can claim the rights of nations; and this they can do only by civilization.

Also I cannot deny that the exclusion of the Chinese from America and Australia is a violation of international right which the Chinese will be perfectly justified in resisting by arms as soon as they feel strong enough. If nations are to limit immigration, inter-marriage with foreigners, and even international trade by tariffs, it had better be done by international law than by arbitrary national force as at present. It will be seen that I am under no delusion as to the freedom of Nationalism from abuse. I know that there are abuses in England which would not exist if she were governed by Germany, and that there will no doubt be abuses in Ireland under Home Rule which do not exist under English rule, just as things have been done under the Irish Local Government Act that the old oligarchical grand juries would not have tolerated. There are, indeed, a hundred horses on which I could ride off if I wished to shirk the main issue. But when all is said, it is so certain that in the long run all civilized nations must at the same time become more dependent one on another and do their own governing work themselves, that if Ireland refused Home Rule now, it would sooner or later be forced on her by England because England will need all her time and political energy for her own affairs when once she realizes that the day for letting them slide and muddling through is past.

LONDON.
19 January 1912.

The Quintessence of Ibsenism

Preface to a revised and enlarged second edition, 1913

In the pages which follow I have made no attempt to tamper with the work of the bygone man of thirty-five who wrote them. I have never admitted the right of an elderly author to alter the work of a young author, even when the young author happens to be his former self. In the case of a work which is a mere exhibition of skill in conventional art, there may be some excuse for the delusion that the longer the artist works on it the nearer he will bring it to perfection. Yet even the victims of this delusion must see that there is an age limit to the process, and that though a man of forty-five may improve the workmanship of a man of thirty-five, it does not follow that a man of fifty-five can do the same.

When we come to creative art, to the living word of a man delivering a message to his own time, it is clear that any attempt to alter this later on is simply fraud and forgery. As I read the old Quintessence of Ibsenism I may find things that I see now at a different angle, or correlate with so many things then unnoted by me that they take on a different aspect. But though this may be a reason for writing another book, it is not a reason for altering an existing one. What I have written I have written [John 29: 22], said Pilate, thinking (rightly, as it turned out) that his blunder might prove truer than its revision by the elders; and what he said after a lapse of twenty-one seconds I may very well say after a lapse of twenty-one years.

However, I should not hesitate to criticize my earlier work if I thought it likely to do any mischief that criticism can avert. But on reading it through I have no doubt that it is as much needed in its old form as ever it was. Now that Ibsen is no longer frantically abused, and is safe in the Pantheon, his message is in worse danger of being forgotten or ignored than when he was in the pillory. Nobody now dreams of calling me a "muck ferretting dog"[1] because I think Ibsen a great teacher. I will not go so far as to say I wish they did; but I do say that the most effective way of shutting our minds against a

---

1. An opprobrious description by the reviewer of *Truth* of attendees of the first English performance of *Ghosts*, presented by the Independent Theatre in London, privately, on 13 March 1891. Portions of the notice were reprinted by Shaw in *The Quintessence of Ibsenism*.

great man's ideas is to take them for granted and admit he was great and have done with him. It really matters very little whether Ibsen was a great man or not: what does matter is his message and the need of it.

That people are still interested in the message is proved by the history of this book. It has long been out of print in England; but it has never been out of demand. In spite of the smuggling of unauthorized American editions, which I have winked at because the absence of an English reprint was my own fault (if it be a fault not to be able to do more than a dozen things at a time), the average price of copies of the original edition stood at twenty-four shillings some years ago, and is no doubt higher now. But it was not possible to reprint it without additions. When it was issued in 1891 Ibsen was still alive, and had not yet produced The Master Builder, or Little Eyolf, or John Gabriel Borkman, or When We Dead Awaken. Without an account of these four final masterpieces, a book entitled The Quintessence of Ibsenism would have been a fraud on its purchasers; and it was the difficulty of finding time to write the additional chapters on these plays, and review Ibsen's position from the point of view reached when his work ended with his death and his canonization as an admitted grand master of European literature, that has prevented me for twenty years from complying with the demand for a second edition. Also, perhaps, some relics of my old, or rather my young conscience, which revolted against hasty work. Now that my own stream is nearer the sea, I am more inclined to encourage myself in haste and recklessness by reminding myself that *le mieux est l'ennemi du bien* [better is the enemy of good], and that I had better cobble up a new edition as best I can than not supply it at all.

I have taken all possible precautions to keep the reader's mind free from verbal confusion in following Ibsen's attack on ideals and idealism, a confusion that might have been avoided could his plays, without losing the naturalness of their dialogue, have been translated into the language of the English Bible. It is not too much to say that the works of Ibsen furnish one of the best modern keys to the prophecies of Scripture. Read the prophets, major and minor, from Isaiah to Malachi, without such a key, and you will be puzzled and bored by the almost continuous protest against and denunciation of idolatry and prostitution. Simpletons read all this passionate invective with sleepy unconcern, concluding thoughtlessly that idolatry means praying to stocks and stones instead of to brass lectern eagles and the new reredos presented by the local distiller in search of a title; and as to prostitution, they think of it as "the social evil," and regret that the translators of the Bible used a much blunter word. But nobody who has ever heard real live men talking about graven images and traders in sex can for a moment suppose them to be the things the prophets denounced so earnestly. For idols and idolatry read ideals and idealism; for the prostitution of Piccadilly Circus read not only the prostitution of the journalist, the political lawyer, the parson selling his soul to the squire, the ambitious politician selling his soul for office, but the much more intimate and widespread idolatries and prostitutions of the private snob, the domestic tyrant and voluptuary, and the industrial adventurer. At once the prophetic warnings and curses take on meaning and proportion, and lose that air of exaggerated righteousness and tiresome conventional rant which repels readers who do not possess Ibsen's clue. I have sometimes thought of reversing the operation, and substituting in this book the words idol and idolatry for ideal and idealism; but it would be impossible without spoiling the actuality of Ibsen's criticism of society. If you call a man a rascally idealist, he is not only shocked and indignant but puzzled: in which condition you can rely on his attention. If you call him a rascally idolater, he concludes calmly that you do not know that he is a member of the Church of England. I have therefore left the old wording. Save for certain adaptations made necessary by the lapse of time and the hand of death, the book stands as it did, with a few elucidations which I might have made in 1891 had I given the text a couple of extra revisions. Also, of course, the section dealing with the last four plays. The two concluding chapters are new. There is no fundamental change: above all, no dilution.

Whether this edition will change people's minds to the extent to which the first did (to my own great astonishment) I do not know. In the eighteen-nineties one jested about the revolt of the daughters, and of the wives who slammed the front door like Nora. At present the revolt has become so general that even the feeblest and oldest after-dinner jesters dare no longer keep Votes for Women on their list of stale pleasantries about mothers-in-law, rational dress, and mixed bathing. Men are waking up to the perception that in killing women's souls they have killed their own. Mr Granville Barker's worthy father of six unmarriageable daughters in The Madras House [1910], ruefully exclaiming, "It seems to me Ive been made a convenience of all my life," has taken away the excited attention that Nora once commanded when she said, "I have been living all these years with a strange man." When she meets Helmer's "No man sacrifices his honor for a woman" with her "Thousands of women have done that for men," there is no longer the old impressed assent: men fiercely protest that it is not true; that, on the contrary, for every woman who has sacrificed her honor for a man's sake, ten men have sacrificed their honor for a woman's. In the plays of Gorki and Tchekov, against which all the imbecilities and outrages of the old anti-Ibsen campaign are being revived (for the Press never learns anything by experience), the men appear as more tragically sacrificed by evil social conditions and their romantic and idealistic disguises than the women. Now it may be that into this new atmosphere my book will come with quite an oldfashioned air. As I write these lines the terrible play with which Strindberg wreaked the revenge of the male for A Doll's House has just been performed for the first time in London under the title of Creditors [Stage Society, 1911–12]. In that, as in Brieux's Les Hannetons [*The Incubus*], it is the man who is the victim of domesticity, and the woman who is the tyrant and soul destroyer. Thus A Doll's House did not dispose of the question: it only brought on the stage the endless recriminations of idealistic marriage. And how has Strindberg, Ibsen's twin giant, been received? With an even idler stupidity than Ibsen himself, because Ibsen appealed to the rising energy of the revolt of women against idealism; but Strindberg attacks women ruthlessly, trying to rouse men from the sloth and sensuality of their idealized addiction to them; and as the men, unlike the women, do not want to be roused, whilst the women do not like to be attacked, there is no conscious Strindberg movement to relieve the indifference, the dull belittlement, the spiteful hostility against which the devotees of Ibsen fought so slashingly in the nineties. But the unconscious movement is violent enough. As I write, it is only two days since an eminent bacteriologist [Almroth Wright] filled three columns of The Times [28 March 1912] with a wild Strindbergian letter in which he declared that women must be politically and professionally secluded and indeed excluded, because their presence and influence inflict on men an obsession so disabling and dangerous that men and women can work together or legislate together only on the same conditions as horses and mares: that is, by the surgical destruction of the male's sex. The Times and The Pall Mall Gazette gravely accept this outburst as "scientific," and heartily endorse it; though only a few weeks have elapsed since The Times dismissed Strindberg's play and Strindberg himself with curt superciliousness as uninteresting and negligible. Not many years ago [1907], a performance of a play by myself [*The Philanderer*], the action of which was placed in an imaginary Ibsen Club, in which the comedy of the bewilderment of conventional people when brought suddenly into contact with the Ibsenist movement (both understood and misunderstood) formed the atmosphere of the piece, was criticized in terms which shewed that our critics are just as hopelessly in the rear of Ibsen as they were in 1891. The only difference was that whereas in 1891 they would have insulted Ibsen, they now accept him as a classic. But understanding of the change of mind produced by Ibsen, or notion that they live in a world which is seething with the reaction of Ibsen's ideas against the ideas of Sardou and Tom

Taylor,[2] they have none. They stare with equal unintelligence at the sieges and stormings of separate homesteads by Ibsen or Strindberg, and at the attack all along the front of refined society into which these sieges and stormings have now developed. Whether the attack is exquisite, touching, delicate, as in Tchekov's Cherry Orchard, Galsworthy's Silver Box and Granville Barker's Ann Leete [*The Marrying of Ann Leete*], or ruthless, with every trick of intellectual ruffianism and ribaldry, and every engine of dramatic controversy, there is the same pettish disappointment at the absence of the old conventions, the same gaping unconsciousness of the meaning and purpose of the warfare in which each play is a battle, as in the days when this book was new.

Our political journalists are even blinder than our artistic ones in this matter. The credit of our domestic ideals having been shaken to their foundations, as through a couple of earthquake shocks, by Ibsen and Strindberg (the Arch-Individualists of the XIX century) whilst the Socialists have been idealizing, sentimentalizing, denouncing Capitalism for sacrificing Love and Home and Domestic Happiness and Children and Duty to money greed and ambition, yet it remains a commonplace of political journalism to assume that Socialism is the deadliest enemy of the domestic ideals and Unsocialism their only hope and refuge. In the same breath the world-grasping commercial synthesis we call Capitalism, built up by generations of Scotch Rationalists and English Utilitarians, Atheists, Agnostics and Natural-Selectionists, with Malthus as the one churchman among all its prophets, is proclaimed the bulwark of the Christian Churches. We used to be told that the people that walked in darkness have seen a great light [Isaiah 9: 2]. When our people see the heavens blazing with suns, they simply keep their eyes shut, and walk on in darkness until they have led us into the pit. No matter: I am not a domestic idealist; and it pleases me to think that the Life Force may have providential aims in thus keeping my opponents off the trail.

But for all that I must not darken counsel. I therefore, without further apology, launch my old torpedo with the old charge in it, leaving to the new chapters at the end what I have to say about the change in the theatre since Ibsen set his potent leaven to work there.

AYOT ST LAWRENCE, 1912–13.

2. English dramatic author of many popular works, including *The Ticket-of-Leave Man* (1863), *Masks and Faces* (with Charles Reade, 1852), and *Our American Cousin* (1858); the latter is remembered as the comedy Lincoln was viewing when assassinated by John Wilkes Booth in 1865.

The Perfect Wagnerite

Preface to the third English edition, 1913

═══════

In 1907 The Perfect Wagnerite was translated into German by my friend Siegfried Trebitsch. On reading through his version in manuscript I was struck by the inadequacy of the merely negative explanation given by me of the irrelevance of Night Falls on The Gods (Die Götter-dämmerung) to the general philosophic scheme of The Ring. That explanation was correct as far as it went; but, put as I had put it, it seemed to me to suggest that the operatic character of Night Falls on The Gods was the result of indifference or forgetfulness produced by the lapse of twentyfive years between the first projection of The Ring and its completion. Now it is clear that in whatever other ways Wagner may have changed, he never became careless and never became indifferent. I therefore inserted in the first German edition a new section in which I shewed how the revolutionary history of Western Europe from the Liberal explosion of 1848 to the confused attempt at a popular and *quasi* Socialist military and municipal administration by the Commune of Paris in 1871 (that is to say, from the literary beginning of The Niblung's Ring by Wagner to the long-delayed musical completion of Night Falls on The Gods) had demonstrated practically that the passing away of the present capitalistic order was going to be a much more complicated business than it appears in Wagner's dramatization.

Since 1907, then, the German edition has been more complete than the English one. I now, after six years' pure procrastination, for which I have no excuse except preoccupation with other work, add the German extension to the English text. [He had, however, added this to the American edition published by Brentano in 1909.] Otherwise the book remains as it was.

I have sometimes been asked why anyone should read a philosophic treatise merely to find out the story of The Ring. I take this opportunity to reply publicly that there is, as far as I know, no reason why anyone should take any trouble in the matter at all unless they want to, and that the degree of trouble must be determined by the degree of want, which, again, will be determined by the wanter's capacity. But this I will say. Even for the purposes of the idlest Bayreuth tourist the story of The Ring must be told as Wagner's score tells it if it is to be of any real use to the visitor who cannot understand what the singers are saying. Anyone can, without knowing a bar of the score, string the events narrated in The Ring together in the order of their occurrence on the stage, add the names of the *dramatis personae* and a description of the scenes, and offer the result as a guide to The Ring. But such a mechanical account of the affair will hinder more than it will help. It will pass over as trivial, or even omit altogether, points to which Wagner has given immense weight and consequence, either by the length or intensity of his direct musical treatment or by the recurrence of themes connected with them; and it will rhetorically emphasize or spread itself descriptively over the more obvious matters which speak for themselves to the spectator and occupy little space and less depth in the musical fabric. People primed with such accounts sit waiting to see the bear or the dragon or the rainbow, or the transformation of Alberic into a snake and a toad, or the magic fire or the swimming feats of the Rhine daughters, and are bored because these exciting spectacles are so unconscionably delayed whilst Wotan, Fricka, Brynhild, Erda, Alberic, and Loki discuss things of which the "synopsis" gives no hint.

Now the story as it is told in this book has its centres of gravity placed exactly where Wagner has placed them in his score. What Wagner has made much of, I have made much of; and I have explained why he made much of it. What he passed lightly over, I have passed lightly over. There is a good deal in The Ring which is on the surface of the score: nobody with ears and eyes can miss its significance at the performance. But there is also a good deal that was at the back of Wagner's mind, and that determined what I have called the centres of gravity; and this, which is neither in the score nor in the stage action, being assumed by Wagner to be part of the common consciousness of mankind, is what I have chiefly attended to. For this, obvious as it was to Wagner, and as it is to anyone who has reflected on human history and destiny in the light of a competent knowledge of modern capitalistic civilization, is an absolute blank to many persons who are highly susceptible to the musical qualities of Wagner's music and poetry, but have never reflected on human destiny at all, and have been brought up in polite ignorance of the infernal depths our human society descended to in the XIX century. Clearly none of your synopses or popular guides or lists of musical themes would be of the slightest use here. That, I take it, is why this little book remains, after some fifteen years, still in demand, and why I have found it necessary to complete it in this edition by a chapter dealing neither with music nor poetry, but with European history. For it was in that massive material, and not in mere crotchets and quavers, that Wagner found the stuff for his masterpiece.

AYOT ST LAWRENCE, 1913.   G. B. S.

Hard Times

Preface to Dickens's novel, in the Waverley edition, 1913

=====

John Ruskin once declared Hard Times Dickens's best novel. It is worth while asking why Ruskin thought this, because he would have been the first to admit that the habit of placing works of art in competition with one another, and wrangling as to which is the best, is the habit of the sportsman, not of the enlightened judge of art. Let us take it that what Ruskin meant was that Hard Times was one of his special favorites among Dickens's books. Was this the caprice of fancy? or is there any rational explanation of the preference? I think there is.

Hard Times is the first fruit of that very interesting occurrence which our religious sects call, sometimes conversion, sometimes being saved, sometimes attaining to conviction of sin. Now the great conversions of the XIX century were not convictions of individual, but of social sin. The first half of the XIX century considered itself the greatest of all the centuries. The second discovered that it was the wickedest of all the centuries. The first half despised and pitied the Middle Ages as barbarous, cruel, superstitious, ignorant. The second half saw no hope for mankind except in the recovery of the faith, the art, the humanity of the Middle Ages. In Macaulay's History of England, the world is so happy, so progressive, so firmly set in the right path, that the author cannot mention even the National Debt without proclaiming that the deeper the country goes into debt, the more it prospers. In Morris's News from Nowhere there is nothing left of all the institutions that Macaulay glorified except an old building, so ugly that it is used only as a manure market, that was once the British House of Parliament. Hard Times was written in 1854, just at the turn of the half century; and in it we see Dickens with his eyes newly open and his conscience newly stricken by the discovery of the real state of England. In the book that went immediately before, *Bleak House*, he was still denouncing evils and ridiculing absurdities that were mere symptoms of the anarchy that followed the industrial revolution of the XVIII and XIX centuries, and the conquest of political power by Commercialism in 1832. In *Bleak House* Dickens knows nothing of the industrial revolution: he imagines that what is wrong is that when a dispute arises over the division of the plunder of the nation, the Court of Chancery, instead of settling the dispute cheaply and promptly, beggars the disputants and pockets both their shares. His description of our party system, with its Coodle, Doodle, Foodle, etc.,[1] has never been surpassed for accuracy and for penetration of superficial pretence. But he had not dug down to the bed rock of the imposture. His portrait of the ironmaster who visits Sir Leicester Dedlock, and who is so solidly superior to him, might have been drawn by Macaulay: there is not a touch of Bounderby in it. His horrible and not untruthful portraits of the brickmakers whose abject and battered wives call them "master," and his picture of the now vanished slum between Drury Lane and Catherine Street which he calls Tom All Alone's, suggest (save in the one case of the outcast Jo, who is, like Oliver Twist, a child, and therefore outside the old self-help panacea of Dickens's time) nothing but individual delinquencies, local plague-spots, negligent authorities.

In Hard Times you will find all this changed. Coketown, which you can see today for yourself in all its grime in the Potteries (the real name of it is Hanley in Staffordshire on the London and North Western Railway), is not, like Tom All Alone's, a patch of slum in a fine city, easily cleared away, as Tom's actually was about fifty years after Dickens called attention to it. Coketown is the whole place; and its rich manufacturers are proud of its dirt, and declare that they like to see the sun blacked out with smoke, because it means that the furnaces are busy and money is being made; whilst its poor factory hands have never known any other sort of town, and are as content with it as a rat is with a hole. Mr Rouncewell, the pillar of society who snubs Sir Leicester with such dignity, has become Mr Bounderby, the self-made humbug. The Chancery suitors who are driving themselves mad by hanging about the Courts in the hope of getting a judgment in their favor instead of trying to earn an honest living, are replaced by factory operatives who toil miserably and incessantly only to see the streams of gold they set flowing slip through their fingers into the pockets of men who revile and oppress them.

Clearly this is not the Dickens who burlesqued the old song of the "Fine Old English Gentleman,"[2] and saw in the evils he attacked only the sins

1. In *Bleak House* Lord Boodle, Lord Coodle and Sir Thomas Doodle are alphabetically ordered generic names (through to Zoodle) for government ministers. The rhyme presumably originated from the term 'Noodle' (numskull), commonly applied by the British to officious individuals, notably politicians.
2. Dickens's pseudonymously signed anti-Tory rhymed lampoon 'The Fine Old English Gentleman: New Version' appeared in the London *Examiner*, 7 August 1841.

and wickednesses and follies of a great civilization. This is Karl Marx, Carlyle, Ruskin, Morris, Carpenter, rising up against civilization itself as against a disease, and declaring that it is not our disorder but our order that is horrible; that it is not our criminals but our magnates that are robbing and murdering us; and that it is not merely Tom All Alone's that must be demolished and abolished, pulled down, rooted up, and made for ever impossible so that nothing shall remain of it but History's record of its infamy, but our entire social system. For that was how men felt, and how some of them spoke, in the early days of the Great Conversion which produced, first, such books as the Latter Day Pamphlets of Carlyle, Dickens's Hard Times, and the tracts and sociological novels of the Christian Socialists, and later on the Socialist movement which has now spread all over the world, and which has succeeded in convincing even those who most abhor the name of Socialism that the condition of the civilized world is deplorable, and that the remedy is far beyond the means of individual righteousness. In short, whereas formerly men said to the victim of society who ventured to complain, "Go and reform yourself before you pretend to reform Society," it now has to admit that until Society is reformed, no man can reform himself except in the most insignificantly small ways. He may cease picking your pocket of half crowns; but he cannot cease taking a quarter of a million a year from the community for nothing at one end of the scale, or living under conditions in which health, decency, and gentleness are impossible at the other, if he happens to be born to such a lot.

You must therefore resign yourself, if you are reading Dickens's books in the order in which they were written, to bid adieu now to the light-hearted and only occasionally indignant Dickens of the earlier books, and get such entertainment as you can from him now that the occasional indignation has spread and deepened into a passionate revolt against the whole industrial order of the modern world. Here you will find no more villains and heroes, but only oppressors and victims, oppressing and suffering in spite of themselves, driven by a huge machinery which grinds to pieces the people it should nourish and ennoble, and having for its directors the basest and most foolish of us instead of the noblest and most farsighted.

Many readers find the change disappointing. Others find Dickens worth reading almost for the first time. The increase in strength and intensity is enormous: the power that indicts a nation so terribly is much more impress-ive than that which ridicules individuals. But it cannot be said that there is an increase of simple pleasure for the reader, though the books are not therefore less attractive. One cannot say that it is pleasanter to look at a battle than at a merry-go-round; but there can be no question which draws the larger crowd.

To describe the change in the readers' feelings more precisely, one may say that it is impossible to enjoy Gradgrind or Bounderby as one enjoys Pecksniff or the Artful Dodger or Mrs Gamp or Micawber or Dick Swiveller,[3] because these earlier characters have nothing to do with us except to amuse us. We neither hate nor fear them. We do not expect ever to meet them, and should not be in the least afraid of them if we did. England is not full of Micawbers and Swivellers. They are not our fathers, our schoolmasters, our employers, our tyrants. We do not read novels to escape from them and forget them: quite the contrary. But England is full of Bounderbys and Podsnaps and Gradgrinds; and we are all to a quite appalling extent in their power. We either hate and fear them or else we *are* them, and resent being held up to odium by a novelist. We have only to turn to the article on Dickens in the current edition of the Encyclopedia Britannica to find how desperately our able critics still exalt all Dickens's early stories about individuals whilst ignoring or belittling such masterpieces as Hard Times, Little Dorrit, Our Mutual Friend, and even Bleak House (because of Sir Leicester Dedlock), for their mercilessly faithful and penetrating exposures of English social, industrial, and political life; to see how hard Dickens hits the conscience of the governing class; and how loth we still are to confess, not that we are so wicked (for of that we are rather proud), but so ridiculous, so futile, so incapable of making our country really prosperous. The Old Curiosity Shop was written to amuse you, entertain you, touch you; and it succeeded. Hard Times was written to make you uncomfortable; and it will make you uncomfortable (and serve you right) though it will perhaps interest you more, and certainly leave a deeper scar on you, than any two of its forerunners.

At the same time you need not fear to find Dickens losing his good humor and sense of fun and becoming serious in Mr Gradgrind's way. On the contrary, Dickens in this book casts off, and casts off for ever, all restraint on his wild sense of humor. He had always been inclined to break loose: there are passages in the speeches of Mrs Nickleby and Pecksniff which are impossible as well as funny. But now it is no longer a question

3. Pecksniff and Sairy Gamp are characters in *Martin Chuzzlewit*. The others appear, respectively, in *Oliver Twist*, *David Copperfield*, and *The Old Curiosity Shop*.

of passages: here he begins at last to exercise quite recklessly his power of presenting a character to you in the most fantastic and outrageous terms, putting into its mouth from one end of the book to the other hardly one word which could conceivably be uttered by any sane human being, and yet leaving you with an unmistakable and exactly truthful portrait of a character that you recognize at once as not only real but typical. Nobody ever talked, or ever will talk, as Silas Wegg talks to Boffin and Mr Venus, or as Mr Venus reports Pleasant Riderhood to have talked, or as Rogue Riderhood talks, or as John Chivery talks.[4] They utter rhapsodies of nonsense conceived in an ecstasy of mirth. And this begins in Hard Times. Jack Bunsby in Dombey and Son is absurd: the oracles he delivers are very nearly impossible, and yet not quite impossible. But Mrs Sparsit in this book, though Rembrandt could not have drawn a certain type of real woman more precisely to the life, is grotesque from beginning to end in her way of expressing herself. Her nature, her tricks of manner, her way of taking Mr Bounderby's marriage, her instinct for hunting down Louisa and Mrs Pegler, are drawn with an unerring hand; and she says nothing that is out of character. But no clown gone suddenly mad in a very mad harlequinade could express all these truths in more extravagantly ridiculous speeches. Dickens's business in life has become too serious for troubling over the small change of verisimilitude, and denying himself and his readers the indulgence of his humor in inessentials. He even calls the schoolmaster McChoakumchild, which is almost an insult to the serious reader. And it was so afterwards to the end of his life. There are moments when he imperils the whole effect of his character drawing by some overpoweringly comic sally. For instance, happening in Hard Times to describe Mr Bounderby as drumming on his hat as if it were a tambourine, which is quite correct and natural, he presently says that "Mr Bounderby put his tambourine on his head, like an oriental dancer." Which similitude is so unexpectedly and excruciatingly funny that it is almost impossible to feel duly angry with the odious Bounderby afterwards.

This disregard of naturalness in speech is extraordinarily entertaining in the comic method; but it must be admitted that it is not only not entertaining, but sometimes hardly bearable when it does not make us laugh. There are two persons in Hard Times, Louisa Gradgrind and Cissy Jupe, who are serious throughout. Louisa is a figure of poetic tragedy; and there is no question of naturalness in her case: she speaks from beginning to end as an

---

4. All are characters in *Our Mutual Friend*, except Chivery, who appears in *Little Dorrit*.

inspired prophetess, conscious of her own doom and finally bearing to her father the judgment of Providence on his blind conceit. If you once consent to overlook her marriage, which is none the less an act of prostitution because she does it to obtain advantages for her brother and not for herself, there is nothing in the solemn poetry of her deadly speech that jars. But Cissy is nothing if not natural; and though Cissy is as true to nature in her character as Mrs Sparsit, she "speaks like a book" in the most intolerable sense of the words. In her interview with Mr James Harthouse, her unconscious courage and simplicity, and his hopeless defeat by them, are quite natural and right; and the contrast between the humble girl of the people and the smart sarcastic man of the world whom she so completely vanquishes is excellently dramatic; but Dickens has allowed himself to be carried away by the scene into a ridiculous substitution of his own most literary and least colloquial style for any language that could conceivably be credited to Cissy.

"Mr Harthouse: the only reparation that remains with you is to leave her immediately and finally. I am quite sure that you can mitigate in no other way the wrong and harm you have done. I am quite sure that it is the only compensation you have left it in your power to make. I do not say that it is much, or that it is enough; but it is something, and it is necessary. Therefore, though without any other authority than I have given you, and even without the knowledge of any other person than yourself and myself, I ask you to depart from this place to-night, under an obligation never to return to it."

This is the language of a Lord Chief Justice, not of the dunce of an elementary school in the Potteries.

But this is only a surface failure, just as the extravagances of Mrs Sparsit are only surface extravagances. There is, however, one real failure in the book. Slackbridge, the trade union organizer, is a mere figment of the middle-class imagination. No such man would be listened to by a meeting of English factory hands. Not that such meetings are less susceptible to humbug than meetings of any other class. Not that trade union organizers, worn out by the terribly wearisome and trying work of going from place to place repeating the same commonplaces and trying to "stoke up" meetings to enthusiasm with them, are less apt than other politicians to end as windbags, and sometimes to depend on stimulants to pull them through their work. Not, in short, that the trade union platform is any less humbug-ridden than the platforms of our more highly placed political parties. But even at their worst trade union organizers are not a bit like Slackbridge. Note, too, that Dickens mentions that there was a chairman at the meeting (as if that were rather surprising), and that this chairman makes no attempt to preserve the usual order of public meeting, but allows speakers to address the assembly and interrupt one another in an entirely disorderly way. All this is pure middle-class ignorance. It is much as if a tramp were to write a description of millionaires smoking large cigars in church, with their wives in low-necked dresses and diamonds. We cannot say that Dickens did not know the working classes, because he knew humanity too well to be ignorant of any class. But this sort of knowledge is as compatible with ignorance of class manners and customs as with ignorance of foreign languages. Dickens knew certain classes of working folk very well: domestic servants, village artisans, and employees of petty tradesmen, for example. But of the segregated factory populations of our purely industrial towns he knew no more than an observant professional man can pick up on a flying visit to Manchester.

It is especially important to notice that Dickens expressly says in this book that the workers were wrong to organize themselves in trade unions, thereby endorsing what was perhaps the only practical mistake of the Gradgrind school that really mattered much. And having thus thoughtlessly adopted, or at least repeated, this error, long since exploded, of the philosophic Radical school from which he started, he turns his back frankly on Democracy, and adopts the idealized Toryism of Carlyle and Ruskin, in which the aristocracy are the masters and superiors of the people, and also the servants of the people and of God. Here is a significant passage.

"Now perhaps," said Mr Bounderby, "you will let the gentleman know how you would set this muddle (as you are so fond of calling it) to rights."

"I donno, Sir. I canna be expecten to't. Tis not me as should be looken to for that, Sir. Tis they as is put ower me, and ower aw the rest of us. What do they tak upon themseln, Sir, if not to do it?"

And to this Dickens sticks for the rest of his life. In Our Mutual Friend he appeals again and again to the governing classes, asking them with every device of reproach, invective, sarcasm, and ridicule of which he is master, what they have to say to this or that evil which it is their professed business to amend or avoid. Nowhere does he appeal to the working classes to take their fate into their own hands and try the democratic plan.

Another phrase used by Stephen Blackpool in this remarkable fifth chapter is important. "Nor yet lettin alone will never do it." It is Dickens's express repudiation of *laissez-faire*.

There is nothing more in the book that needs any glossary, except, perhaps, the strange figure of the Victorian "swell," Mr James Harthouse. His pose has gone out of fashion. Here and there you may still see a man—

even a youth—with a single eyeglass, an elaborately bored and weary air, and a little stock of cynicisms and indifferentisms contrasting oddly with a mortal anxiety about his clothes. All he needs is a pair of Dundreary whiskers,[5] like the officers in Desanges's military pictures,[6] to be a fair imitation of Mr James Harthouse. But he is not in the fashion: he is an eccentric, as Whistler was an eccentric, as Max Beerbohm and the neo-dandies of the *fin de siècle* were eccentrics. It is now the fashion to be strenuous, to be energetic, to hustle as American millionaires are supposed (rather erroneously) to hustle. But the soul of the swell is still unchanged. He has changed his name again and again, become a Masher, a Toff, a Johnny and what not; but fundamentally he remains what he always was, an Idler, and therefore a man bound to find some trick of thought and speech that reduces the world to a thing as empty and purposeless and hopeless as himself. Mr Harthouse reappears, more seriously and kindly taken, as Eugene Wrayburn and Mortimer Lightwood in Our Mutual Friend. He reappears as a club in The Finches of the Grove in Great Expectations. He will reappear in all his essentials in fact and in fiction until he is at last shamed or coerced into honest industry and becomes not only unintelligible but inconceivable.

Note, finally, that in this book Dickens proclaims that marriages are not made in heaven, and that those which are not confirmed there, should be dissolved.

5. Lord Dundreary is the title character in Tom Taylor's *Our American Cousin*. The stage make-up affected by the original performer (E. A. Sothern), consisting of silky whiskers divided to form two extended points, set a new fashion in London.
6. Louis-William Desanges, English-born French artist, specialized in paintings on military subjects and in equestrian portraits.

Index to Volume I

by David Bowron

———

Other than in the entry under his name, Shaw is referred to as S. Insignificant references to persons or works mentioned in Shaw's text and/or in the footnotes have not been indexed.